PUBLIC POLICY, CRIME, AND CRIMINAL JUSTICE

Barry W. Hancock
*School of Public and
Environmental Affairs
Indiana University, South Bend*

Paul M. Sharp
*Department of Sociology
Auburn University at Montgomery*

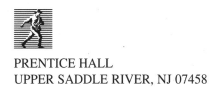

PRENTICE HALL
UPPER SADDLE RIVER, NJ 07458

Library of Congress Cataloging-in-Publication Data

Hancock, Barry W., 1954–.
  Public policy, crime, and criminal justice / Barry W. Hancock,
Paul M. Sharp.
      p.   cm.
  Includes bibliographical references.
  ISBN 0-13-235516-7 (pbk. : alk. paper)
  1. Criminal justice, Administration of—United States.   2. Law
enforcement—United States.   3. Corrections—United States.
4. Juvenile justice, Administration of—United States.   5. Crime—
United States.   I. Sharp, Paul M,   II. Title.
HV9950.H38   1996
364.973—dc20

96-20605
CIP

Editorial/Production Supervision,
    Interior Design, and Electronic Paging: *Naomi Sysak*
Acquisitions Editor: *Neil Marquardt*
Cover Designer: *Miguel Ortiz*
Manufacturing Buyer: *Ed O'Dougherty*
Managing Editor: *Mary Carnis*
Director of Production: *Bruce Johnson*

©1997 by Prentice-Hall, Inc.
A Simon & Schuster Company
Upper Saddle River, New Jersey 07458

Printed in the United States of America

10 9 8 7 6 5 4 3 2 1

ISBN 0-13-235516-7

Prentice-Hall International (UK) Limited, *London*
Prentice-Hall of Australia Pty. Limited, *Sydney*
Prentice-Hall Canada Inc., *Toronto*
Prentice-Hall Hispanoamericana, S.A., *Mexico*
Prentice-Hall of India Private Limited, *New Delhi*
Prentice-Hall of Japan, Inc., *Tokyo*
Simon & Schuster Asia Pte. Ltd., *Singapore*
Editora Prentice-Hall do Brasil, Ltda., *Rio de Janeiro*

CONTENTS

The Courts

Corrections

Juvenile Justice

PART THREE
TRENDS IN PUBLIC POLICY, CRIME AND CRIMINAL JUSTICE, 371

Epilogue, 442

PREFACE

■ ■

An anthological work requires careful selection, editing, and a fastidious blending of pedagogical materials and original works into a congruent whole. This synergistic approach helped us achieve our major goals as we produced *Public Policy, Crime, and Criminal Justice*. Certainly, our most important goal was to create, through original sources, a solid foundation of knowledge about public policy and crime in an up-to-date manner. Consequently, we selected articles that represent some of the best ideas, thinkers, and genres within the crime and criminal justice policy arena. We are especially proud of the cohesive style achieved by the selection of not only superb articles but an organizational format that groups these readings into traditionally recognized categories.

A second goal was to fill a void that we feel has existed for far too long: the creation of a text that addresses, with original works, the policy dimensions of crime and criminal justice specifically rather than supplementally. The articles in this text allow students to broaden their understanding of a particular area not through another's interpretation of materials, but by reading the author's original writing. We have noticed some movement away from traditional textbook approaches in criminal justice courses, and there is little doubt policy concerns have been anything but primary concerns in these formats. Our hope is to be a part of the efforts to broaden the students' knowledge and experience in courses dealing with public policy and crime through this anthology. Of course, this is not to imply that there is no need for textbooks for many courses, but rather to suggest a trend toward more in-depth understanding of the policy processes that help shape the system of justice in America.

Our final goal, the addition of pedagogical materials, was achieved by the development of questions placed at the end of each reading in the anthology. These "Questions for Discussion" integrate the reading materials into major points and weave readings one to another. This provides added consistency and flow to the total work and allows for *Public Policy, Crime, and Criminal Justice* to be adopted as a primary or supplemental text. This learning tool is intended to integrate the reading into your thinking through either open class discussion, exercises, or individual assignments. Each reading serves as a beginning point for further enhanced learning or as an overview of a particular policy issue.

ORGANIZATION OF THE WORK

Public Policy, Crime, and Criminal Justice is organized into three major parts. Part One, "Public Policy and Crime," consists of seven articles that lay the foundation on which the anthology is built. Beginning with the public policy process and covering topics such as family, drugs, race, and science, Part One is essential to understanding historical and political realities as these processes shape and often determine policy regarding crime. This grouping of articles illuminates the often dark background of events and processes that have created and even recreated the system in which justice now presides.

Part Two, "Public Policy and Criminal Justice," is a large selection consisting of seventeen readings, which we've divided into five subsections for purposes of organizational and topical clarity. Specifying the elements of the system first, we further divide readings into the categories of law enforcement, courts, corrections, and juvenile justice. By organizing in this fashion, we are able to cover the traditional components of the criminal justice system as each relates to policy within that particular component and the system as a whole.

"Trends in Public Policy, Crime, and Criminal Justice," Part Three, presents the final six readings in the anthology and represents some leading ideas regarding future crime policy. As a collective, these reading are the most provocative and thought provoking since they poignantly argue past mistakes, current circumstances, and future directions in crime and criminal justice public policy.

ACKNOWLEDGMENTS

We wish to express our gratitude to those who contributed to the planning, design, publication, and many other tasks involved in the production of this anthology. *Public Policy, Crime, and Criminal Justice* was accepted openly by Robin Baliszewski, senior editor at Prentice Hall, and we appreciate the care and attention she has given to this work. The production team members have dealt easily with the many details of such a work, and we thank them for the patience and professionalism with which they went about their tasks. We again owe a tremendous debt of gratitude to Lynn Sharp for her assistance in securing permissions and layout of the manuscript. Without her help, this anthology would have arrived much later and in less than superb condition.

Finally, we would like to challenge students at all levels who encounter this work to glean all that they can here and then move on to other information. As we enter the twenty-first century, it is imperative that that there be new leadership and positive change in our attempts to ameliorate the social problems related to crime and criminal justice. Understanding the many facets of the structure and process of crime policy is the first step toward making any significant change.

Barry W. Hancock
Paul M. Sharp

PART ONE

PUBLIC POLICY AND CRIME

■ ■ ■ ■ ■ ■ ■ ■ ■ ■ ■ ■ ■ ■ ■ ■ ■ ■ ■ ■

INTRODUCTION

A policy is a plan of action. Public policy regarding crime is really no more than a plan of action targeting the various crime phenomena of a society. Crime policy has taken on perhaps more importance in the twilight of the twentieth century than at any other point in our nation's history. More than any of the other factors regarding crime policy, the contradictory outcomes of these policies have produced the crisis of public faith in the criminal justice system that we are now witnessing. As most Americans are painfully aware, the United States has two shameful distinctions: (1) an incarceration level that is the highest in the industrial world, now exceeding one million persons in prisons or jails and approaching five million persons under some form of criminal justice custody; and (2) a homicide rate that is also a worldwide record, and expectations are that it will increase over the next decade. Just imagine our horror if an external enemy were to invade the United States and kill 25,000 or more people each year. The homicide rates for teenaged males, children under age fourteen, and even more tragic, preschoolers up to age 4, have reached record levels. It is as if we are experiencing a nightmare from which we cannot awaken.

Our nation has shifted policies from reform to punishment and waffled on consistent crime policy to the detriment of the citizenry. The fear of crime and the lack of personal safety are now top concerns, leading such issues as economics, education, and health. In many ways, we are witnessing a crime control system that cannot, or perhaps will not, respond to the outcry for effectiveness. Although we continue to spend tremendous sums of time, money, and energy on the crime problem, we are not achieving the major goal of increasing public safety. Perhaps the problems are larger than we have been lead to believe or that the system cannot solve all problems faced by citizens.

As a nation, the United States has often formulated crime policies that emphasize one or more of the following five major goals: (1) retribution, (2) incapacitation, (3) deterrence, (4) rehabilitation, and (5) restitution. It is our contention that the crises of public faith in the system of justice have come about because of a lack of congruity of the various components that make up the system. This, of course, should startle no one and may be stating the obvious. Although this may be common knowledge, the question is "Why hasn't the system been changed?" The structural imbalances among the various parts of the system are especially problematic and likely not to change without major paradigmatic shifts in the ways in which we envision our system of justice.

A poorly operating system of criminal justice, brought on by goal incongruence and imbalance, leads to diminished credibility in which justice is undermined. Agenda setting in criminal justice has often been based on reactive approaches to street-level crime while virtually ignoring white-collar, governmental, and organized crimes. The basic fairness of the system is undermined when these agendas are followed. Street crime became a focus in the 1960s with the civil rights movement and police responses to control what was seen as public disorder. The fear of crime rose at a much faster rate than the actual level of crime. Politicians, especially, often exploited this fear so as to build up the criminal justice system, and resources, both human and financial, were diverted away from various programs and into the new "war on crime."

Of course, many groups help shape public policy, and crime is one of the most popular for legislative, executive, and judicial manipulation and debate. During the 1980s, for example, crime policies shifted away from reform and rehabilitation toward retribution and incapacitation. These policies were not, however, followed with any consistency by all components of the system. Criminal justice policies are often changed and influenced during implementation. The autonomy of various agencies produces goal conflicts that may cause the total system to function ineffectively.

Beyond the conflicting group and lack of consistent achievement, the four basic elements of the implementation process often do not work harmoniously. The four elements include: (1) law enforcement, (2) prosecution, (3) adjudication, and (4) correction. The effectiveness of any set of goals cannot be realized without a synergy of the elements of implementation. Some of the greatest crises in the system are due to this uneven grinding of the wheels of justice.

Although the implementation of policies is more often than not affected by every component in a long line to finality, several important factors are worth considering as we begin our readings in public policy and crime. Resources must be available before any crime-related policy has a chance at implementation. The political environment must be balanced in favor of certain types of policies, or nothing will or can happen. In most respects, the social and economic conditions must be ready for new policies and the methods by which policies are implemented must be carefully evaluated.

As a student of policy as it relates to crime and criminal justice, it is wise to remember that policy is often difficult to define and even more difficult to explain because of the processual nature of policy. In other words, policy is often what people claim it to be rather than a narrowly defined set of plans. Policy is always in motion and moves from side to side depending on the many political, social, and economic influences.

With these ideas in mind, we chose "The Public Policy Process in the United States," by William P. Hojnacki, to serve as your introduction to the various factors that define and shape public policy. How public policy is defined; in what context policy is formulated, adopted and implemented; and the competing interests that affect policy decisions are crucial to understanding the complex dynamics of policy creation and its far reaching and long-term effects.

The historical relationship between criminological research and public policy is the focus of our second selection. In "Public Policy and Criminology: A Historical and Philosophical Reassessment," James F. Gilsinan recommends we begin to view the interrelations between criminology, science, and social policy. The contradictory demands of science and of public policy have created a quandary for many criminologists that has lead to an ineffective, if not denuded, linkage between science and policy. Gilsinan points out that criminology historically has never been confined to the ivory tower but instead has always been linked to policy concerns. Without doubt, criminological research has affected policy both directly and indirectly. Many contradictions and anomalies of the discipline of criminology, and its linkage to public policy, must be understood and appreciated if the knowledge-generating processes of our science are to be seriously linked to policy. Gilsinan argues that criminology and public policy are related hermeneutically. Understanding this linkage will, Gilsinan argues, narrow the gap between policy and the practice of social science.

Two seasoned criminologists, Michael Gottfredson and Travis Hirschi, in "Science, Public Policy, and the Career Paradigm," argue that scientific criminology and sound public policy should reject the "career approach" to crime. This approach might best be replaced by the "theories of crime approach" because the career paradigm has failed to organize the facts about crime in a meaningful way. The implications of this kind of suggestion are immense and extensive. The system of criminal justice has been moving in the direction of controlling habitual, career criminals for some time now, and policy, especially sentencing policy, has been most influenced by this movement.

In "Crime, Justice, and the Social Environment," Elliot Currie claims violent crime is an American epidemic. Currie creates a superb foundation for students to better understand the crime problem and policy reactions to these and other social problems. The punishment ethic that replaced rehabilitative ideology has, in Currie's words, "failed, massively and tragically." This conservative revolution in American criminal justice did not fail for a lack of application, because of foundational principles that were wrong. If we are to revitalize the nation toward true justice, we must begin to see crime as a social problem inextricably intertwined with child poverty, infant mortality, inadequate public services, and extremes of economic inequality.

George B. Palermo and Douglas Simpson eloquently point out, in "At the Roots of Violence: The Progressive Decline and Dissolution of the Family," that the present-day family often does not pass on to its members those traditional high moral values of honesty and responsibility. Moral values and honesty, they argue, are at the core of good citizenship and high self-esteem. When this breakdown in primary socialization combines with an epidemic of drug addiction and serious unemployment, we have the keys for understanding the upsurge in violence in America. The roots of violence are to be found in what happens to children in the earliest years of their lives, not in the symptomology of reactive solutions to social problems. The solutions to our massive problems of violence and crime are to be found in socializing children with unselfish citizenship. Reintegration of the family is the key to stabilizing our nation's fall from greatness.

Our sixth selection, "Racial Disparities in the Criminal Justice System: A Summary," by Joan Petersilia, concludes that the sentencing stage produces a greater differential treatment of minorities than any of the other stages in the criminal justice system. Petersilia points out that, in certain states, judges typically impose heavier sentences on Hispanics and blacks than on whites and that these minorities typically spend more time incarcerated.

Disparities such as these undermine justice and lead to dilemmas that are not easily solved. Any policy reformation or change in sentencing structure must invariably address the issues involved in assuring equal treatment if the system of justice expects to create and maintain public confidence.

The question of the relationship between drug use and criminal behavior has been a policy concern for years. Lana Harrison and Joseph Gfroerer, in "The Intersection of Drug Use and Criminal Behavior: Results from the National Household Survey on Drug Abuse," share some very valuable information with us in this fine piece of research. Research findings suggest such things as drug use and criminal behavior, especially property crime, are much more common among teens and young adults than they are among other age groups. No doubt, the highest crime rates are consistently found among the heaviest drug users, whereas the lowest rates are found among those who use neither alcohol nor illicit drugs.

1

THE PUBLIC POLICY PROCESS IN THE UNITED STATES

William P. Hojnacki

School of Public and Environmental Affairs
Indiana University, South Bend

■ ■ ■ ■ ■ ■ ■ ■ ■ ■ ■ ■ ■ ■ ■ ■ ■ ■ ■ ■

The public policy process in the United States is one of the more confusing aspects of American government and politics. There is little agreement, even among respected political scientists, on what the salient parts of this process are. At least a half dozen theories try to explain how it is supposed to work.[1] The confusion is exacerbated by the difficulty that exists in even defining the term. Again, different political scientists have offered multiple definitions. There are, however, some common threads that run through these different definitions.

The goal here is not to resolve all the theoretical disagreements that political scientists may have, but to identify those aspects of this process that are meaningful to lay observers of it and those individuals who participate in it. The objective here is to put the public policy process into a context that practitioners and ordinary citizens can understand.

PUBLIC POLICY DEFINED

From all those offered, the definition of public policy I like best is the somewhat simplified statement that "public policy is whatever the government chooses to do or not to do."[2] Although, as the author of this definition, political scientist Thomas Dye suggests it may not accommodate everything that everyone would consider public policy. However, it comes close and captures what most people, especially political practitioners, think about when they consider public policy.

Even this simplified definition, however, needs further elaboration. It implies some conditions about what is or is not public policy that are not obvious. There are at least four important characteristics that government activity (or lack of activity) must have before it can be considered public policy.

The first and perhaps most obvious characteristic is that only governments and those individuals who can legitimately act in the name of government can make and implement

Reprinted by permission of the author.

public policy. In order for any action or activity to be public policy, it must have the authority of government at some level behind it.

The second characteristic, drawn from the word *chooses* in Dye's definition, is that public policies are not random acts by either government agencies or elected or appointed government officials. They are deliberate courses of action (or inaction) designed to achieve some predetermined goals and objectives.

Third, public policies are indeed "to do's"; they are not what is merely stated to be public policy, or what is planned, but what is actually being done. Often, there is a gap between what is said to be public policy and what the reality of that policy may be. This gap may contribute to the confusion about what is or is not public policy.[3]

The fourth characteristic is that government, and those who act in the name of government, must be consistent over time; it is not something that happens only occasionally or arbitrarily. A zealous policy officer who chooses on his own accord to strictly enforce a stated speed limit does not automatically alter a more generally accepted policy of a higher level of tolerance, even if strict enforcement of the speed limit has the authority of government behind it. True public policies are not subject to arbitrary interpretation of individuals regardless of their official capacity.

With these four characteristics in mind, it is appropriate to look at the negative side of public policy: when a unit of government chooses not to do something. The point is that choosing not to do something is a legitimate public policy choice only if the choice is in the realm of possibility. Most cities, for instance, do not have policies regarding foreign espionage. The absence of such policies does not mean that cities condone spying. It simply means that foreign espionage is beyond what is a legitimate area of policy concern. On the other hand, for a city to choose not to undertake a solid waste recycling program is a legitimate negative policy decision. Such recycling programs are normally within a city's jurisdiction. The same characteristics apply to negative policy decisions as to positive ones.[4]

PUBLIC POLICY CONTEXT

Public policy is the product of the political system. The way that public policy in the United States is formulated, adopted, and implemented is somewhat different from how it is done in almost every other country in the world because the American political system is different. Many of these differences can be traced to the uniqueness of the Constitution of the United States. At least three important sets of provisions in the U.S. Constitution profoundly affect the way the public policy works in the United States.[5]

The first, and arguably the most important, set of Constitutional provisions in terms of the public policy process are the ones that outline the system of separation of powers among the three main branches of government: executive, legislative and judicial. The importance of these provisions stems from the interdependence among the three branches that the Constitution mandates. The powers of each branch are indeed separate, but no branch can exercise its powers without the cooperation of the other two. It truly is a system of checks and balances that in reality requires a considerable amount of political skill to get anything done. The framers of the Constitution wanted a strong central government but did not want it dominated by a small number of "interests." They succeeded.

Each branch tends to serve different constituencies. Senators represent states, whereas members of the House of Representatives serve small, generally more homogeneous, districts. The president and vice president are the only people elected by the country as a whole. The judiciary is appointed by the president (for life) but only "with the advice and consent of the Senate." Further, each branch is given a different set of responsibilities, and within the legislative branch, different responsibilities are divided between the House and the Senate. Hence, no one group or even a coalition of groups (or "interests") can dominate the policy process.[6]

The importance of the separation of powers provisions of the U.S. Constitution is multiplied because each of the fifty states has tried, with varying degrees of success, to copy this doctrine in its own state constitution. Even local units of government often try to follow a similar organizational pattern although it is often difficult for local government to achieve the same type of checks and balances that exists in the federal government.[7]

The second set of factors that emanate from the Constitution is the federal system itself. The Constitution divides major governmental responsibilities between the federal government and the states. The relationship between the federal government and the states constantly changes, but the essential fact is that despite what, on occasion, appears to be an overwhelming federal dominance of the public policy process, most of what affects citizens on a day-to-day basis takes place as a result of state and local political activity, not as a result of what the federal government does. It is the states, not the federal government, that have the generalized "police power" function of protecting the health, safety, and morals of the population. For instance, there is no federal law per se against murder.

It is state laws and local ordinances adjudicated through state court systems that affect most citizens most of the time. It is state and local government that has primary responsibility for such things as education, streets and highways, and public recreation. Although the federal government does provide funding for a large number of programs, it is the states and their local units of government that have primary responsibility for implementing them.

The importance of the federal system to this discussion of the public policy process is that the federal government is responsible for only part of it. In fact, there are more than 80,000 units of government of various forms in the United States. Each is a public policy process unto itself, and at the same time, each is part of the larger policy process that encompasses the whole country.[8]

The third set of factors that comes from the Constitution and affects the public policy process is the emphasis the Constitution puts on individual rights and responsibilities. The Constitution limits what government at all levels can do. Neither the states nor the federal courts have been reluctant to strike down inappropriate government policies and programs. Simply put, government at all levels can do some things and not others. This idea is carried forward at the state level. Most states attempt to regulate in very precise ways what it is that local units of government can and cannot do. These restrictions have a profound effect on the public policy process and contribute to the confusion about it.[9]

POLICY TYPES

Another way to look at public policy is in terms of types or categories of public policy. They can, for instance, be viewed in terms of who is affected by them. From this perspective, policy can be seen as falling into one of two broad categories. The first category, or type, encompasses policy that affects certain segments of a political jurisdiction's population. Policies in this category would include municipal zoning ordinances, state laws dealing with specific public works projects, or federal policies on price supports for certain agricultural commodities. The second category is what some political scientists call "areal." These are policies that, more or less, have an impact on the entire political jurisdiction equally. Included here would be support for the police and fire departments at the local level, state-level policies dealing with environmental issues, and the foreign policy of the federal government. Taxation issues are areal policies that cut across all levels of government.[10]

Another way to look at public policies is to see them in terms of the degree to which they are substantive or procedural. As James E. Anderson states: "Substantive policies involve what government is going to do, such as the construction of highways or the payment of welfare benefits. Procedural policies, in contrast, involve who is going to take action or how it is going to be done."[11] Procedural policies also involve governmental organizational matters such as how a state legislature or a city council functions.

A third and perhaps more useful way to classify policy is in terms of how it impacts on society. In this regard, policy can be seen as falling into one of four categories: distributive, redistributive, regulatory, or self-regulatory.

Distributive policies involve the delivery of public goods and services such as water from the water works, the creation of public access sites on rivers and streams, and U.S. mail delivery. Distributive policies may be geared to either specific segments of the population or the population at large. All levels of government adopt distributive policies of one form or another.

Redistributive policies are designed to redistribute various forms of wealth among different segments of the population. The most obvious forms of redistributive policies are the federal-sponsored "entitlement" programs such as veterans benefits, Medicare and Medicaid health care programs, and the food stamp program. Although all levels of government can adopt redistributive policies, it is primarily the federal government that takes responsibility for redistributing the nation's wealth. State and local governments, however, are usually the ones that carry out these programs.

Regulatory policies are designed to control the behavior of individuals, groups, and organizations, including corporations. These policies range from the criminal codes that all levels of government adopt to specific regulations like zoning ordinances at the local level and speed limits by state legislatures. Virtually all the policies adopted by such agencies as the Federal Communication Commission and the Interstate Commerce Commission are regulatory.

Self-regulatory policies also seek to control the behavior of individuals, groups, and organizations; however, they are policies that the affected parties themselves seek. The most important self-regulatory policies are the licensing requirements that state governments impose on various professional and nonprofessional occupational groups. Such groups might include barbers, teachers, plumbers, and lawyers. Local, state, and national civil service requirements can also be seen as self-regulatory policies.[12]

WHO MAKES PUBLIC POLICY?

To say that public policy is a product of the political process still does not account for who plays a role in the formulation, adoption, and implementation of public policy. The simple answer to the question of who makes public policy is that anyone who is in a position to make and carry out decisions is also in a position to make policy. Such individuals may range from the president of the United States to governors and mayors, and on down to police officers, welfare case workers, and other street-level bureaucrats who have some discretion in carrying out their assigned duties. Generally, when we think about policy, we understand it to be made by the major political branches of government, most importantly (but not exclusively), the executive branches and the legislative bodies of government at all levels.[13] Also important are the quasi-judicial regulatory agencies which, after receiving a legislative mandate to oversee certain types of activities, have wide discretion in making their own rules, enforcing them, and then judging whether there has been compliance to the rules. Examples here include the role that the Food and Drug Administration plays in the pharmaceutical industry, the role a state-level utility regulatory commission plays in setting utility rates, and the role a local zoning board has in land use planning.[14]

Although prosecuting attorneys, police chiefs, and probation officers can be found in the policy loop, the role of the judiciary is muddled. Officially, judges do not make policy except to the extent they have a role in court administration. Judges are supposed to only interpret the laws and apply them to specific circumstances. From a practical perspective, however, courts often have a significant impact on both the public policy and substantive public policy that borders on actually making policy.

It was the U.S. Supreme Court that changed that nature of state public policy making when it ruled in the one-man, one-vote case, *Mapp* v. *Ohio* that state legislatures must proportionally represent the population they serve.[15] In the legendary *Miranda* decision, in which the court ruled that persons arrested for serious crimes must be informed of their Fifth Amendment rights at the time of their arrest, the policies of virtually every police department in the United States were changed.[16] In similar, if less dramatic ways, other federal and state court decisions have had an impact on the way public policy is made and administered.[17]

THE POLICY SYSTEM

The system diagram on page 10 is adapted from one offered by Robert Lineberry and Ira Sharkansky to reflect their observations of how public policy is created, adopted, and implemented in an urban political system.[18] It was derived from a classic political systems model first developed by political theorist David Easton.[19] The diagram is utilized

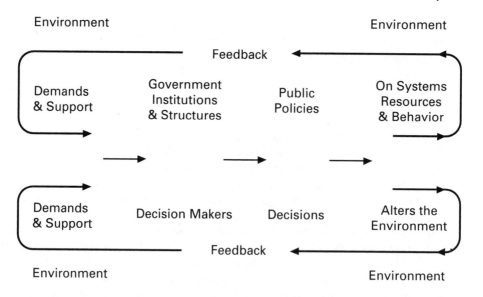

here, not because it somehow accounts for all the factors that can have an impact on how policy is made or implemented, but because it helps organize thinking about this process. The system also emphasizes that the public policy process is an ongoing, virtually never-ending, process, where different issues are being confronted at different places at different times. Further, systems function within systems. In any given state, for instance, hundreds of local political systems may be operating simultaneously and, in some cases, inter-changeably within the larger state political system. We know that at least fifty state political systems are in place that function under the political system that is the U.S. government. It is precisely because of the multiplicity of political processes in the United States that the idea of trying to organize them systematically is useful.

The model used here could be any one of the thousands of political systems that exist in the United States. The environment, as it is depicted here, is unique to whatever unit is being analyzed. It reflects all factors—social, political, economic, physical, and geographic—in which the unit of government functions. It includes the prevailing economic system, which encompasses manufacturing, agriculture, mining, retailing, service providers, finance and banking, as well as organized and unorganized workers. Indeed, it includes all the entities that contribute to the socioeconomic makeup of the particular society. The environment also includes the full range of racial, ethnic and religious groups represented in the area under analysis, and the public and private networks of educational, cultural, and health care institutions. In short, the environment includes all the factors that could have an impact on how the government functions and how public policy is made. The political system considers nothing that does not at some point originate in the environment.

It is the environment that initially generates the inputs, those forces that seek to influence the course of public policy. Because politics is a social activity, inputs come from the socioeconomic mix of the environment. Political scientists call these forces political demands. In short, they are ideas that are generated by citizens reflecting what they want the government to do differently. Literally thousands of citizens come up with these ideas every day. Even if they are good ones, individually, the ideas do not mean very much. In most cases, regardless of how good an idea might be, before it can be considered a political demand, it must become widely accepted; it must get support. Inputs in this context combine the "demands" that individuals make with widely accepted support for those demands.

The conversion process, as shown here, is the mechanism of government. It is labeled the conversion process to connote what it does rather than what it is and because governments come in so many different forms—especially when subunits such as a local human rights commission can be analyzed independently of the larger municipal government of which it may be a part. A conversion process may be as small and simple as a neighborhood council or as large and complex as the federal government itself. It is these mechanisms, however, that convert inputs into outputs.

The outputs are public policy. Again, these policies may be simple declarative statements reflecting what the government chooses to do or not to do on some matter, or they may be highly complex legislative or executive initiatives designed to achieve multiple objectives over an extended time. When looking at outputs, however, at least one other distinction needs to be made: the difference between outcomes and impacts.

Outcomes represent what the government has chosen to do, for instance, setting the speed limit at 55 mph. Impacts refer to what happens as a result of the outcome, for example, lower fuel consumption and reduced traffic fatalities. Impact in this context refers to the changes the public policy has on the environment.

Actually analyzing outputs, both outcomes and impacts, is complicated because of the need to occasionally draw a distinction between short-term and long-range policies. Even though it may be possible to see the impact of short-term policy initiatives quickly, it may take years to understand the impact of long-range policy choices.[20]

In most units of government, especially larger and more complex units, important policies tend to come packaged with both short-term and long-range implications. A city government may, for instance, adopt a series of policies designed to deal with the problems of deteriorating housing. This is the long-range policy. It might then undertake a series of short-term policy decisions such as rehabilitating some houses, demolishing others, and developing new park land as a way of ultimately achieving the long-range policy. It may, however, be difficult on occasion to see the relationship between short-term policies and long-range policy objectives. For instance, it may be difficult to see how a short-term decision of demolishing existing house stock contributes to a long-range policy of providing better housing for low-income families.

Feedback, as it is shown here, represents the extent to which public policy actually does alter the environment so that future inputs are altered as well. Public policies, for instance, that are designed to lower the unemployment rate, and do so, change the political demands that initiated the original policy decision.[21]

WORKING OUTSIDE THE SYSTEM

This system view implies that all public policy must come through governmental channels. It is, however, possible in some instances to bypass governmental decision making altogether. Even though the U.S. Constitution is silent on the question of "direct democracy," it is part of the tradition of English Common Law and has been incorporated into the political decision-making process of many states and local communities. The history of the New England town meeting predates the Constitution. Although the town meeting still exists in many places in the New England states, other states and communities have adopted more modern versions of direct democracy that can bypass the formal government-controlled public policy process. These efforts come in the form of initiative, referendum, and (indirectly) recall.

Initiative is a process whereby citizens who have political demands, and reasonably widespread support for those demands, can circulate petitions to put certain matters on the ballot so that all the voters of a jurisdiction can vote on the matter. If the vote is successful, the matter becomes public policy with any formal legislative or executive action.[22] Such matters might include spending on a public works project or an initiative to ban pornographic bookstores. California is particularly famous for its ballot propositions coming from citizen initiatives. The objective of a citizen initiative is to hold a referendum on the question at hand.

Referendums simply are instances where citizens get to vote on issues directly. Initiatives require a referendum to be successful, but in many places there are other ways referendums can take place. For instance, in some states, all proposed amendments to the state constitution require a referendum, and in some communities, local legislative bodies have the option of putting an issue on the ballot or deciding it themselves. In still other cases, referendums are held as advisory votes that are not binding on a legislature, but serve as a barometer of public sentiment on a controversial issue.

Recall refers to the removal of elected officials before their normal term of office expires. Recall occurs as the result of an initiative and referendum in which voters are asked to decide whether an elected official should be retained in office. Recall as such is not part of the public policy process, but because of the threat it possesses to elected officials, it can have an impact on the public policy process. Provisions for initiative referendum and recall vary substantially from state to state and community to community.[23]

INFLUENCING THE POLICY PROCESS

The vast majority of public policy initiatives comes through normal legislative, executive, and regulatory agency channels. Thus, from the perspective of citizens, the question of influencing the public policy process is one of attempting to influence the political process in general, or the legislative process in particular. There are two important parts: (1) how society organizes itself to formulate inputs to the policy process; and (2) how the government processes these inputs.[24]

In terms of the question of societal organization, it is important to keep in mind that the United States is a highly pluralistic and geographically dispersed society. The mix of inputs varies substantially from place to place and depends heavily on the size and complexity of a particular political unit. A local labor union or a chamber of commerce might virtually control the political process of a small town or country but have almost no influence in the larger state or national political arena. However, levels and types of influence are not all circumstantial. There are indeed some identifiable patterns on how society organizes itself to exercise political influence.

Although different political scientists have offered different models on how the public policy process reflects the makeup of society, in general, these views fall into one of two basic categories. One is that society's elites dominate the policy process. The other is the pluralist model that in essence says that public policy is the result of a "playing out" of conflict between different groups within society that individually reflect distinct economic or social interests.[25] These two schools of thought, in general, are derived from two classic studies of community power structures that came to opposing conclusions.

One of these studies was Floyd Hunter's research in Atlanta, Georgia, in the early 1950s, from which he concluded that community elites were the dominant force in community decision making. The other study was Robert Dahl's research in Hartford, Connecticut, in which he concluded that community decision making was the result of pluralistic-based intergroup conflict.[26] Other studies have reinforced one perspective or the other, thus perpetuating the debate.[27]

A comparative study of Kalamazoo, Michigan, and South Bend, Indiana, two cities of similar size, was undertaken in the mid-1970s. It was found that whereas elites did dominate decision making in Kalamazoo, public policy in South Bend was the outgrowth of group conflict.[28] The primary conclusion that can be drawn from these and other studies is that well-positioned elites are more likely than others to influence the public policy process, but their capacity to do so is highly circumstantial. The base support of Kalamazoo's elites was substantially stronger than the base of support of South Bend's elites. Further, a great deal depends on how political institutions are configured to process the demands and the support for these demands generated by elites or other competitive interests.

A summary of findings of a wide range of studies focusing on community decision making would be that the extent to which a community is homogeneous or heterogeneous seems to influence who can exercise power. Elites are more likely to dominate homogeneous communities than ones that contain many different ethnic, racial, and religious minorities. Also important is the extent to which elites compete with others or function in a unified way. In a similar vein, organized labor, depending on its strength, contributes to a pluralistic policy process, except where it is the community elite, such as occurs in a few blue-collar suburbs.

There also appears to be a correlation between partisanship and pluralistic decision making. Elites tend to dominate communities that have nonpartisan elections or weak political parties. Similarly, elites tend to dominate in communities that feature at-large or, at least, very large legislative districts. Communities that elect council or commissioner members from small single-member wards or districts tend to be more pluralistic. And cities that feature "strong mayor" forms of government tend to be more pluralistic than cities that have commission, council-manager, or "weak mayor" forms of government.[29]

POINTS OF POWER

Discussions about political power usually begin, perhaps for obvious reasons, with an analysis of economic-based interests. Although, to be sure, people do become interested in politics and public policy matters for social, religious, environmental, or other reasons, it seems that the dominant concerns emanate from individuals and groups that have an economic stake in the process. There is little that the government does that does not cost somebody something. When such proposals do appear, they tend to draw the attention of those who are slated to pay the bill. Ultimately, almost everyone is affected economically either as a producer, consumer, or taxpayer.

It is economic "special" interests that are most often talked about when lobbyists are criticized: big business, big labor, trade associations, and others. These groups, of course, are not the only ones who undertake lobbying. Across the country, literally thousands of groups, organizations, businesses, and individuals try to influence the course of government.

As for professional lobbying, "special" interest groups can be divided into four different, if somewhat overlapping, categories. These categories reflect both the nature of different organizations and the types of activities they undertake. Most lobbyists concentrate their efforts on influencing legislators, but some work on administrative agencies and executive branch personnel as well.[30]

Corporate Interests

Large corporations are probably the most intense and pervasive lobbyists at all levels of government in the country. Depending on what the government does or does not do, they often have millions of dollars at stake. They are the best organized and best financed lobbyists in Washington, D.C., and in state capitals around the country. Big companies operate either on their own, or through trade associations, or both. At the national level, they lobby both the Congress and the administrative agencies where the regulations that inevitably follow legislation are written.[31]

Although instances where these corporate interests are blatantly corrupt are rare, they are often portrayed as unprincipled. They function with large well-paid staffs who attempt to influence every phase of the political process. They become intermittently involved with the political campaigns of candidates for both legislative and executive offices, especially at the national level. Through corporate PACs (political action committees), they channel large amounts of money into the campaign coffers of sympathetic candidates and sometimes provide advice and technical assistance as well. After being elected, these interests often find ways to entertain officer holders and provide them with the opportunity to earn extra money by paying them to make speeches at meetings and conventions. These interests also provide legitimate services to office holders by doing research for them and using their "good offices" to broker deals between different interests.

These interests also try to lobby administrative agencies in that it is these agencies who are responsible for writing the rules and regulations needed before any new legislation is carried out. They are aided in this effort by the fact that in many instances high-level (politically appointed) administrators actually come from the affected businesses and industries and because many of the paid lobbyists formerly were with the agencies or compatible congressional committees.

The power of these interests comes both from the fact that they have a great deal of money at their disposal and because they tend to be a reliable, ever-present force. It also helps that because of the nature of their lobbying activities they are usually able to operate below the level of public visibility, and thus public officials associating with them is not normally a matter of controversy.

Corporate interests are easy targets for reformers, but part of their power comes from the fact that in various places they do provide thousands of jobs and major capital investments. They also produce the goods and services that American consumers want. The linkages may sometimes be difficult to see, but these interests can claim to represent constituents as well.[32]

Membership-Based Interests

The second category of special interest groups draw their strength from the fact that they represent large number of members. The most obvious organizations that fall into this category are labor unions and groups like the American Association of Retired Persons (AARP) and National Educational Association (NEA). Other organizations that fall into this category include the Fraternal Order of Police, American Legion, American Bar Association, and American Medical Association. Although most of these organizations are by no means poor, they, in general, cannot match the resources of the corporate interests. Organizations in this category draw their strength from their members and the willingness of their members to become politically active. The ability of these groups to influence the course of public policy depends on the size of the organization, the geographic distribution of their members, and the intensity with which the members are committed to its public policy agenda.

Operationally, groups in this category function in much the same way as do the corporate interests: using PACs to contribute to campaigns and helping public officials in every way they can. But because they need to be more visible in their activities than corporate lobbying efforts and because they are responsible to a membership, they cannot be as free with their money or as blatant in wooing officials as the corporate interests can be.

The biggest problem that groups in this category face is that, because they depend on members, if the membership drops or the public's attention is diverted, their strength is diminished. The power of organized labor is considerably reduced because the number of people who belong to unions is considerably reduced.[33]

Single Issue Groups

Groups like the National Rifle Association (NRA) and the National Right to Life Organization, which focus their attention on a narrow range of concerns, can be very effective at some levels of the policy process. These organizations are also membership based and depend, almost exclusively, on intense commitment of these members to the issues they are supporting or opposing for their effectiveness. Because the groups are "cause" oriented, they tend to concentrate their efforts on the electoral process rather than on administrative or regulatory concerns. They concentrate most of their resources on electing supporters and defeating opponents. At the same time, most of the money they raise is spent trying to recruit more public support rather than trying to "buy" the support of legislators who are already in office.

A few groups like the National Rifle Association gain national recognition for their efforts. For other groups, the record is less spectacular. The effectiveness of these groups is limited because influence is so strategically linked to the size and commitment of their membership base, and the level of visibility of the issues with which they are concerned. When the public's attention is diverted, interest in their cause drops, as does their membership and resources, and hence, their effectiveness.[34]

Environmental advocacy groups, for instance, can be reasonably effective as long as environmental concerns are on the public's mind. But when the public's attention turns to other matters, environmental advocacy groups tend to lose members and consequently their political clout. And because groups in this category often find it difficult to maintain a high level of support over an extended period, their influence, even at peak strength, is diminished. Elected officials often find their help unreliable.

Public Interest Groups

Public interest groups can be considered a separate special interest category because they cannot easily be placed in the first three categories. Some (like Common Cause) are membership based, others (like GreenPeace) are essentially single interest, and still others (like the National League of Cities or the U.S. Conference of Mayors) are brokers for other groups. What they have in common is claiming that they lobby in the public interest rather than for particular private interests. In general these "PIGs" as they are sometimes called, tend to be a small part of overall lobbying efforts and tend to be only marginally effective. Operationally, they function much like the groups in the other categories but tend to have limited public support and considerably fewer resources with which to work.[35]

Although lobbying as it is depicted with these four categories does occur at all levels of government, the types of activities described here are more formal and more visible at the state and national levels of government than at the local level. Most apparent at the local level are small groups of people who organize themselves in more informal ways to influence public policy.

Cities, towns, and countries are, because they are more homogeneous, more likely than states to be dominated by a small number of businesses, institutions, or individuals. In places like Ann Arbor, Michigan, and College Station, Texas, there is little doubt that the dominant political force is the local university. Similarly, the historical landscape of America is famous for its one-industry cities like Detroit (automobiles), Pittsburgh (steel), and Akron, Ohio (rubber). Although the makeup of the American economy has, in most places, reduced the political influence of particular industries in particular cities, most cities still have something of a dominant, political, elite force based on whatever there is that drives the local economy.

Local media can be influential because they often have nearly a complete monopoly on local news coverage and thus can choose which stories to cover and which to ignore. The editorial board of a newspaper in a one-newspaper town—and one-newspaper towns are now more common than not in the United States—can be very influential. Interestingly, however, this influence usually extends only to the local elite, not to the population as a whole. Most people do not read the editorial page.

The influence of the local media is diluted in public policy debates because, in all but the largest cities, local media outlets usually lack the resources or the inclination to do true investigative reporting. Further, because the local media tend to depend heavily on local business for advertising revenue, there is a tendency to be cautious in reporting on local events that make big advertisers look bad.

There is a distinct trend for most larger communities to become more pluralistic, but few are so pluralistic as to be devoid of a community power structure altogether.[36] The owners and managers of any community's largest employers still tend to have the most power in the community, especially on matters that affect them directly. They are usually most concerned about such things as zoning, public works projects near their facilities, and land use planning in general. The more dominant an employer is, the more influence it is likely to exercise. It also makes a difference if a community is where the home office of a company is located. Business and industry leaders tend to be much more involved in their "home town" than in communities where they merely have a plant or branch operation. Branch managers seldom have the same roots in a community as the officers of a locally owned concern; hence, their capacity to influence local public policy matters is often limited.[37]

Next to the owners and managers of large employers in terms of wielding influence are the principals of banks and other financial institutions. Banks are often large employers in their own right. The power of bankers comes from their role in providing investment capital for local business and industry, and as the primary provider of home mortgages and other financial products to local residents. Critical to the political role that bankers often play in local communities is the makeup of their boards of directors. It is on these boards that local business, industrial, and institutional leaders meet and often plot collective action on one project or another. The bankers who work (officially at any rate) for these boards are often the only ones who know what other important persons in the community are doing, and therefore, how to play one off against another.

Like business and industrial leaders in general, the influence of bankers depends on their size, whether or not they are locally owned, and the extent to which there is competition in the field. The president of a medium-size bank in a highly competitive environment is going to have less influence than the president of a small bank that dominates the local financial market.[38]

Third on the power list, and again varying considerably from community to community, are the leaders of local institutions like hospitals, colleges and universities, and foundations. In addition to often being large employers with large capital investments, the boards of directors of these institutions, like banks, usually comprise other community leaders. How influential the leaders of these institutions are depends on the size and stature of the institution. The influence of the president of a large university in a small town is huge, whereas the influence of the president of a small college in a large city is minimal. Similarly, the Upjohn Foundation has the reputation of being very influential in Kalamazoo, Michigan, but the Rockefeller Foundation, despite its international reputation, is reported to exercise scant influence on the public policy process in New York City.[39]

It is possible for individuals who lack a formal institutional or industrial base to exercise power as well, but they usually need some claim to fame. Heirs of old family fortunes can be influential, but not automatically so. They must be willing to spend time and some of their money in appropriate ways before their influence can be felt. Interestingly, representatives of old-line families are often unwilling to pay such a price.

The level of influence exercised by the leaders of such groups as labor unions, chambers of commerce, and various forms of citizen groups depends, as might be expected, on both their strength in the community and the strength of the previously noted power configurations. In a one-company town, the union can never be as powerful as the company whose workers it represents. Chambers of commerce tend to reflect the business community they represent, and whatever power they may appear to have is usually, in reality, the power of the companies that fund it rather than the chambers themselves.

The influence of neighborhood group leaders or the leadership of other forms of citizen groups depends on three factors. One of these factors is the extent to which a community is truly pluralistic and where, therefore, elite influence is diminished. The second is the extent to which the groups represented by these leaders are able to exercise serious influence on the outcome of local elections. The third is the group leader's energy, commitment, and capacity to articulate real community concerns. Civil rights activists Martin Luther King, Jr., and Jessie Jackson were able to use their personal dynamism to build on an essentially weak political base to become enormously influential individuals at all levels of the public policy process.[40]

The political machines of large U.S. cities are legendary in American politics. Indeed, there was a time when Tammany Hall in New York, or Mayor Richard Daley in Chicago, or Governor David Lawrence of Pennsylvania could wield exceptional political power. Although local political party leaders can, in some places, exercise some level of influence, the days of the political machines are largely over, replaced by civil service systems (instead of political patronage) and modern media-based campaign techniques. Further, even from a historical context, there is considerable doubt about how much influence the party bosses actually had on public policy issues.[41]

Political parties are still an important part of the political landscape, but their influence on public policy matters is largely indirect. The primary interest of any political party is to get its candidates elected. Parties do, of course, adopt platforms, but these tend to be vague, generalized statements that provide little guidance to policy makers.

The major impact of political parties on the public policy process comes in the organization of state and national legislative bodies.[42] Most legislative bodies in the United State are organized along party lines, and occasionally, the political party caucus in a legislative body will take positions on various issues, and votes are taken which all loyal party members are supposed to support. What is important about political party positions votes in legislative chambers is that it is the legislators themselves that determine the party's position on various issues in their own caucuses, not party leaders outside the legislatures. Modern party leaders tend to have very little influence on the public policy process at any level of government.

In short, loosely knit political parties provide an umbrella over the public policy process but are not usually active participants in it at any level. At the same time, of course, party leaders do not live in isolation. They are often linked to other interests such as business, labor- or community-based groups, and they will, in these related capacities, attempt to use the party influence to steer the public policy process in one direction or another.[43]

CONCLUSION

Public policy is whatever the government chooses to do or not to do. The question is how government makes these choices. The formal decision-making process that governmental units employ represents only part of the answer. The other part comes from the way society organizes itself to generate the political demands to which the government must respond.

The public policy process in the United States is different from similar processes in other countries because the American political system is different. These differences, initially, stem from the U.S. Constitution, which establishes an elaborate network of checks and balances between the main branches of government, maintains the federal system, and restricts what government at all levels can do. Given that the United States is a pluralistic and geographically diverse country, the public policy process is designed to discourage any group or small number of groups from dominating the process while encouraging a high level of interaction among different individuals, groups, and organizations. In reality, it takes considerable political skill and perseverance to get anything of significance through this process.

The argument of who is able to exercise influence in the process and who is not is unending. The existence of 50 states and some 80,000 units of local government complicates the argument. In the United States, we do not have just one public policy process, but thousands. The literature indicates that society's socioeconomic elites do have an advantage in influencing this process, but they have by no means a monopoly. Influence is highly circumstantial.

The public policy process in the United States is not perfect. Legitimate citizen demands are sometimes sidetracked, whereas the private concerns of special interests are promoted. At the same time, no other society processes the political demands of its citizens as well as the United States. As confusing as it might be, the way the public policy process works in the United States today probably comes very close to what the framers of the Constitution wanted it to be.

NOTES

1. PLANO, Jack C., Milton GREENBERG, Roy OLTON and Robert E. RIGGS (1973) *Political Science Dictionary*. Hinsdale, Ill.: Dryden Press, p. 311.

2. DYE, Thomas (1981) *Understanding Public Policy* (4th ed.). Englewood Cliffs N.J.: Prentice-Hall, p. 1.

3. See James E. ANDERSON (1984) *Public Policy-Making* (3rd ed.). New York: Holt, Rinehart and Winston, Chapter 4.

4. See DYE (1981), op. cit., pp. 2–3.

5. The U.S. Constitution establishes the relationship between the different branches of the federal government. The procedures that the federal government follows come from both the Constitution and from procedures that were adopted early in the Republic's history. For instance, there is no mention in the Constitution of political parties, yet political parties came very quickly to dominate the legislative process. See Everett Carl Ladd (1985) *The American Polity: The People and Their Government*. New York: W.W. Norton, Chapter 5.

6. Interests, as the term is used here and elsewhere, refer to any ideological, economic, social, religious, or any other type of group that wants the government to behave in a way that benefits its interest. See Ladd (1981), op. cit., Chapter 5.

7. WINTER, William O. (1981) *State and Local Government in a Decentralized Republic*. New York: Macmillan, pp. 40–59.

8. Ibid., pp. 60–64.

9. Ibid., pp. 71–76.

10. Areal in this context refers to public policy that affects nearly everyone in a given geographic area.

11. ANDERSON (1981), op. cit., p. 113.

12. Ibid., pp. 113–118.

13. Ibid., pp. 29–33.

14. HAYES, Michael T. (1992) *Incrementalism and Public Policy*. New York: Longman, pp. 54–55.

15. *Mapp* v. *Ohio* 307 U.S. 643 (1961).

16. *Miranda* v. *Arizona* 348 U.S. 436 (1966).

17. ANDERSON (1981), op. cit., p. 118.

18. LINEBERRY, Robert and Ira SHARKANSKY (1978) *Urban Politics and Public Policy* (3rd ed.). New York: Harper and Row, p. 15.

19. EASTON, David "An Approach to the Analysis of Political Systems." *World Politics* (9), (April 1957), pp. 387–400.

20. LINEBERRY and SHARKANSKY (1978), op. cit., pp. 10–12.

21. ANDERSON (1981), op. cit., pp. 57–65.

22. LINEBERRY and SHARKANSKY (1978), op. cit., p. 13.

23. WINTER (1981), op. cit., pp. 295–297.

24. COCHRAN, Clarke E., Lawrence C. MAYER, T. R. CARR and N. Joseph CAYER (1993) *American Public Policy: An Introduction* (4th ed.). New York: St. Martin's Press, pp. 7–10.

25. ANDERSON (1981), op. cit., pp. 15–16.

26. See Floyd HUNTER (1953) *Community Power Structure*. Chapel Hill: University of North Carolina Press; and Robert Dahl (1961) *Who Governs? Democracy and Power in an American City*. New Haven, Conn.: Yale University Press.

27. WINTER (1981), op. cit., pp. 31–34.

28. HOJNACKI, William P. (1977) "Kalamazoo, Michigan and South Bend, Indiana: A Comparative Analysis of Policy Outcomes." Unpublished doctorial dissertation, University of Notre Dame.

29. See Charles M. BONJEAN, Terry N. CLARK, and Robert LINEBERRY (1971) *Community Politics: A Behavioral Approach*. New York: Free Press. This classical anthology looks at a wide range of factors that influence how local units of government process inputs.

30. LADD (1985), op. cit., pp. 351–353.

31. Ibid., p. 356.

32. GRANT, Daniel R., and H. C. NIXON (1982)*State and Local Government in America* (4th ed.). Boston: Allyn and Bacon, pp. 177–183.

33. LADD (1985), op. cit., pp. 360–364.

34. Ibid., pp. 365–368.

35. Ibid., pp. 357–359.

36. As big cities become more pluralistic, surrounding suburbs tend to become more homogeneous.

37. See William A. SCHULTZE (1974) *Urban and Community Politics*. North Scituate, Mass.: Duxbury Press, Chapter 10.

38. Ibid; see also HOJNACKI (1977), op. cit.

39. See Thomas J. SCHOENBAUM (1988) *Waging Peace and War: Dean Rusk in the Truman, Kennedy and Johnson Years*. New York: Simon & Schuster. Rusk, prior to his government service, was the president of the Rockefeller Foundation. Also see Hojnacki, op. cit.

40. SCHULTZE (1974), op. cit., Chapters 4 and 5.

41. MEYERSON, Martin, and Edward C. BANFIELD (1969) "A Machine at Work." In Edward C. Banfield (ed.), *Urban Government: A Reader in Administration and Politics*. New York: Free Press, pp. 169–179.

42. WINTER (1981), op. cit., pp. 115–119.

43. LADD, Everatt Carl, Jr. (1970) *American Political Parties: Social Change and Political Response*. New York: W.W. Norton, pp. 205–228.

QUESTIONS FOR DISCUSSION

1. List and discuss the types of categories of public policy. Provide examples to support your response.

2. Three methods of bypassing governmental decision making are identified by the author. Discuss these methods.

3. How is the policy process influenced? How are partisanship and pluralistic decision making related to this process? In what way are these characteristics evident in your community? Cite examples.

4. Special interest groups may be divided into four different, though overlapping, groups. List and discuss these groups and what role each plays in political power.

5. Although political parties remain an important part of the political landscape, their influence on public policy is largely indirect. Explain.

2

PUBLIC POLICY
AND CRIMINOLOGY
A HISTORICAL AND PHILOSOPHICAL REASSESSMENT

James F. Gilsinan

Saint Louis University

■ ■ ■ ■ ■ ■ ■ ■ ■ ■ ■ ■ ■ ■ ■ ■ ■ ■ ■

This article briefly reviews the history of the relationship between criminological research and public policy in order to explore more fully the nature of the links between social science and policy. A postpositivist critique leads to the conclusion that the distinction between science and policy, fact and value has been overdrawn. This article presents a methodology for accommodating postpositivist thought, thereby linking policy with criminology more effectively. Viewing criminology as part of a policy hermeneutic provides a way of managing the tension involved with a science/policy link that moves beyond the debate among policy pragmatists (Wilson), scientific purists (Cressey), and methodological incrementalists (Gottfredson).

A number of authors have noted the quandary created for criminologists by the seemingly contradictory demands of science and of public policy (Cressey, 1978; Gottfredson, 1982). Wilson (1975) argues that the dilemma is caused by the different goals of science and of policy: the former seeks ultimate causes about which the latter can do little. He goes on to suggest that to be effective, criminal justice researchers must abandon their search for fundamental causal relationships and instead adopt the stance of policy analysts searching for ways to improve system efficiency.

This call for pragmatism has been countered by calls for purity. Cressey (1978), for example, suggests that criminologists would be better off "taking up low paying posts in ivory towers, monasteries, and similar think tanks" and sharpening their scientific skills. This course is preferable to becoming "policy advisors in this repressive war on crime." Yet even this plea does not abandon the hope of influencing policy. Cressey concludes his commentary by noting that if these scientists then produced some reasonable generalizations, "politicians might listen to them, just as politicians listened to Bentham, Beccaria, Voltaire, and even Freud" (189).

James F. Gilsinan. "Public Policy and Criminology: A Historical and Philosophical Reassessment." *Justice Quarterly* 8:(2): 201–206. Reprinted by permission of the Academy of Criminal Justice Sciences.

Cressey's final comment is interesting because three of the four individuals he cites as having influence on policy were not scientists but philosophers or pundits. The fourth, Freud, has been criticized constantly for his lack of scientific method and rigor. This anomaly cautions against an escape to either pure pragmatism or pure science in order to manage the tensions generated by research on criminal justice policy. Both may exist only in myth. To act as if they exist in fact may well prevent the development of sound generalizations that have both scientific and policy significance.

In this article I attempt to move beyond the dichotomous views of theory and policy represented above. I do so by considering theoretical and methodological positions that capture more accurately both the real-world conditions of the policy process and the various ways in which knowledge is actually produced. I then suggest how these positions can be incorporated into an ongoing tradition in criminology, namely, a search for policy relevance.

THE LESSONS OF HISTORY

Although the lessons of history are said to be ambiguous, at least three points become clear from a historical review of criminological theory. First, the concern for policy relevance has been constant. From the incorporation of Beccarian principles into the criminal laws of many European nations (Jones, 1986) through the rejection of the Italian School's reformed penal codes by the Chamber of Deputies under Mussolini (Jones, 1986) to the policy advocacy of American criminologists from Thrasher to Wilson (Gilsinan, 1990), criminological theory has never been confined to the ivory tower.

A second lesson of history is that impacts of policy, both direct and indirect, have occurred because of the work of criminological researchers. To cite only one example, Cloward and Ohlin's (1960) *Delinquency and Opportunity: A Theory of Delinquent Gangs* contained a key idea that led to Lyndon Johnson's War on Poverty and the development of the Office of Economic Opportunity (Sundquist, 1969). The book attempts to integrate two distinct theoretical and policy approaches: Merton's Durkheimian focus on societal pressures that lead to deviance and Sutherland's concentration on social structural features that encourage the selection and evolution of particular forms of criminal conduct (Gilsinan, 1986). Sutherland, in turn, expanded on some of Shaw and McKay's earlier works. The integration of these divergent policy/theory approaches allowed the national government a role in the typically local issues of delinquency and crime control. Income transfers, civil rights laws, and an increase in training and educational support for the economically disadvantaged could expand the legitimate opportunities available, thereby decreasing recourse to illegitimate structures. Such policy prescriptions were anchored in a long tradition of criminological research and theorizing, which Cloward and Ohlin synthesized.

Finally, most of the theoretical explanations of crime and criminal behavior have been subject to severe criticisms regarding their scientific adequacy. This situation has created a seeming paradox. Scientific adequacy appears to constitute neither a necessary nor a sufficient condition for use in policy. Indeed, if one were to compare the policy impacts of the philosophically based criminologists listed by Cressey with those of their modern, "scientifically" oriented counterparts, an inverse relationship would appear to exist between scientific adequacy and policy use.

How can the paradoxes and anomalies of our discipline's history in the realm of public policy be explained? Obviously, the canard that facts always become subservient to ideology in the policy arena is inappropriate because a challenge to scientific adequacy must of necessity challenge the factual basis of many theories. Which "facts" from the various theories would we hold sacrosanct—biological determinism, the poverty-crime link, social learning, opportunity structures? The answer, of course, is none of these. Nor, as several authors have noted (Gottfredson, 1982; Hirschi and Selvin, 1967), does the scientific method require statements of perfection; it requires only statements of probability. Thus biology, poverty, social learning, and opportunity structures may explain some of the variance in crime patterns, some of the time, under particular conditions.

Scientific inadequacy is not synonymous with a nonscientific approach. To confuse the two is to accept the myth of science rather than its practice. By definition, scientific statements are assumed to be inadequate or incomplete; the null hypothesis is rejected only rarely. What may distinguish social science most clearly from laboratory science is that such acceptance or rejection takes place more often in public, in the glare of policy debate and application. This point suggests the need to reconsider the place of policy in the procedures of criminology. A historical review points to a symbiotic relationship that can be broken only at considerable risk to the science elements of criminology. Policy is not simply something on which criminologists advise. Rather, it forms a significant link in the knowledge-generating processes of our science.

The significance of this link has not been appreciated because from Lombroso onward, criminology largely has accepted and participated in the positivist paradigm of knowledge generation. Recent developments in the postpositive and critical literature of science provide a mechanism for integrating policy processes more fully with the processes of knowledge discovery within criminology. We turn to these developments below.

FACTS AND VALUES

Thomas R. Dye (1978) defines public policy simply as "whatever governments choose to do or not to do." The numerous schemes for depicting the elements of science are considerably more complex, but a five-unit framework is common. Scientific theory consists of that which is to be explained (the dependent variables), that which is used to explain (the independent variables), systematic procedures for gathering information (a method), assumptions about the nature of knowledge (epistemological premises), and cultural–political links (persuasive force) (Gilsinan, 1972; Matthews, 1989).

The myth of science stresses the first two elements of the scientific enterprise, creating the illusion of an isomorphic relationship between the articulations of scientific theory and the natural world. Scientific statements therefore are viewed as having denotative meaning—i.e., describing a particular object exactly.

When criminologists approach the policy process with the stance of detached, truth-seeking scientists, the role seemingly advocated by Cressey, they attend only to these first two elements. Moreover, they leave little room for other actors in the policy process (Bozeman and Landsbergen, 1989); thus the "choosing" done by government officials is dictated by an authoritarian rather than a democratic process.

Scientists themselves, when engaging in scientific discourse with others in the field, tend to be concerned with the third element, method. They recognize that apparent findings are subject to the vagaries of the procedures used in discovering them. Thus meaning is connotative as well as denotative in that it points beyond the thing itself to the methods used in understanding it. This is clearly the level at which Gottfredson (1982) approaches the tensions generated by linking policy with criminology. Unfortunately, as pragmatists like Wilson have argued, methodological sophistication and nuances seem to inhibit rather than to encourage the use of scientifically generated knowledge by policy makers, particularly when that knowledge concerns issues of criminal justice.

Philosophers of science focus on the last two elements of theory because they recognize that scientific statements inevitably are enmeshed in a larger web of philosophical, cultural, and political assumptions (Habermas, 1975). Therefore such statements gain meaning not only from their denotative and connotative elements, but also from their relationships with the broader culture. Unfortunately, criminologists often fail to recognize the importance of relational meaning when discussing the management of tensions within criminological practice. Attending specifically to relational meaning as an element of science allows policy applications to be viewed as integral to criminology. For valid criminology, the scientists and the policy analyst must be the same person.

From this perspective, protagonists in the debate on how to manage tensions created by the criminology–policy link share a much greater area of agreement than either they or others might suspect. Both camps—the purists and the pragmatists—accept a fundamental distinction between policy and science. This distinction is a variation on the thirteenth-century problem of double truth, which highlighted the conflict between conclusions based on the natural logic of Aristotle and conclusions based on religious belief (MacClintock, 1967). One solution was to separate the world of logic and fact (the Aristotelian world) from the world of revealed knowledge and dogma. The seeming contradictions between the two then were no longer problematic because each world had different ways of developing and crediting knowledge.

A more recent, secularized version of this distinction has been described as the "separate sphere" doctrine (Hawkesworth, 1988). Simply put, the doctrine describes a fundamental difference between the world of fact and the world of value. The former is knowable through the empirical, observational processes of science; the latter is not. Value premises are not available to scientific manipulation and proof, and therefore are left to the realm of philosophy, ethics, politics, or theology.

This assumption of separate spheres makes the integration of science with policy problematic. Thus, whether science can be useful to policy makers as a means of efficiently furthering particular values (the technological view proffered by Wilson) or as a means of generating new knowledge to counteract the purely political (i.e., irrational) basis of much crime control policy (the "trickle-down" use of science advocated by Cressey), the dilemma remains: How does one speak truth to power (Wildavsky, 1979)? Nor, as noted, is the dilemma resolved by Gottfredson's (1982) call to recognize that scientific statements are always incomplete and subject to the limitations of the methods employed to generate them. Shared assumptions about scientific knowledge as "factual," "verifiable," and capable of "falsification," and about policy as "value-laden," function to place the scientist and the policy maker firmly in two separate worlds, each with its own language and its own methods of warranting what constitutes knowledge.

Developments in postpositive theory suggest that the perception of an immutable, inherent gap between policy and science is the result of an immutable, inherent gap between policy and science is the result of faulty epistemology. Thus Popper (1959) argues that verification is not possible within the positivist paradigm because the observational strategy on which it is based will always be limited. Simply adding observations does not preclude a future in which an observed regularity could be absent. In other words, scientific statements are always incomplete, with no hope of ever being otherwise. Therefore, Guba and Lincoln (1981) have suggested that concerns about external validity and generalizability are overemphasized in social science methods. Generalization is not possible, and all hypotheses are working hypotheses subject to modification in a particular research setting.

Popper attempts to rescue the rational basis of science by relying on falsification as the key scientific method. Yet, as Hawkesworth (1988) demonstrates, falsifiability is also impossible within the positivist paradigm. Any claim of a counter-instance can be refuted by suggesting that the example is not a true counter-instance or is not relevant to the theory being tested. Moreover, examples of falsification themselves can change in the future, and thus at some later time can act in the manner predicted by the theory being tested. Finally, as Kuhn (1970) has shown, scientists are not inclined to abandon theories, regardless of how many counter-instances are discovered.

The debate surrounding the deterrent effect of the death penalty, specifically the use of econometric models for tracking such an effect, illustrates nicely the problematic nature of verification and falsification in practice. Ehrlich (1975) critiqued Sellin's (1959) research on the death penalty by arguing in part that the supposed lack of a deterrent effect is not shown because what was observed was inappropriate to the hypothesis being tested. Sellin focused on a comparison between homicide rates in states with death penalty statutes and those in states without such statutes. Ehrlich instead posited that actual use of the penalty, rather than its statutory presence, is the correct phenomenon to be observed.

Ehrlich's econometric model, which incorporates an imposition factor and which seemingly demonstrates a deterrent effect, was criticized in turn by numerous other scholars (McGahey, 1980). They stated that his model was not a true negation of the original non-deterrence hypothesis because it was based on a number of faulty assumptions, including an overweighting of more recent homicidal rates. In an early response, Ehrlich (1975b) argued that his critics did not understand his model and therefore that their falsifications were not relevant.

This description of verification and falsification in practice, together with the philosophical critiques of the concepts, challenges the notion of separate spheres for fact and for value. Facts are not unmediated images of reality, but are constructed and can be understood only in the context of relational meaning. They are neither denotative nor simply connotative; thus the correspondence theory of truth embedded in the assumptions of the positive paradigm is false. Recent ethnographies of laboratory sciences (Knorr-Centina, 1983) and comparisons between laboratory and social science procedures (Gilsinan and Volpe, 1984) also demonstrate that "facticity" is a construct dependent on the environment in which it emerges. Within this epistemological framework, then, the gap between scientific and policy processes becomes much narrower and requires a reorientation of criminological practice.

IMPLICATIONS FOR PRACTICE

From a review of our own history and recent developments in postpositive thinking, it appears that criminology and public policy are related hermeneutically. Science provides a means of understanding policy issues in a particular way, but at the same time, the very stuff of our science is defined by a set of political, historical, and social contexts that furnish the linguistic and cultural frameworks to make science itself understandable. Criminology has shared and therefore continues to share in the paradox of the hermeneutic circle: in order to bring a scientific understanding to the problem of crime and its control, criminologists already must understand something about crime and its control. This "something" is shaped by policy debates and public (i.e., cultural) understandings, which in turn allow for scientific understandings, which contribute to further public understandings. In short, public policies regarding crime provide the context of meaning that we require in order to grasp meaning more adequately and more scientifically.

Criminology has not been related to public policy vertically, as purists would suggest it should be, nor horizontally, as pragmatists would suggest, but in circular fashion. The implications of this circular relationship for practice can be gathered from the writings of presupposition theorists and from some of the currently applied methods of criminologists and other social scientists.

Presupposition theorists (for example, deHaven-Smith, 1988; Hawkesworth, 1988) substitute a coherence or congruence theory of truth for a correspondence theory. This substitution recognizes that it is possible to make multiple interpretations of the world, of theory, of data, of policy prescriptions without falling into the relativist trap of claiming that all such phenomena have equal truth value. Because the world is partially "out there" and is not simply a subjective projection of our minds, there are rational ways of assessing the relative claims of various theories and/or policies on the basis of experience. To do so, however, requires a conscious effort to traverse the hermeneutic circle. This effort will result in a surfacing of assumptions, of presuppositions which then can be compared logically, and whose implications can be tested empirically. One can relate examples of proofs or counterinstances back to assumptions and their logical derivatives to assess whether they truly represent the phenomenon being tested, the policy goals being articulated, or the program intervention as perceived.

Criminological theory cannot avoid rhetorical terms—that is, the language categories which affect its persuasive powers and provide it with specific, culture-bound meanings. Unfortunately, by ignoring the dimension of relational meaning that forms an element of our science, we tend to leave the construction of the crime problem to others (Barak, 1988). As a result, both pragmatists and purists engage in activity from a considerably weakened scientific base. The "what" to be explained or manipulated is controlled by others. In order to know what "what" we should focus on, a hermeneutical, relational view requires applying as many different rhetorics (theories) as possible to a particular phenomenon. In the first passage around the hermeneutic circle, then, the emphasis is not on eliminating competing explanations of phenomena, but on observing different definitions of problems and different solutions in order to discover their varying impact on both scientific understanding and policy outcomes.

Paris and Reynolds (1983) illustrate this first step by comparing the work of Wilson (1975) with that of Silberman (1978) and articulating the assumptions about crime, human behavior, and the efficacy of various interventions contained in each scholar's thought. They discover that the "what" on which each theory focuses is different; this difference leads in turn to both contrary policy prescriptions and opposing judgments regarding adequate proofs for policy efficacy. The influence of the different "value slopes" in each "theory" therefore demonstrates that the differences between them are more ideological than scientific. Recognizing such ideological components allows the authors to introduce the concept of rational ideology—that is, a coherent system of thought which is underdetermined but is open to contrary proofs, either logical or empirical. They contrast this system with irrational ideologies which are not available to refutation by experience (i.e., they are undetermined) and to scientific theory which is fully determined.

Although I suggested here that the development of scientific theory in the sense of a fully determined body of knowledge is problematic, it is clear that Paris and Reynolds's concept of a rational ideology fits with the epistemology of science for which I argue. Moreover, the concept allows policy and criminology to share a much greater degree of linkage in their processes of knowledge production. The question now becomes "How can the tendency toward irrational ideology be countered?" Clearly, arguments between liberal and conservative criminologists, couched in terms of data and theory without admissions of "value slopes" and ideological commitments, move toward irrational and thus unresolvable ideological debates.

This first passage around the hermeneutic circle reveals the value premises of macro theoretical orientations and policy frameworks, thereby allowing agreement or at least discussion about desirable goals and what will constitute a warrant of their achievement. This process can be illustrated further by considering the different meanings given to the Eighth Amendment phrase "cruel and unusual punishment" in the landmark capital punishment case *Furman* v. *Georgia*.

In 1972 the Supreme Court, by a vote of 5 to 4, declared in *Furman* v. *Georgia* that "the imposition and carrying out of the death penalty...constitutes cruel and unusual punishment in violation of the Eighth and Fourteenth Amendments." The differences between the majority opinion and the dissent hinged on the meanings assigned by each side to the phrase "cruel and unusual."

According to the majority, the world *cruel* was tied to public opinion as expressed by a willingness to inflict the punishment. Thus the term is not interpreted in a fixed historical context but instead is linked to evolving public standards. Justice Brennan, concurring with the majority, writes:

> When an unusually severe punishment is authorized for wide-scale application but not, because of society's refusal, inflicted save in a few instances, the inference is compelling that there is a deep-seated reluctance to inflict it. Indeed, the likelihood is great that the punishment is tolerated only because of its disuse (*Furman:* 384).

Brennan warrants this statement by reference to juries and their decisions. In dissent, Chief Justice Burger agrees that the terms of the Eighth Amendment need to be interpreted in light of evolving standards, but that the measure of the standard is the legislatures:

> There are no obvious indications that capital punishment offends the conscience of society to such a degree that our traditional deference to the legislative judgment must be abandoned (*Furman:* 433).

Because of the two different ways in which "cruel" is defined, one in terms of decisions to impose and the other in terms of decisions to legislate, different kinds of information are used to demonstrate the validity of each position. In this context it is misleading to refer to the exchange as two sides of a single argument.

The participants are linguistically in two different worlds. Therefore no amount of empirical data will suffice to "prove" the validity of one assertion over the other. The same difficulty is apparent when the term *unusual* is considered.

Justice Douglas, in a concurring opinion, also defines the term *unusual* in the context of application, but with the added dimension of selective or arbitrary factors associated with imposition. Thus he writes:

> It would seem to be incontestable that the death penalty inflicted on one defendant is "unusual" if it discriminates against him by reason of his race, religion, wealth, social position, or class, or if it is imposed under a procedure that gives room for the play of such prejudices (*Furman:* 351).

This definition of the term allows for the citing of data dealing with discriminatory application of the penalty. The data so cited consist of statistics showing the existence of ethnic disparity regarding who receives the penalty (see, for example, *Furman:* 357).

The dissent changes the definition of the term slightly, but significantly. "Unusual" is distinguished from "routine"; thus numerical indicators are removed as valid warrants for the unusualness of the punishment. A punishment could be nonroutine and yet usual if it expresses a community sentiment in a particular case. Chief Justice Burger expounds this point:

> Given the general awareness that death is no longer a routine punishment for the crime for which it is made available, it is hardly surprising that juries have been increasingly meticulous in their imposition of the penalty...

> There is no empirical basis for concluding that juries have generally failed to discharge in good faith the responsibility described in Witherspoon—that of choosing between life and death in individual cases according to the dictates of community values (*Furman:* 435–36).

By separating "routine" from "unusual" and adding a dimension of community values to the latter, the dissent has created a linguistic reality that allows the data cited by the majority to prove a point opposite of what was intended. Few applications of the penalty indicate careful decision making, and the presence of any cases resulting in the death penalty affirms a community standard—i.e., something that is not unusual.

Once the linguistic underbrush is cleared, the values underlying each argument are exposed. This dissent values a state's rights approach, preferring to leave to the legislatures the question of the appropriateness of the punishment. Chief Justice Burger notes:

The five opinions in support of the judgment differ in many respects, but they share a willingness to make sweeping factual assertions, unsupported by empirical data, concerning the manner of imposition and effectiveness of capital punishment in this country. Legislatures will have the opportunity to make a more penetrating study of these claims with the familiar and effective tools available to them as they are not to us.

The highest judicial duty is to recognize the limits on judicial power and to permit the democratic processes to deal with matters falling outside of those limits (*Furman:* 445).

The differing judicial philosophies lead to a linguistic structuring of "facts" in a way that negates the possibility of empirical proof for one side or the other in the argument. Therefore calls for better data seldom result in changed positions. This last point is illustrated by a footnote in the Chief Justices' dissent:

To establish that the statutory authorization for a particular penalty is inconsistent with the dictates of the Equal Protection Clause, it is not enough to show how it was applied in the distant past. The statistics that have been referred to us cover periods when Negroes were systematically excluded from jury service and when racial segregation was the official policy in many States. Data of more recent vintage are essential (*Furman:* 436.)

Data of the kind called for were reported in the 1987 decision *McCleskey* v. *Kemp*. By this time, however, such data were considered irrelevant.

Researchers can learn three lessons from this first trip around the hermeneutic circle:

1. Improved data are not germane to the issue at this point; thus warrants of truth value need to be based on logical rather than empirical principles.

2. Criminology as a discipline must pay closer attention to linguistic constructs before attempting any kind of evaluation procedure or application (for other examples of this kind of analysis see Sudnow, 1965; Molotch and Boden, 1985; Manning, 1986; Gilsinan, 1989).

3. Calls for improved data are often symbolic. Thus when such data are forthcoming, value positions and arguments fail to change.

These lessons underscore another paradox of hermeneutic analysis: If empirical data are to be relevant in an argument, the parties first must reach an essential agreement on value premises and linguistic usages. To put it another way, there can be no argument unless there is agreement. Only then can a second trip around the hermeneutic circle prove fruitful.

Chen and Rossi's (1981) "Multi-goal, theory driven" strategy for evaluation represents a hermeneutic approach that begins with a theoretical basis for assessing policy outcomes. This procedure assists in the avoidance of irrational ideological blind spots.

The authors emphasize the advantage of such an approach for both utilitarian and theoretical concerns:

Certainly both social science and policy are better served by the ability of the completed evaluation to decide among competing understandings of the social problems or treatments involved. *Hence, all the outcomes deemed possible by social science theory and knowledge should constitute the pool out of which outcomes are to be selected for evaluation testing* (p. 46; emphasis mine).

This use of theory avoids the problems inherent in adopting a single theoretical stance or, worse, an atheoretical stance when assessing policy interventions. It also provides a means for moving a policy argument beyond ideologically mired discussions of data. This point can be illustrated by further review of uses of data by the Supreme Court in decisions on capital punishment.

In *Gregg* v. *Georgia*, Justice Stewart wrote as follows for the majority:

> Statistical attempts to evaluate the worth of the death penalty as a deterrent to crimes by potential offenders have occasioned a great deal of debate. The results simply have been inclusive…

> Although some of the studies suggest that the death penalty may not function as a significantly greater deterrent than lesser penalties, there is no convincing empirical evidence either supporting or refuting this view…

> The value of capital punishment as a deterrent to crime is a complex factual issue the resolution of which properly rests with the legislatures, which can evaluate the results of statistical studies in terms of their own local conditions and with a flexibility of approach that is not available to the courts (*Gregg*: 2930–2931).

If we assume that the call to resolve the complexity of the deterrence issue is sincere, the approach suggested by Chen and Rossi is appropriate. Social science theory generates a number of possible outcomes resulting from the imposition of the penalty. Deterrence, as typically defined, would constitute only one of these outcomes. Other related possibilities would include an increase in the homicide rate due to identification with the executioner rather than with the executed (Bowers and Pierce, 1980), increases or decreases in prison violence around the time of an execution, increases or decreases in staff discontent, increases or decreases in emotional trauma for the surviving victim, and so on. One could even test the legislators' knowledge and ability regarding research data and could examine the decision-making process by which legislators chose to reenact the death penalty after *Furman* (Toder, 1983).

In the final journey around the hermeneutic circle, the most promising theories would be subject to testing through the creation and/or evaluation of a specific program application. Daniel Glaser (1980) demonstrated how this could be done.

Glaser, applying Sutherland's different association theory, reevaluated delinquency programs that were based on individual or group therapy "talk" models of intervention. By classifying participants according to theoretical rather than demographic or administrative categories, Glaser demonstrated that previously "ineffective programs" in fact had an effect, and in the direction predicted by the theory. For example, individual counseling and psychotherapy programs were most effective for young adults whose criminal careers were not well advanced, particularly when such programs fostered anticriminal definitions through vocational guidance.

Glaser's work underscores two important concepts. First, it provides a model of practice whereby theory and application (i.e., policy) can work in consort. Unfortunately,

because relatively little work has been done at the first level of hermeneutic analysis, successful treatment programs are not easily warranted as obtaining desirable outcomes.

Second, Glaser's work shows how criminologists must be critical of the categories of clients typically available in policy interventions. Demographic and administrative eligibility criteria should not necessarily constitute the categories used to assess program performance. These categories should come from theory, particularly if the theories themselves have been assessed and flow from the second level of hermeneutic analysis.

SUMMARY AND CONCLUSION

Criminal justice researchers are engaging increasingly in ideological debates about their proper role in policy. These debates, however, are couched in theoretical and research categories that cloud rather than enlighten the premises under which the proponents labor. Thus, the discipline moves toward an undetermined ideology—that is, an ideology unchangeable by argument based on experience or logic.

Through the systematic articulation of value premises and the recognition that criminological theory is an example of an underdetermined or rational ideology, the gap between policy and the practice of social science can be narrowed considerably. This recognition in turn will lead us to appreciate how the discipline has been part of a policy hermeneutic. Thus our history can be recognized as one in which the public exposure and debate of ideas has forced a sharpening of definitions, procedures, and conclusions. This history has tended, however, to be interpreted within a framework of mythic science, in which earlier theories simply are decried for their scientific inadequacy. Little attention has been paid to their contribution to policy, and in turn to how policy applications have contributed to the discipline's development. At this point, past failures highlighted by public exposure seem to be propelling the discipline toward the making of oversimplified choices.

Criminology, however, provides neither an ivory tower nor a pragmatic bureaucracy to which to escape because historically each has been intertwined inexorably with the other. To leave the control of relational meaning solely to politicians or to leave denotative and connotative meaning solely to persons isolated from the culture in which their knowledge is to be applied is to abandon a tradition that has encompassed both policy relevance and scientific advancement.

REFERENCES

BARAK, GREGG (1988) "Newsmaking Criminology: Reflections on the Media, Intellectuals, and Crime." *Justice Quarterly* 5 (4):564–587.

BOWERS, WILLIAM J. and GLENN L. PIERCE (1980) "Deterrence or Brutalization: What Is the Effect of Executions?" *Crime and Delinquency* 26 (4):453–484.

BOZEMAN, BARRY and DAVID LANDSBERGEN (1989) "Truth and Credibility in Sincere Policy Analysis: Alternative Approaches for the Production of Policy-Relevant Knowledge." *Evaluation Review* 13 (4):355–379.

CHEN, AUEY-TSYH and PETER H. ROSSI (1981) "The Multi-Goal, Theory Drive Approach to Evaluation: A Model Linking Basic and Applied Social Science." In H. E. Freeman and M. A. Solomon (eds.), *Evaluation Studies Review Annual*, Vol. 6. Beverly Hills, Calif.: Sage.

CLOWARD, RICHARD A. and LLOYD E. OHLIN (1960). *Delinquency and Opportunity: A Theory of Delinquent Danger*. New York: The Free Press.

CRESSEY, DONALD R. (1978) "Criminological Theory, Social Science, and the Repression of Crime." *Criminology* 16 (2):171–191.

DE HAVEN-SMITH, LANCE (1988) *Philosophical Critiques of Policy Analysis: Lindblom, Haberman, and the Great Society*. Gainesville: University of Florida Press.

DYE, Thomas R. (1978) *Understanding Public Policy*. 3rd ed. Englewood Cliffs, N.J.: Prentice Hall.

EHRLICH, ISAAC (1975) "The Deterrent Effect of Capital Punishment: A Question of Life and Death." *American Economic Review* (June): 397–417.

_____ (1975b) "Deterrence: Inference and Evidence." *Yale Law Journal* (December): 209–227.

GILSINAN, JAMES F. (1972) "Symbolic Interactionism and Ethnomethodology: A Comparison." *Rocky Mountain Social Science Journal* 10 (1):73–93.

_____ (1986) "Book Review of Miller and Ohlin, *Delinquency and Community: Creating Opportunities and Controls.*" *Journal of Criminal Law and Criminology* 77 (2):481–484.

_____ (1989) "They Is Clowning Tough: 911 and the Social Construction of Reality." *Criminology* 27 (2):329–344.

_____ (1990) *Criminology and Public Policy: An Introduction*. Englewood Cliffs, N.J.: Prentice Hall.

GILSINAN, JAMES F. and L. CARL VOLPE (1984) "Do Not Cry Wolf Until You Are Sure: The Manufactured Crisis in Evaluation Research." *Policy Sciences* 17:179–191.

GLASER, D. (1980) "The Interplay of Theory, Issues, Policy and Data." In M. Klein and K. Teilmann (eds.), *Handbook of Criminal Justice Evaluation*. Beverly Hills, Calif.: Sage, pp. 123–142.

GOTTFREDSON, MICHAEL R. (1982) "The Social Scientist and Rehabilitative Crime Policy." *Criminology* 20 (1):29–42.

GUBA, E. and LINCOLN, Y. (1981) *Effective Evaluation*. San Francisco: Jossey-Bass.

HABERMAS, JURGEN (1975) *The Legitimation Crisis*. Boston: Beacon.

HAWKESWORTH, M. (1988) *Theoretical Issues in Policy Analysis*. Albany: State University of New York Press.

HIRSCHI, TRAVIS and H. SELVIN (1967) *Principles of Survey Analysis*. New York: Free Press.

JONES, DAVID A. (1986) *History of Criminology: A Philosophical Perspective*. Westport, Conn.: Greenwood.

KNORR-CENTINA, K. D. (1983) "New Developments in Science Studies: The Ethnographic Challenge." *Sociology* 16:153–177.

KUHN, THOMAS (1970) *The Structure of Scientific Revolutions*. Chicago: University of Chicago Press.

MACCLINTOCK, STUART (1967) "Averroism." In Paul Edwards (ed.), *The Encyclopedia of Philosophy*. Vol. 1. New York: Macmillan, pp. 223–226.

MANNING, PETER F. (1986) "Signwork." *Human Relations* 39:283–308.

MATTHEWS, FRÈD (1989) "Social Scientists and the Culture Concept, 1930–1950: The Conflict between Processual and Structural Approaches." *Sociological Theory* 7 (1):87–101.

McGahey, Richard M. (1980) "Dr. Erhlich's Magic Bullet: Econometric Theory, Econometrics, and the Death Penalty." *Crime and Delinquency* 26 (4):485–502.

Molotch, Harvey and D. Boden (1985) "Talking Social Structures." *American Sociological Review* 50:273–288.

Paris, David C. and J. Reynolds (1983) *The Logic of Policy Inquiry*. New York: Longmans.

Popper, Karl (1959) *The Logic of Scientific Discovery*. New York: Basic Books.

Sellin, Thorsten (1959) *The Death Penalty*. Philadelphia: American Law Institute.

Silberman, Charles (1978) *Criminal Violence, Criminal Justice*. New York: Random House.

Sudnow, David (1965) "Normal Crimes: Sociological Features of the Penal Code in a Public Defender's Office." *Social Problems* 12:255–276.

Sunquist, James L. (1969) "Origins of the War on Poverty," in *On Fighting Poverty*, J. Sunquist, ed. New York: Basic Books, pp. 11–12, 29–30.

Toder, Harry (1983) "Capital Punishment Legislation in Missouri." Unpublished doctoral dissertation, Saint Louis University.

Wildavsky, Aaron (1979) *Speaking Truth to Power: The Art and Craft of Policy Analysis*. Boston: Little, Brown.

Wilson, James O. (1975) *Thinking about Crime*. New York: Basic Books.

CASES

Furman v. *Georgia* 408 U.S. 238 (1972).

McCleskey v. *Kemp* 107 S. Ct. 1756 (1987).

Gregg v. *Georgia* 428 U.S. 169 (1976).

QUESTIONS FOR DISCUSSION

1. Gilsinan notes that there are seemingly contradictory demands of science and public policy. What are these demands? Cite examples to support your response.

2. There are at least three ways, historically, that public policy has been influenced by criminological theory. What are these? Cite examples, from your reading, to support your response.

3. Some have assumed that the methods of scientific inquiry and formulating public policy are not reconcilable. Gilsinan believes that they are reconcilable. Why?

4. "Criminology has not been related to public policy vertically, as purists would suggest it should be, or horizontally, as pragmatists would suggest, but in circular fashion." Explain. Cite examples to support your response.

5. How did Glaser's study of differential association (1980) demonstrate how criminology and public policy could complement each other in addressing issues of crime?

3

SCIENCE, PUBLIC POLICY, AND THE CAREER PARADIGM

Michael Gottfredson
Travis Hirschi
University of Arizona

■ ■

The career model reappears with some consistency in the history of criminology. It consistently fails, however, to organize the facts about crime in a meaningful way. As a consequence, we predict that criminology will once again abandon career models in favor of theories of crime.

Research in the 1970s confirmed, for example, the existence of the career criminal. Following up on this important insight the Institute supported surveys to gauge the impact of the high-rate offender on crime and criminal justice operations. From this basic knowledge came the idea of focusing criminal justice resources selectively on the career criminals. Today, the concept of the career criminal is entrenched in criminal justice—a dramatic rethinking of policy and practice. Now research is examining ways to identify these offenders more accurately, moving toward the recommendation of one recent study that concluded that public safety would clearly benefit from incarcerating a larger proportion of high-risk probations and prisoners, and for longer periods of time. (James K. Stewart, director, National Institute of Justice, 1987: iii).

Our paper, "The True Value of Lambda Would Appear to be Zero" (Gottfredson and Hirschi, 1986), sought to "introduce some small degree of tension into [an] otherwise complacent system" that had, we thought, "limited thinking about crime to the repetition of pretentious slogans," ignored research contrary to its assumptions, and proposed to lead public policy about crime in the wrong direction. We were concerned, too, that important theoretical traditions in criminology and even the social scientific approach to crime itself were being demeaned by the career paradigm. Our paper, "The Methodological Adequacy of Longitudinal Research on Crime" (Gottfredson and Hirschi, 1987a), argued that the popularity of the longitudinal study was not justified on methodological grounds and that it in fact reflected the narrow conceptual stance of the career paradigm. Our analysis of selective incapacitation, the policy often used to justify career research, likewise found this policy to be without empirical or considered theoretical support (Gottfredson and Hirschi, 1988).

The response by Alfred Blumstein, Jacqueline Cohen, and David Farrington (this volume) does little to reduce the concerns expressed in our papers. On the contrary, it pays little attention to the substance of our views, and it largely repeats the distinctions and even the figures and tables that have come to be associated with the career paradigm. Moreover, it continues the tradition of ignoring research whose conclusions argue against application of career terminology.

In this paper, we try to explain better why we believe that scientific criminology and sound public policy should reject the career approach to crime. Because we have dealt before with research design and policy issues, we consider here the conceptual foundation of the criminal careers paradigm and its implications for theory and analysis. In doing so, we try to avoid a blow-by-blow response to the details of Blumstein et al.'s defense of career research.[1]

THE CAREER MODEL AND ITS PARAMETERS

Whether applied to dentistry, college teaching, or crime, the concept of a career implies several things. It suggests a beginning, as in "When did you become a teacher?", and an end, as in "When did you quit teaching?" Given a beginning and an end, the career concept also implies variable duration or length, as in "How long did you (or how much longer do you plan to) teach?" Once given, careers may be characterized along many dimensions, such as area of specialization (for example, logic and the scientific method), amount of time and effort devoted to them (half time), level of accomplishment (professor) productivity (.19 article a year), current direction (down), overall shape (peaked early), and time out for other activities (sabbatical, administration, jail). Once the decision to apply career terminology has been made, it is relatively straightforward to construct a career model and to outline the research necessary to estimate its "parameters" (see Blumstein and Cohen, 1987: Fig. 2; Blumstein et al., 1978, 1986: Fig. 1-1).

In our view, the concept of a *career* is not particularly problematic, and we have no quarrel with its application to dentists and professors. The question here is not whether career implies beginning, middle, end, and a minimum level of activity, it is whether the concept is applicable in some positive way to the study of crime. As far as we can see, Blumstein et al. do not bring to the career concept meanings derived from a conception of crime or a theory of criminality. Rather, they simply announce a decision to apply it to crime. The wisdom of this decision must be judged by its consequences.

When the Gluecks introduced career terminology, the idea appeared to have potential merit. In the 1930s, it was reasonable to guess that individual offenders might engage in more serious crimes or at least in more specialized crimes as they grew older. In the 1930s, it was reasonable to assume that concepts of onset, duration, and desistance might lead to better understanding of the crime problem. Not that the Gluecks had much choice in the matter. In the early days, they were stuck with samples restricted to offenders. Following offenders over time and wondering about their "careers" was one way to escape the clearly unacceptable one-shot case study design implicit in their sampling procedure. (The absence of a control group continues to plague career methodology, and the solution adopted today is that adopted by the Gluecks—that is, to produce variation in the dependent variable by following the same people over time.)

Fifty years later, it is not reasonable to wonder whether individual offenders engage in progressively more serious offenses as they grow older. Research on the topic shows that they do not (for example, Glueck and Glueck, 1940, 1968). It is not now reasonable to assume that offenders tend to specialize in particular types of crime. Research shows that they do not (for example, Blumstein and Cohen, 1979: 585; Hindelang et al., 1981; Wolfgang et al., 1972: 163). It is no longer possible to suggest that partitioning offenders into juveniles and adults makes fresh and meaningful the specialization question. It does not (Glueck and Glueck, 1968: Ch. 14). It is no longer possible to assert that these questions have been ignored. They have not.

So, the suggestion that criminology comes to these questions *de novo*, without benefit of prior experience, prepared only to absorb important breakthroughs soon to be made possible by the career paradigm, is no longer fresh. On the contrary, it ignores 50 years of research addressed precisely to the questions it raises. Put briefly, we see no *empirical* support for the view that the time has come to apply career terminology to the study of crime.

Conceptually, the situation is no better. Serious, direct efforts to apply career concepts to crime are, in our view, discouraging, to say the least (see, especially, Wootton, 1959: Ch. 5). Nonetheless, we have tried to understand the meaning of the large body of data gathered with these concepts in mind (Hirschi and Gottfredson, 1983). Our conclusions from this effort have not been addressed by Blumstein and his colleagues. They have, however, been considered by others. For example, David Greenberg (1985: 1–2), in an article otherwise critical of our point of view, says this about our discussion of "onset":

> They provide a new interpretation of what the delinquency literature calls "early age of onset." Noting the existence of a strong negative correlation between age of first involvement in delinquency and the frequency and severity of delinquent acts in later years, several investigators have suggested that early onset leads to deeper, continuing involvement [citations omitted]. Hirschi and Gottfredson point out that if all groups share a common age distribution, young offenders will be disproportionately drawn from those groups whose level of involvement is high, as is true of older offenders. Thus no special explanation of age of onset is needed, beyond that of why some groups have higher levels of involvement in crime than others.

As Greenberg notes, our model accounts for "desistance" and "persistence" as well as "onset," and thus it accounts for all of the parameters of the career model. In doing so, it denies the validity of the career concept as applied to crime.

We have never considered the career parameter question conceptually simple, as our earlier discussion (Hirschi and Gottfredson, 1983: 573–579) will attest, nor has the field (see, again, Wootton, 1959: Ch. 5). But logical criticism of the career concept (see Hirschi, 1969: Ch. 4) is now coupled with a direct, parsimonious, and consistent alternative interpretation of the meaning of its parameters. Add to this research results inconsistent with expectations derived from the career model, and it seems to us that an especially heavy conceptual and empirical burden falls on those who would urge continued exploration of career parameters.

The substantive and statistical distinctions of the career model are not new. Nor do they appear to have been productive of insight in their earlier incarnations. (The Gluecks, given credit by Blumstein and his colleagues for introducing the career idea to criminology, made little use of career terminology in their later, better, and more influential works [Glueck and Glueck, 1950, 1968].) It appears that the ability to import a model and make distinctions (disaggregate, decompose) based on it should not be confused with evidence for the specific value of the model in question. With this thought in mind, we will apply the career distinctions introduced by Blumstein and his colleagues to data and thereby illustrate their potential contribution to an understanding of the nature of crime.

THE EMPIRICAL STATUS OF THE PARTICIPATION–FREQUENCY DISTINCTION

The concept of a career leads to interest in factors affecting career choice or entry. Once entry has been addressed, attention shifts to differences among those within the career itself. As applied to crime, the career concept leads one to focus on the differences between those who commit at least one criminal act and those who do not (called "participation" by Blumstein et al.), and on differences in criminal activity among those active in crime during a particular period (called "lambda" or "frequency"). To justify this distinction, Blumstein et al. assert that the correlates of participation *may* be different from the correlates of lambda.

Before examining new data on the distinctions introduced by the career model, let us consider their logical status. Standard research determines the offensivity of people by counting the number of criminal acts they have committed in a specified period. The aim is to account for variation in the measure of offensivity. Ordinarily, researchers assume that the causes of one offense are the same as the causes of others, that is, that "crime" or "criminality" is a continuous variable. (They of course need not assume that the difference between 20 and 30 acts is 10 times greater than the difference between 2 acts and 3.) They also typically assume that the causal system producing offensivity is likely to remain stable over time unless acted upon by an outside force. Such assumptions have well-known statistical and theoretical advantages and are susceptible to direct, meaningful tests. Researchers vary in where they draw the line between offenders and nonoffenders, and in how many levels of offenders they wish to acknowledge. The actual decisions on these issues are typically guided by inspection of the data and by previous research. Measurement decisions thus depend on the research question, the method of measurement, and the frequency of the offense in the population at issue. As a result they are made prior to examination of the data only with great risk. (Therefore, Blumstein et al.'s pronouncement of the *possibility* of a distinction among measures of crime is not proof of the utility of the distinction.)

The data we use are from the Richmond Youth Project (Hirschi, 1969), which collected police records and self-report data on 2,587 males and self-report data on females. The official data are counts of offenses recorded in police files, whatever the subsequent disposition of the case. The large sample and the large number and seriousness of the offenses recorded and reported are sufficient to allow examination of the major parameters of the career model.[2]

These data include the full range of offenders and nonoffenders typically of interest to criminologists, rather than a sample selected for its relevance to the career model. (In the data presented by Blumstein and Cohen, 1979, and again by Blumstein et al., 1986, there is reason to fear that sampling procedures are responsible for the results; see Gottfredson and Hirschi, 1986.) We can therefore use them to test the value of the distinctions advocated by Blumstein et al. to criminology as a whole.

These distinctions are illustrated with actual data in Table 1. Column 1 represents the number of offenses committed by males in the sample. This column, commonly called a "frequency distribution," is, in career terminology, "incidence" (I). Blumstein et al. would decompose this distribution on the grounds that it *may* be misleading. Following their logic, column 2 divides the sample into two groups, those who have and those who do not have a recorded offense. In career terms again, this distribution is called "participation" (P). Participation is said by Blumstein et al. to be of interest in prevention or in theories of deviance or trivial offending but to have little value in research focused on the effects of criminal justice policy.

Column 3 shows the distribution of offenses among those who have committed offenses—"frequency" (F) or lambda (λ). The central distinction of the career model can thus be represented by the formula: $F = I$, where $I \geq 1$, or $P \neq \varnothing$. The difference between the two measures is that one includes the value $\varnothing$, nonoffenders, while the other does not. Where interest centers on the causes of the difference between $\varnothing$'s (nonoffenders) and any other number (offenders, however defined), lambda does not apply (as implied by the title of our paper critical of this measure).

At the bottom of column 3, we divide the number of offenses (3,067) by the number of offenders (957) to produce an oft-mentioned lambda, the average number of offenses per active offender, for the sample as a whole (3.2). Since lambda is advocated because it allows study of *individual* offenders, the frequent focus on this average lambda is puzzling. If the lambda of interest must vary from individual to individual, we compute such a lambda by counting the number of offenses committed by each offender during the reference period by dividing by 1. Since column 3 lists the number of offenses committed by offenders, it provides the requisite information. Those with scores of 2 have a lambda of 2, those with scores of 3 have a lambda of 3, and so on. The reader will note that individual lambdas are also found in column 1 when nonoffenders are removed.

Our procedure uses the number of offenses committed by an offender during a specific period to estimate the number of offenses he or she has committed during that period. Blumstein et al. appear to suggest that lambda is more esoteric or arcane than our procedure would imply. If, after all, lambda is nothing more than an offense count—even if calculated separately for crime "types"—it would hardly seem to justify its own research agenda, let alone radical restructuring of criminology. What, then, do Blumstein et al. have in mind?

Note that in their rejoinder, Blumstein et al. use *our* definition of lambda as an *average* number of criminal acts for all offenders during a specified time period. Note, too, that the lambdas accepted and calculated by Blumstein et al. are also averages that apply to all offenders in the sample at a particular age. In contrast, our lambdas in Table 1 are disaggregated, individual-level measures, the level of measurement said to justify lambda in the first place. It turns out the lambdas reported in the literature are group means that *ignore* individual variability (Blumstein and Cohen, 1979; Blumstein et al., 1986). These lambdas are often a function of shifts in the definition of the sample (see Blumstein et al., Table 1) or of artifactual methods of counting (see Gottfredson and Hirschi, 1986: note 5). Although constants describing groups may have theoretical and policy significance, we would not grant those created by sorting and sifting samples the status of scientifically discovered and generally applicable laws.

Another "career parameter" often mentioned by those endorsing the perspective is the seriousness of the crimes counted. Robbery, burglary, and assault are cited as being of

TABLE 1   MEASURES OF INCIDENCE (I), PARTICIPATION (P), AND FREQUENCY (λ) BY OFFENSE TYPE AND SOURCE OF DATA (MALES AGED 13–18, RICHMOND, CALIFORNIA)

| | Official Records | | | | | |
| | All Offenses | | | Serious Offenses[a] | | |
Number of Offenses	I	P	(λ)	I	P	(λ)
0	1,630	1,630	—	2,280	2,280	—
1	396	957	396	214	307	214
2	211	—	211	41	—	41
3	111	—	111	33	—	33
4	66	—	66	5	—	5
5	49	—	49	6	—	6
6 or more	124	—	124	8	—	8
Total Sample	2,587	2,587	957	2,587	2,587	307
Total Offenses/ Offenders	3,067	957	3,067	509	307	509
Mean	1.19	.37	3.20	.20	.12	1.66

| | Official Records | | | Self-Reports[b] | | |
| | Theft | | | | | |
	I	P	(λ)	I	P	(λ)
0	2,220	2,220	—	724	724	
1	232	367	232	643	1,757	643
2	73	—	73	482	—	482
3	23	—	23	343	—	343
4	18	—	18	171	—	171
5	6	—	6	79	—	79
6 or more	15	—	15	39	—	39
Total Sample	2,587	2,587	367	2,481	2,481	1,757
Total Offenses/ Offenders	660	367	660	3,949	1,757	3,949
Mean	.26	.14	1.80	1.59	.71	2.25

[a]Robbery, burglary, assault (see Hirschi, 1969: 298–99).

[b]Six-item scale, with reference period "ever." Responses coded "yes" or "no" (see Hirschi, 1969: 54–62).

particular interest to this perspective. Column 4 thus lists the count of these offenses for the sample as a whole. Obviously, this count, too, can be transformed without difficulty into its participation and lambda equivalents (columns 5 and 6).

Before subdividing further the distribution of crime, let us examine the consequences of the distinctions already introduced for the correlates of crime. Those familiar with the statistical implications of restricting the range of the dependent variable for correlation coefficients can predict the results of this exercise. They will be impressed if the career paradigm is sufficiently strong to shine through statistical tendencies to the contrary. They will also be impressed if the career paradigm successfully predicts *for no theoretical reason* results contrary to established statistical tendencies.

Table 2 depicts 7 common correlates[3] and their relation to 12 measures of crime based on distinctions used by Blumstein and his colleagues to justify the career paradigm. Crime is measured first with official records (columns 1–9) and then with self-reports (columns 10–12). The number of cases on which the correlations are based varies from measure to measure (the range of sample sizes is shown at the bottom of each column). (Sex is shown only for self-report data.) Pearson's r and gamma are reported for each comparison. (Unless otherwise noted, Pearson's correlations in the table are significant at the .05 level. The sample is described in Table 1.)

Inspection of the correlations in Table 2 yields two conclusions: First, they are substantively the same from one career measure to another. Contrary to Blumstein et al.'s predictions, and to the general thrust of the career model and its stated research agenda, the researcher could here focus on incidence, participation, or even on lambda and its various definitions without concern.

We grant variation in the correlation coefficients in Table 2. We assert only that the direction, pattern, and relative magnitude of the correlations are much the same for all measures. In general, then, and decidedly contrary to the predictions of the career "paradigm," substantive conclusions about the causes and correlates of crime in Table 2 do not depend on career distinctions. Second, there is one important, easily predictable limitation to our conclusion: Generally, as one moves from participation to frequency to lambda to serious lambda, the correlations become smaller, eventually approaching insignificance as sample sizes also decline. Both problems are especially marked for "serious lambdas." The conclusion is inescapable: The career paradigm would have us pursue ever smaller correlations based on ever-smaller sample sizes, with nothing but a statistical test to tell us whether the results are meaningful.

If we ask, "Would researchers studying *participation* measures be misled about the correlates of lambda?" the answer would be "no." In other words, to the extent this research is generalizable (and the findings of Table 2 are among the most heavily replicated in the field), findings based on standard measures are fully applicable to "active offenders," "serious offenders," "career criminals," and indeed to all of the categories and types of offenders said to be worthy of special study by advocates of the career model. Advocates of this model, thus, have no reason to question the relevance of prior research to questions of the utility and validity of their own "paradigm."

Prior research agrees with Table 2 that the correlates of crime are robust over method of measurement, crime types, crime seriousness, and even limitations of range. In fact, substantial consensus on the basic correlates of crime has developed in the face of considerable dispute about their theoretical meaning. This seems to us to place a heavy burden on those who argue that the correlates of crime depend on distinctions among incidence, prevalence, and frequency. Thus if Blumstein et al. (1986: 67–76) wish to argue that the correlations of race, sex, and age with *participation* differ from their correlations with *frequency*, it seems only reasonable to ask them to explain in some detail why their research appears contrary to

TABLE 2   CORRELATIONS (PEARSON'S R AND GAMMA) BETWEEN OUTSIDE VARIABLES AND INCIDENCE (I), PARTICIPATION (P), AND FREQUENCY (λ) MEASURES OF CRIME (RICHMOND YOUTH PROJECT DATA)

		Official Records					
		All Offenses			*Serious Offenses*		
Outside	*Variable*	*I*	*P*	*(λ)*	*I*	*P*	*(λ)*
Race	r	.21	.25	.16	.17	.20	.10
	gamma	.46	.51	.24	.57	.58	.16
Smoke	r	.21	.25	.15	.14	.16	.06*
	gamma	.47	.52	.28	.47	.48	.21
Drink	r	.20	.23	.16	.14	.16	.09*
	gamma	.44	.48	.16	.46	.47	.26
Date	r	.14	.21	.07	.10	.11	.10*
	gamma	.38	.42	.10	.34	.34	.32
GPA	r	−.21	−.28	−.13	−.15	−.18	−.07*
	gamma	−.35	−.38	−.17	−.36	−.37	−.10
Friends	r	.21	.26	.14	.15	.16	.15
Picked Up	gamma	.37	.41	.21	.37	.38	.30
Number of Cases		1,858–	1,858–	699–	1,858–	1,858–	206–
		2,587	2,587	957	2,587	2,587	307

		Official Records			*Self-Reports*		
		Theft					
		I	*P*	*(λ)*	*I*	*P*	*(λ)*
Race	r	.24	.27	.19	.04	.02*	.04
	gamma	.67	.67	.42	.06	.03	.08
Smoke	r	.16	.15	.17	.35	.23	.30
	gamma	.42	.42	.27	.51	.58	.44
Drink	r	.16	.15	.15	.41	.26	.36
	gamma	.42	.43	.15	.60	.69	.51
Date	r	.11	.11	.12	.29	.22	.22
	gamma	.31	.31	.22	.40	.46	.34
GPA	r	−.13	−.14	−.11	−.15	−.10	−.13
	gamma	−.27	−.28	−.18	−.14	−.15	−.12
Friends	r	.16	.18	.10	.43	.29	.36
Picked Up	gamma	.38	.39	.13	.46	.53	.39
Number of Cases		1,858–	1,858–	250–	1,784–	1,784–	1,274–
		2,587	2,587	367	2,481	2,481	1,757
Sex	r				.28	.25	.21
	gamma				.48	.51	.43
Number of Cases					2,201	2,201	1,370

Note: The three measures of crime are defined and their distributions shown in Table 1.

*Correlation not significant at .05 level.

the vast body of criminological research on these topics. We have attempted to show (in our 1986 paper) how particular artifacts of the Blumstein and Cohen design could lead to the conclusion that frequency (as they define it) has no correlates. (Clearly, if frequency is constructed as a constant for all members of the sample, it can have no correlates.) Similarly, we have offered theoretical reasons to expect the correlates of frequency and participation to be the same. In this respect, we are not alone. In our reading, virtually all theoretical traditions in criminology assume that "criminals" are subject to the same causal forces as "noncriminals." In our reading, the time has gone when criminology would look for features unique to the criminal to explain his or her behavior.

If we ask, "Would researchers who prefer self-report measures be misled by the comparisons in Table 2?" the answer would again be "no." We note that the data in Table 2 are also unkind to a "serious crime" emphasis; the table shows that all offenses are more predictable than the so-called serious offenses. Of course, the pattern of correlations is again much the same, which suggests that serious offenses are simply a subset of all offenses. (It may, for some purposes, sound better to engage in the study of serious offenders, but such purposes should not be confused with the purposes of science.)

We could continue making distinctions in the dependent variable, subdividing it by "crime type," for example. Ordinary research procedure would not, however, recommend further division since the distinctions already in the table have proved to be inconsequential—with, if anything, a slight tendency to mislead about the correlates of "crime." (Note that the "theft" correlates behave identically to those already discussed.) We make this point to show that criminology is capable of disaggregation without the career model and that science is not necessarily on the side of disaggregation or of those who blame the field's *alleged* lack of knowledge on its failure to conduct "crime-type" analyses: "The traditional approach is also deficient because crime is dealt with as a unitary phenomenon without distinguishing the diverse ways in which causal factors might affect individual offenders" (Blumstein and Cohen, 1987: 985). Rather than castigating the field for failure to attend to individual offenders and offenses, it would be more constructive for Blumstein and Cohen to provide empirical examples of the advantages of their point of view.

Interestingly, Blumstein et al. summarize our point of view as a testable hypothesis that turns out to be consistent with Table 2: "If they [Gottfredson and Hirschi] are right, all criminal career features will be interrelated, and the correlates and predictors of participation, for example, will have to be the same as the correlates and predictors of frequency and career length." At the same time, they summarize their own point of view as a testable hypothesis that turns out to be inconsistent with the data in Table 2. "In the criminal career approach, by contrast, the different criminal career features can each have different correlates and predictors and they are not necessarily interrelated" (p. 5).

AGE AND CRIME

Fundamental to our concern with the career paradigm and its implications is the relation between age and crime (Hirschi and Gottfredson, 1983). We earlier mentioned the logical implications of a relation between age and crime for the parameters of the paradigm, implications that do not depend on the validity of our invariance thesis. This point is obscured by defenders of the career paradigm (see Farrington, 1986, and the virtually identical discussion in Blumstein et al., this volume: 8–14), who apparently see in the invariance issue a device for deflecting attention from the implications for their work of the *current* age distribution of crime in the United States. It would be more constructive for them to attend to the logical and statistical problems introduced by this distribution than to the invariance thesis, a thesis that is not necessary to falsify the career hypothesis. However, since the invariance thesis has been raised by Blumstein et al., we are happy to defend it once again.

For a critique of the standard theoretical explanations of the age effect summarized by Farrington (1986), we refer the reader to our earlier work (Hirschi and Gottfredson, 1983, 1986). Our point then and now is simply that criminology is better off when it stops pretending it has explained correlations it has not explained. The empirical challenge to our invariance thesis has come down to a search for statistical variation in the age distribution of crime with respect to such things as mode, level, or skew. As conducted by Blumstein et al. (and by Farrington, 1986), this search is unguided by theoretical purpose. As a result, it tends to lead to the improper conclusion that nonsubstantive and unexplained variations in the age distribution of crime bear on the invariance thesis. Such a conclusion was plainly anticipated by extensive discussion in our 1983 paper, and it is an unreasonable caricature of our position to suggest that it denies the possibility of change in the level of crime between 1965 and 1980 or trivial shifts in the modal age for a particular "crime type."

Still, it is clear that Farrington (1986) and Blumstein et al. do not share our perceptions of similarity and difference (see also Table 2). We tend to see similarity where they see difference. We believe our bias can be justified by its consequences. For example, the conclusion that the age distribution of crime is substantially invariant leads directly to several propositions about crime that can themselves be validated (see Hirschi and Gottfredson, 1983, 1986, 1987). The contrary conclusion of Farrington (1986), and now Blumstein et al., is that the age distribution of crime varies from year to year, place to place, crime type to crime type, and group to group. Observation of such statistical variation does not necessarily lead anywhere, and it does not require the scientific conclusion that trivial variation is more meaningful than the fundamental similarity in the distributions at issue. For example, three-quarters of a century ago, Goring (1913) found statistically significant differences in age distributions and concluded that such differences were scientifically trivial. Farrington (1986) replicated Goring's results, but reached the opposite conclusion. We agree with Goring, and with Guttman (1977: 92), who notes that "a test of statistical significance is not a test of scientific importance":

> No one has yet published a scientific law in the social sciences which was developed, sharpened, or effectively substantiated on the basis of tests of significance. The basic laws of physics were not facilitated this way. Estimation and approximation may be more fruitful than significance in developing science, never forgetting replication.

In our view, the question for criminology is whether the glass is 97 percent full or 3 percent empty, whether to pursue the important implications of a remarkably robust age effect or to continue to revel in the statistical noise generated by atheoretical research.

But the decline in crime with age is the fact directly relevant to the validity of the career paradigm. In our paper critical of this paradigm, we painted a picture of the criminal "career" we thought consistent with research. In this picture, the serious, predatory offenses said to be of interest to the career paradigm are in fact typically committed by young people, some of whom go on committing some of them for a while, but most of whom spend their declining years (late 20s) running afoul of the authorities over alcohol, drugs, and family squabbles. Our research is not the source of this picture. In perhaps their last word on the subject, after a lifetime of research on it, Glueck and Glueck (1968: 151–152) report among *delinquents* a "substantial reduction in criminalism, especially of the more serious kind" during the 25–31 age range, and they note that those offenders who do not during this period "achieve…maturity…tend to commit petty misdemeanors often associated with *disintegration* of organism and morale (emphasis in original)."

Blumstein et al. suggest that such *empirical* descriptions of criminal careers do not bear on the validity of the career construct because the features of the criminal career must be determined *empirically!* They then summarize earlier research of the Gluecks (Glueck and Glueck, 1940) showing essentially the same age pattern the Gluecks reported 28 years later. In the Blumstein et al. summary, however, the Gluecks' data "suggest distinct career paths for different crime types" and make it "possible to distinguish changes in frequency from changes in participation"—with the conclusion that frequency is not a function of age in the way participation is a function of age.

Since this conclusion contradicts our reading of research in the field and straightforward extrapolation from our Table 2, we must examine it further. How can it be said that in the Gluecks' data *participation* alone accounts for the decline in the rate of criminal activity with age? The Gluecks were apparently interested in the same kind of question for they computed several distinct "lambdas." One such lambda we might call a "serious-offense-participation lambda," since it divides the active offender population into two groups, those who commit serious offenses and those who do not. This lambda (the percentage of serious offenders among active offenders) takes the values 75.6, 77.4, 56.6, and 47.8 in the four periods identified in Blumstein et al.'s Table 1 (see also Glueck and Glueck, 1940: 317, Table 18). Such results led Glueck and Glueck (1940: 89) to report that "with the passing of years there was, among our…1,000 delinquents, *both a decline in criminality and a decrease in the seriousness of the offenses of those who continued to commit crimes* (emphasis in original)." Those who defend lambda because of its connection to serious crime cannot dismiss as trivial a marked decline in serious crime with age among active offenders, especially when it occurs in data introduced by them.

The Gluecks' data are corroborated by other sources, as we have shown (Gottfredson and Hirschi, 1986). No response to the data contrary to their position is offered by Blumstein et al. Thus, we need only quickly illustrate the range of data directly consistent with our notion that offenders share the general age distribution of crime.

Offenders in prison (presumably people of special interest to the criminal justice system) commit fewer "infractions" as they grow older, a clear "lambda" effect in a setting relatively free of the extraneous influences and ceiling effects of the outside world (Hirschi and Gottfredson, 1983: 561–562; see also Glueck and Glueck, 1940: 319). Research on offenders in the community also provides a large literature ignored by Blumstein et al. in their search for evidence that "lambda" remains constant with age for offenders. This literature repeatedly shows that offenders, even serious offenders, reduce the level of their criminal activity as they age. The parole follow-up literature, easily construed as research on serious offenders, has always found steep declines in offending as parolees age (see, for example, Glaser, 1964: 474), so much so that age is typically included as a major predictor of success on parole. In fact, the Base Expectancy Measure (perhaps the most thoroughly validated prediction instrument in criminology) gives age one of the largest weights of the variables in the instrument (cited in Gottfredson and Gottfredson, 1980: 258; see also Gottfredson and Ballard, 1965). When a large sample of California parolees was followed for 8 years after release, and only those still free in the community considered, the violation rate for "major new offenses" declined precipitously with number of years since release (Gottfredson and Gottfredson, 1980: 265).

Perhaps the most thorough recent study specifically addressing the question of the stability of lambda over age is reported by Haapanen (1987). Haapanen collected 15-to-20-year follow-up data on a large sample of serious offenders in California. His conclusions (p. iii) are direct, to the point, and contrary to the claims of Blumstein et al.:

> Our longitudinal data allowed us to look not only at simple indices of involvement in crime but also at "career" characteristics, such as breadth of involvement and the extent of repetition for particular crime types. These analyses showed that for this large sample of serious offenders, both the kinds of crimes for which they were arrested and the rate of arrest clearly differed by race and clearly declined with age.[4]

The Blumstein et al. position that crime does not decline with age among active offenders, or that crime *may* not decline with age among active offenders, is advanced in the face of much evidence to the contrary.

Is the distinction between criminal careers and career criminals really a distinction between science and policy? The search for a career criminal is as old as criminology. Whatever the details of the definition, it refers ultimately to some combination of criminal acts by individuals over time. Blumstein and Cohen (1987: 1986) start with the idea of a criminal career, which, they say, is "merely a metaphor for the longitudinal process," and report no difficulty in deriving the career criminal from this concept: "It is...important to distinguish the concept of criminal careers from the policy-oriented reversal of that phrase, the 'career criminal,' which refers to offenders whose criminal careers are of such serious dimension that they represent prime targets for the criminal justice system." We are said to pay insufficient attention to the distinction between career criminals and criminal careers. How did we lose the apparently clear distinction central to the career paradigm?

> The criminal career approach, however, is more appropriate in research that focuses more narrowly on serious offenses, where participation is more limited and the distinction between active offenders and nonoffenders is important. Our preference for the criminal career approach is based partly on our concern for the more serious predatory crimes such as robbery and burglary...(Blumstein et al., this volume: 6).

> A different approach to incapacitation, based on criminal career patterns, may avoid some of the problems associated with selective incapacitation. This approach relies on recent empirical research on criminal careers (see, for example, Blumstein and Cohen, 1979...)...*The goal is to identify classes of offenders who, on average, would remain active at high rates.* In

Blumstein and Cohen's analysis (1979...) of criminal career patterns for arrestees in Washington, D.C., convicted robbery and burglary defendants emerged as prime candidates for incapacitation (Cohen, 1983: 5, emphasis added).

[R]ecent interest in the crime control effects of incapacitation has underscored the importance of developing estimates of λ (Cohen, 1986: 294).

Well, the criminal career "metaphor" is apparently hard to distinguish from a particular research design and a preference for focusing research attention on what Blumstein and Cohen themselves refer to as "the prime targets of the criminal justice system." We may be forgiven for thinking we saw policy interest in such statements when, we are now told, no such interest exists. However, we are not alone. The law enforcement community, criminal justice research agencies (see the quote from Stewart, *supra*), and indeed members of the National Research Council's Panel on Research on Criminal Careers appear to believe that the goal of career research is to locate real, live career criminals (whatever they may be called) and to treat them accordingly:

The National Academy of Sciences, in a lengthy project...supported by the National Institute of Justice, *Criminal Careers and Career Criminals*, has brought these data together....It is one of the best and the most immediately practical emanations of social science research that's come to this field. For the first time from this there emerges the serious possibility of distinguishing the likely intensive repeaters from the likely desisters and adjusting our responses at the level of policing, prosecuting, and sentencing accordingly (Morris, 1987).

As this statement from a member of the criminal careers panel suggests, some would claim that knowledge sufficient to direct policy is already in hand ("one of...the most immediately practical emanations of social science"). We strongly disagree. If, however, such "knowledge" exists, we believe the time has come to share it with the academic community.

In our view, it is academically illegitimate to criticize a body of knowledge on the basis of its putative policy implications (see Gottfredson and Hirschi, 1987b). Unfortunately, this view has not tended to characterize the work of those pursuing the career paradigm:

A significant factor inhibiting the growth of knowledge about criminal careers has been that traditional research focuses on developing correlates of crime....Not surprisingly, many indicators of social deprivation are associated with crime, among them low income, high population density, and high minority racial composition. Knowing of such associations, however, is not very helpful. The strong mutual association among these correlates provides little guidance on their relative individual contributions to crime, and such partitioning is crucial in order to isolate and identify useful social investments to address these presumed causes (Blumstein and Cohen, 1987: 985).

Obviously, whatever the truth of the dubious assertion that traditional causes of crime have no policy implications, this purported lack of utility bears no connection to their status as causes of crime. We think career criminal public policies are without merit. As we hope is clear from this paper, however, we also believe that independent of its policy prescriptions, the career paradigm is of limited value to the scientific study of crime.

CONCLUSION

As we read their response to our papers, Blumstein et al. seem to want it all ways. They want an important distinction between their "criminal career" approach and the policy-oriented hunt for the career criminal at the same time they justify the former by the latter. They want to suggest that their perspective is compatible with traditional criminology at the same time they declare traditional criminology fundamentally defective and misleading. They claim to be open to all research designs yet they develop a "model" whose "parameters" require longitudinal data. They claim to be open to a variety of prevention and intervention policies yet they develop a model so narrow that the criminal justice system alone can be the focus of public policy toward crime. They complain that their critics mock knowledge and obfuscate findings. We are all in favor of science, but believe the line between science and scientism is worthy of respect. In this regard, consider the presentation in *Science* of formulas for the computation of career length (Blumstein and Cohen, 1987: 986), the explanation of the value of scientific notation (their note 6), the extended discussions of elementary issues of research design, and the laborious statistical exercises that eventually produce smaller constants from larger ones, as though it mattered (their note 22). Finally, consider their Figure 6, which illustrates the relation between age and average years of schooling in the 1980 census. This figure is presented to show the dangers of cross-sectional data and the need for longitudinal data in inferring age effects. We believe it shows better the dangers of approaching criminology unaccompanied by substantive concepts. Even Martians with questions about the earthly relation between age and education would not conduct longitudinal research, nor would they take a cross-sectional census of the population of the United States. They would, instead, ask some *one* of the millions of people in the society likely to know the answer to their question, knowing full well that such "informant interviewing" is a perfectly adequate and incredibly efficient device for answering some questions. By the same token, in our view, those genuinely interested in the "parameters" of the career "model" would today conduct neither inefficient cross-sectional nor immensely inefficient longitudinal research. They would, instead, ask someone who knows. In our view, almost any "traditional" criminologist would do.

NOTES

1. We remain convinced that our critique of Blumstein and Cohen's (1979) research procedures is correct, that our use of Farrington's data is appropriate, and that our assessment of the claims for longitudinal research will not be answered by listing the features of this passive observational design. We advise interested readers to consider our arguments in their original form, not as they have been phrased by Blumstein et al.

2. These data were collected in an area with a high crime rate. The distribution of officially recorded offenses is much like that reported by Wolfgang et al. (1972) in Philadelphia. The self-report instrument has been extensively used, and its validity has been established by subsequent research (Hindelang et al., 1981: 108). The sample appears to include about as many robberies and burglaries as the Blumstein and Cohen (1979) sample selected to allow study of active offenders, and it contains many more serious offenses and offenders than the Farrington et al. (1985) longitudinal survey of 411 boys in London. We do not think all this is relevant, but would like to assuage the fears of those who prefer to work with "serious offenders."

3. The "outside variables" in table 2 are defined as follows: race (0 = white; 1 = black); smoke (0 = do not smoke; 1 = smoke); drink (0 = do not drink alcohol; 1 = drink); date (0 = do not date; 1 = date); GPA (decile scores of cumulative school-recorded grade point average in English); friends picked up (self-reported number of friends ever picked up by the police [don't know treated as "missing"]; (5 = four or more).

4. Haapanen's conclusions about the prospects for selective incapacitation are equally straightforward and equally contrary to policies based on identification and capture of the career criminal. For additional recent data documenting the decline in crime for serious offenders as they age, see Peterson et al., 1980). See also McCord and McCord (1959: 158), who show a marked decline in convictions during the early 20s for offenders in the Cambridge–Somerville sample.

REFERENCES

BLUMSTEIN, ALFRED and JACQUELINE COHEN. (1979). "Estimation of Individual Crime Rates from Arrest Records." *Journal of Criminal Law and Criminology 70*: 561–585.

_____. (1987). "Characterizing Criminal Careers." *Science 237*: 985–991.

BLUMSTEIN, ALFRED, JACQUELINE COHEN, and DANIEL NAGIN (eds.). (1978). *Deterrence and Incapacitation*. Washington, D.C.: National Academy Press.

BLUMSTEIN, ALFRED, JACQUELINE COHEN, JEFFREY A. ROTH, and CHRISTY VISHER. (1986). *Criminal Careers and "Career Criminals,"* Vol. 1. Washington, D.C.: National Academy Press.

COHEN, JACQUELINE. (1983). "Incapacitating Criminals: Recent Research Findings." *Research in Brief*. Washington, D.C.: National Institute of Justice.

_____. (1986). "Research on Criminal Careers." In Alfred Blumstein, Jacqueline Cohen, Jeffrey A. Roth, and Christy Visher, *Criminal Careers and "Career Criminals,"* Vol. 1. Washington, D.C. National Academy Press.

FARRINGTON, DAVID. (1986). "Age and Crime." In Michael H. Tonry and Norval Morris (eds.), *Crime and Justice: An Annual Review of Research* (Vol. 7). Chicago: University of Chicago Press.

FARRINGTON, DAVID, BERNARD GALLAGHER, LYNDIA MORLEY, RAYMOND ST. LEDGER, and DONALD J. WEST. (1985). *Cambridge Study in Delinquent Development: Long Term Follow-up, First Annual Report to the Home Office*. Cambridge: Cambridge University.

GLASER, DANIEL. (1964). *The Effectiveness of a Prison and Parole System*. Indianapolis, Ind.: Bobs-Merrill.

GLUECK, SHELDON and ELEANOR GLUECK. (1940). *Juvenile Delinquents Grown Up*. New York: Commonwealth Fund.

_____. (1950). *Unraveling Juvenile Delinquency*. Cambridge, Mass.: Harvard University Press.

_____. (1968). *Delinquents and Nondelinquents in Perspective*. Cambridge, Mass.: Harvard University Press.

GORING, CHARLES. (1913). *The English Convict*. Montclair, N.J.: Patterson Smith.

GOTTFREDSON, DON and KELLY BALLARD. (1965). *The Validity of Two Parole Prediction Scales*. Vacaville, Calif.: Institute for the Study of Crime and Delinquency.

GOTTFREDSON, MICHAEL and DON GOTTFREDSON. (1980). *Decisionmaking in Criminal Justice*, Cambridge, Mass.: Ballinger.

GOTTFREDSON, MICHAEL and TRAVIS HIRSCHI. (1986). "The True Value of Lambda Would Appear to Be Zero: An Essay on Career Criminals, Criminal Careers, Selective Incapacitation, Cohort Studies, and Related Topics." *Criminology 24*: 213–234.

_____. (1987a). "The Methodological Adequacy of Longitudinal Research on Crime." *Criminology 25*: 3.

_____. (1987b). *Positive Criminology*. Newbury Park, Calif.: Sage.

_____. (1988). "Career Criminals and Selective Incapacitation." In Joseph E. Scott and Travis Hirschi, *Controversial Issues in Criminology and Criminal Justice*. Newbury Park, Calif.: Sage.

GREENBERG, DAVID. (1985). "Age, Crime, and Social Explanation." *American Journal of Sociology 91*: 1–21.

GUTTMAN, LOUIS. (1977). "What Is Not What In Statistics." *The Statistician 26*: 81–107.

HAAPANEN, RUDY A. (1987). *Selective Incapacitation and the Serious Offender: A Longitudinal Study of Criminal Career Patterns*. Sacramento, Calif.: California Department of the Youth Authority.

HINDELANG, MICHAEL, TRAVIS HIRSCHI, and JOSEPH WEIS. (1981). *Measuring Delinquency*. Beverly Hills, Calif.: Sage.

HIRSCHI, TRAVIS. (1969). *Causes of Delinquency*. Berkeley: University of California.

HIRSCHI, TRAVIS and MICHAEL GOTTFREDSON. (1983). "Age and the Explanation of Crime." *American Journal of Sociology 89*: 552–584.

_____. (1986). "The Distinction Between Crime and Criminality." In Timothy Hartnagel and Robert Silverman (Eds.). *Critique and Explanation*. New Brunswick, N.J.: Transaction Books.

_____. (1987). "Causes of White Collar Crime." *Criminology 25*: 4.

McCORD, WILLIAM and JOAN McCORD. (1959). *Origins of Crime*. Montclair, N.J.: Patterson Smith.

MORRIS, NORVAL. (1987). "Putting Research to Work for the Courts." Keynote address to National Institute of Justice Conference, "Presiding in Criminal Courts," Phoenix, Arizona. Tape T264-2, Washington, D.C., National Institute of Justice.

PETERSON, MARK, HARRIET BRAIKER, and SUZANNE POLICH. (1980). *Doing Crime*. Santa Monica, Calif.: Rand.

STEWART, JAMES K. (1987). "Foreword." *In Research Program Plan Fiscal Year 1988*. Washington, D.C.: National Institute of Justice.

WOLFGANG, MARVIN, ROBERT FIGLIO, and THORSTEN SELLIN. (1972). *Delinquency in a Birth Cohort*. Chicago: University of Chicago Press.

WOOTTON, BARBARA. (1959). *Social Science and Social Pathology*. New York: Macmillan.

QUESTIONS FOR DISCUSSION

1. Why is it not appropriate to use the term *career criminal* in the study of crime?

2. According to the authors, how does the career paradigm for understanding crime demean traditional criminology and social science approaches to studying crime? Cite examples to support your response.

3. Why, according to the authors, is it difficult if not impossible to separate "participation" from "frequency" when considering an individual as offensive?

4. How are age and crime related to the career paradigm? What are the difficulties with using age and crime as a predictor of criminal careers?

5. Is the distinction between criminal careers and career criminals a distinction between science and policy? Explain.

4

CRIME, JUSTICE, AND THE SOCIAL ENVIRONMENT

Elliott Currie

■ ■ ■ ■ ■ ■ ■ ■ ■ ■ ■ ■ ■ ■ ■ ■ ■ ■ ■ ■

No one should doubt that violent crime constitutes an American epidemic. Crime—and the violent drug trade with which it's often connected—have brought tragedy and devastation to America's cities, especially to poorer and minority communities. The continuing massacre on the streets, brought home daily by gruesome portraits in the newspapers and on the TV screen, has produced a climate of fear and outrage—and stimulated an increasingly punitive response. Legislators have pressed for stiffer prison terms, harsh mandatory sentences for drug offenders, the death penalty for drug dealers and violent children. Public officials have rushed to spend ever-growing proportions of their limited budgets on prisons and jails: this year, the states' spending on corrections rose faster than any other category of expenditure—twice as fast, for example, as money for schools.[1] President Bush's much-touted antidrug strategy, announced at the close of the 1980s, was topheavy with spending for corrections, proposing several times as much federal funding for prison cells as for drug treatment programs. In this climate, many Democratic officeholders have scrambled to appear even "tougher" on crime and drugs than the Republican administration.

All of this may give the illusion of momentum against the crime and violence that plague America in the last years of the twentieth century. It does not, however, offer a realistic remedy. For what's generally ignored in the legislative stampede for more punishment is that we have been systematically following similar policies for many years; and those policies have failed, massively and tragically. In this article, I'll describe the dimensions of that failure, and sketch the outlines of an approach to violent crime that can be both effective and progressive.

I

The basic thrust of American crime policy in recent years dates roughly from the beginning of the 1970s, with the emergence of what we can fairly call the "conservative revolution" in criminology. That revolution was only one facet of a much broader transformation in American social thought and policy on domestic issues. To place it in context, we need to look briefly at what had come before. During the 1950s and 1960s, a more broadly liberal understanding of crime and criminal justice was dominant in the United States, at least on the intellectual level—though it had less consistent impact on the way the criminal justice system worked in practice.

What most characterized the mainstream of liberal thinking in that era—what I'll call here is "liberal realism"—was the fundamental understanding that crime was a *social* problem. As the President's Commission on Law Enforcement and the Administration of Justice— established by Lyndon Johnson in 1966—put it, "Crime is a social problem that is deeply interwoven with almost every aspect of American life." In particular, violent crime on the American level—which the commission recognized was far worse than in other industrial societies—was a symptom of basic social inequalities that had been allowed to fester for too long. This was not just a simple matter of widespread unemployment and poverty, but of a deeper and more disturbing disintegration of basic social institutions, especially for the urban poor: "The social institutions generally relied on to guide and control people in their individual and mutual existence," the commission wrote, "simply are not operating effectively in the inner city." In particular, "every effort" needed to be made to strengthen the family, now "often shattered by the grinding processes of urban slums." The commission accordingly declared that the most important single objective the nation should pursue if it wished to "significantly" reduce crime was to "seek to prevent crime before it happens by assuring all Americans a stake in the benefits and responsibilities of American life."[2]

The commission didn't neglect the problems and needs of the police, courts, and prisons. But it did not simply call for more of them. Instead it focused on what it regarded as the key failing of the justice system in general, and the prisons in particular: they were not doing much to prepare offenders for purposive, constructive lives on the outside. Indeed, if anything, the prisons often rendered them less fit to return to society when they came out than when they went in. The most pressing need was for a "substantial upgrading" of the correctional system, and its reorientation "toward integration of offenders into community life."[3]

The conservative "revolution" stood these themes on their head. It defined crime as largely a criminal justice problem, and it rejected both social explanations of the causes of crime and social solutions to it. By the mid-1970s, that "revolution" had come to dominate American thinking and policy on crime to an astonishing degree. It had dethroned social explanations of the causes of crime, cast the idea of the rehabilitation of offenders into the category of the antique and faintly disreputable, relegated the belief that social programs might help prevent crime to the margins of public discourse, and simultaneously elevated the idea that crime could be best reduced by deterrence and incapacitation to a central place in social policy.

The thrust of the conservative argument was hardly new. It reached back to the social Darwinism of the nineteenth century, and beyond. Crime, in this view, was caused by the absence of sufficient punishment. Often this was couched in the framework of the belief in a "wicked" human nature, as the conservative Harvard scholar James Q. Wilson put it in a hugely influential book, *Thinking About Crime*, in the mid-1970s.[4]

In the United States in recent years, conservatives argued, a pervasive permissiveness had worn down most of the institutional controls of the darker human appetites—

permissiveness spawned by the misguided ideals of liberalism and the hedonistic and indulgent culture of the 1960s. To understand the spread of crime in America, therefore, we needed to look to the indulgent, "child-centered" family and school and, above all, to the leniency of the criminal justice system. Crime could only be held in check if that system punished offenders with sufficient certainty, swiftness, and severity. But in the United States we had largely abandoned those aims in favor of an overemphasis on the rights of criminals.

The other side of this argument was the contention that the adverse social factors invoked by liberal criminologists to explain America's stunningly high crime rate were either irrelevant or, in some cases, worked in the opposite direction from what liberals believed. Conservative criminologists denied that there were strong connections between crime and such key staples of the liberal explanation as economic deprivation, social inequality, and inadequate labor markets: at the extreme, some went so far as to deny that there were social causes of crime at all. Others argued that the liberal explanations were themselves partly to blame for rising crime: the emphasis on social causes of crime had eroded the sense of individual responsibility.

These arguments drew ammunition from the undeniable fact that, though our incarceration rate remained far higher than other countries, it had fallen during the 1960s—just as crime rates were rising. Even more important, the conservative argument was boosted by what its advocates often described as a basic "paradox" of crime in the 1960s—by what the British criminologist Jock Young calls the "etiological crisis."[5] What Young means is that the liberal view of the causes of crime, and of appropriate remedies for it, was undermined by the apparent paradox that crime rates rose just when a number of things which, by this view, ought to have reduced crime were improving substantially—at least on paper and in the aggregate. Incomes were rising, unemployment (on the national level) was falling, and we were beginning to devote significant governmental resources to social programs for the disadvantaged. If the liberal view was correct, conservatives gleefully argued, crime should have fallen; that it didn't do so opened the door to a view that blamed the rise in crime primarily on the leniency of the criminal justice system (and to a lesser extent the family and the schools) while arguing that liberal programs were at best irrelevant, at worst part of the deepening culture of permissiveness and indulgence that bred crime.

But the conservative revolution likewise began to sputter in its tracks in the mid-1980s, when it became apparent to all but the most ideologically stalwart that the model wasn't working. Despite the huge increases in incarceration we witnessed in the 1970s and 1980s, criminal violence remained devastatingly high, and in many places rising; whole communities were shredded and turned nightmarish by drugs and gang violence. This was, after all, one of the largest experiments in social engineering we've ever seen in the United States (though it was rarely acknowledged as such); and so its failure has been an event of considerable moment. Let's step back for a moment and consider the magnitude of the changes the "revolution" has brought—and the magnitude of the crisis it has left us.

On the criminal justice side, the effect of the conservative revolution is most starkly evident in the rapidly rising rate of incarceration in the United States. We tripled the prison population nationally from the early 1970s to the present, and the rate of increase was even greater in some states. Between 1980 and 1987 *alone*, the prison population increased by 210 percent in Alaska, 179 percent in California, 146 percent in New

Jersey, 142 percent in Arizona.[6] By the end of 1988, as the number of Americans behind bars in state and federal prisons, local jails, and public juvenile facilities on any given day approached the one-million mark, that population amounted to a "city" of the incarcerated nearly the size of Detroit. Outside the prison walls, the number of those under the control of parole or probation authorities—almost triple the number behind bars, and increasingly under stringent conditions like home detention and electronic monitoring—rose by 95 percent between 1980 and 1987 alone.[7] And since these are aggregate numbers, they don't convey the degree to which the correctional system has come to loom over the daily life of what we euphemistically describe as "high-risk" communities. Almost one in four black men between the ages of twenty and twenty-nine were in custody, on probation, or on parole on any given day in the late 1980s.[8] Nor should it be thought that these increases simply correspond to equal increases in the crime rate, with which the criminal justice system is struggling to keep up. On the contrary, the level of imprisonment *per crime* has risen sharply—for violent crimes and burglary, by 72 percent between 1980 and 1986 nationwide, *192 percent* in New York, 127 percent in California.[9]

The other side of the conservative revolution was the systematic withdrawal of social supports and public services from the most distressed communities and most disadvantaged families in America, justified by the vague assertion that doing so would free the forces of the private market economy to provide for them what government intervention had not. I can only note here some of the most significant of those changes. Between the end of the 1970s and the mid-1980s alone, the average welfare benefit under the Aid to Families with Dependent Children program (AFDC) fell by a fifth, while the proportion of poor children receiving those benefits fell from 72 to 60 percent: the proportion of low-income families brought above the federal poverty line by some combination of AFDC, Social Security, and unemployment insurance fell from above one in five to one in nine—casting about half a million families into poverty. Meanwhile, there were simultaneous and severe cuts in public medical and social services. From 1978 to 1984, federal spending on maternal and child health care and community health centers dropped by a stunning 32 percent. Between 1981 and 1988, federal funding under the Title XX Social Services Block Grant—which supports, among other things, child abuse prevention and child protective services—fell by a third.[10]

But it has by now become starkly clear that this course of action has not revitalized America's cities, or transformed and motivated the urban underclass, or taken back the streets. On the contrary, no one needs to be reminded of the tragic, sometimes nearly incomprehensible social disintegration and violence that still confront us in the streets and homes of so many of our cities. The FBI's Uniform Crime Reports show overall violent crime up by almost 45 percent from 1978 to 1988. After a lull in the early 1980s, violence has risen relentlessly, almost mimicking the similar rises in incarceration. Overall violent crime rose 4 percent from 1984 to 1985, 12 percent from 1985 to 1986, 5 percent from 987 to 1988. Aggravated assaults rose 6 percent from 1984 to 1985, a startling 15 percent from 1985 to 1986, another 9 percent over the next two years. A number of cities—New York and Washington prominent among them—attained all-time high numbers of homicides in 1988—despite the 192 percent increase in prison admissions per violent offense in New York and a 106 percent increase in the District of Columbia.[11] The rises in crime in the mid-to-late 1980s, moreover, also took place in spite of the continued shrinking of the proportion of the American population in the younger, more crime-prone age groups, a result of the "baby bust" of the 1960s and early 1970s. That decline, as many criminologists predicted, should have lowered the crime rate—and probably did, other things being equal. But other forces kept it up stubbornly.

The conservative revolution, then, didn't fail for lack of implementation. It failed because its premises were wrong. The conservative explanation of America's crime rate depended on the assertion that the criminal justice system in the United States was extraordinarily lenient—at least by implication, more so than that of other countries. But in fact the United States imprisoned a far higher proportion of its citizens than any advanced industrial society outside the Soviet bloc, even in the 1960s. By the beginning of the 1980s we were incarcerating up to ten times the proportion of the Netherlands and several times that of other European nations; and we were suffering homicide rates not less than three and up to ten times higher.[12]

Our high and rapidly increasing levels of incarceration also cast doubt on the more specific conservative argument that an excessive concern with the rights of criminals was "hobbling" the courts. Those doubts were confirmed by careful studies of what actually went on in the criminal courts (most recently, a survey by the American Bar Association) which repeatedly showed that the proportion of criminal cases "lost" because of procedural restrictions was minuscule.[13]

The other central conservative assertion—that crime had little or nothing to do with the social and economic deficits and distortions of American society—also depended on evidence that, to put matters politely, was less than robust. Conservative writers often tried to evade these links between crime and social structure in part by denying that there was anything unusual about America's crime rate. James Q. Wilson, for example, rejected the idea that high rates of crime were linked to particular kinds of social organization on the ground that "virtually every nation in the world, capitalist, socialist, or communist, has experienced in recent years rapidly increasing crime rates."[14] But the assertion was misleading on two counts: a number of countries, including Japan and several European nations, had *not* experienced sharp rises in violent crime: and even those that had were left with rates of serious criminal violence so far below our own that the differences vastly outweighed the similarities. Faced with the weakness of that argument, some conservatives have more recently begun to argue that differences between countries (and between groups within them) in crime may be partly due to biological characteristics—that they reflect what Wilson and the psychologist Richard Herrnstein describe as "underlying distributions of constitutional factors."[15] But neither Wilson and Herrnstein nor anyone else has been able to turn up "constitutional" factors that can explain why violent crime is so much higher in the United States than in Europe, in Detroit than in Toronto, or in the 1980s than in the 1950s.

Meanwhile, study after study continued to affirm the connections between America's crime rate and its high levels of economic insecurity and inequality. Those connections, to be sure, were often more complex than liberal criminologists had generally believed in the 1950s and 1960s. Evidence that a simple connection existed between crime and the national level of unemployment, for example, was not strong. But there *was* strong evidence that the experience of being trapped in a life without the prospect of stable or dignified work was closely linked to crime. Likewise, the most careful research rarely turned up *simple* links between levels of poverty and levels of crime; what it more clearly showed was a strong connection between extremes of social and economic *inequality* and high levels of criminal violence.[16]

These findings help explain the apparent "paradox" of rising crime amidst the prosperity of the 1960s which was so important to the conservative argument. For the broad statistics portraying rising incomes and employment for the nation as a whole masked the deepening marginalization of some groups in American society—especially the minority poor in the inner cities—who were increasingly denied the fruits of the "affluent" society which, with great frustration, they saw growing all around them. And those findings also help us understand why the net effect of the conservative revolution has been to increase violent crime, not reduce it. For even the huge increases in incarceration could not contain the violent results of years of policies that systematically aggravated so many of the social factors known to be implicated in crime: policies that increased inequality, eliminated vast numbers of stable, well-paying jobs, and magnified the economic and social stresses on American families.

II

The failure of the conservative strategy against crime offers an opening for the development of an approach adequate to the genuine crisis that confronts us—one that both builds on and goes beyond the lost mainstream of what I've called "liberal criminology." The heart of that revitalized approach must be a reaffirmation of the central idea that crime is indeed a *social* problem—one that, on its devastating American level, is rooted in deep strains and contradictions in our social structure. It is not by accident that the United States has by far the highest rates of serious crime in the developed world while standing out among industrial societies on a host of other troubling measures—child poverty, infant mortality, inadequate public services, extremes of economic inequality. Mounting a serious attack on the violence that plagues us means confronting those multiple social deficits head-on.

That kind of "social-environmental" strategy must include measures to address the problems of individuals and families "at risk," but must also move beyond them to the tougher level of social control over the larger forces now increasingly undermining American communities and placing families "at risk" in the first place. As that suggests, there can be no "quick fix" for the American crime problem. The level of social devastation in the communities that have been most affected by the destruction of solid labor markets, the withdrawal of preventive social services, and the flood of hard drugs is now beyond anything we've seen before in this country; and it will require responses of a breadth and depth we've not yet seriously contemplated.

Let me sketch out some of the most crucial—and most promising—of those responses. Some of those I'll list involve changes in the criminal justice system; others move beyond it. Some of them involve interventions on the close-in level of families and individuals;

others address more complex and longer-range issues of community stability, of political economy, and even of culture. Some are long term; others could have an immediate impact on crime and the fear it creates. The list is meant to be illustrative, not exhaustive; I want simply to draw, in broad brushstrokes, what I think ought to be some key priorities for a progressive agenda on crime.

1. We need to devote more resources to *public safety* in the cities. There is a crying need for more community protection in the face of the twin crises of violence and rugs in recent years—both to reduce the intolerable risks to residents of inner-city neighborhoods and to create enough breathing room to enable longer-term strategies against crime and community deterioration to be put in place. We need to insist that communities have a fundamental right to the best protection against violence and fear we can offer; and that the erosion of resources for public safety that has often resulted from the fiscal starvation of the cities is unacceptable. That means more, and more visible, law enforcement. But it isn't enough simply to call for more money for local law enforcement without thinking through more clearly what we want law enforcement to accomplish—and how it will be made more accountable to community concerns.

   The most important priority for enhanced public safety in the cities isn't to produce more arrests; we already arrest far more people—especially for minor drug offenses—than the courts can handle. The most important priority should be to protect neighborhood residents from violence and intimidation by dealers and from predation by drug users; secondarily, to disrupt local drug markets and drive them underground, or out of the community. No one imagines that this is anything other than a short-term strategy, which under current conditions is most likely to divert and displace, rather than to eliminate, the problem. But short-term displacement can have an important function in an emergency situation. Dealing can be driven away from residential areas and schools and off the public streets, where it is both harder to find and less likely to pose risks to the community.

   To do this we'll need to spend more. But we can increase the reach of that spending by civilianizing more police tasks and by developing effective civilian patrols that work closely with local police. We have some encouraging evidence that community patrols can significantly improve the sense of security in a neighborhood, given sufficient resources.[17] We should explore them more consistently.

2. We need a commitment, real rather than rhetorical, toward accessible, nonpunitive *drug abuse treatment* for those who need it—both within and outside the criminal justice system. Like our approach to the family, the way we think about hard drugs has been deeply shaped by broader ideological agendas rather than a level-headed reading of the evidence. Some variants of what I've called liberal criminology often failed to take the drug problem seriously, finding more to worry about in the public reaction to drug abuse than in the effects of hard drugs themselves on communities and individuals—particularly the disadvantaged who were (and are) the chief victims of the spread of hard drugs. The Reagan administration put most of its cards on strategies—especially interdiction and harsh mandatory sentencing—that had

already proven spectacularly unsuccessful, while slashing resources for drug treatment. The Bush administration's drug plan promised a slight tilt of federal resources away from interdiction, deterrence, and incapacitation toward treatment and prevention. But it also adamantly refused to raise new revenues to pay for more treatment—and promised to aggravate the drug-crime problem by taking scarce resources from other preventive social programs to cover the costs of the drug "war."

But the problem goes deeper than financing. An effective strategy against hard drugs cannot simply throw new money at the existing treatment system; it must also reform that system and redefine its aims. We need to ensure that treatment is of high quality, intensive, accompanied by serious outreach to addicts, by after-care that supports them once out of treatment, and by advocacy in the community for their broader needs with respect to housing, health care, and employment. We've learned that it's not that hard to get people off drugs; what's hard is to *keep* them off, and that tougher goal must be a main thrust of a progressive drug policy. Addicts typically come to treatment with many other social and personal disadvantages; if these underlying problems aren't addressed, we perpetuate the recycling of addicts from treatment to the social conditions that bred their addiction in the first place, and back again—as the conventional treatment system too often does today.

3. I've suggested that we should push for expanded drug treatment within the criminal justice system as well as in the community. The marginal cost of providing treatment to offenders in institutions, in particular, is very low—and the potential returns in reduced crime and increased chances of success on release are very high. But there is a more general principle here. We should reaffirm and strengthen the Crime Commission's insistence that our chief need is to *upgrade* the correctional system and reorient it toward helping offenders, where possible, to become productive and contributive—not simply to expand its capacity to contain the consequences of social neglect. The commonsense idea that we should do something constructive with people after they've broken the law fell out of fashion, almost into oblivion, in the 1970s. But there is growing evidence for a more encouraging view.[18]

One of the most glaring failings of the conservative approach to the justice system has been its gutting of the services—both inside and outside the system itself—that could help offenders toward more productive lives. The lack of resources has especially crippled the potential of probation and parole. A National Institute of Justice survey in 1988 found that the great majority of probation and parole agencies were unable to offer the community resources offenders needed. Eight out of ten mentioned the lack of sufficient drug programs and housing referrals; seven out of ten included job training, mental health services, and alcohol programs. "Serious questions must be raised," the study concludes, "about the system's present capacity to absorb additional offenders. Large and difficult caseloads coupled with a lack of staff and a shortage of community resources reflect a criminal justice subsystem strained to its limits."[19]

We should aim higher. On the most immediate level, we can begin to deliver more consistently the *basic services* many young offenders often need. Within the juvenile justice system in particular, we should finally insist that more constructive use be made of the time that young offenders are under supervision. We ought to think of that time as a resource, which we may profitably use to see to it that they leave a little smarter, a little healthier, a little more sober than they came in. This is particularly important given what some research suggests about the links between low skills and poor verbal abilities and serious delinquency.[20] We know how to raise those skills, and we should insist that no young person is left languishing idle and illiterate in any juvenile institution in the country.

4. We need a much greater commitment to *family-support programs*, and, especially, real rather than rhetorical support for comprehensive programs against child abuse and domestic violence. The debate over the family's role in crime and delinquency has been shaped, even more than other criminological issues, by the shifting ideological currents of recent years. The liberal criminology of the 1950s and 1960s tended to shy away from acknowledging the family's importance as a crucible of character formation. The conservative criminology of the 1970s and 1980s revived interest in the family's role in developing character and competence, but also detached the family and its functioning from the social and economic forces that powerfully affected it. A revitalized progressive criminology must recognize that the family is both a crucial shaping force and one that is in turn shaped by forces far larger than itself. That recognition is especially important in the face of the massively increased strains on American families in the past fifteen years under the impact of adverse economic shifts and conservative social policy. Accordingly, we will need both a genuinely pro-family economic policy at the national level—about which more in a moment— and far greater attention to interventions at the level of individual families.

Since the 1970s, there has been encouraging evidence that family-support programs can improve childbearing skills; we also have promising results from innovative programs for child-abusing families. But once again, if the emerging evidence on what we *could* do is encouraging, the level of implementation is not. In the case of child abuse, it is pitifully weak: we are quite simply allowing a massive and at least partly preventable tragedy to play itself out in soul-shattering ways, on children whose other social and economic disadvantages render them both vulnerable and largely invisible. This is not only a major crime in itself, but one which tends disturbingly often to recapitulate itself as many abused children become abusive parents in their turn.[21] To be sure, there is nothing inevitable about that progression, as the developmental psychologists Joan Kaufman and Edward Zigler have reminded us. But their own best estimate suggests that perhaps a third of severely abused children are likely to become severely abusive parents—a rate six times that of the population as a whole.[22]

Meanwhile, children at high risk of abuse have also been among the worst— if least vocal—victims of the conservative Darwinist approach to social policy. The Reagan years saw massive cutbacks in federal funding for child-abuse prevention and child protective services, forcing much of the responsibility for the problem onto states and localities just when their resources were shrinking and the risks to children—from rising family poverty, homelessness, parental drug abuse—were sharply increasing. Any serious anticrime strategy must work to reverse that legacy— and to repair, where possible, the damage it has caused.

5. We should also expand *health and mental health services* for vulnerable children—and their parents—including high-quality prenatal and postnatal care. We should do this anyway, but there's good reason to believe that it can be a meaningful part of a comprehensive, "ecological" strategy against crime and delinquency. The evidence is complex, but suggestive, that childhood injuries to the central nervous system and severe, untreated psychiatric problems (often related to child abuse) may be implicated in some of the most troubling and destructive forms of delinquency.[23] In their study of fourteen juveniles condemned to death for especially brutal crimes, for example, Dorothy Lewis and her colleagues conclude that these children are typically "multiply handicapped": they "tend to have suffered serious CNS injuries, to have suffered since early childhood from a multiplicity of psychotic symptoms, and to have been physically and sexually abused." At the same time, "the clinical and legal services necessary to try to uncover these vulnerabilities are *routinely unavailable* to this population of juveniles"—much less, of course, the services necessary to even begin to *treat* them.[24]

6. We should expand high-quality, intensive *early childhood education* along the model of Head Start and the Perry Preschool project. There is by now a consensus that these programs are one of the most effective (and cost-effective) means we have of preventing delinquency; they also produce other positive results, including improved jobs and earnings and reduced welfare dependency.[25] There is indeed some evidence that these programs have a positive effect on the psychological and social functioning of *parents* as well as children.[26] But the proportion of eligible children served by these programs is now about 18 percent.

It's important not to claim *too* much for these programs. Their advocates sometimes place excessive expectations on approaches to the problems of inner-city children which do not confront the larger social and economic context in which those problems originate. And they share a traditional American tendency to overemphasize educational solutions to social problems.[27] A preschool on every ghetto corner won't overcome the structural disintegration of the surrounding communities—a disintegration whose sources lie well beyond the disadvantaged child and family, beyond the local community, and beyond the reach of the school, and which may intensify in the coming decades. But on their own terms, these programs have demonstrated their effectiveness; we should expand them.

III

The accumulating evidence suggests that all of these measures can be important in reducing crime, if they are done with the necessary seriousness and intensity. But a serious anticrime strategy must also be bold enough to confront the deeper and often more complex social deficits that underlie the widespread disintegration of family and personality in the United States—and that will, if left unaddressed, surely cripple and compromise even our best efforts to work with vulnerable individuals and families. Here, therefore, are three long-term goals for the twenty-first century. All of them are worthy of support for many reasons—but not least because they have the potential to alter the context of individual and family development in ways that promise to diminish crime.

First, we must move to *reduce inequality and social impoverishment.*

We know that the gap between affluent and poor has been increasing in the United States—in part because of widening differences in earnings among people who work, in part because of the reductions in income support I've touched on above.[28] And the bare figures on the growing income gap understate the growth in inequality because they do not include the bifurcation of social services that has simultaneously taken place—the withdrawal of the public sector from the poor and the near-poor, especially the young. We will need to reverse this trend—not least because the evidence continues to grow, from both cross-national and domestic studies, that extremes of inequality—especially when coupled with excessive mobility and the fragmentation of community and family life—are fertile ground for the growth of violent crime.[29] Reducing inequality is a tall order: but it's not an impossible one. Many other nations have done it. And though we can't simply transfer their approaches to our own very different social and historical context, we can learn much from their experience that is vital to our own efforts to create a society that is both more just and more secure.

So far, our hesitant legislative efforts to mitigate the extremes of inequality in the United States have met with stiff resistance. Witness the recent legislative battle to restore the value of the minimum wage, which has fallen close to 30 percent in real terms since the 1980s. The fight for a decent minimum floor on earnings should continue, but we also need to do much more; ultimately, to move toward what in Scandinavia is called a "solidaristic" wage policy—one that raises the floor enough to ensure every working adult the means to a dignified livelihood—and to narrow the demoralizing and criminogenic abyss between affluent and poor.[30]

That strategy should include—as it has, for example, in Sweden—an explicit effort to raise the earnings of women closer to those of men, in order to reduce the intolerable deprivations faced by families headed by single women in the United States and to provide the indispensable material foundation for other efforts to enhance family life—and to reduce the toll of domestic violence. As it stands, low-income women are especially likely to be trapped in a cycle of repeated assaults in the home, because they have few realistic options on the outside to help them move out from under abusive relationships. Improving those options by increasing women's capacity for self-support is an essential complement to other strategies, in the community and the justice system, against domestic crime.

Second, and closely related to the reduction of inequality and deprivation, we should move toward an *active labor market policy* aimed at upgrading the work available to disadvantaged Americans. Again, there is strong evidence that poor jobs—unstable, dead-end, with low wages—are linked to many kinds of crime. And the effects tend to accumulate when several generations remain trapped with few opportunities beyond those jobs, in good part because of long-term, corrosive effects on the mediating institutions of family and neighborhood.[31] That being the case, it's difficult to feel sanguine about the much-touted high rate of job creation in the United States in recent years, for it's painfully clear that an increasing proportion of those jobs has been low-wage and often part-time.[32] This kind of economic "growth" can do little or nothing to address the roots of social pathology among those now disadvantaged by low earnings and shattered links to more sustaining and stable livelihoods.

As we move toward the next century, we'll have to acknowledge—as some European countries have long done—that a sufficient supply of good, stable jobs does not flow automatically from the operation of the private market, but requires active intervention by government. In the United States, the most critical need is for publicly supported, community-oriented job creation, particularly in the provision of essential public services to disadvantaged communities. Among other things, a serious commitment to public job creation would help us accomplish some of the key anticrime strategies I've just advocated—expanded early education, improved childhood mental-health services and family support programs, expanded and enhanced drug treatment. *Without* a public policy to create community-sustaining jobs, those crucial services will inevitably be skimpy and starved of enough resources to do their jobs. *With* that policy, we could begin to build a viable economic infrastructure in "high-risk" communities that could serve as the base for overall economic development—while simultaneously delivering the basic reparative and socializing services without which neither social peace nor economic development in those communities will be possible.

That kind of community-service-driven economic development could also, importantly, provide challenging and rewarding roles in the community for young people now ensnared by the lures of the inner-city drug culture. The negative job shifts of the past fifteen years have substantially diminished the number of truly rewarding jobs they can hope for, while creating vast numbers of low-paying jobs in the private retail and service economy that typically lead nowhere—and that cannot offer a compelling alternative to the multiple attractions of dealing and delinquency. A broad, serious commitment to hire the young to help transform their stricken communities *could* offer an alternative. For the appeal of the drug trade in the inner city is not just money; it's also challenge and respect. If we fail to provide those, we can be assured that the urban young will find them where they can.

Let me emphasize that this is a more difficult and long-term task than most criminologists have been willing to acknowledge. Liberal criminologists have sometimes implied that simply reflating the national economy to bring down the overall unemployment rate, or launching another summer job program for ghetto kids, could overcome the accumulated effects on family and personality of several generations of long-term economic deprivation and social impoverishment—and the relentless influence of a broader culture of predatory consumption. That's an unrealistic hope. I believe there is still time to turn that complex of adversities around. But no one should underestimate how hard it will be.

Third, we should work toward a genuinely *supportive national family policy*.

There is much rhetoric about "strengthening the family" in the United States. Beneath it is the reality of an ongoing disaster for American families, especially those in the bottom third of the income distribution, increasingly put at the mercy of a destabilizing and destructive economic and social environment. And the adverse forces in that environment—growing economic deprivation, excessive mobility, the retreat of accessible housing, the corrosive effects of alcohol and drugs—are by no means confined to the inner cities. They now reach upward well into parts of the old "middle" strata of American society. Left alone, those forces are likely to intensify in the future. I've argued that we should put more resources into supportive programs for "high-risk" children and families; but if we make no simultaneous effort to control the forces that undermine families in the first place, we'll be stuck continually at the level of picking up the pieces.

The employment and income policies I've just suggested are themselves key elements of a humane and progressive family policy for the next decades. But we also need national policies devoted specifically to reducing the stresses caused by the present conflicts between family and work. It's well known that we are one of the only remaining countries in the advanced industrial world that doesn't officially recognize the human, social, and even economic value of freeing up time for working parents to spend with families and children.[33] Our traditional practice has been to squeeze every ounce of paid working time out of parents in the service of private economic gain and to resist fiercely the rather innocuous idea that private business bears some responsibility for the impact of the conditions of work on their employees' families. Our first effort at national legislation in this direction, which would have mandated companies to provide up to ten weeks of *unpaid* leave, over two years, to parents at the birth of a child or in the event of a child's illness (some European countries mandate a paid leave of up to several months) has at this writing died once again in Congress, a casualty of the view that it represented unwarranted government interference in the economy.

But the reality is that our lack of a humane national policy to mitigate the conflicts between family and work—a lack which distinguishes us, again, from virtually every other advanced society—amounts to a massive subsidy to private business, in that it requires the rest of us to pay for the social costs of the resulting strains on families—the costs of physical and mental illness, domestic violence and delinquency. We will need to press not only for a family leave policy that finally drags us, kicking and screaming, into the last third of the twentieth century, but also, more broadly, for the idea that Americans who work have a fundamental right to sufficient family time—in order, among other things, to make possible the attentive and unharried care of the young.

IV

Some may object that these strategies go well beyond the customary boundaries of criminology. But a strategy against crime that can hope to make headway against the deepening crisis of America's cities must transcend the disciplinary and bureaucratic fragmentation that now cripples both our thinking and our policy toward crime. Our conventional approach is to isolate crime and criminal justice from their social setting—to think of "crime policy" as something quite separate from a family policy, an employment policy, an antipoverty policy. Nothing could be more fruitless. In human societies, as in the natural environment, things are *connected* to each other. What we do (or don't do) in the realm of economic policy in particular has a profound impact on the social institutions through which individuals are brought up healthy or damaged, compassionate or unfeeling, contributive or predatory. Making a serious attack on criminal violence, in the home and on the street, means restoring the integrity of that social environment by harnessing our material and technological resources to ends more supportive of community, family, and human development. And it means challenging some long-standing cultural attitudes that are deeply implicated in the devastating levels of violent crime in American society. We often think of culture as rigid and unchangeable—a permanent fact of life. But in the last generation alone we've seen major changes in American culture: in the way we think about the social role of women, or the status of people of color; in the way we think about our relationship to the natural environment or about health and nutrition. For the next generation, we should aim for changes or comparable magnitude in some aspects of American culture that may now seem set in stone: the degree of social deprivation and inequality we tolerate; the degree of violence we consider normal and acceptable in the course of childrearing— or of marriage; the level of access to social and health services we deem to be the minimum responsibility of civilized society; the relative balance of private gain versus cooperative endeavor as esteemed personal motives, of private economic "choice" versus the stability and socializing competence of communities and families.

Just as we have now—belatedly—begun to understand that we cannot systematically ravage or neglect the natural environment, or our bodies, without terribly destructive and self-defeating consequences, so we should come to understand that the *social* environment requires a level of sustenance and stewardship far beyond what can be provided as a residual product of economic growth. The big job for progressives in the coming years will be to place the integrity of the social environment firmly at the top of the political and intellectual agenda, and keep it there.

There is some encouraging evidence that the stark consequences of a decade of neglect have produced at least the stirrings of a reaction against the hard conservative Darwinism of the 1980s. By the end of the decade, majorities of the American public, according to opinion polls, supported greater investment in educational, employment, and health care strategies to help the disadvantaged into more productive roles in American life. And they were more willing to pay for those strategies than to pour more resources into an already bloated military. Opinion research also suggests that what the public most wants is for crime to be prevented before it happens; and that they tend to believe that crime is most often caused by remediable social problems.[34]

Nor have the implications of continuing urban disintegration been lost on those whose job is to govern the cities, or to do business in them. *Business Week* magazine, in a 1988 cover story on what it called the crisis of "human capital" in America, warned that "The U.S. may now be entering an era when neglect of the bottom half of society begins to threaten the welfare of the entire nation."[35] The magazine went on to propose substantially increased public spending—for preschool education, prenatal care, intensive job training for the disadvantaged young, and more. In the same year, *U.S. News and World Report*—again, a magazine not previously noted for its bleeding-heart sympathies—chided the Reagan government for offering "too many promises, too little help" to the children of the inner cities.[36] The Committee for Economic Development, an influential policy-making voice for America's corporate elite, similarly urged billions of dollars in new funding for Head Start, child health care, and other active public policies for high-risk children.[37] Even George Bush, in his 1988 campaign for the presidency, called on the nation to "invest in children," while the Republican party platform called for "large" increases in funding for Head Start.

Skepticism about the depth of some of these claims is in order, of course; especially those made in the midst of a presidential campaign. Nevertheless, I believe the shift from the hard, unalloyed "free-market" social Darwinism of the Reagan years is a real one.

But it is also a fragile one: There are other, less encouraging, possible responses to the continuing violence in America's streets. One troubling possibility is that we could go backward. We could adopt the view that the failure of our recent strategies toward street crime—and toward the problems of the "high-risk" urban poor generally—indicates that the problems are much more intractable than we had supposed. We might locate the source of this intractability in the biological or cultural insufficiencies of those who still fail to make it into the increasingly elusive mainstream of American society. And we might use that explanation to justify a kind of urban triage: an even greater withdrawal of resources from the most stricken communities and a tacit policy of allowing them to spiral still further downward, while unleashing the repressive power of an expanded criminal justice system to contain the resulting violence and disorder. I don't think that will happen; I think its potential social costs are too enormous and too widely understood. But I don't think it's inappropriately alarmist to bring it up as a possibility. It is, after all, not so far removed from the strategy we've in fact been following for some years. It should be clear that none of these possible outcomes are inevitable: the prospects for the safety of our cities and for the integrity of our criminal justice system in the coming decades will depend crucially on our ability to build a broad, lasting, and effective movement for social change.

NOTES

1. "States Spending Fastest on Jails," *The New York Times*, August 9, 1989.

2. President's Commission on Law Enforcement and the Administration of Justice. (1967). *The Challenge of Crime in a Free Society*, Washington, D.C., Government Printing Office, p. vi.

3. Ibid., p. 183.

4. Wilson, James Q. (1975). *Thinking About Crime*, New York: Random House.

5. Young, Jock. (1988). "Recent Developments in Criminology." In *Developments in Sociology*, ed. M. Haralambos. London: Causeway Press.

6. U.S. Bureau of Justice Statistics. (1988). *Prisoners in 1987*. Washington, D.C., Government Printing Office, p. 3.

7. Calculated from *Statistical Abstract of the United States, 1987*. (1988). Washington, D.C.: U.S. Government Printing Office, p. 173, and U.S. Bureau of Justice Statistics, *Correctional Populations in the United States, 1987*. (1989). Washington, D.C.: U.S. Department of Justice, cover chart.

8. Mauer, Marc. (1990). *Young Black Men and the Criminal Justice System*, Washington, D.C.: The Sentencing Project, p. 1.

9. Bureau of Justice Statistics, op. cit., p. 6.

10. U.S. Congress, House Select Committee on Children, Youth, and Families. (1988). *Children and Families: Key Trends in the 1980s,* Washington, D.C.: Government Printing Office, p. 44; Center on Budget and Policy Priorities. (1988). *Impact of Government Benefit Programs*

Declines, Adds to Number of Poor Families, Washington, D.C.: U.S. Congress, Office of Technology Assessment. (1987). *Healthy Children: Investing in the Future*, Washington, D.C.: Government Printing Office, p. 43; Center on Budget and Policy Priorities. (1988). *Still Far From the Dream*, Washington, D.C., p. 37.

11. Federal Bureau of Investigation, *Uniform Crime Report 1988*. Preliminary Annual Release, April 1989.

12. U.S. Bureau of Justice Statistics. (1988). *International Crime Rates*, Washington, D.C.: Government Printing Office, p. 5.

13. American Bar Association. (1988). *Criminal Justice in Crisis*, Washington, D.C.

14. Wilson, op. cit., p. xiii.

15. Wilson, James Q., and Richard J. Herrnstein. (1985). *Crime and Human Nature*, New York: Simon and Schuster, p. 88.

16. For a review of this research, *see* Currie, Elliott. (1985). *Confronting Crime: An American Challenge*, New York: Pantheon Books, chaps. 4 and 5.

17. One community patrol in New York City is described in Milton S. Eisenhower Foundation. (1990). *Twenty Years Later: Progress on the Unfinished Agenda*, Washington, D.C.

18. For a review on the rehabilitation of offenders, *see* Gendreau, Paul, and Robert Ross. "Revivification of Rehabilitation: Evidence from the 1980s," *Justice Quarterly*, vol. 4, no. 3, September 1987.

19. U.S. National Institute of Justice. (1988). *Difficult Clients, Large Caseloads Plague Probation, Parole Agencies*, Washington, D.C., p. 8.

20. *See, e.g.,* Berlin, Gordon, and Andrew Sum. (1988). *Toward a More Perfect Union: Basic Skills, Poor Families, and Our Economic Future*, New York: Ford Foundation.

21. Gelles, Richard J., and Murray A. Straus. (1988). *Intimate Violence*, New York: Simon and Schuster.

22. Kaufman, Joan, and Edward Zigler. "Do Abused Children Become Abusive Parents?" *American Journal of Orthopsychiatry*, vol. 57, no. 2, April 1987.

23. *See,* Lewis, Dorothy O., et al. "Biopsychosocial Characteristics of Children Who Later Murder: A Prospective Study," *American Journal of Psychiatry*, vol. 142, no. 10, October 1985.

24. Lewis, Dorothy O., et al. "Neuropsychiatric, Psychoeducational, and Family Characteristics of 14 Juveniles Condemned to Death in the United States," *American Journal of Psychiatry*, vol. 145, no. 5, May 1988.

25. Beruetta-Clement, J.R., et al. (1987). "The Effects of Early Educational Intervention on Crime and Delinquency in Adolescence and Early Adulthood." In *Prevention of Delinquent Behavior*, ed. John D. Burchard and Sara N. Burchard, Beverly Hills, Calif.: Sage.

26. Parker, Faith, Chaya S. Piotrowski, and Lenore Peay. "Head Start as a Social Support for Mothers: The Psychological Benefits of Involvement," *American Journal of Orthopsychiatry*, vol. 57, no. 2, April 1987.

27. Cf. Woodhead, Martin. "When Psychology Informs Public Policy: The Case of Early Childhood Intervention," *American Psychologist*, vol. 43, no. 6, June 1988.

28. For a general discussion of these trends, see Currie, Elliott, Robert Dunn, and David Fogarty. (1988). "The Fading Dream: Economic Crisis and the New Inequality." In *Crisis in American Institutions*, ed. Jerome Skolnick and Elliott Currie, Glenview, Ill.: Scott, Foresman/Little,

Brown; Harrison, Bennett, Chris Tilly, and Barry Bluestone. (1986). "Rising Inequality." In *The Changing American Economy*, ed. David Obey and Paul Sarbanes, New York: Basil Blackwell.

29. *See generally*, Currie, *Confronting Crime*, chap. 5; most recently, Avison, William R., and Pamela Loring. "Population Diversity and Cross-national Homicide Patterns; the Effects of Inequality and Heterogeneity," *Criminology*, vol. 24, no. 4, 1986.

30. On the Swedish experience, *see* Rehn, Gosta. "Swedish Active Labor Market Policy: Retrospect and Prospect," *Industrial Relations*, vol. 24, Winter 1985.

31. *See generally*, Sviridoff, Michele, and Jerome McElroy. (1985). *Employment and Crime: A Summary Report*, New York: Vera Institute of Justice; Currie, *Confronting Crime*, chap. 4.

32. Bluestone, Barry, and Bennett Harrison. "The Grim Truth About the Job Miracle," *The New York Times*, February 1, 1988; Levitan, Sar, and Elizabeth Conway. "Shortchanged by Part-time Work," *The New York Times*, February 27, 1988.

33. Hopper, Pauline, and Edward Zigler. "The Medical and Social Science Basis for a National Infant Care Leave Policy," *American Journal of Orthopsychiatry*, vol. 58, no. 3, July 1988.

34. *See, e.g.*, Doble, John, and Keith Melville. "The Public's Social Welfare Mandate," *Public Opinion*, January/February 1989; Morin, Richard, "A Sea Change on Federal Spending," *Washington Post*, National Weekly Edition, August 28–September 3, 1989. On the public view of crime prevention, *see* Doble, John. (1987). *Crime and Punishment: The Public's View*, New York: Public Agenda Foundation.

35. *Business Week*. September 19, 1988, p. 103.

36. *U.S. News & World Report*. November 7, 1988.

37. Committee for Economic Development. (1987). *Children in Need: Investment Strategies for the Educationally Disadvantaged*, New York.

QUESTIONS FOR DISCUSSION

1. Compare the conservative and liberal views of the causes and solutions to crime.

2. List and discuss the six key priorities outlined by Currie for responding effectively to crime. Are these reasonable approaches to the social problem of crime? Why?

3. How does Currie propose to reduce inequality and social impoverishment?

4. Discuss Currie's proposal for a supportive national family policy.

5. Why must strategies against crime go beyond the customary bounds of criminology and criminal justice?

5

AT THE ROOTS OF VIOLENCE
THE PROGRESSIVE DECLINE
AND DISSOLUTION OF FAMILY

George B. Palermo
Douglas Simpson

■ ■

The authors reflect on the origin of the family and its traditional dynamic force in the social and moral education, and in the affective support and protection of its members. They expound on their thesis that since the institution of the family is progressively crumbling under the pressures of ever changing socioeconomic events, people feel more insecure and frustrated. It is their belief that the present day family often does not pass on to its members those traditional high moral values of honesty and responsibility so important for good citizenship and self-esteem, and that the above, compounded by unemployment and the widespread presence of psychoactive drugs in our streets, may be a basic factor in the upsurge of violence and criminal behavior in our homes and our cities. Sociological and psychological thoughts are offered in support of their theories on the importance of the family as a germ-cell of society. Even though violence in the streets is multifactorial and the too easy availability of guns and the drug culture are certainly important factors, the authors believe that the progressive disintegration of the family and its value deficit are basic to the problem of disruptive violence in our streets. They envision a modern functional family whose members uphold personal responsibility together with cultural, religious, and moral values. They believe that their adherence to the above values would enable them to be better motivated and disciplined for good citizenship. Crime would then be fought at its roots.

HISTORICAL NOTES

Existentialism proposes as the basis of human life a dynamic adaptational psychobiological force, and changing cultural and social patterns, and continuous scientific discoveries are its obvious expressions (Lavine, 1984). Humans and the human family have been, and are, subject to this dynamic force. The original functions of the human family as a group that preexisted the *civitas* were to maintain order and readiness for defense, and to carry out, even though in a microstructure, the essential functions of the later State. Studies

Reprinted by permission of the publisher.

of Babylonian, Assyrian, Egyptian, Islamic, Indian, Greek, and Roman early civilizations strongly support this assertion. The early Roman family was patriarchal and authoritarian and, as in the primordial family, the father had the power of life and death over family members to such an unconscionable degree that unwanted children were exposed in public or abandoned, and family name and industriousness were more important than blood. We are told that strict rules were to be observed by the family members who gave up a certain amount of freedom for a portion of security. It was only during the middle and late Medieval era when the church championed the nuclear family that "family" began to denote "a complex ramified community whose essential function was one of protection" (Rouche, 1987, p. 464) and its fabric allowed "large numbers of children…[to have] frequent contact with the elderly whose words were heeded by the young" (Duby, Barthelémy, and LaRoncière, 1987, p. 169). Throughout history, the structure of the family was so strongly rooted and so well accepted that not even the social upheaval of the French revolution was able to destabilize it. It was a natural institution. "The newest political idea of the day was probably that the family is the basic cell of society. Domesticity had a fundamental regulatory function; it played the role of the hidden god" (Perrot and Martin-Fugieri, 1987, p. 100).

In more recent times, however, families—and in this case we take into consideration those in the Western Hemisphere—stable and united for many years, fully supporting of and supported by the Judeo-Christian tradition, have been shaken at their roots by a multitude of socioeconomic factors, radical social changes and rejection of previous religious conformism. The concept of the family as a psychobiological group, matriarchal or patriarchal in type, basic component of society, has tended to crumble and at times has reached dissolution. Fortunately, the process is not widespread, and the majority of families are still united.

Originally, the family provided for the needs of its members, and also offered certain protective boundaries. Eventually, it was recognized that the structure of the family should not be a fixed and static one, but that "[It] can and must vary widely to fit into, and assure the continuity of, the very divergent societies of which it is a subsystem" (Lidz, 1963, p. 3). Its functions are basic and vital for society. It helps its members to internalize institutions and teaches them *social and moral values* and responsible roles. It passes on to them basic adaptive techniques proper to their culture, as well as the *sense of social responsibility* so important for proper human development and humane, civic interaction. Also, as a basic component of society, the family is bound to play a role in the dissolution of cultures when it no longer carries out its basic functions.

SOCIOLOGICAL REFLECTIONS

A family is as healthy as its members, and factors leading to a healthy family and its maintenance are numerous. Scott and Scott (1983) state that while trust, affection, autonomy, and initiative are basic psychological components for the formation of a lasting group, the presence of a good genetic and psychogenetic pool, of a private and a mutual territory for the spouses, and the existence of a family myth that provides symbolism, values, and structure seem to be essential to it. It is evident that, "A family without values is a non-directed, goal changing, grasping small group" (Scott and Scott, 1983, p. 73).

Today, social violence is soaring. Its presence is multifactorial. It occurs both in communities and within the single family. There, within the home, the clash between spouses or live-in members often proves to be highly disruptive to physical and emotional well-being. Many members of society, both young and old, show the negative consequences of family violence and of its effect on the family group. They show difficulty in adaptation, communication, and in establishing relationships, and children may not be helped to develop their inborn capacities. "Many of our insecurities in living and the instabilities of individuals surely arise from the contemporary family's difficulties in finding a secure structure and satisfactory ways of raising children" (Lidz, 1963, p. 28).

The ever-increasing succession of new expedients to the problem of living, the secularization of religion, the industrial, and postindustrial revolutions with their migration of workers—blue and white collar alike, the fear of losing a job or the anxiety of not finding one, and an overstressed personal autonomy and hedonistic goals contribute to social confusion and irresponsible living. Many people, possibly overwhelmed by sociocultural changes and devoting their energy to personal needs and desires, distance themselves from one another, and this lack of communication at times leads to a different family structure, a new family structure or no family at all. The one-part family has appeared on the social scene and is steadily growing in number. Statistics speak clearly about the decline of the institution of the traditional family. "According to the Census Bureau half of all marriages end in divorce. Births to single mothers now make up one-quarter of total births. One in four Americans over age 18 have never married" ("Married with Children," 1992). Married couples with children under age 18 make up 25.9% of American households; married couples with children, 29.4%; people living alone, 25.05%; unrelated people living together, 4.7%; other families without children, 6.5%; other families with children, 8.5%. It is a statistical fact that married couples with a child under age 18 have become a shrinking minority. In 1970, married couples with a child under 18 constituted 40.3% of all American households; that became 30.9% in 1980 and a mere 25.9% in 1991. Concentrations of families made up of a married couple with children are "primarily in areas with large numbers of Hispanic, Indian, or Mormon families, in parts of Appalachia and some suburbs" ("Married with Children," 1992).

A closer look at today's family shows that the paternal figure has often been deprived of authority as in a society of bees, and perhaps as a consequence of the misinterpretation of some of Freud's psychological theories.

One can portray many present-day families, even those nuclei still apparently intact, regardless of race, age group, or socioeconomic status, as groups of separate, individual members within a hypothetical circle. Each of the family members looks toward a different horizon—almost staring into infinity. That infinity often equates to emptiness, solitude, and frustration, and frustrated emotional needs are often at the basis of aggressive behavior.

As stated by Parsons, "Society is a system of inter-related parts" (Collins and Makowsky, 1980, pp. 205–206), and the idea that at the basis of a wholesome and stable society there should be a functional interdependence of its parts seems quite logical and acceptable. However, during the past 50 years drastic and rapid economic and value changes have taken place, contributing to a lack of stability of family structure and emotional ties. Reproduction, biological maintenance, socialization, social control, status placement and emotional maintenance are no longer the prerogative of a family nucleus (Goode, 1960). "The three pillars of *gemeinschaft*—blood, place (land), and mind, or kinship, neighborhood, and friendship...all encompassed in the family...united in spite of all separating factors" (Nisbet, 1966, p. 75) seem to have lost their importance, and communities have been supplanted by what sociologists call *gesellschaft*—a society, held together by codified laws and certificated advisors—from financial counselors to mental therapists.

Not only have people and their families changed, but so have the architectural design of modern cities and towns. The public square, seat of people's encounters and ever ongoing democratic conversation (Hill et al., 1990), is no longer present. Parks are often unusable because of the fear of human violence, and cold, consumer-oriented malls, expressions of an object-oriented, robotized society, have poorly replaced them. Neatly packaged and promoted consumerism has facilitated the progressive alienation of people from one another and a void is felt in this still orderly and extremely envied American way of living. The decline of human values and wholesome relationships leads to a rush to own material objects that will fill the days and hopefully will lend meaning to existence. In many families, both parents must work just in order to maintain a marginal family menage. In other families, however, both spouses work in order to possess more things.

Even forms of communication have changed. They have evolved from the direct personal contact of meetings, discussions, and letters to the remote, electronic means of the telephone, answering machine, and Fax. To the extent that people are still drawn to common areas (for example, to shop) there is little chance that actual contact or communication will occur, and the contact that occurs will be with mirror-image individuals. People experience a sense of loss and an increasing inability to relate to one another. Human isolation is ubiquitous.

In a frenetic tempo of life the child, at times still an infant, is often placed in a preschool kindergarten, and there, like a partially abandoned being, attempts to socialize with other similarly frustrated children, all of them frustrated in their most important affective needs. An increasing number of children are being born into homes where no family, in the traditional sense of the word, has been established, or into homes where the family, because of divorce or separation, dissolves soon after birth. Because children learn parenting and other skills by observation and experience, we have a generation of children being raised without adequate role models. This is a particular problem for black children. Male black children, especially, often have to make the transition from boyhood to manhood under the guidance of a woman or mother. In his book *The Truly Disadvantaged*, black sociologist Wilson shows that in 1940, toward the end of the Great Depression, only 17.9% of black American families were headed by women, and, in those that were, the reason was usually that the husbands were dead. By 1988, the percentage was more than 50 and rising, but widowhood was no longer the cause (Hamill, 1988).

Not only may children suffer because of the loss of parents to the needs of two-income families, but an erosion of grandparent–grandchild relationships has also become common. The elderly, simply by their presence in the family, have always taught the young about suffering and humanness. They taught about death and the meaning of our existence. Once a powerful source of values and meaning, the elderly are now often shoved to one side in order that other family members can seek out the "good life," and they are unable to pass on to the younger generation the experiences of their lives. The affective alienation of the young and the old has been beautifully rendered in the poem "The Little Boy and the Old Man" (Silverstein, 1983), in which each describes his respective, and similar, loneliness.

Lidz's (1963, p. 37) statement of 30 years ago, "A larger proportion of the population is married than ever before," contrasts with the above-mentioned common occurrence in today's society—the one-parent family. The one-parent family, however, still holding good socio-moral values, should not be regarded in a negative way, even though "It becomes increasingly evident scientifically, as it has been through common sense, that children require two parents with whom they interact and who optimally are of opposite sexes in temperament and outlook, but who together form a parental coalition complementing and completing one another" (Lidz, 1963, p. 34).

One could certainly wonder whether emancipation and individualism have contributed to excessive egocentrisim and to a gradual dissolution of the nuclear family. That the world changes because people change is normal. It is the acceptable consequence of people's becoming more aware of themselves, their environment, their position in life. They become better educated, more constructive, more interested in creating a better world to live in for both themselves and for their children. But too drastic and sudden a social change such as society has experienced during the past few decades has created chaos, insecurity, and directionless activity for many. A supervening discomfort and anxiety became fertile ground for drugs, and crime followed, unconscionable, and motiveless.

AT THE BASIS OF SOCIAL VIOLENCE

Violence is often the express of frustration and hostility, at times generated by a profound dissatisfaction with the business of life. Unchecked by moral values, it may erupt and become highly destructive. Those basic moral values which serve to direct one's personal or group libidinal energy constructively are usually learned in the family that upholds them, and their importance is reinforced by civic laws. The functions of the family should lie primarily in offering to its members the affective, social, and educational arena that promote the personal and social growth and emotional stability of its members. As the nonfunctioning or noncoordination of the various organ systems creates sickness in the human body, so the disruption of the family is producing a nonfunctioning society. To this effect, Zimmerman's various parallels on the relation between family and society through the centuries, and his ideas of a possible connection between the decline of the modern family and the general breakdown of society is quite appealing (Goode, 1960).

People may be manipulated by social systems. Today, a good percentage of them seem to direct themselves, inappropriately and unsuccessfully, toward those ever-changing goals that culture and society incessantly manufacture for them. Bureaucracy, extreme rationalism, and utilitarianism have reduced "man to a pure subject, an organism with behaviors that can be predicted, manipulated, and controlled" (Kendall, 1990). Frustrated individuals and a similarly frustrated society alternate in a fruitless search for an existential answer. *Social frustration creates insecurity, hostility and confusion, and all too often hostility and violence find their outlet in the family itself.* Within the home, people are victimized by their own family members. "[T]he one place on earth where they should feel safe and secure has become a place of danger" (Herrington, 1984, p. iv). More unconscionable violence floods our streets.

Families should be the result of togetherness, sharing, love, work, lack of selfishness, and awareness of the physical, emotional, and spiritual needs of their members and of others. Healthy families help to form healthy communities. The family may find it difficult to keep itself healthy when the woman or mother has been drawn into the large cauldron of competitive work outside the home, and the man or father must often procure a second job. That does not mean, however, that it is not possible. It only means that the family may be under more stress. Achieving better material goods is part of the American heritage. "The achievement society cannot love a man or a woman who is without zeal" (Watson, 1991, p. 113). Fear of failure and abhorrence of idleness and boredom have contributed to the development of a society of workaholics and worried overachievers. They are the frustrated possessors of fleeting "goods." They seem to "look both upward and downward, applauding and reproaching themselves daily and hourly for their success in having climbed so far, their failure in not having climbed further" (Watson, 1991, p. 116). De Tocqueville already noticed that Americans had "a cloud habitually upon their brow...forever brooding over advantages they do not possess" (Watson, 1991, p. 114). The above can still be observed a century and a half later.

Today, almost half of the working class is composed of women, some by choice, considering it, correctly, their right to pursue their chosen career, and some by necessity. Many of these women are mothers. That is in tune with present sociocultural mores. One should be aware of the impact that this present-day social reality will have on the structure, functioning, and nurturing of the family and the development of resentment, frustration, and a hostility in many people. The child may feel deprived of parental affection and possibly that he or she is a secondary consideration to his or her parents' position in society. The child's formative years, often controlled by a series of commercial arrangements, leave the strong impression that there are no relationships in society other than those that are contracted. The parents themselves also become prey to guilt feelings and restlessness. The child may grow up with no concept of warm, human, spontaneous relationship, and, in some instances, a lack of parental presence may throw them into unhealthy streets where crime is high.

Basic cultural patterns are usually maintained through the family, its socialization and its moral education. Respect and duties toward self and others should be taught in the family and not by superficial conditioning of laws and policing. Families often seem to lack the emotional cohesiveness necessary for good personal and social growth and are no longer that "zone of immunity to which we may fall back or retreat, a place where we may set aside arms and armor needed in the public place, relax, take our ease, and lie about unshielded by the ostentatious carapace worn for protection in the outside world. This is the place where the family thrives, the realm of domesticity" (Duby, 1987, p. viii). In this atmosphere of increasing alienation many people, full of conscious and subconscious frustration, move around and about like automatons. They are under pressure—inner and outer, and run through the days, the months, and the years like goal-directed projectiles, going through life almost unaware of the world of affective interaction. Frequently, solitude makes them prey to inner anxiety and agitation and *frustrated rebelliousness*.

Is this the consequence of our technological discoveries? If that is the case, then one should realize that either technology is not good for society or that society is not making good use of technology. A technological society may tend to create a mechanical type of cooperation among its robotized members. Life becomes more organized but also more monotonously Orwellian. Monotony may also breed the upsurge of disruptive interests. Present-day social engineering and an ultrarational approach to life have created the image of a "[t]runcated…man, a less than fully human" (Kendall, 1990, p. 105) who, by logical consequence, will dehumanize anyone who comes in contact with him. It is a fact that present-day messy urban realities are a source of deep dissatisfaction and frustration for the majority of people. Daily, people must contend with the aggressive tempo of urban life—its traffic, its lack of jobs, its costly housing, increasing prostitution, use of drugs or sudden, uncalled-for, violent behavior. Does this social panorama breed frustration, rebellion, and violence in the family and society? Probably so. Does it justify violence in our society? Certainly not.

SUGGESTIONS AND CONCLUSIONS

Laws are in a continuous flux in an attempt to rectify the personal and social confusion that often breeds crime and violence, forgetting that "Legislation cannot save society. Legislation cannot rectify society…[T]he law that would work…is the successful embodiment of unselfish citizenship" (Wilson, 1915). If our assumption is correct, that the dissolution of the family is one of the major factors at the roots of violence in our homes and neighborhoods, the reintegration of the family in a modern and functional structure, upholding high moral values, is central to the stabilization of present-day society. We believe that responsibility and civic duties are as important as personal or group rights but that, more basically, human beings should become more humane in their dealings with one another. Indeed, "the duties of a person towards others are the same as his duties towards himself…Natural obligation is absolutely unchangeable" (Wolff, 1955, pp. 1234–1235). If the family group will emphasize the values of honesty, respect, love, and responsibility for others, criminality and violence in our homes and chaotic streets may be lessened. As a consequence of that, the number of prisoners in our jails, many of them young people— social offenders and victims themselves of early emotional and affective deprivation—will diminish. "[T]runcated beings…inevitably end up being mired in social disorder, because their souls are disordered and spiritual disorder leads, in the end, to social disorder" (Kendall, 1990, p. 106). As roots are essential for the growth of good, healthy trees so "[f]amilies stand at the center of society…[and] building our future must begin by preserving family values" (Reagan, 1984, p. 11). In the midst of present-day social confusion, it is of comfort to know that the majority of American families are still united, loving, and responsible. These families silently and stoically oppose their disintegration because they believe in those traditional values passed on to them by previous generations. Myriad low-income families are successfully protecting their members from the ravages of drugs, alcohol, and violence because they are honest, civil, and moral. It is the lack of values in a rapidly changing society that creates the propensity to crime in an individual, not poverty, and the family is an essential supporting structure for both the young and the old. Ackermann clearly pointed this out: "The essence of life is change, growth, learning, adaptation to new conditions, and creative evolution of new levels of interchange between persons and environment…The matrix of human relationship, whether healthy or sick, is the family…[and] intrapsychic equilibrium cannot be divorced from interpersonal equilibrium" (Ackerman, 1966, p. 203). The family is a natural social group, preexisting any state organization, with a proper set of internal rules, rights, and duties, destined to carry out a function that goes beyond personal interests to favor the interests of the group. We believe that a new, modern, well-integrated, wholesome loving family, enriched by the knowledge and experience acquired in the recent past, may be the agency capable of eliminating, at its roots, that sense of despair and confusion that leads to the violence that often seems to be dominant in our streets and in many homes. Even though its structure may, at times, be different from the traditional mold, the family will benefit from retaining traditional values. We certainly wish to take issue with the statement that "contrary to popular opinion, there is no scientific evidence for the application of our Euro-American concepts of family, house, home or household to the entire known spectrum of human domestic arrangements" (Harris, 1971, p. 266). We believe, indeed, that in confronting the problems facing today's families, it would be wise to take popular opinion into consideration, as well as clinical experience, statistical and scientific evidence (especially when it has to do with things of the heart), deep feelings, and values. We like to look at people not just as cold data. The majority of people are sensitive, and, sensibly, they know how much they suffer, how alienated they feel, how frightened they are, how capable or incapable they are to change axioms that serve to manipulate their actions and reactions. People know what they want and the average American citizen does not deny the natural importance of the family and its value system in our society.

Recently, the political scene has raised the issue of family values, and the press and public opinion have dealt with it extensively. However, it seems to us that a great deal of confusion exists concerning the meaning of the term. We believe that a family unit is primarily an entity that holds people from a similar biological background together, generally residing under the same roof until the children reach late adolescence. It developed naturally for protective and nurturing reasons and has been found to be essential for a smoother running of communities and states. However, when we talk about family values we mean a family, regardless of its structure and membership, holding within itself the values of love, respect, and responsibility for self and others, a part of those larger values that have come to be known as human rights and duties. These values are handed down from generation to generation and are exemplified in the sacred books of the world's religions. We, as a society formed by family groups, have made those values an integral part of our *modus vivendi* to the point that a family, in its purest sense, is not a family unless those values are an integral part of it. Without them, it is just an aggregation of people, held together by biological, nurturing, and defensive factors. The present-day upsurge of violent crimes perpetrated by adolescents whose age ranges from 14 to 17 may be an example of the partial failure of the family to pass on to its children good values to live by, or of the family giving them mixed value messages.

Freud understood that people in general have a certain "inclination to aggression" (Freud, 1950, p. 114) and he thought of the family as the "germ-cell of civilization" (Freud, 1950, p. 116) essential to counteract man's aggressive instinct. In *Civilization and Its Discontents*, he beautifully expressed that the human aggressive instinct, which we consider to be at the basis of family and societal violence, opposes the course of civilization: "[C]ivilization is a process in the service of Eros whose purpose is to combine single human individuals, and after that families, then races, peoples and nations, into one great unity, the unity of mankind…[but] man's natural aggressive instinct, the hostility of each against all and of all against each, opposes this programme of civilization" (Freud, 1950, p. 122). Sixty years later a pastoral voice reaffirmed the importance of the family in facing the present violent destructive trend: "It is necessary to go back to seeing the family as the sanctuary of life. The family is indeed sacred: it is the place in which life, the gift of God, can be properly welcomed and protected against the many attacks to which it is exposed, and can develop in accordance with what constitutes authentic human growth. In the face of the so-called culture of death, the family is the heart of the culture of life" (John Paul II, 1991, p. 76). That should be true for a two-parent family, the single-parent family, and for any group that considers itself a family.

Halting the progression of the dissolution of the family should be a concerted effort involving sociologists, educational and religious leaders, politicians, and parents. The reintegration of the family unit in some areas may be helped by the presence of the "man of the house" thus far kept away by certain regulations of welfare legislation. Fathers should not be forced out of the home as an eligibility requirement; we should not encourage additional births by benefit structures that reward subsequent pregnancies; we must stop contributing to the abandonment of all hope for employment and self-sufficiency. The combination of these systemic defects is a moral tragedy, and a lack of parental guidance and moral support contributes to indolence, crime, and violence. Organized religion should also become more involved and accept leadership in this crusade, while a "'social-environment'…'human-ecological'…strategy which includes interventions on the level of individuals and families 'at risk' [should be implemented]…to exert social control over those larger forces which now are increasingly undermining communities" (Currie, 1989). We believe it possible that by tackling these many factors, society will be able to effectively diminish the wave of violence in the country and people will have directed their energies constructively and purposefully and their social conscience will be at ease. Imbert stated that "In the long term, the solution [to social violence] will almost certainly lie in a greater sense of social responsibility, instilled through family, school, church, and all those other institutions which share the burden of the moral development of society" (Imbert, 1990, p. 425).

REFERENCES

ACKERMAN, N. W. (1966). "Family Therapy." In S. Arieti (Ed.), *American Handbook of Psychiatry* (Vol. 3, pp. 201–212). New York: Basic Books.

COLLINS, R., and M. MAKOWSKY. (1989). *The Discovery of Society*. New York: Random House.

CURRIE, E. (1989). "Confronting Crime: Looking Toward the Twenty-First Century." *Justice Quarterly, 6*, 5–25.

DUBY, G. (1987). "Foreword." In P. Aries and G. Duby (Gen. Eds.), P. Veyne (Ed.), *A History of Private Life* (Vol. 1, p. viii). Cambridge, Mass.: Belknap Press of Harvard University Press.

DUBY, G., D. BARTHÉLEMY and LA RONCIÈRE. (1987). "Portraits." In P. Aries and G. Duby (Gen. Eds.), P. Veyne (Ed.), *A History of Private Life* (Vol. 2, p. 169). Cambridge, Mass.: Belknap Press of Harvard University Press.

FREUD, S. (1950). *The Standard Edition of the Complete Psychological Works of Sigmund Freud* (Vol. 11, J. Strachey, Trans.). London: Hogarth Press.

GOODE, W. (1960). "The Sociology of the Family." In R. Merton, L. Broom, and L. Cottrell, Jr. (Eds.), *Sociology Today. Problems and Prospects* (pp. 188–190). New York: Basic Books.

HAMILL, P. (1988, March). "America's Black Inderclass: Can It Be Saved?" *Esquire.*

HARRIS, M. (1971). *Culture, Man and Nature.* New York: Crowell.

HERRINGTON, H. (1984, September). In *Attorney General's Task Force on Family Violence. Final Report* (p. iv). Washington, DC: U.S. Government Printing Office.

HILL, J., R. FLEMING, E. PLATER, R. ZYBERK, J. WINES, and E. ZIMMERMAN. (1990, July). "Whatever Became of the Public Square?" *Harper's Magazine*, pp. 49–60.

IMBERT, P. (1990). "Policing a Violent Society." *Journal of the Royal Society of Medicine, 83,* 425–426.

John Paul II. (1991, May 1). *On the Hundredth Anniversary of Rerum Novarum—Centesimus Annus.* Encyclical Letter, Publication No. 436-8. Washington, D.C.: United States Catholic Conference.

KENDALL, G. (1990). "Bureaucracy and Welfare: The Enslavement of the Spirit." *Social Justice Review*, May/June, pp. 104–107.

LAVINE, T. (1984). *From Socrates to Sartre—The Philosophical Quest.* New York: Bantam Books.

LIDZ, T. (1963). *The Family and Human Adaptation.* New York: International University Press. Married with children: The waning icon. (1992, August 23). *The New York Times*, Section 4, p. 2.

NISBET, R. (1966). *The Sociological Traditions.* New York: Basic Books.

PERROT, M., and A. FUGIER-MARTIN. (1987). "The Actors." In P. Aries & G. Duby (Gen. Eds.), P. Veyne (Ed.), *A History of Private Life* (Vol. 4, p. 100). Cambridge, Mass.: Belknap Press of Harvard University Press.

REAGAN, R. (1984, September). In *Attorney General's Task Force on Family Violence. Final Report* (p. 11). Washington, D.C.: U.S. Government Printing Office.

ROUCHE, M. (1987). "The Early Middle Ages in the West." In P. Aries & G. Duby (Gen Eds.), P. Veyne (Ed.), *A History of Private Life* (Vol. 1, pp. 464–465). Cambridge, Mass.: Belknap Press of Harvard University Press.

SCOTT, E., and K. SCOTT. (1983). "Healthy Families." *International Journal of Offender Therapy and Comparative Criminology, 27,* 71-78.

SILVERSTEIN, S. (1983). "The Little Boy and the Old Man." In *Poetry for Children.* New York: Random House.

WATSON, G. (1991). "The Decay of Idleness." *The Wilson Quarterly*, Spring. pp. 110–116.

WILSON, W. (1915, May 31). Memorial Day address. Arlington, Va.

WOLFF, C. (1955). "Duties Toward Others." In D. Runes (Ed.), *Treasury of Philosophy* (pp. 1234–1236). New York: Philosophical Library.

QUESTIONS FOR DISCUSSION

1. What has been the historical function of the family? What modern-day factors have presented families with a significant increase in stress?

2. How are the progressive disintegration of the family and the increase in violence related? Cite examples to support your response.

3. When identifying the genesis of violence in our society, much of the focus has been on discouraging violence with tougher laws and more severe punishments. Will this approach work? Cite examples to support your response.

4. If Palermo and Simpson are correct, implementing changes in social policy that strengthen families should have an immediate and long-term effect in reducing violence. Do you agree or disagree? Why?

5. Other than the family unit, are there any social institutions that may be able to fight the rising tide of violence in society? If so, in what ways?

6

RACIAL DISPARITIES IN THE CRIMINAL JUSTICE SYSTEM

A SUMMARY

Joan Petersilia

■ ■

This article summarizes a comprehensive examination of racial discrimination in the criminal justice systems of California, Michigan, and Texas. In each of those states, judges typically imposed heavier sentences on Hispanics and blacks than on whites convicted of comparable felonies and who had similar criminal records. Not only did these minorities receive harsher minimum sentences but they also served more time. It is chiefly at the sentencing stage where differential treatment is most pronounced. I discuss what could account for differences in sentencing, and suggest areas for future policy and research attention.

The United States criminal justice system allows policemen, prosecutors, judges and parole boards a great deal of discretion in handling most criminal cases. The statistics on minorities in prison have convinced many people that this discretion leads to discrimination. These statistics are, indeed, alarming.

As Figure 1 shows, blacks make up only 12% of the United States population, but 48% of the prison population. This seemingly outrageous disparity has prompted allegations that the police overarrest minorities, prosecutors pursue their cases more vigorously, judges sentence them more severely, and corrections officials make sure they stay incarcerated longer than whites. However, it is difficult to believe that discrimination in the United States is so vast as to produce such a disparity. Logic suggests and statistics show that much of this disparity is simply due to the much greater prevalence of crime among minorities than among whites. As Alfred Blumstein (1982) recently concluded, "racial differences in arrest alone account for the bulk of racial differences in incarceration."

The facts about traditional street crimes support this conclusion. An astonishing 51% of black males living in large cities are arrested at least once for an index crime during their lives, compared to only 14% of white males. Fully 18% of black males serve time in prison or jail,

Joan Petersilia, "Racial Disparities in the Criminal Justice System: A Summary," *Crime and Delinquency* (Vol. 3, No. 1), pp. 15–34, copyright © 1985 by Sage Publications, Inc. Reprinted by permission of Sage Publications, Inc.

either as juveniles or adults, compared with 3% of white males (Greenfield, 1981). Murder is the leading cause of death for young black males and is almost as high for young black females.

Crime is a fact of life in the ghetto. Blacks and other minorities must cope with both crime and the criminal justice system much more than whites, with devastating effects on families, employment, and self-respect. This situation raises a vital question for criminal justice research: Does the American judicial system intensify the problem by discriminating against minorities in any way? The central issue for this study is not whether blacks and Hispanics (in the general population) commit a disproportionate amount of crime, but whether, once arrested, the criminal justice system compounds the problem by treating them differently from whites.

The National Institute of Corrections supported this two-year study to answer three basic questions:

1. Does the criminal justice system treat minorities differently from whites?

2. If so, does that treatment reflect bias or the extent and seriousness of minority crimes?

3. If the treatment reflects bias, how can that be corrected?

This article summarizes the study's main findings and policy implications. However, because the study deals with a complex and sensitive issue, interested readers are urged to read the full report, *Racial Disparities in the Criminal Justice System*, which describes the data, methodology, and findings in consider, technical detail.[1]

FIGURE 1   **Racial Distribution in the United States and the Prison Population**

STUDY MOTIVATION

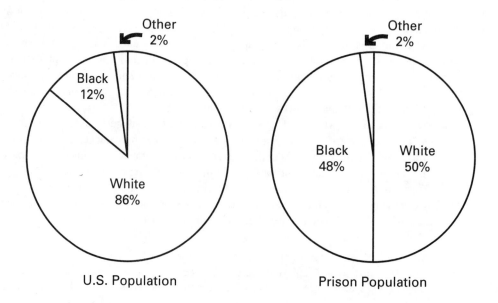

U.S. Population   Prison Population

DATA AND METHODS

Over the last three decades, social science researchers have addressed repeatedly the possibility of racial discrimination. Studies have offered evidence both for and against racial bias in arrest rates, prosecution, conviction, sentencing, corrections, and parole. There are many reasons for these contradictions. Some studies have databases too small to permit any generalization. Others have failed to control for enough (or any) of the other factors that might account for apparent racial discrimination. Most studies have looked at only one or two levels of the system. And no studies have examined criminals' prearrest contact with the system— the point at which many believe the greatest racial differences in treatment exist.

We attempted to overcome those shortcomings by using data from official records and prisoner self-reports, by examining the evidence for discrimination throughout the criminal justice system, and by controlling for the major variables that might create the appearance of discrimination. Whenever the data were sufficient to do so, we used multiple regression analyses of system decisions and criminal behavior to control for the most obvious variables.

The study data came from two sources: the California Offender-Based Transaction Statistics (OBTS) for 1980, and the Rand Inmate Survey (RIS). The OBTS is a computerized information system maintained by the California Bureau of Criminal Statistics. It tracks offenders from arrest through sentencing (or presentencing release). Once an offender enters the system, a number of social and legal variables are recorded (for example, sex, race, age, prior record, criminal status, and the original arrest offense). The OBTS also records the date of arrest and offense, conviction offense, date and point of disposition, type of proceeding, type of final sentence, and length of prison sentence.

The Rand Inmate Survey consists of data obtained from a self-administered questionnaire completed by a total of 1380 male prison inmates in California, Michigan, and Texas in 1978. Together, these three states house 22% of the national population of state prisons. In each state, the survey procedures produced a sample of inmates whose characteristics approximated the statewide intake of male prisoners. The self-reports elicited information about inmates' crimes, arrests, criminal motivations, drug and alcohol use, prior criminal record, participation in prison programs, institutional infractions, and the like.[2]

Because self-reports inevitably raise questions about the respondents' veracity, the survey was constructed to allow for both internal and external validity checks. The questionnaire included pairs of questions, widely separated, that asked for essentially the same information about crimes the respondents had committed and about other topics. This made it possible to check for internal quality (inconsistency, omission, and confusion). Over 83% of the respondents filled out the questionnaire accurately, completely, and consistently. The responses were not anonymous, and the official records serve not only as part of the analysis but also as an external check on the validity of the self-reports. Although the external check revealed more inconsistencies than the internal check, 59% of the respondents had an external error rate of less than 20%. However, for most disparities, the records were as questionable as the respondents' veracity. Records are often missing or incomplete, through no fault of the prisoners.[3]

The Rand Inmate Survey data permitted us to examine racial differences in crime commission rates—as opposed to arrest rates—and the probability of arrest. This information gave the study a considerable edge over much prior research because it provided a standard for assessing charges that minorities are overarrested. It also enabled us to examine questions of discrimination in corrections and length of sentence served, and of racial differences in crime motivation, weapon use, and in-prison behavior.

TABLE 1   SUMMARY OF STUDY FINDINGS

Element Studied	Evidence of Racial Differences[a]
Offender Behavior	
Preference for different crime types	+
Volume of crime committed	0
Crime motivation	++
Type of weapon preferred and extent of its use	++
Victim injury	+
Need for drug and alcohol treatment	0
Need for vocational training and education	+
Assessments of prison program effects	0
Arrest	
Probability of suffering arrest	0
Whether arrested on warrant or probable cause*	+
Probability of having case forwarded to prosecutor*	+
Prosecution and Sentencing	
Whether case is officially filed*	+
Type of charges filed*	0
Reasons for nonprosecution*	+
Whether the case is settled by plea bargaining*	+
Probability of conviction*	0
Type of crime convicted of*	0
Type of sentence imposed*	++
Length of sentence imposed	+
Corrections	
Type of programs participated in	0
Reasons for not participating in programs	0
Probability of having a work assignment	0
Length of sentence served	++
Extent and type of prison infractions	++

Sources: The OBTS for starred (*) items: the Rand Inmate Survey for all others.

a. 0 = none; + = suggestive trend; ++ = statistically significant.

MAJOR FINDINGS

As Table 1 indicates, we found some racial differences in the criminal justice system's *handling* of offenders, but few statistically significant racial differences in *criminal behavior* of active offenders. However, strong trends in some of the data raise important issues for policy and future research.

Racial Differences in Case Processing

As for racial differences in the disposition process, the OBTS data revealed an interesting pattern in California. As Table 2 shows, at the front end of the process, the system seems to treat white offenders more severely and minority offenders more leniently; at the back end, the reverse is true.

White suspects are somewhat more likely than minority suspects to be arrested on warrant, and considerably less likely to be released without charges. Whites are also more likely than blacks or Hispanics to have felony charges filed. However, a greater percentage of whites arrested on felony charges are subsequently charged with misdemeanors, whereas blacks and Hispanics are less likely to have the seriousness of their cases thus reduced.

Once charged, offenders of all races have about the same chance of being convicted of a felony, but white defendants are more likely than minorities to be convicted by plea bargain. In contrast, minority defendants are more likely than whites to have their felony cases tried by jury. Although plea bargaining, by definition, ensures conviction, it also ensures a reduced charge or a lighter sentence, or both. Moreover, prior research indicates that defendants receive harsher sentences after conviction by juries. These differences may contribute to the racial difference in sentencing. The study found that after a misdemeanor

TABLE 2   RACIAL DIFFERENCES IN CASE PROCESSING

Stage	*Percentage At Each Stage*		
	White *(N = 90, 865)*	*Black* *(N = 58, 683)*	*Hispanic* *(N = 39, 753)*
Arrested "on warrant"	9	6	6
Arrested "on view"	91	94	94
Released without charges	20	32	27
Felony charges filed	38	35	35
Misdemeanor charges filed	41	33	37
Felony convictions	20	20	19
Convicted by plea bargain	92	85	87
Tried by jury	7	12	11
Sentenced to probation	21	15	12
Sentenced to prison	6	8	7

Source: OBTS data for 1980.

conviction, white defendants had a greater chance than minority defendants of getting probation instead of jail. After a felony conviction, minority defendants were somewhat more likely to get prison instead of jail sentences.

These aggregate findings treat all felonies as if they were the same. If minority defendants had committed more serious felony offenses and had more serious prior records, we would expect their treatment to be more severe. Actually, minorities in the 1980 OBTS did have more serious prior records; a greater proportion of them had been charged with a violent crime; and a greater number were on probation or parole. However, by controlling for these factors using multiple regression techniques, we determined that the racial differences in postarrest and sentencing treatment still held.[4] White arrestees were more likely than minorities to be officially charged following arrest. Black arrestees were more likely to have their cases dismissed by police or prosecutor. After charges were filed, the conviction rates were similar across the races, but more black defendants than whites or Hispanics were sentenced to prison.

Length of Court-Imposed Sentence Using RIS Data

Our analysis of the OBTS data yielded evidence of racial disparities in postarrest release rates and in type of sentence imposed. The latter, especially, seems to substantiate charges that the criminal justice system does sentence minorities to prison more often than it does whites. But what of sentence length? Critics have also repeatedly claimed that judges sentence minorities to longer terms. Although the scope of the study did not permit us to analyze all aspects of case processing in all three states, it did allow us to analyze and compare length of court-imposed sentences. Considering the seriousness of the issue, we preferred to use the Rand Inmate Survey data rather than limit the findings to one state.

To establish the minimum and maximum sentence imposed by the court for each inmate who completed the Rand Inmate Survey, we consulted his official corrections records. We used this information in separate regression analyses for the three states to assess possible racial disparities in those sentences. The regression models controlled for

TABLE 3   ADDITIONAL MONTHS IMPOSED AND SERVED FOR MINORITIES

State	Court Imposed Sentence	Length of Sentence Served
California		
Blacks	+1.4 months	+2.4 months*
Hispanics	+6.5 months*	+5.0 months*
Michigan		
Blacks	+7.2 months*	+1.7 months
Hispanics	(small sample)	(small sample)
Texas		
Blacks	+3.7 months	+7.7 months*
Hispanics	+2.0 months	+8.1 months*

*Statistically significant

race, age, type of conviction crime, and number of previous juvenile and adult incarcerations. In all three states, we found that prior criminal record was not significantly related to *length* of court-imposed sentence. However, sentence length was significantly related to age and type of conviction crime. Further, the regression results indicate that, controlling for the defendant's age, conviction crime, and prior record, race made a difference in each state.

Although the relative lengths are not consistent for particular groups or states, these findings support charges that minorities receive longer sentences. In all three states, minority status alone accounted for an additional one to seven months in sentence length (see Table 3).

CORRECTIONS AND LENGTH OF SENTENCE SERVED

From arrest to sentencing, the system duly records most major decisions involving offenders. Consequently, it is rather easy to examine racial differences in handling. However, once a person is sentenced to prison, he is potentially subject to a range of decisions that are not systematically recorded. Prison guards and staff make decisions that influence strongly the quality of an offender's time in prison, and parole boards and other corrections officials decide how long that time lasts. The possibility of discrimination enters into all these decisions, but length of time served is the only one certain to be recorded. In other words, corrections is a closed world in which discrimination could flourish.

That charge has frequently been brought against the system, and the steady increase of prison racial problems makes it imperative to examine the treatment that different races receive in prison and at parole. We examined prison treatment and length of sentence served using the Rand Inmate Survey and the official records of our sample, where available. Our analysis revealed some racial differences for participation in work and treatment programs, but they were largely determined by the prisoners, not by guards or staff.

To create a larger framework for assessing possible discrimination, the study established criteria for identifying inmates who needed education, vocational training, and alcohol and drug treatment programs. We then compared the percentage who had need with the percentage that participated for each racial group.

Although there were no significant racial differences in the overall rate of program participation, there were some differences in participation, relative to need. In all three states, participation matched need most closely for education. In all three states, a greater percentage of minorities than of whites were identified as having high need for education. However, in Texas, blacks received significantly less education treatment. Moreover, in two of the study states, blacks had a significantly higher need for vocational training than whites or Hispanics, but did not have significantly higher participation rates. Compared with the other racial groups, blacks who needed alcohol treatment had a significantly lower participation rate.

Nevertheless, the reasons respondents gave for *not participating* suggested that minorities were discriminating against the programs, not vice versa. Prisoners most often said they were "too busy" or "didn't need" to participate; few said that they did not participate because staff discouraged them. The findings for work assignments were similar.

We found, however, that although minorities received roughly equal treatment in prison, race consistently made a difference when it came time for release. In Texas, blacks and Hispanics consistently served longer than whites—and the disparity was appreciably larger than the disparity in court-imposed sentences. In California, blacks served slightly longer sentences, but the disparity largely reflected the original sentencing differences. In Michigan, the parole process evidently worked in favor of blacks. Although their court-imposed sentences were considerably longer than those of whites, they did not actually serve longer (Table 3).

CRIME COMMISSION RATES AND PROBABILITY OF ARREST

To estimate whether minorities are overarrested *relative to the number of crimes they actually commit*, analysts need comparable "prearrest" information—variety of crimes committed, incidence of crime or crime commission rates, and the probability of arrest— for white and minority arrestees. Although official records provide information on the crimes for which people are arrested and convicted, they provide no information on the number of other crimes these offenders commit. To overcome this problem, we used data from the RIS on the actual types and number of crimes that offenders reported committing in the 15-month period preceding their current imprisonment. Inmates also reported on the number of arrests for each kind of crime they had committed during the same period. Using this information, we estimated each offender's annualized crime rate. Our purpose was to estimate separately the range of crime types in the different racial groups, and then to estimate the probability that a single crime would result in arrest for members of that group. We found strong evidence that *in proportion to the kind and amount of crime they commit*, minorities are not being overarrested.[5]

There are racial differences in the range of crime *types* committed:

- More Hispanics reported committed personal crimes—both personal robberies and aggravated assault.
- More whites and Hispanics reported involvement in both drug dealing and burglary.
- Significantly more whites committed forgery and credit card and auto thefts.

We found few consistent, statistically significant, differences in *crime commission rates* among the racial groups. However, there were differences in rates for two particular crimes.

- Blacks reported committing fewer burglaries than whites or Hispanics.
- Hispanics reported fewer frauds and swindles than whites or blacks.
- Black and white offenders reported almost identical rates of robberies, grand larcenies, and auto thefts.
- Black and white offenders were involved in more drug deals than Hispanics, but the differences were not statistically significant.

That last finding illustrates the difference between range of criminality and incidence of crime. The findings on range indicate that more Hispanics than blacks reported being involved in at least one drug deal. However, the annualized crime rates, which represent incidence, indicate that once involved in drug dealing, blacks committed more of it than Hispanics did.

Even though minorities are not overarrested relative to the number of crimes they commit, it is still possible that they have a higher *probability* than whites of being arrested for those crimes. Critics of the system have argued that this explains why blacks are "over-represented" in the arrest and prison populations. We found, however, that the probability of being arrested for a crime is extremely low regardless of race. For example, only 6% of the burglaries, 21% of the business robberies, 5% of the forgeries, and less than 1% of the drug sales reported by these offenders resulted in arrest. This finding held for all racial groups. We found no statistically significant racial differences in arrest probability for the crimes we studied with the exception of personal robbery. For personal robbery, blacks and Hispanics did report suffering more arrests relative to the number of crimes they committed.

MOTIVATION, WEAPON USE, AND PRISON BEHAVIOR

Motivation, weapon use, and prison behavior seem likely to influence the impression a prisoner makes on probation officers, judges, and parole boards. Using RIS data, we examined these characteristics for racial differences that might help explain the differences we observed in sentencing and time served. The statistically significant differences were few and not very helpful in explaining those decisions.

All three racial groups rated economic distress as the primary motive for committing crime, with "high times" second and "temper" third. However, there was only one statistically significant difference in motivation: Whites rated "high times" much higher than blacks and Hispanics did. Nevertheless, there were some other, suggestive, differences. Blacks rated economic distress considerably higher than high times, whereas whites rated it only slightly higher. This suggests that socioeconomic conditions among blacks may be more consistently related to crime than they are among whites. That comes as no particular surprise; but if probation officers, judges, and parole boards see unemployment as an indicator of recidivism—rather than as a mitigating circumstance in crime—blacks or any unemployed offenders are likely to receive harsher sentences and serve longer.

In weapons use, the data revealed a few clear racial differences, but if those differences influence sentencing or parole decisions, they do so inconsistently. Hispanics are more likely than whites to be sent to prison and to stay there longer, and Hispanics show a statistically significant preference for using knives in all crimes. Moreover, they indicated a greater tendency to injure their victims seriously. In contrast, the proportion of blacks in prison for burglary is considerably higher than the proportion of blacks arrested for that crime. Yet, in our sample, blacks were the least likely to be armed during burglaries. Indeed, they were less likely than whites to use guns and less likely than Hispanics to use knives. If these differences indicate that blacks are less violent and, perhaps, less "professional" than other groups, probation officers and judges apparently do not recognize it. Our findings on prison violence raise similarly conflicting suggestions.

The percentage of inmates with behavioral infractions differs markedly across states—significantly for five of the seven infraction types we studied. We therefore examined each state separately. Racial differences were pronounced for prison behavior. However, in all three states, age was most strongly, and negatively, correlated with higher infractions. Younger prisoners in all three states got into the most trouble. Younger prisoners in all three states got into the most trouble. After age came race, but not consistently for all states. In California, white inmates had the highest infraction rate; in Texas, blacks did. The high-rate infractors had the following profiles:

- California: a young white inmate who has had limited exposure to treatment programs, and who currently has no prison work assignment.
- Michigan: a young inmate serving for nonviolent crime.
- Texas: a young black inmate with few serious convictions, who has had limited exposure to treatment programs and currently has no prison work assignment.

Racial differences in prison behavior had no apparent relation to length of sentence served. In California, whites have significantly higher infraction rates than blacks. In Texas, the reverse is true. Yet, in both states, blacks serve longer sentences. (In Michigan, where there were no statistically different racial differences in prison behavior, race also had no bearing on length of time served.)

We again advise the reader that, whenever the data were sufficient to do so, our analyses of system decisions and criminal behavior controlled for the major variables that could reasonably account for apparent racial differences. Because of data limitations, however, we were unable to control for all important factors such as strength of the evidence. We also want to stress again that both our findings and our conclusions reflect data from only three states. Further, our self-report data come from prisoners, and conclusions drawn from those data are not applicable to the criminal population at large.

EXPLAINING DISPARITIES IN CASE PROCESSING AND TIME SERVED

Our analysis of the RIS data found that minorities are not overrepresented in the arrest population, *relative to the number of crimes they actually commit*, nor are they more likely than whites to be arrested for those crimes. Nevertheless, the OBTS analysis raised a question that the study could not answer: If blacks and Hispanics are not being overar-rested, why are police and prosecutors so much more likely to get them go without filing charges? One possibility is that the police more often arrest minorities on "probable-cause" evidence that subsequently fails to meet the filing standards of "evidence beyond a reasonable doubt."

Prior research may shed some light on this phenomenon. Earlier studies have shown that arrests depend heavily on witnesses' or victims' identifying or carefully describing the suspect (Greenwood, Chaiken, and Petersilia, 1977). Prosecutors may have a more difficult time making cases against minorities "beyond a reasonable doubt" because of problems with victim and witness identifications. Frequently witnesses or victims who were supportive at the arrest stage become less cooperative as the case proceeds. Witness problems may be more prevalent in minority defendant cases.

In addition to "evidentiary" problems, the study found another racial difference in case processing that may help explain a small proportion of the high release rates for minorities. A slightly higher percentage of white suspects than blacks were arrested with a warrant in the study period. Because the criteria for issuing warrants are essentially the same as the criteria for filing charges, cases involving warrants would be less likely to develop evidentiary problems after arrest. However, there is only a 3 percentage point difference between whites and minorities for warrant arrests.

Nevertheless, the difference raises a provocative question. Why are the police more hesitant to arrest white than minority suspects without a warrant? From the release rates, it appears that the police and prosecutors have a harder time making a "fileable" case against minorities. Yet, by getting warrants more often to arrest whites, the police implicitly indicate that the reverse is true. Or they may assume that minority suspects are less likely than white suspects to make false arrest charges or other kinds of trouble if a case is not filed.

Whatever their reasons, the racial differences in warrant arrests and release rates suggest that the police operate on different assumptions about minorities than about whites when they make arrests. Other study findings tend to reinforce the suggestion that the system regards minorities differently. Controlling for the factors most likely to influence sentencing and parole decisions, the analysis still found that blacks and Hispanics are less likely to be given probation, more likely to receive *prison* sentences, more likely to receive longer sentences, and more likely to serve a greater portion of their original time.

Possibly, the racial differences in type and length of sentence imposed reflect racial differences in plea bargaining and jury trials. Fully 92% of white defendants were convicted by plea bargaining, compared with 85% for blacks and 87% for Hispanics. Those numbers imply the percentage that engaged in plea bargaining since, by nature, plea bargaining virtually ensures conviction. However, it also virtually guarantees a reduced charge and/or lighter sentencing. Defendants who go to trial generally receive harsher sentences, and our study found that only 7% of whites prosecuted in Superior Court were tried by jury, compared with 12% for blacks and 11% for Hispanics.

However, even if these mechanisms did account for the apparent racial differences in sentencing, the implication of bias simply shifts to another node in the system. Why should minorities plea bargain less and go to jury trial more than whites? If the differences represent defendants' attitudes and decisions, then the system is not actively responsible for this racial difference. If these differences reflect decisions by prosecutors or decisions by default, then the issue of bias returns.

The suggestion that the system regards whites and minorities differently may enter into sentencing in another way. Judges may hesitate to send white defendants to prison for two reasons. First, research indicates that in prisons where whites are the minority, they are often victimized by the dominant racial group, whether black or Hispanic. In most states, blacks now outnumber whites in the prison population. Second, judges may regard whites as better candidates for rehabilitation.

INFORMATION USED IN SENTENCING AND PAROLE

Putting aside the ambiguity of findings about post-arrest release, the study found strong racial differences only in length and type of sentence imposed and length of time served. If there is discrimination in the system, it is inconsistent. Minorities are no more likely than whites to be arrested or convicted of crimes or to be treated differently by corrections. Yet, they are given longer, harsher sentences at conviction and wind up serving longer terms than whites in two of our study states. It may be possible to explain these inconsistencies by considering who makes decisions at key points in the system and what kinds of information they use to make those decisions.

As the accused moves through the system, more information about him is attached to his folder and that information is weighted differentially. Police and prosecutors are primarily concerned with "just desserts." Their legal mission is to ensure that criminals are convicted. They concentrate on the information they need to make arrest and conviction stick—primarily information about the crime and about the offender's prior record—according to strict legal rules. Judges also consider the nature of the crime and prior record in weighting just desserts, but they are further concerned with the defendant's potential for rehabilitation or recidivism. In other words, will returning him to society through probation or a lighter sentence endanger society? In deciding on probation, jail, or prison for an offender, they consider his conviction crime, prior record, and his personal and socioeconomic characteristics.

To provide the latter material, probation officers in most counties prepare a presentence investigation report (PSR), which contains a sentence recommendation. Probation officers are more concerned with analyzing and understanding the person and his situation, and they tend to deemphasize the legal technicalities necessary to assess guilt and convictability. The PSR describe factors such as the subject's family background, marital status, education and employment history, past encounters with the law, gang affiliation, and drug and alcohol abuse. In most states, it is the key document in sentencing and parole decisions. Its recommendations are generally followed by the sentencing judge, and its characterization of the defendant becomes the core of the parole board's case-summary file.

The influence of the PSR may help explain the racial differences in sentencing and time served. Minorities often do not show up well in PSR indicators of recidivism, such as family instability and unemployment. As a result, probation officers, judges, and parole boards are often impelled to identify minorities as higher risks.

These conjectures are supposedly by the comparison between length of sentence imposed and time served. In California, determinate sentencing practices make length of time served depend primarily on length of sentence imposed. Thus, racial differences in time served there, especially for Hispanics, reflect racial disparities in sentencing. Minority defendants also receive longer sentences than whites in Texas, and parole decisions there lengthen those sentences even more, relative to time served by whites. In Michigan, we found a reverse effect. Blacks received sentences 7.2 months longer than white defendants, but they served roughly equal time.

This contract can perhaps be explained by the parole practices in Texas and Michigan. Texas has a very individualized, highly discretionary, parole process that incorporates the full range of an inmate's criminal history and personal and socioeconomic characteristics. Since 1976 Michigan parole decisions have been based almost exclusively on legal indicators of personal culpability such as juvenile record, violence of conviction crime, and prison behavior. Evidently, this practice not only overcomes racial disparities in time served, but also even overcomes racial disparities in sentencing. Nevertheless, overcoming racial disparities in sentencing is neither the primary, nor perhaps the proper, concern of parole boards. Their major responsibility is to decide whether an inmate can safely be returned to society. By putting aside the socioeconomic and other extra-legal indicators of recidivism, they may be setting potential recidivists loose.

ASSESSING THE INDICATORS OF RECIDIVISM

If the indicators of recidivism are valid, the criminal justice system is not discriminating against minorities in its sentencing and parole decisions; it is simply reflecting the larger racial problems of society. However, our research suggests that the indicators may be less objective (and certainly less "race-neutral") than past research and practice have indicated.

The overrepresentation of minorities in aggregate arrest statistics has tended to obscure the fact that the criminal justice system and criminal justice research are, nevertheless, dealing with a criminal population that is half white and half minority. Unless minorities in *that* population have had higher recidivism rates than whites, there is no reason why minorities should consistently be seen as presenting a higher risk of recidivism. There is clearly a much higher *prevalence* of crime within the minority portion of the national population—that prevalence largely accounts for their equal representation with whites in the criminal population. But there is no evidence that they have a higher recidivism rate.

The Rand Inmate Survey data indicate that, once involved in crime, whites and minorities in the sample had virtually the same annual crime commission rates. This accords with Blumstein and Graddy's (1982) finding that the recidivism rate for index offenses is approximately 0.85 *for both whites and nonwhites*. Thus, the data suggest that large racial differences in aggregate arrest rates must be attributed primarily to differences in *ever becoming involved in crime at all* and not to different patterns among those who do participate.

Under these circumstances, any empirically derived indicators of recidivism should target a roughly equal number of whites and minorities. The reason this does not happen may be the relative sizes and diversity of the base populations. The black portion of the criminal population draws from a population base that is much smaller and more homogeneous, socioeconomically and culturally. That is, black criminals are more likely than their white counterparts to have common socioeconomic and cultural characteristics. The white half of the criminal population comes from a vastly larger, more heterogeneous base. Individuals in it are motivated variously, and come from many different cultural, ethnic, and economic backgrounds. Consequently, the characteristics associated with "black criminality" are more consistent, more visible, and more "countable" than those associated with white criminality. Moreover, because *prevalence* of crime is so much higher than incidence of crime (or recidivism) among minorities, characteristics associated with prevalence of crime among blacks (for example, unemployment, family instability) may overwhelm indicators of prevalence for the entire criminal population. They may also mask indicators of recidivism common to both blacks and whites.

The findings on criminal motivation and economic need lend support to this hypothesis. Blacks rated economic stress much higher than "high times" and much higher than "temper" as their motive for committing crime. They also rated it more highly than either whites or Hispanics did. Moreover, the black inmates were consistently identified as economically distressed by the study's criteria for economic need. These findings imply that socioeconomic characteristics are more consistent and more consistently related to crime among blacks than they are among whites. Considering that blacks make up approximately half of the criminal population, their characteristics may have the same effect on indicators of prevalence and recidivism that the extremely high crime rates of a few individuals have on average crime rates.

This is a real vicious circle. As long as the "black experience" is conducive to crime, blacks will be identified as potential recidivists, will serve prison terms instead of jail terms, will serve longer time, and will thus be identified as more serious criminals.

IMPLICATIONS FOR FUTURE RESEARCH AND POLICY

These findings and conclusions suggest some important research needs and policy initiatives. Among the research priorities are the following:

- Documenting the reasons for postarrest/prefiling release rates and controlling for race of the offender and type of arrest
- Analyzing postarrest problems with witnesses to discover whether and how the race of the suspect and/or of the witnesses affects cooperation
- Determining the relation of plea bargaining and jury trials to race, and why minority defendants are less likely to plea bargain
- Establishing the reasons why minorities receive and serve longer sentences, paying particular attention to effects that length of court-imposed sentences, gang-related activities in prison, and prison infractions have on time served

Although these and other issues deserve research attention, we believe that understanding why recidivism indicators more often work against minorities has particular priority. The system is moving to heavier reliance on these indicators precisely to render sentencing and parole decisions more objective. Paradoxically, just the opposite may result if, as we suspect, some of these indicators overlap with race in ways largely unrelated to recidivism.

Definitive policy recommendations will not be possible until some of these research tasks are completed, but three interim policy initiatives may be useful:

- Police and prosecutors should take into account the obstacles to filing charges after minority arrests, particularly the problems with witnesses, and try to find ways of ensuring that prearrest identifications will hold firm.

• Plea bargaining needs close monitoring, perhaps by a single deputy, for indications that minority defendants are consistently offered less attractive bargains than whites.

• Until the quality and predictive weight of recidivism indicators can be tested, probation officers, judges, and parole boards should give more weight to indicators of personal culpability than to indicators based on group classifications, such as education and family status.

Although this study shows that minorities are treated differently at a few points in the criminal justice system, it has not found evidence that this results from widespread and consistent racial prejudice in the system. Racial disparities seem to have developed because procedures were adopted without systematic attempts to find out whether they might affect various races differently. Consequently, future research and policy should be concerned with looking behind the scenes at the key actors in the system and their decision-making process, primarily at the kind of information they use, how valid it is, and whether its use affects particular racial groups unfairly.

NOTES

1. Copies of the complete report can be obtained by writing Joan Petersilia, The Rand Corporation, Santa Monica, California, 90406-2078.

2. For researchers with a special interest in Rand's inmate survey itself, a discussion of the method and content and a description of the objectives are detailed by Mark Peterson et al. (1982).

3. For a complete discussion of the validity of the Rand Inmate Survey, see Chaiken and Chaiken (1982) and Marquis and Ebener (1981).

4. Previous research using the OBTS file has shown significant differences in the processing of defendants from different counties and arrested for different crimes. Consequently, for the regression analysis, we wanted a sample from the same county and charged with the same crime. We were able to obtain a large homogeneous sample (n = 6652) by selecting defendants who were charged with robbery in Los Angeles County in 1980.

5. The Rand Inmate Survey has certain limitations as a means of calculating crime rates and of detecting racial differences in these rates. All the respondents were in prison and the sample was chosen to represent each state's male prison population. Therefore, it is not appropriate to view these crime rates as applicable to offenders in the community. They refer only to a cohort of incoming prisoners in the states chosen for this study. Selection effects and other factors cause these rates to be substantially higher than those for "typical" offenders (Rolph, Chaiken, and Houchens, 1981).

REFERENCES

BLUMSTEIN, A. (1982). "On the Racial Disproportionality of United States Prison Populations." *The J. of Criminal Law and Criminology* 73:3.

BLUMSTEIN, A. and E. GRADDY. (1982). "Prevalence and Recidivism in Index Arrests: A Feedback Model Approach." *Law and Society Rev.* 16:2.

CHAIKEN, J. and M. CHAIKEN. (1982). *Varieties of Criminal Behavior*. Santa Monica, Calif.: Rand Corporation, R-2814-NIJ.

GREENFELD, L. (1981). "Measuring the Application and Use of Punishment." Washington, D.C.: National Institute of Justice.

GREENWOOD, P., J. CHAIKEN, and J. PETERSILIA. (1977). *The Criminal Investigation Process*, Lexington, Mass.: D.C. Heath and Company.

MARQUIS, K. and P. EBENER. (1981). *Quality of Prisoner Self-Reports: Arrests and Conviction Response Errors*. Santa Monica, Calif.: Rand Corporation, R-2637-DOJ.

PETERSON, M. et al. (1982). *Survey of Prison and Jail Inmates Background and Method*. Santa Monica, Calif.: Rand Corporation, N-1635-NIJ.

ROLPH, J., J. CHAIKEN, and R. HOUCHENS. (1981). *Methods for Estimating Crime Rates of Individuals*. Santa Monica, Calif.: Rand Corporation, R-2730-NIJ.

QUESTIONS FOR DISCUSSION

1. According to the author, racial disparities exist at the arrest stage of the criminal justice process. Discuss these disparities.

2. It appears that the criminal justice system treats white offenders more severely in the early stages of processing and minorities more leniently. At the later stages of the process, the reverse is true. What evidence is provided in this article to support this claim?

3. What did this study find with regard to racial differences in types of crimes committed and differences in crime commission rates?

4. What explanation is given for the disparities in case processing and time served?

5. Based on the findings of this research, the author makes several suggestions for research priorities and for policy initiatives. What are these suggestions? Can you think of any other areas for research and policy initiatives? Explain.

7

THE INTERSECTION OF DRUG USE AND CRIMINAL BEHAVIOR

RESULTS FROM THE NATIONAL HOUSEHOLD SURVEY ON DRUG ABUSE

Lana Harrison
Joseph Gfroerer

■ ■ ■ ■ ■ ■ ■ ■ ■ ■ ■ ■ ■ ■ ■ ■ ■ ■ ■

In 1991, questions on involvement in criminal behavior and being arrested and booked for a crime were added to the National Household Survey on Drug Abuse (NHSDA) to ascertain the relationship between drug use and criminal behavior. Analysis shows that drug use is a strong correlate of being booked for a criminal offense, but age is the more important correlate of criminal involvement. There were few differences in models predicting violent as opposed to property crime, although minority status was a more important predictor of violent crime, and poverty was a more important predictor of property crime. Cocaine use was the most important covariate of being booked for a crime in large metropolitan areas that were oversampled in the 1991 NHSDA.

The National Household Survey on Drug Abuse (NHSDA) has tracked patterns of licit and illicit drug use among the general household population since 1971. This article provides a broad overview of the study, highlighting its methodology and results. In 1991, questions were added to the NHSDA on both self-reported criminal involvement and criminal behavior that resulted in being arrested and formally booked for a crime. This article examines the relationship between licit and illicit drug use and criminal behavior in the general population. Rates of criminal behavior derived from the NHSDA are presented, and the relationship between criminal behavior and drug use is examined using crosstabulations and logistic regression analysis. The article concludes with a discussion of the results.

Lana Harrison and Joseph Gfroerer, "The Intersection of Drug Use and Criminal Behavior: Results from the National Household Survey on Drug Abuse," *Crime and Delinquency* (Vol. 38, No. 4), pp. 422–443, copyright © 1992 by Sage Publications, Inc. Reprinted by permission of Sage Publications, Inc.

DRUG USE AND CRIMINAL BEHAVIOR

Research has consistently demonstrated a high degree of correlation between drug use and criminal behaviors (Nurco, Hanlon, Kinlock, and Duszynski, 1989; Speckart and Anglin, 1985; Hunt, Lipton, and Spunt, 1984; Inciardi, 1986; Wish and Johnson, 1986). Studies show high levels of drug use among incarcerated populations (Innes, 1988; Harlow, 1991). Likewise, studies of narcotic addicts (Nurco, Hanlon, Kinlock, and Duszynski, 1988; Anglin and Speckart, 1988) and heavy cocaine users (Johnson, Elmoghazy, and Dunlap, 1990; Inciardi and Pottieger, 1991; Gfroerer and Brodsky, 1992) have shown that these individuals are also frequently involved in criminal offenses. However, research shows that the principal criminal activity of many drug addicts is selling drugs. Only a small number are actively engaged in nondrug crimes (robbery, burglary, shoplifting, other larcenies, prostitution, and so on) on a regular basis (Ball, Shaffer, and Nurco, 1982; Johnson et al., 1990). There is no firm evidence of a causal relationship between drug use and crime. The general conclusion reached by a number of researchers is that deviant behaviors such as drug use and criminal offenses occur within the context of a general deviance syndrome (Osgood, Johnston, O'Malley, and Bachman, 1988; Elliott, Huizinga, and Ageton, 1985; Jessor, Chase, and Donovan, 1980; Kaplan, Martin, Johnston, and Robbins, 1986; Akers, 1984). Those likely to engage in one form of deviant behavior (for example, crime) are also likely to engage in other forms of deviant behavior (for example, drug use).

Another explanation for the correlation between drug use and crime, particularly property crime, is the economic motivation due to the high cost of illicit drugs. The relationship must also be considered in the context of the pharmacological properties of the drug. For example, there is virtually no research indicating that cannabis use leads to crime for economic gain. Likewise, alcohol, because of its legality and low cost, also does not lead to crime for economic gain. But there is evidence that opiate use leads to crime for economic gain. (There is also some evidence that cocaine use leads to crime for economic gain.) Research shows that narcotic addicts greatly increase their level of criminal offending during periods of elevated narcotic use (Nurco et al., 1988; Anglin and Speckart, 1988). McGlothlin (1978) has shown that income from property crime escalates with increasing narcotic use. Research further indicates that nonproperty crime does not covary with levels of narcotic use, suggesting that the relationship between narcotic use and crime is attributable to economic motivations (Anglin and Speckart, 1988; Watters, Reinarman, and Fagan, 1985).

The relationship between drug use and violent crime has not been well researched. However, the available research suggests that drug addicts commit few violent offenses (Hunt et al., 1984; Ball et al., 1982). Goldstein, Brownstein, and Ryan (1992) show that the vast majority of murders linked to drugs are due to systemic violence engendered by the drug trade. They propose that violence is inherent to the drug distribution system. For example, a person selling drugs may be assaulted or even killed when he tries to shortchange his customers or fails to pay his supplier. They conclude that drug users are more likely to finance their drug use by working in the drug distribution business than by engaging in violent predatory theft (Goldstein, Brownstein, Ryan, and Bellucci, 1989), suggesting that violence is peripherally related to drug abuse. There appears to be a hierarchy of criminal activity among drug abusers, with drug dealing as the preferred means of support, followed by property crimes and, infrequently, violent acts (Harrison, forthcoming).

Studies of incarcerated populations have shown high rates of drug use among criminal offenders. For example, in 18 of the 23 cities included in the Drug Use Forecasting Study in 1990, 50% or more of those who had been recently booked on criminal charges tested positive for some illicit drug. Cocaine, by a large margin, was the drug that booked arrestees were most likely to test positive for, followed by cannabis and opiates (National Institute of Justice [NIJ], 1991). A national study of jail inmates in 1989 found that 30% of jail inmates reported daily illicit drug use in the month prior to committing the offense that led to their incarceration. Over a quarter (27%) of the convicted inmates reported they were under the influence of an illegal drug when they committed the offense leading to their incarceration (Harlow, 1991).

MEASURING DRUG USE AND CRIME IN THE UNITED STATES

Although there is comparatively good information on drug use among incarcerated criminals, and some information on criminal offending among drug abusers, little is known about the relationship between drug use and criminal behavior among the general population. There is information on both drug use and crime rates at the national level, but not on the intersection of these behaviors.

The National Household Survey on Drug Abuse (NHSDA), sponsored by the National Institute on Drug Abuse (NIDA), has been conducted periodically since 1971 to provide estimates of the prevalence, consequence, and patterns of drug use and abuse in the United States. The National Crime Survey (NCS), which measures criminal victimization, has been conducted annually by the Bureau of Justice Statistics (BJS) since 1973 (see BJS, 1992a for a more complete description of the NCS). The respondent universe for both the 1991 NHSDA and NCS was the noninstitutionalized civilian population age 12 years and older in the United States. This includes residents of households, noninstitutional group quarters (for example, shelters, rooming houses, dormitories), and residents of civilian housing on military bases. Persons excluded from the universe include those with no fixed address, active military personnel, and residents of institutional quarters, such as jails and hospitals. The 1991 sample size for the NHSDA was 32,594 respondents. The NCS included a sample of about 95,000 persons in 1990.

The NHSDA sample design incorporates varying selection probabilities that result in oversampling of blacks, Hispanics, and young people. Special samples of about 2,500 respondents were also selected in each of six large metropolitan areas in 1991 (Chicago, Denver, Los Angeles, Miami, New York, and Washington, D.C.). Through intensive callback procedures, response rates in the NHSDA have been uniformly high. The 1991 screening response rate was 96.5% and the interview rate was 84.2%, for a total response rate of 81.3%.

The NHSDA interview takes about an hour to complete and employs procedures to maximize honest reporting of illicit drug use. Data are collected on the recency and frequency of use of various licit and illicit drugs, demographic characteristics, problems associated with drug use, and drug abuse treatment experience. Respondents use self-administered answer sheets for all drug-related questions so that responses are not revealed to interviewers.

Respondents place completed answer sheets in an envelope with no name or address information. The envelope is sealed at the end of the interview, and respondents are invited to accompany the interviewer to the nearest mailbox to mail it.

In 1991, the NHSDA added questions about criminal behavior. Using a self-administered answer sheet, respondents were asked whether they had committed any of a number of deviant activities within the past year. The series of questions is adapted from a scale that has frequently been used in surveys to measure delinquency, and yields information on a number of illegal criminal behaviors (Osgood, Johnston, O'Malley, and Bachman, 1989). Respondents were also asked if they had been booked during the past year for any of a number of offenses. The offenses include the Federal Bureau of Investigation's (FBI) Crime Index offenses (murder/homicide, forcible rape, robbery, aggravated assault, larceny or theft, motor vehicle theft, burglary, and arson), as well as a few individual offenses that have a high rate of arrest such as driving under the influence (DUI).

TRENDS IN DRUG USE AND CRIMINAL BEHAVIOR

The analysis reported in this article is based on a preliminary 1991 NHSDA data file. Measures of drug use and criminal behavior clearly show that these behaviors are more prevalent among young adults and youth. The NHSDA typically provides estimates of drug use prevalence among three age groups: youth (age 12–17), young adults (age 18–25), and older adults (age 26 and older). The highest rates of illicit drug use are found among young adults, followed by youth. The highest rates of alcohol and tobacco use are also found among young adults, but older adults have higher rates of use of the licit drugs than youth. Criminal victimization, as measured by the NCS, shows the highest rates of criminal victimization among 16–24 year olds, followed by those age 12–15. Arrests for serious crime are also highest among youth and young adults (BJS, 1988).

The trends in past-year use for several of the illicit drugs and alcohol among young adults age 18–25 are shown in Figure 1. Prevalence rates for both alcohol and illicit drugs increased during the 1970s, reaching a peak in 1979 and decreasing thereafter. Trends for 12–17 year olds show similar peaks in 1979. However, among older adults, marijuana and cocaine prevalence continued to increase after 1979, reaching the highest levels in 1982 (marijuana) and 1985 (cocaine).

Criminal victimization shows a trend somewhat similar to the trend in drug use among 18–25 year olds (Figure 2). Household crimes, personal theft, and violent crimes all reached their high points around the turn of the decade, although the trend in violent crime shows less variation and a gradual increase since 1986. As noted earlier, research suggests less correlation between violent crimes and drug use than between property crimes and drug use.

The similarity in trends between drug use and property crimes evident in these surveys may be entirely coincidental, but it is likely that it is related to the maturing of the baby boom generation. During the late 1970s and early 1980s, the last of this cohort reached young adulthood, the prime age for involvement in criminal behavior, illicit drug use, and a number of other deviant behaviors (Easterlin, 1978). Rates of drug use have been found to increase with age until the early 20s, then decrease thereafter (O'Malley, Bachman, and Johnston, 1988;

FIGURE 1:   **Trends in Past Year Drug Use Among Young Adults 18–25 Years Old: 1974–1991**

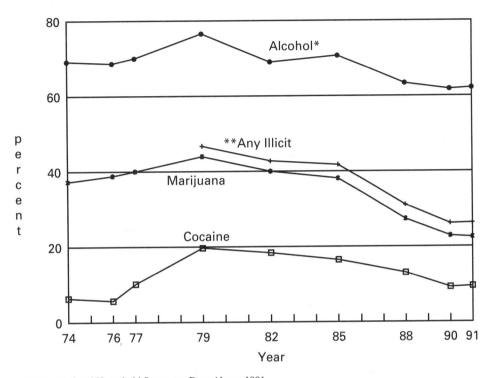

Source: NIDA, National Household Survey on Drug Abuse, 1991.

*Past month alcohol use.

**Composite measure of any illicit only available since 1979.

NIDA, 1991). Involvement in illegal behavior has also been found to increase with age, with rates peaking at about 17 and decreasing by two thirds by age 23 (Osgood et al., 1989). Data from the FBI's 1990 Uniform Crime Report show the highest arrest rates in the 18–20 year old age group (FBI, 1991). These data suggest that crime rates are greatly affected by the relative proportion of the population in the late teens to early 20s (Osgood et al., 1989). The data also indicate that involvement in deviant activities is highly related to the aging process.

1991 NHSDA PROVISIONAL ESTIMATES OF DRUG USE AND CRIMINAL BEHAVIOR

Provisional data from the 1991 NHSDA indicate that 37.1% of the general population age 12 and older reported at least one occasion of illicit drug use in their lifetime, with 12.8% reporting some use in the past year and 6.2% some use in the past month. The most prevalent of the illicit drugs was cannabis, with 33.4% lifetime prevalence, 9.6% past-year

FIGURE 2:   **Trends in Victimization Levels: 1973–1991**

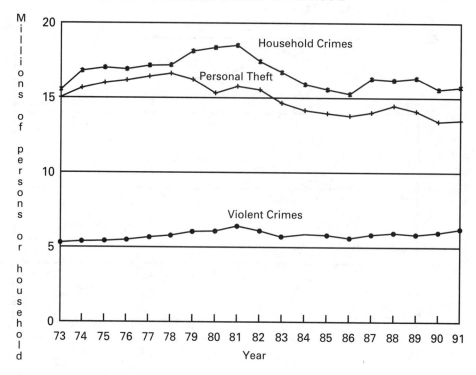

Source: BJS, National Crime Survey.
*Does not include murder or kidnapping.

prevalence, and 4.8% past-month prevalence. The nonmedical use of a psychotherapeutic drug was reported by 12.1% of the population (lifetime prevalence). About 4.5% had used a psychotherapeutic drug for other than medical reasons in the past year, and 1.5% reported past-month use. The lifetime prevalence rate for cocaine was 11.7% with annual prevalence at 3.1%, and past-month prevalence at 0.9%. Alcohol and tobacco were used at much higher rates than any of the illicit drugs. About half the population had used alcohol in the past month, and 4.6% had been drunk. Nearly three quarters (73%) had tried cigarettes in their lifetime, and over a quarter (26.7%) reported smoking in the past month. Higher rates of illicit drug use are found in Metropolitan Statistical Areas (MSAs), which are generally comprised of a very large city and the surrounding community. Other subgroup differences show males reporting higher rates of illicit drug use than females, and Hispanics reporting lower rates of drug use than either whites or blacks.

The provisional population estimates (12 years of age and older) and percentages of the population reporting engaging in the various delinquent/criminal behaviors during the past year are shown in Table 1. The most frequently reported crime was DUI, which 9.6% (or 19.4 million) of the population self-reported. Involvement in a physical fight was reported by 6.7% of the population or 13.7 million people. Shoplifting or stealing from a

TABLE 1   PAST YEAR DELINQUENCY/CRIMINAL BEHAVIOR AMONG U.S. POPULATION AGE 12 AND OLDER: 1991 PROVISIONAL DATA

	Percentage	Population Estimate
Any violent crime	7.0	14,198,300
Used weapon or force to get money from a person	0.3	573,242
Physical fight or hit someone	6.7	13,671,200
Hurt someone badly enough to need bandages or doctor	1.8	3,678,800
Used weapon to get something from a person	0.3	705,459
Any property crime	5.8	11,818,900
Steal from a store	2.9	5,846,260
Take money or property (other than from a store)	2.8	5,728,250
Purposely damaged or destroyed property	2.3	4,744,430
Motor vehicle theft	0.4	801,875
Breaking and entering	0.5	1,086,080
Other		
Drive under the influence	9.6	19,446,900
Sold drugs	0.9	1,831,710
Anything else to get in trouble with police	3.3	6,686,060

store was reported by 2.9% of the population, and 2.8% reported taking money or property (other than from a store).

The population estimates and prevalence rates for being arrested and formally booked for various offenses within the past year are shown in Table 2. Less than 1% of the population report being booked for any of the offenses in the past year. This is much lower than the proportion who disclose they have engaged in illegal activities that potentially could have resulted in their being booked. Consistent with FBI arrest data and the delinquency items, respondents most frequently report being booked for DUI. More people report being booked for a property offense than a violent offense, which is consistent with FBI arrest data but different from the pattern observed for self-reported criminal behavior.

The rates of drug use and criminal behavior by age group are shown in Table 3. Consistent with previous research and other data sources, the 1991 NHSDA shows that rates of drug use and arrest increase with age generally peaking in the late teens to early 20s and then decreasing steadily. The composite measures of involvement in property crime and violence have the highest rates among youth 15–17 years of age, and the highest rate of arrest for a property crime is found among 15–17 year olds. (Property and violence are broad categories encompassing several behaviors. See Table 1 for the behaviors comprising *property* and *violence*, and Table 2 for the offenses included under *booked violence* and *booked property*.)

THE CORRELATION BETWEEN DRUG USE AND CRIMINAL BEHAVIOR

The rates of delinquency/criminal behavior and being booked for criminal offending by various categories of alcohol and drug use are shown in Tables 4 and 5. The analysis is restricted to those 18–49 years old. Those over 50 are excluded because there are precipitous drops in alcohol use, drug use, and criminal behavior after age 50. Youth age 12–17 years are not included because there is a different pattern observed with respect to both drug use and criminal behavior for this age group.

In general, rates of criminal behavior are higher for populations more heavily involved in drug use. The lowest rates of criminal behavior are found among those who did not use alcohol or illicit drugs during the past year. Rates are higher among those who report getting drunk monthly, generally even higher for users of both alcohol and marijuana (with no use of any other illicit drugs), and substantially higher for persons who report using alcohol, marijuana, and cocaine in the past year.

The relationship between drug use and criminal behavior was further investigated using logistic regression models that controlled for confounding factors such as age, which could account for the apparent correlations between drug use and criminal behavior seen

TABLE 2   PAST YEAR ARRESTED AND BOOKED AMONG U.S. POPULATION AGE 12 AND OLDER: 1991 PROVISIONAL DATA

	Percentage	Population Estimate
Booked for any violent crime	0.4	910,055
Murder, homicide[a]	0.0	12,077
Forcible rape[a]	0.0	3,264
Robbery[a]	0.0	99,871
Aggravated assault[a]	0.2	335,638
Other assault	0.3	525,843
Booked for any property crime	0.7	1,457,730
Larceny or theft[a]	0.3	684,925
Other property offense (fraud, vandalism)	0.2	321,294
Motor vehicle theft[a]	0.1	164,789
Burglary or breaking and entering[a]	0.2	438,848
Other		
Arson[a]	0.0	23,254
Drive under the influence	0.9	1,845,900
Drug sale/possession	0.2	474,648
Drunkenness	0.4	778,424
Other	0.4	896,923

[a]FBI Crime Index Offenses.

TABLE 3   DRUG USE AND CRIMINAL BEHAVIOR BY AGE GROUP AMONG U.S. POPULATION AGE 12 AND OLDER (PERCENTAGE REPORTING BEHAVIOR IN PAST YEAR): 1991 PROVISIONAL DATA

	Age Group								
	12–14	*15–17*	*18–21*	*22–25*	*26–29*	*30–34*	*35–49*	*50+*	*All ages 12+*
Alcohol use	25.0	55.4	82.3	83.4	80.8	80.9	75.2	56.4	68.1
Drunk monthly	0.7	5.0	8.2	6.6	8.2	5.0	5.5	2.4	4.6
Cannabis use	3.4	16.7	26.5	22.4	15.7	13.6	7.9	1.1	9.6
Cocaine use	0.6	2.5	6.7	8.8	5.9	4.5	2.8	0.6	3.1
Violence	27.5	31.2	20.4	10.7	5.8	4.1	3.2	0.3	7.0
Property	18.8	27.5	18.6	9.0	5.4	3.5	2.2	0.5	5.8
Booked violence	0.6	1.0	1.7	1.0	0.7	0.4	0.3	0.3	0.4
Booked property	1.0	2.9	2.7	1.8	0.8	0.4	0.3	0.1	0.7

in Tables 4 and 5. Four dependent variables were used for these models: involvement in property crime, involvement in violent crime, being booked for a property offense, and being booked for a violent offense in the past year. For each dependent variable, two separate models were run, one for the portion of the sample in the six oversampled metropolitan areas in the 1991 NHSDA and one for the remainder of the national sample. This was done because the sample design (and probabilities of selection) were substantially different in the six over-sampled areas when compared to the rest of the sample. This strategy also allowed the inclusion of a variable indicating whether residents in the six cities lived in low socioeconomic (SES) areas, based on the 1980 census values of the sample segments' mean housing values and rents. Except for the SES variable, all eight models included the same set of independent variables. All models were restricted to 18–49 year olds.

Results of the logistic regression modeling are shown in Tables 6 and 7. The adjusted odds radio for each variable in the model is reported. The odds ratios reflect the likelihood of a positive response on the dependent variable relative to that for the defined reference group, after controlling for all the other variables included in the model. Adjusted odds ratios greater than 1.0 indicate an increased likelihood of criminal behavior, and those less than 1.0 indicate a decreased likelihood. The rank correlation statistic c provides a measure of the overall significance of the model, which ranges from 0.5 (no predictive accuracy beyond chance alone) to 1.0 (perfect predictive accuracy) and is loosely analogous to the R^2 statistic in ordinary linear regression. All of the models provide a reasonably good fit.

Even after controlling for other variables such as age, race, income, education, and marital status, all three drug-use indicators (getting drunk monthly, using marijuana in the past year, and using cocaine in the past year) were significantly related to criminal behavior. This result was found in all eight models, and odds ratios were generally higher for the drug use variables than for demographic and SES variables. Cocaine use was the strongest

TABLE 4   PAST YEAR DELINQUENCY/CRIMINAL BEHAVIOR BY ALCOHOL AND DRUG USE AMONG THOSE AGE 18–49 (PERCENTAGE COMMITTING CRIME): 1991 PROVISIONAL DATA

	Alcohol and Drug Use			
	None (N = 4,801)	*Alcohol Only (N = 11,492)*	*Drunk Monthly[a] (N = 1,259)*	*Alcohol and Cannabis Only (N = 1,786)*	*Alcohol, Cannabis, andd Cocaine (N = 890)*
Any violent crime	2.7	4.8	6.3	14.6	26.1
Used weapon or force to get money from a person	0.0	0.1	0.6	0.4	b
Physical fight or hit someone	2.5	4.7	11.5	14.0	23.3
Hurt someone badly enough to need bandages or doctor	0.7	1.1	3.2	4.7	9.2
Used weapon to get something from a person	0.2	0.1	0.3	1.3	b
Any property crime	1.7	3.8	8.0	13.0	24.7
Steal from a store	0.5	1.5	3.3	5.8	15.5
Steal money or property	1.1	1.8	3.3	6.5	15.0
Purposely damaged or destroyed property	0.5	1.1	4.2	4.7	11.4
Motor vehicle theft	0.1	0.2	0.1	0.5	4.3
Breaking and entering	0.1	0.3	0.4	0.7	4.1
Other					
Driving under the influence	0.1	12.3	33.3	30.8	57.2
Sold drugs	0.0	0.1	0.2	2.2	15.1
Anything else to get in trouble with police	1.4	2.5	4.6	9.1	22.2

a. Drunk monthly in past year, but no illicit drug use.

b. Low precision, no estimate reported.

predictor of being booked for a violent crime or a property crime in the six cities, with odds ratios of 6.18 and 4.92, respectively. However, in all other models the three drug use variables were about equally as important predictors of criminal behavior and being booked, with odds ratios ranging from 1.60 to 3.23.

Consistent with data in Table 3 and prior research, age is highly significant in several of the models, and the pattern of odds ratios indicates a decreasing rate of criminal behavior with increasing age. However, the relationship between age and offending was different for involvement in criminal behavior and being booked for criminal behavior. In general, age (being 18–21 years old) was the strongest predictor of involvement in violent and

TABLE 5   PAST YEAR ARRESTED AND BOOKED BY ALCOHOL AND DRUG USE AMONG THOSE AGE 18–19 (PERCENTAGE BOOKED FOR CRIME): 1991 PROVISIONAL DATA

	Alcohol and Drug Use				
	None (N = 4,801)	Alcohol Only (N = 11,492)	Drunk Monthly[a] (N = 1,259)	Alcohol and Cannabis Only (N = 1,786)	Alcohol, Cannabis, andd Cocaine (N = 890)
Booked for any violent crime	0.4	0.3	1.3	0.9	3.9
Murder, homicide	b	b	b	b	b
Forcible rape	b	b	b	b	b
Robbery	0.0	0.0	0.3	b	0.2
Aggravated assault	0.2	0.1	0.1	0.3	2.0
Other assault	0.2	0.2	0.9	0.6	2.4
Booked for any property crime	0.2	0.4	0.4	1.9	6.3
Larceny or theft	0.1	0.1	0.1	1.0	3.2
Other property offenses (fraud, vandalism)	0.1	0.2	b	0.1	1.4
Motor vehicle theft	b	0.0	0.0	0.5	0.6
Burglary or breaking and entering	0.1	0.1	0.3	0.3	2.4
Other					
Driving under the influence	0.1	0.9	3.6	2.6	10.5
Drug sales/ possession	0.0	0.1	0.2	0.6	4.1
Drunkenness	0.1	0.2	1.2	1.4	2.4
Arson	b	b	b	b	b
Other	0.0	0.4	0.6	1.7	2.8

a. Drunk monthly in past year, but no illicit drug use.

b. Low precision, no estimate reported.

property crime, whereas cocaine use was the strongest predictor of being booked for these crimes. The only exception was in the six-city property crime model, in which being 18–21 (relative to being 35–49) years old was equally as important as cocaine use in being booked for a property crime. The 18–21 year old age group was the only age group that was significantly related to being booked for a violent or property crime, once other variables were controlled.

The demographic variables were all generally significant. Gender was a significant predictor in all eight models, indicating that males were much more likely than females to

TABLE 6 LOGISTIC REGRESSION RESULTS FOR MODELS OF VIOLENT CRIME AMONG THOSE AGE 18-49 (ADJUSTED ODDS RATIO): 1991 PROVISIONAL DATA

	Six Major U.S. Cities[a]		U.S. Excluding Six Major U.S. Cities	
	Violence	Booked Violence	Violence	Booked Violence
Drunk monthly (during past year)	2.21****	3.23****	2.14****	2.26****
Cannabis (past year)	2.25****	2.99****	2.06****	1.87****
Cocaine (past year)	2.54****	6.18****	1.60****	2.50****
Age 18–21[b]	4.93****	2.11*	5.60****	2.17**
Age 22–25[b]	2.42****	1.43	2.96****	1.70
Age 26–29[b]	1.77****	1.16	1.71****	1.20
Age 30–34[b]	1.69****	.97	1.42**	1.30
Male	1.96****	1.76**	2.19****	2.45****
Black[c]	1.55****	2.79****	1.52****	2.70****
Hispanic[c]	.79*	1.89*	.81**	1.63*
Unmarried	1.11	.78	1.54****	2.25***
High school dropout	1.46****	1.44	1.52****	2.60****
Poverty (household)[d]	1.13	.90	.98	.70
Low SES (area)[e]	.84*	1.36		
Predictive accuracy of full model (c)	.79	.87	.80	.84

a. Includes Chicago, Denver, Los Angeles, Miami, New York, and Washington, D.C. MSAs.

b. The reference group is the 35–49 year old age group.

c. The reference group is nonblack, non-Hispanic.

d. 1990 poverty level as calculated by the U.S. Census Bureau based on number of residents in household and total family income.

e. Defined as the third of the urbanized area segments with the lowest median housing value and rent (based on 1980 U.S. Census).

*$p < .10$; **$p < .05$; ***$p < .01$; ****$p < .001$.

be involved in criminal behavior. Blacks were more likely to report engaging in, as well as being booked for, violent crime. However, being black was a stronger predictor of being booked for a violent crime than it was for actually committing a violent crime. Blacks were not more likely to commit property crimes, but outside the six cities, they were more likely to be booked for property crimes. Hispanics were less likely to be involved in property crime, but no less likely to be booked for property crime. Hispanics were also somewhat less likely to engage in violent crime, but somewhat more likely to be booked for violent crime. Marital status was not significant in any of the six-city models, but it was significant in three of the non-six-city models.

TABLE 7   LOGISTIC REGRESSION RESULTS FOR MODELS OF PROPERTY CRIME AMONG THOSE AGE 18–49 (ADJUSTED ODDS RATIO): 1991 PROVISIONAL DATA

	Six Major U.S. Cities[a]		U.S. Excluding Six Major U.S. Cities	
	Property	Booked Property	Property	Booked Property
Drunk month (during past year)	2.16****	1.62*	1.64****	1.72***
Cannabis (past year)	2.80****	2.25***	2.80****	3.06****
Cocaine (past year)	2.91****	4.92****	1.84****	2.84****
Age 18–21[b]	4.80****	4.89****	5.44****	1.94**
Age 22–25[b]	2.22****	1.99	2.45****	1.51
Age 26–29[b]	1.30	1.75	1.73****	.64
Age 30–34[b]	1.52	2.32*	1.48**	.73
Male	1.61****	2.61****	1.79****	1.60**
Black[c]	.98	1.33	.93	1.71****
Hispanic[c]	.77**	.59	.67****	.91
Unmarried	1.09	.94	1.58****	1.37
High school dropout	.92	1.77**	.91	1.93****
Poverty (household)[d]	1.40****	1.73**	1.25***	.98
Low SES (area)[e]	.91	1.31		
Predictive accuracy of full model (c)	.79	.87	.80	.80

a.   Includes Chicago, Denver, Los Angeles, Miami, New York, and Washington, D.C. MSAs.

b.   The reference group is the 34–49 year old age group.

c.   The reference group is nonblack, non-Hispanic.

d.   1990 poverty level as calculated by the U.S. Census Bureau based on number of residents in household and total family income.

e.   Defined as the third of the urbanized area segments with the lowest median housing value and rent (based on 1980 U.S. Census).

$*p < .10; **p < .05; ***p < .01; ****p < .001.$

The SES level of the sampled segment (i.e., block) was generally not significant in the four six-city models. (This measure, classifying segments according to their average housing values and rents based on 1980 Census data, is an indicator of the SES of the neighborhood in which the respondent resides.) However, analysis showed that living in a household below the 1990 poverty level was generally a significant correlate of involvement in property crime, but not violent crime.

Being a high school dropout was not significant in the models of involvement in property crime, but it was significantly related to being booked for a property crime. Dropouts were significantly more likely to report engaging in violent crime, but they were only more likely to be booked for a violent crime in the non-six-city model.

Further analysis of the relationship between drug use and crime was conducted, using criminal behavior as an independent variable in logistic regression models. When involvement in property crimes was added as an independent variable in the violence and booked-violence models, it became the most important predictor (data not shown), indicating a high degree of correlation between involvement in property and violent crimes. In general, the other variables found significant in these models were the same ones that were significant in models without property crime as a predictor (see Table 6), but the size of the odds ratio for drug use and age were reduced. When involvement in violent crime was added as an independent variable to the property and booked-property models, it also became the most important predictor. Significant variables shown in Table 7 generally remained significant in these models as well, with similar reductions in odds ratios for age and drug use variables. These results indicate that the criminal behavior variables are even more closely related to each other than they are to drug use. However, in the booked-violence and booked-property models, the odds ratios for cocaine use were similar to the odds ratios for the independent crime variable added to these models.

DISCUSSION

The results of these analyses based on the 1991 NHSDA preliminary file show that drug use in general, and cocaine use in particular, are the most important correlates of being booked for property and violent crimes. Drug users (including those getting drunk at least once a month) are more likely to be booked for offenses than nondrug users, especially in major cities. Drug users are also more likely to engage in property and violent crime, but age is perhaps an even stronger correlate of involvement in crime. Age (being 18–21) is only as strong a predictor as cocaine use for being booked for a property crime in the six cities. These findings suggest that although age is a strong correlate of engaging in criminal activity, with an inverse relationship from the early 20s on, drug use is the stronger correlate of actually being booked for a criminal offense.

This does not mean, however, that drug use causes crime. It would likewise be appropriate to say that age causes involvement in property and violent crime. What we can say is that drug use and criminal behavior are highly correlated. We can also say that age is highly correlated with criminal behavior, but it is generally not as highly correlated with being booked and charged for a criminal offense once drug use and other demographic and

SES variables are controlled. Drug use, and especially cocaine use, is highly related to being booked and charged for an offense, and this is more true in the six cities than in the remainder of the United States.

Perhaps one of the more interesting findings is the robustness of the drug use-criminal behavior relationship. Whereas previous research demonstrates the relationship among heavy drug users, narcotic addicts, and incarcerated populations, our analysis shows that the relationship is strong even in the general population, based on those who report the activity at least once in the past year. Also, separate logistic regression models found similar results in both the six major cities and in the remainder of the United States.

Drug use and criminal behavior are also activities that decline with age. The analyses confirm the "maturing out" of criminal behavior and although no controls were introduced (Table 3), drug use also decreases with age. Both drug use and criminal behavior tend to peak in the general population in the late teens to early 20s.

Previous research showing that drug abusers are more likely to engage in property crimes than in violent crimes is not supported by our analysis. We found drug use to be a strong correlate of both violent and property crime in the general population. Furthermore, the use of cannabis, getting drunk monthly, and the use of cocaine were equally important in predicting criminal involvement. These results lend support to the general deviance theory.

Some interesting patterns emerged in the minority status and socioeconomic variables in the logistic regression models. Being black was a risk factor for involvement in violent crime but not property crime. Similarly, high school dropouts were more likely to be involved in violent crime but not property crime. On the other hand, poverty status was a significant predictor of involvement in property crime but not violent crime. Living in a low income area did not predict involvement in crime. Hispanics were less likely than whites to be involved in property and violent crime. In the booked-violence and booked-property models, however, odds ratios for minority status and high school dropout variables were larger than in the corresponding models of involvement in violence and property crime. In these models, blacks were found to be more likely than whites to be booked for property crimes. Hispanics were found to be more likely than whites to be booked for violent crimes. Because our outcome variables were composite measures that did not account for the specific types of crimes committed, this finding is difficult to explain. However, it could be an indication of differential arrest practices. Additional research is needed to explain the relationship between minority status and being booked for violent and property crimes.

Based on our analysis, the NHSDA does appear to have adequately sampled persons involved with the criminal justice system. FBI data on arrests provide some indication of the accuracy of NHSDA estimates of criminal behavior. According to the 1991 NHSDA preliminary data file, the number of persons booked for an FBI Index Crime during the past year was 1.05 million. The number of bookings cannot be obtained from the NHSDA because persons may be arrested more than once for the same charge. However, by counting respondents multiple times when they report multiple types of FBI Index Crimes, an estimate of arrests can be derived from the NHSDA. Although it does not account for multiple arrests for the same charge, this calculation yields an estimate of 1.76 million, about 60% of the 2.92 million arrests estimated by the FBI in 1990. The NHSDA appears to get better coverage of persons arrested for some offenses than for others. Estimates of the number of people booked for DUI, drunkenness, burglary, and motor vehicle theft in the NHSDA are similar to the FBI estimates of arrests for these offenses. For some of the less frequently committed crimes such as murder/homicide, forcible rape, and arson, there is less congruence.

At least part of the difference in the NHSDA and FBI estimates is due to individuals being incarcerated for their crimes. According to the BJS, 32% of felony offenders (in larger cities) were incarcerated for their crime (1991). Federal courts report that 63% of charged arrestees are released (meaning 37% are detained), and 70% are released sometime prior to trial (BJS, 1992b). Therefore, the NHSDA should only be getting a proportion of the arrestees who have been booked and charged for offenses, because the survey does not include those who are incarcerated (for more than a few weeks). Taking these factors into consideration, the NHSDA estimate of 1.76 million for the sum of the FBI Index Crimes appears to be consistent with the FBI estimates on arrests, indicating that undercoverage and underreporting bias are small in the NHSDA.

There appears to be some underestimating of individuals on probation or parole in the NHSDA. As with the other criminal justice-related questions, respondents are asked to report on the past year, that is, whether they have been on probation or parole at any time in the past year. Adding the point-prevalence estimates for probationers and parolees on January 1, 1990, to the number of entries in 1990 (Jankowski, 1991) shows that the NHSDA estimates are only about 56% of the probationers and 60% of the parolees. However, some proportion of probationers and parolees are rearrested and incarcerated and therefore would not be eligible for the NHSDA sample. Of those leaving probation in 1990 whose subsequent whereabouts were known, 19% were reincarcerated and 3.3% were discharged to custody, detainer, or warrant. Half of parolees were reincarcerated, and 1.1% were discharged to detainer or warrant (BJS, personal communication).

Therefore, although incarcerated criminals are excluded from the NHSDA, those engaging in criminal behavior and those who have been booked on criminal charges are not entirely missed. There may be a small amount of underreporting and undercoverage, but the estimates from the NHSDA show reasonably good coverage of unincarcerated persons involved in the criminal justice system. Estimates of drug use in the population based on the assumption that the NHSDA completely misses frequent drug users in the criminal population are therefore subject to substantial bias (cf. Wish, 1990–1991; U.S. Senate Judiciary Committee, 1990).

Estimates of drug use from the NHSDA may also be subject to bias because respondents may not accurately report incriminating or deviant behaviors, and undercoverage of drug-using populations may occur. For drug abuse data, there are no good independent criterion data that can be used to validate the NHSDA estimates. Urine tests are most frequently used to validate self-reported drug use, but they have a narrow window of detectability: generally less than 72 hours. Even so, in a review of self-report validation studies primarily using urinalysis, Mieczkowski (1990) found that most studies concluded drug use is accurately self-reported 70% to 90% or more of the time. Many of the respondents included in these types of studies were drawn from criminal justice populations (Mieczkowski, 1990). These individuals may have greater reason to conceal their drug use than members of the general population. Furthermore, a methodological study looking at the difference between interviewer-administered and self-administered questionnaire strategies on the NHSDA found a significantly higher rate of drug use was reported under the self- versus interviewer-administered conditions as drug use became more proximal, that is, little impact on lifetime rates but more on past year, and even more on past month (Turner and Lessler, 1992). This suggests that rates of accurate reporting of drug use in the past 72 hours as validated by urinalysis may not be generalizable to drug use measured in the past month, past year, or lifetime. Because the NHSDA uses methods to maximize confidentiality and anonymity and our analysis was restricted to drug use in the past year, there is ample evidence to suggest the results are valid. But this is obviously an area that needs more research.

This article supports the conclusions of prior research showing a high degree of cor- relation between drug use and criminal behavior. However, analyses show that age is more strongly related to engaging in crime, whereas drug use is more strongly related to being booked for a criminal offense. It may be that drug users engage in more risk taking with regard to their criminal activity, which places them at greater risk for being apprehended and booked. It may also be that upon questioning by police, drug users are more likely to display behavior that results in their being booked. Although the analysis is not definitive, it supports the conclusion reached by a number of researchers that both drug use and criminal behavior are part of a general deviance syndrome, and those likely to engage in one type of deviant behavior are likely to engage in others as well. Knowing that this relationship exists, the question becomes: What can be done to curb deviant adaptations? Prevention/intervention strategies must be targeted to youth, as they are most at risk for involvement in deviant behaviors, but it should also be recognized that youth tend to curb their own involvement in deviant activities as they age (see Greenwood, 1992). Strategies to reduce criminal behavior should be differentially targeted to males. Risk factors for violent crime appear to be dropout status and being black, which provides clues about where to target prevention/intervention strategies. Poverty status is a risk factor for property crime, which also provides an indication of where to target prevention/intervention strategies.

REFERENCES

AKERS, RONALD L. (1984). "Delinquent Behavior, Drugs, and Alcohol: What is the Relationship?" *Today's Delinquent 3*:19–46.

ANGLIN, M. DOUGLAS and GEORGE SPECKART. (1988). "Narcotics Use and Crime: A Multisample, Multimethod Analysis." *Criminology 26*:197–233.

BALL, JOHN C., JOHN W. SHAFFER, and DAVID N. NURCO. (1982). "The Day-to-Day Criminality of Heroin Addicts in Baltimore—A Study in the Continuity of Offense Rates." Revised paper pre- sented to the American Society of Criminology.

Bureau of Justice Statistics. (1988). *Report to the Nation on Crime and Justice*. Washington, D.C.: U.S. Department of Justice.

_____. (1991). *Compendium of Federal Justice Statistics, 1988*. Washington, D.C.: U.S. Department of Justice.

_____. (1992a). *Criminal Victimization in the United States: 1990*. Washington, D.C.: U.S. Department of Justice.

_____. (1992b). *The Prosecution of Felony Arrests, 1988*. Washington, D.C.: U.S. Department of Justice.

EASTERLIN, RICHARD A. (1978). "What Will 1984 Be Like? Socioeconomic Implications of Recent Twists in Age Structure." *Demographics* 15:397–432.

ELLIOTT, DELBERT S., DAVID HUIZINGA, and SUZANNE S. AGETON. (1985). *Explaining Drug Use and Delinquency*. Beverly Hills, Calif.: Sage.

Federal Bureau of Investigation. (1991). *Crime in the U.S.—1990*. Washington, D.C.: U.S. Department of Justice.

GFROERER, JOSEPH G. and MARC BRODSKY. (1992). *An Analysis of Frequent Cocaine Users and Their Treatment Utilization.*

GOLDSTEIN, PAUL J., HENRY H. BROWNSTEIN, and PATRICK J. RYAN. (1992). "Drug-Related Homicide in New York: 1984 and 1988." *Crime & Delinquency* 38:459–476.

GOLDSTEIN, P. J., H. H. BROWNSTEIN, P. J. RYAN, and P. A. BELLUCCI. (1989). "Crack and Homicide in New York City, 1988: A Conceptually Based Event Analysis." *Contemporary Drug Problems* Winter: 651–687.

GREENWOOD, PETER W. (1992). "Substance Abuse Problems Among High-Risk Youth and Potential Interventions." *Crime & Delinquency* 38:444–458.

HARRISON, LANA D. (Forthcoming). "The Drug-Crime Nexus in the USA." *Contemporary Drug Problems.*

HARLOW, CAROLINE WOLF. 1991. *Drugs and Jail Inmates, 1989.* Washington, D.C.: U.S. Department of Justice.

HUNT, DANA E., DOUGLAS S. LIPTON, and BARRY SPUNT. (1984). "Patterns of Criminal Activity Among Methadone Clients and Current Narcotics Users Not in Treatment." *Journal of Drug Issues* Fall: 687–701.

INCIARDI, JAMES A. (1986). *The War on Drugs: Heroin, Cocaine, Crime and Social Policy*. Palo Alto, Calif.: Mayfield.

INCIARDI, JAMES A. and ANNE E. POTTIEGER. (1991). "Kids, Crack and Crime." *Journal of Drug Issues* 21:257–270.

INNES, CHRISTOPHER A. (1988). *Drug Use and Crime*. Washington, D.C.: U.S. Department of Justice.

JANKOWSKI, LOUIS A. (1991). *Probation and Parole*. Washington, D.C.: U.S. Department of Justice.

JESSOR, RICHARD, J.A. CHASE, and JOHN E. DONOVAN. (1980). "Psychosocial Correlates of Marijuana Use and Problem Drinking in a National Sample of Adolescents." *American Journal of Public Health* 70:604–613.

JOHNSON, BRUCE D., ELSAYED ELMOGHAZY, and ELOISE DUNLAP, (1990). "Crack Abusers and Noncrack Drug Abusers: A Comparison of Drug Use, Drug Sales, and Nondrug Criminality." Paper presented at the American Society of Criminology meetings.

KAPLAN, HOWARD B., STEPHEN S. MARTIN, ROBERT J. JOHNSTON, and CYNTHIA A. ROBBINS. (1986). "Escalation of Marijuana Use: Application of a General Theory of Deviant Behavior." *Journal of Health and Social Behavior* 27:44–61.

McGLOTHLIN, WILLIAM H. (1978). "The Etiologic Relationship Between Drug Use and Criminality." In *Research Advances in Alcohol and Drug Problems*, Vol. 4, edited by Y. Israel, F. Glaser, H. Kalant, R. Popham, W. Schmidt, and R. Smart. New York: Plenum Press.

MIECZKOWSKI, T. (1990). "The Accuracy of Self-Reported Drug Use: An Evaluation and Analysis of New Data." In *Drugs and Crime and the Criminal Justice System*, edited by R. Weisheit. Cincinnati: Anderson.

National Institute on Drug Abuse. (1991). *Drug Use Among Youth: Findings From the 1988 National Household Survey on Drug Abuse*. Washington, D.C.: U.S. Department of Health and Human Services.

National Institute of Justice. (1991). *Drug Use Forecasting Drugs and Crime 1990 Annual Report*. Washington, D.C.: U.S. Department of Justice.

NURCO, DAVID N., THOMAS E. HANLON, TIMOTHY W. KINLOCK, and KAREN R. DUSZYNSKI. (1988). "Differential Criminal Patterns of Narcotic Addicts over an Addiction Career." *Criminology* 26:407–423.

_____. (1989). "The Consistency of Types of Criminal Behavior Over Preaddiction, Addiction, and Nonaddiction Status Periods." *Comprehensive Psychiatry* 30:391–402.

O'MALLEY, PATRICK M., JERALD G. BACHMAN, and LLOYD D. JOHNSTON. (1988). "Period, Age, and Cohort Effects on Substance Use Among Young Americans: A Decade of Change, 1976–86." *American Journal of Public Health* 78:1315–1321.

OSGOOD, D. WAYNE, LLOYD D. JOHNSTON, PATRICK M. O'MALLEY, and JERALD G. BACHMAN. (1988). "The Generality of Deviance in Late Adolescence and Early Adulthood." *American Sociological Review* 53:81–93.

_____. (1989). "Time Trends and Age Trends in Arrests and Self-Reported Illegal Behavior." *Criminology* 27:389–417.

SPECKART, GEORGE and M. DOUGLAS ANGLIN. (1985). "Narcotics and Crime: An Analysis of Existing Evidence for a Causal Relationship." *Behavioral Sciences and the Law* 3:259–282.

TURNER, CHARLES F. and JUDITH T. LESSLER. (Forthcoming). "Effects of Mode of Administration and Wording on Reporting of Drug Use in the NHSDA." In *Survey Measurement of Drug Use: Methodological Studies*, edited by C.F. Turner, J. T. Lessler, and J. C. Gfroerer. Washington, D.C.: U.S. Department of Health and Human Services.

U.S. Senate Judiciary Committee. (1990). *Hard-Core Cocaine Addicts: Measuring—and Fighting—the Epidemic—A Staff Report Prepared for the Use of the Committee on the Judiciary United States Senate.* Washington, D.C.: U.S. Government Printing Office.

WATTERS, JOHN K., CRAIG REINARMAN, and JEFFREY FAGAN. (1985). "Causality, Context, and Contingency: Relationships Between Drug Abuse and Delinquency." *Contemporary Drug Problems* Fall:351–373.

WISH, ERIC D. (1990–1991). "U.S. Drug Policy in the 1990s: Insights From New Data From Arrestees." *International Journal of the Addictions* 25:377–409.

WISH, ERIC D. and BRUCE D. JOHNSON. (1986). "The Impact of Substance Abuse on Criminal Careers." In *Criminal Careers and "Career Criminals,": Vol 2.*, edited by A. Blumstein, J. Cohen, J. A. Roth and C. A. Visher. Washington, D.C.: National Academy Press, pp. 52–88.

QUESTIONS FOR DISCUSSION

1. Research has consistently shown that there is a strong relationship between drug use and criminal behavior. Based on your reading, provide a brief review of the research on the relationship between drug and crime presented by the authors.

2. What new evidence does this article provide to validate the correlation between drugs and crime? Cite examples to support your response.

3. Discuss how demographic variables, such as gender, race, marital status, and socioeconomic status, are related to property and violent crime.

4. Why is age important when considering the increases and decreases in crime? Cite examples.

5. Age is more strongly related to engaging in crime, whereas drug use is more strongly related to being booked for a criminal offense. What reasons do Harrison and Gfroerer cite for these phenomena?

PART TWO

PUBLIC POLICY
AND CRIMINAL JUSTICE

■ ■ ■ ■ ■ ■ ■ ■ ■ ■ ■ ■ ■ ■ ■ ■ ■ ■

INTRODUCTION

The criminal justice system comprises several entities that are collectively viewed as a whole. The police, courts, corrections, and juvenile justice components are the formal crime control agencies that have evolved into this collective. Public policies regarding the system are often directed at the entities and rarely upon the whole. For example, historical periods have witnessed police reform that has vacillated between crime control and due process. Correctional and court reform policies have followed similar courses. It has become almost commonplace for one component to suddenly be the focus of reform efforts depending on a particular political agenda rather than serious evidence.

The vacillation from one component to another has usually come about through reactive political agendas that call for directional changes toward either greater due process or crime control. Rarely has middle ground been found on which the expectations of the system are based on something other than nebulous goals and, as a result, hit-or-miss outcomes. These processes have lead to a diminishment of public faith in the system of criminal justice despite the highest spending levels in history.

Implementation of criminal justice policy begins with the law enforcement component. This is an extremely complicated process, and police personnel are increasingly in danger of violence and stand on the front lines of public safety. The level of drug use and trade alone is unbelievable, and law enforcement cannot possibly keep up with the negative social fallout. Although many believe policing should move toward community-based policing systems under local control, the real explosion in the police force has been in the area of private policing groups. This may create further problems in which those who can afford private protection will be safe, whereas the public may become increasingly fearful.

The court system and especially sentencing policies have created some of the most difficult problems in the entire criminal justice system. Again, a lack of congruence among the various components has lead to most of these problems. The reactive politics of the "get tough" philosophy have increased sentence length and types in a net-widening process that is tantamount to general incapacitation.

As with the other components of the criminal justice system, correction swings from rehabilitation to retribution and follows a crooked path toward goal attainment, yet seldom arrives. Corrections routinely is blamed for a plethora of social ills for which it is not responsible and which it cannot solve. Corrections is not the great social redeemer of social ills for which some believe it should be held accountable. Clearly, we must slow the rate of incarceration in the nation through the development of an effective, multifaceted correctional system.

The newest component, known as juvenile justice, is the most enigmatic element in criminal justice. If it is enigmatic, it is also problematic in that age of culpability and the child-saving movements have created unique and complicated reactions regarding children and teens. Along with historical processes that have changed youth statuses and roles, the state as a superparent has been attempting to intervene for amelioration purposes. The enigmatic persona is further enhanced by youth violence and serious crime involvement fueling the sharpest increases in the overall crime rates.

"Public Policy and Criminal Justice" is a lengthy section that encompasses the major components of the criminal justice system, and due to this fact, we have added five sub-categories to this part that we feel add clarity and organizational consistency for the student and instructor alike.

The Criminal Justice System

Malcolm M. Feeley leads us into the second part of this anthology with "Two Models of the Criminal Justice System: An Organizational Perspective." Feeley introduces the "goal" and "functional-systems" models as primarily focused on *goal* activities and *means* activities, respectively. Each component of the criminal justice system may be structured primarily for organizational effectiveness, the goals model or, for needs assessment, the means model. In considering any reform of a system as vast as the justice systems in America, Feeley recommends several excellent ideas in delineating the organizational model.

The conflict of goals in any system is often hailed as problematic or antithethical to the general survival of the particular system. Kevin N. Wright, however, argues, in "The Desirability of Goal Conflict Within the Criminal Justice System," that a monolithic system of justice geared toward goal integration and uniformity ignores the sociopolitical reality in which the system exists. Allowing goal conflict to exist in the system not only offers checks and balances, but allows flexibility and stability over time.

Law Enforcement

An astute veteran of criminology, William J. Chambliss delves into the sociopolitical aspects of law enforcement in "Policing the Ghetto Underclass: The Politics of Law and Law Enforcement." The crime control industry has exploded over the last twenty years with the creation of what Chambliss calls a "moral panic" over crime issues. The combination of political, media, and law enforcement concerns has fueled the panic and the diversion of substantial resources away from education, welfare, and other social services.

"A paradigm of operational control" is how Geoffrey P. Alpert and William C. Smith refer to law enforcement in "Developing Police Policy: An Evaluation of the Control Principle." The history of policymaking has been, Alpert and Smith argue, one of reaction rather than a guide to thinking. To be effective, policies must include such things as workability in the real world, training, evaluation, and examples of behavior.

Following Alpert and Smith are John E. Eck and William Spelman in "Who Ya Gonna Call? The Police as Problem-Busters." This selection discusses the history and policies regarding police–community relations and programs designed to get the police closer to the community. Police units and departments must return to problem solving as a basic criterion rather than focusing solely on improved management. More clearly defining problems, collecting information from a larger variety of sources, and searching for creative solutions to problems serve as excellent recommendations.

"Transforming the Police," by Stephen D. Mastrofski and Craig D. Uchida, argues that no other institution has been the object of reform more often than the police. This article reviews three highly regarded works in policing, each with a varying view of the reforms needed to cause police transformation.

The Courts

Marcia R. Chaiken and Jan M. Chaiken approach a most important subject of debate in "Priority Prosecution of High-Rate Dangerous Offenders." A subject of serious debate inside and outside the justice system, most programs targeting habitual offenders argue selective incapacitation in one form or another. A fair amount of evidence suggests that persistent, high-rate offenders account for over half of the crime rate. Targeting this type of offender, it is argued, would have a significant impact on the total crime reduction process. Most often, however, these programs have not been consistently organized and administered.

Should the courts have latitude in influencing public policy? Christopher E. Smith, in "The Capacity of Courts as Policy-Making Forums," examines several intriguing elements in answering this question. Further questions about the courts' legitimacy and capacity combine to create a lively debate. Smith presents cases for and against court-based policy forums and further shows the intricate complexities involved. Information from the characterization of issues to judicial capacity is covered in this most important reading.

The conflicts within the court system are examined by G. Larry Mays and William A. Taggart in "Court Clerks, Court Administrators, and Judges: Conflict in Managing the Courts." The rationality of managing versus antibureaucratic philosophies of judges and lawyers appears to be an inherent problem. Major problems exist in relation to case-flow management, financial issues, policy and planning issues, communications problems, and conflict over authority.

The dilemma of the public loss of faith in the system of justice is often placed at the doorstep of the court. Edward E. Rhine in "Sentencing Reform and Correctional Policy: Some Unanswered Questions" provides some valuable insights into why we have such a dilemma. The reform of sentencing is perhaps the most significant issue facing the justice system. Reform efforts must consider the linkage between sentencing and correctional populations, the linkage and integration of rehabilitation and punishment, and finally, the role of parole boards in the future.

Corrections

The "get tough on criminals" philosophy is now several decades old. Don C. Gibbons, in "The Limits of Punishment as Social Policy," points out that this philosophy has not produced a safer society. In fact, we now have the distinction of having the highest incarceration rate of any society in the free world. Despite this incarceration rate, we also stand as one of the most criminalized societies in the free world. Crime is often found among people who are trapped in the secondary labor market or chronically unemployed. Gibbons goes on to point out that crime control policies are often a schizoid combination of therapeutic and punitive approaches. The real questions to be answered in crime control policies are do they work, and how much do they cost?

Alida V. Merlo and Peter Benekos present some serious food for thought in "Adapting Conservative Correctional Policies to the Economic Realities of the 1990s." The "get tough" approaches, begun in the 1980s, are not only influencing the budgeting processes in all jurisdictions, but may in fact become the most serious drain on state resources by chipping away at education and other budgets. With more than $20 billion a year being spent on prisons, the economic realities are staggering. The authors point out several alternatives and suggest we reverse the trend of overincarceration or face economic crises.

Although myths abound in relation to crime and criminals, Joseph W. Rogers argues that one stands out above all others. In "The Greatest Correctional Myth: Winning the War on Crime Through Incarceration," Rogers points out that the use of imprisonment as a solution to rising crime rates is not working. The issues raised by Roger are really at the center of the debates about how we should proceed in dealing with crime control in our country.

Juvenile Justice

John J. Wilson and James C. Howell present our twenty-first selection with "Serious and Violent Juvenile Crime: A Comprehensive Strategy." Juvenile crime, especially serious and violent juvenile crime, has increased at an alarming rate, and evidence increasingly suggests that a small percentage of youths are responsible for almost 75 percent of these types of crime. Any strategy aimed at slowing this rate must include both prevention and the systems' response to youth crime.

"Youth Gangs and Public Policy," by C. Ronald Huff, summarizes recent findings regarding youth gangs and points out several relevant policy issues from these findings. Youth gangs are, of course, symptomatic of many social problems facing our country. The "feminization" and "juvenilization" of poverty are especially important for students to understand if the human infrastructure is to be rebuilt.

The family crisis in America influences every aspect of our social structure. The increasing illegitimacy rate, the number of children below the poverty line, and the growing numbers of dysfunctional families combine to negatively affect the nation. Kevin N.

Wright and Karen E. Wright, in "A Policy Maker's Guide to Controlling Delinquency and Crime Through Family Interventions," make several recommendations for change. What is important is that they focus on preventive measures rather than reactive responses.

We conclude this section on juvenile justice with some future orientation in "Emerging Trends and Issues in Juvenile Justice," by Michael F. Aloisi. As we've seen in other readings and evidence, a major trend has been to get tough on juvenile offenders. The most important issues revolve around which juvenile offenders will be treated with greater harshness and which will be treated as youth in need of help from the formal system. Clearly, a small number of offenders create the greatest concern for the public, whereas the majority of them need only minimum intervention.

8

TWO MODELS
OF THE CRIMINAL JUSTICE
SYSTEM
AN ORGANIZATIONAL PERSPECTIVE

Malcolm M. Feeley

■ ■

Despite the scholarly and popular interest in the administration of criminal justice, there are few *theoretical* discussions of the process. Consequently, this paper is an attempt to develop an explicit theoretical framework by which the practices in the administration can be depicted and explained. In it I characterize the criminal justice system in terms of the theory of large-scale organizations, and then examine some of the tasks of administration in terms of established concepts and criteria supplied by this perspective. Following Etzioni, by organization I mean "social units devoted primarily to the attainment of specific goals" (1961). In this case, the formal task of the criminal justice system is to process arrests, determine guilt or innocence, and in the case of guilt, to specify an appropriate sanction. The major actors in the organization include the defendant, prosecutor, defense counsel, judge, arresting officer, court clerk, and to varying degrees, other persons such as witnesses, additional policemen, clerks, parole officers, court psychiatrists and social workers, and the defendants' families and friends. A system of the administration of justice, whether it is adversarial or inquisitorial, entails the key elements of organization: institutionalized interaction of a large number of actors whose roles are highly defined, who are required to follow highly defined rules and who share a responsibility in a common goal—that of processing arrests.[1]

In this discussion, I will outline two models of, or approaches to, organizational analysis and then use them to characterize and evaluate much of the recent systematic research on the administration of criminal justice. Finally, some of the concerns raised by the theories of large-scale organizations generally, but which have been overlooked by students of the administration of justice, will be examined.

TWO MODELS OF ORGANIZATION AND A MODIFICATION

At the risk of oversimplification, let me suggest that a good portion of the systematic studies of the administration of justice in the United States can be classified into two general models of organization—models which I have adapted from Etzioni's discussion of organizational analysis. They are the *goal model* and the *functional-systems model* (1960). The former, he argues, is an approach which is concerned primarily with "organizational effectiveness," in which the criteria for the assessment of effectiveness is derived from organizational goals (Etzioni, 1960: 257). Thus the announced public goals of an organization are usually regarded as the "source for standards by which actors assess the success of their organization" (Etzioni, 1960: 257). This approach, its adherents claim, facilitates an "objective" analysis because it does not insert the observer's own values, but takes the "values," that is, the goals, of the organization as the fixed criteria of judgment. On the other hand, Etzioni (1960: 259) identifies what he has termed the functional-systems model of organizational analysis. It is sharply distinguished from the goal model in that:

> The starting point for this approach is not the goal itself, but a working model of a social unit which is capable of achieving a goal. Unlike a goal, or a set of goal activities, it is a model of a multi-functional unit. It is assumed *a priori* that some means have to be devoted to such non-goal functions as service and custodial activities, including means employed for the maintenance of the unit itself. From the viewpoint of the system model, such activities are functional and increase the organizational effectiveness.

The key difference between the models, Etzioni argues, is that the latter approach is more open-ended in its analysis of the function and "needs" of an organization than is the former, and the researcher is likely to be more attentive to a wide range of influencing factors and as a result apt to show a less biased point of view.

In applying this very general typology to an analysis of approaches to the study of the administration of criminal justice, I have made certain adjustments. In particular it seems appropriate to join the *goal model* with Weber's *rational-legal* model of organization, and produce what I call a *rational-goal model* of the criminal justice system. Etzioni has identified the key distinction between these two models. The rational model "differs from the goal model by the types of functions that are included as against those that are neglected. The rational model is concerned almost solely with *means* activities, while the goal model focuses attention on *goal* activities" (Etzioni, 1960: fn. 16, 263). In the administration of criminal justice, however, it is possible to join these two models, because means and goals merge. While on a highly abstract level, the goal—as opposed to the means—of the criminal justice system might be stated in terms of achieving justice, this goal has no clear empirical referent or context by itself. In the dominant tradition of the West at least, the goal, justice, usually requires meaning in a normative, legal, and empirical context, only when operationalized in terms of procedure, that is, means.[2] Thus, particularly in the administration of justice, the means become the end, at least in terms of viewing "organizational effectiveness" and "formal goal activities."[3]

THE RATIONAL-GOAL MODEL

There is a large body of research focusing primarily upon means or formal goals of the administration of criminal justice. Although there is no consensus or common methodology among the writers adopting this rational-goal approach, their common theme is a primary concern with formal rules. One approach in this type of research is the logical analysis of the interrelationship of the rules of criminal procedure in order to identify and overcome problems of ambiguity, fairness, and discretion. These studies are analogous to the analysis and continuous refinement of formal organizational schema. Another form of research this model uses is the empirical description of practices in the administration of justice, which is then contrasted to the formal rules and goals of the system in an attempt to identify and measure discrepancies between reality and ideal.

This preoccupation with formal goals and rules has as its most eloquent theoretical spokesman Max Weber, who regarded the organization of the administration of justice in the West as the prime example of rational organization. According to Weber, the drift of history in the West has been an ever-increasing reliance upon rational modes of thinking, organization, and authority (1954). In terms of organization this has resulted in a system of depersonalized, rule-bound, and hierarchically structured relationships, which produce highly predictable, rationalized, and efficient results. The system of the administration of justice, he argued, is an excellent example of this phenomenon (Weber, 1954: 350):

> Above all, bureaucratization offers the optimal possibility for the realization of the principle of division of labor in administration according to purely technical considerations, allocating individual tasks to functionaries who are trained as specialists and who continuously add to their experience by constant practice. "Professional" execution in this case means primarily execution "without regard to person" in accordance with calculable rules. The consistent carrying through of bureaucratic authority produces a leveling of differences in social "honor" or status, and consequently, unless the principle of freedom in the market is simultaneously restricted, the universal sway of economic "class position." The fact that this result of bureaucratic authority has not always appeared concurrently with bureaucratization is based on the diversity of the possible principles by which political communities have fulfilled their tasks. But for modern bureaucracy, the element of "calculability of its rules" has really been of decisive significance...Bureaucracy provides the administration of justice with a foundation for the realization of a conceptually systematized rational body of law on the basis of "laws" as it was achieved for the first time to a high degree of technical perfection in the late Roman Empire.

On the formal level, and from a broad perspective, most legal scholars would tend to concur with this characterization of the administration of justice in the West.[4] However, on a more specific level, does this rational goal model characterize the actual organization of criminal justice? Weber has characterized the major components of all organizations as: (1) a continuous organization of official functions bound by rules; (2) a specific sphere of competence, i.e., a sphere of obligations, in the division of labor to be performed by a person who is provided with the necessary means and authority to carry out his tasks; (3) the organization of offices following the principle of hierarchy; and (4) a set of technical rules and norms regulating the conduct of the offices (Etzioni, 1964: 43).

These conditions applied to the organization of the administration of criminal justice imply an elaborate apparatus which processes arrests according to highly defined rules and procedures undertaken by "experts" who perform the functions ascribed to them by highly defined formal roles, under a rigorous division of labor, and who are subject to scrutiny in a systematic and hierarchical pattern. This model seems to be the dominant view or ideal of the criminal justice process held by appellate judges and lawyers, and many of the academic students of the courts. Much of their discussion and research, therefore, has centered on the problems with the formal rules of operation, that is, increasing the "rationality" by minimizing discretion and arbitrary administration, through specifying with increasing precision the roles of the actors. Lawyers under the auspices of the American Bar Association go to great lengths to articulate and refine the precise role of the advocate in criminal justice; many appellate court decisions are attempts at further defining and refining the rules and roles for the various actors in the organization; law journals and appellate court opinions are filled with discussions of the proposals for rules to minimize discretion and more completely define the rules of procedure; and social scientists continue to point out that no one is following the formal rules.

One form of planning by utilizers of the rational-goal model is to examine and explicate the operative rules to determine whether or not they are internally consistent. Abraham Goldstein's discussion of the rules of criminal procedure is an excellent example of this type of analysis (1960). He attempts to show by logical analysis and example that certain alterations of the rules of criminal procedure have the effect of undercutting other, more generalized and basic rules and norms of "equality" among the parties. Since the system is conceived of as a meticulous application of highly defined and prescribed rules, Goldstein can convincingly argue this point, that certain alterations in procedure undercut the power of the defense and thereby weaken or destroy the more fundamental rule of "balanced advantage" between the adversaries. An analogy is that the equilibrium or balance of power in a game of chess is disturbed if a new rule permits White additional moves that are not granted to Black.

The rational-goal approach has not, however, concerned itself entirely with speculative and logical analysis of the rules and norms of the system; it has an empirical component as well. As Etzioni has noted, one of the major objects of the empirical studies adopting a goal model approach is to measure organizational "effectiveness" by contrasting observed, actual behavior with the stated, formal goals of the organization, and a good deal of social science research has followed this pattern.

Lefstein, Stapleton, and Teitelbaum's study of juvenile court judges' compliance to the *Gault* decisions is one example of this research (1969). Their basic format was to outline the requirements and implications of the *Gault* and related decisions, and then identify the extent to which the actual practices of judges in various jurisdictions and types of cases conformed to them. While they have demonstrated quite convincingly that the *Gault* decision had a major impact on the administration of juvenile justice, their optimism regarding the eventual full compliance to the standards of that decision seems somewhat unwarranted when one considers the practices of the actors in the administration of justice generally. What is not found in this study is an examination of the variety of factors, goals, and incentives operative (and likely to remain so) for the various individual actors in the system. A skeptical social scientist might well ask of a lower court judge, "So the Supreme Court handed down a decision, why should it affect you?" A full analysis of the dynamics of compliance and a theory of organization effectiveness would have to address itself to this question which assumes that the Supreme Court decision is just one of a number of factors affecting the system.

Likewise some of the studies reporting the impact of the *Miranda* decision on police behavior follow a similar format (Wald, et al., 1966–67, and Medalie, et al., 1968). The requirements specified in the decision are regarded as the formal goals and then actual behavior is observed and contrasted with them. The studies report different levels of compliance and acceptance on the part of the police, but generally note a low level of effectiveness. Various factors are raised and suggested as possible bases for this less than complete compliance. The "newness" of the decision is one such mentioned factor. Another is the generally hostile attitude of the police toward the new requirements. These factors, however, are not examined systematically, nor are they—and others—incorporated into a dynamic model of organization which considers the multiplicity of goals and incentives operating simultaneously within the system.

My criticism of these types of empirical studies echoes Etzioni's criticism of the goal model approach in general. The preoccupation with a set of formal goals and the observation of behavior primarily in terms of how it squares with these goals (or how the rules have altered previous patterns of behavior) is not conducive to theory building and the explanation of the observed patterns of behavior. It tends to produce a *unidimensional* picture of the process by placing undue emphasis on one set of goals and rules without adequately considering other factors which are, perhaps, equally important in shaping the behavior of the actors in the system. The shortcomings of this approach will become more evident as the functional-systems model is explicated and examples of it are discussed.

FUNCTIONAL SYSTEMS APPROACHES

Turning to the second model, the functional-systems model, a substantially different conception of organization is employed. A different set of practices tends to be focused on, and there is a far greater and explicit concern for "explaining" the behavior of the actors (as opposed to simply "contrasting" it). Etzioni has lumped together a wide variety of studies under the rubric of systems models, and here too, there is a wide variation in the approaches to the analysis of criminal justice which I have placed in this category. There are, however, a number of common and distinguishing characteristics and assumptions which are shared by most of them. They all tend to view the organization of the administration of criminal justice as a system of action based primarily upon *cooperation, exchange,* and *adaptation,* and emphasize these considerations over adherence to formal rules and defined "roles" in searching for and developing explanations of behavior and discussing organizational effectiveness. Rather than being the primary focus of attention, formal "rules" and "disinterested professionalism" are viewed as only one set of the many factors shaping and controlling individuals' decisions, and perhaps not the most important ones. The efficacious "rules" followed by the actors are not necessarily the ideal, professional rules; and the goals they pursue are not necessarily the formal "organizational" goals posited by the researcher or even the "public" goals posited by the leaders of the organization.

Rather the "rules" the organization members are likely to follow are the "folkways" or informal "rules of the game" within the organization; the goals they pursue are likely to be personal or subgroup goals; and the roles they assume are likely to be defined by the functional adaptation of these two factors. These three features of the organization then are the objects to be accounted for, and the functional-systems approach is likely to begin to identify and examine the adaptation of the actors to the environment, the workload and the interests of the persons placed within the system, that is, other goals of the actors within the organization.

The idealized perspective of the *rational organization* pursuing its single set of goals is replaced by a perspective of the set of *rational individuals* who comprise the system, in this case the prosecutor, defense counsel, police, defendant, clerks, and so on, pursuing their various individual goals. Unlike the rational-goal model, this model explicitly recognizes the "normality" of, and emphasizes the reality of, conflict between formal organizational goals, and the goals of the individual actors within the organization. According to this model, the "authority" of legal rules and "professionalism" is not automatically assumed to be efficacious. A more complete system of incentives is required.

In order to account for the actual behavior and practices of the organization, the scholars who to varying degrees utilize this functional-systems model of organization describe the actual process and then begin to identify and examine the causes and conditions of the patterns of behavior of the various actors. In doing this, they focus on the working conditions the system of controls, incentives, and sanctions at the disposal of the various actors, and the larger environmental effects of the system. However, beyond these very general sets of concerns, there is little in common among the scholars who use this functional systems approach of criminal justice administration.

As with the rational-goal method, analysts utilizing a functional-systems model also tend to be motivated by normative concerns, but they are more likely to move beyond the contrasting of ideal goals with actual practices, to search for and identify the factors contributing to the observed practices. While perhaps personally accepting one set of goals for the system and giving expression to their own values, the functional systems approach is at least open enough to allow for and acknowledge the existence of other goals and not accept as "normal" the perfect coincidence of normal organizational goals with the goals of the individual actors within the system. Thus the perspective not only lends itself to accurate description of actual behavior but also begins to attempt to identify and account for the causes and conditions leading to this behavior.

Herbert Packer's recent book, *The Limits of the Criminal Sanction* (1968), dramatically illustrates one of the major points of the functional-systems analysts. There can be many "goals" operating simultaneously—and at odds with each other—within any single system of organization, so that even to speak of "the formal goals" of an organization is likely to be misleading. He convincingly argues that there are at least two major sets of distinctly antagonistic values (the "due process" model and the "crime control" model) held by different actors responsible for administering criminal justice. One set emphasizes "due process," strict adherence to legal rules, and a full-fledged adversary relationship; the other emphasizes effective "crime control" for the community, and tends to minimize the concern for formality and individual rights. One's assessment of the "effectiveness" in achieving the "system's goals" would obviously depend upon which of the two sets of goals or models of values he subscribes to. Clearly any analysis of organizational behavior must be open-ended enough to identify and deal with the multiplicity of goals, values, and incentives of the various actors comprising the system. To do otherwise is likely to lead into the trap of reification and away from social theory.

Another body of research using a type of functional-systems approach tends to rely on an exchange model, adapted in varying degrees from Peter Blau's theoretical perspective (1964). The works of Jerome Skolnick (1966), Herbert Packer (1968), Abraham Blumberg (1967), and George Cole (1970) all tend to utilize this framework. The most widely read work by any of these scholars is Skolnick's *Justice Without Trial*. While it is primarily an analysis of the functioning of the police in the realm of law enforcement, it does touch on police–prosecutor–court relationships, and characterizes them as participating in an elaborate exchange and bargaining system. However, in a related study, he focuses directly on the administration of criminal justice, and in particular on the roles, behavior, and relationships of the public defender and the prosecuting attorney (1967). For purposes of analysis, he has suggested that all institutions are based either on norms of cooperation or norms of conflict, and that a major task of the social analyst is to identify and analyze means for countering these forms. That is, in an organization such as the family or corporation, a major concern is maintenance of cooperation and procedures for cooperation, and in other organizations, such as the sporting event or the adversary system, a major concern is maintenance of the institutionalized conflict and procedures for the conflict. In both sets of institutions, Skolnick argues, the social analyst is interested in identifying the "deviation" from these norms of corporation or conflict and the conditions and principles accounting for such deviation (Skolnick, 1967: 53). Thus his analysis focuses on the institutionalized and structural pressures to reduce the conflict between prosecutor and defense attorney, on the resulting functional adjustments, and also on the normative justifications that support these new practices which seem to violate the *formal* norms of conflict.

Skolnick (1967: 53) identifies the main pressures for "deviant" cooperation in this system as *administrative concerns* of each of the sets of actors (for example, the defense attorney wants to get the best deal for his client and also handle it in the most expeditious manner; the district attorney has many publics to satisfy, an enormous amount of work, and opportunity for a great amount of discretion in selecting cases and charges to develop). As a result, a strong tendency toward cooperation develops in the relationship that is theoretically portrayed as a zero-sum game. Strong informal norms to enhance the smooth functioning of the system itself replace the norms of conflict and adversarial relationship (Skolnick, 1967: 55). Thus, the main cause for the "deviation" from the conflict norms Skolnick identifies as administrative *convenience*, brought about through an elaborate exchange system of mutually advantageous benefits. Additionally, he notes that the prosecuting and defense attorneys (almost always young, inexperienced and idealistic lawyers) are usually "successfully" socialized into this through an elaborate system of informal controls, or are transferred out.

The main device in which all parties share an interest of administrative convenience is in settlement by a plea of guilty. This serves the administrative purposes of saving time, effort, and—the actors all usually emphasize—in "getting a better deal" for the accused. It also has the effect of replacing the adversary system's norm of "presumption of innocence" with a norm of "presumption of guilt." Skolnick, however, argues in regard to this point that cooperation does "not demonstrably impede the quality of representation," a phrase which is unfortunately quite vague.[5] The operating norms—which rationalize this "deviant" behavior—at least from the public's or layman's perspective—are those of "administrative efficiency" and the "interests" of the accused in securing a reduced sentence.

Similar themes are taken up by other writers, who supply additional evidence to support a functional-systems model of the administration of criminal justice. Cole, in an analysis of the defense counsel/prosecutor relationships in Seattle, describes a similar system of mutually advantageous exchanges which function to displace conflict with cooperation, and produce a smooth-running system which seeks to maximize the administrative and personal goals of the individual actors rather than the formal organizational goals of due process. Stefan Kapsch (1971), in an interesting analysis which characterizes the plea bargaining by prosecution and defense as a mixed-strategy game—rather than the zero-sum game of adversary theory—emphasizes the administrative goals (the reduction of decision-making costs) being served by this substitution of cooperation for conflict, and also goes on to develop an explicit justification for the practice.[6]

Another well-known study of the administration of justice—and virtually the only recent full-length sociological analysis of the operations of a criminal court—is Blumberg's book on the New York City criminal justice system (1967). Despite his strong adherence to the principles enunciated in the "formal organizational goals" and particularly full-fledged adversary proceedings, Blumberg undertakes a functional analysis attempting to identify *causes and conditions* leading to the actual practices. He does this by conceptualizing the organization (the court, as he terms it) as an elaborate system of exchanges by persons who can mutually benefit by cooperating. In a highly decentralized and complex organization, his model assumes that each of the actors will pursue more immediate goals and interests, and hence either the personal interests of the individual actor or the goals of and pressures for "production" and "efficiency" from his immediate supervisors and peer group will determine his actions. Thus, for example, the prosecutor's office wants high "batting averages," the defense counsel wants to handle cases as quickly as possible either for financial reasons or, in the case of the public defender, for administrative efficiency, and judges are constantly pressed to clear their calendars.

Blumberg identifies two main factors leading to the "displacement" of the formal, organizational goals by this system of mutual adjustment and exchange (1967).

> Intolerably large case loads of defendants which must be disposed of in an organizational context of limited resources and personnel....As a consequence an almost irreconcilable conflict is posed in terms of intense pressures to process large numbers of cases on the one hand, and the stringent ideological and legal requirements of "due process" of law on the other hand. A rather tenuous resolution of the dilemma has emerged in the shape of a large variety of bureaucratically ordained and controlled "work crimes" short cuts, deviations and outright rule violations adopted as court practices in order to meet production norms (Blumberg, 1967a: 22).

Thus he has identified the press of large case loads and the strains on the actors as perhaps the chief reason for the systematic violations and/or tendencies to deviate from the prevailing ideological rules and norms of the adversary system. This makes it literally impossible for the actors to perform their prescribed roles, even if they wanted to. While it is no doubt accurate to identify a crushing case load as one of the factors necessitating functional adjustments and violations of the due process norm, the implication of Blumberg's argument seems to be that, in the absence of heavy case loads, the actors would "naturally" tend to perform their "proper" adversarial roles as defined by the full-fledged fight theory of the adversary system, and as outlined in some of the rational-goal models of the process.

This position is in at least partial conflict with Skolnick's and Cole's analyses of the conditions for cooperation (as opposed to institutionalized adversarial conflict), which emphasize the structural factors of long-term interaction, acquaintanceships, and a variety of personal and administrative factors (including handling of heavy case loads) as the primary factors contributing to a system of cooperation and exchange. Also, there is some evidence to indicate that rapid processing of defendants (and presumably "corner-cutting" by the actors in the system) occurs in situations where the workload of the court is not pressing (Mileski, 1971). Thus I suspect that Blumberg has somewhat overstated the importance of heavy case loads, and perhaps as well, overinflated the efficacy of "professional norms" of lawyers, norms which he feels most criminal lawyers have been "forced" to abandon for the purposes of court-dictated expediency.

Blumberg is also interested in the defense counsel, whom he argues is ideally supposed to assume a highly defined "professional" role as advocate and champion of his client, but in fact is usually found—like the prosecutor, judge and other court personnel—to respond to more direct and immediate incentives than those of "professional duty" (Blumberg, 1967a: 28).

> The strong incentive of possible fee motivates the lawyer to promote litigation which would otherwise never have developed. However, the criminal lawyer develops a vested interest of an entirely different nature in his client's case: to limit its scope and duration rather than to battle. Only in this way can a case be profitable...In effect, in his role as double agent, the criminal lawyer performs an extremely vital and delicate mission for the court organization and the accused. Both principals are anxious to terminate the litigation with a minimum of expense and damage to each other.

This argument appears reasonable, and Skolnick's reports tend to corroborate it to some extent. However, one still wishes here that Blumberg had been more careful and systematic in collecting and evaluating his data and presenting his arguments on the incentives of defense counsel. His discussions of the two factors which undercut the full-fledged adversary role of the defense counsel, the heavy case load and the financial incentive to quick disposition of cases, tend to contradict each other. On one hand, he argues, the court, in an attempt to cope with the heavy case load, has "co-opted" the defense counsel and "forced" him into acting the part of a "confidence agent" in convincing his client to plead guilty. On the other hand, the discussion of the financial incentives indicates that regardless of the judge's and prosecutor's interests, it is still in the self-interest of the defense counsel to seek a quick termination of the case through a plea of guilty since he is usually paid a flat fee for representation. Consequently, the less time a case takes, the higher the volume of his income. If the financial incentive is an important one, then one would expect the defense counsel to willingly press for pleas of guilty regardless of case load before the court. Furthermore, it is not unreasonable to expect that up to a point, as case load diminishes, the defense counsel's desires for quick and cursory disposition of cases would tend to increase. If business is slackening, then one must hustle even more to maintain volume. Systematically gathered and presented evidence would go a long way toward resolving these rival plausible hypotheses and unsupported assertions. Still, on the whole, one is given the distinct impression from the works of Blumberg, Skolnick, and Cole that the defense counsel is not so much an unwittingly co-opted agent used by the self-serving court bureaucracy, as he is one of the key figures in an elaborate system in which everyone, including himself, has certain commodities to exchange in the pursuit of his own interests.

There is still another set of factors which has been identified and examined by many of the scholars adopting the functional-systems approach. This is the enormous amount of discretion possessed by most of the actors in the criminal justice system, and in particular, the police and prosecutor. Most analysts subscribing to the rational-goal model of the system make little mention of this, tending to emphasize the rational administration according to specified rules and assume that it is an "attainable goal." Likewise, many "reformers" and advocates of increased "professionalism" (that is, rule-following) avoid dealing squarely with the problem posed by discretion. Among those scholars who have focused on this problem, Joseph Goldstein (1969), Packer (1968), and Skolnick (1967) are the most prominent. What they have all noted is that the administrators of justice have tremendous leeway in defining a situation, a vast array of competing rules in their arsenal, and are placed in a situation where it is frequently physically impractical (if not literally impossible) to enforce or administer all, or perhaps even most, of the rules all of the time.

This problem of discretion has two main components: first is the problem of the sheer magnitude of substantive laws and procedural rules; second is the inherent ambiguity of rules. A moment's reflection tells us that this is physically impossible and undesirable in anything approaching a democratic society to attempt to enforce all rules— both substantive criminal law and due process norms in the administration of justice—all the time. There are simply too many rules, and it would require a police state, a totalitarian bureaucracy, and a highly costly apparatus to begin even to approach total enforcement. Therefore, given the virtual impossibility of faithful adherence to and enforcement of all the rules, there is considerable room for discretion in the enforcement and administration of the rules. Discretion in such circumstances is inevitable, and because of the low visibility of most of the criminal activities and administration, it falls primarily on the hands of the police and prosecutors, and is not subject to much public attention and continuous supervision.

The second component of discretion—the ambiguity of rules and the subsequent leeway in defining an action—is more complex and perhaps more philosophically intriguing. For instance, if a person is arrested for burglary, he could also be charged with intent to commit burglary, illegal possession of burglary tools, illegal entry, possession of stolen property, and numerous other criminal violations. In short, a single action can be defined and interpreted in a number of ways. The ambiguity of "facts," of course, further complicates the picture and enhances discretionary practices. The process of selecting which "facts" to consider and which "rule" to apply to define the activity is in itself a discretionary matter of considerable importance. The variety of available "legal" alternatives allows the actor a wide latitude for discretion, and of course a very valuable commodity to bargain with in the system of exchange. In this view, the interpretation and use of the rules themselves are viewed as instruments of rationalization, not application. That is, the rules are selected and used as weapons or supports at the whim of, and in the particular interests of, the various actors in the system. Thus ambiguity and discretion are inherent to the very nature of all elaborate systems of rules, and "force" enforcement and administrative officials—the so-called rule appliers—into a position of making "lawless" decisions. This poses a major problem in the administration of justice, as Herbert Packer (1968: 290) has noted:

> The basic trouble with discretion is simply that it is *lawless*, in the literal sense of that term. If police or prosecutors find themselves free (or compelled) to pick and choose among known or knowable instances of criminal conduct, they are making a judgment which in a society based on law should be made only by those to whom the making of law is entrusted.

To the extent that this in fact is the case—for the reasons just outlined—a faithful adherence to the rational-goal model of the criminal justice system is *impossible* in practice and in principle.

CONSIDERATIONS FOR REFORM

While analysts using the rational-goal model have tended to emphasize the set of formal goals, ideals, and rules which they suggest should be operating in the administration of justice, and have examined the consequences of nonperformance of these goals in terms of the normative ideals and consequences to individual rights, they have frequently ignored the factors and conditions contributing to the displacement, violation, and non-performance of these goals, ideals and rules.[7] On the other hand, the functional-systems approach has gone a long way toward identifying the causes and conditions accounting for the observed behavior, and toward demonstrating that there is no particular reason to expect individual behavior to coincide with the behavior prescribed by the formal goals of the system. Formal rules and norms obviously affect and guide the behavior of the actors, but they are only one set of considerations among several.

It is therefore unreasonable to expect a perfectly "effective" system for administering criminal justice. This, of course, does not preclude the adopting of policies and practices which incrementally increase the system's "effectiveness." Additional rules of clarification and procedure, reducing the reliance on the criminal sanction, more and better trained personnel, more space, and improved calendars, are all frequently mentioned as measures of reform, and there is little question that their adoption would result in improvement. However, running through such proposals is the assumption that if these steps were taken, the actors in the system would somehow *naturally* begin to assume stronger commitments to the formal goals and rules of the system and act accordingly. This tends to underestimate, I think, the very real and strong individual and subgroup incentives, goals, and values, and underestimates as well the saliency of the "crime control model" as the operative normative ideal among many persons involved in the system. Clearly it is more than a problem of overcoming workload so that good men can do good work. There exist strong competing norms and incentives which act at cross-purposes to the system's formal goals and norms. The task of institutionalized reform rests squarely on the generation of mechanisms which strengthen the position of the organizational goals and norms vis-à-vis the competing subgroup and individual goals.

At this point, it is particularly useful to return to the concerns of the theorists of large-scale organizations, and begin to consider some of the structural features of the system, particularly the compliance-inducing mechanisms. What emerges from the analysis of the operations of the criminal justice system is a clear picture of an organization which has highly specified rules and goals, but has virtually no instruments by which to enforce them. Rather than the highly rationalized rule-bound and bureaucratically structured system that Weber depicted the process to be, one finds a highly decentralized and decidedly nonhierarchial system of exchange, in which there are virtually no instruments to supervise practices and secure compliance to the formal goals of the organization. In the absence of such efficacious compliance securing mechanisms, institutionalized long-term reform is unlikely.

Only two mechanisms are institutionalized to induce actors to comply with the formal rules and goals of the criminal justice system—normative inducements accruing from *professionalism* and the *appellate procedure*—and neither is very effective in relation to the countervailing incentives.

Appeal to the normative considerations of professionalism is a key source of control in many organizations composed of highly trained and skilled personnel, and in many instances is a highly successful instrument. Certainly the guild-like pride and clannishness of the legal professional generally and bar associations in particular act as a powerful influence on lawyers. Legal training is marked with a continuing emphasis on the professional responsibilities of the lawyer and one might expect all these factors to act as a substantial "professionalizing" influence on the actors in the criminal justice system. However, a great many students of professional organizations have noted that the importance of professional norms—in the absence of direct supervision and other formal means of control—are not as powerful as they are popularly believed to be.

This downward revised assessment would particularly seem to be the case in the administration of criminal justice. There is little disagreement among knowledgeable observers that the criminal lawyer—including the office of prosecutor, defense lawyer, and not infrequently the criminal court judge as well—holds the status of anchor-man within the legal profession. This certainly acts to reduce the importance of the norm of "professionalism" as a compliance-inducing mechanism. Likewise, the low visibility of the administration of criminal justice and the generally "low" status of its clients tends to further erode the "professional" environment and leads to a lack of concern on the part of the more prestigious legal professional organizations and public generally, further undercutting one of the major sources of inducement to professionalism.

The other mechanism—the only formal one— institutionalized to induce compliance to formal organizational norms on the part of the actors within it is the appellate process, and the continuing opportunity for appeal. This, however, is a highly ineffectual instrument in that it is relatively passive, extremely expensive, can be instituted only at the insistence of a convicted defendant, and usually only if it is pressed by his defense counsel. At best it is a passive instrument, which might function to curb some of the most flagrant violations of administration, but is hardly a powerful and systematic instrument of control in most instances.

In short, what one finds in the system of criminal justice is a highly formalized and defined set of rules, norms, and goals, but also an organization which possesses no corresponding set of incentives and sanctions which act to systematically enforce them. Any far-reaching discussion of reform and proposals for change in the administration within the American system of criminal justice would have to deal with this problem of the nature and distribution of compliance-including mechanisms.[8] Ironically, it seems to lead to a solution requiring more bureaucracy, not less.

NOTES

1. I have been criticized on this point by some persons who argue that the American adversary system cannot be considered an "organization," and in fact is designed explicitly to avoid "organizational" and "bureaucratic" processing of cases on a routine basis. The argument is that the adversary system protects individual rights by institutionalizing the lack of an organization to "process" cases, in contrast to (to varying degrees) many of the countries relying on inquisitorial methods. While there are certainly differences between European and American practices in the administration of criminal justice, I think that these differences are easily contained within an organizational framework. One system may be more centralized and hierarchically organized than another, but in all cases there is a group of institutionalized interacting roles which in principle are expected to work together (whether through conflict or cooperation) toward a common set of goals.

2. Herbert Packer (1968) makes a similar point in his discussion of the two models of criminal justice, the "due process" model and the "crime control" model. He suggests that among academic lawyers, the former tends to be regarded as the "goals" of the system. Likewise, John Rawls has made a similar point (1958).

3. No doubt one of the major reasons for concentrating almost exclusively on "means"—aside from their connection with the concept of justice—in analyzing the activities of the criminal justice system is that there is no way of measuring effectiveness in terms of deciding guilt or innocence, another activity which might reasonably be identified as the "goal" of the organization. That is, if one posed this as the goal of the organization, there would be no reliable measure which would allow him to contrast the "ideal" with the actual in that there is no way of always knowing *factual* guilt or innocence.

4. This position, on a general level, reflects Maine's (1963) celebrated observation that the "movement of the progressive societies has hitherto been a movement from Status to Contract." Likewise, similar division of labor and specialization of the administration of justice has been demonstrated systematically in the work of Schwartz and Miller (1964) and Schwartz (1954). On the other hand, many scholars question the extent to which all this has in fact taken place. The legal realists have rather successfully demonstrated the ambiguity of legal rules and the flexibility of rule-application (Llewellyn, 1964). Likewise, the judicial behaviorists have rather convincingly demonstrated a relationship between judicial backgrounds and judicial behavior (see Schubert, 1965, and Nagel, 1970). Also, Friedman (1966)

has challenged and at least modified Weber's arguments regarding the nature of "rational" legal reasoning, and along with Joseph Goldstein (1969) and others has shown the increasing utilization of discretionary, nonrule specified powers within the "modern" law. Kadi-like justice seems not to have disappeared either in theory or in fact.

5. At any rate, this argument should have been dwelt on in more depth. He offers no real evidence for it, nor does he attempt to operationalize "quality of representation," and it remains an undemonstrated assertion. It is, I think, an example of the conservative bias, that is, the acceptance of the *status quo* once one "understands" it, which if not inherent in the logic of functional analysis generally is certainly reflected in a good deal of functionalist literature.

6. I think that his is a tortured reading of the traditional theory of the adversary system and the administration of justice, but nevertheless it is one of the new thoughtful discussions of the practices—one that moves away from implicit normative support of the practices, and begins to offer an explicit justification of them.

7. This language assumes that if there is widespread consensus that these are, in fact, the actual goals of the organization, and that they once were—or could have been—achieved. Packer's persuasive analysis of the two models of criminal justice points up the existence of a multiplicity of goals within the organization, and shows that they frequently lead to cross purposes.

8. For an elaboration of the problem of individual incentives and compliance-inducing mechanisms, see my discussion of law as a "public good," and the subsequent problem for an explanation of individual incentives and compliance (Feeley, 1970). For a general exposition of the problem of incentives and compliance to organizational goals by "rational actors," see Downs (1967).

REFERENCES

BLAU, P. (1964). *Exchange and Power in Social Life*. New York: John Wiley.

BLUMBERG, A. (1967). *Criminal Justice*. Chicago: Quadrangle Books. (1967a). "The Practice of Law as a Confidence Game." *Law and Society Review 1*:15–29.

COLE G. (1970). "The Decision to Prosecute." *Law and Society Review 4*: 331–345.

DOWNS, A. (1967). *Inside Bureaucracy*. Boston: Little Brown.

ETZIONI, A. (1960). "Two Approaches to Organizational Analysis: A Critique and a Suggestion." *Administrative Science Quarterly 5*: 257–278.

_____. (1961). *A Comparative Analysis of Complex Organizations*. New York: Free Press.

_____. (1964). *Modern Organization*. Englewood Cliffs: Prentice-Hall.

FEELEY, M. (1970). "Coercion and Compliance." *Law and Society Review 4*: 505–519.

FRIEDMAN, L. (1966). "On Legalistic Reasoning—A Footnote to Weber." 1966 *Wisconsin Law Review* 148–171.

GOLDSTEIN, A.S. (1960). "The State and the Accused: Balance of Advantage in Criminal Procedure." *Yale Law Journal 69*: 1149–1199.

GOLDSTEIN, J. (1969) "Police Discretion Not to Invoke the Criminal Process: Low Visibility Decisions in the Administration of Justice." *Yale Law Journal 69*: 543–594.

KAPSCH, S. (1971). *The Adversary System and the Assistance of Counsel*. Unpublished Ph.D. Thesis. Department of Political Science, University of Minnesota.

KLONOSKI, J. and R. MENDELSOHN (Eds.). (1970). *The Politics of Legal Justice*. Boston: Little Brown.

LEFSTEIN, N., V. STAPLETON, and L. TEITELBAUM (1969). "In Search of Juvenile Justice." *Law and Society Review 5*: 491–563.

LLEWELLYN, K. (1960). *The Common Law Tradition*. Boston: Little Brown.

MAINE, H. (1963). *Ancient Law*. Boston: Beacon Press.

MEDALIE, R.J., et al. (1968). "Custodial Police Interrogation in Our Nation's Capital: The Attempt to Implement *Miranda*." *Michigan Law Review 66*: 1347–1422.

MILESKI, M. (1971). "Courtroom Encounters." *Law and Society Review 5*: 473–538.

NAGEL, S. (1970). *The Judicial Process from a Behavioral Perspective*. Chicago: Dorsey.

PACKER, H. (1968). *The Limits of the Criminal Sanction*. Stanford, Calif.: Stanford University Press.

RAWLS, J. (1958). "Justice as Fairness." *Philosophical Review 67*: 164–197.

SCHUBERT, G. (1965). *The Judicial Mind*. Evanston, Ill.: Northwestern University Press.

SKOLNICK, J. (1966). *Justice Without Trial*. New York: John Wiley. (1967). "Social Control in the Adversary System." *Journal of Conflict Resolution 11*: 52–67.

SCHWARTZ, R.D. (1954). "Social Factors in the Development of Legal Control," 63 *Yale Law Journal* 471–491; and J. MILLER (1964). "Legal Evolution and Societal Complexity." *American Journal of Sociology 70*: 159–169.

WALD, M.S., et al. (1966). "Interrogations in New Haven: The Impact of *Miranda*." *Yale Law Journal 76*: 1521–1648.

WEBER, M. (1954). "Rational and Irrational Administration of Justice." In Max Rheinstein (Ed.), *Max Weber on Law in Economy and Society*. Cambridge, Mass.: Harvard University Press.

QUESTIONS FOR DISCUSSION

1. Feeley combines Weber's rational-legal model of organizations with Etzioni's goal model to produce what he calls a "rational-goal model." What is the difference between the rational model and the goal model of organizations? Is it possible to join the two models? Why?

2. Explain how the rational-goal model applies to criminal justice organizations. Cite specific examples to support your response.

3. Explain the functional-systems model approach to criminal justice organizations. Cite specific examples to support your response.

4. According to Feeley, "a faithful adherence to the rational-goal model of the criminal justice system is *impossible* in practice and in principle." Why?

5. What suggestions are made to reform the effectiveness of organizations for administering criminal justice? Cite specific examples.

9

THE DESIRABILITY OF GOAL CONFLICT WITHIN THE CRIMINAL JUSTICE SYSTEM

Kevin N. Wright

■ ■

CONFLICTING GOALS IN THE NON-SYSTEM

Experts in the field of criminal justice have recently displayed a growing obsession with the idea of creating a monolithic system for the administration of justice. This obsession is reflected in a diversity of writings, yet a common theme can be found throughout the literature: if criminal justice is to fulfill its function of crime control, then a transformation must occur which will create a rational, well-integrated system in which a common set of goals can be pursued through a compatible set of strategies and techniques.

One source of this trend is found in the various theoretical and philosophical treatises which are intended to serve as a framework for revamping the criminal justice system. Duffee (1980: 4) has succinctly described the nature of these works:

> Whether the analysis of criminal justice has been done by radicals, liberals or conservatives, most analysts from van den Haag, to Packer, to Quinney have assumed that centralized planning and program development dealing with criminal justice can or could influence significantly the frequency with which crime is committed, the proportion of offenders who are apprehended, and the degree to which punishment for crimes would feed back upon the political, economic and social conditions which give rise to crime and the means with which society responds to it.

Radicals such as Quinney (1969; 1974 and 1977) and Chambliss (1969; 1971; 1972; 1975 and 1979) generally perceive the existing system to be coherent in that the system functions to protect the interests of the powerful, and individuals are punished for the inequities of society. Change of the system is considered in terms of broader social change but is aimed at creating a new form of coherence. Conservatives such as Packer (1968, van den Haag (1975), and Wilson (1975) and liberals such as Clark (1971) and Menninger (1969), on the other hand, generally perceive the existing system as lacking coherence and continuity in that a single set of goals is not pursued. Each indicates, however, that coherence could be built into the system and the problem of crime control resolved.

Reprinted with permission from *Journal of Criminal Justice*, Vol. 9, pp. 19–31, Kevin N. Wright, "The Desirability of Goal Conflict Within the Criminal Justice System," (1980), Elsevier Science Ltd., Pergamon Imprint, Oxford, England.

A second source of advocacy for a monolithic system can be found in the structural analyses of the organizational aspects of the criminal justice system as reflected in the work of Skoler (1977) and Kellogg (1976). These assessments focus on the inability of the "system" to function as a true system, that is, one which is coherent and well integrated and has a unitary set of goals. Consequently, this group of analysts refer to the criminal justice system as a "non-system." Criminal justice is characterized by conflicting goals, a lack of integration, and overlapping jurisdictions which promote inequities of justice and create inefficiencies which result in higher costs of operation:

> Official decisions affecting the criminal offender are made by a patchwork of separate juris-
> dictions, in a system of independent prosecutors, judges, prison administrators, and parole and
> probation officers. Respective policies vary arbitrarily from place to place, or even from time
> to time within the same place. Sentencing decisions with in the same jurisdiction, not to mention
> among different ones, vary widely with the attitudes of individual judges. Decisions are based
> upon limited and inconsistent information, generally without adequate explanation to benefit
> other officials in the decision-making process. (Kellogg, 1976: 50)

In fact, the components of criminal justice are characterized as being noncooperative and even hostile toward one another. It has been suggested that the inability of the criminal justice system to function as a true system results in a fragmented output and often an undesirable outcome (Skoler, 1977; Kellogg, 1976; O'Neill, et al., 1976: 4–17).

Unlike the theoretical and philosophical treatises which propose frameworks for revamping the system, the structural analysts focus their attention on remedial structural changes. In other words, the structural analysts concentrate on the mechanics of change rather than the content and direction of change within the system. Various proposals (see Skoler [1977] for a comprehensive review) have been made to alleviate the problems of conflict and fragmentation within the criminal justice system. Such suggestions range from integration and cooperation to direct unification of the system. However, more attention has been given to the former than the latter. Statewide and comprehensive planning and fiscal incentives have been advocated as mechanisms for integration. Structural change has also been suggested as a mechanism for integrating the components. Reorganization of state government is quite often cited as a potentially effective method of structural change. Skoler (1977: 289) has even suggested that the "fragmented, duplicative, and uncoordinated character of criminal justice services" can best be resolved through the consolidation and unification of the system's components. Services should be combined and centrally administered.

The inherent desirability of creating a monolithic system for the administration of justice, however, deserves further consideration. As suggested above, the lack of integra-tion, coordination, and goal and technique compatibility within the criminal justice system seems to be quite inefficient and ineffective. The system lacks the rationality associated with systemic organization. Additional assessment, however, may not support this conclu-sion. Proposals for unification seem to ignore the environment in which criminal justice exists. Furthermore, there are at least three reasons why goal conflict within the systems is desirable. The purpose of this article is to consider these factors in order to assess the desirability of a monolithic system.

THE SOCIOPOLITICAL ENVIRONMENT

The theoretical and philosophical treatises and the structural analyses which advocate a monolithic criminal justice system seem to have conveniently ignored the sociopolitical environment in which the system exists. Such an oversight may be helpful in gaining public attention to one's ideas but is most unfortunate from a practical and pragmatic standpoint. The essence of a system as complex as criminal justice simply cannot be understood from the perspective which considers it as an isolated system. Nor can any proposal for significant planned change of the system claim any validity without considering the effects and constraints of the environment on that system.

In order to understand fully the implications of this idea, it is necessary to assess what type of a system criminal justice is. Numerous authors (Emery and Trist, 1965; Terryberry, 1968; March and Simon, 1958; Cyert and March, 1963) have argued that there are at least two types of social systems: simple and complex. In a simple system, goals can be specified, tasks to accomplish those goals can be undertaken, and progress can be monitored so that the system is self-regulating. These activities are possible because the internal and external environments of the system are relatively stable. It is this model of the criminal justice system which the theoretical and structural analysts noted above have used. A complex system, on the other hand, does not exist in stable environments but rather finds itself in a complex and rapidly changing, or turbulent, environment which produces unpredictable changes within the system itself. This situation precludes rational, long-range, and macro-planned change. Because the environment is turbulent, and thus drastically and dynamically affecting the system, it is simply impossible to identify and specify a set of goals and to bring about some change to remodel the system (Emery and Trist, 1965, Terryberry, 1968). Duffee (1980: 101) has made a very strong case that criminal justice is in fact a complex system:

> There is a wide variety of information available pertaining to the fact that criminal justice is not a monolithic, commonly conceived routine exercise. Criminal justice may well have different meanings in different places, or behave differently under contrasting conditions. Before we attempt to change actual operating agencies so that they might conform to a unitary motive of criminal justice operation, we may wish first to ask why such variations occur, whether these variations are functional equivalents, or whether the contrasting practices provided to the locality in which they are observed contributions to social order that might be lost if all criminal justice agencies behaved appropriately to the expectations of the analyst.

Duffee goes on to argue that criminal justice is, in fact, an institution much like the family or religion, and that its existence and what happens to it are unrelated to goal accomplishment.

Just as Duffee noted that there is a wide variety of information which indicates that criminal justice is not a monolithic system, there is, in particular, considerable information which indicates the political nature of criminal justice. Both conservatives and radicals concur that the basis of criminal justice, criminal law, is generated within an interest structure (see Pound, 1943; Quinney, 1969: 20–30). Society is characterized by an interest structure in which various kinds of interests are distributed throughout that structure. Laws are the product of different interest groups vying for power to see their interests represented or realized. Theorists differ, however, in their perceptions concerning the output of the process as to whether the result is a product of compromise or domination.

Beyond the law, the actual administration and allocation of justice can also be viewed within the political context. Cole (1973: 15–16) has provided one of the most concise reviews of this idea:

> Rather, like all legal institutions, the criminal justice system is "political" since it is engaged in the foundation and administration of public policies where choice must be made among such competing values as the rights of defendants, protection of persons and property, justice and freedom. That various groups in society interpret these values differently is obvious. Decisions result from the influence of the political power of decision makers and relative strength of competing elites.

Cole (1973: 16) continues by nothing that there is a wide range of discretion within the administration of justice. Laws are often ambiguous, and full enforcement of them is neither possible nor desirable. Decisions must, therefore, be made within the context of the community and its interest structure. Legal personnel, judges, and prosecutors, must operate within a political environment. Their decisions must rest on the selection among competing dispositions which reflect dominant political interests. The actions of police executives are similarly influenced by the political nature of the position. To summarize, "in many ways the administration of criminal justice is a community affair; political influentials and interest groups work to ensure that the law will be applied in ways consistent with their perception of local values" (Cole, 1973: 17). (For an excellent discussion of the political reality of the administration of justice, see Chapter 4, "The Making of Criminal Justice Policy" in Levine, Musheno, and Palumbo, 1980.)

Suggestions to create a monolithic, unified system deny the very existence of an interest structure characterized by a specific distribution of power. Therefore, to analyze the criminal justice system as if it did not exist within a political environment seems to be particularly naive. There are actors within the system who have a vested interest in its organization and operation, as well as influential persons within the community who want to see their particular interests represented. We know that interests vary from area to area. What is "justice" in an urban area may not be similarly perceived in a rural area. We know that what is "justice" to a police officer may not be "justice" to a young offender and his or her liberal public defender.

Radicals, to a degree, seem to understand the political context of the administration of justice in that their proposals for change are couched in terms of broader social changes. They realize that massive change in the system rests on social change. For example, the proponents of prison abolition fairly consistently advocate such change within a proposal for the creation of a society characterized by pervasive equality. (See Hawkins, 1976; 5–12 for a review of the abolitionist movement.) Radicals, however, often fail to consider the likelihood of drastic social change.

Liberals, conservatives, and structural analysts virtually ignore the political environment. They propose massive change in the system without considering the possibility that actors within the system as well as politically influential persons would resist that change. They fail to see that criminal justice is as it is for a reason, that there is a certain rationality in the seemingly structural irrationality of the system. (See Diesing's *Reason in*

Society [1962] for a discussion of this conceptualization of rationality.) To create a mono-lithic, unified system would require a compatible set of values to serve as its basis; our complex society is not constituted in such a manner. Individuals working in the various components of the system, personnel in various jurisdictions, and influence bearers who have an interest in the administration of justice are extremely unlikely to agree on a single set of values. Levine, Musheno, and Palumbo (1980: 38, 150) in their introductory text-book make this fact clear when they conclude:

> In short, the public interest is constantly being defined and redefined. The balance among its various facets is always shifting. As is true in any area of public policy, the choice of ideals in criminal justice is the result of an unpredictable, ever-changing and very intricate political process....This often means that only incremental rather than sweeping changes can be made.

Furthermore, there are at least three reasons why goal conflict and fragmentation are advantageous to the processes and functioning of the system. Conflict makes it possible to represent and protect different societal interest, establishes a system of checks and balances, and promotes a smoothly operating offender-processing system.

REFLECTIVE DIVERSITY

Underlying the ideas of unification and the creation of a monolithic system for the administration of justice is an assumption that there is a compatible set of values, or if you please, a single culture, whence unification can proceed. As suggested above, there is con-siderable theoretical and empirical evidence that indicates the existence of a diversity of values within the criminal justice environment. The fragmentation and lack of integration within criminal justice would thus seem possibly to allow different interests to be incor-porated into the system. As such, different societal interests may be reflected or represented by the different, and often conflicting, goals within criminal justice. This idea has been verified on a number of different levels.

First, the representatives of different interests can be seen among different jurisdic-tions. Wilson's study of the police (1968) indicated that styles of law enforcement vary from community to community. While the day-to-day routine of police work was not directly affected by political influence, the political culture of the community was found to influence directly the style and policies of the department. Similarly, Levin (1980) found in his study of criminal courts that the handling of defendants varied according to the political culture of the community. The lack of consistency between judicial decisions in Pittsburgh and Minneapolis was explained by their different political systems. If it is assumed that the political culture and public interests vary from area to area, then the seemingly fragmented system of justice may serve to fulfill those diverse interests. This conclusion is reflected in the research of both Wilson and Levin. For example, the influence of both middle- and lower-class culture in Pittsburgh as opposed to a predominantly middle-class cultural influence in Minneapolis was found to be reflected in judicial practices.

On a second level, different interests can be represented by the fragmentation and inconsistencies within a single component. This situation is evidenced in the corrections' search for an alternative to rehabilitation. Certain issues are advocating community supervision and reintegration, while other groups stress increased incapacitation and retribution. These considerations are further complicated by new demands for lowering state budgets with correspondingly rising cost of incarceration and demands for the protection of the rights of offenders. Trends seem to be toward greater use of community supervision with simultaneous specification of mandatory sentences for particularly "fear-invoking" offenses. We thus see quite different and conflicting interests being considered, incorporated, and implemented within corrections.

A study by Cole (1980) of the Office of the Prosecuting Attorney in King County, Washington, also supports the contention that different interests are represented within the seemingly conflicting processes of a single agency. Cole's research indicated that the prosecutor's office could be viewed as an organization within an exchange system that operated in a marketlike fashion. The decision to prosecute or not to prosecute could occur at various times during processing and was often based on the influence of a variety of officials. In this manner, the prosecutor could only exercise discretion within the exchange framework. As Cole (1980: 166) points out, "the police, court congestion, organizational strains, and community pressures are among the factors that influence prosecutorial behavior."

In a most informative paper, Ohlin (1974) has outlined the manner in which conflicting interests influence organizational objectives and policy. (While Ohlin focused his analyses on correctional organizations, his ideas seem to be applicable to all criminal components.) Ohlin notes that interest groups arise when they feel that particular issues will directly affect them. The group may perceive that existing or possible activities will serve as a means to the achievement of its own objectives, it may be threatened by some existing or proposed activity, or it may view support of some issue as a way to fulfill some other obligation to another group. (See Bauer, 1968: 17 for a discussion of obligatory activities which develop between interests groups.) A group's involvement in a particular issue will be determined by the advertency, saliency, and potency of the issue to that group. If the issue or activity is deemed important enough for the interest group's involvement or influence, the group can either try to obtain representation in the decision-making process or to support or penalize the organization for its particular decision. Over time and issues, the influence of various interest groups will change. As Ohlin (1974: 149) describes, "the old, routinized ways of doing things gradually create problems. These problematic situations become the focus of new conflicts of interest, out of which new patterns of activity emerge."

The activities of an organization cannot be understood without considering the influence of interest groups. In that policies and activities of the organization reflect the influence of different interest groups, they may appear actually to conflict with one another, yet that conflict may be necessary in mediating among conflicting values within the community. The nature and activities of the organization may vary considerably as control passes from one group to another and as the interest structure shifts. Such dynamics are imperative for organizational survival in a complex environment.

On a final level, it would also seem possible that different interests are represented by the different components of criminal justice. Unfortunately, there is a lack of empirical analysis of this possibility, yet some support for the proposition can be inferred from what we know about the system. As suggested throughout this article, it is certainly reasonable to suggest that various aggregates of society desire different things from the justice system. The American Friends Service Committee seems to have a very different set of values than law-and-order traditionalists such as the International Association of Chiefs of Police. In attempting to see that their respective values are realized, these two groups advocate very different justice policies. However, each group tends to concentrate the exertion of its influence on a different component of the system, corrections and law enforcement, respectively. In responding to the interests of these and similar groups, it is quite possible for the components to focus on different and conflicting goals.

It is clear that criminal justice incorporates a number of different goals, including crime prevention, public tranquility, justice, due process, efficiency, and accountability (Levine, Musheno, and Palumbo, 1980: 19–35). It is also known that the components differentially incorporate these goals into their operations. For example, it is often noted that the police tend to be more concerned with efficiency than due process, while the courts tend to focus on due process over efficiency. The different orientations of the police and the courts may very well make it possible to represent different interests within the community.

The apparent incoherence of the criminal justice goals does seem to serve a useful function when we view the environment in which the system exists. That environment is characterized by different values and interests. The fragmentation among jurisdictions, the goal conflict within a single component of the system, and the conflict among components allow different interests to be incorporated into the system. As we will see in the following section, the existence of goal conflict allows for continual mediations of interest and adaptability of the system.

MEDIATIONS OF INTEREST AND SYSTEM ADAPTATION

A second advantage of conflicting goals within the criminal justice system is that they promote a process of checks and balances within the system. Fragmentation ensures that no single component of the system can dominate all other components, nor can any unitary interest be overemphasized. The various components can and do influence the operations of the other elements.

As Coser (1956) has demonstrated, conflict establishes and maintains a balance of power within the structure of the system. To make oneself understood and to achieve at least partial realization of goals, power must be exercised. Specifically, one's interest will not be considered in the negotiating process unless that individual's presence is felt. As Coser (1956: 137) has stated, "struggle may be an important way to avoid conditions of disequilibrium by modifying the basis for power relations....Conflict, rather than being disruptive and dissociating may indeed be a means of balancing and hence maintaining a society as a going concern." In an environment which is characterized by a high degree of diversity of interest, conflict may well serve to produce an equilibrium, a balance, rather than a state of disequilibrium. Interest groups are forced continually to negotiate and compromise. Differences are thus mitigated, and the system changes and adapts over time. Given the high diversity of attitudes about justice and its administration, the conflicts and fragmentation within the criminal justice system probably provide the only means of maintaining equilibrium among the various interest groups. Thus, a strong law enforcement orientation can exist in a system which is also committed to a program of diversion. Lack of specificity is thus an effective device that allows various and diverse interests to be presented.

Lack of integration allows the system to adapt to special problems. For example, in reacting to public sentiment, a local prosecutor may attempt to see that a particular offender is sentenced to a very long period of incarceration. Other than promoting the goal of retribution, such a sentence may be incongruent with other criminal justice goals. In a fragmented system, corrections may modify the prosecutor's action through some form of early release. The correctional decision as such directly conflicts with the values and goals of the local prosecutor and the public which he or she represents but may be consistent with contemporary trends of corrections and justice.

Blumstein and Cohen (1973) have suggested that levels of punishment are consistent over time within cultures. They contend that as crime increases the boundaries of criminality and severity of punishment will be modified in order to maintain a consistent level of punishment. Lack of unification within the criminal justice system seems to serve a similar function. Discretion, such as corrections mediating a prosecutor's long sentence, allows for an equalization process to occur. In this manner, the motivation of police is modified by the decision of the courts as to what crimes will be prosecuted. Corrections monitors and modifies court decisions by implementing forms of early release, thus mitigating the overemphasis of incapacitation and retribution. The police and the courts monitor correctional decisions by being particularly attuned to previous offenders. This interactive process within the system makes it possible, at least to some degree, to maintain levels of punishment at consistent levels.

It is important to realize that the influence which components exert on one another is less than total domination. Because of the circular nature of influence, each component has the ability to modify the output of every other component and consequently that influence can be reciprocated. Also, no single component can totally reverse or change the action or activity of another component. Therefore, influence is limited to a specific extent. In this manner, the courts' insistence on police practices which are consistent with due process does not eliminate the law enforcement orientation toward efficiency. Efficiency is simply pursued within the boundaries of the courts' influence. This reality is critically important in that different components may represent different interests. The provision for diversity prevents any single interest from becoming dominant. Unification and the pursuit of a monolithic system would reduce discretion and limit the ability of the system to respond to aberrations and peculiarities. Fragmentation, on the other hand, allows the components to check the behavior of one another and to promote a balanced or equitable system of justice.

Thus, by allowing different interests to be present within an agency or a component, conflict may be played out and resolved among different jurisdictions and among the different components. Negotiation and mitigation may occur. Allowing fragmentation to exist and conflict to surface provides the system with the ability to adapt and evolve over time. Specifically, the system can experiment; it can act and react to the influence of different social interests. The impetus and implementation of change develops slowly with a unified and monolithic system; a more fragmented system can rely on and use conflict as an impetus for change.

OFFENDER PROCESSING

The final advantage of goal conflict and fragmentation within the criminal justice system is that they may actually promote and support rather than retard and hinder the processing of offenders. This suggestion is contrary to most contemporary claims. For example, Kellogg (1976: 50) suggests that "the system functions best when all of its parts most rationally and consistently assess offenders and their offenses, match these with the most appropriate responses, and administer the activities required to maintain the process." To the contrary, the lack of unity may be essential for the smooth operation of offender processing whereby the system is able to move a person through its various stages.

Recent research behind criminal justice consolidation has questioned the assumptions, theory, and evidence and has suggested that polycentricity is actually better than unity and centrality. Skoler (1977: 300) has summarized the works of these researchers as follows:

> They cite, variously (and persuasively), emerging knowledge on organizational design and behavior, the cost and inefficiency of layered and complex public bureaucracies, new insights on where economies of scale and public service systems are illusory or nonexistent, and a theory of governmental responsiveness and efficiency which suggests greater "payoff" from less orderly, sometimes overlapping, and locally autonomous service units than from large, centralized, policy-uniform hierarchies. New theories of organizational behavior seem to suggest that large centralized organizations are less effective than smaller more autonomous organizations.

Ostrom and Parks (1973), in examining the merits of small versus large police departments, found that the public generally favors small departments, that efficiency is not gained with greater departmental size after a certain point, that fragmentation of agencies within a metropolitan area does not necessarily reduce the service, and that bureaucratization may reduce effectiveness more than increase it (Skoler, 1977: 300). There seems to be little evidence that suggests that bigger, more centralized, and more unified systems or organizations are better; most evidence runs to the contrary.

In an attempt to unify a system, it is difficult, if not impossible, to anticipate all idiosyncrasies and probable changes and to formulate rules which will accommodate these future events. A nonunified system can change and make necessary adaptations to events which were not anticipated. Similarly, it is difficult to conjecture how the interest structure will develop and be modified in the future. A formalized and necessarily unified system will have difficulty in adapting to these changes.

Hasenfeld (1974: 67–68) noted that the components of the criminal justice system depend on each other for validation of their claimed competence. The police depend on the conviction of apprehended offenders by the courts in order that their action be effective. The criteria that the police use for deciding which suspects to introduce formally into the system are partially defined by the behavior of the courts. Lack of unification within the system provides for the interaction between the various elements of the criminal justice system in this manner and allows the system to make changes in order to maintain a smooth flow of clients. As the use of marijuana became more widespread, the system adapted: courts ceased prosecuting users, and the police responded by no longer arresting minor offenders.

CONCLUSIONS

Based on the arguments made above, the long-term implications of increased integration and unification cannot be regarded as favorable. Unification would create inequities to the extent that any new structure could not accommodate the diverse interests which currently have an impact on the system. The complex and dynamic process of negotiation which occurs within the decision-making environment of offender processing would accordingly be limited. Any system which exhibits high diversity, even in the form of fragmentation, allows conflicts to be played out and resolved on a continual basis. Any degree of centralization and unification, on the other hand, promotes rigidification and creates bureaucracy, which is known to be an inefficient structure for change. A more unified criminal justice system would be more static, less able to respond to various interests. Greater investments of time and energy would be required to change the system.

As Coser has shown, conflict provides system stability rather than reduces it. The dynamic quality of a fragmented criminal justice system promotes a balance of power between antagonistic interests as it encourages adaptation and change. As societal attitudes and values fluctuate, the system can make corresponding changes. Unification would limit the ability of components to adjust their outputs to specific individual cases, to changes that occur over time, and to overreactions and mistakes by the other components. Furthermore, the balance which results from the exertion of influence on components by other components would be limited.

REFERENCES

BAUER, R. A. (1968). "The Study of Policy Formation: An Introduction." In R. A. Bauer and K. J. Gregen (eds.), *The Study of Policy Formation*. New York: Free Press, pp. 1–26.

BLUMSTEIN, A., and J. COHEN (1973). "A Theory of the Stability of Punishment." *Journal of Criminal Law and Criminology 64*: 198–207.

CHAMBLISS, W. J. (1969). *Crime and the Legal Process*. New York: McGraw-Hill.

CHAMBLISS, W. J. and R. B. SEIDMAN. (1971). *Law, Order and Power*. Reading, Mass.: Addison-Wesley.

_____. (1972). "The State, the Law and the Definition of Behaviors as Criminal or Delinquent." In D. Glazer (ed.), *Handbook of Criminology*. Chicago: Rand-McNally.

CLARK, R. (1971). *Crime in America*. New York: Irwin and Schuster.

COLE, G. F. (1973). *Politics and the Administration of Justice*. Beverly Hills, Calif.: Sage.

_____. (1980). "The Decision to Prosecute." In G. F. Cole (ed.), *Criminal Justice: Law and Politics*. North Scituate, Mass.: Duxbury, pp. 155–166.

COSER, L. A. (1956). *The Functions of Social Conflict*. Glencoe: Free Press.

CYERT, R. M. and J. G. MARCH (1963). *A Behavioral Theory of the Firm*. Englewood Cliffs, N.J.: Prentice-Hall.

DIESING, P. (1962). *Reason in Society*. Westport, Conn.: Greenwood Press.

DUFFEE, D. (1980, reissued 1990). *Explaining Criminal Justice.* Prospect Heights, Ill.: Waveland Press, Inc.

EMERY, F. E. and E. L. TRIST (1965). "The Causal Texture of Organizational Environments." *Human Relations 18*: 21–31.

HASENFELD, Y. (1974). "People Processing Organizations: An Exchange Approach." In Y. Hasenfeld and R. A. English (eds.), *Human Service Organizations.* Ann Arbor: The University of Michigan Press, pp. 60–71.

HAWKINS, G. (1976). *The Prison: Policy and Practice.* Chicago: The University of Chicago Press.

KELLOGG, F. R. (1976). "Organizing the Criminal Justice System: A Look at 'Operative' Objectives." *Federal Probation 40*: 50–56.

LEVIN, M. A. (1980). "Urban Politics and Policy Outcomes: The Criminal Courts." In G. F. Cole (ed.), *Criminal Justice: Law and Politics.* North Scituate, Mass.: Duxbury, pp. 336–361.

LEVINE, J. P., and M. C. MUSHENO and D. J. PALUMBO (1980). *Criminal Justice: A Public Policy Approach.* New York: Harcourt Brace Jovanovich.

MARCH, J. G. and H. A. SIMON (1958). *Organizations.* New York: John Wiley.

MENNINGER, K. (1969). *The Crime of Punishment.* New York: Viking.

OHLIN, L. E. (1974). "Conflicting Interests in Correctional Objectives." In Y. Hasenfeld and R. A. English (Eds.), *Human Service Organizations.* Ann Arbor: The University of Michigan Press, pp. 135–152.

O'NEILL, M. E., R. F. BYKOWSKI and R. S. BLAIR (1967). *Criminal Justice Planning.* San Jose: Justice Systems Development.

OSTROM, E. and R. PARKS (1973). "Suburban Police Departments: Too Many and Too Small?" In Masotti and Hadden (Eds.), *The Urbanization of the Suburbs*, Vol. 7. Beverly Hills, Calif.: Sage.

PACKER, H. (1968). *The Limits of Criminal Sanction.* Stanford, Calif.: Stanford University Press.

POUND, R. (1943). "A Survey of Social Interests." *Harvard Law Review 57*: 1–39.

QUINNEY, R. (1969). *Crime and Justice in Society.* Boston: Little, Brown.

_____. (1974). *Critique of Legal Order: Crime Control in Capitalist Society.* Boston: Little, Brown.

_____. (1977). *Class, State and Crime.* New York: Longman.

SKOLER, D. L. (1977). *Organizing the Non-System.* Lexington, Mass.: Lexington Books.

TERRYBERRY, S. (1968). "The Evolution of Organizational Environments." *Administration Science Quarterly 12*: 490–613.

VAN DEN HAAG, E. (1975). *Punishing Criminals: Concerning a Very Old and Painful Question.* New York: Basic Books.

WILSON, J. Q. (1968). *Varieties of Police Behavior.* Cambridge, Mass.: Harvard University Press.

_____. (1975). *Think About Crime.* New York: Basic Books.

QUESTIONS FOR DISCUSSION

1. Whatever their theoretical positions, many experts believe that the criminal justice system must become a well-integrated system with common goals, strategies, and techniques. Why?

2. Discuss the sociopolitical environment of criminal justice. Provide examples of how this "environment" affects the policies and responses of criminal justice agencies.

3. An assumption, typically made, is that a common set of values exist that underlies criminal justice policies and practices. Wright asserts that the system is characterized by "reflective diversity." What is the basis for his assertion? Provide specific examples of Wright's position.

4. An advantage of conflicting goals in the criminal justice system is that they promote a system of checks and balances. Explain.

5. How is offender processing enhanced by conflicting goals in the criminal justice system? Cite examples.

10

POLICING THE GHETTO UNDERCLASS

THE POLITICS OF LAW AND LAW ENFORCEMENT

William J. Chambliss
George Washington University

■ ■ ■ ■ ■ ■ ■ ■ ■ ■ ■ ■ ■ ■ ■ ■ ■ ■ ■ ■

For the past several years, my students and I have been riding with the Raid Deployment Unit (RDU) of the Washington, D.C. Metropolitan Police. In response to the urban riots of the 1960s Washington, D.C., like many other cities, established specialized riot control units within the police department.[1] These units were specially trained to respond quickly and with force to the threat of riots or urban disturbances. Even in the United States, riots do not happen that often. For the police, the "war on drugs" provided a functional equivalent to riots: the crisis of inner-city drugs and violence.

In all, we spent more than 100 hours riding with members of the RDU and other police officers. These observations and discussions with police officers stimulated the reflections that follow on the state of law enforcement in U.S. cities and the impact it is having on the public's perception of crime and the lives of those most affected.

THE RAPID DEPLOYMENT UNIT

Members of the RDU are described by other police officers as the "Dirty Harrys" and "very serious bad-ass individuals." The RDU is deployed in teams of three patrol cars with two officers in each car. While each car may patrol in different areas, they are never so far from one another that they cannot be summoned on short notice to converge in one place. They patrol what Wilson (1987, 1993) calls the urban ghetto: that is, the area of the city where 40 percent of the black population lives below the poverty level.

The RDU organizes its efforts at crime control around three distinct activities: the "rip," vehicular stops, and serving warrants.

The "Rip"

The "rip" involves the use of undercover agents to buy drugs and to identify the person who sold the drugs. Obviously, it is the goal of undercover agents to maintain their cover. How can an undercover agent identify a drug seller to uniformed officers without revealing his or her identify as an undercover agent to the drug seller? The following field notes illustrate how this is done:

RIPS: CASE NO. 1

"It is about 1730 hours on a hot summer day in 1992. Rapid Deployment Unit (RDU) is patrolling the Seventh District. The 7th district police are doing drug raids called 'rips.' An undercover officer approaches a person suspect of dealing drugs and makes a buy of $10 worth of crack cocaine. The officer then walks away. Another undercover officer is watching. The second officer radios uniformed officers and gives a brief description of the offender. The uniformed officers move in and arrest the suspect. The suspect is then taken to a remote street corner where he is photographed and told to look out into traffic. Various cars drive by. One of the cars is being driven by the officer who made by the buy. He looks at the apprehended suspect and positively identifies him."

The purpose of this elaborate process is to maintain the secret identity of the undercover officer. If the suspect were arrested, immediately the undercover officer would be compromised in the community.

Most "rips" do not go as smoothly as the one described. Suspects often flee or enter a building before the uniformed police can make an arrest:

RIPS: CASE NO. 2

"It is 10:25 at night when an undercover agent purchases $50 of crack cocaine from a young black male. The agent calls us and tells us that the suspect has just entered a building and gone into an apartment. We go immediately to the apartment; the police enter without warning with their guns drawn. Small children begin to scream and cry. The adults in the apartment are thrown to the floor, the police are shouting, the three women in the apartment are swearing and shouting 'You can't just barge in here like this…where is your goddam warrant?' The suspect is caught and brought outside. The identification is made and the suspect is arrested. The suspect is sixteen years old.

While the suspect is being questioned one policeman says:

'I should kick your little black ass right here for dealing that shit. You are a worthless little scumbag, do you realize that?'

Another officer asks:

'What is your mother's name, son? My mistake…she is probably a whore and you are just a ghetto bastard. Am I right?'

The suspect is cooperative and soft spoken. He does not appear to be menacing or a threat. He offers no resistance. The suspect's demeanor seems to cause the police officers to become more abusive verbally. The suspect is handled very roughly. Handcuffs are cinched tightly and he is shoved against the patrol car. His head hits the door frame of the car as he is pushed into the back seat of the patrol car. One of the officer comments that it is nice to make a "clean arrest."

When asked whether it is legal to enter a home without a warrant, the arresting officer replies:

"This is Southeast [Washington] and the Supreme Court has little regard for little shit like bursting in on someone who just committed a crime involving drugs....Who will argue for the juvenile in this case? No one can and no one will."

RIPS: CASE NO. 3

A "rip" is made involving an older (34 year old) black male.

"It is after midnight and the suspect enters a local strip bar. Three patrol cars race up the street and jump the curb to block the entrance. In the process one officer on foot who is nearly hit by a patrol car jumps and tears up his knee on the wet pavement. Three patrol cars surround the front of the establishment. The arrest team charges in the front door with their weapons drawn. The officers retrieve the suspect and drag him out to the hood of the patrol car. The suspect might have walked of his own volition but is never given the opportunity. The suspect denies any wrongdoing and becomes upset and confused by the arrest. He appears to be slightly intoxicated or high on drugs. He is forced to sit down on the front bumper of one of the patrol cars. He is instructed to sit on his handcuffed hands with his legs crossed. The suspect says: 'What is this shit? This is all a bunch of bullshit man. You guys don't got shit on me man. Kiss my ass.' One of the officers responds by forcefully shoving the suspect against the grill of the car. The officer places his flashlight against the side of the suspect's face and presses it hard into the suspect's cheek:

'Listen shorty, you say once more word and that's your hospital word. I will lay you out in a heartbeat so shut your damn mouth.'"

Rips account for approximately one third of the RDU's arrests. Another 50 percent of their arrests come from vehicular stops and the remainder from serving warrants, observations made of transactions taking place on the street, and responding to telephone calls and tips received through police headquarters.

Vehicular Stops

The RDU patrols the ghetto continuously looking for cars with young black men in them. They are especially attentive to newer-model cars, Isuzu four-wheel drive vehicles, BMWs, and Honda Accords, based on the belief that these are the favorite cars of drug dealers. During our observations, however, the RDU officers came to the conclusion that drug dealers were leaving their fancy cars at home to avoid vehicular stops. It thus became commonplace for RDU officers to stop any car with black men in it.

There is a nod to legality in vehicular stops in that the officers look for a violation in order to justify the stop:

Field Notes: As we pass a new-looking BMW with two black men in it the driver of the patrol car says to his partner: "Joe, check out that car for violations." The partner says quickly: "Broken tail light, hit the horn." The siren is put on and the car pulls over.

Any minor infraction is an excuse: going through a yellow light, not stopping completely at a stop sign, or having something hanging from the rear-view mirror (a violation of which almost every car in the southeast section of the city is guilty). In addition, I was told confidentially by some of the officers, though neither I nor any of my students ever observed it, that if the officers feel strongly that they should stop a car, they will stop it and break a taillight as they approach the car.

> "This is the jungle…we rewrite the constitution every day down here.…If we pull everyone over they will eventually learn that we aren't playing games any more. We are real serious about getting the crap off the streets."

Once a car is stopped the officers radio for backup. The two other cars in the area immediately come to the scene and triangulate the suspect's car: one car comes in close behind, and the two other cars form a V in front of the suspect's car.

Vehicular stops occur on an average of every twenty minutes throughout the shift. From our observations, illegal drugs, guns, weapons, or someone who is wanted by authorities are found in only 10 percent of the cars stopped. The officers themselves believe that they find serious violations in "about a third" of the vehicular stops. The following cases typify vehicular stops.

VEHICULAR STOP: CASE NO. 1

> "12:15 A.M. A car is spotted with a broken headlight. The patrol car pulls over the vehicle and runs the license plate number through the computer. One officer approaches the vehicle from the rear and another approaches on the opposite side of the car. Both officers have their Glocks (guns) drawn. Momentarily the car is surrounded by two other patrol cars triangulating the stopped car. One officer goes to the window of the car and says: 'Good evening. My name is officer _____. I am with the Rapid Development Unit. Our job is to remove guns and drugs from the streets. Do you have any guns or drugs on your person or inside the vehicle?' The driver of the car says there are none. The officer requests permission to search the car. The individual refuses the officer's request.
>
> The officer begins pressuring the driver with threats: 'You know what happens if you refuse to obey a police officer's request?' The driver says nothing, shrugs and gets out of the car. The car is searched and nothing is found. A check is made for outstanding warrants of everyone in the car. There are none. The suspects are released with a warning to 'never let me catch you with anything, you understand?'"

VEHICULAR STOP: CASE NO. 2

> "After midnight. The driver of the patrol car points out a car driven by two young black men. He tells his partner to check for violations. The partner says, 'pull 'em over. Broken taillight.'
>
> The officers call for backup. Two other RDU patrol cars arrive and the suspect's car is surrounded by the three cars. Two officers approach the car on each side. The driver rolls down his window and the officer asks to see his license, which is given without comment. The officer on the other side of the car asks to see some identification of the passenger and is given his driver's license. The licenses are given to a third officer who removes himself to his car to check for warrants and to check the license plate of the car.
>
> The officer on the driver's side asks: 'Can we search your car?' The driver says 'No.' The officer then says, 'You know what will happen if you refuse a police officer's request?' The driver

then says 'OK, you can look.' Both occupants are told to get out of the car and the car is searched. The officers find nothing.

Apparently satisfied that there are no drugs or guns in the car, the officer says: 'OK. You can go; but don't let us catch you with any shit, you understand?' The driver nods yes, everyone returns to their cars."

VEHICULAR STOP: CASE NO. 3

"Another vehicular stop takes place at 12:17 that follows the same pattern. Again there are two black men in the car. The officers approach the car with their guns drawn and tell the occupants to get out of the car. One officer points to a small piece of white paper on the back seat. The driver of the car is extremely nervous. He keeps putting his hands into his pockets, then pulling them out. He seems to be trying to push his hand through his pants pockets.

'What's in your pants?' The driver responds, 'Nothin', man. nothin'.'

Officer: 'Empty pockets, quick.'

The driver seems confused but complies. An envelope containing perhaps two grams of crack cocaine is handed to the officer who opens the packet, smirks and tells the driver to put his hands on the top of the car. The officer on the other side of the car follows suit. Both men are handcuffed and taken to the patrol car. No one says anything."

The RDU does not patrol the predominantly white sections of Washington, D.C. Observations of policing in this area of the city reveal an entirely different approach by the police. There are no "rips" and no vehicular stops unless there is a clear violation. Officers are not looking for cars with black drivers. If a car is stopped other cars are not called as backups, and the officer handles the infraction on his or her own.

VEHICULAR STOP: CASE NO. 4

"9:15 P.M. A rusted 1978 Bonneville Pontiac is spotted and the officer witnesses the vehicle making erratic lane changes. The officer follows at a distance of about 100 yards. The vehicle attempts to go through a yellow light which turns red before the vehicle gets through the intersection. The officer hits his siren and pulls the car over. He calls in the license plate number and advances to the driver's side of the car. He has no other officer with him, only the observer. His gun is not drawn. The officer notifies the driver of the offense and he begins to search the car visually. The suspect is asked, 'Can I search your car?' The suspect says yes but the officer declines the offer. The suspect is written up for running a red light, is told to have a good evening, and is released."

Search Warrants

The RDU's third major activity is carrying out search warrants. Based on information received from informants, undercover agents, or observations a warrant is issued by the court to search an apartment or home for various reasons:

WARRANTS: CASE NO. 1

"Five RDU officers enter an apartment about 10:45 P.M. Before entering the officers draw their guns, break down the door and rush in. The suspect is spotted, guns are pointed at him and he is told to 'lie down, NOW.' The suspect is handcuffed and taken outside. An elderly woman begins screaming and crying. She tells the officers to put their guns away. An officer goes to her, his gun still drawn, and tells her to 'shut up or I'll pop you in the jaw.' He physically forces her to lie down on the floor face down. The officers leave the apartment, put the suspect in the car and take him to the precinct for booking."

Observations indicate the police carry out warrants differently in the predominantly white section of Washington, D.C.:

WARRANTS: CASE NO. 2

A warrant is issued by the court for the arrest of a suspected drug dealer wanted for assault and attempted murder. The third district police are in an excited state over the pending arrest. An anonymous tip has provided them with information as to the suspect's whereabouts and a discussion at the station lays out a plan for making the arrest. Twelve officers are dispatched to the house where the suspect is supposedly living. Seven officers surround the house and five others approach the front door. Most, but not all, of the officers have their guns drawn. In the dark it is not possible to see all of the officers, but of those observable three had guns drawn and two do not. It is a few minutes past 1 A.M. when the officers approach the front door. The doorbell is rung and the team leader shouts, "Police, open up." Everyone appears to be on edge. There is no response to the knock or the command. The officers break open the door. Flashlights are shining in every corner, behind further and into people's eyes. A terrified elderly woman stands at the top of the stairs and asks what is going on. One of the officers approaches her with calmness and no gun drawn, speaks to her in a low voice, and gently removes her from the house to be watched by the team outside. The suspect is found in the basement behind a water cooler. He is identified and handcuffed. As he is being led from the house one officer says to him, "You sure have a pretty face, buddy boy. See you at the country club."

THE CONSEQUENCES

The prison population in the United States increased by 167 percent between 1980 and 1992, with the greatest percentage increase in drug law violations (see Table 1). The United States today incarcerates a higher percentage of its population than any country in the world: a dubious distinction formerly held by the USSR and South Africa (see Figure 1). And it is minorities, especially young African Americans and Latinos, who are disproportionately arrested, convicted, and sentenced to prison. In 1991, African-American males between the ages of 15 and 34 made up 14 percent of the population and more than 40 percent of the people in prison. White males made up 82 percent of this age group but less than 60 percent of the prison population (Statistical Abstracts, 1993). Blacks accounted for more than 40 percent of the inmates in state and federal prisons (Table 2).

In Washington, D.C. and Baltimore, 40 to 50 percent of all black males between the ages of 18 and 35 are either in prison, jail, on probation or parole, or there is a warrant for their arrest (Mauer, 1990; Miller, 1992). Arrests and convictions for drugs play an increasingly important part as a source of criminal convictions. Nearly 30 percent of all state and over 55 percent of all federal prisoners in 1992 were convicted on drug violations (Maguire, Pastore, and Flannagan, 1993). Two-thirds of all drug arrests in 1992 were for possession,

TABLE 1   CHANGE IN STATE AND FEDERAL PRISON POPULATIONS: UNITED STATES, 1980–1992

Year	No. of Inmates	Percent Change
1980	329,821	—
1981	369,930	12.2
1982	413,806	25.5
1983	436,855	32.5
1984	462,002	40.1
1985	502,752	52.4
1986	545,378	65.4
1987	585,292	77.5
1988	631,990	91.6
1989	712,967	116.2
1990	773,124	134.4
1991	824,133	149.9
1992	883,593	167.9

Source: Darrell K. Gilliard, "Prisoners in 1992." Bureau of Justice Statistics, U.S. Department of Justice, Washington, D.C.

FIGURE 1   COMPARATIVE PRISON POPULATIONS IN SELECTED COUNTRIES, 1990 RATE PER 100,000

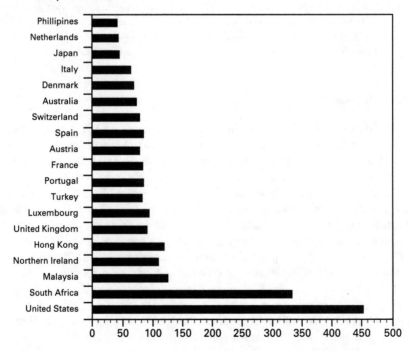

Sources: Nils Christie, *Crime Control as Industry*, London: Routledge, 1993:29 and Australian Institute of Criminology, "Incarceration Rates for the United States, South Africa, and the Soviet Union in Comparison to Europe and Asia," Melbourne: 1991.

and only one-third were for the sale or manufacture of drugs. African Americans account for more than 40 percent of all drug arrests (Maguire, Pastor, and Flannagan, 1993) despite the fact that self-report surveys show that, except for crack cocaine, whites are three to five times as likely to use drugs as blacks (Bureau of Justice Statistics, 1993a; see Table 3). Thus more whites than blacks use illegal drugs and more than 80 percent of the population is white. But 66 percent of the inmates in state prisons convicted of drug offenses are black, and only 33 percent are white (Maguire, Pastor, and Flannagan, 1993).

Effects on Family and Education

The intensive surveillance of black neighborhoods, and the pattern of surveillance of white neighborhoods has the general consequence of institutionalizing racism by defining the problem of crime generally, and drug use in particular, as a problem of young black men. It further ghettoizes the African-American community and destroys any possibility for normal family and community relations. Young African-American and Latino men are defined as a criminal group, arrested for minor offenses over and over again, and given criminal records which justify long prison sentences. The culture of the black community and the black family is then blamed for high rates of illegitimate children and crime. Crime control policies are a major contributor to the disruption of the family, the prevalence of single parent families, and children raised without a father in the ghetto, and the "inability of people to get the jobs still available" (Anderson, 1993; Wilson, 1987, 1993).

But the consequences go beyond the destruction of family and community in the ghetto. Scarce resources are transferred from desperately needed social programs to criminal justice. For the first time in history, state and municipal governments are spending more money on criminal justice than education (Figure 2; Chambliss, 1991). Nationwide, expenditures on criminal justice increased by 150 percent between 1972 and 1988, while expenditures on education increased by 46 percent. Between 1969 and 1989, per capita spending on criminal justice in U.S. cities (municipal expenditures) rose from $34 to $120, and county expenditures as a percentage of total budget rose from 10 to 15 percent between 1973 and 1989. State expenditures showed even greater increases, rising tenfold from per

TABLE 2   STATE AND FEDERAL PRISONERS BY RACE, 1991

State Prisoners	
White Non-Hispanic	35.4%
Black Non-Hispanic	45.6%
Hispanic	16.7%
Other	2.4%
Federal Prisoners	
White	65.5%
Black	31.7%
Other	2.8%

Source: *Sourcebook of Criminal Justice Statistics*. eds. Kathleen Maguire, Ann Pastore, and Timothy J. Flanagan. 1992 Bureau of Justice Statistics, U.S. Department of Justice, Washington, D.C.: USGPO, 1993:622, 634.

TABLE 3   SELF-REPORTED DRUG USE BY TYPE OF DRUG AND RACE

	Race and Ethnicity		
	% White	% Black	% Hispanic
Heroin	74.5	14.8	10.7
Cocaine	62.0	23.4	14.6
Crack Cocaine	49.9	35.9	14.2
Marijuana	75.1	17.5	7.3

Source: Bureau of Justice Statistics, "Drugs, crime and the criminal justice system," 1992 U.S. Department of Justice, Washington, D.C.: NCJ 133652:28.

capita expenditures on police and corrections of $8 in 1969 to $80 in 1989 (Figure 2). State government expenditure for building prisons increased 593 percent in actual dollars. Spending on corrections—prison building, maintenance, and parole—has more than doubled in the last ten years (Chambliss, 1991; Maguire and Flannagan, 1990; Maguire, Pastore, and Flannagan, 1992).

The number of police officers in the United States doubled between 1980 and 1990, and in 1994 the Senate passed a bill, strongly supported by President Clinton, that proposes

FIGURE 2A   **COMPARISON OF PER CAPITA MUNICIPAL EXPENDITURES ON CRIMINAL JUSTICE AND EDUCATION 1968–1989 (IN MILLIONS)**

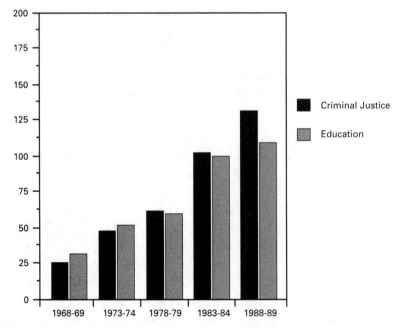

Source: U.S. Department of Commerce: Bureau of Census. City Government Finances: 1968–1969, 1973–1974, 1978–1979, 1983–1984 and 1988–1989.

FIGURE 2B   COMPARISON OF PER CAPITA COUNTY EXPENDITURES ON EDUCATION AND CRIMINAL JUSTICE, 1980–1988 (IN MILLIONS)

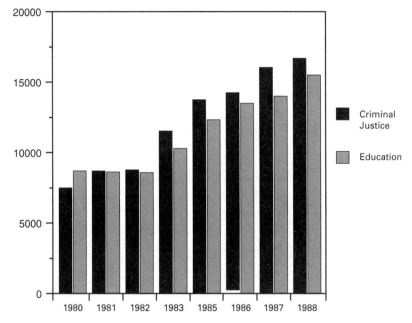

Source: U.S. Department of Commerce: Bureau of Census. County Government Finances: 1983–1984 and 1988–1989.

adding another 100,000 police officers. This is a continuation of a policy begun under the Reagan administration that has seen the federal government increase its allocation of resources for criminal justice without a pause. The War on Drugs, with a budget of $1 billion in 1981, received $13.4 billion in 1993. The government added 700 FBI agents in 1990, an increase of 25 percent, while teachers have been fired in states already suffering from large classes and poor facilities. Welfare for the poor also is severely cut. In real dollars, the Aid to Dependent Children program's cash contribution to a mother with two children and no outside employment dropped from $7,836 in 1982 to $4,801 in 1991.

WHY?

Many reasons have been proposed for the rapid increase in expenditures on criminal justice (or, in the words of Nils Christie, the growth of "the crime industry") in the United States (Christie, 1993). One explanation is the alleged increase in crime. There is a general perception that crime, especially violent crime, has increased. The notion of a crime increase is a perception, apparently created by the law enforcement establishment, the media, and politicians. But this is not supported by the facts. The best available data, the findings of victim surveys conducted every year since 1973, show that the crime rate has not changed significantly in the last 20 years (Figure 3).

Victim surveys show also that it is very unlikely that anyone will be the victim of a crime in any given year. More than 90 percent of respondents report that neither they nor any member of their household was the victim of a criminal offense. Indeed, over a lifetime it is unlikely that most people will be the victim of a serious offense. The risk of being a victim of a violent crime in any given year is less than 3 percent (Bureau of Justice Statistics, 1992b).

Creating the perception

The news media and law enforcement agencies use "crimes known to the police," as reported in the FBI's Uniform Crime Reports (UCR), to demonstrate an increase in the crime rate. By the manipulation of data through gimmicks (such as a "crime clock" and percentage increases that appear large because the base is small), the FBI distorts the reality of crime rates and the severity of the crime problem. The most often cited FBI data are the "crimes known to the police," which consist of crimes reported by the police and crimes reported to the police. Bogess and Bound conclude from their comparison of data from the Uniform Crime Reports and data from the National Crime Victim Survey that most of the increase in

FIGURE 3   RESPONDENTS REPORTING BEING THE VICTIM OF CRIME BY TYPE OF CRIME

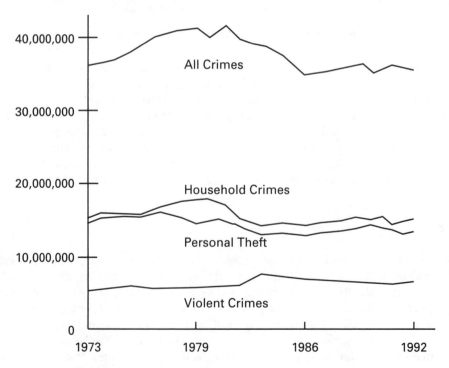

Victimization Trends, 1973-92
Number of Victimizations

Source: Bureau of Justice Statistics, 1992. "Criminal victimization, 1992." Washington, D.C.

crime reported by the FBI between 1975 and 1992 is attributable to an increase in the reporting of crimes to the police, not an increase in the incidence of crime (Bogess and Bound, 1993). Furthermore, "the large increase in the incarceration rate [between 1980 and 1992] is attributable primarily to an increase in the likelihood of incarceration given arrest," *not* to an increase in arrests or, inferentially, the crime rate (Bogess and Bound, 1993).

For example, the 1992 UCR reported a dramatic increase in the murder rate between 1988 and 1992. The FBI used the report to demonstrate a crime rate increase. What the report failed to mention was that between 1980 and 1987 the murder rate actually declined and the 1992 rate was below that of 1980 (Figure 4). That the murder rate has shown no appreciable increase since the 1980s is particularly noteworthy given the fact that the weapons in use today are more efficient than ever before. Pistols have been replaced with rapid firing automatic weapons that leave a victim little chance of escaping with a wound.

The Seriousness of Crime

If the crime rate has not increased, perhaps the astronomical increase in crime control expenditures and the number of people in prison can be explained by an increase in the seriousness of crime. Data from victim surveys and studies of prison inmates contradict this interpretation as well. For every type of crime reported by victims, the least serious crime is

FIGURE 4   U.S. MURDER RATE, BY RACE: 1976–1992

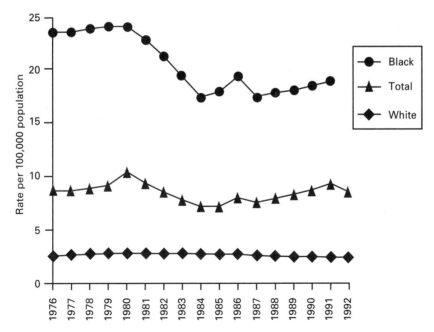

Note: Race specific data is for single victim/single offender murders.

Source: Current Population Reports, P25-1095; Crime in the U.S. and Statistical Abstract of the U.S., various years.

the most common (Table 4). Larceny without contact occurs more than 20 times as often as larceny with contact, and simple theft accounts for the vast majority of crimes reported every year. Attempted crimes are reported twice as often as completed crimes (Bastian, 1992; Table 4).

About 50 percent of respondents who report being the victim of a crime do not report the crime to the police. When asked why, more than half of the victims say that the crime was "not important enough" or that "nothing could be done about it" (Bureau of Justice Statistics, 1992b).

As for the people in prison, Austin and Irwin's survey found that more than 50 percent of the prisoners in state and federal prisons are in for offenses that opinion surveys show the general public thinks are "not very serious crimes" (Austin and Irwin, 1989; Figure 5). A recent study by the Bureau of Justice Statistics found that more than 20 percent of the inmates in federal prisons were in for drug offenses with no history of violent crime or other felonies (Bureau of Justice Statistics, 1994). This indicates that the growth of the crime industry is not due to the seriousness of the crimes.

Crime and Public Opinion

Another explanation for the growth of the crime industry is that lawmakers are merely responding to public opinion. In explaining the creation of President Lyndon Johnson's crime commission and the spate of anticrime legislation in the 1960s, James Q. Wilson argues that public opinion forced political action. He cites the Gallup Polls in support of this conclusion:

In May 1965 the Gallup Poll reported that for the first time "crime" (along with education) was viewed by Americans as the most important problem facing the nation (Wilson, 1975:65).

Wilson goes on to say:

In the months leading up to the Democratic National Convention in 1968—specifically in February, May and August—Gallup continued to report crime as the most important issue…(Wilson 1975:65-66).

Wilson's argument is problematic. The Gallup Polls never showed that crime was perceived by the respondents as the most important problem facing the nation. Every year

TABLE 4   ESTIMATED RATE OF VICTIMIZATION BY SERIOUSNESS OF OFFENSE, 1992 RATE PER 1,000 PERSONS AGE 12 OR OLDER OF PER 1,000 HOUSEHOLDS

More Serious Offense		Less Serious Offense	
Larceny with Contact	2.4	Larceny without Contact	60.6
Aggravated Assault	8.0	Simple Assault	17.5
Assault Attempted without Weapon	5.8	Assault Attempted without Weapon	12.1
Robbery with Injury	1.6	Robbery without Injury	2.3
Attempted Robbery without Injury	.5	Attempted Robbery without Injury	1.5

FIGURE 5   NATIONAL ESTIMATE OF THE SEVERITY OF CRIMES COMMITTED BY PERSONS ADMITTED TO STATE AND FEDERAL PRISONS

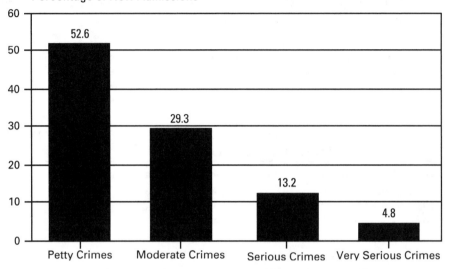

Source: James Austin and John Irwin, *Who Goes to Prison?*, San Francisco: National Council on Crime and Delinquency, 1991.

since 1935 the Gallup Poll has asked a sample of Americans "What do you think is the most important problem facing the county?" Between 1935 and 1993, crime rarely appears as one of the most important problems mentioned, and in the nearly 60 years the poll has been taken, crime is never chosen over other issues as "the most important problem facing the country." In 1989 and 1991, "drugs" and "drug abuse" is frequently mentioned but only once (April 1990) is it the most often chosen. Even when "drugs" is mentioned, crime in the April 1990 poll is seen as "the most important problem" by only 2 percent of the population (Gallup Poll, 1989, 1990, 1991).

Wilson's claim that public opinion forced politicians to pass wide-ranging criminal law legislation in the 1960s is simply not supported by the data. In August 1968, a public opinion poll showed for the first time in 20 years that "crime, lawlessness, looting and rioting" was perceived by 29 percent of those asked as one of "the most important problems facing the nation." In the same poll, 52 percent of those surveyed mentioned the Vietnam War as the most important problem facing the United States, and 20 percent mentioned race relations as the most pressing issue facing the nation (Gallup, 1972:2107). In fact, between 1935 and 1993, crime was never mentioned as "the most important problem" facing the country in Gallup Polls. (see Table 5).[2]

One cannot conclude from these polls that crime is not an important issue, but it is safe to say that it is rarely seen as the most important issue. This is particularly significant given a concerted political effort on the part of conservative politicians since the 1960s to create what Cohen calls "a moral panic" over crime (Cohen, 1980).

CREATING MORAL PANIC

Crime became a national political issue for the first time in 50 years with the presidential campaign of 1964 when the Republican candidate, Barry Goldwater, sounded the alarm (Cronin et al., 1981:18):

> Our wives, all women, feel unsafe on our streets. And in encouragement of even more abuse of the law, we have the appalling spectacle of this country's Ambassador to the United Nations (Adlai Stevenson) actually telling an audience—this year, at Colby College—that, 'in the great struggle to advance human civil rights, even a jail sentence is no longer a dishonor but a proud

TABLE 5   THE MOST IMPORTANT PROBLEM MENTIONED IN GALLUP
POLLS FROM 1935 TO 1990

1935	Unemployment	1965	Vietnam, race relations
1936	Unemployment	1966	Vietnam
1937	Unemployment	1967	Vietnam, high cost of living
1938	Keeping out of war	1968	Vietnam
1939	Keeping out of war	1969	Vietnam
1940	Keeping out of war	1970	Vietnam
1941	Keeping out of war, winning war	1971	Vietnam, high cost of living
1942	Winning war	1972	Vietnam
1943	Winning war	1973	High cost of living, Watergate
1944	Winning war	1974	High cost of living, Watergate, energy crisis
1945	Winning war	1975	High cost of living, unemployment
1946	High cost of living	1976	High cost of living, unemployment
1947	High cost of living, labor unrest	1977	High cost of living, unemployment
1948	Keeping peace	1978	High cost of living, energy problem
1949	Labor unrest	1979	High cost of living, energy problem
1950	Labor unrest	1980	High cost of living, unemployment
1951	Korean war	1981	High cost of living, unemployment
1952	Korean war	1982	Unemployment, high cost of living
1953	Keeping peace	1983	Unemployment, high cost of living
1954	Keeping peace	1984	Unemployment, fear of war
1955	Keeping peace	1985	Fear of war, unemployment
1956	Keeping peace	1986	Unemployment, fear of war
1957	Race relations, keeping peace	1987	Fear of war, unemployment
1958	Unemployment, keeping peace	1988	Budget deficit, drug abuse
1959	Keeping peace	1989	Drugs, poverty, homelessness
1960	Keeping peace	1990	Budget deficit, drugs
1961	Keeping peace	1991	Economy, poverty, homelessness, drugs, unemployment
1962	Keeping peace	1992	Economy, unemployment
1963	Keeping peace, race relations		
1964	Vietnam, race relations		

achievement.' Perhaps we are destined to see in this law-loving land people running for office not on their stainless records but on their prison record (*New York Times*, September 4, 1964:13).

Goldwater's hue and cry did not strike a resonant chord in the U.S. public. As the *Newsweek* editors observed:

> Remarkably late in the campaign, Barry Goldwater was still a candidate in search of an issue that could score a voting breakthrough...[He] did all he could to press the issue of law and order (*Newsweek*, October 19, 1964:27–34).

Gallup Polls taken at the time depict a public more concerned about war, civil rights, poverty and unemployment than crime. Nonetheless, conservative Democrats and Republicans continued to press the issue of crime control after Goldwater's defeat. They focused their attention on Supreme Court decisions such as *Miranda*, *Gideon* and *Escobedo* which gave the accused the right to legal counsel, protection against coerced confessions and the right to remain silent unless a lawyer was present. Congressman Ford and Senators McClellan, Stennis, Ervin, Hruska, Thurmond, Bible and Lausche (a formidable conservative block of five Democrats and three Republicans) sponsored the Omnibus Crime Control and Safe Streets Act that legalized wiretapping and "bugging" by federal agents and local police without requiring a court order, authorized trial judges to admit confessions as voluntary after considering "all factors," thus emasculating the Miranda decision, and exempted law enforcement agencies from having to meet the requirements of the 1964 Civil Rights Act therefore allowing federal grants to be given to law enforcement agencies even if they were guilty of racial discrimination (Chambliss and Sbarbaro, 1993).

In the 1968 presidential campaign (Nixon vs. Humphrey), Richard Nixon and his running mate, Spiro Agnew (both later to be accused of serious crimes themselves), continued the effort to create a moral panic over "law and order." Nixon attacked the Johnson administration's focus on social conditions as the cause of crime:

> By way of excuse, the present Administration places the blame on poverty. But poverty is just one contributing factor....The truth is that we will reduce crime and violence when we enforce our laws—when we make it less profitable, and a lot more risky to break them (*New York Times*, October 25, 1968:34).

Along with Johnson, Nixon held the Supreme Court responsible for the crime problem. He assailed some of the court's decisions as having "tipped the balance against the peace forces and strengthened the criminal forces" (*New York Times*, September 30, 1968:1).

The Republican and conservative Democrat campaign was apparently somewhat successful for, as noted above, in August 1968 a public opinion poll showed for the first time in 20 years that "crime, lawlessness, looting and rioting" was perceived by 29 percent of those asked as one of "the most important problems facing the nation." It is arguable, however, that the success of the campaign to make crime a major political issue came at a time when riots in the cities and violent demonstrations were taking place throughout the country and "crime" was only mentioned by a significant number of respondents when it was collected together with lawlessness, riots, and looting. In any case, the public's concern was short-lived, for crime is not mentioned again among the top two or three problems facing the country until 1989 when "drugs" is seen as one of the nation's most important problems.

The years following the Nixon presidency have witnessed a continued assault on civil liberties and an expansion of federal authority in crime control. The Reagan and Bush administrations hammered away at the issue of crime and created the "war on drugs," complete with a "drug czar" and the expenditure of billions of dollars for crime control. Although the public was slow to respond to the barrage, as the Gallup Polls show, in 1989 "drugs" was perceived as one of the two "most important problems facing the country" (Table 5).

The politicization of crime by conservative politicians occurred at a time when the country was deeply divided over the Vietnam War and civil rights. In this historical context, crime became a smokescreen behind which other issues could be relegated less important. Crime served as well as legitimation for legislation designed primarily to suppress political dissent and overturn Supreme Court decisions (Chambliss and Sbarbaro, 1993).

In addition to these political forces, and partly because of them, the crime control industry emerged as a powerful lobby. Law enforcement agencies control the information available about crime and, as noted above, manipulate the data to serve their purposes. In their effort to create moral panics, and thereby increase their budgets and power, law enforcement agencies are happily joined by the media always hungry for stories that will increase their audience. Indeed, the media has become so dependent on crime news in recent years that in 1993 crime was the most frequently reported subject on television news (Media Monitor, 1994). Between 1990 and 1993, the number of crime stories appearing on ABC, CBS, and NBC evening newscasts increased from 737 to 1,698.

The crime industry has become so powerful, it is virtually immune from the budgetary cuts experienced by other public services during the recent recession. On those rare occasions when a mayor or governor suggests cutting justice expenditures or even holding steady the number of police officers, propaganda, politicking and arm twisting by police officer associations (often called "benevolent" associations rather than trade unions) and lobbyists with vested interests in supply equipment and prison facilities quickly reverse the decision. In Prince George's County, a suburb of Washington, D.C., for example, when there was talk of layoffs and pay cuts for police the police officer's association hired a public relations firm and ran television commercials citing increasing crime rates and accusing the county executive of handcuffing police officers with proposed budget cuts. The union spent more than $10,000 in one week on television and newspaper advertisements, and the politicians acquiesced, canceling the proposed budget cuts.

With their newfound success as lobbyists and self-perpetuating bureaucracies, however, law enforcement agencies face some formidable organizational problems, the most important being how to justify their claim to more and more of the tax payer's dollars. Manipulating data, creating moral panics, and feeding the media crime stories can only go so far. Eventually, arrests must be made, successful prosecutions carried out, and people sent to prisons. For these symbols of effective law enforcement the large population of poor black males is the perfect bureaucratic solution. For here is a population without political clout, with few resources to successfully defend against criminal charges, and a public image as a group in which crime is endemic. Enforcing the law in the black ghetto enables the police, as one officer expressed it, to "rewrite the constitution every day."

A police officer's career and even his annual income is determined by the number of "good collars" he makes. A "good collar" is an arrest for what is defined as a serious violation of the law that culminates in a conviction. Drug arrests qualify. They are among the easiest convictions, the most difficult to defend, and often lead to the longest prison terms as a result of mandatory sentences. But they are organizationally effective only if the person arrested is relatively powerless. Arrests of white male middle class offenders (on college campuses for example) are guaranteed to cause the organization and the arresting officers strain, as people with political influence and money hire attorneys for their defense. Arrests of poor black men, however, create only rewards for the organization and the officer since the cases are quickly processed through the courts, a guilty plea obtained, and the suspect sentenced. Organizations reward role occupants whose behavior maximizes rewards and minimizes strains for the organization. In a class society, the powerless, the poor, and those who fit the public stereotype of "the criminal" are the human resources needed by law enforcement agencies to maximize rewards and minimize strains. It is not surprising, but sociologically predictable, then, that doubling the number of police officers in the last 10 years has tripled the number of people in prison and jail, filled these institutions with minor offenders, exacerbated the disproportionate imprisonment of minorities, and institutionalized racist beliefs that make being a young black man synonymous with being criminal.

SUMMARY AND CONCLUSIONS

In the last 20 years, the crime control industry has experienced unprecedented growths in the United States. The number of police officers has doubled and, since 1980, the prison population has increased by more than 160 percent. This heady growth has taken place at a time when federal, state, and municipal budgets have been severely strained and other public services cut.

The reasons often given for the diversion of resources from education, welfare and other social services to criminal justice is that a rising crime rate necessitates it and the public demands it. Analysis of crime rates reveals, however, that despite the propaganda of law enforcement agencies and the impression perpetrated by the media, the crime rate in the United States has not changed significantly in the past 20 years. Nor do public opinion polls support the idea that crime has ever been one of the problems perceived as "the most important" facing the country.

The creation of a moral panic over crime was brought about by a coalition of political, law enforcement, and media interests that accounts for the growth of the crime industry. First are the political interests of politicians from Goldwater to Clinton in making crime (and drugs) a public issue to gain electoral advantage over their opponents and to serve as a smokescreen or diversion from issues fraught with political danger, such as confronting the budget deficit or health care. Second, a coalition of conservative Democrats and Republicans used crime as a smokescreen to (a) detract from more controversial issues such as Vietnam and civil rights and (b) legitimize the passage of laws that provided law enforcement agencies with more efficient means of suppressing social interest.

Political interests coalesced in the 1970s and 1980s with the growth of a crime industry lobby consisting of organizations representing the interests of police and correctional officers alongside firms profiting from prison construction, the sale of weapons, technology, and equipment to law enforcement agencies. The media contributed its part to the creation of a moral panic and young black males particularly, and minorities generally, paid the price in the form of intensive police surveillance, imprisonment, and institutionalized racism.

Reversing the process will prove to be more difficult than instituting it. Political leaders will have to show the kind of courage shown by Lyndon Johnson and Hubert Humphrey who defied the conservative platform's call for more police and harsher penalties with pleas for more public spending on schools and jobs. Law enforcement agencies will have to change their reward system to emphasize community policing and rewarding officers who do not have to make arrests to their communities, rather than rewarding those who do. And the media will have to assume some responsibility for educating rather than sensationalizing. Social scientists can play a critical role by conducting studies of law enforcement in the communities most affected and communicating the results to policymakers and the public. It is unlikely, however, that any of these changes will take place so long as we continue to criminalize drugs and provide an incentive for police officers and prosecutors to entrap and arrest people for the possession or sale of small amounts of drugs. The longer it takes, the more lives will be lost and the more the United States will move toward a society permanently divided by race and class into communities that are quasi police states patrolled by RDU-type police units in search of crime and communities where minor infractions of the law are treated, as they should be, as tolerable indiscretions.

NOTES

1. According to FBI statistics, approximately 10 percent of law enforcement personnel are now employed in specialized police units. In 1992, such specialized units accounted for 25 percent of police departments' budgets (Maguire, Pastore, and Flanagan, 1992).

2. Contrary to Wilson's claims, crime was *not* reported in the Gallup Poll of May 1965 as the most important problem; in May 1965, the Gallup Poll did not even ask what respondents thought was the most important problem facing the nation. But in June 1965 the question was asked and the responses were as follows: Vietnam, 23 percent; civil rights, 23 percent; threat of war, 16 percent; prestige abroad, 9 percent; spread of world communism, 9 percent; juvenile delinquency, 2 percent (Gallup Poll, 1965).

   It is a gross distortion of fact to say, as Wilson does, that "in February, May and August [of 1968] Gallup continued to report crime as the most important issue." Gallup did not ask the question in February. In May 1968, the question was asked and only 15 percent of the respondents named crime including riots, looting, and juvenile delinquency as the most important problem, but 42 percent named Vietnam and 25 percent race relations. In August, crime, etc. is mentioned by 29 percent as the most important problem, but the Vietnam War is seen as the most important problem by 52 percent (Gallup, 1968).

REFERENCES

ANDERSON, ELIJAH. (1993). "Abolish Welfare—Then What?" *The Washington Post*, December 31:A23.

AUSTIN, JAMES, and JOHN IRWIN. (1989). *Who Goes to Prison?* San Francisco: The National Council on Crime and Delinquency.

BASTIAN, LISA D. (1992). "Criminal Victimization, 1992." Bureau of Justice Statistics, U.S. Department of Justice, Washington, D.C.

BOGESS, SCOTT, and JOHN BOUND. (1993). "Did Criminal Activity Increase During the 1980's? Comparisons Across Data Sources." Research Report No. 93-280. Population Studies Center, University of Michigan, Ann Arbor, Mich.

Bureau of Justice Statistics. (1992a). "Drugs, Crime and the Criminal Justice System." U.S. Department of Justice, Washington, D.C., NCJ 133652:28.

_____. (1992b). "Criminal Victimization in the United States: 1973–1990." U.S. Department of Justice, Washington, D.C.

_____. (1994). "Drug Offenders in Federal Prison." U.S. Department of Justice, Washington, D.C.

CHAMBLISS, WILLIAM J. (1991). *Trading Textbooks for Prison Cells*. Alexandria, Va.: National Center on Institutions and Alternatives.

CHAMBLISS, WILLIAM J., and EDWARD SBARBARO. (1993). "Moral Panics and Racial Oppression." *Socio-Legal Bulletin*, Melbourne, Australia.

CHRISTIE, NILS. (1993). *Crime Control as Industry*. London: Routledge.

COHEN, STANLEY. (1980). *Folk Devils and Moral Panics: The Creation of the Mods and Rockers*: New York: St. Martins Press.

CRONIN, THOMAS E., TANIA Z. CRONIN, and MICHAEL E. MILAKOVICH. (1981). United States Crime in the Streets. Bloomington, Ind.: Indiana University Press.

GALLUP, GEORGE. (1993). *The Gallup Poll: Public Opinion, 1935–1993*. Wilmington, Del.: Scholarly Resources.

MAGUIRE, KATHLEEN, and TIMOTHY J. FLANAGAN, (eds.). (1990). *Sourcebook of Criminal Justice Statistics 1990*. Washington, D.C.: Bureau of Justice Statistics.

MAGUIRE, KATHLEEN, Ann PASTORE, and TIMOTHY J. FLANAGAN, (eds.). (1993). *Sourcebook of Criminal Justice Statistics*. U.S. Department of Justice, Bureau of Justice Statistics 1990. Washington, D.C.: USGPO, 1993.

MAURER, MARK. (1993). *Young Black Men and the Criminal Justice System: A Growing National Problem*. The Sentencing Project, Washington, D.C.

Media Monitor. (1994). *1993: The Year in Review: TV's Leading News Topics, Reporters, and Political Jokes*. Center for Media and Public Affairs. Washington, D.C.: January/February.

MILLER, JEROME M. (1992). *Search and Destroy: The Plight of African American Males in the Criminal Justice System*. Alexandria, Va.: National Center on Institutions and Alternatives.

Newsweek. (1964). "The Curious Campaign—Point by Point," October 19.

Statistical Abstracts of the United States. (1993). *The National Data Book*. Washington, D.C.: U.S. Department of Commerce.

WILSON, JAMES Q. (1975). *Thinking About Crime*. New York: Basic Books.

WILSON, WILLIAM JULIUS. (1987). *The Truly Disadvantaged: The Inner City, the Underclass, and Public Policy*. Chicago: University of Chicago Press.

_____. (1993). *The Ghetto Underclass: Social Science Perspectives*. New York: Sage Publications.

QUESTIONS FOR DISCUSSION

1. Describe the three distinct activities of the Rapid Deployment Unit (RDU) in Washington D.C.

2. Discuss the characteristics of the prison population in America. Do patterns of bias exist in which individuals are incarcerated? Provide examples.

3. What effects does intensive surveillance in black neighborhoods have on the family and education? Has the criminal justice system institutionalized racism? Explain.

4. Allegedly, there has been an increase in crime. Explain how this perception is created by law enforcement, the media, and politicians.

5. What suggestions are made by Chambliss to reverse the ineffective and harmful initiatives of the existing approach to crime?

11

DEVELOPING POLICE POLICY
AN EVALUATION OF THE CONTROL PRINCIPLE

Geoffrey P. Alpert
William C. Smith

■ ■

Law enforcement is a paradigm of operational control. Virtually every aspect of policing is subject to some combination of either law, policy, guideline, directive, rule or general order. By the very nature of the police function, such a tight rein appears to be critically necessary. Conventional wisdom is that police agencies must exercise strict control over their officers. As policing has become more complex there has been a tendency to over-regulate the officers' actions. Creating complex policies, procedures and rules has become the customary method of controlling the discretion of police officers. It is the purpose of this paper to explore the context and role of police policymaking and to address the need to authorize discretion rather than strictly control officers' behavior in any area of policing. The first section describes the legal parameters of policy and the differences among policies, procedures and rules. The second section reviews the areas that need strong policies and the areas that need only broad guidance. The third section includes a brief comment on the need to assess policies. The final section includes examples of the components of policy.

LEGAL PARAMETERS OF POLICY

The primary mission of police is the protection of life. However, it would be naive to regard policymaking as driven only by that altruistic principle. Other forces, including public preferences, the desire for uniform quality of performance and liability prevention, all direct policy. Realistically, the police policymaking process is governed by the principles of risk management and liability.

The history of policymaking has been one of reaction. Traditionally, policies have been produced in a response to a problem. In recent years, however, policymakers have received a backhanded judicial incentive to review and revise their policies. When the U.S. Supreme Court in *City of Canton, Ohio* v. *Harris* (1989) recognized "delivered indifference" as the benchmark for municipal policy deficiencies, it created a financial necessity for agencies to review, revise, and sometimes develop policies (Alpert, 1989).

To understand the judicial incentive, a quick review of the history of police civil liability is necessary. Until the early 1960s, police civil liability was unremarkable and basically limited to claims of negligence (Kappeler, 1993; del Carmen, 1991). The United States Supreme Court's decision in *Monroe* v. *Pape* (1961) had effectively alleviated concerns held by municipalities that they were proper defendants for citizens' civil rights claims brought under 42 USC Section 1983. This atmosphere continued until the Court's 1978 decision in *Monel* v. *New York City Department of Social Services* (1978). The Court in *Monel* effectively overruled *Pape* and opened the floodgates for Section 1983 actions against municipalities, thereby giving plaintiffs access to the deep pockets of the local treasury. The linchpin of the *Monel* decision was that the policy of a municipality, as a moving force behind a plaintiff's injury, could result in municipal liability. In essence, the courts were evaluating the behavior of the police and were involved in judicial rulemaking (Alpert and Haas, 1984). Since *Monel*, additional refinements of the "policy" rule have resulted in municipal liability concerns regarding police "custom" and "practice."

Noteworthy among these refinements are cases which have held that an elected county prosecuting attorney who provided advice to the police is a "policymaker" of a county for purposes of attaching liability (*Pembaur* v. *City of Cincinnati*, 1986) and one case in which an unchecked pattern of violence was held to be attributable to a sheriff's policy of inadequate training (*Davis* v. *Mason County*, 1991).

Although local municipalities have been put under great pressure to address policy issues, state agencies and their employees have felt some sense of insulation from the threat of lawsuits brought pursuant to Section 1983. This belief has persisted even though the Supreme Court's enthronement of the "deliberate indifference" standard in *City of Canton* v. *Harris* (1989). The sense of security was brought about by the ostensible protection of the Eleventh Amendment which precludes suits against states in a federal court and by judicial interpretations which extended the protection to federally created causes of action which could be brought in state court. Indeed, the Supreme Court held as recently as 1989 in *Will* v. *Michigan Department of State Police* that state actors in their official capacities enjoyed immunity from suit under Section 1983 even when brought in state court. Prior to *Will*, the holding in *Howlett* v. *Rose* (1987) conferred the same immunity in federal court Section 1983 actions. As a result of this reasoning, state law enforcement and their officials have enjoyed greater immunity than their local law enforcement counterparts in Section 1983 cases where "official capacity" actions have been involved.

The 1990s, however, have brought about a rethinking of the status of such immunity. In *Hafer* v. *Melo* (1991), the United States Supreme Court allowed an elected official to be sued under Section 1983 for what were alleged by her to be "official capacity" actions. The significance of the case lies in its discussion of the distinctions between actions taken in a personal capacity and those performed in official capacity. The operational consequence of the case is pressure on all law enforcement executives to review their various methods of control, including policies, lest such control methods be deemed to constitute personal capacity actions.

Policies, Procedures, and Rules

A *policy* is not a statement of what must be done in a particular situation, but it is a statement of guiding principles which must be followed in activities that fall within either specific organizational objectives or the overall police mission. A policy is a guide to thinking. A *procedure* is the method of performing a task or a manner of proceeding on a course of action. It differs from policy in that it specifies action in a particular situation to perform a task within the guidelines of policy. A procedure is a guide to action. A *rule* is a managerial mandate which either requires or prohibits specified behavior. A rule is a mandate to action. These various control mechanisms are designed to address a multitude of needs, including the need for regulation and uniformity of police activities.

The National Advisory Commission on Criminal Justice Standards and Goals, Report on Police (1973:54) provides an excellent discussion of the differences among written policies, procedures and rules.

> Policy is different from rules and procedures. Policy should be stated in broad terms to guide employees. It sets limits of discretion. A policy statement deals with the principles and values that guide the performance of activities directed toward the achievement of agency objectives. A procedure is a way of proceeding—a routine—to achieve an objective. Rules significantly reduce or eliminate discretion by specifically stating what must and must not be done.

As an example, this notion has been translated by the Metro-Dade Police Department in Miami, Florida, which has defined policy as "principles and values which guide the performance of a departmental activity. Policy is not a statement of what must be done in a particular situation; rather, it is a statement of guiding principles which should be followed in activities which are directed toward attainment of objectives" (1989:5).

These directives, in varying degrees, establish discretionary parameters for officers to perform day-to-day operations in a manner consistent with the philosophy of the administration and command staff. Policies, based upon relevant laws and philosophy, serve to control officers' behavioral choices.

THE NEED FOR CONTROL IN POLICE ACTIVITIES

Law enforcement agencies must have rules, regulations, training, supervision and structured accountability to guide and control the broad discretionary powers of their officers. However, as officers are confronted daily with a variety of complex situations, discretion is necessary (Adams, 1990). Discretion must be guided by legal strictures and administrative philosophy rather than by adrenaline-charged, split-second decisions. Written and enforced directives are necessary for the proper management of law enforcement functions because of structural, personal and situational factors that affect behavioral choices. These directives are formulated by determining objectives and identifying the principles or ideas which will best guide the officer in achieving them (Alpert and Dunham, 1992).

The objectives and methods of police departments are affected by the laws, the communities they serve, their parent political system, the fraternal associations, unions, professional police associations and other general and special interest groups (Sheehan and Cordner, 1989:465). A policy indicates to the officers and the public the agency's philosophy in the area of concern and also provides a set of standards by which it can be held accountable (see Alpert and Dunham, 1992). As James Auten (1988:1–2) has noted:

To do otherwise is to simply leave employees "in the Dark" in the expectation that they will intuitively divine the proper and expected course of action in the performance of their duties…Discretion must be reasonably exercised within the parameters of the expectations of the community, the courts, the legislature and the organization, itself.

Similarly, Robert Wasserman informs us (1982:40):

When written policy statements are not available (or not well disseminated), the police agency and the administration run considerable risk that some police actions will be completely alien to a segment of the community. This result can be aggravated conflict between police and the community, resulting in political demands for major measures to ensure accountability on the part of the police organization.

Wasserman warns the police administrators to create and disseminate policy directives before a problem occurs and the public holds the police and other government officials accountable. Policies and procedures must cover general duties and obligations as well as methods to achieve them. In other words, law enforcement agencies must have regulations, provide training and supervision, and hold officers accountable for their actions.

Deciding upon which activities and tasks requires strong control, or fundamental guidance requires a comprehensive understanding of the role and function of police in society. One aspect of that insight is the increasing educational level of the police. During the past few years, more educated persons are joining the police force, and many officers are raising their level of education. At a time when police are becoming more educated, the requirements of the police are becoming more complicated. No longer do the police simply respond to calls for service. The renewed emphasis on community-oriented policing and problem-solving policing requires officers to think and plan rather than just respond (Alpert and Dunham, 1992). That is, officers are being educated and trained to use good judgment and discretion in many situations. However, in some critical areas, officers need strong policies and training.

Identification of Policy Areas

There is little doubt that some police activities require closer supervision and control than others. Although much of the police function may occur in areas of high public visibility, neither logic nor necessity mandate that every activity or decision be subject to strict agency directive or control. The crucial task is to identify those behaviors which should be value driven and those which must be control driven. Obviously, behavior which, if improperly carried out, is likely to result in severe injury or death must be subject to control-driven policies.

David LeBrec (1982) has designed a graphic which helps understand and explain the categories of risk (see Figure 1).

Simply put, the police functions which are high-risk and low-frequency require strong policies, formal procedures and explicit rules. The high-frequency, low-risk functions can be discharged with minimal guidance and a strong system of shared values (Greene et al., 1992). The use of force or deadly force can be considered a high-risk, low-frequency activity, and police pursuit driving can be considered a high-risk, high-frequency activity (Alpert and Fridell, 1992). These functions require the most extensive policies, training, and overall guidance (Alpert and Smith, 1991).

FIGURE 1   CATEGORIES OF RISK

	High	Low
High	High Frequency High Exposure	Low Frequency High Exposure
Low	High Frequency Low Exposure	Low Frequency Low Exposure

EXPOSURE

There are police activities which require specific direction but not to the extent required for use of deadly force or pursuit driving. In fact, some of these activities, if subjected to a strict control policy, may result in officer behavior which is detached, dispassionate, or cold. For example, police response to domestic violence incidents requires not only tact but the ability to read a situation and respond in the interests of all parties. Such a complicated behavioral scenario would be virtually impossible to regulate by a strict control policy. However, certain important procedural issues must be controlled by this type of policy, including statutory requirements concerning the timing and substance of the police response to a domestic abuse call, arrest requirements as well as the coordination of efforts among officers, investigators, and victim service agencies (Buzawa and Buzawa, 1992).

Many of these police tasks must be considered as an art, requiring a fluid response and not a mechanical reaction. Policing requires a variety of behavioral alternatives. That is, officers need wide discretion in those areas of their work not directly and immediately involved in the protection of life or defense against injury. Discretion must not be based on "gut reaction" or a whim but requires extensive quality preservice and inservice training. In order for officers to choose an appropriate response (discretionary choice), they must be trained in the options available. A critical part of the training must focus on ethics, values, and morals. Value-driven guidelines are preferred in areas not directly involved in the protection of life or defense against injury (Green et al., 1992).

An example of a police function requiring only summary guidance is telephone contact with the public. Police administrators have no need to instruct their officers and civilians who answer the telephone to read a written statement. They should, however, require officers to be pleasant, cooperative, and provide assistance. Further, a policy in this area should direct the officer or civilian to collect certain information. The Metro-Dade Police Department (1989:32) provides the following direction:

Telephone Communications: The telephone is the primary method by which police services are requested. All incoming telephone calls must be answered promptly to provide the desired quality of service.

Telephone Courtesy: When answering the telephone, an employee should identify the unit and himself, and ask to be of assistance. Employees should make every attempt to supply requested information and assistance or refer party to proper agency.

Answering the telephone is a high-frequency, low-risk function. Obviously, officer discretion is important as long as it fits within the general guidelines of the agency. The examples of force, response to domestic violence and answering the telephone establish points on a policy-control continuum. Police agencies must determine which functions require the most stringent control and which require structured guidelines or summary guidance only. Using the examples discussed above, Figure 2 provides an illustration of the continuum of policy control.

A valuable example of this determination process can be taken from private industry. Private companies are increasingly minimizing formal rules and placing importance on value training and discretionary behavior (Cordner, 1989). Moore and Stephens (1991) suggest more reliance on what Kenneth Andrews (1980) labeled "The Corporate Strategy." This strategy refers to the identification of an objective(s), design of the organizational character, and allocation of resources to achieve the objectives under potentially adverse circumstances. While there are numerous differences between the public and private sectors which complicate the transfer of technology and operational philosophies, private enterprise offers an innovative direction worthy of analysis (Cordner, 1989; Moore and Stephens, 1991).

When concepts derived from the private sector are transferred to police management, the following issues arise. Officer discretion is appropriate if defensible and valid hiring and fitness-for-duty evaluations are employed. During training, focus should be shifted to allow officers greater creativity in dealing with "nontextbook" scenarios where human emotion, pride, or dignity are at issue. It is critical that police officers learn to deal with members of the public as fellow human beings rather than as participants in situations. It is necessary not to program an officer's response to a preconceived scenario but to permit a response that incorporates training and preparation. In other words, the control principle must not be permitted to escape its bounds and take reason and compassion hostage. Perhaps the area of policing in which there is the greatest need for control is the use of force.

An Example of Force

In 1970, Egon Bittner noted that the unique feature of the police is their power to use force and deadly force limited only by law and policy. Further, the significance of this power, he argued, includes its omnipresent potential and threat (1970). No other occupational group

FIGURE 2   CONTINUUM OF POLICY CONTROL

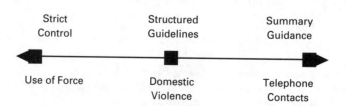

LEVELS AND EXAMPLES

possess this authority. Although police use of physical force is not a frequent event, its abuse is by human means irreversible and by any legal means incapable of compensation. In other words, it is the classic low-frequency, high-risk event (Friedrich, 1980; Fyfe, 1988).

Although a relatively low-frequency event, accusations of excessive force are among the most common and highly visible complaints made against police officers. The proliferation of control mechanisms in this and other areas has been fueled by the nature and ever-increasing number of civil liability actions filed against the police (for example, Rodney King). The absence of meaningful policy and training in critical function areas may serve as an invitation to sue where the absence is proximately related to a plaintiff's injury. Other explanations for increased control range from the traditional and generalized perception of need by the command staff to specific needs, including administration discipline and the accreditation movement. In effect, it could be safely said that the extent of policy within a police agency is linked to the intensity of its mission and its potential exposure to liability. In sum, the police who are given the authority to use force over others must be subject to significant restraint in its application. Officer discretion must be guided by implementing a structured policy and providing extensive and continuous training to remove the need to make split-second decisions. This discretion may be cultivated by the following strategies: the articulation and acceptance of organizational values, internal inspections and audits of incidents, community feedback, an interactive style of policing, and an appropriate system of discipline (Alpert and Dunham, 1992; Alpert and Fridell, 1992).

An unintended consequence of strict control policies, however, is their expansion into areas where such structure may be disadvantageous to both law enforcement and the public it serves (Cordner, 1989). Cordner notes that, "The prevailing wisdom in modern police administration is that policies and rules are needed to govern every contingency and every substantial aspect of operation and management" (1989:17). The critical question becomes: Is a strict-control policy model effective for all behavior, or has the current trend of developing policies for most police functions set forth on a faulty premise?

Proposing Boundary Limitations

As discussed above, the use of deadly force may be low-frequency but is high-risk. The current paranoia over civil liability and the need to improve relations with members of the community have caused many police agencies to implement a strong system of oversight and superficial accountability of daily police operations. On the one hand, some policymakers, by addressing each important police function, believe that they are insulated from personal or institutional liability. On the other hand, some believe this strategy merely decreases officers' discretion without any corresponding immunity (del Carmen, 1991). From either position, a strong-control form of management ignores a critical aspect of the police function: human interaction. Further, a program of extensive regulation by policy likely conveys to officers a message of distrust and engenders a stifling of creativity. The critical issue is to identify the acceptable limits for strict-control mechanisms.

Proposed boundaries may be drawn at those activities which are oriented to *protection of life* and *defense against injury*. While the principal mission of the police is the protection of life, not every activity in the duty day is directed toward this goal. A useful inquiry in identifying those police functions which are life preserving and which defend against injury is accomplished by asking whether the activity involved will likely cause severe injury or death if improperly discharged. In other words, a behavioral threshold should be created so that, once crossed, strict control would be appropriate. This concept, in its purest sense, should create little controversy, for it is precisely the approach which is underscored in the majority of police agencies. For example, few would argue that discharge of a firearm, vehicular pursuit of an offender, or the use of a baton or Taser must be subject to strenuous control. The stark reality is that such behaviors are relative infrequent although their criticality is great. What is proposed is that police officers be afforded the opportunity in less than critical areas, such as the ones mentioned above, to participate in a belief system where their discretionary actions reflect a legitimate desire to serve the public.

Recently, Cohen and Feldberg (1991:148–149) identified three factors which provide police officers with sufficient information to operate successfully in a law-enforcement agency.

> The practical ingredients an individual needs in order to have free moral choice in matters of professional conduct are an understanding of the values that inform his or her profession, the intention to live up to the values and an environment that supports those values and discourages behavior that is contrary to them.

Basically, appropriate departmental policies, training, and a powerful accountability or disciplinary system will create an environment that establishes the mission and philosophy of the agency. If an officer is trained in those values and guidelines and chooses to follow them, he or she will be able to use discretion appropriately. Hopefully, this training and understanding will help officers make the appropriate behavioral choices and mirror what Cohen and Feldberg have called the "free moral choice in matters of professional conduct" (1991:148).

ASSESSING THE EFFECTIVENESS OF POLICIES

Police officers perform a wide variety of functions, and the agencies in which they work are traditionally organized in a paramilitary structure with a specific chain-of-command. This structure and function suggests a need for a strong-control type of management. The evolution of many policy manuals is based upon the negative reinforcement of behavior. Many policy directives are stated negatively, and it is often difficult to measure their effectiveness since police performance measures are typically based upon positive behaviors. The difference between what is measurable and the behavior recommended by the majority of policies creates serious "bean-counting" or methodological problems for evaluation (Spelman, 1988). As Cordner notes (1989:19), "No experiments have been conducted to test the effectiveness of written rules and guidelines. There simply is not much agreement about how to define or measure the effectiveness of a policy agency."

Rather than evaluate the effectiveness of a proposed policy, many administrators have made policy changes as a response to officers' mistakes. This process has created in many agencies a compilation of guidelines, regulations, and rules that prohibit behavior that has been found inappropriate or in violation of the law. Some aspects of policy or a rule may be attributed to a specific officer or situation. Often, these rules are fondly named after the officer or event.

While this approach appears solid, it creates a situation that may be too limiting and challenges officers to circumvent the language of the policy. In other words, control-oriented management can lead to a macro-management approach by always limiting behavioral alternatives with rules.

A superficial assessment of this "prohibition" approach may yield a positive result. However, an in-depth analysis would likely come to a different conclusion. The consequences of the approach are a loss of police services, reduced morale among the officers, and an environment that stifles creative police work. Gary Cordner notes (1989:18):

> The question of most importance is whether extensive written directives make police organizations more effective. Do rules and regulations improve the quality of police service? Do they contribute to police goal attainment?

These questions raise very important issues that remain unanswered. The next section addresses the elements that should be included in an appropriate and defensible policy.

ELEMENTS OF MODELS POLICIES

The development of police policies should reflect the values of the command staff *and community* and should include input from officers at all levels. Policies should incorporate the following principles:

1. Be workable in real-world situations.
2. Be adaptable to training.
3. Be written in a positive manner.
4. Refer to or incorporate relevant laws.
5. Be pretested to assure that all officers understand the specific intent and consequences of noncompliance.
6. Include inservice training, as a matter of record, for all officers and supervisors.
7. Provide examples of behavior.

Many departmental policies have been developed properly, include these principles, and provide excellent direction and guidance to their officers. Other agencies do not have policies or have such weak policies that they provide no real direction. As a response to the problems of developing and refining policies, the International Association of Chiefs of Police (IACP) established a National Law Enforcement Policy Center. Through the auspices of the Center, the IACP developed the most comprehensive compilation of model policies and background papers (Issues and Concepts) justifying their views (National Law Enforcement Policy Center, 1991). This compilation includes policies on some of the most difficult issues facing law enforcement in the 1990s. The model policies include protection of life issues with little discretion such as the use of force, deadly force and pursuit driving as well as areas permitting wide discretion, such as a policy to control a confidential fund.

The model policies were developed to provide general guidance. A disclaimer states that the models must be reviewed and adjusted to individual departments. The requirement to adjust these models must be emphasized. Different jurisdictions and environments need different direction to produce the best policing. However, any agency would benefit from the outline and background papers prepared by the Policy Center. Fortunately, there are many commonalities among police policies for high-risk activities. These include a policy's *first* principle, that an officer's primary responsibility is to protect lives. Since many police activities are potentially dangerous, and because officers are likely to react to the heat of the moment, an overall *mission statement* must be included as a first element and as a reminder in policies guiding high-risk activities. Beyond the mission statement, the IACP models provide an excellent design for developing an agency's policy. For example, the model policy regarding use of force is detailed and includes the following headings or elements:

A. Purpose

B. Policy (statement of philosophy)

C. Definitions

D. Procedures

    1. parameters for use of deadly force

    2. parameters for the use of nondeadly force

    3. training and qualifications

    4. reporting uses of force

    5. departmental response (administrative review)

By adding a mission statement to this outline, a department will have an excellent foundation for a policy. It is important to acknowledge the threat new policies may have on some departments' officers.

If a new philosophy is incorporated in a policy or a more structured response is required from an officer, effective training to the policy is required. Effective training may include the reading, understanding, and discussion of a policy for low-risk activities. However, in high-risk activities, beyond the understanding of the language of the policy, practice and simulation or role-playing decision-making skills may be necessary to avoid what the United States Supreme Court has called "deliberate indifference."

Accountability

Just as police policies are divided among several levels based upon their consequences, accountability of officers must also be structured. Officers who make contact with citizens are usually asked to take notes on the meeting to preserve any information that was provided. Officers who are involved in automobile accidents will have to complete a mandated accident reporting form. Officers who must control a suspect with force to effect an arrest should be responsible for completing a "control of persons" report. If deadly force is used, an officer must complete a form describing the why, where, and how. It is important to hold accountable any officer who has been involved in some low-risk and all high-risk activities. Writing an analytical critique is the first step. This process serves several purposes: first, the information contained in a critique can help determine if the action was necessary and conducted within the departmental policy; second, critiques will help determine if specific training is needed; third, critiques will help determine if a change in policy is needed; and fourth, an analysis of the data generated in these reports will reveal trends and demonstrate specific risk factors. As a second step, the agency must assign supervisory personnel to evaluate these reports to determine if a violation has occurred and suggest that the officer face disciplinary action.

An agency's disciplinary system is a critical reinforcer of its policies and rules. It is important that an agency's policies are followed and that an appropriate disciplinary scheme is established for violations. An important function of the disciplinary action is the message that is sent to others when an officer is disciplined or when he or she is *not* disciplined for a policy violation. All officers must understand the importance of the rules and regulations and the consequences for violating them. For example, if an officer is involved in a preventable accident, it is important to have a disciplinary scheme established. The first violation may result in a letter to the file, whereas a second violation may require some remedial training. A third violation may result in a change of duty so the individual does not have an opportunity to use force to control a suspect. At some point a department will have to take more drastic action and those steps must also be made known to the officers. A policy without a disciplinary system will not be taken as seriously as one which includes a system of discipline. Similarly, a disciplinary system that can be subverted or manipulated will not serve as a deterrent. There is no room for "winking" at a violation and excuse poor judgment or deliberate actions which result in a violation of policy.

This concept has been summarized by The United States Commission on Civil Rights which found that (1981:158):

> Once a finding sustains the allegations of wrongdoing, disciplinary sanctions commensurate with the seriousness of the offense that are imposed fairly, swiftly, and consistently will most clearly reflect the commitment of the department to oppose police misconduct. Less severe action such as reassignment, retraining, and psychological counseling may be appropriate in some cases.

CONCLUSION

Creating meaningful mechanisms of control, including the development of police policies, is a process of integrating a wide variety of interests. To be effective, policy must address the legitimate concerns of the public as well as the law. In balancing these issues, due attention must be paid to future flexibility and the process of refinement and change.

Police activities range from low-criticality to high-criticality and low-frequency to high-frequency. Police officials must identify which activities require strict control-oriented policies and which require only summary guidance. In other words, the style of policy will vary according to a continuum of control. In addition, there must be training to the policy, control, and supervision of the activities and a system of discipline that holds the officers and agency accountable for the behavior.

The determination of the type of policy to be employed in any given duty function must be based upon the command staff's realization and understanding of law enforcement as a service to the public. Investiture of discretion to officers in low-criticality areas after proper training in ethics, values, and morals may go a great distance in bridging intermittent gaps between the police and the community. By the same token, high-criticality functions will necessitate strict control policies to guide them to protect the public safely in an effective and efficient manner.

REFERENCES

ADAMS, THOMAS. (1990). *Police Field Operations*. Englewood Cliffs, N.J.: Prentice-Hall.

ALPERT, GEOFFREY P. (1989). *"City of Canton v Harris* and the Deliberate Indifference Standard." *Criminal Law Bulletin* 25:466–472.

ALPERT, GEOFFREY P. and ROGER G. DUNHAM. (1992). *Policing Urban America*. Prospect Heights, Ill.: Waveland Press.

ALPERT, GEOFFREY P. and LORIE FRIDELL. (1992). *Police Vehicles and Firearms: Instruments of Deadly Force*. Prospect Heights, Ill.: Waveland Press.

ALPERT, GEOFFREY P. and KENNETH HAAS. (1984). "Judicial Rulemaking and the Fourth Amendment: Cars, Containers and Exclusionary Justice," *Alabama Law Review* 35:23–61.

ALPERT, GEOFFREY P. and WILLIAM SMITH. (1991). "Beyond City Limits and into the Wood(s): A Brief Look at the Policy Implications of *City of Canton v Harris* and *Wood v Ostrander." American Journal of Police* 10:19–40.

ANDREWS, KENNETH. (1980). *The Concept of Corporate Strategy*. Chicago: Irwin.

AUTEN, JAMES. (1988). "Preparing Written Guidelines." *FBI Law Enforcement Bulletin* 57:1–7.

BITTNER, EGON. (1970). *The Functions of Police in Modern Society*. Rockville, Md.: National Institute of Mental Health.

BROOKS. LAURE. (1989). "Police Discretionary Behavior: A Study of Style." In R. Dunham and G. Alpert (Eds.) *Critical Issues in Policing*. Prospect Heights, Ill.: Waveland Press, pp. 121–145.

BROWN, MICHAEL K. (1981). *Working the Street: Police Discretion and the Dilemmas of Reform*. New York: Russell Sage Foundation.

BUZAWA, EVE and CARL BUZAWA (Eds.). (1992). *Domestic Violence: The Criminal Justice Response*. New York: Greenwood Press.

COHEN, HOWARD and MICHAEL FELDBERG. (1991). *Power and Restraint: The Moral Dimension of Police Work*. Westport, Conn.: Praeger.

CORDNER, GARY. (1989). "Written Rules and Regulations: Are They Necessary?" *FBI Law Enforcement Bulletin*. July:17–21.

DAVIS, KENNETH C. (1975). *Police Discretion*. St. Paul, Minn.: West Publishing Co.

DEL CARMEN, ROLANDO. (1991). *Civil Liabilities in American Policing*. Englewood Cliffs, N.J.: Brady.

FRIEDRICH, ROBERT. (1980). "Police Use of Force: Individuals, Situations and Organizations." *Annals of the American Academy of Political and Social Science* 452:82–97.

FYFE, JAMES. (1988). *The Metro-Dade Police—Citizen Violence Reduction Project*. Washington, D.C.: Police Foundation.

GREENE, JACK, GEOFFREY P. ALPERT, and PAUL STYLES. (1992). "Values and Culture in Two American Police Departments: Lessons from King Arthur." *Contemporary Criminal Justice* 8:183–207.

LABREC, DAVID. *Risk Management: Preventive Law Practice and Practical Risk Management Methods for the 1980s*. Paper presented to the Annual Meeting of the National Institute of Municipal Law Officers. Miami, Florida, 1982.

KAPPELER, VICTOR. (1983). *Critical Issues in Police Civil Liability.* Prospect Heights, Ill.: Waveland Press.

Metro-Dade Police Department. (1989). *Metro-Dade Police Department Manual—Part I.* Dade County Florida.

MOORE, MARK and DARREL STEPHENS. (1991). *Beyond Command and Control: The Strategic Management of Police Departments.* Washington, D.C.: Police Executive Research Forum.

National Advisory Commission on Criminal Justice Standards and Goals. (1973). *Report on Police.* Washington, D.C.: United States Government Printing Office.

National Law Enforcement Policy Center. (1991). *A Compilation of Model Policies.* Arlington, Va.: National Law Enforcement Policy Center.

SHEEHAN, ROBERT and GARY CORDNER. (1989). *Introduction to Police Management.* Cincinnati: Anderson.

SPELMAN, WILLIAM. (1988). *Beyond Bean Counting.* Washington, D.C.: Police Executive Research Forum.

The United States Commission on Civil Rights. (1981). *Who Is Guarding the Guardians?* Washington, D.C.: The United States Commission on Civil Rights.

WASSERMAN, ROBERT. (1982). "The Government Setting." In Bernard Garmire (Ed.) *Local Government Police Management.* Second Edition. Washington, D.C.: International City Management Association, pp. 30–51.

CASES

City of Canton, Ohio v. *Harris*, 489 U.S. 378 (1989).

Davis v. *Mason County*, 927 f.2d 1473 (9th. Cir. 1991).

Monroe v. *Pape* 365 U.S. 167 (1961).

Monel v. *New York City Department of Social Services* 436 U.S. 658 (1978).

Pembaur v. *City of Cincinnati*, 475 U.S. 469 (1986).

Will v. *Department of Michigan State Police* 491 U.S. 58 (1990).

Howlett v. *Rose* 469 U.S. 356 (1990).

QUESTIONS FOR DISCUSSION

1. Summarize the legal parameters of policy as it relates to the police.
2. How do procedures and rules differ from policy? Cite an example to support your response.
3. How are categories of risk related to policy formation? Cite examples to support your response.
4. There is little agreement on how to measure the effectiveness of police agencies. Why?
5. List and discuss the elements of a model policy for police agencies.

12

WHO YA GONNA CALL?
THE POLICE AS PROBLEM-BUSTERS

John E. Eck
William Spelman

■　■　■　■　■　■　■　■　■　■　■　■　■　■　■　■　■　■　■

Charlie Bedford couldn't sleep. Most nights, his residential Newport News street was quiet, marred only by the low rumble of an occasional truck on Jefferson Avenue two blocks away. But lately, Friday and Saturday nights had been different: groups of a dozen or more rowdy teenagers kept him awake, with their loud music and their horseplay. There had been no violence. But there had been some vandalism, and the kids seemed unpredictable. More disturbing, the kids came from another section of town, miles away. One sleepless Friday night it became too much. Charlie Bedford called the cops.[1]

Problems like Mr. Bedford's plague many urban neighborhoods. Disorderly behavior and other incivilities make life difficult for residents while creating fears of more serious harm. Wilson and Kelling (1982) have suggested that without intervention, citizens' fear may spark disinvestment in neighborhoods, leading to decay, more crime, and more fear. Because of concerns like these, incivilities have become a focus of researcher interest and police action.[2]

The increased interest in social order, fear, and community policing is the latest development of a continuing discussion about the role of the police in the community. The last two decades have seen a variety of proposals to bring the police closer to the community—community relations units, team policing, neighborhood watch, and foot patrol, among others. At the same time there has been equal interest in police operational effectiveness especially with regard to crime control; directed patrol, case screening, crime analysis, and differential response were but a few of the ideas proposed and tested. For the most part, these two lines of thinking have developed independently. But we can help the Charlie Bedfords of our communities by combining the two areas. To see why, let us take a closer look at what might be called "community policing" and "crime control policing."

COMMUNITY POLICING

Largely as a result of the riots of the 1960s, police began to examine their ties to the communities they served. Black and Hispanic communities were concerned largely so with controlling police use of force. The police were concerned with defusing the dissension, creating a more favorable image for themselves. Perhaps because these aims were politically charged, these first attempts were formal, involving new bureaucratic structures such as community relations units and civilian review boards. Both were limited: community relations units had little effect on the behavior of street officers; line officers objected so strenuously to civilian review boards that most were dismantled or rendered impotent shortly after they were implemented (Goldstein, 1977).

Dissatisfied, some police administrators began efforts aimed at bringing police closer to people. The most ambitious of these efforts, team policing, typically involved a radical restructuring of the police bureaucracy. The hierarchical structure of policing was to be abandoned; decision making was to be decentralized; police officers were to be well-rounded generalists, rather than specialized technicians. These operational changes were to put police decision making closer to the communities served. In practice, team policing proved too hard to implement, and few efforts survive today. But three team policing strategies survived: storefront police stations, foot patrol, and community crime watch.

Storefront police stations put police officers in the community at all times, forcing them to deal with the public constantly. And, presumably, members of the public would be more willing to walk into a station located in an unpretentious setting in their own neighborhood if they wished to provide information or make a complaint. Storefronts were often well accepted by the communities they served, and increased the amount of communication between police and citizens. There were indications that they helped to reduce fear of crime, too. But officers who did not staff the storefronts often regarded these jobs as "public relations," far removed from "real police work."[3]

Foot patrols cast police in the most traditional of roles. Because they are in direct contact with the public at almost all times, foot officers become informal authority figures wielding the (usually) discreet threat of force to get results (Kelling, 1987). The bulwark of policing at the turn of the century, foot patrols were enjoying a comeback as early as the mid-1960s. The trend has become more pronounced in the last few years. Evaluations of foot patrol programs conflict over whether they reduce serious crime (Trojanowicz, n.d.; Police Foundation, 1981; Williams and Pate, 1987). However, they agree that foot patrols lead to increased contact between police and citizens, often leaving the citizens feeling safer and more satisfied with their police services. Perhaps more important, foot patrol officers learned more about the neighborhood's problems; the best foot patrol officers tried to resolve them.

Finally, community crime watches emerged as an important means of police–citizen communication in the 1970s. At first, police just provided citizens with crime prevention information. Later, police grew more ambitious, and tried to organize communities. Organized communities were supposed to exert more control over rowdy youths and wayward adults, thus reducing illegal and threatening behavior. Despite some initial successes (for example, Cirel, et al., 1977), crime watch programs have led to few sustained crime reductions nor do they seem to make people feel much safer. Indeed, there are indications that the organizing tactics usually used by police leave people more afraid than before (Lavrakas, 1985; Rosenbaum, 1987).

Most evidence suggests that storefronts, foot patrols, and crime watches do little to control crime. But they are all successful in creating communication between the police and the public, and sometimes they have made people feel safer. Surely this is a gain, particularly in light of research that suggests that citizens may be more harmed by fear of crime than by victimization itself (Taub, Taylor, and Dunham, 1984; Greenberg, Rohe, and Williams, 1984). To the degree that fear of crime is a vague and somewhat irrational sense of unease, sighting an officer on foot, in a local station, or standing before a neighborhood meeting can help to reduce it. But most research indicates that fear of crime is quite rational, grounded in reasonable perceptions of vulnerability (Skogan, this issue; Fowler and Mangione, 1974). To the degree that fear of crime is rational, we can expect that fear will return to its prior levels, so long as the conditions that cause it do not change. Indeed, there are indications that fear-reduction strategies based on increased police–public communication are only effective in the short run (Fowler and Mangione, 1983).

The community policing projects also showed the disparity between the problems people face and the problems police attack. Most citizens' concerns are not directly related to crime. Trash on the streets, noise, abandoned and ill-maintained buildings, barking dogs, and the like form the bulk of calls for police service. In many areas, residents judge these problems to be more serious than street crime (Spelman, 1983). Still, police are oriented to crime control. Given the attention police have paid to crime over the years, one would expect that they would have learned to control it. In fact, the opposite is true.

CRIME CONTROL POLICING

Also as a result of the riots of the 1960s, researchers began to examine the ability of the police to control crime. Over the next two decades, researchers steadily undermined five basic premises of police crime control practice.

First, the Kansas City Preventive Patrol Experiment questioned the usefulness of random patrol in cars (Kelling, et al., 1974). Second, studies of response time undermined the premise that the police must rapidly send officers to all calls (Kansas City Police Department, 1980; Spelman and Brown, 1984). Third, research suggested, and experiments confirmed, that the public does not always expect fast response by police to nonemergency calls (Farmer, 1981; McEwen, Connors, and Cohen, 1984). Fourth, studies showed that officers and detectives are limited in their abilities to successfully investigate crimes (Greenwood, Petersilia, and Chaiken, 1977; Eck, 1982). And fifth, research showed that detectives need not follow up every reported unsolved crime (Greenberg, Yu, and Lang, 1973; Eck, 1979). In short, most serious crimes were unaffected by the standard police actions designed to control them. Further, the public did not notice reductions in patrol, response speed to non-emergencies, or lack of followup investigations.

Random, unmanaged patrol operations did not seem to work. Special units, although occasionally successful, were expensive and could not be used routinely. But, police administrators reasoned, perhaps the problem was not that patrol and investigation tactics did not work. Perhaps they just needed to be managed better.

Research was showing that patrol officers and detectives had time available that could be better used (Gay, Schell, and Schack, 1977; Greenwood, Petersilia, and Chaiken, 1977). And additional time could be created since citizens did not notice changes in patrol or detective operations. To free up patrol officer time, differential police response strategies were developed. Citizen calls that could be handled over the phone, through the mail, or by the caller appearing at a police station were diverted from patrol officers to civilians. Nonemergency calls requiring an officer received a scheduled response instead of an immediate dispatch (Farmer, 1981; McEwen, Connors, and Cohen, 1984). To free up detective time, crimes that had no leads, short of murder or rape, were no longer investigated once a patrol officer had completed the initial investigation. Managers would direct investigative efforts so that the free time could be used effectively in the fight against crime (Eck, 1982). To direct these efforts, information about crime and criminals was needed. Crime analysis seemed to be the answer.

Crime analysis units used police records describing initial and follow-up investigations, arrests of offenders, and police encounters with suspicious persons to analyze the nature of crime and criminals (Reinier, Greenlee, and Gibbens, 1976). The crimes that analysts reviewed were usually burglaries, robberies, and, in a few agencies, rapes and auto thefts. Crime analysts looked for patterns. They plotted the locations and times of burglaries to direct patrol officers to the most likely targets. They mapped robberies to deploy stakeouts by patrol officers and detectives. They collated offender descriptions to identify suspects for detectives. In some agencies, crime analysts even gave information about crime patterns to neighborhood watch groups.

These efforts showed that collecting and analyzing information about crimes may improve police operations. But it is doubtful whether they reduce crime (Gay, Beall, and Bowers, 1984). Crime analysis units have too many limitations to have more than a marginal influence on crime, or any other problem. One limitation is particularly critical: crime analysis is an attempt to find out where to apply established police responses. The responses are set because problems are understood, the same responses are used on widely differing problems. Instead, the aid should be to understand a problem, and then determine what is needed to solve it.

Street operations do need more and better management. In order to manage, police managers need better information about local problems. But they must understand the problem before designing a solution. They must look for solutions to such problems as vandalism, rowdy behavior, drug use, drunkenness, and noise.

Community policing has used the same responses—foot patrol, storefront stations, and neighborhood watch—to address a wide variety of community concerns. Crime control policing has applied another standard set of procedures—patrol, investigations, surveillance, and stakeouts—to a wide variety of crime problems. In neither form of policing has there been a systematic attempt to tailor the responses to the characteristics of each particular problem.

Sergeant Hogan was on duty when Mr. Bedford called. He assigned the problem to Officer Paul Summerfield. Summerfield suspected that the source of the problem might be a roller skating rink. The rink had been trying to increase business by offering reduced rates and transportation on Friday and Saturday nights. At two in the morning, as he drove north along Jefferson Avenue to the rink, Summerfield saw several large groups of youths walking south. Other kids were hanging around the rink. Summerfield talked to several of them and found that they were waiting for a bus. The other kids, he was told, had become impatient and begun the three-mile walk home. Summerfield talked to the rink owner. The owner had leased the bus to pick up and drop off kids who lived far from the rink. But there were always more kids needing rides at the end of the night than the bus had picked up earlier.

Officer Summerfield returned to the skating rink early the next evening. He saw fifty or so youngsters get out of the bus rented by the skating rink. But he saw others get out of the public transit buses that stopped running at midnight. And he saw parents in pajamas drop their kids off, then turn around and go home. Clearly the rink's bus would be unable to take home all the kids who would be stranded at closing time. Summerfield left, perplexed.

PROBLEM-ORIENTED POLICING

How could Officer Summerfield solve this problem? Herman Goldstein has described an approach that could help (Goldstein, 1979). According to Goldstein, police have lost sight of their objectives in their efforts to improve management. They must begin focusing on problems the public expects them to solve. Problems are "the incredibly broad range of troublesome situations that prompt citizens to turn to the police." Management improvements, though important, are only a means for improving police capacities to solve problems. Goldstein described three, key elements of this problem-oriented approach.

First, problems must be defined more specifically. Broad legal definitions, such as burglary or robbery, should be replaced by descriptions that include such characteristics as location, time, participants' behaviors and motivation, and so on.

Second, information about problems must be collected from sources outside the police agency and not just from internal sources. The officers who have to deal with problems are a good source of information that is seldom exploited. But businesses, other government agencies, and private citizens can often provide data needed to understand problems fully.

Third, police agencies must engage in a broad search for solutions, including alternatives to the criminal justice process. The best solutions often involve public and private individuals and organizations who have a stake in seeing the problem resolved.

The Baltimore County Police Department and the Newport News Police Department have begun to implement problem-oriented policing. Let us look at how these agencies diagnose problems and try to resolve them.

Baltimore County.   Two sensational murders within a week brought fear of violent crime among Baltimore County residents to a head in August, 1981. The incidents were unrelated and unlikely to be repeated, and the murderers were soon caught and eventually imprisoned for their acts. Still, the public's concern did not subside. In response, the Baltimore County Council provided its police department with 45 new officers.

Realizing that these officers would be spread very thin in a 1,700-officer department, Chief Cornelius Behan and his command staff decided to concentrate them into a special, 45-officer unit to combat fear of crime—the Citizen-Oriented Police Enforcement Unit (COPE).

In 1981, no one knew much about fighting fear of crime. As a result, COPE officers confined their activities in target neighborhoods to directed patrol, motorcycle patrol, and community crime prevention. Despite some modest successes, COPE managers were dissatisfied with their efforts. Chief Behan had given them a charge to be innovative; so far, they had done little that had not been done many times before.

Gary Hayes, the late Executive Director of the Police Executive Research Forum and a friend of Chief Behan's, was asked to help. Hayes arranged for Herman Goldstein to train COPE supervisors in the theory and practice of problem solving. Almost immediately, COPE began to take on a sense of direction it had lacked in its first year of operation.

COPE's approach to problem solving relies heavily on a unique combination of creativity and standard procedures. A problem is usually referred to COPE by another unit of the police department, or by another county agency. An initial assessment of the nature of the problem is made, and one officer is assigned to lead the solution effort. COPE officers then conduct a door-to-door survey of residents and businesses in the problem neighborhood. The officers also solicit other opinions: patrol officers, detectives, and officials from other agencies are often important sources of information. The results are used to define the problem more specifically and to identify aspects of the problem the police never see.

The COPE officers assigned to solve the problem then meet to consider the data they have collected and to brainstorm possible solutions. Next they design an action plan, which details the solutions to be attempted and a timetable for implementing them. Once the solutions are in place, COPE officers often conduct a second survey to see whether they have been successful.

Three years after its inception, these procedures have become the COPE unit's primary approach to reducing fear. But this is not the only method of solving problems; in Newport News, a complementary approach was designed.

Newport News.   In 1984, the National Institute of Justice funded the Police Executive Research Forum to develop and test a new approach to crime analysis. Darrel Stephens, then Chief of the Newport News, Virginia, Police Department, was particularly interested in this approach and he invited the Forum to test it in his agency. Like the COPE unit, this project relies heavily on Goldstein's problem-oriented approach, and Goldstein consulted with the project staff and officials of the Newport News Police.

There are several differences between the Newport News Police Department's project and the Baltimore County COPE project. First, problem-oriented policing is an agencywide strategy in Newport News. All department members, including supervisors, are responsible for identifying, analyzing, and solving problems. Second, any type of problem is fair game, whether it is crime, fear, or another disorder. Third, less emphasis is placed on procedures in Newport News. Instead, a department task force under the guidance of Chief Stephens developed a "problem analysis model," a set of guidelines for data collection and thinking.

But the Newport News approach has many similarities with Baltimore County's. Both departments emphasize careful definition and analysis of problems prior to developing solutions. Evaluating solutions is also stressed. In both departments, supervisors encourage officers analyzing problems to look beyond the police department for information. This means talking to residents, businesspeople, offenders, city agency personnel, and anyone else who could know something about the problem. Similarly, supervisors encourage officers to work with people and organizations outside policing to develop solutions. Criminal justice responses, although not discouraged, are seen as only one option among many.

PROBLEM-ORIENTED POLICING AT WORK

Let us look at how these two agencies have handled several common problems. Much attention has been devoted to crime and fear in residential neighborhoods, so we will first look at two problems of this type. Problems occur in nonresidential areas as well; we next describe an effort to solve a problem occurring in a downtown area with few residents and little commercial activity. Finally, some problems are not confined to a small geographic area but affect people everywhere. As our last case study shows, the problem-oriented approach can be applied equally well to problems like these.

Neighborhood Problems

Loch Raven Apartments (Baltimore County).   Residents of the Loch Raven Apartments were shocked and frightened when beset by a spate of street robberies in 1984. While patrol officers and detectives tried to solve the crimes, COPE was called in to deal with the problem of fear. Officer Wayne Lloyd was assigned to lead the effort.

Officer Lloyd first coordinated a door-to-door survey of Loch Raven residents. He found that most of the residents were elderly women who felt particularly vulnerable to street attacks. Most were unwilling to leave their apartments after dark. Their feelings were exacerbated by the conditions of the complex: many street and building lights were broken; unkempt trees and shrubs created many hiding places; rats, stray dogs, and unrepaired structural damage all contributed to the feeling—widespread among residents—that they were trapped.

Reasoning that many solutions were needed for so complex a problem, Lloyd and his colleagues found a way to get almost everyone involved. Representatives of two local neighborhood associations agreed to help Loch Raven Apartments residents form their own association. The police convinced a variety of organizations to assist the new neighborhood group: a local printer produced crime prevention information, free of charge; a local church donated its meeting facilities; a local baker contributed free donuts. Other agencies helped in other ways. Alerted to the poor lighting situation, Baltimore Gas and Electric repaired its street lights and installed new ones. The walkways and hallways of Loch Raven Apartments were visited by representatives of numerous local agencies, including the Animal Control, Health, Fire, and Housing Departments. The apartment manager bowed to the accumulated pressures and began to refurbish the buildings.

Perhaps because of the deterrent effect of patrolling dog catchers, building inspectors, and the like, the string of robberies stopped completely. Burglaries in the complex, running at a rate of six per month prior to the COPE unit's intervention, dropped to one every two months; it has remained at that level ever since. Perhaps most important, COPE provided the residents with better living conditions and a new Community Association that can help them obtain further improvements.

As the Loch Raven case illustrates, the police can draw upon the resources of many other public and private agencies in their problem-solving efforts. These "hidden Allies" may only need guidance as to where they can be most effective. In this case, a variety of agencies respected the COPE unit's opinion that Loch Raven was a trouble spot that deserved their attention.

The Belmont Treehouse (Baltimore County).   No one ever seemed to use the Belmont Community Park. Casual passersby would rarely see a child in its playground, or a jogger on one of the park's tree-shaded walks. Had they looked closely, they might have seen the reason: rowdy youths frequented one corner of the park. They used drugs and drank, and resisted all attempts by patrol officers to remove them. Neighborhood residents kept their children—and themselves—far away, fearing intimidation and exposure to alcohol and drugs. Residents had complained to various local government agencies for years with no response. Finally, one of the residents read about COPE in his community newspaper and called the unit.

COPE officers Sam Hannigan and James Chaconas were assigned to handle the Belmont problem. Their survey of neighborhood residents revealed that the problem did not focus on the park, after all; instead, it centered on a shed, dubbed the "treehouse," that older youths had constructed in the vacant, wooded lot next door. The treehouse was often used as a crash pad and drinking place by a few, local teenagers.

Hannigan and Chaconas felt that the public nature of the drinking and drug abuse was mostly responsible for the residents' fears. So, at the suggestion of several neighborhood residents, they decided to make the drinking and drug abuse level visible by removing the treehouse.

Their first efforts went nowhere. The County Road Department agreed that the treehouse posed a hazard and was in violation of city codes. They refused to take the problem seriously, however, since no one lived there. The Health and Fire Departments felt the same way. Even if they had been willing to condemn the shack, the formal process would have taken months.

Instead, the officers decided to work with the owner. They searched through tax records to find the owner of the vacant lot. When interviewed at his home, the owner readily admitted that the treehouse was a nuisance and a hazard, and that he had no use for it whatever. Still, he feared retaliation from the kids who had constructed it, and was unable to pay the costs of demolishing the building.

Hannigan and Chaconas discussed the situation with Central COPE Lieutenant Veto Mentzell. They agreed that the two officers should demolish the treehouse themselves. Two employees of the County Roads Commission agreed to help out. Next Saturday morning, the four, armed with saws and sledgehammers, quickly reduced the treehouse to rubble. Then they carted the pieces to a waiting county truck and took them to the dump.

The kids still drink and use drugs, and most of them have stayed in the neighborhood. They now meet in private places, however, where they are not visible to their neighbors. Most important, residents are no longer subject to their unpredictable, loud, and threatening behavior. The Belmont Neighborhood Association reports that residents are less fearful. One tangible result of the fear reduction is that, for the first time in years, the park is filled with children.

The Belmont case shows that an apparently intractable problem—here, fear created by teenage drinking and drug abuse—can be ameliorated with a little analysis and through some simple actions. The Treehouse case took two weeks from start to finish. The key was to accept the neighborhood's definition of the problem (threatening public behavior) rather than the usual police definition (illegal drinking and drug abuse).

A Nonneighborhood Problem

Not all problems occur in areas used by people who have common concerns. Some parts of cities have no real community of interest. Our next example shows how the problem-oriented approach can be applied in this sort of area.

Thefts from vehicles (Newport News).   For years, thefts from vehicles parked near the Newport News Shipyards have constituted around 10% of all index crime reported in Newport News. In 1984, 738 such thefts were reported; dollar losses from the thefts—not including damage to the vehicles—totaled nearly $180,000. Patrol Officer Paul Swartz was assigned to analyze the issues involved and to recommend solutions. He reviewed offense and arrest reports for the parking lot area going back three years and began tracking current cases. Because of these efforts, he was able to identify several parking areas where large numbers of thefts had taken place. These theft-prone areas became the focus of patrol officers' efforts. Swartz also interviewed patrol officers and detectives familiar with the area and talked to members of the shipyard's security force. As a result, Swartz identified a couple of brothers who stole from vehicles in the northern lots, and a few individual offenders who stole in the southern lots.

Swartz gave the descriptions of the known offenders to the officers patrolling the lots. These officers began to stop and talk to suspects when they were seen in the area. Meanwhile, Swartz interviewed several thieves already convicted and sentenced for breaking into vehicles in these parking lots. He promised the offenders that nothing said in the interviews would be used against them. Swartz learned that drugs were a prime target of the northern thieves, but stereo equipment and auto parts were also targets. They especially looked for "muscle" cars, cars with bumper stickers advertising local rock and roll stations, or cars with other evidence that the owner might be a marijuana smoker or cocaine user (for example, a roach clip or a feather hanging from the rearview mirror). The southern thieves did not focus on drugs, but instead concentrated on car stereo equipment and auto parts. Swartz also learned the names, descriptions, and addresses of other thieves; he confirmed that a few were particularly frequent offenders. This information was passed on to other street officers, who made several in-progress arrests. The detectives and the prosecutor worked to ensure that the most frequent offenders were convicted and sentenced to several months in jail.

As of this writing, the department is still developing a long-term solution to this problem. It will probably include working with the shipyard and its workers to develop a theft prevention strategy. In the interim, there has been a 55% decrease in the number of these thefts since April, 1985 (from 51 per month to 23 per month), when the field interrogations and arrests for the repeat offenders began.

This is an example of using previously untapped information. Some street officers had knowledge of who was involved in the thefts, but this information was never put to use until Swartz began his analysis. Offenders were another source of information that had not been used before. As with the community problems described above, collecting information about nonneighborhood problems gives the police the ability to design a response that has a good chance of solving the problems. In this case, the solution involved standard police practices, but they were the practices that fit the need.

A Jurisdictionwide Problem

In addition to problems occurring in small geographic area, police must deal with problems that affect their entire jurisdictions. Among these problems are some of the most troublesome issues confronting the police: juvenile runaways, drunk driving, and spouse abuse, for example. The last example describes how an officer dealt with a jursidiction-wide problem.

Domestic violence (Newport News).   Marvin Evans was a Newport News homicide detective. He was also a member of the task force that designed the department's approach to problem-oriented policing. Frustrated with investigating murders after they had been committed, Evans decided to find a way to prevent them. His analysis of homicide data indicated that most occurred in the southern part of the city; but, more important, half were the direct result of domestic violence, and half of these cases involved couples who had come to police attention previously. When Evans reviewed national research on domestic violence, he found that his findings were typical. This encouraged him to look into the handling of these cases locally. So he began interviewing counselors at the local woman's shelter, assistant state's attorneys, judges, ministers, and anyone else who had an interest in the problem.

Since his fellow officers had an important role in dealing with this issue, he sought their views. Evans used a survey to determine how officers handled domestic cases and their knowledge of the available options. He found that officers were unaware of the fact that they could file a complaint that could result in a warrant, even if the victim refused. He found that officers did not like handling domestic violence cases because those officers who did handle these cases spent many frustrating hours processing them.

So Evans decided to bring together a group of interested people who could design a better way of handling these cases. This group included representatives of the local women's shelter, the state attorney's office, the circuit court, churches, the local newspaper, the Army, and other organizations, as well as the police.

The result of their efforts was a comprehensive plan for handling family violence in the city. The objective was to keep families together while showing both the abuser and the victim how to handle stressful situations without resorting to violence. Although a mandatory arrest policy was adopted for specific types of circumstances (incidents involving injuries, the presence of a weapon, or a prior history of violence, for example), arrest was not seen as an end in itself, but as a means to provide treatment that could preserve the valuable aspects of the families involved. To support this tragedy, the state attorney's office and the court agreed that they would not drop charges if the victim refused to prosecute. Instead they would use the threat of legal sanctions to get both parties into counseling.

The program was pretested in the fall of 1985, and officers were instructed on its operation. In January, the program was officially begun, and in February the local news-paper published a 20-page, special section on domestic violence. Virtually all aspects were covered, from the causes of domestic violence as seen by victims, offenders, and researchers, to the responses to domestic violence by the police, courts, and counselors.

This example shows that line officers can identify problems, conduct an analysis, and organize a communitywide response. In this case, the solution included the entire city. In addition to mobilizing many private and public organizations to help reduce domestic killings and assaults, Evans was able to convince the local newspaper to show the public what they could do to curb domestic violence.

SUMMARY

As these cases illustrate, the problem-oriented approach can be applied to a wide variety of problems. Problem solving can assist in the resolution of neighborhood problems, but it is equally applicable to problems that affect areas with no residential population or to citywide problems. Problem-oriented policing relies on and supports community policing, but it is not synonymous with community policing.

Moreover, the experience of Baltimore County and Newport News shows that police officers have the skill and interested needed to conduct thorough studies of problems and do develop creative solutions. Training and management direction can improve officers' problem diagnosis and analysis skills. And officers involved in problem solving seem to enjoy improving the quality of life of the citizens whom they serve. For many, problem solving is more satisfying than traditional police work because they can see the results of their work more clearly (Cordner, 1985).

The case studies also demonstrate that police have the time available to handle their current workload and to solve problems as well. Differential patrol response, investigative case screening, and similar practices can free up time for nontraditional activities.

The additional free time can be structured in a variety of ways. Baltimore County adopted one approach—it created a special unit. Newport News adopted a different approach—it had all department members solve problems part of the time. In Newport News, problem-solving time was structured in two ways. For a few problems, an officer was temporarily assigned to attack the problem full time. (For example, Officer Swartz was assigned full time to the parking lots problem.) For most others, an officer was assigned to handle the problem in addition to his or her other duties. (Detective Evans created a domestic violence program while investigating homicides, for instance.) Each of the three methods offers its own set of costs and benefits, and it is too soon to tell which methods are best. Most likely, different methods will work better for different problems and police agencies.

Finally, the case studies make it clear the problem-oriented policing is a state of mind, and not a program, technique, or procedure. The keys are clear-headed analysis of the problem and an uninhibited search for solutions. These can be achieved by applying standard operating procedures (as is typically the case in Baltimore County) or a looser analytic model (as in Newport News). There probably is no single best method for developing this state of mind. The best method for any given agency will depend on the characteristics of the agency.

Long-Run Considerations

As problem-oriented policing becomes standard practice in more and more departments, we can expect to see three other fundamental changes in the way police do business. The problem-oriented police department will probably have to change its internal management structure. The role of the police will change, and with it their relationship with the community and other parts of the city bureaucracy. Finally, although problem solving creates the opportunity for greatly increased benefits, it also brings with it the potential for increased risks. Let us consider these long-run considerations in more detail.

Management structure.   As we have emphasized, the point of problem solving is to tailor the police response to the unique circumstances of each problem. Inevitably, this means that decision-making authority must be decentralized; the discretion of line officers and their supervisors—those members of the department who know most about each problem—must increase. As a result, we can expect that mid- and upper-level managers will need to develop new methods of structuring this increased discretion.

Decentralized authority will affect all levels of the hierarchy, but it will probably affect line supervisors—sergeants—the most. As a result, agencies adopting a problem-oriented approach will have to provide much more extensive policy guidance and training to their sergeants. Problem solving puts a dual burden on these officials. On the one hand, they must make many of the tough, operational decisions. Line supervisors—those members of the department who know most about each of their officers, set priorities among different problems, facilitate work with other divisions of the police department and outside agencies, and make sure their officers solve the problems they are assigned. On the other hand, the sergeants must also provide leadership, encouraging creative analysis and response. So a first-line supervisor under problem solving might come to resemble the editor of a newspaper, or the manager of an R & D unit, more than an army sergeant.[4] Indeed, in Baltimore County there are indications that these changes are beginning to happen (Taft, 1986).

Police role.   It is almost certain that problem solving will influence the police officers who undertake it to reconsider their role in society. As we have described, identifying, studying, and solving problems requires that officers make more contacts with people and organizations outside the police agency. As they do this, they will become exposed to a wider variety of interests and perspectives. Many officers will discover that they can accomplish more by working with these individuals and groups. As a consequence, they will begin to take a broader, more informed view of the problems they must handle.

This is all to the good, but few improvements are without complications. A police agency taking on a complex problem may find itself in the midst of a contentious community power struggle. This could undermine the authority of the agency in other, less controversial areas. As a result, police agencies may avoid important but controversial problems. On the other hand, the problem-oriented police agency may find that it must get involved in controversial problems to avoid favoring one side over another.

Political problems will probably not be limited to police–community relations. Solving problems will require police agencies to work closely with a host of other public agencies as well. This raises the issue of "turf." Other public agencies may view a problem-solving endeavor as encroachment, rather than collaboration. This is especially likely when the problem is largely due to the failure of another agency to do its job. Even if police are successful in avoiding conflict with other agencies and with the public, problem solving will almost certainly increase the political complexity of managing a police agency.

Increased risks and benefits.   The case studies described above suggest that police agencies who taken on a broader, problem-solving role can be more effective than before. But they may also do more harm than before, either through inadvertent mistakes or through outright abuses of authority.

Even creative responses based on careful analysis will sometimes fail. Some responses may even make matters worse. This has always been true of police work or the work of any government agency. Currently, however, failures to handle calls adequately seldom result in difficulties for the public at large. Few people are involved in each incident, and the scope of police intervention is usually very limited. The consequences of a failure to solve a problem may be much more serious: problems involve many people; ill-advised responses may have far-reaching social implications.

Abuse of authority presents an even thornier issue. The police will be actively intervening in situations they had previously left alone, presenting more opportunities for abuse.

At the same time, however, the problem-oriented approach encourages police to analyze problems in detail and solicit the cooperation of outside organizations and individuals before responding. This will help reduce the likelihood of both errors and abuses. In addition, because problem-oriented policing emphasizes noncoercive responses, inappropriate use of force and sanctions should become less likely. Mistakes and abuses will persist, of course; whether they are more or less benign than present mistakes and abuses remains to be seen.

In any case, it is clear that the limits of police authority will become more and more an issue as problem solving becomes standard practice. Who will set these limits? The short answer is, some combination of the same actors who already set and enforce police standards: informal pressure from private citizens in their contacts with individual officers, elected officials, the staff of other public and private agencies, and the police themselves. What limits will be established is an open question, considered at greater length elsewhere (Goldstein, 1987). One thing is certain: problem solving will require a new consensus on the role, authority, and limitations of the police in each jurisdiction that tries it.

Full implementation of problem solving will be a slow and sometimes difficult process. No agency will be able to "adopt" problem solving simply by making a few changes in standard operating procedures or just by telling officers to go to it. If it becomes a fad—if police managers try to implement it too quickly, without doing the necessary spadework—problem-oriented policing will fail. As Charlie Bedford's case shows, however, careful planning can yield great benefits for an agency that works to solve its community's problems.

Officer Summerfield consulted Sergeant Hogan. They agreed that the skating rink owner should be asked to bus the kids home. Summerfield returned to the rink and spoke with the owner. The owner agreed to lease more buses. By the next weekend, the buses were in use and Summerfield and Hogan saw no kids disturbing Mr. Bedford's neighborhood.

Sergeant Hogan summed it up: "Look, we can have the best of both worlds. People here can get their sleep and the kids can still have fun. But we can't do it by tying up officers and chasing kids every Friday and Saturday night. There has to be a way of getting rid of the problem once and for all."

NOTES

1. This case study and those that follow are true. Names of citizens have been changed, but names of police officials and places have not been. The information on which these case studies are based came from two projects being conducted by the authors. The Newport News study was funded by the National Institute of Justice under grant 84-U-CX-0040. The Baltimore County project was funded in part by the Florence V. Burden Foundation.

   The opinions expressed in this article are those of the authors, and not necessarily those of the National Institute of Justice, the Burden Foundation, the police agencies described, or the Police Executive Research Forum.

2. See, for example, Skogan and Maxfield (1981); Skogan, this issue; Police Foundation (1981); Williams and Pate, this issue; Brown and Wycoff, this issue.

3. For descriptions and evaluations of the effectiveness of storefronts in Detroit and Houston, see Holland (1985); and Brown and Wycoff, this issue.

4. For examples of supervision in an R&D unit and a high-tech firm, see Kidder (1981) and Auletta (1984). For a broader discussion of this management style, see Drucker (1985) and Peters and Waterman (1982).

REFERENCES

AULETTA, KEN. (1984). *The Art of Corporate Success: The Story of Schlumberger.* New York: Penguin.

BROWN, LEE and MARY ANN WYCOFF. (1987). "Policing Houston: Reducing Fear and Improving Service," *Crime & Delinquency* 33, 1.

CIREL, PAUL, PATRICIA EVANS, DANIEL McGILLIS, and DEBRA WITCOMB. (1977). *Community Crime Prevention Program, Seattle, Washington: An Exemplary Project.* Washington, D.C.: Department of Justice, National Institute of Justice.

CORDNER, GARY W. (1985). *The Baltimore County Citizen Oriented Police Enforcement (COPE) Project: Final Evaluation.* Final Report to the Florence V. Burden Foundation. Baltimore: Criminal Justice Department, University of Baltimore.

DRUCKER, PETER F. (1985). *Innovation and Entrepreneurship: Practice and Principles.* New York: Harper & Row.

ECK, JOHN E. (1979). *Managing Case Assignments: The Burglary Investigation Decision Model Replication*. Washington, D.C.: Police Executive Research Forum.

_____. (1982). *Solving Crimes: The Investigation of Burglary and Robbery*. Washington, D.C.: Police Executive Research Forum.

FARMER, MICHAEL (Ed.). (1981). *Differential Police Response Strategies*. Washington, D.C.: Police Executive Research Forum.

FOWLER, FLOYD J., Jr., and THOMAS W. MANGIONE. (1974). "The Nature of Fear." Center for Survey Research Working Paper. Boston: Center for Survey Research, University of Massachusetts and Joint Center for Urban Studies, Massachusetts Institute of Technology and Harvard University.

_____. (1983). *Neighborhood Crime, Fear and Social Control: A Second Look at the Hartford Program*. Washington, D.C.: Government Printing Office.

GAY, WILLIAM G., THOMAS M. BEALL, and ROBERT A. BOWERS. (1984). *A Four-Site Assessment of the Integrated Criminal Apprehension Program*. Washington, D.C.: University City Science Center.

GAY, WILLIAM G., THEODORE H. SCHELL, and STEPHEN SCHACK. (1977). *Prescriptive Package: Improving Patrol Productivity, Volume I, Routine Patrol*. Washington, D.C.: Government Printing Office.

GOLDSTEIN, HERMAN (1977) *Policing a Free Society*. Cambridge, Mass.: Ballinger.

_____. (1979). "Improving Policing: A Problem-oriented Approach." *Crime & Delinquency 25*: 236–258.

_____. (1987). "Toward Community-Oriented Policing: Potential Basic Requirements and Threshold Questions." *Crime & Delinquency 33*, 1.

GREENBERG, BERNARD, OLIVER S. YU, and KAREN LANG. (1973). *Enhancement of the Investigative Function, Volume 1, Analysis and Conclusions*. Final Report, Phase I. Springfield, Va.: National Technical Information Service.

GREENBERG, STEPHANIE W., WILLIAM M. ROHE, and JAY R. WILLIAMS. (1984). *Safe and Secure Neighborhoods: Physical Characteristics and Information Territorial Control in High and Low Crime Neighborhoods*. Washington, D.C.: Government Printing Office.

GREENWOOD, PETER, and JOAN PETERSILIA, and JAN CHAIKEN. (1977). *The Criminal Investigation Process*. Lexington, Mass.: D.C. Heath.

HOLLAND, LAWRENCE H. (1985). "Police and the Community: The Detroit Ministration Experience." *FBI Law Enforcement Bulletin 54* (February): 1–6.

Kansas City Police Department. (1980). *Response Time Analysis: Volume II—Part 1 Crime Analysis*. Washington, D.C.: Government Printing Office.

KELLING, GEORGE L. (1987). "Acquiring A Taste For Order: The Community and Police." *Crime & Delinquency 33*, 1.

KELLING, GEORGE, TONY PATE, Duane DIECKMAN, and CHARLES E. BROWN. (1974). *The Kansas City Preventive Patrol Experiment: A Technical Report*. Washington, D.C.: Police Foundation.

KIDDER, TRACY. (1981). *Soul of a New Machine*. New York: Avon.

LAVRAKAS, PAUL J. (1985). "Citizen Self-Help and Neighborhood Crime Prevention Policy." In *American Violence and Public Policy*, Lynn A. Curtis (Ed.). New Haven, Conn.: Yale University Press.

McEWEN, J. THOMAS, EDWARD F. CONNORS, and MARCIA I. COHEN. (1984). *Evaluation of the Differential Police Response Field Test*. Alexandria, Va.: Research Management Associates.

PETERS, THOMAS J. and ROBERT H. WATERMAN. (1982). *In Search of Excellence: Lessons from American's Best-Run Companies*. New York: Warner.

Police Foundation. (1981). *The Newark Foot Patrol Experiment*. Washington, D.C.: Author.

REINIER, G. HOBART, M. R. GREENLEE, and M. H. GIBBENS. (1976). *Crime Analysis in Support of Patrol*. National Evaluation Program: Phase I Report. Washington, D.C.: Government Printing Office.

ROSENBAUM, DENNIS P. (1987). "The Theory and Research Behind Neighborhood Watch: Is It a Sound Fear and Crime Reduction Strategy?" *Crime & Delinquency 33*, 1.

SKOGAN, WESLEY G. (1987). "The Impact of Victimization on Fear." *Crime & Delinquency 33*, 1.

SKOGAN, WESLEY G. and MICHAEL G. MAXFIELD. (1981). *Coping With Crime: Individuals and Neighborhood Reactions*. Beverly Hills, Calif.: Sage.

SPELMAN, WILLIAM. (1983). *Reactions to Crime in Atlanta and Chicago: A Policy-Oriented Reanalysis*. Final report to the National Institute of Justice. Cambridge, Mass.: Harvard Law School.

SPELMAN, WILLIAM and DALE K. BROWN. (1984). *Calling the Police: Citizen Reporting of Serious Crime*. Washington, D.C.: Government Printing Office.

TAFT, PHILIP B., Jr. (1986). *Fighting Fear: The Baltimore County C.O.P.E. Project*. Washington, D.C.: Police Executive Research Forum.

TAUB, RICHARD D., GARTH TAYLOR, and JAN DUNHAM. (1984). *Patterns of Neighborhood Change: Race and Crime in Urban America*. Chicago: University of Chicago Press.

TROJANOWICZ, ROBERT C. (n.d.). *An Evaluation of the Neighborhood Foot Patrol Program in Flint, Michigan*. East Lansing: Neighborhood Foot Patrol Center, Michigan State University.

WILLIAMS, HUBERT and ANTONY M. PATE. (1987). "Returning To First Principles: Reducing the Fear of Crime in Newark." *Crime & Delinquency 33*, 1.

WILSON, JAMES Q. and GEORGE L. KELLING. (1982). "Broken Windows: The Police and Neighborhood Safety." *The Atlantic Monthly* (March): 29–38.

QUESTIONS FOR DISCUSSION

1. Contrast and compare community policing to crime control policing. Provide examples for each type of policing style.

2. What is problem-oriented policing? How does this type of policing differ from the community and crime control styles of policing?

3. Discuss how problem-oriented policing addresses "fear" in a residential neighborhood.

4. How might problem-oriented policing effectively deal with nonneighborhood and jurisdiction wide problems? Provide examples to support your response.

5. In the future we can expect to see three fundamental changes in the way police do business. Discuss changes in management structures, police roles, and increases in risks and benefits.

13

TRANSFORMING THE POLICE

Stephen D. Mastrofski
Craig D. Uchida

■　■　■　■　■　■　■　■　■　■　■　■　■　■　■　■　■　■　■

Problem-Oriented Policing, by Herman Goldstein. New York: McGraw-Hill, 1990.

Policing Domestic Violence: Experiments and Dilemmas, by Lawrence W. Sherman. New York: Free Press, 1992.

Above the Law: Police and the Excessive Use of Force, by Jerome H. Skolnick and James J. Fyfe. New York: Free Press, 1993.

There has been no American institution so intensely and continuously the object of reform in the last hundred years as the police. Here we have three books by distinguished scholars, each arguing forcefully for the need to change anew the American way of policing. The books differ sufficiently in topical focus and method of analysis that some, including the authors, might regard the three as strange bedfellows. Yet they are compatible in several respects about what ails contemporary police and what should be done about it. All find fault with various aspects of the form of police professionalism ascendant in post–Second World War America, and all seek a police more open to innovation, experimentation, and evaluation. Although all four authors are scholars, the books are pitched primarily to policy makers and practitioners, a group with whom they have had active involvement throughout their careers.

Together, the volumes offer insight into avenues of police reform in the next century. Our essay focuses on the theme of change that runs through them. We first comment on the observations and arguments of each book and then suggest a framework to discern the larger implications of change they advocate.

THE TRANSFORMATION OF PROGRESSIVE REFORM

If, as historian Robert Fogelson (1977) argues, progressive police reform was "at a standstill" by 1970, it is certainly on the move today. In the last two decades, new engines of police progressivism have arisen (e.g., Police Foundation, Police Executive Research Forum, National Organization of Black Law Enforcement Officers) and older ones (e.g., the

Stephen D. Mastrofski and Craig D. Uchida, "Transforming the Police," *Crime and Delinquency* (Vol. 30, No. 3), pp. 330–358, copyright © 1993 by Sage Publications, Inc. Reprinted by permission of Sage Publications, Inc.

Federal Bureau of Investigation, the International Association of Chiefs of Police) are even endorsing a new vision of progressivism. That vision now goes by the term *community policing*, which has been viewed with favor by presidential administrations as diverse as those of Reagan, Bush, and Clinton, and it enjoys increasing federal financial support as a vehicle to improve American police. The community policing movement is still in its formative stage, and its direction not entirely clear, but it appears to pervade the thinking of the most visible fountains of reform rhetoric in academe, think tanks, police professional associations, and the leadership of the largest police departments in the nation.

The forces behind the emergence of the community policing movement are diverse, and many individuals have contributed to its conceptual development. First, among these, however, is Herman Goldstein. Receiving his initiation in American policing under the tutelage of the eminent police reformer, O. W. Wilson, Goldstein has, over the years, been the most perceptive observer of the limitations of Wilson's form of progressivism. Through a series of books and monographs, Goldstein has offered the most comprehensive critique of contemporary policing and the most cogent and striking departure from the trend of increasing legalization and bureaucratization that has marked the trajectory of modern American policing (Reiss, 1992).

Of the three books reviewed here, Goldstein's is the broadest in scope. His is an argument for a radical restructuring of police organization and practice. His *Problem-Oriented Policing* fleshes out a line of thought about American policing that first appeared in a 1979 journal article on the topic. He contends that policing is too focused on internal efficiency matters and insufficiently concerned with the impact of the organization's efforts on substantive problems in its work environment. Police are too reactive to that environment, continuously responding to calls for service without exercising initiative to prevent or reduce the underlying problems that generate those calls. The police fail to develop and draw upon two important resources for handling these problems: the community and the rank-and-file within the department. Finally, organizational reform has been too piecemeal, ignoring the capacity of the police subculture to subvert reforms and failing to offer a coherent plan for change that addresses the necessary scope of structure, policy, and practice.

Goldstein's corrective to this state of affairs is problem-oriented policing (p-o-p). P-o-p focuses on what Goldstein calls "substantive" problems—those conditions in their *external* environment that police are expected to manage, change, promote, or inhibit. Broadly speaking, these things have traditionally included crime and disorder although Goldstein envisions a role that incorporates a broader range of concerns of the community. This vision is reminiscent of early American police whose diverse responsibilities have been narrowed over the years by the emergence of other specialty occupations and municipal services (Fogelson, 1977; Walker, 1977), but Goldstein adds two important new features. First, police and their efforts are to be judged by their impact on those substantive problems. The ultimate measure of success must be some improvement in those aspects of the environment targeted for results. Second, police must attempt to discern patterns in the multitude of individual incidents presented to them and then to distinguish among these in ways that make sense—not to the rest of the legal system, but to those in the department and community who must find solutions to those problems. Although problems might be defined on any scale, Goldstein shows a preference for problems narrowly, rather than globally, defined. That is, he wants police to disaggregate problems (in terms of offender characteristics, victim characteristics, geography, and so on) so that they are sensitive to the complexities of the problem environment, a sensitivity which is the first step to understanding causes and identifying effective responses.

This requires an organization with the capacity for systematic empirical inquiry, one that is not bound by conventional criminal offense categories and one with sufficient flexibility to alter its mode of inquiry as it learns from its efforts. This inquiry must include a careful detailing of the interests of various segments of the community who have some stake in the problem, the strengths and weaknesses of the department's current efforts relevant to the problem, a search for alternatives that might prove more effective, and empirical evaluation of the effectiveness of any solution implemented.

To enact this vision of policing, Goldstein proposes a number of specific transformations. He advocates what might be termed a "managed democratization" of policing, by giving the community and the rank-and-file officers central roles in identifying and selecting problems for police intervention. Those closest to the problems are presumed to be in the best position to inform organizational priorities, the ultimate determination of which remains with department managers, who are responsible for striking a balance among multiple and often conflicting interests. Indeed, participatory management and decentralized decision making are key structural features of problem analysis and impact evaluation.

Since creativity is valued, Goldstein urges police administrators to encourage nontraditional responses to problems, to eschew the habits of punitive bureaucracies by rewarding successful innovations and not penalizing those officers whose good-faith efforts fail. He suggests a variety of approaches that are alien to most contemporary police but whose prospects seem promising: strategic targeting of people and places that generate problems, working closely with other government and private agencies, using mediation and negotiation to resolve conflicts, educating and informing the public, reinforcing other institutions of social control (e.g., the family, neighborhood, school officials), altering the physical environment, enforcing civil and regulatory laws, and more discriminate use of the criminal sanction. He calls for a police whose identify is not tied closely and exclusively to the criminal justice system but who, in fact, became a police more adept at using many other systems of problem prevention and control. Even more radical is the proposition that police themselves become *the* catalysts for kindling community consciousness about what problems exist and for mobilizing the fragmented, turf-sensitive, red-tape-entangled urban service behemoths.

To ensure that police have the capacity to engage effectively in these activities, the department must recruit and train officers with the skill and disposition to conduct empirical inquiry and engage in the many nonarrest, alternative problem-solving strategies. Supervisors must become educators and facilitators, not pencil-pushing bureaucrats whose principal function is to review reports and fill out work schedules. And the department must develop its research and planning capacity—to gather and analyze the information necessary to support the problem-solving endeavors of officers on the street.

Among the most challenging and revolutionary p-o-p proposals is weaning the police, at least to some extent, from the reactive, calls-for-service system by which most department resources are allocated. P-o-p activities will require that officers have blocks of time free from the responsibility to respond to calls, which can be secured by shedding some of that workload, using less intensive response alternatives (e.g., mail-in reports and telephone report takers), and "smoothing" techniques that postpone some police responses to give the organization greater control over the distribution of its workload.

Among the past decade's proliferation of books and essays promoting some version of community policing, Goldstein's work stands as a model of comprehensiveness, conceptual depth, and, especially, balance. Where some advanced a limited, uninspiring program for change (e.g., more foot patrol, more civilians, more ministations, more neighborhood meetings), Goldstein offers a transformation so striking that, if fully implemented by the next century's end, a time traveler from the present would scarcely recognize it as policing. Where some offer flimsy or facile methods of engaging the community in this process (e.g., conducting opinion surveys), Goldstein wrestles with the enduring challenge of responding to majority interests without traversing minority rights. Where some sell the new reforms with shameless hucksterism that makes all manner of outlandish even-cures-warts claims, Goldstein acknowledges and engages the risks that his proposals entail.

Having noted the immense debt that contemporary American policing owes to Goldstein's invigorating work, we suggested that his proposals deserve much greater scrutiny than they have thus far received. Two questions deserve serious consideration: whether p-o-p should be pursued and whether it can in fact be achieved. This is not an appropriate forum for a comprehensive discussion of either question, but we consider here the implications of one aspect of Goldstein's plan, how it would transform the governance of police.

One of the themes of Goldstein's writings on American police is that they are poorly governed, to the extent that they are governed at all (Mastrofski, 1988b). The good government reforms initiated in the early 20th century eventually produced the *appearance* of centralized, rational control of urban police, but the various institutions signifying control (rules and regulations, formal records, steep supervisory and administrative hierarchies, squads of specialists, etc.) have been remarkably ineffectual in giving police administrators much additional control over what police officers do and what the agency accomplishes. At the same time, as the power of local political parties ebbed and urban political power became fragmented among multiple interests, police leaders were fairly successful in buffering their organizations from the direct manipulation of electoral politicians. Further, authority for control of the police became fragmented among multiple specialist bodies that each assumed responsibility for only a piece of the larger picture (the mayor, city council, civil service, labor relations boards, the courts, civilian review boards, training standards councils, etc.). While this may have reduced the opportunities for certain forms of systematic police corruption, it also made them less responsive to external governance by those segments of the population most likely to experience police control firsthand. The consequences can be seen in the highly publicized civil disorders of the 1960s and early 1970s. Thus police administrators, the linchpin of policy accountability, remained largely irrelevant to the actual control of their agency's everyday work, while their organizations became disconnected from the traditional channels of control.

Goldstein's p-o-p is a blueprint for how to establish both external and internal accountability—with police management at the center. One should not be misled by the effusive rhetoric about empowering the community and the rank-and-file officers that characterizes the arguments of some p-o-p's most ardent disciples. Successfully executed, Goldstein's is a plan to empower, above all, police management. But doing so requires that police organizations devise mechanisms for both the community and the rank and file to participate constructively in the policy-making process. This requires that administrators give up two of their security blankets: the appearance of top-down internal command and control and many of the bulwarks against external, community involvement in departmental affairs.

The benefits of this move to participatory management are (a) improved community and employee morale and commitment to the organization and (b) a vastly enhanced managerial capacity to obtain, analyze, and use information about the organization's practices and environment. Most important, p-o-p is a rationale for police management to decouple resource allocation from reactive, incident-driven processes—over which management exerts little control—and enables it to rationalize priority setting for the agency. Problems are selected for police attention based upon their scope, severity, and the prospects of successful intervention. Problem solving, as an organizing tool, enhances managers' capacity to orchestrate the focus of employee activity and to monitor success.

Moving away from reactive policing also enables police to spend time in dialogue and debate with various segments of the community in virtually all phases of this process, but the nature of that role is clearly defined: the community proposes, but police management disposes.

In fact, Goldstein argues for a police leadership that takes a much more visible "political" role that good government advocates have in the past found anathema. Police chiefs must lead, exhort, organize and negotiate with diverse interest groups, the general public, and other government actors. Their domain is no longer restricted to public safety but extends to virtually all facts of the quality of urban life. Problem-solving police are expected to work with, indeed to mobilize and coordinate (for the cause of public order and safety), many other service bureaucracies: schools, child care and family services, recreation, sanitation, public works, code enforcement, transportation, public and mental health, welfare, the courts, probation and parole, and so on. And they are to integrate the efforts of the private sector, such as traditional institutions of social control (the church, neighborhoods), civic groups, and businesses. The logic of p-o-p reinvests police with the responsibility for seeing that communities are policed in the original, broad sense of administration that ensures the public's general welfare—one that predates the emergence of a full-time police occupation housed in municipal bureaucracies (Lane, 1992, p. 5).

Although Goldstein does not say so explicitly, such a recommendation certainly resonates with the view (supported by considerable evidence and the current popularity of Perotism) that traditional mechanisms of urban governance are simply "not tending the store." Making local government work is an undeniably laudable ambition, but whether it should, or could, be reinvented in this way is open to debate.

There is, of course, the liberal's concern about the concentration of power in one institution, especially one that has a near monopoly on the legal use of force (Bittner, 1970). One can make a counterargument, however, that the ability of local urban governments to address worsening problems has deteriorated to such an extent, and the mechanisms of control become so diffuse, that there is no great danger of the police chief becoming the new urban "boss."

Goldstein suggests that the principal safeguard for this concentration of power in the police is openness throughout the problem-solving process. This volume does not provide a systematic discussion of how such openness might be achieved, nor does it indicate how the knowledge derived from such exposure might be used to prevent and correct errors. The openness challenge is of such magnitude that it deserves a volume of its own, replete with careful attention to the many ways that ostensible mechanisms of openness can be perverted, co-opted, and manipulated.

Problem-Oriented Policing is mostly about transforming the police, but to accomplish accountability that is both profound and enduring, it will be more important to transform the political environment of the police department. That, we believe, is a challenge that extends well beyond the capacity and will of the police to accomplish. There can be no police–community partnership without vital community institutions with which police can link, and the police alone can neither create nor sustain such institutions. The 1970s brought hope to some of a resurgence of neighborhood-based grass-roots political organizations, but, at best, the most successful of those in our large urban areas achieve domain over a diminished and diminishing resource base. If center cities are to revitalize, they must come to grips with metropolitan and regional economic and political forces.

And there will be no problem solving on a broad scale involving the wide range of municipal, metropolitan, state, and federal agencies as long as municipal services are organized along the lines of what Theodore Lowi called the "New Machines" (1969). These are the professionalized agencies that run the city, headed by career bureaucrats, each hegemonous over "*islands of functional power*, before the modern mayor stands impoverished" (p. 200)—likened by Lowi to the premier of a French Fourth Republic confronting an assortment of obstreperous parties in the National Assembly:

> The plight of the mayor, however, is worse: at least the premier could resign. These modern machines, more monolithic by far than their ancient brethren, are entrenched by law and supported by tradition, the slavish loyalty of the newspapers, the educated masses, the dedicated civic groups, and, most of all, by the legitimized clientele groups enjoying access under existing arrangements. (1969, p. 201)

Indeed, by the late 1960s, it was clear that urban government had become decentralized—but functionally instead of geographically. Yet Goldstein's problems defy the functional boundaries of urban bureaucracy and require a geographic responsiveness that has in no small part evaporated from the big city scene. One wonders whether the police are really the folks to spearhead a movement to mobilize the urban polity and the catalyst to restructure the panoply of urban services. These challenge are of such magnitude that they, too, deserve an entire problem-solving volume of their own, lest p-o-p be rendered a blueprint for a lovely edifice that cannot be built.

Ultimately, Goldstein sets forth a vision of a police organization free of the traditional legalistic and bureaucratic filters that shape decision-makers' understanding and interpretations of the work environment. It is an organization that thinks, grows, and learns—what Lawrence Sherman in *Policing Domestic Violence* approvingly calls a "smart" police department (p. 251). It is to Sherman's vision that we now turn, one which elaborates a process by which police agencies might achieve this status.

TRANSFORMING THE SCIENCE OF POLICING

The phrase "police science" not infrequently begets smirks when used before audiences of accomplished researchers in traditional disciplines that enjoy some status as "hard" sciences, and this is so even among those "softer" social sciences, which are themselves further down the pecking order of the research community. Indeed, August Vollmer's (1930) aspiration for a police profession grounded, like medicine, in science still seems a distant goal by any candid appraisal (Bayley and Bittner, 1989). That is not to say, however, that advances in the science of policing have not been forthcoming, and there is no more ardent a pursuer of this objective on the current scene than Lawrence Sherman, whose prolific research career has been devoted largely to empirical exploration of law enforcement's capacity to control crime.

Sherman's *Policing Domestic Violence* is an in-depth examination of a relatively narrow range of criminal offenses. In the broader context set by Goldstein's p-o-p, it is an exploration of the causes and consequences of violence between inmates but is mostly an assessment of the deterrent effects of arresting offenders compared to nonarrest alternatives, such as counseling or separating disputants. The book reviews a wide range of empirical research on domestic violence, focusing especially on the author's own experimental evaluations of the deterrent effects of arrest, and those of other scholars.

Sherman's book has two parallel themes: understanding the impact of police practices on domestic violence and how that knowledge should be used to inform public policy. Although the book offers some theoretical speculation about the causal processes involved in domestic violence, these are subordinate to the assessment of the relative merits of policy alternatives. These assessments in turn rely heavily upon the author's own well-publicized research on misdemeanor domestic violence in Minneapolis and subsequently in Milwaukee, as well as studies by others in Charlotte, Colorado Springs, Metro-Dade, and Omaha—all field experiments sponsored by the National Institute of Justice.

The gist of the findings are these. The 1984 Minneapolis study, which received tremendous dissemination in the press and among police, found that arresting the suspect was substantially more effective in reducing repeat domestic violence than just sending the offender away or mediating/arbitrating the dispute, although the strength of these differences, and the likelihood that they differed by chance, depended upon the method of measuring results (police records vs. follow-up victim interviews). These findings were used to support efforts to implement mandatory domestic violence arrest laws and policies, which were widely adopted around the nation. The Minneapolis experiment, the first fielded to assess specific offense intervention strategies, had several limitations, however, and the National Institute of Justice subsequently sponsored similar studies to see if the finding would be replicated with strengthened designs at other sites.

The five spouse assault replication studies reviewed by Sherman suggest that the impact of arrest is far more complicated than many had assumed from the Minneapolis study. The effects of arrest varied by city, actually *increasing* domestic violence in Omaha, Charlotte, and Milwaukee in the long run, after showing some initial deterrent effects. Only Omaha produced evidence of an effective innovation: having the prosecutor issue an arrest warrant when the offender was absent from the scene at the time of the initial police response. Evidence of deterrent effects on Colorado Springs and Metro-Dade was mixed, depending upon the measures of results used. Secondary data analysis revealed that, in Milwaukee, Colorado Springs, and Omaha, the effects of arrest depended upon the type of suspect. Those with a stake in conformity (e.g., those with jobs) tended to be deterred, but those without such a stake actually became *more* violent if arrested (a backfire effect).

These and other findings from the domestic violence evaluations illuminate several moral dilemmas which structure most of the book:

1. Arrest reduces domestic violence in some cities but increases it in others.

2. Arrest reduces domestic violence among employed people but increases it among unemployed people.

3. Arrest reduces domestic violence in the short run but can increase it in the long run.

4. Police can predict which couples are most likely to suffer future violence, but our society values privacy too highly to encourage preventive action.

5. Unreplicated experiments can inform policy making, but further experiments may lead to different conclusions (pp. 18–20).

Wrestling with these dilemmas brings Sherman to a number of conclusions, among which are:

1. Repeat mandatory arrest laws, substituting instead police discretion that is "structured" by departments listing acceptable options (both arrest and nonarrest) and requiring frequent training that updates police on the latest research on what works under what circumstances.

2. Allow warrantless arrests for misdemeanor domestic violence.

3. Encourage the issuance of warrants for absent offenders.

4. Do not hold police civilly liable for failure to prevent serious domestic violence because of failure to make an arrest in prior misdemeanor assaults (because there is no demonstrated causal connection between the latter and the former).

5. Police should continue experimentation with approaches to handling chronically violent couples.

6. Vigorously pursue research and development on the control of domestic violence (pp. 22–24, 252–260).

He concludes with an agenda for future research and development, one that stresses the need for experiments, quasi experiments, and replication.

The second theme of *Policing Domestic Violence* is how research can and should be used to shape public policy. Sherman begins with a forceful argument that policy on this and other issues of crime control and police effectiveness is best informed by the use of controlled experiments because, when properly executed, they provide the greatest confidence in discerning the strength of the causal relationship between the test policies and the measured outcomes. This constitutes an extension of an argument set forth in a review of *Problem-Oriented Policing*, in which he takes Goldstein to task for insufficiently attending to the need for rigor in evaluation of problem-solving efforts (Sherman, 1992). An enthusiastic supporter of Goldstein's vision of a police organization that thinks about what results it can produce, Sherman faults Goldstein for failing to pay serious attention to the need for rigor in measuring those results. Sherman acknowledges that the degree of rigor (and, therefore, effort) expended on evaluating a problem-solving strategy must depend upon a number of practical considerations, as well as the scope and seriousness of the problem, but he strongly cautions against the dangers of drawing conclusions based on studies with weak design and shaky data. To illustrate these risks, his critique focuses on Goldstein's laudatory exposition of a nonexperimental evaluation of the police response to a spate of convenience store robberies in Gainesville, Florida. He briefly outlines the many unexamined threats to the study's finding of deterrent effects from the problem-solving effort. He urges that big problem-solving efforts receive proportionately rigorous evaluation efforts that can come to grips with rival hypotheses that might account for evaluation results.

One can read *Policing Domestic Violence* as Sherman's idea of what p-o-p *can* produce when the resources and commitment are available to hold problem-solving efforts to high social science standards for internal validity. The irony is that much of Sherman's own book is given to the defense and reinterpretation of the Minneapolis experiment and its external validity in light of the mostly contrary findings of subsequent replication attempts. As Sherman notes, the major drawback to even the best conceived and executed experiments is the question of their generalizability, the assessment of which is possible only through replication at other sites and times, with different types of offenders and victims, and so on.

In any event, replications can easily produce findings that differ significantly from preceding research, a leitmotif of this volume, which serves as the basis for the author's current prescriptions for changing public policy on domestic violence. It would, indeed, be a significant shift for state law and local policies to be determined by the conclusions of scientific studies, something that Sherman acknowledges in assessing the nationwide impact of the high-visibility Minneapolis study. He argues that the study was more a convenient tool of change agents active at that time (e.g., feminist groups and other battered women's advocates) than itself an independent force for change.

If policy makers are to use science to inform their decisions, then, Sherman argues, they must recognize that definitive and enduring answers to "What works?" are improbable, and that, as new information emerges, new or different policy directions are likely to seem preferable. As a contribution to policy analysis, Sherman attempts to come to grips with the features of social science and policy that are so frequently at odds: the typically high degree of uncertainty in the former and the compulsion to do something about public problems in the latter. We give Sherman high marks for illuminating the current state of research on the problem of domestic violence, but we find his prescriptions for resolving the policy dilemma he sets forth less compelling.

The "replication dilemma" is the most difficult issue, in our view, yet it is the one which troubles Sherman the least: "There are strong grounds for always taking research into account when making policy, no matter how limited and provisional the research may be" (p. 22). The most perplexing aspects of this dilemma are deciding (a) how demanding we should be of research in terms of quality and quantity before using it to determine policy and (b) what policy implications to derive from a given body of knowledge.

Sherman argues that it was entirely appropriate to make policy recommendations based on the unreplicated Minneapolis study in 1984. He claims that the state of knowledge on the three options of arrest, advice, and separation was "equipoise," that none of these enjoyed stronger theoretical or evidentiary superiority, so the evidence from his study — with all of its limitations—was a sufficient basis for recommendations. While the logic of the equipoise argument seems unassailable, there is no reason to wonder about the frequency with which it can be applied in criminology and police problems generally, and there is certainly some basis to doubt its validity for misdemeanor domestic violence in 1984. Even if we assume that no policy option enjoyed an empirical or theoretical advantage at that time, based on *science*, one might still acknowledge that there other, *nonscientific* sources of knowledge about the issue that should have been considered.

Here we speak of the knowledge of the police themselves, experienced in the practice of their craft. Indeed, as Sherman notes, the Minneapolis findings were at odds with prevailing craft views, and they were subsequently received quite skeptically by that community, as well as by many researchers. Sherman himself seems to give credence to nonscientific craft knowledge when he attempts to resolve several of the policy dilemmas; he suggests that, based on evidence currently available, officers can and should be trusted to make clinical decisions in the field about whether to arrest in misdemeanor domestic assault situations. We do not suggest that the Minneapolis findings should have been ignored, only that the playing field was not so level as Sherman claims. We do not wish to romanticize the infallibility of craft wisdom, for after all, bleeding the patient was once the treatment of choice when medicine was based only on craft. But many prescientific medical practices have been supported by scientific research, and in this case the nonarrest treatment options failed to provide a true test of the best the police craft had to offer.

Deciding just how far to go toward an arrest policy is the second aspect of the replication dilemma Sherman discusses. The Minneapolis researchers suggested that at least certain barriers to arrest should be removed (allowing warrantless arrests) and that "police should probably employ arrest in most cases of minor domestic violence" (p. 98). Sherman suggests that the principal impediment to making the strongest (mandatory) pro-arrest recommendation was the generalizability of the findings across different groups of people, but that the problem was not sufficiently great to prevent an arrest-preferred recommendation. This argument shows a striking inconsistency, for without specifying the conditions under which backfiring is likely to occur (something that could not be done with the Minneapolis data), a preferred arrest policy could do nearly as much damage as a mandatory arrest policy. One simply cannot compensate for a generalizability problem by compromising between treatment options. One should not confuse differences among research subjects with differences among treatment regimens.

The replication dilemma is a daunting challenge for social science, and Sherman is to be commended for wrestling with it. However, the book falls short in providing the kinds of principles that should guide policy analysis. Sherman's is an unconvincing bias to action in what he regards as a knowledge vacuum, even if the evidence is weak. His calculus repeatedly gives heaviest weight to opportunities lost by *not* acting on findings and tends to ignore or undervalue the potential costs of those policies—both in terms of backfiring and in terms of lost opportunities to pursue other options. Sherman argues that trial and error based on the best evidence currently available is the best way to proceed. That is to say that, rather than taking the failure to find substantial support for the Minneapolis findings in subsequent replications as a lesson learned about premature and imprudent recommendations, he transforms vice to virtue, suggesting that such practice is a rule that future policy analysis should adopt.

The perils of this practice are evident in one of the recommendations set forth in this volume. Based on the findings of a deterrent effect in Omaha when warrants were issued for absent offenders, Sherman encourages law enforcement officials to adopt this policy— despite the explicit unwillingness of the Omaha researchers to do so. Sherman finds this single study compelling, despite the absence of a persuasive theoretical explanation for why the threat of an arrest (as experienced through notification by letter that a warrant had been issued) would show so decisive a deterrent effect when the actual experience of an arrest failed to do so in the same study.[1] And even without a test for backfire effects in the offender-absent experiment, Sherman rather cavalierly concludes, "there is little reason to predict that the method would backfire" (p. 257)—despite the fact that in all three of the *arrest* experiments where interaction effects with the offender's stake in conformity were explored, backfire effects *were* found. A fair and prudent reading of the available evidence reported in this book would seem to weigh the risks and costs of the offender-absent warrant procedures as too great to pursue without further testing.

Finally, there is a practical limitation to Sherman's take-the-best-evidence-and-run-with-it approach to policy making. It will inevitably generate a policy zigzagging that requires of police departments and policy makers a much greater flexibility than is evident in most communities. It suggests a societal willingness to submit social policy to the vagaries of social science that simply is not there at present. When policies about the application of criminal sanctions change, they do so principally because they are responding to substantial societal shifts in the degree of moral outrage or tolerance toward a given act, not scientific evidence about the impact of those sanctions, to be sure a source of frustration to the author of *Policing Domestic Violence* (p. 265).[2] The feasibility of Sherman's approach thus rests with the willingness and capacity of society or its change agents to revolutionize the fundamental mechanisms by which support for police is mobilized. Later, we will turn to the prospects for effecting such changes in the police environment.

THE LEGAL TRANSFORMATION OF POLICE

If Sherman and Goldstein search for ways to make police more effective at solving problems, Skolnick and Fyfe seek ways to keep police from creating them. Both authors have published extensively on various aspects of police misbehavior and have distinguished themselves a scholars and experts who wish to hold police accountable, first and foremost, to the rule of the law. Their book, *Above the Law*, focuses on a topic much in the news of late. The authors set for themselves the tasks of understanding the occasions for excessive force, how its occurrence can be explained, and how it can be remedied. The Rodney King incident and the Los Angeles Police Department are at the epicenter of the authors' arguments, although they draw on cases from other cities, as well as historical, legal, and social science studies.

Their argument in a nutshell is this. Current patterns in police abuse of their authority to use physical force can be traced through America's history to vigilante justice (especially lynchings), abuse forms of in-custody interrogation of suspects (the "third degree"), and the inept, biased, and oppressive handling of large civil disorders. Although police excessive force occurs today in a variety of forms and contexts, it shares with these antecedents an underlying fear and disdain of outgroups, such as racial minorities, the underclass, and the unconventional. That is, police brutality today is a means for the amplification, under color of law, of some of American society's worst impulses.

According to Skolnick and Fyfe, policing serves as particularly fertile ground for the enduring expression of these proclivities because of (a) the culture of policing that isolates officers from those they are sworn to serve, (b) the well-ingrained vision of the police as soldiers engaged in anything-goes war against crime, and (c) police leaders who have achieved virtual autonomy from local electoral reins of government and who reinforce rather than discourage the above two inclinations in their subordinates. The answers to these problems are (a) administrative reforms, such as reducing the high degree of special units in police agencies; (b) using civil suits and civil rights prosecutions to punish departments as well as individuals who fail to correct abuse of force problems; (c) establishing stronger accountability to the public through civilian review boards; and (d) a variety of initiatives to renew the police, such as reorienting department policies to protection of life, implementing community and problem-oriented policing, civilianizing certain police functions, and a police cadet corps that puts more college-educated people in uniform.

The authors' assertion about the driving force behind police abuse of their coercive authority suggests a profound and disturbing problem, not just for American police, but for all of American society:

> America is, culturally speaking, two countries. One is urban, cosmopolitan, and multicultural. It suffers disproportionately from crime, gang violence, poverty, and homelessness. The other is suburban, relatively safe, relatively prosperous, and—most important—unicultural...America is a divided nation, and cops are perched perilously on the divide. (pp. xi, xv)

Their analysis suggests that police brutality persists, in no small part, because it is a contemporary manifestation of America's racist, classist history, in which police have been, and remain, active participants. They allow that both society generally and the police specifically have curbed some of the most abusive aspects of this past, but that the King episode and other evidence suggest that these forces are still at work.

The Skolnick/Fyfe vision of a transformed police is one of an institution that takes the lead, that guides us to what Lincoln called the "better angels of our nature." Theirs is a vision of a lawful police who place highest value on the protection of human life, whether the wronged or the wrongdoer's. Their challenge is to find ways to refashion police to fit this mold when so many social forces pressure them to follow their and society's "lesser" angels.

Despite their powerful opening indictment of the broader social forces at work in America, Skolnick and Fyfe focus on what is wrong with the *internal* matters of police organization: the police culture, the police mission, and the top police leadership. The authors argue that the way to making policing better than society's lesser angels is to find ways to make police more open to their "better" ones. This is to be accomplished by demolishing those features of the organization that have obstructed access to police by various institutions of improvement. They note, with approval, that some barriers have already been lowered. For example, appellate court rulings in the late 1970s have substantially increased citizens' access to civil remedies against *departments* that fail to address excessive force through adequate policies, supervision, and training. Among those obstructions advocated for future demolition are agency specialization that places high value on cops as warriors against crime, chiefs' autonomy from external control, a disciplinary system that relieves supervisors of any responsibility for reviewing and correcting instances of excessive force, and recruitment practices that keep the police force from being racially and culturally representative of the community it serves. New or revitalized institutions of police improvement advocated by the authors include a U.S. Department of Justice that is energized to respond thoroughly and vigorously to civil rights complaints, civilian review boards, hierarchical accountability for officer performance, strengthened professional review of excessive force complaints, community and problem-oriented policing, civilianized "para-police," and more college-educated people.

Notably absent from their prescriptions for change are broad programs to transform the underlying race, cultural, and social class schisms that they identify as the root of the excessive force problem. Theirs is a plan to ensure that the police do not exacerbate these problems, but, inasmuch as possible, serve to meliorate them, providing in a less-than-just society a refuge of justice under law, not above it. If it has become fashionable in the 1990s to embrace gingerly a constrained hopefulness about the capacity of government to address problems such as these, *Above the Law* is well timed. Whether it makes a convincing case is another matter.

At the outset, the reader needs a good sense of what excessive force means, yet such a definition is not forthcoming. The authors distinguish two types of excessive force: brutality, which is "conscious and venal," and unnecessary force, which is due to "ineptitude or insensitivity" (p. 19). Although they provide a useful discussion of what constitutes force and its various levels (pp. 37–42), they fail to offer a clear definition of "excessive," thus rendering hazy all discussion of what it means for police to be excessively forceful.

The book's title and tenor lead the reader to presume that by excessive force Skolnick and Fyfe mean that force not authorized by law. Such an approach would seem to call for careful attention to the various ways in which the law illuminates what constitutes excessive force, but such a discussion is not offered, even though experts, including the authors, acknowledge that the law is neither simple nor clear about what police force is and is not permissible (Bittner, 1970; Reiss, 1968; Cheh, 1992).

The book's implicit legal definition of excessive force also excludes consideration of another, and in many respects, more rigorous standard of performance—that of the craft of policing (Bittner, 1983).[3] Klockars (1992) suggests that "'excessive force' should be defined as the use of any more force than a highly skilled police officer would find necessary to use in that particular situation" (p. 10). Setting aside the practical difficulties of knowing in advance what a highly skilled officer would actually do in a given situation, we find Klockars's definition more useful because, like Bittner, he refuses to be satisfied with what merely passes legal muster. It allows any system of training, review, and correction to address what undoubtedly accounts for the far more frequent instances of unnecessary use of force (the consequences of which can be as dire as the illegal use of force)—even if they are not as morally deplorable.

The many cases of egregious misuse of force vividly detailed in *Above the Law* will surely excite outrage in all but the most enured readers, but in a sense, they constitute the "easy" cases that come from bad or twisted cops in administrative environments that quite predictably communicated a sense of tolerance of such behavior. It is not enough to flush from policing these officers and their commanders who permit it, for if we could do so, we would still leave unattended the much greater amount of unnecessary force that occurs among the well-intentioned.

One might also expect in a work of this scope that some effort would be undertaken to estimate the frequency with which police apply excessive force. While this is an undeniably difficult task, there is research dating back to the mid-1960s that provides some sense of the incidence of police use of force generally and excessive force in particular (see Adams, 1992, for a review). Unfortunately, no such estimates are offered in *Above the Law*, except to suggest that in Los Angeles the problem must be rampant if Rodney King's police assailants could deliver their blows before twenty-some officers without fear of being reported.

Several chapters of *Above the Law* place police excessive force in a historical perspective. The chapter on lynchings argues that some instances of police brutality today are analogous to vigilante justice of the past: both are shielded by legal authority,[4] both are expressions of fear and hatred of outgroups, and both justify their actions as a corrective to a legal system unable to act properly (p. 24). Although they amply illustrate these parallels, they do not show the historical linkages that they claim exist—how and why lynching was transformed into contemporary forms of police brutality. This is unfortunate, for there may be something to learn from this about how certain undesirable police practices evolve or "mutate." Their analysis only supplies evidence of some correlation or historical similarities; the etiology remains opaque.

They do a better job with the evolution of police practice in in-custody interrogations—from the brutal third degree of the past to the psychologically sophisticated and deceptive techniques of contemporary interrogation. The disappearance of the third degree is credited to the work of blue ribbon commissions and reformers, and especially to appellate courts that over several decades forbade brutal interrogation practices. Despite their obvious conviction that the courts played a critical role in what they regard as a success story, the authors draw no lessons to apply to contemporary police, and they make no effort to reconcile this assessment with one expressed later, that "the general conception of the courts' influence on police activity is exaggerated" (p. 194). If courts could bring about the demise of the third degree, could they now do the same for other forms of excessive force?

The authors' discussion of the causes of police brutality does more to present propositions that actually submit them to empirical test. It is virtually impossible to test the proposition that the "police culture" is a cause of brutality because, as the authors describe it, it has lone been a pervasive aspect of all American police organizations. The war-on-crime ethos may be more readily testable since it seems likely that there is significant variation from department to department in the degree to which management exhorts and reinforces the "thin blue line" mentality. And certainly, the extent to which autonomous, insular, rogue chiefs account for high rates of excessive force is testable although there will be few cities that can currently match the three cases discussed in this book (Daryl Gates in Los Angeles, Harold Breier in Milwaukee, and Frank Rizzo in Philadelphia). If reliable cross-department data on police use of excessive force are ever developed, these macro-level explanations can be tested.

However, the more remarkable phenomenon is the great degree of variation in use of force that arises among individual officers—even in the same department. Unfortunately, *Above the Law* does not give much attention to these individual-level explanations of police violence. The most well-developed theories in this area are by Toch, Grant, and Galvin (1975) and Muir (1977). These researchers find, in certain police officers, a psychological predilection to expressive violence although neither approach has been rigorously tested with large numbers of officers in a variety of departments.[5] The validity of employee screening and selection programs relies upon the merits of "predispositional" theories such as these, so there is ample policy as well as scholarly justification to explore these theories.

The authors' agenda for reform is a set of eclectic proposals loosely bound by the thread of "openness" (p. 266). A few enjoy a measure of empirical support; several enjoy little or none. One of the proposals for which the authors make a good case is the need for a vigorous effort by top police management to clarify and strengthen use of force policies, accompanied with the necessary structural reforms (accountability for performance up the chain of command, an effective internal fact-finding process, and strict, but nonarbitrary discipline). Most of the hard evidence of this comes from studies of the use of lethal force (see Sherman, 1983; Geller and Scott, 1990, for a review). Skolnick and Fyfe note that translating administrative reform into real changes at the street level requires some luck (a crisis that enables a chief to shake things up), a supportive external environment, and a great deal of skill in taking advantage of such opportunities. Their comparison of Patrick Murphy's effectiveness in fighting corruption in New York and the ineffectiveness of Vollmer in Los Angeles and Wilson in Chicago is instructive because it makes clear just how necessary political savvy is in effecting substantial organizational change.

On the other hand, a number of proposals in *Above the Law* are not very convincing although many are fashionable among reformers today. Community and problem-oriented policing have become the most popular touchstones of police progressivism although most of the literature focuses on their potential for reducing crime and disorder, not correcting police behavior (but cf. Toch and Grant, 1991). Skolnick and Fyfe also see in these reforms the potential to reduce excessive force, but absent from their brief discussion is an articulation of how their adoption will transform those aspects of street-level decision making that are relevant to officers' use of force. This is indeed problematic because, if anything, community policing would seem to place street-level officers at greater risk to be responsive to vigilante values in "defended" neighborhoods (Bayley, 1988, p. 232; Mastrofski, 1988a, p. 50). Some discussion of how the "rule of the community" can be reconciled with the "rule of law" would have been welcome.

Others have offered a bare-bones description of how community policing is expected to reduce police brutality, arguing that community policing will provide an effective antidote to police stereotyping, which begets unnecessary police violence associated with race and lifestyle characteristics of citizens (Trojanowicz, 1991). Detailed knowledge of the people on the beat is undeniably a prerequisite to achieving economy in the use of force (Muir, 1977, chap. 10; Mastrofski, 1983), but there still remains the challenge of finding ways to impart the moral imperative of economy in the use of force, and the skill to do it. Much of the book places responsibility for moral motivation on the police chief, but the authors appear to have overlooked an opportunity to discuss the state of the art of using force effectively but minimally. Had they given less space to condemning obviously deplorable police practices and more to specific methods for preventing and correcting a wide range of excessive force situations, the police readership of this volume might be more receptive to it. Critical to such a discussion is understanding how police officers obtain and use information in situations that could erupt into violence. Academic discussions of this are available (Binder and Scharf, 1980; Reiss, 1980), and could be profitably translated into language that the nonacademic audience of *Above the Law* could appreciate. Further, a consideration of the merits of various violence reduction and avoidance techniques would seem to be essential to reducing excessive force that is legal but, nonetheless, more than necessary.

One of the specific proposals made by Skolnick and Fyfe is to reduce the degree of specialization within a police force. They assert that specialized crime control units focus on only a narrow aspect of policing, becoming obsessed with generating impressive statistics instead of solving community problems, and are more willing to take legal shortcuts to look good, thus increasing the incident of excessive force. If that is so, it seems to us that these faults are due more to failures of top management and unit leadership than anything inherent in specialization. If specialization has an impact because it focuses officers' energies and attention, it can be used as easily to sensitize and reward officers for economy in the use of force as it can to facilitate abuse of authority.

Their support for civilian review boards is even more puzzling because they acknowledge that evidence suggests that such boards are unlikely to improve the quality of fact-finding or disciplinary action for citizens' abuse-of-force allegations. The basis for their recommendation is that the public wants it and will trust it more than it will trust a strictly internal review process (p. 230). This is a remarkable recommendation in light of the favorable consideration they give professional review of officer performance by boards of peers who come from *outside* the department (pp. 196–198). One wonders why the authors would find a Simi Valley civilian review board's decisions on these matters preferable to those of a Simi Valley jury's.

There is evidence to support the authors' point that civilian review is neither as punitive of police defendants as its opponents claim nor as productive in rooting out police brutality as its advocate assert (Perez and Muir, 1992). Civilian review will undoubtedly enhance the legitimacy of the police oversight process in many communities, at least for a while, but will probably have little consequence for the quality of justice. That is because the major challenge in reviewing most complaints about police excessive force is establishing the facts, the proliferation of amateur video recorders notwithstanding. Here the authors' concluding recommendation is routine police videotaping of high-risk situations. This proposal will likely receive considerable attention because it offers an appealing technical solution, but this sort of evidentiary tool can be manipulated and misleading (Surette, 1992). Perhaps the weakest link in the evidence-gathering chain is that which immediately follows the incident (interviews of participants, witnesses, and physical evidence) at the scene—for which first-line supervisors are responsible, but not necessarily well prepared or motivated to do a thorough job. If reformers devoted as much effort to improving this part of the process as they do mulling the meaning of evidence (by whatever body of reviewers), more than community relations might be improved.

Among the more baffling of their proposals for addressing the excessive force problem are civilianizing some police service to citizens and the police cadet corps. Using civilians for certain activities (routine report taking, serving as translators) has obvious cost-cutting advantages, but the authors fail to demonstrate how this will reduce the incidence of excessive force.[6] The cadet corps idea rests on the assumption that forces leavened with more college-educated youth will be less inclined to abuse their authority to use force. This is a hypothesis that, as far as we know, enjoys no substantial empirical support (Mastrofski, 1990) although it comports with the middle-class assumption that a liberal college education makes a significant contribution to civilizing the nation's youth. It seems quite appropriate to characterize, as the authors do, the cadet corps as police "gentrification" (p. 262), but it is not at all clear that a gentrified police will have the kind of appreciation and understanding of the streets, neighborhoods, and cultures most at risk to experience excessive police violence. The risk in the push to require a baccalaureate to get a badge is that reformers and their audiences will be deluded that college education is the sine qua non of good policing. At present, the contributions of a college education to police performance are undocumented although it will undoubtedly continue to serve as one of many "circumlocutions" that help us accommodate to the uncomfortable paradox of needing an institution that has the authority and capacity for "nonnegotiable" violence in a society that places highest value on achieving peace by peaceful means (Bittner, 1970).

TRANSFORMING POLICE ORGANIZATIONS AND THEIR ENVIRONMENTS

The three volumes reviewed above offer an interesting overview of the larger picture of police reform at the end of the 20th century. A useful framework for showing the relationship of these volumes to each other comes from organizational theory, differentiating organizations by their environments. Because environments apply pressure to organizations, they heavily influence how the organizations are structured, how they present themselves, and what activities they undertake to secure and sustain resources and legitimacy. Police organizations, like others, exist in certain kinds of environments, and it is the character of these environments that is the target for change of police reform advocates such as those reviewed above. To understand the meaning of the transformations they propose, as well as their prospects, we first need to review briefly different types of environments, drawing heavily on the general overview provided by Scott (1992, chap. 6).

Two dimensions of organizational environment are *technical* and *institutional*, each referring to a different kind of pressure to which an organization must respond if it is to survive:

> *Technical environments* are those in which organizations produce a product or service that is exchanged in a market such that they are rewarded for effective and efficient performance. These are environments that foster the development of rationalized structures that efficiently coordinate technical work....By contrast, *institutional environments* are characterized by the elaboration of rules and requirements to which individual organizations must conform in order to receive legitimacy and support. In institutional environments, organizations are rewarded for utilizing correct structures and processes, not for the quantity and quality of their outputs. (Scott, 1992, p. 132)

Some organizations exist in environments where the technical dimension is strongly developed, but the institutional environment is weak. General manufacturing firms, for example, tend to operate in such an environment. The firm's product and performance are well defined, and the technical knowledge about how to produce the product (transforming inputs to outputs) is well established. Organizations in this environment succeed to the extent that they meet the technical demands of that environment, which may involve coping with the availability of resources, fluctuations in market demand, how the competition is organized, and so on.

The reverse image of this environment is the strong institutional/weak technical environment. Here the nature of the organization's product or service and what constitutes performance are not readily specified in ways that are easy to confirm empirically; the technical capacity of such organizations to produce this service is not known or well established. However, these organizations succeed in their well-developed institutional environment to the extent that they conform to structures (procedures, programs, and policies) that are widely accepted as being right even though the relationship of these structures to actual performance is not well established. Types of organizations that fall into this category include schools, mental health clinics, legal agencies, and other human service agencies that operate in a noncompetitive context—including police departments.

Some organizations operate in environments that are strongly developed in both their technical and institutional aspects: utilities, banks, and general hospitals, for example. They must produce tangible products and services requiring a high degree of technical sophistication. The appraisal of performance is relatively straightforward in terms of effectiveness and reliability. However, there are equally strong pressures to conform to certain symbolic forms that are accepted as right: for example, structures that signify organizational accountability (hospital uniforms and job titles and that differentiate workers by rank and function) and structures that signify professional accountability (medical malpractice review panels).[7]

Crank and Langworthy (1992) offer an in-depth discussion of police organizations' highly developed institutional environment. The quantity and quality of services provided by police are hard to document, at least in terms of the "mission" that has been used to obtain resources and legitimacy since the 1930s, crime fighting (Manning, 1977). Crime prevented or eliminated is hard to measure, and it is harder still to establish what police efforts have to do with it. Effectiveness and efficiency in crime control have little meaning in a noncompetitive environment. Police departments represent a class of organizations that Meyer and Zucker (1989) characterize as "permanently failing" because, despite their inability to demonstrate technical efficiency and effectiveness, they usually survive. Police departments, therefore, achieve legitimacy by responding to what have become widely held expectations about certain structures that signify such performance: for example, specialist crime squads, crime control technological paraphernalia and strategies (e.g., preventive patrol and 911 rapid response systems), steep supervisory hierarchies (to give the appearance of top-down control), and elaborated rules and reports. Indeed, the mere presence of a police officer in the neighborhood is highly desired by the public and has become synonymous with public safety.[8] Despite the absence of evidence to document the merits of these structures in a technical sense, certain myths evolve (many promulgated or "enacted" by the police themselves) that justify the activities and structures of police organizations to their environment.

All three books reviewed in this essay question the myths that have for some time served as the basis of the police response to their institutional environment. Goldstein's critique of "traditional" police management, street-level tactics, and organizational structures constitutes an effort to weaken the environmental pressure for the institutionally elaborated aspects of departmental "operating efficiency"—such as the obsession with fast response times that seldom improve the prospects of making an arrest or reducing crime. His proposal for a problem-oriented police, if accomplished, would require the transformation of the character of the police technical environment. His vision of a results-oriented police, one whose performance is measured in terms of the extent to which it solves specific community problems, is clearly a call to develop the technical environment of police.[9]

Sherman's perspective also seeks to strengthen the technical environment of policing. His book deflates the short-lived but eagerly embraced (at least by some) myth that police arrests are an effective specific deterrent to misdemeanor spouse abuse.[10] The volume constitutes an example of how to expand police science and knowledge about the technical capacity of police to solve one type of problem.

On the other hand, Skolnick and Fyfe's proposals call, not for a transformation of the police technical environment, but for a transformation of the police institutional environment. The Rodney King incident crystalizes for them a legitimacy crisis faced by police around the country. Crank and Langworthy (1992, pp. 355–360) note that periodically police departments experience crises of legitimacy, such as the King episode, and that the crises are generally resolved by the ritual degradation and dismissal of the chief whose leadership personified the old institutional norms—to be replaced by one whose reputation was built on the new ones, such as community policing (p. 359).

It is neither police effectiveness nor efficiency that shapes the Skolnick/Fyfe support of community and problem-oriented policing and the array of other reforms they suggest, but rather conformance to the rule of law, a central theme of the Wickersham Commission's recommendations, and one that subsequently sustained progressive reformers for some time (Klockars 1988, p. 241). Skolnick and Fyfe revisit and urge the revitalization of the law as a sustaining institutional structure in the police environment. They prescribe a variety of programs and strategies to accomplish this, such as community policing, p-o-p, and civilian review boards. Ironically, enthusiasm for these reforms grows precisely *because* of the perceived failures of the rule of law. Whether these new institutional forms are robust enough to satisfy simultaneously both of these contradictory themes remains to be seen,[11] but one cannot appreciate too much the power of institutional forms that can be all things to all people.

What are the prospects for such transformations as those advanced in these three volume? Unfortunately, organizational theory is not as well developed on the evolution of environments as one might wish, and there is a hesitancy to generalize a priori about the general direction of change without empirical investigation (Scott, 1992, p. 148). But considered in the broader framework described above, the strengthening of policing's technical environment, for which Goldstein and Sherman call, requires prodigious change. It is a change not unlike the radical transformation of the general hospital's environment in the early to mid-20th century, a product of the larger set of forces at work on the medical profession (Starr, 1982).

Police leaders who encourage the community to hold their feet to the fire of actually solving problems must have well-defined, measurable outcomes or products and the knowledge and technology to accomplish them with some degree of reliability. Police organizations do seem to be awakening to the desirability of research and evaluation although the resources and efforts are modest in nearly all (Klockars and Harver, 1993). And not much beyond its infancy is the scientific research base of policing and criminology, which has of late done more to discredit the old police crime control technologies than validate new alternatives. This suggests that, at least for the foreseeable future, p-o-p and community policing cannot serve as *technical* sources of legitimacy. Police chiefs who market their p-o-p and community policing programs strictly on the basis of performance are likely to raise public expectations well beyond their organization's capacity to deliver, exposing them to their own crises of legitimacy.

The greater likelihood is that police will embrace the new reforms and use them as new institutional myths to replace the old ones, sustaining the police in a time of resource scarcity and threats to "reinvent" government. Indeed, several scholars have suggested that community policing is ideally suited and timed to do this (Bayley, 1988; Klockars, 1988; Manning, 1988; Mastrofski, 1988a). If police cannot reduce crime, they can at least get credit for reducing the fear of crime, making people feel better about their neighborhoods and their police even if they are no safer. Putting police and public safety at the nexus of community organizing is an ideal strategy to ensure that the police do not lose in the contest over what remains in the dwindling municipal treasuries of center cities and even suburbs. As many cities become increasingly culturally heterogeneous, differences in the quality and quantity of police service are justified by "customizing" services and "solving problems."

We do not mean to imply that all or even most police chiefs and elected officials will undertake these reforms out of some cynical motivation to manipulate appearances (although some will). Most will do so out of the desire to make police, and local government generally, work better. But the intense public pressure for problem-solving government will likely come hard aground on the shoals of limited capacity. The police, whose services are much valued by taxpayers, have no clearly demonstrated crime control capacity in the way that various medical organizations can demonstrate their contributions to health. Police enjoy large budgets because they perform to standards that are institutionally elaborated: simply being there when we call for them, for example. Eschewing these institutional structures without the organizational infrastructure and technology to accomplish problem solving seems likely to drive the police to enact and embrace new institutional forms that in themselves signify a department that is doing the "right things": civilian review, ministations, foot and bicycle patrol, drug education programs, crime prevention community partnerships, total quality management, and so on.

The great risk in pursing, as Sherman suggests, a rigorous program of empirical evaluation is that either measures and standards of performance will be trivialized or these new programs will be shown to be not so effective either. The latter is a risk that is absolutely necessary if policing is to experience a sustained period of substantial technical improvement, but we doubt very much that those technical gains will be what sustains police organizations during that time. The art for police leadership will be finding ways to advance in the technical domain, with all the risks that innovation, experimentation, and evaluation raise, while at the same time shaping and meeting the expectations of whatever new institutional forms are necessary to sustain their organization.

NOTES

1. The Omaha researchers offered three post hoc theories, were able to conduct an empirical assessment of two, and found support for neither. The third was not testable within this study. It was that the warrant served as a "sword of Damocles," that the unknown and unexpected penalty associated with the warrant was more threatening than an already-experienced immediate arrest. Interestingly, only half of the group that received such a warrant were actually arrested.

2. One might argue that there is precedence in the field of medicine for the achievement of public policy driven by scientific findings. Although there are many instances where this is apparently so (e.g., the decline in smoking due to the intensive publicity about health risks), it has been persuasively argued that the fundamental structure and practice of American medicine has been driven at least as much by social forces as science (Starr, 1982).

3. Muir (1977) notes that police craftsmanship places a high value on economy in the use of force, even when greater force is legally justifiable. This is not just for the protection of the public, but because coercion, especially in its physical manifestations, carries high risks for the officer for backfiring immediately or at some future time.

4. On the face this claim would appear to be false, since vigilantes are by definition volunteer citizens acting to suppress and punish crime without any legal authority to do so. However, Skolnick and Fyfe argue that in many instances police officers participated in mob actions, condoned them, or declined to intervene.

5. The best study to date, with data of limited value for these purposes, finds little support for the notion that officers' characteristics or attitudes have a substantively significant effect on the officer's inclination to use or abuse force (Worden, 1992).

6. See Klockars (1988) for a review of the limitations of civilianization as a community policing strategy.

7. There are organizations that operate in environments that are weakly developed in both their technical and institutional aspects (e.g., restaurants, health clubs, and child care), but they are irrelevant to our discussion.

8. The most recent visible manifestation of the institutionalization of this perspective is given in the Clinton administration's proposal to "put 100,000 additional cops on the street" during its term.

9. Goldstein does not propose to make the technical environment of the police more competitive although other p-o-p advocates argue that it is a "corporate strategy" for maintaining "market share" in the face of competition from private sector security (see Manning, 1992, for a discussion).

10. As we noted earlier, Sherman points out that the transformation of this myth into mandatory arrest laws was due more to its conformance with what reformers accepted as correct. The resistance of these laws to adapt to the findings of the new, more extensive scientific evidence reinforces the notion that the institutional environment of police remains far better developed than its technical environment.

11. For a discussion of the compatible and incompatible elements of community policing and the rule of law, see Mastrofski and Greene (1993).

REFERENCES

ADAMS, KENNETH. (1992). "Measuring the Prevalence of Police Abuse of Force." In *And Justice for All*, William A. Geller and Hans Toch (Eds.). Washington, D.C.: Police Executive Research Forum. Unpublished manuscript.

BAYLEY, DAVID H. (1988). "Community Policing: A Report From the Devil's Advocate." In *Community Policing: Rhetoric or Reality*, Jack R. Greene and Stephen D. Mastrofski (Eds.). New York: Praeger, pp. 225–238.

BAYLEY, DAVID H. and EGON BITTNER. (1989). "Learning the Skills of Policing." In *Critical Issues in Policing: Contemporary Readings*, edited by Roger G. Dunham and Geoffrey P. Alpert. Prospect Heights, Ill.: Waveland, pp. 87–110.

BINDER, ARNOLD and PETER SCHARF. (1980). "The Violent Police-Citizen Encounter." *Annals* 452:111–21.

BITTNER, EGON. (1970). *The Functions of the Police in Modern Society*. Rockville, Md.: National Institutes of Health.

_____. (1983). "Legality and Workmanship: Introduction to Control in the Police Organization." In *Control in the Police Organization*, Maurice Punch (Ed.). Cambridge, Mass.: MIT Press, pp. 1–11.

CHEH, MARY M. (1992). "Judicial Review of Alleged Police Brutality: State of the Criminal and Civil Law." In *And Justice for All*, William A. Geller and Hans Toch (Eds.). Washington, D.C.: Police Executive Research Forum. Unpublished manuscript.

CRANK, JOHN P. and ROBERT LANGWORTHY. (1992). "An Institutional Perspective of Policing." *Journal of Criminal Law and Criminology* 83:338–363.

FOGELSON, ROBERT F. (1977). *Big City Police*. Cambridge, Mass.: Harvard University Press.

GELLER, WILLIAM A. and MICHAEL S. SCOTT. (1990). "Deadly Force: What We Know." In *Thinking About Police: Contemporary Readings*, Carl B. Klockars and Stephen D. Mastrofski (Eds.). New York: McGraw-Hill,, pp. 446–476.

GOLDSTEIN, HERMAN. (1977). *Policing a Free Society*. Cambridge, Mass.: Ballinger.

_____. (1979). "Improving Policing: A Problem-Oriented Approach." *Crime & Delinquency* 25:236–258.

KLOCKARS, CARL B. (1988). "The Rhetoric of Community Policing." In *Community Policing: Rhetoric or Reality*, Jack R. Greene and Stephen D. Mastrofski (Eds.). New York: Praeger, pp. 239–258.

_____. (1992). "A Theory of Excessive Force and Its Control." In *And Justice for All*, William A. Geller and Hans Toch (Eds.). Washington, D.C.: Police Executive Research Forum. Unpublished manuscript.

KLOCKARS, CARL B., and WILLIAM E. HARVER. (1993). "The Production and Consumption of Research in Police Agencies in the United States." Report to the National Institute of Justice, Grant #90-IJ-CX-0031, March.

LANE, ROGER. (1992). "Urban Police and Crime in the Nineteenth-Century America." In *Modern Policing*, Michael Tonry and Norval Moris (Eds). Chicago: University of Chicago Press, pp. 1–50.

LOWI, THEODORE J. (1969). *The End of Liberalism: Ideology, Policy, and the Crisis of Public Authority*. New York: Norton.

MANNING, PETER K. (1977). *Police Work: The Social Organization of Policing*. Cambridge, Mass.: MIT Press.

_____. (1988). "Community Policing as a Drama of Control." In *Community Policing: Rhetoric or Reality*, Jack R. Greene and Stephen D. Mastrofski (Eds.). New York: Praeger, pp. 27–45.

_____. (1992). "Economic Rhetoric and Policing Reform." *Criminal Justice Research Bulletin* 7:1–8.

MASTROFSKI, STEPHEN. (1983). "Police Knowledge of the Patrol Beat: A Performance Measure." In *Issues for the Eighties*, Richard R. Bennett (Ed.). Bevery Hills, Calif.: Sage, pp. 45–64.

_____. (1988a). "Community Policing as Reform: A Cautionary Tale." In *Community Policing: Rhetoric or Reality*, Jack R. Greene and Stephen D. Mastrofski (Eds.). New York: Praeger, pp. 47–67.

_____. (1988b). "Varieties of Police Governance in Metropolitan America." *Politics and Policy* 8:12–31.

_____. (1990). "The Prospects of Change in Police Patrol: A Decade in Review." *American Journal of Police* 9:1–79.

MASTROFSKI, STEPHEN D., and JACK R. GREENE. (1993). "Community Policing and the Rule of Law." In *Police Innovation and Control of the Police*, David Weisburd and Craig D. Uchida (Eds.). New York: Springer-Verlag, pp. 80–102.

MEYER, MARSHALL W., and LYNNE ZUCKER. (1989). *Permanently Failing Organizations*. Newbury Park, Calif.: Sage.

MUIR, WILLIAM K., Jr. (1977). *Police: Streetcorner Politicians*. Chicago: University of Chicago Press.

PEREZ, DOUGLAS, and WILLIAM K. MUIR, Jr. (1992). "Administrative Review of Alleged Police Brutality." In *And Justice for All*, edited by William A. Geller and Hans Toch (Eds.). Washington, D.C.: Police Executive Research Forum. Unpublished manuscript.

REISS, ALBERT, JR. (1968). "Police Brutality—Answers to Key Questions." *Trans-action* 5:10–19.

_____. (1980). "Controlling Police Use of Deadly Force." *Annals* 452:122–133.

_____. (1992). "Police Organization in the Twentieth Century." In *Modern Policing*, M. Tonry and N. Morris (Eds.). Chicago: University of Chicago Press, pp. 51–98.

SCOTT, W. RICHARD. (1992). *Organizations: Rational, Natural, and Open Systems*, 3rd ed. Englewood Cliffs, N.J.: Prentice-Hall.

SHERMAN, LAWRENCE W. (1983). "Reducing Police Gun Use: Critical Events, Administrative Policy and Organizational Change." In *Control in the Police Organization*, Maurice Punch (Ed.). Cambridge, Mass.: MIT Press, pp. 98–125.

_____. (1992). "Book Review: Problem-Oriented Policing." *Journal of Criminal Law and Criminology* 82:690–707.

STARR, PAUL. (1982). *The Social Transformation of American Medicine*. New York: Basic Books.

SURETTE, RAY. (1992). *Media, Crime and Justice: Images and Realities*. Pacific Grove, Calif.: Brooks/Cole.

TOCH, HANS, and J. DOUGLAS GRANT. (1991). *Police as Problem Solvers*. New York: Plenum.

TOCH, HANS, J. DOUGLAS GRANT, and R. T. GALVIN. (1975). *Agents of Change: Study in Police Reform*. Cambridge, Mass.: Schenkman.

TROJANOWICZ, ROBERT. (1991). "Community Policing Curbs Police Brutality." *Footprints* 3:1–3.

VOLLMER, AUGUST. (1930). "The Scientific Policemen." *American Journal of Police Science* 1:8–12.

WALKER, S. (1977). *A Critical History of Police Reform: The Emergence of Professionalism*. Lexington, Mass.: Lexington Books.

WORDEN, ROBERT E. (1992). "The 'Causes' of Police Brutality." In *And Justice for All*, William A. Geller and Hans Toch (Eds.). Washington, D.C.: Police Executive Research Forum. Unpublished manuscript.

QUESTIONS FOR DISCUSSION

1. Discuss the progressive reform that has been occurring in police organizations over the last two decades. Provide examples to support your response.

2. Discuss how transforming science and research can positively affect policing. Provide examples.

3. In what ways will the legal system contribute to changes in police work, particularly regarding police misconduct and brutality? Provide examples.

4. Discuss the difference between technical and institutional environments in police organizations.

5. Although it is difficult to predict how police organizations and the environment will change, the authors suggest several possible ways that police organizations are most likely to proceed. Discuss these possible changes.

14

PRIORITY PROSECUTION OF HIGH-RATE DANGEROUS OFFENDERS

Marcia R. Chaiken
Jan M. Chaiken

■ ■

This article examines a special prosecution program known as the career criminal program. The authors examine the specific practices used by this program to help prosecutors meet their goals. Chaiken and Chaiken seek to determine if the criteria used to determine a priority prosecution were consistent across jurisdictions and to assess which criteria were the most effective in classifying a case for priority prosecution. Prosecutors' reactions to priority prosecution programs are also examined.

Faced with high caseloads, long delays in the courts, and public demand for swifter and more effective justice, criminal justice practitioners must make hard choices in allocating resources. This *Research in Action* summarizes the results of a recent study conducted by the authors under the sponsorship of the National Institute of Justice.[1] It provides research findings about information district attorneys can use to focus attention on dangerous offenders who commit crimes at high rates.

The study examined official record data available to prosecutors in two jurisdictions to learn which items of information most accurately identified offenders as high-rate (committing crimes frequently) and dangerous (committing violent crimes). While much of the information usually available to prosecutors was found useful for identifying high-rate dangerous offenders, the study revealed that other commonly used information can be misleading or ineffective for purposes of identification. As with all studies based on data from a small number of jurisdictions, these findings require replication in other jurisdictions before they can be considered generally applicable.

PRIORITY PROSECUTION PROGRAMS

Almost all prosecutors deal with a wide variety of criminal offenders. They must regularly decide what kinds of offenders or offenses are to receive attention from the best or most experienced attorneys or from staff members with specialized training or knowledge. District attorneys around the country have established a variety of priority prosecution programs. Some focus on major narcotics dealers, organized crime figures, arsonists, or sex offenders; others concentrate on offenders whose victims are children, or on cases likely to entail lengthy or complex trials.

A popular form of priority prosecution program—and the type upon which our research focused—is commonly known as career criminal prosecution. The earliest career criminal programs were established over 10 years ago and were targeted primarily to habitual offenders who had extensive records of felony convictions.[2] Since then, more than a hundred U.S. jurisdictions have adopted some form of priority prosecution for career criminals.[3]

Most types of priority prosecution programs are intended to help prosecutors meet the following goals:[4]

- Conviction on the most serious applicable charge—for example, conviction for burglary rather than possession of stolen property.
- Increased likelihood of incarceration of convicted offenders.
- Increased length of sentence.
- Increased pretrial detention.
- Reduced time until the case is disposed.

The specific practices used in prosecutors' priority prosecution programs vary among jurisdictions. However, the following procedures are commonly followed:[5]

- Close cooperation with police officers. Police alert prosecutors to arrestees who appear to warrant priority prosecution. In turn, to ensure the technical soundness of cases, attorneys advise police about practices such as obtaining warrants and collecting evidence.
- Screening of defendants. Records of defendants charged with or wanted for specific types of serious crimes are reviewed to determine if they meet specified criteria for priority prosecution.
- Assignment of experienced attorneys to prosecute cases selected for priority prosecution.
- Vertical prosecution. The same attorney is assigned to the case from the time it is first accepted for prosecution until the case is completed.
- Coalescing of cases. The same attorney is assigned to all pending cases involving the same defendant.
- Close supervision of selected cases by a senior prosecutor. Senior attorneys, typically program directors, frequently monitor the progress and procedures used in cases chosen for priority prosecution.
- Curtailment of plea negotiations. Attorneys seek prosecution for the most serious crime charged and do not allow "bargaining" for guilty pleas to lesser crimes and shorter sentences.
- Caseload reduction. Attorneys prosecuting priority cases are assigned relatively few other cases to prosecute.

DEFINING "CAREER CRIMINALS"

Although prosecutors in existing career criminal programs try to target certain types of defendants for priority prosecution, there is no uniform understanding across the country of what is meant by a "career criminal." In reality, three overlapping types of offender profiles could be called career criminals:

- Persistent offenders, also known as long-term offenders or habitual offenders, are those who commit crimes over a long period of time. This study included as persistent offenders all the offenders who had been committing crimes for at least one-third of their lifetimes.

- High-rate offenders are those who commit numerous crimes per year whenever free to do so (whether they have been doing so for many years or relatively recently). For example, an offender who commits 104 burglaries per year (an average of 2 burglaries per week) when not locked up is a high-rate offender.

- Dangerous offenders are those who commit crimes of violence, often injuring their victims. The study included in this category all those who were high-rate robbers or who had assaulted, threatened with a weapon, shot at, or tried to cut, beat, or strangle another person.

While some offenders fit into more than one category, others do not. For example, a 30-year-old who has committed occasional burglaries since age 17 would be categorized as a long-term persistent offender but not necessarily either high-rate or dangerous. A person who had committed three assaults, two robberies, and a burglary in the past month, however, would be both high-rate and dangerous.

In response to changing public concerns and growing research knowledge, many career criminal prosecution programs have gradually begun to focus on offenders who are both high-rate and dangerous. High-rate dangerous offenders—and how to identify them— are the topics of the remaining sections of this [article]. These offenders should receive career criminal prosecution whether or not they have been involved in crime for a long time. The high-rate dangerous offenders are a small proportion of all felony defendants.

Although some prosecutors still have programs for dealing with habitual offenders, some research evidence indicates that many criminals who persistently cycle in and out of the criminal justice system are not worth special attention from prosecutors: these offenders may commit relatively few crimes but get caught nearly every time they do.[6]

IDENTIFYING HIGH-RATE DANGEROUS OFFENDERS

The first step in priority prosecution of high-rate dangerous offenders is to select appropriate cases. Some cases are so obvious that little attention needs to be given to selection decisions. A defendant charged with 10 or 12 eye-witnessed robberies clearly qualifies as high-rate and dangerous. Most cases are not so clear cut. For example, should a defendant arrested for two separate robberies on the same day be classified as a high-rate dangerous offender? What of the defendant who held up five victims at gunpoint at a local convenience store at midnight? Selections often must depend on information obtained from several sources, such as rap sheets (records of past arrests and convictions), the police officer's arrest report, or the investigating police officer's report.

In some jurisdictions, selection decisions must follow strict guidelines established by State law or local regulations. (When the number of defendants who qualify under law exceeds program capacity, prosecutors may then use additional information to define a subset of defendants who will actually receive priority prosecution.)

In other programs the guidelines are less formal, and prosecutors have wider discretion in choosing candidates for priority prosecution. While some guidelines and discretionary information currently used to make priority prosecution decisions are in fact helpful in identifying high-rate dangerous offenders, this study found that other information is redundant or misleading.

Clearly, if prosecutors knew exactly how many and what types of crimes an offender had committed, classification would be simple. Instead, only limited data exist; a rap sheet, for example, will report only arrests and convictions—not crimes committed successfully and without detection. In a sense, then, the task in identifying high-rate dangerous offenders is one of using limited data to draw inferences about actual (but unreported) behavior. Simply stated, do the rap sheet and other available data create a profile of a person who—if all the unreported facts were known—would in fact be high-rate dangerous?

Which factors in the official sources commonly available to prosecutors most accurately identify those offenders who are in fact high-rate and dangerous? To answer this critical question, the research:

1. Analyzed information available to prosecutors for identifying arrested persons for priority prosecution.
2. Statistically compared it to data obtained from confidential self-reports from convicted offenders.

The accuracy of data from the self-reports was controlled to the maximum extent possible. Respondents were assured of confidentiality. Repetitive questions were used to check consistency of response. Analyses controlled for self-reports that did not contain consistent data.

INTERVIEWS WITH PROSECUTORS

In-depth research studies were carried out in Los Angeles County, California, and Middlesex County, Massachusetts. Selection procedures were also reviewed with prosecutors from a wide and diverse group of additional jurisdictions.

The Los Angeles Career Criminal Division exemplifies programs that operate under fairly rigid and restrictive selection rules and are carried out by a limited number of attorneys who follow cases from their initiation.

Priority prosecution cases in Middlesex County, by contrast, can be handled by a large number of designated senior assistant attorneys (not just those in a special unit).

Broader selection guidelines are used to target high-rate dangerous offenders, and cases can be selected for priority prosecution at any stage of their processing.

The two study sites also differ in size, resulting in differing levels of selectivity. The Los Angeles County District Attorney's Office is the largest in the United States, processing more than 100,000 criminal cases a year. Its Central Branch office, the locus of this study, handles the bulk of the county's most serious offenses. The Middlesex County office serves 54 cities and towns near Boston. It ranks number 42 in size among district attorneys' offices (in terms of the volume of cases handled) and processes 35,000 criminal cases a year.

In Los Angeles, the Career Criminal Division concentrates on a relatively small number of robbery and burglary defendants. In Middlesex County, a subset of defendants charged with robbery, burglary, rape, aggravated assault, homicide/murder, and drug sales receive priority prosecution.

In both sites, interviews and observation of attorneys who select cases for priority prosecution revealed the criteria they use in making their judgments and the procedures they follow. Attorneys then examined anonymous versions of cases that had previously been eligible for possible priority prosecution in either their own county or the other study site. Their responses were analyzed to determine the extent to which judgments were consistent between the two sites. This procedure also verified that the information about defendants and their offenses claimed to be taken into account actually had been taken into account.

The criteria used in the two study sites were also presented to career criminal program directors from many other counties in California for comments or additions. During the course of the study, researchers met informally with prosecutors from other States and discussed the information they used to select career criminals.

DEFENDANTS' REPORTS OF OFFENSES AND RECORDED DATA

The study collected data from and on 500 male defendants who were ultimately convicted. The sample included nearly all defendants selected for priority prosecution during the study period; they made up 17 percent of the sample. The remaining defendants selected for the study did not receive priority prosecution, but their charged offense—for example, robbery or burglary—was one of those targeted by the priority prosecution attorneys.

By examining records in these defendants' case folders, the study was able to code hundreds of items of data about them, their criminal history, and the instant offense. Since the researchers found the data in criminal justice agency records, obviously prosecuting attorneys had access to the same information. The wording of California State career criminal legislation, observations and interviews with prosecuting attorneys, and the results of prior research determined which items of data were coded.

Immediately after their cases were disposed, all defendants who had been selected for the study completed self-report questionnaires. The questionnaires asked about 10 types of crimes (e.g., robbery, burglary, assault)[7] that they might have committed in the period preceding their arrest, and their frequency of committing each of them.

Because the veracity of self-reports on these sensitive topics is questionable, analytical techniques have been developed to permit drawing valid conclusions from such data.

Although some of the respondents were untruthful in their survey responses, the quality of the defendants' data was the same or slightly better than that of data previously collected in similar surveys of jail and prison inmates who had several months to adjust to incarceration before completing the questionnaire.[8]

Although 500 defendants were interviewed, 12 were excluded from the study because they did not provide any usable self-report information about the numbers or types of crimes they had committed. Official record data were obtained for 452 of the remaining respondents; these 452 constitute the sample used in the analyses that compare official record data with self-reports.

WHAT THE STUDY FOUND

The study resulted in 10 major findings:

Finding 1.   Prosecutors evaluate separately the three dimensions of a defendant's criminality: rates of committing crimes, dangerousness, and persistence. They also consider other aspects of seriousness.

The prosecutors interviewed did not think of serious offenders as a homogenous category. Instead, they often judged separately whether a particular defendant committed crimes at high rates, whether he was dangerous, and then whether he was a persistent offender.

Additional categories of seriousness, not specifically addressed by the study, were also considered in some cases. For example, defendants were considered serious offenders worthy of priority prosecution if their crimes reflected "professionalism," such as careful planning involving several defendants for extremely high criminal gain. Other defendants considered serious enough for priority prosecution were involved in crimes receiving intense coverage by the media.

Finding 2.   Defendants who were identified as high-rate and dangerous by prosecutors in one site were also identified as high-rate and dangerous by prosecutors in the second site.

Despite wide differences in the selection criteria and procedures in the two study sites, the defendants actually selected for priority prosecution were remarkably similar across the two sites. However, the Los Angeles County prosecutors had a more restrictive view of the type of offender that is high-rate and dangerous. After the attorneys had reviewed the same group of anonymously presented cases, every defendant designated as high-rate and dangerous by the Los Angeles attorneys was also so characterized by the Middlesex County Attorneys. But the Middlesex County attorneys also evaluated as high-rate and dangerous some defendants who were considered less serious by the Los Angeles attorneys.

Finding 3.   Written office guidelines concerning selection criteria for "career criminals" promote consistency in deputy district attorneys' judgements about the kinds of defendants who are high-rate dangerous offenders.

The evaluations of the prosecutors are clearly shaped by their department policies. The more inclusive evaluations of the Middlesex County attorneys reflect the district attorney's policy of casting a wide net to prevent serious offenders from escaping punishment. The more restrictive evaluations of the attorneys in Los Angeles reflect their concentration on the most serious offenders among the many offenders who have committed serious crimes.

The study found that in offices where selection of "career criminals" must be justified using established criteria, attorneys have developed a consistent mental model of the information that is relevant for judging a defendant to be high-rate or dangerous. The career criminal selection criteria they work with daily enter into these judgments and into their general understanding of criminal behavior. The Middlesex County attorneys, who did not use mandated selection rules, were found to have varied views about what information indicates a defendant is high-rate or dangerous.

Finding 4.   Long-term persistent offenders may or may not be high-rate dangerous offenders. Habitual criminality should not be confused with high-rate dangerous criminality.

The study found that thinking about offenders in terms of persistent or habitual criminal behavior is probably more confusing than productive. Many different measures of "a rap sheet as long as your arm" are valid indicators of persistence, but they bear little relationship to the type of offender the priority prosecution units would like to target.

Some indicators of persistence are also indicators of high-rate or dangerous behavior, but if they are not listed in the findings below, they are not as strong as the listed factors. Other indicators of persistence, such as a large number of adult arrests for burglary, actually were found to be counterindicators of high-rate dangerous behavior.

Finding 5.   While some existing guidelines for identifying high-rate dangerous offenders are valid and useful, greater accuracy may be obtained through a two-stage screening process.

The study found that information used because of formal rules or State laws does help focus resources on high-rate, dangerous, and persistent offenders. Moreover, some of the discretionary criteria applied by prosecutors increase the accuracy of these selections. Additionally, other information available but not generally used by prosecutors can be used to hone even finer selections. In all, 31 indicators of high-rate dangerous offenders were found.

The research indicated that the best way to use this information in identifying high-rate dangerous offenders is to ask questions in two stages: First, who is high-rate? Then, of those, who is high-rate dangerous? The first stage is less accurate than the second, but the two stages together result in a practical and useful selection method.

Finding 6.   The strongest official-record indicators of high-rate offending in the two study sites were found if a defendant:

- Had a prior adult conviction for robbery, burglary, arson, forcible rape, sex crime involving a child, kidnapping, or murder.
- Was currently charged for three separate criminal transactions of burglary.
- Was wanted by the authorities for failure to complete a previous sentence (probation, parole, prison, or jail).
- Was on parole when arrested.
- Had one or more adult arrests for receiving stolen property.

- Was on pretrial release (bail or own recognizance) when arrested.
- Was known to have a drug problem.

The above indicators are listed generally in order of the accessibility and acceptability of the information to prosecutors for decisionmaking purposes.

Despite this, all the indicators, taken together, were not strongly associated with high-rate offending. The study sample, which included many defendants who had already been chosen for priority prosecution, contained a larger proportion (43 percent) of offenders classified as high-rate than is commonly found in offender populations. Yet, in common with earlier research,[9] this study did not find many items of information that are available to prosecutors and that validly and decisively distinguish high-rate offenders from others. One of the strongest of these indicators was the California legislatively mandated criterion listed first above (prior conviction for robbery, burglary, arson, etc.).

Several factors in the list are used as bases for enhancing sentences in some jurisdictions. Judges may impose longer sentences on convicted offenders who have failed to complete a previous sentence or who have violated their terms of parole or pretrial release. These factors may be particularly pertinent for triggering priority prosecution in those jurisdictions.

These seven indicators can be used to divide defendants into subgroups having widely divergent probabilities of being high-rate. In fact, defendants in the study sample who had any three or more of these characteristics had a greater than 90-percent chance of being high-rate. The selection rule based on this method was found to have very few false positives. Less than 2 percent of low-rate offenders in the sample would be classified as high-rate by this rule. But the selection rule would have many false negatives. It would not identify most defendants who are actually high-rate. For this reason, prosecutors who use these seven listed factors as a rough "first stage" screen for high-rate offenders should require no more than two of the seven factors to be positive.

Although in the study information about a defendant's drug problem could have been entered in the official records from various sources—such as probation reports or pretrial release investigation reports—more accurate information can be obtained from urine test results. However, a single positive drug test at the time of arrest may provide misleading information. The majority of arrestees test positive in many jurisdictions,[10] but only a small percentage of arrestees are high-rate offenders. Rather, the result of drug tests might be assembled over a period of time, covering multiple arrests. Defendants who have a persistent history of positive drug tests could then be considered to have a drug problem in the sense intended here—relatively long-term use of opiates or other addictive drugs.

Finding 7.   Once a group of high-rate offenders was identified, the subset of high-rate dangerous offenders could be identified using a small number of criteria that include elements of the instant crime. The criteria for such determination are the following:

- The defendant was wanted by the authorities for failure to complete a previous sentence.
- A knife was brandished or used to injure someone in the instant offense.

- A victim in the instant offense was female.
- The offense was committed to an outside public location (e.g., street, alley, parking lot).
- The defendant had one or more juvenile convictions for robbery (armed or unarmed).

These criteria are strongly related to high-rate dangerous offending, in contrast with the situation for high-rate offending (Finding 6). Further, they are much more powerful than personal characteristics (e.g., age at first arrest, race, employment) over which the defendant has little control at the time of arrest.

Although prosecutors have available to them numerous valid indicators of dangerousness, the five official-record items listed above are statistically nearly equal in value to using all valid indicators of high-rate dangerous offending found in the study. It may therefore be superfluous to collect information about all the possibly relevant data items and evaluate them as a means of screening defendants for priority prosecution.

Other factors—strong in themselves but not adding any significant information after taking the above five indicators into account—included victim injury and multiple current charges for robbery.

Purse-snatches or strong-arm street robberies are often considered by police and prosecutors to be less serious than inside robberies with the use of a gun. However, neither commission of crimes inside buildings nor gun use was found to distinguish high-rate offenders from others, or dangerous from less dangerous offenders.

All indicators of high-rate dangerous behavior identified in the study were drawn from criminal justice agency records. The defendants' self-reports were used only to classify them as high-rate, dangerous, persistent, or not.

Finding 8.   Several factors that are commonly perceived as indicative of high-rate dangerousness in fact proved not to be, and in some cases were counterindicators.

Our study found 23 factors not to be associated with high-rate dangerous offending. Examples include:

- Display or use of a gun to threaten a victim.
- Alcoholism.
- Number of prior arrests for drug distribution or possession.
- Number of adult convictions for assault, burglary, auto theft, robbery, or receipt of stolen property.
- Record of previous probation or parole revocations.
- Record of previous incarceration.

While prosecutors may wish to assign such cases for priority prosecution on other grounds, these findings suggest that such factors are not in themselves dependable indicators of high rate dangerousness or of persistence.

Finding 9.   Some factors may preclude the selection and priority prosecution of defendants who are in fact dangerous offenders:

- An instant charge for a crime that can carry only light penalties. Even if the defendant is recognized as a high-rate dangerous offender due to past violent offenses, prosecutors would be legally unable to obtain a severe sentence for a minor new offense. For example, the study found a defendant with a long juvenile and adult record for robberies and assaults who was not recommended for priority prosecution because the current charge involved a single breaking and entering in an unoccupied business establishment. The case was satisfactorily handled by the assistant district attorney who originally received it, and priority prosecution resources could not have yielded a more severe sentence.
- Constraints on resources for prosecution. In Los Angeles, because Career Criminal Division attorneys had high caseloads, they could not prosecute some defendants evaluated as high-rate and dangerous. This constraint was not present in Middlesex County, where a large number of senior prosecutors handled priority cases.
- Constraints on resources leading to inadequate identification of priority prosecution candidates. In both sites, because records for screening defendants were inadequate, some high-rate dangerous offenders "slipped through the cracks." Later, when presented with anonymous profiles corresponding to these overlooked offenders, prosecutors accurately identified them as high-rate and dangerous. The study showed that in most cases the original oversight occurred because official record information was not available at the time of screening or was fragmentary. In some cases the necessary information was located in another office in the same building as the district attorney's office.

Timely availability of critical official-record information is a problem to prosecutors throughout the country. In a recent survey sponsored by the National Institute of Justice,[11] 58 percent of district attorneys noted difficulty in obtaining early information on defendants' backgrounds.

Since the study indicated that a small number of official-record items can help distinguish high-rate dangerous defendants, prosecutors who lack rapid access to official records should develop systematic date retrieval systems focusing on these few specific items.

Finding 10.   The most criminally active defendants in Middlesex County, Massachusetts, and the most criminally active defendants in Los Angeles County commit crimes at essentially the same rates.

Although fewer people in Middlesex County than in Los Angeles are prosecuted for robbery each year, the most active 30 percent of robbers in Middlesex County commit essentially the same number of robberies as the most active 30 percent of robbers in Los Angeles County. Similarly, the 30 percent most active defendants in both jurisdictions who committed burglary, forgery, fraud, and drug dealing also committed these crimes at essentially the same rates. Car theft proved an exception. The most active car thieves in Los Angeles committed four times as many thefts as their counterparts in Massachusetts.

RECOMMENDATIONS

The study was limited to two jurisdictions; replication of the findings in other jurisdictions should precede any limitation of a jurisdiction's selection criteria to the factors found in this research alone. However, the broad implications of the findings fit the results of other research, and so several recommendations can be drawn from them.

Prosecutors planning priority prosecution programs should target dangerous offenders who commit crimes at high rates. The offenders can be identified more accurately than high-rate offenders who are not dangerous, and the crimes they commit are more serious. The high-rate dangerous offenders are also more serious than some of the habitual offenders who are continually cycling through the criminal justice system.

Selection for priority prosecution can be enhanced by systematic searches of record information, including rap sheets and other records of prior arrests and convictions, offense reports, arrest reports, and—whenever relevant—reports of other criminal justice agencies with whom the defendant had prior contact (probation, parole, police, pretrial release, courts). To promote consistency in selection, jurisdictions can develop standard office selection guidelines that include factors associated with high-rate dangerous criminality, like those described above in findings 6 and 7, along with any other criteria that are considered important locally.

Prosecutors can prepare a checklist of factors that should be taken into account when selecting offenders for priority prosecution. Such a checklist assists in defining office policy and helps screening attorneys identify the small percentage of defendants likely to be high-rate dangerous. This eliminates unnecessary effort looking for official-record items that apparently do not contribute to the screening process. The checklist also flags cases that at the time of screening lack a key piece of information for selection purposes.

Prosecutors who have adopted such a checklist should review the list with both police and judges. If they do not, the criminal justice system risks operating at cross-purposes by having prosecutors target offenders having certain characteristics (for example, being addicted to drugs at the time of the crime) while police or sentencing judges consider the same characteristics to be mitigating factors.

In addition to a checklist, jurisdictional policies should allow screening prosecutors discretion in recommending priority prosecution based on other information. The study found that while defendants who have many of the characteristics listed in Findings 6 and 7 were very likely to be high-rate and dangerous, other defendants also were high-rate dangerous. Some kinds of circumstances, not readily captured in a checklist, indicate to the screening attorney that the case involves a high-rate or dangerous offender. Cases selected for exceptional reasons could be subjected to higher level review within the district attorney's office.

NOTES

1. Chaiken, Marcia, and Jan Chaiken, *Selecting "Career Criminals" for Priority Prosecution*, report to the National Institute of Justice. 1987, NCJ 106310. This research report is summarized in an *Issues and Practices* publication intended for prosecutors: Chaiken, Marcia, and Jan Chaiken. *Redefining the Career Criminal: Priority Prosecution of High-Rate Dangerous Offenders*. National Institute of Justice. 1990, NCJ 124136. (Contact National Institute of

Justice/NCJRS. Box 6000, Rockville, MD 20850, telephone 800–851–3420 or 301–251–5500, to obtain a copy.)

2. A felony is a more serious crime than a misdemeanor. Generally, conviction of a felony can result in imprisonment for 1 year or more.

3. Phillips, Joel L., and Lynne P. Cannady, *The Effectiveness of Selective Prosecution by Career Criminal Programs*. EMT Associates, Inc., Sacramento, California, 1985.

4. Ibid.

5. Ibid.; Bureau of Justice Assistance, *Career Criminal Prosecution Program*. Program Brief, Washington, D.C., March 1985; Chaiken and Chaiken, see note 1.

6. The proportions shown in the figure are based on defendant survey data from the two study sites.

7. Chaiken, Marcia, and Jan Chaiken. "Who Gets Caught Doing Crime?" Bureau of Justice Statistics Discussion Paper, U.S. Department of Justice, Washington, D.C., 1985: Williams, Terry M., and William Kornblum, *Growing Up Poor*, Lexington Books, Lexington, Massachusetts, 1985.

8. Specifically, defendants were asked to report about incidents within the past 2 calendar years (excluding incarcerated periods) in which they had committed burglary; committed business robbery or other robberies or muggings; hurt or killed someone during a burglary or robbery; assaulted someone not during a burglary or robbery; committed motor vehicle theft or other theft; committed forgery, fraud, or credit card offenses; or dealt drugs (made, sold, smuggled, or moved drugs).

9. For details of these comparisons, see appendix B of the *Issues and Practices* report cited in note 1.

10. Chaiken, Jan, and Marcia Chaiken. *Varieties of Criminal Behavior*, The RAND Corporation, Santa Monica, California, R–2814–NIJ, August 1982; Rolph, John, and Jan Chaiken, *Identifying High-Rate Serious Criminals From Official Records*, the RAND Corporation, R–3433–NIJ, 1987; Blumstein, Alfred, et al., *Criminal Careers and "Career Criminals,"* National Academy Press, Washington, D.C., 1986.

11. Wish, Eric D., Mary A. Toborg, and John Bellassai, *Identifying Drug Users and Monitoring Them During Conditional Release*, National Institute of Justice, U.S. Department of Justice, 1988, NCJ 114730. (Contact National Institute of Justice/NCJRS, Box 6000, Rockville, MD 20850, telephone 800–851–3420 or 301–251–5500, to obtain a copy.)

QUESTIONS FOR DISCUSSION

1. What are the goals of most priority prosecution programs?

2. What are the three types of offender profiles used to identify career criminals? Why do the authors suggest that prosecutors need to identify high-rate dangerous offenders? Explain.

3. What were the strongest indicators of high-rate offending found in both study sites?

4. What factors that are commonly perceived to be indicative of high-rate dangerousness proved not to be or were not indicated?

5. What are the recommendations made by the Chaikens, based on the results of their study?

15

THE CAPACITY OF COURTS AS POLICY-MAKING FORUMS

Christopher E. Smith

■ ■

In any given case, questions may be raised about whether it is proper under the American system of government for courts to influence the development of public policy. This issue about the legitimacy of judicial policy making is not, however, the only fundamental controversy underlying the role of courts in policy formulation and implementation. There is also a continuing debate regarding courts' capabilities for producing public policy. Even if it is legitimate for courts to affect public policy, do they have the necessary resources and characteristics to formulate and implement policy? In essence, are courts structured to be capable forums for good policy decisions? As noted by Donald Horowitz, the issues of courts' legitimacy and capacity for policy making are related:

> [The issue is not] whether the courts *should* perform certain tasks but...whether they *can* perform [those tasks] competently.
>
> Of course, legitimacy and capacity are related. A court wholly without capacity may forfeit its claim to legitimacy. A court wholly without legitimacy will soon suffer from diminished capacity.[1]

Questions about courts' legitimacy and capacity can be examined separately, but both elements need to exist for effective judicial policy-making.

Social science research on judicial decision making has shown that judicial decisions are shaped by the same kinds of personal and political influences that affect decisions in other branches of government. Judges' decisions are not dictated by "law." Judges are legal precedents and theories in their written opinions to justify the decisions that they make, but their attitudes, values, political ideologies, and policy preferences exert significant influence over their decisions. For example, scholars who study the Supreme Court have concluded that justices' "policy preferences serve as a powerful force shaping how they view cases and choose among alternative policies."[2] Studies of other courts demonstrate a strong correlation between judges' political party affiliations and the decisions that they make on civil rights and other cases.[3] Republican and Democratic judges tend to decide cases differently because they possess differing attitudes, values, and policy preferences. Although these political influences that shape judicial decision making are similar to the

Reprinted by permission of the publisher.

underlying influences that affect legislators and executive branch officials, decision-making processes within the judicial branch are structured differently than parallel processes in other governmental institutions. The judicial process involves different actors and different kinds of information. Decision makers in the judiciary possess role concepts and authority that differ from those of elected officials. The 1950s, 1960s, and 1970s were decades of swiftly accelerating policy-making activities by judges. In the aftermath of those decades, some commentators believe that courts did not go far enough, but others believe, in the words of one critic, "the dream of the 1960s and 70s that activist courts can be the agents of social progress has worn very thin."[4] The contradictory assessments of the consequences of judicial policy making frequently stem from divergent analyses of the capacity of the judiciary to develop and implement beneficial public policies.

ARGUMENTS ENDORSING COURTS AND GOOD POLICY-MAKING FORUMS

In a well-known article in the *Harvard Law Review*, Abram Chayes presented several arguments advancing the idea that the judiciary may have some important institutional advantages for policy-making tasks.[5] Although Chayes was not alone in raising the idea that courts may be well-suited to the task of policy making, his arguments provide a good illustration of the justifications presented on behalf of courts' policy-making capacity.

Courts are arguably good forums for policy making because judges are, relative to other governmental officials, insulated from interest groups, political parties, and other direct partisan political influences. In the federal courts in particular, judges do not need to worry about reelection. Unlike other actors within the government system, federal judges are structurally positioned to undertake the course of action that they see as most beneficial to society without any significant personal risk from political backlash. Moreover, judges have a traditional role of striving to be as neutral as possible when considering competing arguments. Although systematic examination of judicial decisions by social scientists can provide evidence that judges' attitudes, values, and policy preferences influence outcomes, judges consciously try to be as fair as they can be when making decisions. Judicial officers' heightened consciousness about striving for fairness contrasts sharply with the motivations of legislators and executive branch officials who openly curry favor with interest groups, voters, and other political constituencies that can help elected officials gain and maintain power within government.

Judges can develop *ad hoc* policies that are tailored to remedy particular problematic situations. Legislatures' policy decisions tend to sweep with a broad stroke across all relevant situations without regard for the subtle but potentially important differences between specific circumstances. By contrast, judges can take particular situational needs and constraints into consideration in carefully designing remedial policies that address specific problems.

The judicial process permits a relatively high degree of participation from interested parties. Unlike the legislative process in which poor and unorganized interests are not represented at all by lobbyists, both sides in a court case are generally represented by professional legal counsel. Additional arguments and evidence may be presented through *amicus* briefs and expert witnesses so that the judge will have access to viewpoints and evidence from all relevant perspectives.

The adversarial structure of the judicial process creates incentives for both sides to bring forward as much favorable information as possible. In the legislative context, sometimes only specific interest groups have the resources and opportunity to testify at legislative hearings in order to make their views heard by legislators. Similarly, administrative agencies within the executive branch are noted for responding to organized political interest groups but not to individual citizens. By contrast, both parties in a court case will bring forward all available favorable information so that the judge can sift through complete presentations of the competing arguments and evidence before rendering a decision. Because attorneys for both parties have ethical and personal incentives to represent their clients zealously in order to win the case, they will leave no stone unturned in bringing relevant information to the court's attention.

Unlike legislative and administrative governmental forums, courts must respond to the issues brought before them. The policy agenda of judges are determined by the cases initiated in court, and judges do not have the same ability as other governmental officials to avoid certain difficult questions while consciously pursuing favored policy issues. Legislators ignore intractable problems and address issues of interest that will generate political benefits for them among the electorate. Judges tackle intractable policy problems because parties bring such issues to court and ask the judiciary to develop solutions. In addition, the judges who hear the complete arguments and evidence are the decision makers in court. Unlike the processes in the legislative and executive branches in which arguments, evidence, and decisions are filtered through layers of different offices and staff personnel, the judicial process provides a relatively nonbureaucratic setting for policy-making decisions.

ARGUMENTS OPPOSING COURTS AS EFFECTIVE POLICY-MAKING FORUMS

Donald Horowitz presented the best known critique of courts' capacity for effective policy making in his book, *The Courts and Social Policy*.[6] Horowitz examined judicial interventions into state and local governmental institutions to highlight the drawbacks affecting judges' effectiveness as policy makers.

Judges cannot select their areas of policy emphasis and, because of the constant flow of their other judicial responsibilities, they cannot give sustained attention to specific issues. Although legislative committees and executive agencies contain experts on various policy issues, judges are not likely to be experts on any public policy issues. Judges are generalists trained in law who gained authority over public policy issues by virtue of becoming judicial officers. Judges are also insulated from the environment affected by their policy decisions because judicial ethics require that judges withdraw from participation in most social and political organizations. Legislators meet regularly with constituents to keep in touch with public opinion and social concerns. Judges keep to themselves within the protective confines of the courthouse. Because they lack expertise and close contacts with affected communities, judges are less able to participate the broader consequences of their decisions. Moreover, the *ad hoc* nature of judicial decisions creates policies that lack the comprehensive, coherent perspective that may be developed in legislative and executive settings through the utilization of policy studies, experts, and long-term planning.

Judges' policy decisions are based upon a skewed sample of problems. Judges address the particular case that happens to arrive before them. The case may be highly unrepresentative of the larger problems affecting that policy issue, yet the specific circumstances underlying the case in question may become the basis for policy decisions that produce detrimental effects upon a variety of other cases. In addition, the issue addressed by the judge is framed by litigants in accordance with their particularistic interests. Therefore the judge has little ability to take a comprehensive view of the policy problem, even if he or she desires to do so. In the adversarial process, the parties have an incentive to hide unfavorable information, and the judge does not have a large enough staff to ferret out complete information. Thus, the judge's decision relies upon the potentially biased and incomplete information submitted by the competing parties. Moreover, even if comprehensive information is obtained, the judge may not be able to utilize relevant information because of constraints imposed by decisions of higher appellate courts that have limited the range of judicial policy choices in a specific issue area.[7]

The process of litigation itself may be an undesirable means to formulate and adjust public policy. Litigation leads to definitive decisions in favor of one party or the other. Such "win or lose" decisions may be an undesirable means of addressing many policy issues. Policy outcomes derived from negotiation and compromise may provide more satisfactory and socially beneficial solutions for society's problems. Thus legislative bodies containing representatives from various segments of society are better suited to develop compromise policies that will gain broad acceptance.

ASSESSING COURTS' CAPACITY AS POLICY-MAKING FORUMS

The foregoing summaries are cast as competing sets of arguments about courts' capacity (or lack thereof) for producing good public policy outcomes. In fact, most authors, including Chayes and Horowitz, discuss the complexity of the capacity issue in greater detail. Yet, these simplified arguments represent the underlying basis for raging disagreements about the effectiveness of judicial policy making. Which set of arguments concerning judges' capacity for effective policy making is closest to the mark? Both viewpoints contain accurate elements, but neither fully captures the actual complex interactions that underlie judicial policy making.

Characterization of Issues

One characteristic of judicial policy making is that issues must undergo a "legalization" process in the hands of lawyers before they can be presented in court. Legal procedures are structured to address issues that fit within the confines of specific dispute categories. Because disputes that do not fit within a recognized basis for legal action cannot be heard by courts, people must transform their claims into legal forms that courts are willing to consider. As Horowitz observes, "[t]he framing of the issue is geared to the litigant and his complaint," which may represent an atypical case, rather than to the broad policy issue that may be affected by a judicial decision.[8] It is necessary to create a narrow focus in litigation for the presentation of evidence and the analysis of issues, and this narrowing process of transforming claims into legal actions may limit the ability of judges to give broad consideration to a policy question. When a homosexual man challenged on privacy grounds the constitutionality of Georgia's law that provides for sentences of up to twenty years in prison for sodomy, even if between consenting adults or married couples within the privacy of their own bedrooms, the majority of justices on the Supreme Court characterized the issue very narrowly: "Does a homosexual have a constitutional right to commit sodomy?"[9] Because of the way the issue was framed, the Court did not consider broadly whether or not such a law represents a good policy. Indeed, after deciding against the claimant, one justice's opinion implicitly informed the claimant that if he had challenged the law as having an excessively severe punishment, the justice might have decided the case differently.[10] Obviously, the justices assessed the policy in accordance with a very narrow characterization of the legal issue (privacy rights of homosexuals) rather than from a broad perspective that considered the law's impact on heterosexuals and the potentially "cruel and unusual" nature of the punishment. Ideally, policy makers should examine an issue comprehensively and not analyze it from one limited, selected angle.

The legalization process also casts policy debates into a framework of individual constitutional "rights." By examining policy decisions as if they are absolute entitlements for individuals, the courts may lack the capacity for flexible development of policy outcomes that maximize the interests of competing actors or that benefit society as a whole.[11] In addition, a "rights" orientation may permit interest groups to capture a public policy issue and thereby control executive branch agencies' ability to administer governmental programs in the interest of society. According to Jeremy Rabkin:

> When different constituencies can challenge so many different aspects of agency operations, private rights or "legally protected interests" no longer seem to be an exception from the general flow of public policy, but rather the essential elements of public policy themselves. In other words, public policy seems to reduce to the legally protected claims of contending groups.[12]

Although this observation raises a serious concern about courts' capacity for comprehensive policy making, it must be considered in light of the capabilities of other governmental branches. Legislative and executive branch actions are not focused upon individuals' "rights," but they are equally susceptible to capture by narrow interest groups. In theory, the accountability of elected officials to the voters will undercut the power of political action committees, interest group lobbying, and close relationships between organized interests and executive branch agencies. In practice, however, many policies produced by legislative and executive decisions are narrowly tailored for specific interests. Thus the risks of narrow policy making by courts are less compelling as evidence of judicial capacity. Moreover, the political system provides constraints upon courts that limit the extent to which judicial policy making may remain uniquely captured by any particular interest.

The legalization process creates opportunities for judges to avoid cases that are initiated in court. Although judges have tackled many difficult issues, they are able to utilize jurisdictional concepts such as "standing," "mootness," and "political question doctrine" to avoid issues that might generate excessive political controversy. When judges focus upon a litigant's "standing," they question whether this is the proper party to initiate a case, and they challenge the litigant's assertion that there was a sufficient injury to meet legal standards for litigation. When he was a circuit court of appeals judge, current Supreme Court Justice Antonin Scalia avoided making decisions on civil rights issues by questioning whether claimants had the proper legal basis for initiating a lawsuit.[13] The issue of "mootness" arises if the case's underlying conflict has ended before the courts have fully considered the case. When the first affirmative action case arrived at the Supreme Court in *DeFunis* v. *Odegaard*,[14] the justices avoided the issue by declaring it moot because the plaintiff had subsequently been accepted into the law school that he was suing for "reverse discrimination." Although affirmative action was a divisive issue, the Supreme Court managed to delay its contact with the controversial issue. The "political question" doctrine has served as a basis of judicial avoidance of many matters, particularly in the area of foreign policy, when the courts declare that the issue should properly be addressed by the legislative and executive branches of government.

How does the legalization process for policy issues affect courts' capacity for policy making? By examining narrow issues there are risks that judges will not analyze issues comprehensively and that the resulting judicial decisions will affect public policy in undesirable or unintended ways. At the same time, however, the legalization process creates opportunities for courts to avoid undertaking policy decisions or to limit the scope of decisions and thereby defer primary decision-making responsibility to the other branches of government.

Access to Information

The adversary system of courtroom combat between competing attorneys has been criticized for the risk it creates that relevant information will not be presented to judges. Although both competing parties are represented by attorneys, the attorneys control the information that is presented to the court. The two parties in the case present all relevant information that is favorable to their cause. They hope that the other side will fail to discover and present information that might to detrimental to their arguments. Thus, the judges may not have access to complete information. As described by Marvin Frankel:

> While the administration of justice is designated as the public's business and the decision-makers are public people (whether full-time judges or lay judges who sit in jury boxes), the process is initiated, shaped, and managed by the private contestants in civil matters....The deciders, though commissioned to discover the truth, are passive recipients, not active explorers. They take what they are given. They consider the questions raised by counsel, rarely any others.[15]

By contrast, the German legal system empowers judges to perform as the primary investigators who question witnesses, seek additional evidence, and otherwise actively pursue complete information.[16]

In addition, judges are not experts on the public policy issues that they shape with their decisions. They are inevitably questions about whether "generalist" judges have the capacity to make good decisions on complex policy issues. Moreover, because judges frequently rely upon "theoretical knowledge" from social scientists' studies, they cannot accurately predict the consequences of their policy decisions.[17] Although these are important criticisms to direct at judicial policy making, do they indicate that courts are incapable of making good policy decisions? Might these same criticisms be directed at other governmental institutions that shape public policy?

Legislatures presumably have access to broader information than courts because issues are not characterized to fit the contours of law and the interests of two specific litigants. In addition, legislatures benefit from the assistance of committee staff members who possess expertise on various policy issues. Legislatures can also hear testimony and receive reports from a wide range of experts without regard for narrow rules of evidence that limit the kinds of information regarded as admissible in court. Although these attributes appear to grant significant advantages to legislatures as policy-making forums, in fact, courts share many of these attributes.

As Stephen Wasby points out, legislatures frequently examine policy issues on a case-by-case basis when a particular problem rises to the top of the legislative policy agenda because of a specific event or circumstances that captures public attention.[18] Thus legislatures do not undertake public policy decisions from a comprehensive perspective either. John Kingdon's research on the policy process in the legislative and executive branches indicates that:

> Problems are often not self-evident by the indicators. They need a little push to get the attention of people in and around government. That push is often provided by a focusing event like a crisis or disaster that comes along to call attention to the problem, a powerful symbol that catches on, or the personal experience of a policy maker.[19]

Judicial policy-making arises from authoritative attention to a specific dispute between two or more contending parties, but legislative policy making may be initiated and shaped by similar circumstances.

In the legislative context, legislators are "generalists" who make decisions with the advice of experts. Similarly, judges utilize the advice of experts to make decisions. The contending parties bring expert witnesses to court, but the judge may also listen to separate experts or appoint "special masters," frequently college professors or attorneys with specific expertise, to provide advice or oversight for difficult policy disputes.[20] Thus judges have the authority to seek additional information in order to examine issues more comprehensively. Whether or not they actually examine policy disputes from a broad perspective is determined by the actions of the judges and litigants in specific cases. The same is true, however, of legislative decisions because legislators often listen only to representatives and experts from selected interest groups before enacting legislation with wide impact.

Although judges are criticized for failing to predict accurately the consequences of their policy decisions, other policy-making institutions are similarly flawed in their capacity to predict effectively the long-term results of particular public policy initiatives.[21] Legislatures and executive branch agencies also rely upon "theoretical knowledge" from social scientists' studies and therefore, like courts, must wait to see the practical effects of public policy decisions.

It is easy to criticize courts for ineffective policy making by examining persistent policy problems that have received judicial attention. An accurate assessment of courts' capacity for policy making can only be gained, however, by examining additional criteria that critics of the courts often fail to evaluate. According to Wasby, analysis of judicial capacity requires attention to both the *comparative capacity* of courts and other policy-making institutions and the *will to proceed* that is characteristic of a particular policy-shaping actor.[22] From a comparative perspective, courts share many of the capacity-reducing disabilities that are characteristic in alternative policy-making forums. In addition, because of their independence from direct control by voters, federal judges, in particular, may have a greater capacity for tackling rather than avoiding difficult controversies.

The Policy-Shaping Process

Critics of judicial capacity assert that judicial policy making is undesirable because court decisions favor one party or the other for policy issues in which negotiation and compromise may be most desirable. This image of the formal judicial process does not, however, accurately reflect the processes of judicial policy making for most cases. The adversarial litigants do not conduct their case preparations in isolation and then meet in a "clash of gladiators" in the courtroom. The actual process of civil litigation is more accurately characterized as "bargaining in the shadow of the law."[23] Lawyers for the contending parties meet continuously throughout the months of preparation for trial in order to obtain information from each other in the pretrial process known as "discovery." Judges encourage and even force the parties to negotiate with each other in an effort to reach a settlement without a judicial decision. The parties "bargain in the shadow of the law" because the threat of a zero-sum decision looms over their heads as the scheduled trial date approaches. Thus most civil cases are processed through negotiated settlements, and relatively few cases actually receive judicial decisions after a trial.

Because of the importance of behind-the-scenes negotiation in the civil litigation process, judges are not merely potential policy makers through their authority to issue judicial decisions, they are also policy shapers through their ability to encourage negotiation between the parties. One well-known article about the role of judges in reforming governmental institutions characterized judges as "power-brokers" who make choices about how to guide the judicial processing of policy disputes.[24] Observers have noted judges' increasing emphasis upon negotiation rather than litigation as the means for processing disputes. Indeed, contemporary judicial officers have been labeled "managerial judges" because they "are meeting with parties in chambers to encourage settlement of disputes and to supervise case preparation. Both before and after trial, judges are playing a critical role in shaping litigation and influencing results."[25]

The negotiation process that underlies judicial policy making creates opportunities for participation by contending parties in the development of compromise policy outcomes that avoid the necessity of a single judge making a choice about the most desirable public policy. A negotiation process may have advantages over other kinds of policy-shaping processes by encouraging presentation of complete information and by inducing opposing interests to work together in formulating results that will receive broad support. Studies of judicial policy making have found that judges utilize negotiation to shape and refine policy outcomes. For example, in Alabama, a federal judge took control of the state's correctional institutions because, among other things, public health inspectors found the prisons to be unfit for human habitation.[26] A study of prison litigation in Alabama found that the state government and the prisoners' advocates engaged in continuing negotiations during the development and implementation of remedies.[27] In studies of judicial policy making concerning several issue areas (i.e., prisons, mental health institutions, housing, school desegregation), Phillip Cooper found that judges played complex roles, which combined negotiation and adjudication, but that judges did not fit any simplistic characterization as judicial policy makers who simply issue decisions after an adversarial trial:

> [J]udges play different roles at different stages of a case. The judge plays a facilitator role in the first part of the remedy crafting process and a ratifier/developer role in the second. In the plan development and negotiation stage, all the judges [in the study] encouraged settlement or, at a minimum, a narrowing of issues. In each case…the judges found points at which they declared limits. When those limits were reached, the process became more formal and the judges became less a facilitator and more a validator or ratifying official who placed the court's imprimatur on specific plans submitted by the parties without regard to voluntary acceptance by the other parties.[28]

The Consequences of Judicial Decisions

There are studies indicating that judges frequently do not foresee the adverse consequences of their decisions. One study, for example, indicates that judicial intervention in prison administration may exacerbate prison violence by altering the established procedures and authority structure within institutions.[29] Commentators also note that judicial policy making often fails to accomplish intended objectives. In urban school desegregation cases, for example, some commentators argue that judicial intervention contributes to deterioration in city school systems as middle-class families leave the city to avoid court-mandated busing programs.[30] Does the existence of adverse consequences from judicial policy making indicate that judges lack the capacity to formulate and implement effective policies? Or do the less-than-completely-successful attempts at judicial policy-making simply indicate that judges' effectiveness is limited by the same kinds of factors that diminish the success of policy initiatives produced by other governmental branches? In fact, court-mandated school desegregation has been successful in increasing educational opportunity and reducing polarization in many communities, especially in county-wide school systems and medium-sized cities which contain a broad mixture of racial and socioeconomic groups.[31] The highly publicized failures of busing programs in the largest cities stem, at least in part, from the Supreme Court's 1974 decision to limit such programs to the confines of rigid and relative arbitrary established school system boundaries within metropolitan areas.[32] The slim five-member Supreme Court majority that constrained the range of desegregation remedies available to district judges was apparently concerned about the massive political backlash that would be generated if affluent suburbanites were forced to participate in developing solutions for the problems affecting predominantly minority urban school systems.[33] There is nothing unique about judges' inability to implement effective remedies for many of the significant problems of urban education. The legislative and executive branches of government have never effectively dealt with these pressing problems either. Judges, however, often feel a greater responsibility to do *something* to enforce constitutional rights when there is evidence that individuals are being victimized by discriminatory government policies and programs.

IMPLEMENTATION OF JUDICIAL DECISIONS

As indicated by the foregoing discussion, courts' capacity for producing good public policy outcomes is flawed. However, the flaws that afflict the judicial branch are not unique. In many respects, elements of the judicial policy-making process are similar to the processes undertaken in other branches (e.g., negotiation, assertion of narrow interests, etc.). Because they share common attributes with the judicial branch, the other branches of government cannot claim that they possess unique or flawless policy-making characteristics. Common weaknesses also exist in the policy implementation process. Public policy decisions are not self-implementing, whether they come from the Supreme Court, Congress, or the president. The president obviously has the greatest ability to implement decisions through control of the executive branch agencies that are responsible for administering governmental programs. However, even the executive branch's desires are affected by the actions of other political actors. As illustrated by the previous sections of this chapter, the inability of the judicial branch to implement public policy outcomes quickly and effectively should be viewed as a flaw with detrimental impacts upon the courts' policy-shaping capacity. This is a flaw that also affects other branches in various ways.

Although courts possess authority and legitimacy, and judicial decisions are enforceable as "law," judicial decisions often do not affect people's lives in the manner intended by the judges who issued those decisions. In 1990, for example, the Supreme Court issued a decision declaring that the Social Security Administration had violated a congressional statute for sixteen years by refusing to pay benefits to children with a variety of disabilities, including Down's syndrome, muscular dystrophy, spina bifida, AIDS, cystic fibrosis, and other chronic illnesses and birth defects.[34] Nine months after the Court's decision, the Social Security Administration had still not acted to pay benefits to the excluded children. Although children in these categories of illnesses and disabilities had prevailed in their policy dispute with the federal government by winning their case in the Supreme Court, they had not gained any benefits from their victory.[35] In such a case, any knowledgeable observer might guess that the children's goals were thwarted by the nature of government bureaucracies, which tend to change and implement policies very slowly. Indeed, this Social Security example is affected by the organizational characteristics of a large government bureaucracy. The difficulties that hinder the implementation of judicial decisions are more complex and pervasive than the simple bureaucratic inertia that is apparent in this example. Judicial policy decisions that affect other issues and actors must undergo a complex implementation process.

Because judicial decisions are not self-implementing, they must pass through the hands of various influential actors in the implementation process before they affect people's lives as public policies. The involvement of actors with varying political attitudes, values, and partisan interests can lead to inconsistent and unpredictable outcomes that diminish judicial officers' ability to ensure that policy decisions accomplish judges' intended goals. In a useful model for illustrating the implementation and impact of judicial policies, Charles Johnson and Bradley Canon identified interpreters, implementers, and consumers who, along with external political actors, determine precisely if and how judges' decisions will affect society.[36]

Interpreters

After judges issue a decision, the judicial opinion and its implications must be communicated and explained to the people who will carry it out. Police officers, for example, cannot follow closely the developing case law affecting search and seizure, *Miranda* warnings, and the other aspects of their jobs that are shaped by judicial decisions. Police officers do not have easy access to judges' opinions on such issues and they do not have the time or training to study and interpret the judges' intended meanings. Thus, other actors assume the task of interpreting and explaining judicial decisions.

The most far-reaching policy pronouncements come from the Supreme Court and other appellate courts. Frequently, if a trial judge makes a decision affecting public policy, the policy is not implemented until the issue has been examined by higher courts on appeal. When appellate courts issue policy decisions, their decisions are often limited to broad announcements that describe the duties of governmental officials or provide directions to officials involved within a particular case. Thus there is uncertainty about how the appellate decision is to apply to other cases with factual circumstances that are similar but not necessarily identical to the case decided by the appellate court. The interpretation and explanation of the judicial policy is developed gradually by the trial judges who must apply the appellate decision to the individual circumstances within new cases that arise concerning that policy issue. In *Brown* v. *Board of Education*, the Supreme Court explicitly acknowledged this interpretation and implementation process by instructing the federal district courts to examine alleged racial segregation within school systems and to develop remedies on a case-by-case basis. In other issue areas, the interpreting role of trial judges is equally inevitable but based on less explicit instructions. When the Supreme Court declared that criminal suspects must be informed of their rights prior to questioning in the *Miranda* decision,[37] trial judges subsequently had to decide precisely when the warnings had to be given, whether the warnings had to be phrased in a precise fashion, whether any questions could be asked of suspects prior to the warnings, and other issues that were not specifically spelled out in *Miranda*. Some of these issues received clarification from the Supreme Court in subsequent appeals, but because not all defendants fully pursue the appeal process or initiate other actions to challenge their convictions, the trial judges' interpretations frequently determined the outcomes of cases.

Other officials may also serve as interpreters. City attorneys advise police departments and school systems about the meaning and implications of judicial policy decisions. State attorneys general interpret decisions and provide instructions to state and local officials about how they must follow judicial policy pronouncements. Interpretation of judicial decisions is not always done by lawyers. Because of their positions within government agencies, people who are not trained in law may have to interpret and explain judicial policies. For example, police chiefs may interpret and explain decisions to patrol officers. School superintendents and principals may explain policies to teachers.

What are the consequences of this interpretation process? The various interpreters may interpret and explain the judicial policies in different ways. Moreover, some interpreters may never even hear about specific judicial decisions, especially if they are in small towns and do not have immediate access to the latest appellate opinions. Thus the actual meaning and implementation of the judicial policy may vary from city to city. The varying interpretations of the judges' intentions may stem from ambiguity in the wording of the judicial decision, mistaken perceptions on the part of interpreters, or even willful efforts by interpreters to shape the meaning of the judicial decision to fit the interpreters' own policy preferences. If city officials object to a judicial decision, they may intentionally interpret it as applying only to a limited range of circumstances. This may force a citizen to go back through the lengthy litigation process again in order to force the officials to follow a precise directive from the courts. In the meantime, the city officials have succeeded in weakening and delaying implementation of a policy that they oppose.

Implementers

Even if judicial policies are explained, they do not affect society according to the judges' intentions unless the officials responsible for carrying out the policies implement the directives properly. The *Miranda* decision, for example, is primarily a symbolic declaration unless police officers follow through with their instructions to inform suspects about the right to counsel and the right against self-incrimination. The success or failure of judicial policies can depend upon whether implementers have heard about the policies, whether they understood the explanations concerning the meaning of policy, and whether they comply with policy directives.

A failure to comply with judicial policies may stem from a lack of understanding or from an intentional effort to subvert the judicial policy. When federal courts issued orders to desegregate public schools, many school systems in the South initially refused to comply. They knew what they were supposed to do, but the judicial policy did not take effect because the implementers disagreed with the policy and intentionally failed to follow the judges' directives. This willful noncompliance was premised upon a hope that other political actors, such as Congress, would combat the courts' decisions and prevent desegregation through a constitutional amendment or other means. Eventually, it took additional judicial decisions to levy fines on school systems, legislative and executive actions to withhold funds, and even the actions of law enforcement officers or military forces to initiate compliance in several cities.

Failure to implement judicial policies can occur in more subtle ways as well. For example, an individual police officer who makes an arrest in an alley with no witnesses present may have the opportunity to treat, or rather mistreat, the suspect in violation of judicial policies governing police behavior. If the suspect asserts that the police officer never informed him of his rights and the police officer says the suspect is lying, the judge will simply decide which witness is more credible. Such decisions are likely to go against a criminal suspect whether or not the suspect is telling the truth.

Alternatively, an individual police officer's failure to follow judicial policies in areas such as search and seizure is likely to stem from a lack of knowledge about the most recent, technical court decisions explaining the nuances of appropriate police behavior. Police cannot be expected to read and understand the most recent judicial decisions, especially because certain areas of law are refined every year by new decisions. There are likely to be weaknesses in the processes for communicating the details of judges' decisions to implementers, and these weaknesses will reduce the effectiveness of judicial policies.

Consumers

The people directly affected by court decisions can also influence their implementation. Consumers may hear about important judicial policy decisions that are reported by the news media, but frequently they have no ability to learn about the most recent court cases. Thus, if the implementers fail to respect the consumers' rights in accordance with judicial directives and the consumers do not realize that their rights have been violated, the judicial policy will not be effectuated because there is no one to complain about the lack of implementation. For example, if a public school teacher in a small town leads prayers in the classroom in violation of the Supreme Court's 1962 decision in *Engle* v. *Vitale*[38] but no students or parents realize that this is improper, no one will complain and seek enforcement of the judicial policy. In addition, if a consumer recognizes a rights violation but is frustrated by resistance from a school system or other government agency, or alternatively, cannot afford to hire a lawyer to seek enforcement in court, the consumer may not follow through with additional efforts to ensure that the policy is fully implemented. In small, homogeneous communities, if the entire community disagrees with a judicial policy, such as the prohibition on organized prayer in public schools, the judicial policy may be repeatedly violated, but no consumer will be interested in pursuing actions to seek implementation of the public policy. Alternatively, consumers' resistance may defeat intended policies if they boycott schools to protest school desegregation or otherwise refuse to supply the public participation essential to the success of the public policy. Thus, consumers play an important role in the implementation, or lack thereof, of judicial policies.

Secondary Groups

There are many external political actors who influence the development and implementation of judicial decisions. The president and state governors are important enforcers of judicial policies. Their commitment, or lack thereof, to the enforcement of judicial decisions can significantly affect whether the judges' intentions are implemented. Interest groups frequently bear the burden of pressing for implementation of judicial decisions. Because the consumers who are supposed to be directly affected by the judicial policies frequently are not aware of court decisions or they lack the resources to seek enforcement of such decisions, interest groups utilize their organizational expertise and resources to initiate additional legal actions, publicize government officials' failure to obey judges' orders, lobby elected officials for enforcement, and otherwise seek to effectuate the judicial decisions that favor their policy preferences. The news media play an important role in disseminating information about judicial decisions so that interpreters, implementers, and consumers learn about recent policy directives. Moreover, the news reports help to keep the judges themselves informed about the consequences of their decisions and thereby influence future judicial decisions, including actions to accelerate implementation. Legislators, scholars, and others are also part of the judicial policy process throughout their actions, which influence and inform the actors most directly responsible for the interpretation and implementation of judges' decisions. Politicians may, for example, lend legitimacy and encouragement to citizens who resist judicial orders, as often occurred in school desegregation cases, and thereby hinder the effectuation of judicial policies.

The Consequences of the Implementation Process

Several scholarly studies provide examples of the effects of implementation process in shaping, changing, and even negating judicial policy making. For example, a study of lower court decisions concerning the public's right of access to judicial proceedings indicated that federal district court judges may resist implementation of Supreme Court decisions, even when there is no public opposition or significant controversy surrounding the judicial policy.[39]

Research on judicial policy making indicates that the sources and quality of information available to implementers vary greatly from one city to another.[40] A study of police departments in Wisconsin in the aftermath of the *Miranda* decision found varying patterns of compliance with the Supreme Court's directive for police to inform criminal suspects of their rights.[41] The more professionalized departments received information about the decision from several sources, including formal conferences and training sessions.[42] Because the quality and completeness of information conveyed to police officers varied from department to department, the implementers in different cities had differing perceptions about the precise requirements of the judicial policy and its desirability. These mixed perceptions led to differing applications of the judicial policy depending upon the knowledge about and commitment to the policy possessed by the police officer making the arrest.

A study of compliance with Supreme Court decisions forbidding organized religious activities within public schools found that in one city "[w]hile superintendents soberly answered mail questionnaires to the effect that their schools were in full compliance with the Court's interpretation of the Constitution, many teachers led pupils in a wide variety of morning and afternoon prayers, Bible reading, and hymns."[43] In this community and other locales where the Supreme Court's policy directives were ignored, no implementer took responsibility for ensuring compliance. Moreover, school officials had little incentive to clash with the local consensus against the policy, especially when there were few consumers, if any, sufficiently interested and able to challenge the lack of compliance.[44]

As these examples demonstrate, judges are not omnipotent. The practical political world that they attempt to shape through their judicial policy making is not readily controllable. Judges' decisions are influenced by the internal and external factors that guide judicial decision making. The consequences of judicial decisions are subsequently shaped by the degree of understanding and cooperation exhibited by the political actors who must implement court decrees. Without a high degree of cooperation and support from executive branch officials and the public, judicial policies may be rendered ineffective.[45]

JUDICIAL CAPACITY

Serious concerns exist regarding the capacity of courts as policy-making forums. The nature of the judicial process creates risks that judicial policy outcomes will be based upon inadequate information and the assertion of narrow legal interests. In addition, the political forces that shape and hinder judicial outcomes in the implementation process undercut the purported effectiveness of courts. Although these issues are cause for concern, a complete assessment of policy-making processes in other branches of government casts doubt upon the proposition that courts are uniquely unqualified for policy-shaping activities. The quality of outcomes produced by courts will vary from court to court and case to case, depending upon the expectations and performance of individual judges and attorneys. Recognition of the flaws in judicial policy-making processes does not provide a basis for simple condemnation or support of courts' policy-making capacity. Observers should seek an understanding of the complexity of the policy-making processes in all branches of government *and* of the branches' interactions with each other in the policy process. Policy outcomes are not "good" or "bad" simply because they were shaped by a particular branch of government. Policy outcomes should be judged on their own merits with a recognition that all branches of government will continue to shape public policy and no branch of government is uniquely capable of developing "good" public policy for all issue areas.

NOTES

1. Horowitz, Donald. (1977). *The Courts and Social Policy* (Washington, D.C.: Brookings Institution), p. 18.

2. Baum, Lawrence. (1989). *The Supreme Court*, 3rd ed. (Washington, D.C.: Congressional Quarterly Press), p. 136.

3. See Christopher E. Smith, "Popularization and Change in the Federal Courts: *En Banc* Decisions in the U.S. Courts of Appeals," *Judicature*, 74 (1900): 133–37.

4. Rabkin, Jeremy. (1989). *Judicial Compulsion: How Public Law Distorts Public Policy* (New York: Basic Books), p. xiii.

5. See Abram Chayes, "The Role of the Judge in Public Law Litigation," *Harvard Law Review*, 89 (1976): 1281–1316.

6. See Horowitz, *The Courts and Social Policy*, pp. 22–67, 255–298.

7. Winter, Jr., Ralph K. Winter. (1979). "The Growth of Judicial Power," in *The Judiciary in a Democratic Society*, (ed.), Leonard J. Therberge (Lexington, Mass.: Lexington Books), p. 60.

8. Horowitz, Donald. (1977). "The Courts as the Guardians of the Public Interest," *Public Administration Review*, 37: 152.

9. *Bowers* v. *Hardwick*, 478 U.S. 186 (1986).

10. Ibid., concerning opinion of Justice Lewis Powell.

11. See Richard Morgan, *Disabling America: The "Rights Industry" in Our Time* (New York: Basic Books, 1984), pp. 3–11, 74–133.

12. Rabkin, *Judicial Compulsions*, p. 20.

13. Wilson, Richard. (1986). "Constraints of Power: The Constitutional Opinions of Judges Scalia, Bork, Posner, Easterbrook, and Winter." *University of Miami Law Review*, 40: 1181.

14. *DeFunis* v. *Odegaard*, 416 U.S. 312 (1974).

15. Frankel, Marvin. (1988). "Partisan Justice." In *Readings on Adversarial Justice: The American Approach to Adjudication* (ed.), Stephan Landsman (St. Paul, Minn.: West Publishing), p. 55.

16. See John H. Langbein, "The German Advantage in Civil Procedure," *University of Chicago Law Review*, 52 (1985): 823–866.

17. Glazer, Nathan. (1978). "Should Judges Administer Social Services?," *The Public Interest*, 50: 79.

18. Wasby, Stephen. (1981). "The Arrogation of Power or Accountability: 'Judicial Imperialism' Revisited," *Judicature*, 65: 215.

19. Kingdon, John W. (1984). *Agendas, Alternatives and Public Policies* (Boston: Little, Brown and Co.), pp. 90–100.

20. Wasby, "Arrogation of Power," p. 215.

21. Ibid.

22. Ibid., p. 216.

23. See Robert H. Mnookin and Lewis Kornhauser, "Bargaining in the Shadow of the Law: The Case of Divorce," *Yale Law Journal*, 88 (1979): 950–997.

24. See Colin S. Diver, "The Judge as Political Powerbroker: Superintending Structural Change in Public Institutions." *Virginia Law Review*, 65 (1979): 43–106.

25. Resnik, Judith. (1982). "Managerial Judges," *Harvard Law Review*, 96: 377.

26. See *Newman* v. *Alabama*, 349 F.Supp. 278 (M.D. Ala. 1972); *Pugh* v. *Locke*, 406 F.Supp. 318 (M.D. Ala. 1976).

27. Yarbrough, Tinsley E. (1984) "The Alabama Prison Litigation," *The Justice System Journal*, 9: 276–290.

28. Cooper, Phillip J. (1988). *Hard Judicial Choices* (New York: Oxford University Press), pp. 337–338.

29. See Geoffrey P. Alpert, Ben M. Crouch, and C. Ronald Huff, "Prison Reform by Judicial Decree: The Unintended Consequences of *Ruiz v. Estelle*," *The Justice System Journal*, 9 (1984): 291–305.

30. Graglia, Lee Lino A. (1976). *Disaster by Decree* (Ithaca, NY: Cornell University Press), pp. 203–283.

31. See Gary Orfield, *Must We Bus?: Segregated Schools and National Policy* (Washington, D.C.: Brookings Institution, 1978), pp. 62–67, 119–126; Meyer Weinberg, "The Relationship Between School Desegregation and Academic Achievement: A Review of the Research." In *The Courts, Social Science, and School Desegregation* (eds.) Betsy Levin and Willis D.

Hawley (New Brunswick, N.J.: Transaction Books, 1977), pp. 241–270; Thomas F. Pettigrew, "A Sociological View of the Post-*Bradley*- Era," *Wayne Law Review*, 21 (1975): 813–832.

32. *Milliken* v. *Bradley*, 418 U.S. 717 (1974).

33. Kluger, Richard. (1975). *Simple Justice: The History of* Brown *v.* Board of Education *and Black America's Struggle for Equality* (New York: Random House), pp. 771–773.

34. Pear, Rober. (1990). "Social Security Stalls Disabled Children Aid," *Akron Beacon Journal*, Nov. 20, 1990. p. A1.

35. Ibid.

36. See Charles A. Johnson and Bradley C. Canon, *Judicial Policies: Implementation and Impact* (Washington, D.C.: Congressional Quarterly Press, 1984).

37. *Miranda* v. *Arizona*, 384 U.S. 436 (1966).

38. *Engle* v. *Vitale*, 370 U.S. 421 (1962).

39. Reid, Traciel V. (1988). "Judicial Policy-Making and Implementation: An Empirical Examination," *Western Political Quarterly*, 41: 509–527.

40. Wasby, Stephen. (1973). "The Communication of Supreme Court's Criminal Procedure Decisions: A Preliminary Mapping," *Villanova Law Review*, 18 (1973): 1086–1118.

41. Milner, Neal. (1970). "Comparative Analysis of Patterns of Compliance with Supreme Court Decisions," *Law and Society Review*, 5: 119–134.

42. Ibid, p. 123.

43. Dolbeare, Kenneth M. and Phillip E. Hammond. (1970). "Inertia in Midway: Supreme Court Decisions and Local Responses," *Journal of Legal Education*, 23: 112.

44. Ibid., pp. 115–116.

45. See Charles S. Bullock, III and Charles M. Lamb, "Toward a Theory of Civil Rights Implementation," *American Court Systems*, 2nd ed., (eds.) Sheldon Goldman and Austin Sarat (New York, Longman, 1989), pp. 559–568.

QUESTIONS FOR DISCUSSION

1. List and discuss at least four arguments favoring courts as policy-making forums.

2. List and discuss four arguments opposing courts as policy-making forums.

3. Although there are arguments for and against courts as policy-making forums, how does the author characterize the issue of the court's involvement in policy making? Provide examples to support your response.

4. Access to information in the adversarial system of justice is a critical issue in deciding judicial outcomes and ultimately policy dictates. Why? Provide examples to support your response.

5. Discuss the application of judicial decisions regarding the following interpreters, implementers, consumers, and secondary groups.

16

COURT CLERKS, COURT ADMINISTRATORS, AND JUDGES
CONFLICTING IN MANAGING THE COURTS

G. Larry Mays
William A. Taggart

■ ■

The United States judicial system has always been seen as providing a forum for settling disputes. The courts, at least ideally, are an arena where parties can contest actions in an orderly, acceptable manner. This textbook view of the judicial process shows the courts and their attendant actors as passively waiting for the next group of combatants to bring their dispute forward. The conflicts are seen as originating with individuals or groups and as arriving in the courts for settlement.

Neubauer (1979) and Einstein and Jacob (1977) have noted the dynamics of the courtroom work group in disposing of cases.[1] However, their emphasis is on those factors promoting cooperation and interdependence in the attainment of dispositions. One feature is overlooked in most discussions of work-group interaction, namely, that the nonadjudicative business of the courts has a distinctly bureaucratic flavor, while the adjudicative business of the courts involves judges and lawyers who have nonbureaucratic, or antibureaucratic, orientations (Saari, 1982).

This article examines one area of inherent conflict in the courts: the rationality of "managing" versus the antibureaucratic philosophies of professionals such as lawyers and judges (Mort and Hall, 1980; Scheb, 1981; Feeley, 1983). As Saari (1982:55) has noted,

> Direct supervision, standardizing work processes, and standard outputs do not work well in a professionally dominated organization. Management styles of a bureaucratic nature are inappropriate for courts, because they cannot control a central process that does not exist.

SURVEY OF COURT MANAGERS

In order to assess the sources of conflict in the courts, especially conflict between judges and court management personnel, a questionnaire was sent to 731 court managers residing in 46

Reprinted with permission from *Journal of Criminal Justice*, Vol. 14, G. Larry Mays and William A. Taggart, "Court, Clerks, Court Administrators, and Judges: Conflict in Managing the Courts" (1986), Elsevier Science Ltd., Pergamon Imprint, Oxford, England.

states.[2] For the sake of convenience, as well as of accuracy, these individuals were identified from the membership rolls of the National Association for Court Administration (NAC) and the National Association of Trial Court Administrators (NATCA). These are the professional organizations most closely identified with court management at the local level in the United States. While this method of identifying the population of court managers is not optimal, other attempts to identify these individuals have proved to be less satisfactory.

In late 1982, the questionnaire was sent to 410 NACA members and 321 NATCA members. From the 731 questionnaires sent (with one postcard follow-up), 407 (55.7 percent) were returned, including 205 (50 percent) of the NACA members and 202 (62.9 percent) of the NATCA members. Thirty of the questionnaires returned were from individuals not directly engaged in court management, bringing the number of usable cases down to 377. Although using a response group of slightly over 55 percent is far from ideal, it was felt that the dearth of empirical research on court management underscored the importance of the information gained.

The survey instrument was divided into two areas: (1) general demographic features of the court managers and courts in which they served and (2) questions dealing with the role of court managers and their relations with others in the courts. The present article focuses on the scope of the court manager's job and the conflicts arising from interaction with the courtroom work group.

THE SCOPE OF COURT MANAGEMENT

A major function of the courtroom work group is to assure that there is a smooth flow of cases through the courts, and all member of the work group bear some responsibility for this function (Einstein and Jacob, 1977). Although the judges are ultimately responsible for the disposition of cases, court managers execute many administrative functions that are directly or indirectly related to case flow.

Mort and Hall (1980: 12) point out that when the first trial-court administrative positions began to appear "there was little doubt or confusion about their exact purpose." The functions of the "professional" court administrator have been assumed to include: case-flow management, personnel administration, budgeting and finance, records keeping, and other housekeeping functions (Butler, 1977; Saari, 1982). Yet it should also be noted that the context and scope of court management is not defined solely by appointed administrators. As Berkson and Hays (1976) note, most courts have de facto court administrators—the court clerks—irrespective of the presence or absence of appointed administrators. In terms of conflict within the courtroom work group, the existence of both court clerks and appointed administrators may serve to exacerbate conflicts.

Given the possibility of administrators and clerks coexisting within the same court and given the fact that judges are ultimately responsible for the management of the courts, it is entirely reasonable to examine first the administrative status of court managers and assess to what extent they act in an administrative capacity. For this reason, respondents were asked who had the primary responsibility—a manager or a judge—for performing four administrative functions. Two of the functions, budgeting and personnel, are commonplace in any organizational setting. The other two functions, case scheduling and jury management, are endemic to the legal process and represent major elements in many intracourt conflicts.

It can be seen in Table 1 that at least half of the managers reported having the primary responsibility for each of the four functions. However, the degree of managerial control was not uniform across functions. The most prevalent function assigned to court managers concerned the budget, for which almost nine out of every ten managers claimed primary responsibility. This function was closely followed by functions involving personnel administration. In terms of jury management and case scheduling, the degree of domination by court managers was not nearly as great. Less than two-thirds claimed primary responsibility for these two functions. Among those managers not having primary control, the consensus was that the four duties were under the direct authority of a judge or judges.

SOURCES OF DISAGREEMENT

Local court managers were asked to name the three most common sources of disagreement between their offices and the judges' offices. Because of the open-ended nature of the question and the broad range of answers, these responses were grouped into sixteen general categories. In turn, the number of first, second, and third mentions within each category were tallied. These absolute frequencies were then used to rank the sixteen categories in descending order from most to least mentions. The top five categories are presented in Table 2. To enhance the analysis, rankings are presented for both elected and appointed managers.

Case-Flow Management Practices

The major source of conflict for both elected and appointed managers was case-flow management. Included in this category were comments concerning: postponement of cases, judges rescheduling the calendar, docketing, judicial assignments, and backlogs. Case-flow management is one of the crucial elements in any court management scheme. However, it is also one of the elements that lie in the ill-defined area between adjudicative and nonadjudicative functions.

TABLE 1   ADMINISTRATIVE RESPONSIBILITY FOR FOUR FUNCTIONS

	Budget		*Personnel*		*Jury Management*		*Case Scheduling*	
	No.	*%*	*No.*	*%*	*No.*	*%*	*No.*	*%*
Manager	325	88.8	319	86.9	215	65.7	202	54.6
Judge	14	3.8	28	7.6	99	30.3	149	40.3
Both	23	6.3	18	4.9	9	2.8	15	4.1
Someone else	4	1.1	2	.5	4	1.2	4	1.1
Total	366	100.0	367	99.9	237	100.0	370	100.0
Missing cases	11		10		50		7	

As was seen in Table 1, case-flow management in much less a universal responsibility for court managers than are budgeting and personnel administration. This comports with Butler's (1977) findings that: (1) case-flow management was one of the ten duties least-delegated by presiding judges and (2) case-flow management was ranked last in a list of the ten administrative duties most frequently mentioned in conjunction with court administration.

Mort and Hall (1980) also found, in a 1978 survey of NATCA members, that case-flow management was one of the six functions least performed by court administrators. Their explanation was that "judges would be reluctant to delegate any duties that might be considered judicial in nature" (1980: 14). They found also that case-flow management, or calendar management as it is often called, ranks second among the areas presenting the greatest problems to trial-court administrators.

It would seem, then, that although case-flow management is defined as one of the primary functions of court managers (see, for example, LaBar, 1975; Butler, 1977; Scheb, 1981; Saari, 1982), it is a leading source of conflict within the courtroom work group.

Financial Issues and Personnel Matters

Although ranked slightly differently by elected and appointed managers, the areas of finances and personnel were considered two of the five major sources of conflict in court management. Financial issues included accounting problems and methods, unbudgeted expenditures, procurement policies, and budget cutbacks. Among the personnel issues identified were employee evaluations, salary disputes, the lack of adequate staff, and the competency of staff.

As noted in Table 1, the vast majority of managers identified financial issues and personnel matters, to a much greater extent than jury scheduling and case management, as

TABLE 2 MAJOR SOURCES OF INTRACOURT CONFLICT FOR ELECTED AND APPOINTED MANAGERS

Elected

1. Case-flow management practices
2. Policy and planning issues
3. Communication problems
4. Financial issues
   Personnel matters

Appointed

1. Case-flow management problems
2. Personnel matters
3. Policy and planning issues
4. Financial issues
5. Authority to administer

being primarily their responsibility. One of the leading reasons for conflict here could easily be the broader political environment of the courts.

A number of writers (Berg, 1972; Berkson and Hays, 1976) have noted the fact that, in a very real sense, the courts frequently are not masters of their own fates. Their budgets are adopted by county or state legislative bodies and their purchasing and personnel procedures (merit systems, for example) are adopted by these same groups. This means that court managers must live by rules not of their own making. There are also internal court procedures and policies allowing judges, and occasionally others, to hire, fire, direct, and compensate their own employees. Additionally, as previously mentioned, there may exist within a court two administrative infrastructures—one for the elected court clerk and one for an appointed administrator.

Both Butler (1977) and Mort and Hall (1980) report that personnel management and financial control are the duties performed most frequently by court administrators, or assigned most frequently by judges. However, Mort and Hall indicate further that these responsibilities rank second and third, respectively, as areas presenting the greatest problems to court administrators.

According to additional comments made by respondents to the questionnaire, both internal and external sources of conflict are evident in the areas of budgeting and personnel. The managers seemed to feel constrained by legislative control, by the state administrative offices of court, and by the wielding of power—often perceived as interference—by judges.

Policy and Planning Issues

A fourth area of common concern, for appointed and elected managers, was policy and planning. Among the responses in this category were poor planning, no goal setting, no standardization of procedures, lack of policy consistency, and reorganization.

Previous studies on the roles and functions of court managers have shed little light on this area of conflict. At least two studies (Mort and Hall, 1980; Saari, 1982), however, seem to indicate that such conflict should be examined along an administration continuum. If the goal of court management is to control, that is, to "routinize," "bureaucratize," and make more rational, then conflict may arise between managers and other professionals, such as judges and attorneys. Efforts to make the courts more manageable may increase the "mounting tension between judicial and administrative roles in trial courts" (Mort and Hall, 1980: 12). Thus the more court managers try to control the courts, the greater the tendency toward a classical bureaucratic model, and, as previously mentioned, Saari (1982: 55) maintains that "management styles of bureaucratic nature are inappropriate for courts, because they cannot control a central process that does not exist."

Authority to Administer

The fifth area of concern for appointed administrators was with what may be called *authority to administer*. Responses here dealt with issues such as: authority not clearly established, delegation of responsibility without authority, lack of major policy-making authority, and changes that must be initiated by the judge(s).

When one looks at what Saari (1982) calls the derivative nature of court administration, this concern of appointed administrators becomes understandable. First, appointed administrators do not enjoy constitutional status, as do elected court clerks in the majority of states, and 82 percent of the responding managers in this study were appointed to their positions by a judge or panel of judges and served at the pleasure of their appointer(s).

Second, the derivative nature of court administration means that the appointed administrator exercises his or her authority as an extension of the judge's (or judges') authority. This "reflected glory" leaves the appointed administrator uncertain of his or her power base, unsure of direction, and perhaps reluctant to exercise policy initiatives. Court administrators must "constantly 'check with judges' to ascertain their wants and needs" (Saari, 1982: 62).

Comments elicited at the end of the questionnaire provide further illumination on the authority-to-administer issue. Several court administrators noted that their judges either failed to provide support or leadership, or, at worst, questioned the need for court administrators. Related to this issue, Mort and Hall (1980) conclude that many judges view court administrators merely as administrative aides, an attitude that might result in the eventual elimination of such positions.

For elected court managers, intracourt communication presents a problem. In response to questions about this area of conflict, elected managers listed problems such as lack of staff meetings, lack of communication, and proper oral or written communications.

It is important to remember that local courts are composed of a number of independent, though interdependent, actors. Judges, prosecutors, public defenders, and clerks are all independently selected, creating the perception of independent political constituencies. As Berkson and Hays (1976) suggest in their study of Florida court clerks, communications problems may result from a lack of meaningful leadership on the part of local judges. This lack of leadership means that the office of court clerk may at times operate almost autonomously.

Given their different methods of selection, it is not unusual for elected and appointed managers to have different perceptions regarding intracourt communication. As a final measure of their perceptions of independent power, elected and appointed managers were asked whether the judge(s) treated them as colleagues, employees, or some other category. The majority of elected clerks (58.9 percent) perceived themselves as colleagues, thus being coequal with the judges. This perception clearly indicates potential communication problems. Of the appointed managers, only 37.1 percent felt they were colleagues with the judges; most (41.4 percent) considered their position as that of a court employee.

Conflict and Administrative Duties

It is quite possible that conflict is a product of confusion over who has the primary responsibility for carrying out a particular set of tasks. That is, the types of conflicts experienced by court personnel may depend on who is in the driver's seat—a judge or a court manager. To assess this possibility, the responses to each of the administrative functions discussed in Table 1 were cross-tabulated with whether or not a respondent mentioned one of the five sources of conflict described above. While the tables produced from this procedure are too numerous to report here, a certain uniformity exists among them: there is no relationship between (1) who has a particular responsibility and (2) sources of conflict.

Thus, for example, managers who had responsibility for budgeting were just as likely as managers who did not perform this task to mention financial issues as a source of conflict. Further, there was no difference in this pattern between appointed and elected managers.

One reason for this lack of relationship between primary authority and sources of conflict resides in the fact that the judges are the ultimate managers of the courts. Conflict arises, from the structural arrangement that gives the judges a central role in the courts. A slightly more complex explanation might arise from considering the dynamics of the court work group. If and when a manager has primary responsibility for a function, any behavior on the part of judges might be interpreted as interference, and conflictual in nature. If, on the other hand, a manager does not have primary responsibility for a task, conflict may arise due to managerial encroachment. In any event, the scope of conflict is not constrained by functional authority.

CONCLUSIONS

Although the courtroom work group is a useful device for examining the organizational dynamics of American courts, many of the assumptions made previously about such groups need to be examined. While the actors in the work group may indeed be interdependent, there are a number of forces at work within the courts that bring these factors into conflict with one another.

Among the major areas of disagreement identified by respondents to this questionnaire were case-flow management practices, policy and planning issues, financial issues, personnel matters, communication problems, and conflict over the authority to administer. Given these areas of disagreement, it appears that there are some common concerns for both elected and appointed managers. By the same token, there seem to be some distinct factors influencing each group.

In the final analysis, the main source of conflict within the courtroom work group may very well be a difference of perspective. The more court managers attempt to control the administrative process, the wider the gap will be between managers, on the one hand, and lawyers and judges, on the other. It must be recognized that these two groups have different perspectives on *what* is to be done and *how* it is to be done.

ACKNOWLEDGMENTS

The authors gratefully acknowledge the Arts and Sciences Research Center at New Mexico State University for funding this project and the executive boards and members of the National Association for Court Administration and the National Association of Trial Court Administrators for their assistance in the research.

NOTES

1. The term *courtroom work group* provides a useful shorthand for denoting judges, attorneys, court reporters, bailiffs, and court management personnel.

2. The generic term *court manager* is used here to include administrators, executives, and clerks, whether appointed or elected.

REFERENCES

BERG, J. S. (1972). "Assumption of Administrative Responsibility for the Judiciary: Rx for Reform." *Suffolk University Law Review* 6: 796–814.

BERKSON, L. and S. HAYS. (1976). "The Forgotten Politicians: Court Clerks." *University of Miami Law Review* 30: 499–516.

BUTLER, B. W. (1977). "Presiding Judges' Perceptions of Trial Court Administrators." *Justice System Journal* 3: 181–198.

EINSTEIN, J. and H. JACOB. (1977). *Felony Justice: An Organizational Analysis of Criminal Courts.* Boston: Little, Brown.

FEELEY, M. J. (1983). *Court Reform on Trial.* New York: Basic Books.

LaBAR, W. (1975). "The Modernization of Court Functions: A Review of Court Management and Computer Technology." *Journal of Computers and Laws* 5: 97–119.

MORT, G. A. and M. D. HALL. (1980). "The Trial Court Administrator: Court Executive or Administrative Aide?" *Court Management Journal* 12–16, 30–31.

NEUBAUER, D. W. (1979). *America's Court and the Criminal Justice System.* North Scituate, Mass.: Duxbury Press.

SAARI, D. (1982). *American Court Management.* Westport, Conn.: Quorum Books.

SCHEB, J. M. (1981). "Florida Conference Examines Education of Court Administrators." *Judicature* 465–468.

QUESTIONS FOR DISCUSSION

1. According to the authors, why is there an inherent conflict "managing" the courts and the professional philosophies of judges and lawyers?

2. Discuss the scope of courtroom workgroups, particularly when managing the smooth flow of cases through the process.

3. Discuss the following list of disagreements in the court. Provide examples to support your response.
   - Case-flow management practices
   - Financial issues and personnel matters
   - Policy and planning issues
   - Authority to administer

4. How do the authors explain the conflict in the court with respect to responsibility, authority, and administrative duties?

5. Based on your reading of this article, how might the relationship between members of the courtroom workgroup be changed to enhance the courts' effectiveness? Provide examples to support your response.

17

SENTENCING REFORM AND CORRECTIONAL POLICY
SOME UNANSWERED QUESTIONS

Edward E. Rhine

■ ■

The years since the mid-1970s have witnessed profound changes in sentencing philosophy and practice in the United States. The philosophy of sentencing in many states has shifted from a reliance on a rehabilitative rationale emphasizing utilitarian goals and a focus on the offender to a "just deserts" rationale emphasizing retribution and the nature of the offense. While the former looks toward the future and what the offender may do, the latter is concerned with the type of crime that has been committed and the sanction that should be imposed commensurate to the severity of the offense.

A variety of factors have contributed to the movement toward sentencing reform, most notably, the politicization of crime control policy and the loss of faith in the capacity of sentencing to effect offender change. The innovations that have since been adopted reflect a fundamental shift to greater determinacy in sentencing. Yet, in contrast to the indeterminate sentence that dominated sanctioning policy from the 1930s through the early 1970s, the sentencing reforms that have been implemented display significant variation in structure. A single comprehensive approach to sentencing comparable to the indeterminate sentencing model has yet to emerge (Tonry, 1987).

Nonetheless, the sentencing reform movement has exerted an enormous impact on the field of corrections. The "get tough" sentencing policies sponsored under its auspices contributed to unprecedented prison population growth in many jurisdictions during the 1980s, a pattern that is likely to continue well into the 1990s. Likewise, the emphasis on tailoring punishment almost exclusively to the nature of the crime has served to devalue concerns with rehabilitation and support for treatment programs. Finally, the preoccupation with narrowly structuring the type of punishment that can be imposed at the time of sentencing has presented a serious challenge to the value, if not the future, of parole.

This chapter will consider sentencing reform in relation to three correctional policy issues that must be addressed in the decade ahead. How these issues are resolved will carry enormous consequences for correctional and parole management administrators. First, should sentencing policy be linked to the management of correctional resources, that is, to

Reprinted by permission of the publisher.

available prison capacity? Second, should (and can) a concern for rehabilitation be integrated within a sentencing model that emphasizes "just deserts"? Third, should parole boards be retained and, if so, what role should they play within a structured system of sentencing? Though some jurisdictions have confronted these issues, the diversity of approaches to sentencing reform has produced wide variation in their responses.

SENTENCING REFORM: PAST AND PRESENT

From the Progressive Era in criminal justice through the start of the 1970s every state and the federal system relied on indeterminate sentencing structures (Tonry, 1987). Judges were given extraordinary latitude to impose terms of confinement subject only to minimum and maximum sentencing limits. Parole boards, in turn, exercised broad discretion in deciding when an inmate should be released from prison. This type of sentencing system reflected a widespread consensus, perhaps honored more in the breach than in practice, that accepted rehabilitation as the governing rationale for imprisonment. As Cullen and Gilbert (1982) note, it assumed that the process of sentencing should contribute to offender reform.

This consensus in sentencing policy manifested a remarkable durability for over four decades. For a variety of reasons, some of which will be discussed here, there was a collapse of the consensus that had long supported indeterminacy as the reigning paradigm in sentencing. (For a succinct review of the reasons for the challenge to indeterminate sentencing codes, see Morris and Tonry, 1990, pp. 20–24.) Within the span of a decade beginning around 1975, every state, the District of Columbia, and the federal government revised or considered replacing indeterminate with determinate sentencing codes (Shane-DuBow, Brown, and Olsen, 1985).

Despite the intensity of focus, as Tonry points out, during this period "the monolith of American indeterminate sentencing dissolved, to be replaced not by another monolith, but by a diverse assortment of sentencing approaches that varied state by state" (1987, p. 6). With growing momentum, one jurisdiction after another increased its criminal penalties, enacted mandatory sentencing laws, and passed or strengthened habitual or repeat offender statutes.

Although the trend toward greater determinacy in sentencing did not result in a common approach, the proponents of the reforms agreed that "justice" and "fairness" should serve as the paramount goals of sentencing (for example, Fogel, 1975; Twentieth Century Fund Task Force, 1976; von Hirsch, 1976). Sentencing systems should be structured to achieve consistency and predictability in outcomes, reduce the disparate treatment often experienced by offenders, and ensure accountability in official decision making.

The sentencing reforms that emerged subsequently may be placed into three general categories. The first major innovation was the development of voluntary sentencing guidelines, by far the single most popular sentencing reform in the United States between 1975 and 1980 (Tonry, 1988, p. 278). More than forty states eventually established voluntary sentencing guidelines projects (Morris and Tonry, 1990, p. 26).[1] Because compliance with the guidelines was largely voluntary and not a matter of statutory or legislative mandate, the various efforts failed to achieve their goals, and in most states, have now been abandoned.

The second pattern of sentencing reform is often referred to as statutory or presumptive determinate sentencing. According to Tonry, a determinate sentencing system is "one in which parole has been abolished and, accordingly, the length of a prison sentence can be known, that is determined, at the time that it is imposed" (1987, p. 77). Though the presumptions governing such sentences varied widely using this definition, ten states adopted some form of determinate sentencing: California, Colorado, Connecticut, Illinois, Indiana, Maine, Minnesota, New Mexico, North Carolina, and Washington.

The trend toward statutory determinate sentencing has ended. No jurisdiction has adopted this approach for several years. Moreover, two states (Minnesota and Washington) have replaced this sentencing scheme with presumptive sentencing guidelines—perhaps the most important of the sentencing reform initiatives undertaken to date.

The third sentencing innovation was introduced in 1972 by Judge Marvin Frankel. Decrying the absence of the rule of law in criminal sentencing, he urged that a sentencing commission be created to establish explicit standards to structure judicial discretion (von Hirsch, Knapp, and Tonry, 1987, p. 461). Three key features were incorporated within the sentencing framework that he proposed: (a) the formation of a permanent sentencing commission to create, monitor, and modify presumptive sentencing guidelines; (b) the development of presumptive sentencing guidelines for judges specifying whom to imprison and for how long; and (c) the creation of a formal mechanism permitting appellate sentence review whenever the sentencing judge departed from the guidelines.

Six years later, in 1978, Minnesota became the first state to form a sentencing commission and subsequently adopt presumptive sentencing guidelines. Other jurisdictions have since followed suit, including Washington, Pennsylvania, and the District of Columbia. In 1983, Florida moved from a system of voluntary to presumptive sentencing guidelines. At the federal level, the U.S. Sentencing Commission was established in 1984. Three years later, it implemented a system of presumptive sentencing guidelines.

In contrast to the demise of voluntary sentencing guidelines projects and a declining interest in statutory determinate sentencing, two to three states per year establish sentencing commissions or their equivalent (Morris and Tonry, 1990, p. 39). Such bodies are currently found in Kansas, Louisiana, New Mexico, Oregon, and Tennessee. Whether they will be successful, however, remains an open issue. Sentencing commissions were created in Connecticut, Maine, New York, and South Carolina, but either they were unable to achieve a consensus on sentencing policy or the guidelines they recommended for adoption failed to win legislative approval (Tonry, 1987, p. 45–75).

The movement toward greater determinacy and equity in sentencing has occurred within a political and legislative arena that has stiffened penalties for criminal convictions and increased the average time served in prison by such means as mandatory sentencing laws, sentencing enhancements, and the abolition of discretionary parole release. In a majority of jurisdictions, sentencing reforms have contributed to and occurred simultaneously with the rapid growth of prison populations. While sentencing commissions in several states have developed presumptive sentencing guidelines that are sensitive to the prison population capacity of the state, others have not. Given unrelenting prison population growth, unless this issue is addressed directly and realistically, the effectiveness of any sentencing reform that is undertaken will be seriously compromised (Tonry, 1988; von Hirsch, 1987).

PRISON POPULATION GROWTH AND THE MANAGEMENT OF CORRECTIONAL RESOURCES

Austin and McVey (1988) report that when the first national census of federal and state prisoners was conducted in 1850 it showed that the nation housed 6,737 inmates. The rate of incarceration was 29 per 100,000 population. Though the incarceration rate increased shortly afterwards through the end of the 19th century until the start of the 1970s, it hovered between 75 and 125 prisoners per 100,000. Thus, for well over a century, the nation's rate of imprisonment showed remarkable stability.

The situation has changed dramatically in a very short period of time. Since 1972 the prison population has grown more rapidly than in any other period since the founding of the penitentiary in the early 1800s (Blumstein, 1988). In 1970, state and federal prisons housed 196,429 prisoners. The rate of incarceration was 96 per 100,000 population (Blumstein, 1988). In 1980, a total of 329, 821 inmates were confined behind prison walls, representing an incarceration rate of 139 per 100,000. Less than 10 years later, on December 31, 1989, the combined prison population was 710,054, while the incarceration rate stood at 274 per 100,000 (Bureau of Justice Statistics, 1990).

This historically unprecedented level of growth has continued unabated. As of June 10, 1990, the prison population had grown by over 80,000 prisoners to a record-breaking total of 755,425 and an incarceration rate of 289 per 100,000. According to the director of the Bureau of Justice Statistics, this increase represents "the largest growth in sixty-five years of prison population statistics" (*USA Today*, 9 September 1990). Current projections indicate that the prison population will continue to grow, perhaps even more dramatically, well into the 1990s (Austin and McVey, 1989; Blumstein, 1989).

The enormous jump in the rate of imprisonment has been accompanied by unparalleled increases in expenditures for corrections. For some time, the costs associated with corrections have been increasing at a significant rate relative to per capita spending by state and local governments for other governmental functions (for example, education, public welfare, hospitals and health care). In fiscal year 1987, the fifty states spent nearly $12 billion on corrections. This figure, which increased 15.6 percent in fiscal year 1988 to $13.9 billion, grew even more to $14.5 billion in fiscal year 1989 (National Association of State Budget Officers, 1989).

The continuing growth in the prison population, combined with the escalating costs, has focused the attention of policymakers and legislators on how to cope with correctional systems that seem to be spinning out of control. In a number of states, especially those which have engaged in massive prison construction programs and have spend hundreds of millions of dollars in an effort to manage the growth, the recognition is spreading that it is not possible nor desirable to continue to expand bedspace to meet the demand (Strasser, 1989).

California offers a telling example. In 1987, the state legislature established a Blue Ribbon Commission to review the corrections crisis and to make recommendations for the future. In 1979, the prison population stood at 22,500. By 1990, it was over 86,000, an increase of over 400 percent (California Blue Ribbon Commission, 1990). According to estimates developed by the commission, there will be over 136,000 inmates by 1994 in a prison system that will have a capacity of 72,000, despite further construction. Likewise, the department of corrections' budget has increased from $300 million in 1980 to roughly $1.8 billion in 1990. By 1994 or 1995, it will exceed $4 billion.

In assessing the causes for the growth, the commission found that the

> proliferation of sentencing and enhancement laws as developed by the legislature has resulted in a "piecemeal" approach to sentencing without attention to any precise sentencing structure. The result has been the development of an extremely complex system which now has become very difficult to administer. (California Blue Ribbon Commission, 1990, p. 6)

Among its recommendations, the commission urged that a Sentencing Law Review Commission (SLRC) composed of representatives from across the criminal justice system be established to review adult and juvenile sentencing issues.

In terms of authority, the SLRC would be empowered to make recommendations to the governor and the legislature on the creation of an ongoing mechanism to monitor the effects of sentencing laws, population "caps," and the financial and administrative impact any changes in the sentencing structure will have on the California Department of Corrections, the California Youth Authority, and local jail populations. It seems evident, however, that unless the SLRC adopts a systemwide sentencing strategy that is tied to prison population growth, the state's correctional crisis will overwhelm any future efforts at sentencing reform.

What is true in California also applies to other jurisdictions that are attempting to cope with the effects of prison crowding and spiraling correctional budgets. Minnesota offers one of the few examples wherein the sentencing commission that was created addressed the need to tailor sentencing policy to prison capacity. The commission adopted a "just deserts" premise to govern the use of imprisonment. With respect to sentencing policy, it decided to use confinement mainly as a punishment for violent, but not property, offenders. Previously, repeat property offenders had been imprisoned while first-time violent offenders received other sanctions (von Hirsch, Knapp, and Tonry, 1987).

The commission likewise determined that a statutory directive stating that it take correctional resources into "substantial consideration" required that it develop sentencing guidelines so that their implementation could be achieved within the limits of the existing capacity of the prison system. Although there has been some "backsliding" in terms of overall compliance with the guidelines' provisions, the commission has been fairly successful in achieving the goals of sentencing reform within the constraints of available correctional resources (Tonry, 1988).

As von Hirsch et al. (1987, pp. 12–13; 69) note, "freezing" prison populations at current levels, or at levels just above or below existing capacity, introduces a measure of realism in debates over how much to punish. It requires that public officials consider what trade-offs they are willing to make to ensure that offenders who most deserve imprisonment are actually confined. In commenting on the willingness of the Minnesota Sentencing Commission to develop guidelines detailing how such trade-offs should be made, Morris and Tonry point out that for the first time policymakers had "to think comprehensively about sentencing, to think about punishments for any single offense in relation to punishments for all other offenses" (1990, p. 49).

The need to link sanctioning policy to prison capacity is more urgent today than it was even five years ago. Several of the sentencing commissions that have been established recently are considering changes in sentencing policies that would, in effect, link punishment to correctional resources (for example, Louisiana). This approach treats prison beds as a scarce source that must be rationally allocated to those offenders who are considered the most serious or violent lawbreakers.

The formation of a sentencing commission and the development of presumptive sentencing guidelines offer a promising vehicle for achieving this linkage. Accomplishing this goal will not occur, however, unless the commission is directed to ensure that the prison population remains within a capacity level deemed appropriate. Other jurisdictions that have created sentencing commissions but without a commitment to tie sentencing policy to correctional resources are facing a serious prison crowding crisis. The most notable example is, of course, the Federal Bureau of Prisons, which is reeling under the impact of the guidelines promulgated by the U.S. Sentencing Commission.

Reserving prison bedspace for those offenders deemed most important to incarcerate represents an essential component of sentencing reform. It does not, however, serve as a rationale for punishment. Nor does it suggest the programs and opportunities that should be provided to inmates during confinement. A notable—albeit intentional—weakness of most sentencing reform initiatives thus far undertaken is their failure to include a commitment to offender rehabilitation as a salient rationale for sentencing.

REHABILITATION AND THE RATIONALE FOR SENTENCING

Though its roots may be traced to the Progressive Era of criminal justice, the ascendancy of the rehabilitative ideal occurred during a period of unparalleled confidence in American institutions following World War II (Zalman, 1987). the belief that offender treatment should be the primary purpose of imprisonment soon came to exercise an ideological hegemony over the field of corrections.

The rehabilitative ideal served as the reigning paradigm in corrections for nearly three decades, from the 1940s through the early 1970s. As was suggested earlier, one of the primary factors contributing to the sentencing reform movement was the marked loss of confidence in the value of rehabilitation (Allen, 1981). Its dramatic decline was precipitated by changes in the social and political order that caused the public, politicians, academicians, and others to lose faith in the capacity of the correctional system to change offender behavior and thereby reduce recidivism (Cullen and Gendreau, 1989; Griset, 1987).

A number of existing studies had already raised questions concerning the impact of treatment programs on subsequent criminal behavior (for example, Wooton, 1959). The now well-known article published in 1974 by Robert Martinson entitled "What Works— Questions and Answers About Prison Reform," however, provided an apparently irrefutable, research-based critique of the capacity of the correctional system to rehabilitate criminal offenders.

Martinson's article and the much longer 1,400-page report on which it was based (Lipton, Martinson, and Wilks, 1975) called into question the entire correctional enterprise with the comment that in terms of programmatic intervention "nothing works." Basing this conclusion on a review of 231 studies evaluating the effectiveness of treatment programs for criminal offenders that were conducted between 1945 and 1967, Martinson dismissed the whole notion of correctional treatment:

> With few and isolated exceptions, the rehabilitative efforts that have been reported so far have had no appreciable effect on recidivism. Studies that have been done since our survey was conducted do not present any major grounds for altering that conclusion. (Martinson, 1974, p. 25).

Martinson (1979) was later to recant the stridency of his original conclusion with supportive qualifications regarding the efficacy of treatment programs. It was perhaps fortuitous that at the same time that this article was published, the National Academy of Sciences confirmed the soundness of the original conclusion (Sechrest, White, and Brown, 1979). Given the credibility accorded these findings, the rehabilitative ideal suffered a profound, if not irreparable, loss of legitimacy.

In response to the seeming ineffectiveness of rehabilitation, as well as widespread criticism of indeterminate sentences, a growing chorus of works urged the adoption of determinate or fixed sentencing structures (for example, American Friends Service Committee, 1971; Fogel, 1975; von Hirsch, 1976). The proponents argued that the primary purpose of sentencing should be retribution, with a focus on the distance offense, and not rehabilitation with its concern for what the offender might do in the future. Von Hirsch argued forcefully for a "just deserts" model wherein disparity would be reduced and equity emphasized within a determinate sentencing structure. Within this framework, comparable sanctions would be imposed on equally culpable offenders commensurate to the severity of their crimes.

The just deserts rationale that was adopted subsequently by a number of states emphasized punishing offenders proportionate to the gravity of their crime. In accordance with this rationale—one featuring deserts and proportionality—the question of what punishment to impose is determined mainly by the seriousness of the offense. Though most jurisdictions opted for a "modified deserts" model in which the offender's prior criminal history factored in systematically at the time of sentencing, the focus moved away from any concern for rehabilitating criminal offenders.

The Sentencing Commission in Minnesota embraced a "modified desert" rationale to govern the decision whether or not to impose a prison sentence. It established a sentencing rationale that stated explicitly that the primary determinant of a prison sentence is the seriousness of the current offense; prior criminal history is given less importance in placing the offender above or below the "in/out" dispositional slope on the presumptive sentencing grid (von Hirsch, Knapp and Tonry, 1987).

Likewise, the presumptive sentencing guidelines system developed in Washington following passage of the Sentencing Reform Act (SRA) reflected a shift in rationale from the offender to the offense. Under SRA, the punishment to be imposed is to be proportionate to the seriousness of the offense and the offender's criminal history (Lovell, 1985). The guidelines, which have been in effect since July 1, 1984, stress equity and predictability in sentencing outcomes.

At the federal level, the U.S. Sentencing Commission was given broad authorization by Congress to craft sentencing guidelines that took into account the seriousness of the offense, deterrence, public protection, and correctional treatment. Instead, the commission chose an exclusively deserts-oriented rationale and presumptive sentencing guidelines that are stingy in their provision for nonprison sentences (Morris and Tonry, 1990). Its guidelines grid includes a detailed specification of the punishment to be imposed based on where the defendant falls in terms of offense level (of which there are 43) and criminal history category (of which there are six). The sentencing structure is designed to be strictly punitive.

As these jurisdictions illustrate, the choice of a rationale for sentencing is critical. Von Hirsch and colleagues point out that how this choice is made "will determine which features of the offense or of the offender should be relied on in determining the punishment" (1987, p. 10). Though they vary to some extent, most jurisdictions that have adopted statutory determinate sentencing or presumptive sentencing guidelines have excluded rehabilitation as a rationale for offender sanctioning. Recent research suggests that this issue may need to be reconsidered.

Future sentencing reform must confront the growing body of evidence that effective correctional treatment is possible. The remarkable pace at which legislators and policy makers moved from the era of "everything works" to the era of "nothing works" suggests that the findings of science and ideology both played a role (Andrews et al., 1990; Cullen and Gendreau, 1989; DiIulio, 1990). With respect to science, the past several years have witnessed the development of a significant body of research reaffirming the value of rehabilitative programs for criminal offenders, as well as principles to enhance the effectiveness of such intervention.[2]

Cullen and Gendreau (1989, p. 31) report that between 1973 and 1987 nearly two hundred studies were conducted evaluating the effectiveness of treatment programs for offenders. Gendreau and Ross (1987) reviewed this literature covering the period 1981 to 1987. The studies they selected had to satisfy certain requirements (for example, quasi-experimental designs, published in edited journals or texts). The types of interventions that were examined varied widely from early/family prevention, traditional probation and parole, work and restitution programs, intensive supervision, substance abuse regimens, and "get tough" approaches (for example, shock incarceration). According to these authors, "it is downright ridiculous to say 'Nothing works.'...Much is going on to indicate that offender rehabilitation has been, can be, and will be achieved" (Gendreau and Ross, 1987, p. 395).

Nonetheless, Gendreau, Ross, Cullen, or others pursuing research on this topic (Zample and Porporino, 1988, 1990) do not argue that adopting rehabilitation as a goal or rationale for offender sanctioning will serve as a panacea for the problem of crime. The accumulating research suggests only that certain programs may reduce the likelihood that certain offenders will commit new crimes when compared to similar groups of nonpartic-ipants. Any programs that are implemented must be multifaceted, use several intervention techniques, and be conducted by qualified staff in supportive environments consistent with therapeutic principles (Ross, 1989).

These findings suggest that rehabilitation should be considered an appropriate rationale for sentencing and incorporated within a presumptive guidelines system—if just deserts concerns for equity and proportionality are also taken into consideration. Rehabilitation may be used as a rationale for selecting specific treatment-oriented sanctions (for example, placement in a residential drug program) within the constraints of fair and proportionate punishments. In accordance with Morris and Tonry (1990), a range of interchangeable punishments may need to be established as presumptively appropriate for cases falling within the same cell on the sentencing grid. Yet, doing so would permit rehabilitative considerations to influence the choice of sanctions to impose at the time of sentencing.

The argument thus far suggests that sentencing reform in the 1990s must confront the need to link sentencing policy to correctional resources and consider restoring rehabilitation as an important though not exclusive rationale for offender sanctioning. Future initiatives must also address and resolve the question of parole.

PAROLE AND THE STRUCTURING OF DISCRETION

Parole is in a period of transition (Bottomley, 1990). Prior to the era of sentencing reform parole boards were given broad discretion to determine when an offender was ready for release—a decision limited only by the constraints of the minimum and maximum sentence imposed by the judge. There were few standards governing the decision to grant or deny parole. Parole boards were considered an integral part of an indeterminate sentencing system that elevated rehabilitation as the central purpose of imprisonment.

The challenge to indeterminacy in sentencing was coupled with an assault on parole as well. In fact, the shift toward greater emphasis on determinacy in sentencing exerted a more far-reaching impact on parole than on any other component of the criminal justice system. With Maine in the forefront, six states either eliminated or severely limited parole release between 1976 and 1979: California, Colorado, Illinois, Indiana, Maine, and New Mexico. From 1980 to 1984 another five states followed suit: Connecticut, Florida, Minnesota, North Carolina, and Washington.

Likewise, with respect to the federal level, the Comprehensive Crime Control Act of 1984 was enacted creating the U.S. Sentencing Commission. This legislation abolished the U.S. Parole Commission, which is scheduled to be phased out in 1997. Certain offenders will continue to be supervised upon their release.

In terms of sentencing reform, the abolition of parole does not necessarily follow the adoption of presumptive determinate sentencing structures (for example, New Jersey) or a shift to presumptive sentencing guidelines (for example, Pennsylvania). In states where sentencing commissions are considered "success stories," however, the discretionary authority of the parole board has been abolished (for example, Minnesota and Washington).

The wave of sentencing reform that began in the 1970s has resulted in a significant diminution of parole boards' discretionary authority to release. Between 1977 and 1988 the percentage of inmates granted conditional or parole release declined from 71.9 percent to 40.3 percent, respectively. Conversely, those released to mandatory supervision jumped sharply from 5.9 percent in 1977 to 30.6 percent in 1988 (Bureau of Justice Statistics, 1989).[3]

Though the impact has been dramatic, the movement to abolish parole appears to have peaked. Since 1984, only one state has eliminated discretionary parole release (Delaware in 1990). Two states that at one point abolished discretionary parole release have recently restored the parole board, Colorado and Connecticut. North Carolina, which placed severe constraints on its parole commission in 1981, has gradually restored some of its previous discretion. Florida, which adopted sentencing guidelines in 1983 and abolished parole, has now returned the function under the new name, Controlled Release Authority.

If enthusiasm for abolishing parole has waned, this is due largely to the pressures generated by prison crowding. Parole boards have long served as the historical "back door keeper" of the American prison system (Garry, 1984; Rothman, 1980). The unprecedented growth in correctional populations, however, has placed enormous pressures on parole boards to serve as the de facto manager of prison population levels.[4] The record-setting increases threaten to undermine recent developments in parole that have significant implications for future sentencing reforms.

One of the more salient, if unrecognized, trends with respect to paroling authorities nationwide has been the movement toward structured parole decision making. In response to widespread criticism in the 1970s over the absence of standards to govern release decisions, some parole boards began to experiment with parole guidelines. The first and best-known guidelines project was initiated by the U.S. Parole Commission (then the U.S. Board of Parole) in 1972 (Gottfredson, Wilkins, and Hoffman, 1978). Gradually, other boards followed suit. An ACA Parole Task Force survey conducted in 1988 found that 23 jurisdictions reported using "formal structured guidelines" (Rhine, Smith, Jackson, Burke, and LaBelle, 1991).

There is no one common definition of what constitutes such guidelines. In some states, a "matrix" approach is used, whereas in others a listing of factors (aggravating and mitigating) informs the decision to grant or deny parole. Various studies of different states' experiences with parole guidelines, however, have concluded that structuring the release decision through guidelines provides a measure of equity (by reducing both sentencing and parole disparities), greater consistency and fairness, and more accountability relative to how parole decisions are made (Tonry, 1987).

Many states that use parole guidelines also include a structured assessment of offender risk. Predicting which inmates may be returned safely to the community has always been a concern of parole boards. Offender risk assessment through the use of objective decision-making tools represents a relatively new development that has occurred simultaneously with the adoption of parole guidelines.

The trend toward managing both discretion and offender risk through the application of structured, decision-making tools represents a significant philosophical shift in the direction of balancing "just deserts" goals with the more traditional crime control concerns. For those offenders subject to the parole board's jurisdiction, presumptive parole guidelines may be integrated within the parameters established by presumptive sentencing guidelines. Though it would be the parole board rather than the sentencing judge that would determine the actual timing of release from confinement, the board would be expected to provide reasons for any departure from the presumptive parole date.

The same reasoning applies to parole revocation. Most of the sentencing reforms thus far have created presumptive sentencing guidelines for those who may be imprisoned. They have not addressed what actions should be taken for noncompliance with the conditions of supervision nor the duration of reconfinement if parole is revoked. Parole boards that have considered these issues have focused mainly on developing schedules for setting future eligibility terms without due regard for grading the seriousness of the parole violation. Formal revocation guidelines may be developed by a sentencing commission or the parole board to cover the types of violations and the presumptive length of confinement that should apply.[5] As with the release decision, the parole board would have to justify departures from the presumptive term of recommitment.

Paroling authorities are uniquely situated in most jurisdictions to balance the goals of fairness, just deserts, and offender risk management at the point of granting or denying parole. Likewise, they occupy a pivotal position relative to establishing fair and just standards to govern the revocation of parole. The rationale and structure that they adopt for decision making, however, may and must be firmly integrated within the principles and framework of determinate sentencing reform.

CONCLUSION

Within the span of less than two decades, sentencing practices across the United States have undergone dramatic change. Despite the variety of approaches that have been adopted, the sentencing reform movement has resulted in greater determinacy and accountability with respect to decision making. The attempt to introduce greater rationality and structure in sentencing practices has not always been successful, however, as evidenced by the number of jurisdictions in which sentencing commissions have been unable to develop presumptive sentencing guidelines or win legislative approval once proposed.

Nonetheless, the framework and principles established under the auspices of sentencing reform will continue to exert a significant influence on whatever innovations are introduced in the future. Moreover, if the emphasis has thus far been on the "in/out" decision with respect to imprisonment, the focus will eventually come to include how to structure sentencing for the vast majority of offenders who receive nonprison terms. According to Morris and Tonry,

> [concerns] for justice and fairness will lead, in time, probably within 25 years, to the creation in most American states of comprehensive systems of structured sentencing discretion that encompass a continuum of punishments from probation to imprisonment, with many intermediate punishments ranged between. (1990, p. 18).

This chapter has considered sentencing reform and correctional policy only in relation to offenders who are presumptively bound for state prison. Given the projected future rate of growth in this population, however, it is imperative that sanctioning policy be linked to prison capacity. Reserving prison bedspace for persons who are viewed as the most deserving of confinement requires that policymakers think realistically about the inevitable trade-offs that must occur when debating overall punishment policy for a given jurisdiction.

The effective management of limited correctional resources must be extended as well to managing constructively offenders' time during confinement. Sentencing reforms to date have chosen to elevate just deserts concerns based on the gravity of the crime and prior criminal history as the predominant rationale for punishment. What happens incidental to incarceration and the value of rehabilitation as a rationale for sanctioning are for the most part excluded from consideration within determinate sentencing models.

In view of the spate of research reaffirming the value of rehabilitation—under appropriate programmatic circumstances—future sentencing initiatives should incorporate offender treatment as one of several rationales for sentencing. Though it may not be possible to integrate philosophically retributionist or just deserts goals with utilitarian or crime control goals, they can and must be balanced as a matter of sensible public policy.

Just as there is growing evidence with respect to the efficacy of correctional treatment, recent surveys suggest that the public believes in and is supportive of rehabilitative programs if such programs do not compromise public safety. A recent study in Alabama (Doble and Klein, 1989) showed particular support for work and reparative programs (for example, community service), while research in Ohio revealed citizen support for inmates earning early release for good behavior and for participation in education and work programs during their confinement (Skovron, Scott, and Cullen, 1988).

Over 750,000 inmates are confined in state and federal prisons across the country, most of whom will eventually return to the community. By virtue of their location in the criminal justice system, paroling authorities are uniquely situated to balance the goals of just deserts and offender risk management through the application of parole guidelines. Such guidelines may be integrated within a structured sentencing framework and cover release and revocation decision making.

As von Hirsch and colleagues (1987, p. 88) point out, the sentencing policies that are adopted within given jurisdictions will exert, at most, a marginal influence on aggregate crime rates. Many factors well beyond the control of the criminal justice system contribute to increases or decreases in the rate of crime. Future sentencing reforms may, however, provide a sensible, just, and effective system of sanctioning to the extent they treat prison bedspace as a finite resource, restore rehabilitation as a justification for sentencing, and support the trend toward structured parole decision making.

NOTES

1. This initiative drew on the development of parole guidelines by the U.S. Parole Commission, a notable project that was aimed at bringing structure and consistency to parole decision making at the federal level (Gottfredson, Wilkins, and Hoffman, 1978).

2. Martinson's review which represents the most widely commented upon empirical basis for debunking the value of rehabilitation, especially as a rationale for sentencing, suggested only that "the statistical evidence was inconclusive based on the best research then available....The data did not admit of confident generalizations one way or the other" (DiIulio, 1990).

3. Inmates who leave prison as supervised, mandatory releases do so when the calendar time they have served plus the accrual of "good time" credits equal their maximum sentence. They

are not on parole though they are normally supervised by a parole officer. Unlike regular parole, mandatory releases remain under supervision only for a period of time equal to the amount of good time deducted. During this limited period, they may be subject to revocation by the parole board for noncompliance with the conditions of supervision.

4. Some paroling authorities have received legislative authority to control the prison population (for example, Georgia), while parole boards elsewhere have been required to release inmates under emergency powers acts (for example, South Carolina). In still other jurisdictions, quota systems have been created wherein the number of inmates released must equal the number of new admissions (for example, Texas).

5. While the concept of intermediate sanctions has been confined largely to the front end of the criminal justice system, between prison and probation (for example, McCarthy, 1987; Morris and Tonry, 1990), it may be extended to cover the back end of the system as well, between prison and parole. Paroling authorities may develop a range of intermediate sanctions that are considered presumptively appropriate for cases falling with the same cell on the revocation guidelines grid.

REFERENCES

ALLEN, FRANCIS A. (1981). *The Decline of the Rehabilitative Ideal: Penal Policy and Social Purpose.* New Haven, Conn.: Yale University Press.

American Friends Service Committee. (1971). *Struggle for Justice.* New York: Hill and Wang.

ANDREWS, D. A., IVAN ZINGER, ROBERT D. HOGE, JAMES BONTA, PAUL GENDREAU, and FRANCIS T. CULLEN. (1990). "Does Correctional Treatment Work? A Clinically Relevant and Psychologically Informed Meta-analysis." *Criminology, 28* (3), 369–402.

AUSTIN, JAMES, AND AARON D. MCVEY. (1988). *The NCCD Prison Population Forecast: The Growing Imprisonment of America.* San Francisco: National Council on Crime and Delinquency.

AUSTIN, JAMES, and AARON D. MCVEY. (1989). "The Impact of the War on Drugs." *Focus.* San Francisco: National Council on Crime and Delinquency.

BLUMSTEIN, ALFRED. (1988). "Prison Populations: A System Out of Control?" In Michael Tonry and Norval Morris (Eds.), *Crime and Justice: A Review of Research.* Chicago: University of Chicago Press, pp. 231–266.

BLUMSTEIN, ALFRED. (1989). "American Prisons in a Time of Crisis." In Lynn Goodstein and Doris L. Mackenzie (Eds.), *The American Prison: Issues in Research Policy.* New York: Plenum, pp. 13–22.

BOTTOMLEY, A. KEITH. (1990). "Parole in Transition: A Comparative Study of Origins, Developments, and Prospects for the 1990s." In Michael Tonry and Norval Morris (Eds.), *Crime and Justice: A Review of Research.* Chicago: University of Chicago Press, pp. 319–374.

Bureau of Justice Statistics. (1989). "Probation and Parole, 1988." Washington, D.C.: U.S. Department of Justice.

Bureau of Justice Statistics. (1990). "Prisoners in 1989." Washington, D.C.: U.S. Department of Justice.

California Blue Ribbon Commission on Inmate Population Management. (1990). *Final Report.* Sacramento, Calif.

CULLEN, FRANK, and PAUL GENDREAU. (1989). "The Effectiveness of Correctional Intervention." In Lynn Goodstein and Doris L. Mackenzie (Eds.), *The American Prison: Issues in Research Policy.* New York: Plenum.

CULLEN, FRANK, and KAREN GILBERT. (1982). *Reaffirming Rehabilitation*. Cincinnati: Anderson.

DIIULIO, JOHN J., Jr. (1990, Fall). "Getting Prisons Straight." *The American Prospect*, pp. 54–64.

DOBLE, JOHN, and JOSH KLEIN. (1989). *Prison Overcrowding and Alternative Sentences: The Views of People of Alabama*. New York: Public Agenda Foundation.

FOGEL, DAVID. (1975). *We are the Living Proof: The Justice Model for Corrections*. Cincinnati: Anderson.

GARRY, EILEEN. (1984). *Options to Reduce Prison Crowding*. Rockville, Md.: National Institute of Justice/NCIRS.

GENDREAU, PAUL, and ROBERT R. ROSS. (1987). Revivification of Rehabilitation: Evidence from the 1980s. *Justice Quarterly 4*. 349–407.

GOTTFREDSON, DON, LESLIE T. WILKINS, and PETER B. HOFFMAN. (1978). *Guidelines for Parole and Sentencing*. Lexington, Mass.: Lexington Books.

GRISET, PAMELA L. (1987). *The Rise and Fall of the Determinate Ideal in New York State* Dissertation. State University of New York at Albany.

LIPTON, DOUGLAS, ROBERT MARTINSON, and JUDITH WILKS. (1975). *The Effectiveness of Correctional Treatment: A Survey of Treatment Evaluation Studies*. New York: Praeger.

LOVELL, DAVID G. (1985). *Sentencing Reform and the Treatment of Offenders*. Seattle, Wash.: Washington Council on Crime and Delinquency, SAFECO Insurance Company.

MARTINSON, ROBERT. (1974). "What Works—Questions and Answers About Prison Reform." *Public Interest, 35*, 22–54.

MARTINSON, ROBERT. (1979). "New Findings New Views: A Note of Caution Regarding Reform." *Hofstra Law Review, 7*, 243–258.

MCCARTHY, BELINDA R., (Ed.). (1987). *Intermediate Punishments: Intensive Supervision, Home Confinement and Electronic Surveillance*. Monsey, N.Y.: Criminal Justice Press.

MORRIS, NORVAL, and MICHAEL TONRY. (1990). *Between Prison and Probation: Intermediate Punishments in a Rational Sentencing System*. New York: Oxford University Press.

National Association of State Budget Officers. (1989). "State Expenditure Report 1989." Washington, D.C.: U.S. Government Printing Office.

National Conference of State Legislatures. (1989). "State Legislatures and Corrections Policies: An Overview." Denver, Co.: National Conference of State Legislatures.

RHINE, EDWARD E., WILLIAM D. SMITH, RONALD W. JACKSON, PEGGY B. BURKE, and ROGER LABELLE. (1991). *Paroling Authorities: Recent History and Current Practice*. Laurel, Md.: American Correctional Association.

ROSS, ROBERT. (1989, April). "Something Works!" *Liaison*. Ottawa, Ontario: Ministry Secretariat, Solicitor General of Canada, pp. 4–12.

ROTHMAN, DAVID J. (1980). *Conscience and Convenience: The Asylum and Its Alternatives in Progressive America*. Boston: Little, Brown.

SECHREST, LEE B., SUSAN O. WHITE, and ELIZABETH BROWN (Eds.). (1979). *The Rehabilitation of Offenders: Problems and Prospects*. Washington, D.C.: National Academy of Sciences.

SHANE-DUBOW, SANDRA, ALICE P. BROWN, and ERIK OLSEN. (1985). *Sentencing Reform in the United States: History, Content, and Effect*. Washington, D.C.: U.S. Government Printing Office.

SKOVRON, SANDRA E., JOSEPH E. SCOTT, and FRANCIS T. CULLEN. (1988). "Prison Crowding: Public Attitudes Toward Strategies of Population Control."*Journal of Research in Crime and Delinquency, 25*, 150–169.

STRASSER, FRED. (1989, January). "Making the Punishment Fit the Crime and the Prison Budget." *Governing*, pp. 36–41.

TONRY, MICHAEL. (1987). *Sentencing Reform Impacts*. National Institute of Justice, U.S. Department of Justice. Washington, D.C.: U.S. Government Printing Office.

TONRY, MICHAEL. (1988). "Structuring Sentencing." In Michael Tonry and Norval Morris (Eds.), *Crime and Justice: A Review of Research*. Chicago: University of Chicago Press, pp. 267–337.

TWENTIETH CENTURY FUND TASK FORCE ON CRIMINAL SENTENCING. (1976). *Fair and Certain Punishment*. New York: McGraw-Hill.

USA Today. (1990, September 4). "Prison Population at Record Level."

VON HIRSCH, ANDREW. (1976). *Doing Justice: The Choice of Punishments*. New York: Hill and Wang.

VON HIRSCH, ANDREW, KAY A. KNAPP, and MICHAEL TONRY. (1987). *The Sentencing Commission and Its Guidelines*. Boston: Northeastern University Press.

WOOTEN, BARBARA. (1959). *Social Science and Social Pathology*. London: George Allen and Unwin.

ZALMAN, MARVIN. (1987). "Sentencing in a Free Society: The Failure of the President's Crime Commission to Influence Sentencing Policy." *Justice Quarterly, 4*, 545–569.

ZAMBLE, EDWARD, and FRANK J. PORPORINO. (1988). *Coping, Behavior, and Adaptation in Prison Inmates*. Secaucus, N.J.: Springer-Verlag.

ZAMBLE, EDWARD, and FRANK J. PORPORINO. (1990). "Coping, Imprisonment, and Rehabilitation: Some Data and Their Implications." *Criminal Justice and Behavior, 17*, (1), 53–70.

QUESTIONS FOR DISCUSSION

1. In the mid-1970s, a shift took place in sentencing policy. Indeterminate models that had been used for forty years were replaced, in many states, by determinate models of sentencing. Discuss the three general categories of sentencing reforms that occurred.

2. What impact has determinate sentencing policies had on the incarceration rate since the 1970s?

3. Why is the need to link sanctioning policy to prison capacity becoming increasingly urgent?

4. Why should rehabilitation and treatment of offenders be an integral part of sentencing options?

5. As determinate sentencing became a paramount model for many states, the importance of parole boards waned. According to the author this trend has had a negative influence on corrections because paroling authorities are uniquely situated to balance goals of fairness, just deserts, and risk management. Discuss.

18

THE LIMITS OF PUNISHMENT AS SOCIAL POLICY

Don C. Gibbons

INTRODUCTION

For the past few decades, American society has been pursuing crime control policies that reflect a central theme, "get tough with criminals." In particular, punitive measures have been urged as the way to deal with "garden variety offenders" who commit offenses such as petty theft, burglary, or larceny, and who come most often from the underclass in American society. "Get tough" policies have been much less frequently urged for inside traders, physicians involved in Medicare fraud, or other upperworld criminals.

Have these punitive crime control policies produced a safer society? Is there less crime in the United States as a result of taking a hard line toward offenders? The answer is that the crime control policies of the past decade or so have produced few positive results. Starting in the early 1970s, markedly increased numbers of people have been warehoused in prisons, so that incarcerated offenders increased from about 200,000 per day to nearly 900,000 per day in this period. But recent data would indicate that imprisonment has neither rehabilitated nor deterred most of those who have been sent to prisons. Most of those who have been imprisoned have been "low rate" offenders rather than "career criminals." We have purchased, at great cost, relatively little reduction in crime through imprisonment.

What about claims that significant shrinkage of crime might be achieved through *selective* incapacitation of those who would appear to be hardened criminals? This proposal bumps up against the obdurate fact that no one has been able to develop techniques that make it possible to select these "high rate" lawbreakers before they have embarked on a pattern of intensive criminal activity.

Massive use of imprisonment is an ineffective social policy and ought to be curtailed for that reason alone. Moreover, widespread use of prisons cannot be defended as a social control policy in a decent society. There is a glaring tension between our beliefs that American society is a model for the rest of the world and that we have the highest incarceration rate of any free world nation.

Instilling fear in offenders or potential lawbreakers through threats of imprisonment or other punitive measures cannot succeed as the central strategy around which the criminal justice system is to operate. There is an urgent need for alternative and less harsh measures to be employed, along with sparing use of imprisonment, for violent offenders. Even more important, the first line of defense against lawbreaking is a society that provides meaningful social and economic rewards for all of its citizens.

GETTING TOUGH WITH CRIMINALS

During the past two decades, opinion polls have repeatedly shown that American citizens perceive themselves to be under domestic siege from "barbarians from within" who threaten to rob them, burglarize their homes, assault them, or make their lives intolerable in other ways. In short, the belief is widespread that a "crime wave" has engulfed in the United States. Many citizens also apparently think that the crime problem can be drastically reduced if our political leaders and those who run the correctional machinery exhibit the firmness and resolve that hard solutions require. Consistent and punitive actions are needed for those who offend against other citizens, so it has been said.

These punitive sentiments have been voiced by criminologists and intellectual leaders in criminal justice as well. Rarely do we hear any of those appeals that were common in the 1950s and 1960s calling for treatment and rehabilitation measures that might help offenders untangle themselves from lawbreaking. Indeed, those who describe criminals in this way have fallen silent and have been replaced by observers who tell us alarming things about "the criminal mind," "career criminals," and the lawless classes in American society. Some also advocate that certain lawbreakers, including violent juveniles, be disposed of entirely through capital punishment. Long prison sentences have been put forth as the cure for the errant ways of hardened "career criminals."

Recent decades have witnessed the spread of such dramatic and punitive responses to crime and criminals as we have moved to "get tough" with domestic enemies. The most visible impact of this hard line is found in the dramatic increase in the number of citizens, adults and juveniles alike, now packed into prisons, training schools and other custodial institutions. This trend is revealed in prisoner statistics for state and federal penal institutions which indicate that from 1958 to 1965 the year-end population count in those institutions hovered around 210,000 people, while from 1965 to 1973 the figure was below 200,000 inmates (Flanagan and McGarrell, 1985, p. 531).

However, beginning in 1973, prison populations began an apparently inexorable growth, starting with 204,211 inmates in 1973, 285,456 prisoners in 1977, and 315,974 in 1980. In the years since 1980, this surge in prison populations has been even more marked. There are currently (late 1989) over 700,000 adults incarcerated in prisons and reformatories—not including those in jails or juvenile institutions, which are also stuffed to overflowing with inmates. Virtually all of the nation's correctional facilities are experiencing severe pressures arising from this massive shift toward incarceration as the linchpin of correctional policy. The end result of warehousing miscreants and lawbreakers is that the United States now has the unenviable distinction of being the leader of the free world in the use of imprisonment as a social policy.

The facts are clear enough—criminal justice policies in American society have hardened markedly in the past decade or so. The increased use of incarceration is simply the most dramatic manifestation of the general shift toward punitive crime control measures. Less clear are the lessons citizens and policymakers ought to draw from such recent experiences. Are the policies validated by evidence indicating that they have reduced crime and protected law abiding citizens from lawbreaking? Or have imprisonment and other hard-line solutions to the crime problem produced few if any tangible results? Clearly, it is time to ask whether current American crime control policies make sense.

CONTROLLING CRIME: FIRST PRINCIPLES

Although the statistical signals are somewhat mixed, recent evidence on reported crime in the United States hints that lawbreaking leveled off in the early 1980s from the peaks observed in the 1970s, but then began to increase again from 1985 to the present (Federal Bureau of Investigation, 1990, p. 48). The hard fact is that crime continues to occur much more frequently in this country than in other nations around the world. The United States stands virtually alone among Western nations in terms of excessive violence among its citizens including robbery, theft, and other criminal activities (Archer and Gartner, 1984; Currie, 1985). Further, there are compelling indications that lawlessness is likely to continue well into the twenty-first century unless drastic steps are taken to curb it (Currie, 1987; Sykes, 1980).

What can be done to control or perhaps even drastically curtail crime in the decades ahead? Before answering this question, we must address a prior one: What are the causes of crime? Unfortunately, there are no simple answers to the mysteries of crime causation. The accumulated criminological wisdom cannot be captured in a few brief paragraphs, but is it possible to limn the contours of that knowledge?

Two quite different views about the causes of criminality can be found in the research produced by criminologists and other students of crime. Beginning with the writings of Lombroso in the 1800s, a number of thinkers urged upon us the conclusion that lawbreakers differ from the rest of us in biological and/or psychological ways. This claim bears a good deal of similarity to beliefs about "the dangerous classes" that were entertained by citizens in the nineteenth century England, with crime being linked to hypothesized biological or psychological defects on the part of criminals. Contemporary versions of this line of thinking range from the patently wrongheaded (Samenow, 1984) to some complex, multifaceted, and at least at first reading, seemingly valid arguments linking biological defects, low intelligence, and psychological inadequacies to crime (Wilson and Hernstein, 1985).

If offenders are psychologically flawed or if they are willfully bad, then threats and punishment make sense, but if this diagnosis is off the mark, some other approach of preventing or curing it is called for.

What about the view of offenders as depraved members of "the dangerous classes"? There is no denying that a few psychologically impaired "monsters" do turn up in the offender population from time to time. John Gacy, Ted Bundy, and Richard Speck come quickly to mind. Few would deny that there are *some* lawbreakers whose behavior can be traced to biological or psychological defects or impairments, but that does not demonstrate the validity of such explanations for crime and criminals in general. Two points stand out. First, those who speak of "the criminal mind" or who link lawbreaking to biological or constitutional factors, low intelligence, and low tolerance for frustration have restricted this picture of the defective criminal to "garden-variety" offenders and have remained silent about upper-world or white-collar criminals to whom such arguments would surely seem not to apply. Second, the evidence in support of these theories, even when applied only to underclass criminals, is weak and unconvincing.

This picture of garden-variety offenders is not entirely out of focus for, not surprisingly, many of them do exhibit personal and social liabilities of one kind or another. Garden-variety lawbreakers are not usually drawn from the most talented or successful groups in society. Lawbreaking is often the work of people who have experienced little success or sense of fulfillment in the world of work, school, or marriage, and who have been cut off from the economic mainstream.

But, the key question is this: Why are there so many candidates for crime and participants in lawbreaking in American society? Is it true, as many criminologists have argued, that crime most often involves people who are trapped in the secondary labor market or are chronically unemployed? Are they individuals who feel the sting of relative deprivation and the victims of racial or ethnic discrimination which cuts them off from job opportunities? Are they the products of ineffective schools located in the inner-city neighborhoods? Have many of them grown up in "problem families" whose difficulties stem mainly from their precarious economic existence, and who reside in urban, inner-city neighborhoods populated by similarly situated families and in which the informal social controls that operate in more affluent neighborhoods are lacking? Most criminologists have concluded that these factors more accurately capture the casual influences in lawbreaking than do the arguments of those who speak of "the criminal mind" or who posit the existence of a criminal class in American society (Currie, 1985; Gibbons, 1987).

There is one point that warrants particular emphasis. Much of the commentary on crime control that turns up in the public arena emphasizes the use of formal measures of social control in order to discourage further criminality on the part of offenders. Probation is one formal sanction on one end of a punitive scale, while imprisonment or execution is one the other pole. However, conformity, including law abiding conduct, is obtained principally through informal social controls—one's internalized standards or conscience, neighborhood influences, and social ties and traditions that bind the members of society together into a law abiding population.

Japan comes quickly to mind as a low-crime society in which law abiding conduct is maintained, not principally by the police or the courts, but by family solidarity and cultural traditions. The Japanese experience shows that where informal social controls are strong, the police and justice system agencies have relatively little work to perform, but where community controls are weak and citizens are atomized or alienated, even draconian measures of formal social control fail to stem the tide of criminality.

Sociological observers in the United States have frequently observed widely varying capabilities of local neighborhoods to deter crime, with high crime areas showing sundered social ties and defective neighborhood social controls (Reiss and Tonry, 1986). The implication of this finding is clear: The search for viable approaches to dealing with the crime problem in American society ought to emphasize measures that strengthen the informal social control mechanisms in our communities, rather than concentrate entirely on ways to strengthen the hand of the state in crime control measures or on tactics that will either attract apprehended offenders into more law abiding ways of behavior or will frighten and intimidate them and drive them out of lawbreaking.

Why are the social influences that discourage criminality weak in some American neighborhoods and strong in others? The causes are the same ones that push some individuals into violent acts and crude and illegal forms of "income retribution" such as robberies or burglaries. Those who have lost out in the struggle for meaningful work and educational opportunities, decent housing, and other less tangible but equally important rewards of American society end up with other disadvantaged citizens in neighborhoods where they are unable to sustain a sense of community and where they are vulnerable to attacks from lawbreakers in their midst.

DIAGNOSING AND CONTROLLING CRIME

A look at the history of crime control measures in Western societies shows that virtually every tactic the human mind could invent to be used in the "war on crime" has been employed somewhere, including such historically important measures as flogging, transporting, imprisoning, or burning the cheeks of offenders. Also, some advocates of "new" approaches to crime control periodically attempt to revive some of the more barbarous of these tactics, for example, those who have recently advocated a return to corporal punishment.

Among criminologists, it was once fashionable to announce that punishment is a futile and immoral policy, but such a pronouncement is too facile. Experiences in South Africa, for example, indicate that an unpopular minority government is quite capable of ruling with an iron fist, at least in the short run. Similarly, who is to say that the Malaysian policy of executing all drug dealers is a failure? Perhaps if we allowed no reduction of murder charges to manslaughter, made no exceptions for second degree murder, and quickly put all convicted murderers to death, homicide rates might drop.

There might be a noticeable reduction in crime if we were to maintain a level of two or three million citizens in prison. But is this the kind of nation in which most Americans want to live—a fortress society? While criminal justice policies that emphasize the draconian punishments may be effective, at least for short periods, severe sanctions raise profound moral and ethical concerns.

Formal social control measures are extremely varied, but they can be sorted into two types. The first, and currently most popular approach, is predicated on modern-day versions of imagery about the dangerous classes that were popular in nineteenth century England. It centers on instilling fear in lawbreakers and potential lawbreakers through tactics of terror and repression, along with sanitizing society, at least temporarily, by preventive detention of so-called career criminals.

Some will protest such labels as tactics of fear and repression or terror as exaggerations at best; after all, Americans do not throw political dissenters in gulags or employ the repressive measures that are too common in South Africa. Perhaps their protest has some merit. On the other hand, a nation that incarcerates nearly a million of its citizens in prisons can hardly be described as a kind and gentle one! Fear, repression, and terror are apt terms for proposals that have been aired to extend capital punishment to juveniles and for policies of throwing a large and ever-increasing number of people in prisons and other custodial institutions.

A rehabilitative posture toward offenders need not excuse them from responsibility for their lawbreaking. Society can and should condemn lawbreaking while refraining from terror tactics.

The second approach, the "society as patient" perspective, assumes that crime is a reflection of societal conditions. This rehabilitation–social integration–preventive position shifts attention away from punishing offenders and toward efforts to alter "criminogenic" features of society, as well as to assist lawbreakers in disengaging themselves from criminal activity.

Proposals focusing on the breakdown of informal social controls and the need to strengthen them, along with other efforts to improve the quality of life in American society so as to provide positive incentives for law abiding conduct, have usually emanated from the liberal part of the American political spectrum. The same is true of programs to provide offenders with job skills, find them rewarding employment, and aid them in various other ways to become reintegrated into their communities. But we need to ask hard questions about which programs work and which ones don't, rather than get bogged down in attaching "liberal" or "conservative" labels.

These two approaches to crime are polar ones, for in the real world everywhere, in both the past and the present, mixtures of crime control practices have been pursued. For example, in England in the 1700s there were 350 capital offenses for which large numbers of people were executed but, at the same time, fewer people were actually put to death than were eligible to be hanged. Many offenders escaped severe punishments through benefit of clergy and other forms of leniency (Thompson, 1975).

Crime control practices in contemporary America are a schizoid combination of therapeutic and punitive approaches. The criminal justice system comes down hard on underclass offenders, filling institutions with hordes of them and lining up large numbers of people to be executed (Cheatwood, 1985). At the same time, our newspapers are filled with reports about financial shenanigans on a large scale by brokerage firms, antitrust activities of major corporations and savings and loan organizations, sleazy and illegal behavior by present and former government officials, and other instances of upperworld crime that result in judicial wrist slapping and other lenient penalties. Similarly, we live in a society that has recently witnessed such countervailing trends as a move to "get tough" with some juvenile offenders at the same time that other programs have been created to divert misbehaving youngsters out of the official juvenile justice system. In the same way, there are two competing views of school violence and delinquent conduct that occurs in schools and about how to respond to it. Some authorities hold that school violence is the work of "rotten kids" and the solution is to throw them out of school, leaving in school only the conformist youngsters who want to learn. Others have written about "rotten schools" that drive youths toward delinquent acts and have recommended reforms in school programs. It is impossible to describe all these divergent programs as part of a coherent and coordinated criminal or juvenile justice system.

EVALUATING CRIME CONTROL POLICIES

There are two basic questions that should be asked about crime control efforts. Do they work, and at what cost? The first question is deceptively simple, asking whether policy A works better than policy B, as measured by such criteria as reduction or recidivism on the part of punished or treated offenders. Although the methodological directions to be pursued in trying to get answers to this query are clear, specific efforts to gauge the impact of correctional intervention efforts have been plagued by a host of problems, producing results that have often been exceedingly equivocal. The issue of the effectiveness or ineffectiveness of the death penalty as a deterrent is an extreme illustration. Some experts claim the evidence shows the inefficacy of the death penalty while others have argued that data show that each execution prevents several other homicides. No wonder some criminologists have been driven to the fuzzy but judicious conclusion—we are not sure what the data really show!

The issue of "at what cost?" is even more thorny. For one thing, there are cost–benefit questions of how much crime reduction is obtained from alternatives, such as incarcerating people as opposed to doing something else with them. Even more troublesome is the issue of the dangers to a free society that may be posed by punitive policies, particularly of the kind currently being pursued. What are the effects on our cherished notions of justice when more and more people are being handed the death penalty and ever-increasing numbers of citizens are being placed in prison, and, especially troubling, the most severe penalties are coming down particularly hard on blacks and other minority group members? Answers to these questions go well beyond simple empirical issues but still must be addressed. If we are to lay claim to being the finest society yet devised, we must examine the moral impact as well as the financial and correctional effects of crime control policies. Policies must be judged by how much justice they deliver as well as their specific impact upon offenders.

NOTHING WORKS—OR DOES IT?

There are three broad periods in the crime experiences of American society since the turn of the century. The first, roughly from about 1900 to the 1940s, was characterized by relatively low crime rates and by punitive approaches to offenders, relieved somewhat by humanitarian gestures. A substantial number of lawbreakers were imprisoned in penal institutions, but the rate of incarceration was relatively low. Most of the prisons of this period made little or no pretense of being in the rehabilitation business; instead, they were convict-run, harsh, and punitive in their programs.

The late 1950s and the 1960s witnessed the rise of "the rehabilitative ideal." Criminologists rushed to announce that punishment was an archaic response to crime and that it would soon disappear. Correctional administrators around the nation gave a good deal of lip service to treatment and intervention as the primary goals of their systems. In a number of states, the authorities moved to wrest control of penal institutions away from convict leaders. Finally, in a few states such as California, concerted efforts were actually mounted to implement the rehabilitative ideal. In the 1950s and 1960s, a variety of experimental ventures were launched to test out new and hopefully more effective programs of correctional intervention.

In the third and most recent period, the exceedingly pessimistic "nothing works" view captured the attention of many correctional policymakers and lay people alike. Public support for treatment and intervention withered away, at least in part because many criminological observers have rushed to embrace the contention that rehabilitation is an idea whose time has gone. We now find ourselves thrown back upon punishment and repression as devices to be employed in a desperate struggle to turn back the tide of lawbreaking.[1]

Robert Martinson (1975) has frequently been credited with or blamed for delivering the bad news that "nothing works," although earlier warnings that all was not well with correctional treatment had been sounded by a number of others (Bailey, 1966; Lerman, 1968; Robinson and Smith, 1971). Also, the negative message about treatment and its lack of impact on offenders has been repeated a number of times since the 1975 report by Lipton, Martinson, and Wilks (Greenberg, 1977; Sechrest, White, and Brown, 1979).

Although advocates of rehabilitation were severely shaken by these assertions that nothing works, some of them refused to endorse this conclusion and instead continued to claim that the picture was not as bleak as first appearances suggested (Halleck and Witte, 1977; Palmer, 1975; Ross and Gendreau, 1980; Shireman, Mann, Larsen, and Young, 1972). Indeed, Martinson himself subsequently confessed to seeing signs of positive results from treatment that he had earlier overlooked (Martinson, 1979; also see Wilson, 1980).

Much of the protreatment argument turned on the contention that the rehabilitative ideal remains valid but that efforts to implement it had been too puny.[2] If more funds were provided for treatment and if better trained workers were employed, intervention efforts would then produce significant results, so it was claimed. Another defense of rehabilitation appeared in a study by Murray and Cox (1979), who argued that the standard measure of program success, namely, complete desistance from further lawbreaking, is too strict or demanding. In their view, programs should be judged in terms of the extent to which they result in *suppression* or misbehavior, that is, the extent to which treated offenders reduce the number of offenses they commit in the post-intervention period.

Another defense of rehabilitation programs is the "different strokes for different folks," or differential treatment, argument. This is the plausible claim that intervention efforts directed willy-nilly at haphazardly chosen collections of offenders are likely to fail. What is called for instead is the matching of specific intervention activities with particular types of offenders.

These are reasonable arguments, as is also the claim that the evaluation studies that have been conducted to date are too few in number, methodologically flawed, and in other ways an inadequate foundation for bold assertions that nothing works. Even so, those who argue that "treatment works" are ultimately obliged to produce positive evidence to buttress that contention. Some of that evidence is now at hand. Some support for rehabilitative ventures can be found in a small book by Greenwood and Zimring (1985; also see Gibbons, 1990), which begins by observing that the surveys of treatment evaluation studies concluding "nothing works" failed to look for differences in impact *within* intervention program types such as milieu treatment or group counseling. Perhaps some programs have been effective while others have been unsuccessful depending on whether they were headed by a charismatic director and staffed by high caliber workers or contained other positive program elements.

Greenwood and Zimring examined a number of programs that seem to hold particular promise. Some of these are addressed to chronic offenders and are operated by private organizations rather than local or state governments. Other promising intervention efforts were identified for predelinquents or less serious lawbreakers, including programs that strive to teach parenting skills to offenders' parents and advocate intensified schooling programs.

Lundman's (1984) critique of various delinquency control ventures is also a source of new ideas regarding intervention and rehabilitation. Also, reports have appeared from time to time concerning ventures such as New Pride, an apparently effective nonresidential, community-based program for juvenile offenders that provides a blend of counseling, alternative schooling, correction of learning disabilities, vocational training, job placement, recreation, and cultural activities (Regnery, 1985).

Many of these new ideas and new programs have to do with juvenile offenders, but there are also recent efforts in rehabilitation of adult offenders. New evidence indicates that instead of being an idea whose time has passed, the full potential of rehabilitation and social intervention has not yet been realized. This is a conclusion to which we shall return, but first we need to examine the punitive policies of the past dozen years in more detail.

THE LIMITS OF PUNISHMENT AS SOCIAL POLICY

The American crime rate began a dramatic move upward in the early 1970s, reached a peak in 1980, apparently began a slight descent in the years from 1980 to 1984, and then turned upward again in the past few years. On the other hand, the daily count of prisoners in adult correctional institutions rose from about 200,000 in 1970 to more than 710,000 at the end of 1989. Indeed, the prison population grew 10 times faster than did the general population between 1975 and 1985.

In addition, the number of felons doing time in jails increased markedly during the same period. Jails have received the overflow that cannot be accommodated in American prisons, most of which contain greater numbers of prisoners than they were designed to hold and many of which are under court order to reduce crowding or alleviate other conditions of inhumane treatment.

The explosion of prison populations was the result of two related processes: More convicted felons were being sent to prison by judges than in earlier periods, and for longer sentences. Crime control through incapacitation of greater numbers of criminals has been the guiding principle of social policies in the 1970s and 1980s. Increased use of incarceration has been joined with efforts to raise the punitive force of lesser penalties handed out to less dangerous offenders. In short, punishment has been the order of the day.

What have we reaped from these policies? In particular, has incarceration had an appreciable effect on crime rates? Is imprisonment a viable social policy?

Although incarceration is widely used in the United States, the extent varies from state to state. In 1987, the District of Columbia had an imprisonment rate of 905 people per 100,000 population, followed by Nevada with a rate of 432 inmates, while at the other extreme, Minnesota and North Dakota had rates of about 60 prisoners per 100,000 population (Jamieson and Flanagan, 1989, p. 613). Statewide index crime rates for the fifty states in 1987 show relatively little correlation with imprisonment rates. Should we conclude from this that imprisonment causes crime? Obviously not, but neither should we assume that increased imprisonment leads to significant reductions in lawbreaking.

A number of criminological researchers have been involved in the past decade or so in complex calculations designed to determine how much reduction in lawbreaking can be attributed to the increased use of imprisonment and to gauge the degree to which criminality can be curtailed through further expansion of prison capacity. The results have not been precise or unequivocal, due largely to the problem of obtaining a valid measure of what these experts refer to as "lambda," that is, the annual rate at which individual offenders commit offenses.

If, in the real world, relatively few offenders commit a large share of the major crimes that occur, and if we have successfully identified those high-rate lawbreakers and have put them in prison, then crime rates should be influenced by imprisonment. But if, on the other hand, a large number of lawbreakers are engaged in sporadic flirtations with criminality and only a very small number of "high-rate career criminals" exist, incarceration of even large numbers of these part-time offenders would have relatively little impact on crime rates.

The truth appears to be closer to the second scenario than to the first. Rates of imprisonment are "driven" by available cell and bed space. In responding to the hue and cry for greater toughness in dealing with offenders, judges have had little trouble in singling out suitable candidates to fill all the cell space made available through expansion of existing facilities or building of new institutions. A relatively small amount of crime reduction is being purchased at an exorbitant cost, both to taxpayers and to many of those who are incarcerated. Finally, estimates of the number of people who would have to be incarcerated in order for significant reductions in crime to occur have indicated that the prison population would have to be at least doubled. No wonder, then, that some authorities have turned to a different and superficially appealing proposal: Don't incarcerate petty offenders on a massive scale; rather, catch budding "career criminals" who seem likely to commit crimes at a high rate before they have embarked on those careers, then selectively incapacitate them and reduce crime rates accordingly (Greenwood and Abrahamse, 1982).

Unfortunately for advocates of selective incapacitation, although perhaps fortunately for the targets of this proposed policy, there are two insurmountable problems with such a policy. To begin with, its supporters have not managed to dispose of the objection that giving much longer sentences to people who are predicted to become career criminals than are handed out to individuals who have committed similar crimes but do not appear to be budding career offenders is inequitable. Even more compelling, sentencing individuals for crimes that they may or may not commit if they are not incapacitated violates the fundamental principle that people are to be punished for their *actual* misdeeds, not ones they might do in the future.

Even if these moral and ethical objections to selective incapacitation could be set aside, there is the practical problem of prediction errors that has not been overcome. No one has managed to develop a prognostic tool for identifying potential career criminals that does not also misidentify a large number of people as potential serious offenders. This "false positive" problem plagues most predictive ventures in criminal justice, whether of career criminals, violent people, or some other kind of lawbreaker. While it might be acceptable for a predictive scheme to generate a number of "false negatives," that is, individuals erroneously identified as unlikely aggressive offenders of career criminals, a system that puts people into prison who do not deserve to be there is another matter entirely. It is for reasons of this kind that enthusiasm for selective incapacitation has waned (for example, see Greenwood and Turner, 1987).

Selective incapacitation is a chimera, as is the hope that a crime can be controlled by general incapacitation. Although it might be possible to make a dent in the crime problem by sentencing two to three million adults at any one time to prison, recent experiences in the United States indicate that such a policy is not going to become a reality. While many citizens might not be reluctant to send a horde of their fellow citizens off to prison if there were no price tag to contend with, they are not willing to pay the massive costs involved in construction and maintenance of prisons. The results from bond elections around the country have demonstrated considerable voter reluctance to fund an ever-expanding prison system.

Prisons have always had enemies in American society, so it is no wonder that many voices have been heard in recent years decrying the rapid and massive expansion of the population of incarcerated citizens. However, some new voices have very recently come from unexpected quarters, lamenting the overuse of prisons. In late 1986, a group of conservative scholars and politicians joined together to call for alternatives to prison, including restitution, community service, and even floggings and beatings. This conservative message differs from the one advanced in this chapter, for it is weighted heavily on the side of harsh sanctions and threats as crime control measures, rather than positive efforts to reintegrate offenders into the social mainstream. Nonetheless, that growing numbers of conservatives have come to see that the financial costs of imprisonment are too high may ultimately be of major significance in directing American society toward more rational and effective criminal justice policies.

NEW DIRECTIONS IN CONTROLLING CRIME

We come now to the final question: What directions should be pursued to create more sensible crime control strategies? The crime problems of American society are serious and cry out for short- and long-term solutions. There are immediate problems posed for criminal justice policymakers by the large numbers of lawbreakers whose misbehavior must be brought under control, often by restrictions imposed upon them as well as by positive intervention efforts. It would be Pollyannaish to argue that we can "break down the walls" and place all offenders under minimum supervision in the community. Liberal and conservative spokespeople alike can find common ground in the search for alternatives to incarceration. Such programs endeavor to (a) maximize the protection of the general public and (b) maximize the chances of offenders being able to untangle themselves from law-breaking conduct.

Those programs currently advocated include intensive supervision programs, some of which involve electronic monitoring of probationers or "house arrest." Electronic monitoring requires the probationer to wear a bracelet of sorts that sends an electronic signal to a central computer. The computer is monitored so ensure that the offender doesn't leave home during specified hours. The probationer is allowed to work or go to school. "House arrest" is a sentence in which the offender is ordered to serve time in his or her own home under the close supervision of a probation officer. Such programs mainly serve nonviolent offenders. (For a review of a number of these programs, see the special issue on intensive probation of *Crime and Delinquency*, January 1990.)

Additionally, fines and restitution programs allow those who commit crimes to work and live at home, while making financial payments for their offenses. At the same time, it saves the jurisdiction the money that would otherwise be used to jail the offender.

Community service programs offer yet another alternative to incarceration by requiring the offender to work a specified number of hours in public service projects. This might include cleaning and maintenance of public recreation areas, providing services for the elderly or disabled, or working with youth groups (Harris, 1979).

Community-based residential centers offer mental health services, supervision, drug and alcohol detoxification treatment, job training programs, and education. These services provide offenders with saleable skills once their sentence is completed and usually cost less than incarceration.

Evidence regarding the effectiveness of community-based control measures is skimpier than we would like, but there are some indications that these techniques do work (for example, see Lilly, Ball, and Wright, 1987). The data are less clear on intervention efforts that endeavor to aid offenders through helping them find employment or that provide other services to them while also maintaining close supervision over them. However, two points need to be emphasized. First, the full potential of community-based sanctions and intervention programs has yet to be realized. Second, the current criminal justice situation in America cries out for the development of new, innovative, and creative approaches to crime control that will free us from the overuse of penal sanctions.

However, we must do much more than simply find cost-effective alternatives to incarceration if we are to produce a less crime-ridden society. Elliott Currie's assessment of the contemporary crime problem and proposals about how to curb it is correct in observing that garden-variety lawbreaking is related more to variations in the *quality* of work available to people than it is to simply being employed or not employed. He is also correct in his diagnoses of deficiencies in the social life of local neighborhoods and communities, negative learning experiences in schools that push people in the direction of criminal misconduct, and other pressures that contribute to criminality. Most of his recommendations for attacking the crime problem center on the same rents and tears in the social fabric:

If we are serious about attacking the roots of this American affliction, we must build a society that is less unequal, less depriving, less insecure, less disruptive of family and community ties, less corrosive of cooperative issues. In short, we must begin to take on the enormous task of creating the conditions of community life in which individuals can live together in compassionate and cooperative ways. (Currie, 1985, pp. 225–228)

Currie's recommendations regarding crime control range widely from narrow to global ones, from tactics of dealing with domestic violence by arresting the offenders to proposals to develop family support programs, family planning services for teenager, improved child care arrangements, high-quality early education programs for disadvantaged children, and locally based counseling programs to deter family violence. He also argues for major alterations in the social and economic fabric of society, such as efforts to upgrade the quality of low-paying jobs as well as raising the pay levels of those jobs. Additionally, he supports programs of permanent job creation in the public and private sectors of the economy and universal and generous income support for families headed by individuals who fall outside the paid labor force.

Proposals to reorder the social priorities in American life are considerably easier to enunciate than they are to bring about (Gibbons, 1990), but it is noteworthy that a number of European countries have already moved a considerable distance in the right directions. The obstacles to bringing about a world less ridden with crime are more political and ideological than anything else. Finally, major reforms in social and economic life in contemporary America represent our best hope for the future.

NOTES

1. Some intellectual support for the hard line on crime control can be found in James Q. Wilson (1975), *Thinking about crime*, New York: Basic Books; Wilson, Ed. (1983), *Crime and public policy* (San Francisco: Institute for Contemporary Studies).

2. Cullen and Gilbert have presented a forceful case for reaffirmation of the rehabilitative ideal. However, their basic argument is that rehabilitation ought to be reaffirmed so that the inhumane, excessive, inequitable punishments that are often advocated by proponents of "deserts" or "justice" models of corrections can be avoided. They urged renewed attention to rehabilitation principally as a play to thwart the hard-line advocates of punitive approaches, rather than stating a case for correctional treatment on its own merits. See Francis T. Cullen and Karen E. Gilbert (1982), *Reaffirming rehabilitation*, Cincinnati: Anderson.

REFERENCES

ARCHER, DANE, and ROSEMARY GARTNER. (1984). *Violence and Crime in Cross-National Perspective*. New Haven, Conn.: Yale University Press.

BAILEY, WALTER C. (1966, June). An evaluation of 100 studies of correctional outcome. *Journal of Criminal Law, Criminology and Police Science, 57*, 153–160.

CHEATWOOD, DERRAL. (1985, October). "Capital Punishment and Corrections: Is There an Impending Crisis?" *Crime and Delinquency*, pp. 461–479.

CURRIE, ELLIOTT. (1985). *Confronting Crime*. New York: Pantheon.

CURRIE, ELLIOTT. (1987). *What Kind of Future? Violence and Public Safety in the Year 2000*. San Francisco, Calif.: National Council on Crime and Delinquency.

Federal Bureau of Investigation. (1990). *Crime in the United States: Uniform Crime Reports, 1989*. Washington, D.C.: U.S. Department of Justice.

FLANAGAN, TIMOTHY J., and EDMUND F. McGARRELL. (Eds.). (1985). *Sourcebook of Criminal Justice Statistics, 1985*. Washington, D.C.: U.S. Department of Justice.

GIBBONS, DON C. (1986, April). "Juvenile Delinquency: Can Social Science Find a Cure?" *Crime and Delinquency*, pp. 186–204.

GIBBONS, DON C. (1987). *Society Crime and Criminal Behavior* (5th ed.). Englewood Cliffs, N.J.: Prentice-Hall.

GIBBONS, DON C. (1990, April). "From the Editor's Desk: A Call for Some 'Outrageous' Proposals for Crime Control in the 1990s." *Crime and Delinquency*, pp. 194–203.

GREENBERG, DAVID F. (1977). "The Correctional Effects of Corrections." In David F. Greenberg (Ed.), *Corrections and Punishment*. Beverly Hills, Calif.: Sage, pp. 111–148.

GREENWOOD, PETER W., and ALLAN ABRAHAMSE. (1982). *Selective Incapacitation*. Santa Monica, Calif.: Rand.

GREENWOOD, PETER W., and SUSAN TURNER. (1987). *Selective Incapacitation Revisited: Why the High-Rate Offenders are Hard to Predict*. Santa Monica, Calif.: Rand.

GREENWOOD, PETER W., and FRANKLIN ZIMRING. (1985). *One More Chance*. Santa Monica, Calif.: Rand.

HALLECK, SEYMOUR, ANN E. WITTE. (1977, July). "Is Rehabilitation Dead?" *Crime and Delinquency*, pp. 372–382.

HARRIS, KAY. (1979). *Community Service by Offenders*. Washington, D.C.: National Institute of Corrections.

JAMIESON, KATHERINE M., and TIMOTHY J. FLANAGAN. (Eds.). (1989). *Sourcebook of Criminal Justice Statistics, 1988*. Washington, D.C.: U.S. Department of Justice.

LERMAN, PAUL. (1968, July). "Evaluative Studies of Institutions for Delinquents: Implications of Research and Social Policy." *Social Work*. pp. 55–64.

LILLY, J. ROBERT, RICHARD A. BALL, and JENNIFER WRIGHT. (1987). "Home Incarceration with Electronic Monitoring in Kenton County, Kentucky: An Evaluation." In Belinda R. McCarthy (Ed.), *Intermediate Punishments, Intensive Supervision, Home Confinement, and Electronic Surveillance*. Monsey, N.Y.: Criminal Justice Press, pp. 189–203.

LIPTON, DOUGLAS, ROBERT MARTINSON, and JUDITH WILKS. (1975). *The Effectiveness of Correctional Treatment: A Survey of Treatment Evaluation Studies*. Springfield, Mass.: Praeger.

LUNDMAN, RICHARD. (1984). *Prevention and Control of Juvenile Delinquency*. New York: Oxford University Press.

MARTINSON, ROBERT. (1975, Spring). "What Works? Questions and Answers About Prison Reform." *The Public Interest*, pp. 22–54.

MARTINSON, ROBERT. (1979, Winter). "New Findings, New Views: A Note of Caution Regarding Sentencing Reform." *Hofstra Law Review, 4*, 250–260.

MURRAY, CHARLES A., and LOUIS A. COX, JR. (1979). *Beyond Probation*. Beverly Hills, Calif.: Sage.

PALMER, TED. (1975, July). "Martinson revisited." *Journal of Research in Crime and Delinquency*, pp. 133–152.

REGNERY, ALFRED S. (1985, September). "Introducing New Pride." *NIJ Reports*, pp. 9–12.

REISS, ALBERT J., Jr., MICHAEL TONRY. (Eds.). (1986). *Communities and Crime*. Chicago: University of Chicago Press.

ROBISON, JAMES, and GERALD SMITH. (1971, January). "The Effectiveness of Correctional Programs." *Crime and Delinquency*, pp. 67–80.

ROSS, ROBERT and PAUL GENDREAU. (1980). *Effective Correctional Treatment*. Toronto: Butterworths.

SAMENOW, STANTON E. (1984). *Inside the Criminal Mind*. New York: Time Books.

SECHREST, LEE, SUSAN O. WHITE, and ELIZABETH D. BROWN. (Eds.). (1979). *The Rehabilitation of Criminal Offenders*. Washington, D.C.: National Academy of Sciences.

SHIREMAN, CHARLES H., KATHERINE BAIRD MANN, CHARLES LARSEN, and THOMAS YOUNG. (1972, March). "Findings from Experiments in Treatment in the Correctional Institution." *Social Service Review*, pp. 38–59.

SYKES, GRESHAM M. (1980). *The Future of Crime*. Rockville, Md.: National Institute of Mental Health.

THOMPSON, E.P. (1975). *Whigs and Hunters*. New York: Pantheon.

WILSON, JAMES Q. (1980, Fall). *What Works? Revisited: New Findings on Criminal Rehabilitation. The Public Interest*, pp. 3–17.

WILSON, JAMES Q., and RICHARD J. HERRNSTEIN. (1985). *Crime and Human Nature*. New York: Simon & Schuster.

QUESTIONS FOR DISCUSSION

1. The author contends that "conformity, including law-abiding conduct, is obtained principally through informal social controls." Explain and provide examples to support your response.

2. There are two types of formal social control measures. List and discuss these measures. Provide examples to support your response.

3. What are the two basic questions that must be asked about crime control policies? Discuss the issues that must be considered when answering these questions.

4. Many have held that "nothing works" with respect to altering offenders' behavior. Is this a defensible position? Why?

5. According to the author, what directions should be taken to create more sensible crime control strategies? Provide examples to support your response.

19

ADAPTING CONSERVATIVE CORRECTIONAL POLICIES TO THE ECONOMIC REALITIES OF THE 1990S

Alida V. Merlo
Westfield State College

Peter J. Benekos
Mercyhurst College

■ ■

This article reviews the impact that the punitive, "get tough" policies of the 1980s have had on corrections. With record-breaking increases in prison populations, legislators and policy makers have had to confront the realities of fiscal constraints while responding to the conservative agenda on crime. The consequence has been to develop and expand alternatives to incarceration which can be both tough on criminals but cheaper than traditional prison punishment. However, intermediate punishments such as intensive probation, electronic monitoring, and shock incarceration may be widening the correctional net. In reviewing these developments, the authors examine ideologies and consequences, and observe that economic considerations will influence corrections policies in the 1990s.

INTRODUCTION

The United States has surpassed all other countries in the world in the number and rate of people incarcerated. According to the Sentencing Project, there are currently 1.1 million offenders in American prisons; and the incarceration rate is 455 per 100,000 (Butterfield, 1992:A16). Unfortunately, there appears to be no end to this trend. It is estimated that the prison population will increase by 30 percent by 1995. The doubling of the number of inmates between 1980 and 1990 has posed significant problems for the federal government and the fifty states (Butterfield, 1992:A16).

This paper examines the conservative policies underlying the record-breaking increases, the resulting dilemma of skyrocketing prison construction costs, and the search for effective alternatives. Ironically, the alternatives to incarceration to which conservatives have been forced to turn bear a strong resemblance to liberal community correctional policies of the

Reprinted by permission of Indiana University of Pennsylvania.

1960s and early 1970s. This merger of conservative and liberal policies is not, however, because of some shared ideological belief. Rather, it is a function of simple economics—Americans cannot afford to continue incarcerating a million people a year.

IDEOLOGIES AND POLICIES OF THE 1980S

The current conservative agenda on crime can be reviewed in the context of the assumptions of correctional ideologies and the objectives of sentencing practices.

Liberal-Rehabilitative Ideology

Since the mid twentieth century, a liberal perspective which emphasized reform and rehabilitation guided correctional policy. Shover and Einstadter explain that efforts to treat and improve offenders were influenced by the assumptions of the "medical model" (1988:24). In this model, crime was viewed as symptomatic of underlying deficiencies which could be diagnosed and corrected with appropriate treatments. The model emphasized the social factors of criminal behavior and relied on therapeutic intervention to rehabilitate the offender (Shover and Einstadter, 1988:25).

The medical model reflected a liberal-optimistic view of human nature and how to confront the problem of crime. For corrections, this required a focus on the individual and on the efforts to change behavior. Since it was "impossible to specify in advance just how much time" was necessary for this treatment to be successful, the concomitant of the medical model was indeterminate sentencing (Shover and Einstadter, 1988:25).

In their study of sentencing reform, Goodstein and Hepburn characterize the indeterminate sentence as the policy which prevailed in the 1900s based on the ideological assumption that individualized treatment of offenders would prevent future involvement in criminal activities (1985:12). The model emphasized an individual sentencing structure that required judicial discretion to determine the needs and circumstances of the criminal. The model required that judges provide broad parameters, that is, indeterminacy, in which correctional specialists and parole board authorities could evaluate treatment progress and determine the appropriate time for release.

This sentencing model is consistent with the liberal perspective on crime policy. It focuses on the rehabilitative goal of corrections and requires discretion for judicial sentencing, correctional treatment, and parole release. By the 1970s, however, critics were questioning the assumptions and the outcomes of the rehabilitative model and were reassessing the goals of sentencing (Fogel 1975; von Hirsch 1976). Several authors (von Hirsch, 1976; Cullen and Gilbert, 1982; Travis, 1982; Hepburn and Goodstein, 1986) have reviewed this period of sentencing history and have observed that disillusionment and dissatisfaction with rehabilitation provided an opportunity for conservative assumptions to be revived.

Conservative-Punitive Ideology

Conservatives viewed rehabilitation as the "coddling of criminals" that conveyed a concern and sympathy for offenders which should be more appropriately directed toward the victims of crime (Shover and Einstadter, 1988:30). Conservatives believed that crime was the result of inadequate control rather than illness. Additional assumptions were that criminal behavior was due to free will, individual choice, and hedonic calculation. Therefore, in order to deter criminals from their evil ways, the conservative perspective emphasized the necessity of structured consequences, that is, punishment.

This conservative deterrence model included elements of retribution, incapacitation, and punishment. With an ideological shift from rehabilitation to deterrence, sentencing policy also shifted from discretion to determinacy and the search for "just desserts." In the effort to get tough, determinate sentencing policy was advocated by supporters who argued that certainty, swiftness, and severity of punishment would serve to deter criminals and reduce crime. Determinate sentencing would require judges to impose sanctions which were commensurate with the crime committed, not with the character of the criminal who committed them. This would reduce judicial and parole board discretion and, therefore, the disparity in sentences and punishments. For different reasons, the issue of "disparity" was a concern to both liberals and conservatives, and provided a common basis for seeking sentencing reform (Travis, 1982).

The shift from indeterminate to determinate sentencing practices and from rehabilitation to deterrence models signaled the emergence of new assumptions and objectives in crime control. Crime was not committed by offenders who were sick, but by criminals who made free-will decisions to commit crime. With this "paradigm" shift in the 1970s and early 1980s, efforts to identify and develop treatment programs were replaced with initiatives to determine the "just" sentences to fit the crimes and to reduce disparity by removing judicial discretion with legislative schedules (Travis, 1982). The result was the development of mandatory sentences, sentencing commissions, and the creation of sentencing guidelines (Blumstein, Cohen, Martin, and Tonry, 1983; Champion, 1989; Lawrence, 1991; Tonry, 1991).

Sentencing Reform

In the social and political context of this conservative approach to crime control, two important developments occurred in the 1980s: (1) get-tough sentencing reforms were implemented and (2) incarceration rates and prison populations increased.

As noted above, the shift from indeterminate to determinate sentencing not only signaled different assumptions but it was also indicative of new sentencing objectives. Sentencing "reforms" were initiated to establish (1) specific terms of incarceration, (2) equity in the sentencing process, and (3) reduction in judicial and administrative discretion (Pennsylvania Department of Corrections, 1991:2). The new principle was "just desserts" and the salient concerns were "honesty," "uniformity," and "proportionality" in sentencing (Katzenelson and McDanal, 1991:1).

In addition to the development of sentencing guidelines in the Federal Court System (Katzenelson and McDanal, 1991), several state legislatures introduced proposals to implement a standardization of punishment and to respond to the public's concern about crime (Aniskiewicz, 1991; Benekos, 1991; Lawrence, 1991). This concern was transformed into, and sustained, a get-tough momentum which also helped to politicize legislative sentencing.

The "lessons of Willie Horton" (The Sentencing Project, 1989) and the 1988 presidential election are recent reminders of how politics can distort policymaking. Throughout the 1980s, the "war" on drugs, the urban gang problem, and the fear of crime and violence were used to justify more severe criminal sanctions. Politicians capitalized on emotional issues and pursued short-term political gains (Aniskiewicz, 1991:8).

Since the 1970s, most states have revised their sentencing codes and several have adopted determinate sentencing. As part of these reforms, penalties were increased and mandatory sentences were legislated (Shover and Einstadter, 1988:51). The punishment frenzy of the 1970s and 1980s reflected conservative ideology and the emphasis on incarceration as the preferred get-tough punishment. As a result, prisons became synonymous with punishment and at the same time prison populations began to increase. While it is "difficult to determine to what extent" the sentencing reform movement contributed to this rise in prison populations (Shover and Einstadter, 1988:52), there is no question that the rate of incarceration and the number of prisoners confined in the United States have increased (Butterfield, 1992). In this context, prison crowding has become an administrative and legislative challenge for the 1990s.

STATE OF CORRECTIONS

Implications of Conservative Correctional Policies

Even though more and more offenders are being sentenced to prison, there has not been any significant decrease in violent crime. According to the *Uniform Crime Reports*, the incidence of murder, rape, robbery and aggravated assault increased in 1990 over the previous year (Federal Bureau of Investigation, 1991). Official crime data from 1980 and 1986 further illustrate the difference noted between 1989 and 1990. The number of index crimes known to the police in 1990 was 8 percent higher than in 1980 and 10 percent higher than in 1986 (Federal Bureau of Investigation, 1991:50). These data exacerbate the public's fear of criminal victimization and the frustration with the status quo. Nationally, it is estimated that one adult in forty-three is under the control (in some form) of correctional authorities (Jankowski, 1991:1).

Not surprisingly, most states cannot keep up with the demand for more prison space. This fact has resulted in overcrowded institutions, inmate lawsuits, court-ordered limits on institutional populations and court-appointed masters. Camp and Camp report that on January 1, 1991, the average federal and state prison system had 25 percent fewer beds than the total number of inmates under its jurisdiction (1991:36). They report that fifteen states had court-appointed monitors or overseers (1991:6), and fourteen states had emergency release procedures (most of them statutory) to deal with overcrowding (Camp and Camp, 1991:20). During 1990, 24,878 inmate lawsuits were filed in thirty-seven states, and 95 class action suits were filed in twenty-nine states (Camp and Camp, 1991:6). Often, the public is unaware of these facts and the efforts to reduce prison populations with "back door" policies. For example, Austin reported that as Florida's prison population increased in 1990, credit for good-time was also increased to the level that prisoners served about one-third of their prison terms (1991:6). In response to prison crowding in Illinois, the legislature doubled the amount of good time which could be awarded with the result that sentences could be reduced by one-half (*Criminal Justice Newsletter*, 1991b:5). And in Texas, the "average prison inmate...serves less than 20 percent of his sentence" (*Criminal Justice Newsletter*, 1991a:6).

Prison overcrowding also impacts local corrections. As prisons attempt to deal with court-ordered limits on population, they funnel more and more inmates into the jails. In 1990, there were 403,019 adult offenders in jail (Jankowski, 1991:5)

The concomitant fiscal and regulatory stress associated with jail overcrowding has resulted in some dramatic reactions. For example, a sheriff in Arkansas transported fifty inmates from his jail to a diagnostic unit in the state prison system. In order to preclude the state prison officials from refusing to accept these felony transfers, he ordered his deputies to chain the thirteen women and thirty-seven men to trees in front of the unit. At that time, approximately 400 felons were being held in county jails in Arkansas awaiting prison beds (Vanagunas and England, 1988:196). Although the sheriff's actions were atypical, they illustrate how prison overcrowding overwhelms local officials and their institutions.

Economic Realities and the Consequences

The consequences of the over-utilization of incarceration sanctions are significant. Mauer contends that it costs $20.3 billion a year for the 1.1 million offenders currently in prison (Butterfield, 1992:A16). Although the costs of construction vary from state to state, some states reported that it cost $110,000 per bed for construction in 1987 (Castle, 1991:1). In 1990 alone, thirty eight states and the federal system reported construction costs in excess of $3.2 billion for 87,664 beds (Camp and Camp, 1991:44).

These figures do not reflect the construction costs for additional facilities and the economic constraints they represent for the public. Camp and Camp report that 812,649 new prison beds are anticipated based upon current and planned construction in the United States (1991:41). For example, Texas voters recently approved a $1.1 billion bond that will enhance the state's prison system over the next four years by adding 25,000 beds (American Correctional Association, 1992:3). Californians spend more than $1 million every day to pay the interest on the money that they borrow to build new prisons (Bennett, 1991:92).

As prison construction costs continue to soar, state and federal budgets continue to shrink. Funding required for prison construction projects simultaneously reduces the appropriations for other projects like education, highways, and waste disposal. Although Americans may fear crime and want to send a strong message to criminals, they are not necessarily prepared to continue to allocate a disproportionate share of their state's limited resources to construct and maintain these institutions (Merlo and Benekos, 1992).

Politics and Policy

In spite of prison crowding, the conservative get-tough rhetoric and legislative "reforms" continue unabated. For example, the omnibus crime package before the Second Session of the 102nd Congress would have imposed the federal death penalty to about fifty additional crimes (*Congressional Quarterly*, 1992:273). One amendment to the Senate version of this bill (S 1241) would have imposed a ten-year mandatory federal prison sentence for using a firearm in a drug-trafficking crime and a twenty-year sentence if the firearm were discharged (Isikoff, 1991:32).

Representative Newt Gingrich (R) promised that his goal in the 102nd Session of Congress was to build more prisons. He contends that America should...

> build enough prisons so that there are enough beds that every violent offender in America is locked up and they will serve real time and they will serve their full sentences and they do not get out on good behavior. (Clymer, 1992:14)

Since polls continue to reveal that the public is concerned about crime and favors the death penalty, politicians will maintain conservative perspectives and talk tough about sentencing (Clymer, 1991). There are three reasons why this politicizing is disconcerting.

The first is that "if promised anonymity, conservatives readily concede there is more symbol than substance in their crime bill" (Clymer, 1991:E5). Get tough legislation is cheap; implementation is not. If these symbolic gestures had no consequence, then legislative policy predicated on the conservative assumptions would not seriously impact on the criminal justice system.

The second concern arises, however, because this politicalization of crime does have a negative impact on the system. Senator Alfonse M. D'Amato (R) of New York sponsored the amendment which would impose mandatory federal sentences on firearm violations. When asked about the impact of this amendment on federal courts, Senator D'Amato expressed disregard for the consequences and said he "could care a hoot" about the burden this legislation would create for the courts (not to mention the prison system) (Isikoff, 1991:32). In short, elected leaders are eager to introduce strategies that sound tough without concern for the feasibility of their implementation.

Third, if the public were adequately apprised of the costs, there is some evidence that it would likely opt for the less costly and less restrictive alternatives (Castle, 1991:2). Research conducted in California suggest that although the public prefers incarceration as the primary method to deal with offenders, it considers the alternatives appropriate sanctions when made aware of their existence and their reduced cost (Bennett, 1991).

This review of ideology and policy in the 1980s can be summarized in the three points. First, the conservative assumptions and crime control policies are prevalent in the legislatures and popular with the politicians. While some researchers have found that the public supports rehabilitative interventions (for example, Cullen, Skovron, Scott, and Burton, 1990), policymakers seem reluctant to embrace the issue.

Second, prison crowding not only distorts and compromises retributive sentencing objectives, it also is expensive public policy which is contributing to state budget problems, while not necessarily providing better public safety to citizens. In other words. "the problem of overcrowded prisons (has) assumed priority over the objectives of determinacy" (Hepburn and Goodstein, 1986:360) and has become a public policy issue of its own.

Finally, in order to reconcile the above concerns (that is, getting tough and dealing with rising costs of imprisonment), initiatives in policies and programs need to offer politicians "a possible way to be tough on crime (and criminals) and at the same time possibly reduce, or at least not exacerbate, prison crowding" (MacKenzie and Parent, 1991:236). The cost of incarceration and the number of offenders returning to prison suggest that the public would be receptive to alternative approaches and intermediate sanctions like private prisons, intensive probation, electronic monitoring and shock incarceration. To that end, legislators and policy makers are exploring these alternatives in the hope that they appeal to conservative voters and ideologies but cost less than existing correctional policies.

ALTERNATIVES AND INTERMEDIATE PUNISHMENTS

Privatization of Prisons and Jails

One way that some government agencies have coped both with the public's demand that more offenders be incarcerated and with dwindling budgets is to involve the private sector. Although federal, state, and local governments have contracted with private providers for services for adult and juvenile offenders for a long time, total reliance on the private sector to own, manage and administer correctional facilities is a departure from that stance. In 1989, there were approximately two dozen adult confinement institutions operated by about twelve companies (Logan, 1990).

Private prisons are frequently advocated as an alternative to the traditional government-owned and -operated facilities because of their anticipated lower construction and administrative costs. However, very little research has actually been conducted on large privately administered prisons to prove that the costs are lower and that private vendors are more effective. Most of the research has examined smaller private facilities in locations where large, state administered maximum security prisons continue to incarcerate more troublesome offenders. In fact, no state has transferred the custody, care, and control of its entire correctional population to the private sector. Even if such a transfer did occur, there is no reason to believe that the private sector could maintain the current increase in prison populations and save the state substantial amounts of money.

In addition to the fact that these facilities may end up costing as much as or more than the government's, there are some important ethical issues associated with the transfer of the state's authority to detain and punish offenders to a private corporation (Bowditch and Everett, 1987; Merlo, 1992). DiIulio (1988, 1990) contends that if there is no moral difference between private corporations' and the state's incarcerating inmates, then there should be no reason to exclude the utilization of private police and private judges. Is the state prepared to have all of its justice components under private control? At a minimum, these costs and ethical concerns suggest that the government ought to exercise caution before embarking on a privatization strategy to address overcrowding and the expensive construction costs of building more prisons.

Intensive Probation and Electronic Monitoring

As the number of offenders in prison has increased, so too has the number of probationers. In 1990, there were 2,670,274 adult offenders on probation (Jankowski, 1991:1). This means that probation caseloads have increased making "it difficult to provide adequate supervision for many of these offenders, who are, in effect, then left unsecured in the communities they victimized" (Stewart, cited in Erwin and Bennett, 1987:1).

The alternative to sending these offenders to prison is to "improve" community supervision. The response has included intensive probation supervision programs and the increasing use of electronic technology (and house arrest) to provide more "control" over offenders (Ford and Schmidt, 1985; Erwin and Bennett, 1987; Morris and Tonry, 1990).

The goals of these intermediate sanctions are to provide some relief to prison crowding and, in comparison to "regular" probation, to increase the level of punishment for offenders (Erwin and Bennett, 1987). Harland and Rosen conclude that due to the increased level of supervision which these "new" programs permit, they emphasize incapacitation and specific deterrence (1987).

In assessing the merits and technological aspects of these alternatives (for example, see Ford and Schmidt, 1985; Morris and Tonry, 1990), it is evident that community supervision has been transformed from a reintegrative to a retributive focus (Benekos, 1990). Studt characterizes this as a shift from service to surveillance (1972).

This get-tough approach with community corrections is a response to prison crowding and an attempt to offer a panacea which is tough on criminals but cheap on taxpayers. The intermediate punishments are promoted as cost-effective, tough sanctions which can help alleviate prison crowding. They are consistent with the conservative influence on the development of alternatives to incarceration. The get-tough model requires deterrence, incapacitation, and punishment, and intensive probation and electronic monitoring fit these objectives.

However, there are problems with these alternatives. Researchers and program evaluators have questioned some of the assumptions and consequences of these intermediate sanctions and alternatives (Byrne, Lurigio, and Baird, 1989; Petersilia and Turner, 1990; von Hirsch, 1990). Reliance on these programs also raises the issues of widening the net, expanding social control, and unrealistic expectations (Morris and Tonry, 1990). Offenders who previously might have been placed on probation or dismissed may now find themselves subjected to electronic surveillance and stricter supervision. The use of sophisticated technological devices does not necessarily preclude criminal activity, and the failure rate may be as high or higher than that of traditional community-based alternatives.

Another development in community corrections is the imposition of "supervision fees" which are viewed as both an additional dimension of punishment and as a way "to help defray the continuing costs of corrections" (Legan, 1991:5). For example, Pennsylvania recently enacted legislation which requires a twenty-five dollar per month supervision fee for any offender who is under state or county probation, parole, or accelerated rehabilitative disposition. Probationers in some states not only pay a monthly supervision fee but also pay for the presentence investigations (Langston, 1988:92). "In part, the fees are designed to make up for reductions in state funds to pay salaries of county probation and parole officers" (Leban, 1991:5).

Although states can generate revenue through these procedures, there is concern that these fees "will turn probation and parole officers into bill collectors, with little time to exercise their parole or probation supervision functions" (Leban, 1991:5). With this theme of fiscal constrains in mind, the "alternatives" momentum has also had an impact on prison programs in the form of "shock incarceration."

Shock Incarceration

If the traditional attitude toward incarceration has been that longer sentences equal more punishment, then the popularity of shock incarceration relies on the view that shorter sentences which provide for tougher conditions of incarceration can be equally punitive. In reaction to prison crowding and the need for more bed space, shock incarceration programs have been adopted as "an alternative to longer prison terms" (MacKenzie and Parent, 1991:225).

In return for these relatively shorter sentences—three to six months of incarceration—shock inmates are exposed to military training and drill, physical exercise, various treatment programs, and hard work. Intensive post-release supervision (or "after shock") is also a feature of the programs (Parent, 1989). Programs are highly structured and demanding in comparison to traditional imprisonment. As a result, not all inmates are eligible or selected for boot camp incarceration, nor do all inmates successfully complete shock programs (Parent, 1989; MacKenzie and Parent, 1991).

Since the early 1980s, when shock incarceration programs began to appear, the number has grown to the extent that several states have at least one program or are planning to implement a boot camp prison (MacKenzie and Parent, 1991). As noted above, the popularity of the boot camp concept primarily reflects the economics of corrections. However, in order to justify the shorter sentences in the conservative, get-tough political climate, the programs must emphasize the punitive as well as the cost-effective nature of shock incarceration (O'Daniel and Wells, 1991:1).

The importance of this punitive theme was also observed by MacKenzie and Parent in their evaluation of the Louisiana Shock Incarceration Program (1991). In considering the value of "intensive treatment" and "drill, hard labor, physical training and strict discipline," they acknowledged the political as opposed to the programmatic reality of boot camp incarceration (1991:236):

> If the program were changed to focus on therapy without the boot-camp atmosphere, perhaps the most important change would be the attitudes of the public and policymakers. It appears that policy makers are willing to trade longer prison terms for offenders for a program such as this if the program incorporates hard labor and strict discipline....A second reason policymakers appear willing to allow the shorter term in boot camp instead of a longer term in prison is because of the punishment aspects of the boot camp.

These intermediate and alternative punishments—private prisons, intensive probation, electronic monitoring, and shock incarceration—are some of the initiatives to deal with prison crowding and the increasing expense of incarcerative policies while upholding conservative objectives. Their acceptance to policy makers and the public depends on their compatibility with conservative ideology regarding crime and criminals. In other words, these sanctions must be tough on criminals but at the same time, safe to the community and less expensive than incarceration (Corrigan, cited in Gordon, 1990:100).

While these and other intermediate punishment programs (IPP) continue to receive popular support, Morris and Tonry are less optimistic that they can achieve their objectives (1990). In their critique of the "alternatives" movement, they maintain that the programs give "false promise of reducing the present overcrowding in American prisons and jails" (1990:4). Not only are they concerned about a widening of the net (as are others, for example, Austin and Krisberg, 1982; MacKenzie and Parent, 1990), but they also perceive the potential for "jurisprudential and political problems" (1990:7). For example, they raise questions regarding enforcement, fair and equitable application to avoid bias, and control of judicial (and administrative) discretion to minimize "disparity and injustice" (7).

If conservatives were simply interested in the cheapest alternatives, they would probably resort to the halfway houses, work release, and probation programs of the early 1970s. However, cost is not the only issue. The liberal ideology that accompanied these programs is not acceptable in today's political climate. Therefore, the search for alternative punishment-oriented programs which are also less costly than incarceration has become the rule. Alternative and intermediate sanctions may deal with only a small percentage of offenders, but the fact that they sound tough and cost less enhances their stature and increases the likelihood of their utilization and acceptance. These observations suggest that quick-fix, politically expedient responses to prison crowding may provoke another generation of policy issues and politicalization of crime and corrections.

CONCLUSION

If trends continue, the record breaking number of offenders in prison and jail, and on probation and parole, will increase all through the 1990s. Such a course implies a departure from the less stigmatizing sanctions of the 1970s, a greater exploitation of public frustration with crime, a greater willingness to punish offenders, and intolerance for even relatively minor crimes. The lack of empirical evidence to support a continuation of these policies does not appear to be an impediment.

Throughout this paper, the authors have argued that during the last twelve years, crime and what to do about it have become more politicized. As a result, conservative assumptions have prevailed and policies have reflected a sterner, tougher America. Second, the incarceration policies of the 1980s increased the rate of imprisonment and the population of offenders confined in jails and prisons. Prisons have failed to deter crime, however, and the recidivism rate among offenders is high. The high costs of this conservative public policy have prompted initiatives to develop alternatives which can alleviate prison crowding, be cost-effective, and still be tough on criminals. The intermediate punishment programs which have been developed rely to a large extent on community corrections to provide surveillance, control, and deterrence. The philosophy of get-tough has been filtered through the economic realities of fiscal limitations, and community punishment has replaced corrections.

These seemingly liberal-sounding alternatives are less costly, but there is no evidence that their usage will actually reduce the number of people incarcerated. They are currently being utilized in conjunction with incarceration and not as a substitute for it. Intermediate sanctions may result in greater increases in the number of people under correctional control, fewer constitutional procedural protections for offenders, and more unbridled discretion for criminal justice professionals.

REFERENCES

American Correctional Association. (1992). "Texas Governor, Voters Approve $1.1 Billion Prison Construction." *On The Line,* January 15:1–6.

ANISKIEWICZ, R. (1991). "The Politics of Prison Reform in Indiana." Paper presented at the annual meeting of the American Society of Criminology, San Francisco.

AUSTIN, J. (1991). "The Consequences of Escalating the Use of Imprisonment." *Corrections Compendium.* (September).

AUSTIN, J. and B. KRISBERG. (1982). "The Unmet Promise of Alternatives to Incarceration." *Crime and Delinquency, 28*:374–409.

BENEKOS, P. (1991). "Public Policy and Correctional Reform: Politics of Overcrowding." Paper presented at the annual meeting of the American Society of Criminology, San Francisco.

_____. (1990). "Beyond Reintegration: Community Corrections in a Retributive Era." *Federal Probation.* (March):52–56.

BENNETT, L. A. (1991). "The Public Wants Accountability." *Corrections Today, 53* (July):92–95.

BLUMSTEIN, A., J. MARTIN S. COHEN, and M. TONRY, (eds.). (1983). *Research on Sentencing: The Search for Reform*, Volumes I and II. Washington: National Academy Press.

BOWDITCH, C. and R. S. EVERETT. (1987). "Private Prisons: Problems within the Solution." *Justice Quarterly, 4* (September):441–453.

BUTTERFIELD, E. (1992). "U.S. Expands Its Lead in the Rate of Imprisonment." *The New York Times* (11 February):A16.

BYRNE, J., A. LURIGIO, and C. BAIRD. (1989). "The Effectiveness of the New Intensive Supervision Programs." *Research in Corrections,* 2(2):1–48.

CAMP, G. M. and C.G. CAMP. (1991). *The Corrections Yearbook—Adult Corrections.* South Salem, N.Y.: Criminal Justice Institute.

CASTLE, M. A. (1991). "Alternative Sentencing: Selling It to the Public." In U.S. Department of Justice, National Institute of Justice Research in Action: 1–5.

CHAMPION, D. (ed.). (1989). *The U.S. Sentencing Guidelines: Implications for Criminal Justice.* New York: Praeger.

CLYMER, A. (1992). "A G.O.P. Leader Aims at 'Welfare State' Values." *The New York Times* (5 January):14.

_____. (1991). "Politicians Take Up the Domestic Issues: Polls Suggest Why." *The New York Times* (15 September).

Congressional Quarterly. (1992). "Status of Major Legislation." 50(5): 273.

Criminal Justice Newsletter. (1991a). "Texas Parole Board under Fire: Prison Crowding Raises Pressure." (1 May) 22:9.

Criminal Justice Newsletter. (1991b). "Illinois 'good time' Law Eased Prison Crowding, Study Finds." (3 June) 22:11.

CULLEN, F. and K. GILBERT. (1982). *Reaffirming Rehabilitation.* Cincinnati: Anderson Publishing.

CULLEN, F., S. E. SKOVRON, J. SCOTT, and V. BURTON. (1990). "Public Support for Correctional Treatment: The Tenacity of Rehabilitative Ideology." *Criminal Justice and Behavior, 17*(1): 6–18.

DiIULIO, J. J. (1990). "The Duty to Govern: A Critical Perspective on the Private Management of Prisons and Jails." In D. C. McDonald (ed.). *Private Prisons and Public Interest.* New Brunswick: Rutgers University Press: 155–178.

_____. (1988). "What's Wrong with Private Prisons." *The Public Interest,* 92 (Summer): 66–84.

ERWIN, B. and L. BENNETT. (1987). *New Dimensions in Probation: Georgia's Experience with Intensive Probation Supervision (IPS).* Washington, D.C.: U.S. Department of Justice. National Institute of Justice. (January).

Federal Bureau of Investigation. (1991). *Uniform Crime Reports for the United States 1990.* Washington, D.C.: U.S. Government Printing Office.

FOGEL, D. (1975). *We are the Living Proof...The Justice Model for Corrections.* Cincinnati: Anderson Publishing.

FORD, D. and A. SCHMIDT. (1985). *Electronically Monitored Home Confinement.* Washington, D.C.: U.S. Department of Justice. National Institute of Justice. (November).

GOODSTEIN, L. and J. HEPBURN. (1985). *Determinate Sentencing and Imprisonment: A Failure of Reform.* Cincinnati: Anderson Publishing.

GORDON, D. (1990). *The Justice Juggernaut: Fighting Street Crime, Controlling Citizens.* New Brunswick, N.J.: Rutgers University Press.

HARLAND A. and C. ROSEN. (1987). "Sentencing Theory and Intensive Supervision Probation." *Federal Probation, 51* (4):33–42.

HEPBURN, J. and L. GOODSTEIN. (1986). "Organizational Imperatives and Sentencing Reform Implementation: The Impact of Prison Practices and Priorities on the Attainment of the Objectives of Determinate Sentencing." *Crime and Delinquency, 32* (3):339–365.

ISIKOFF, M. (1991). "The Senate's Crime Bill with Hidden Costs." *The Washington Post National Weekly Edition.* (July 29–August 4): 32–33.

JANKOWSKI, L. (1991). *Probation and Parole 1990.* Washington, D.C.: U.S. Department of Justice. Bureau of Justice Statistics. (November).

KATZENELSON, S. and C. McDANAL. (1991). "Sentencing Guidelines and Judicial Discretion in the Federal Court System." Paper presented at the annual meeting of the American Society of Criminology, San Francisco.

LANGSTON, D. C. (1988). "Probation and Parole: No More Free Rides." *Corrections Today, 50* (August):90–93.

LAWRENCE, R. (1991). "The Impact of Sentencing Guidelines on Corrections." Paper presented at the annual meeting of the Academy of Criminal Justice Sciences, Nashville.

LEBAN, J. (1991). "Prison Society Supports a Stay in Implementing Supervision Fees for Parolees and Probationers." *Corrections Forum,* (December):5.

LOGAN, C. H. (1990). *Private Prisons: Cons and Pros.* New York: Oxford University Press.

MacKENZIE, D. and D. PARENT. (1991). "Shock Incarceration and Prison Crowding in Louisiana." *Journal of Criminal Justice, 19*(3):225–237.

McCARTHY, B. (1987). *Intermediate Punishments: Intensive Supervision, Home Confinement, and Electronic Surveillance.* Monsey, N.Y.: Criminal Justice Press.

MERLO, A. V. (1992). "Ethical Issues and the Private Sector." In P. J. Benekos and A. V. Merlo (eds.). *Corrections: Dilemmas and Directions.* Cincinnati: Anderson Publishing Company: 23–36.

MERLO, A. V. and P. J. BENEKOS. (1992). "The Politics of Corrections." In P. J. Benekos and A. V. Merlo, (eds.). *Corrections: Dilemmas and Directions*. Cincinnati: Anderson Publishing Company: ix–xvii.

MORRIS, N. and M. TONRY. (1990). *Between Prison and Probation: Intermediate Punishments in a Rational Sentencing System*. New York: Oxford University Press.

O'DANIEL L. and B. WELLS. (1991). *Boot Camp: A Viable Alternative to Prison for the Male Hispanic Offender*. Paper presented at the annual meeting of the Academy of Criminal Justice Sciences, Nashville.

PARENT, D. (1989). *Shock Incarceration: An Overview of Existing Programs*. Washington, D.C.: U.S. Department of Justice. National Institute of Justice. (June).

Pennsylvania Department of Corrections. (1991). *Sentencing Reform Proposal*. Camp Hill, Pa..

PETERSILIA, J. and S. TURNER. (1990). *Intensive Supervision for High-Risk Probationers: Findings from Three California Experiments*. Santa Monica, Calif.: Rand.

The Sentencing Project. (1989). *The Lessons of Willie Horton: Thinking about Crime and Punishment for the 1990s*. Washington, D.C.

SHOVER, N. and W. EINSTADTER. (1988). *Analyzing American Corrections*. Belmont, Calif.: Wadsworth Publishing.

STUDT, E. (1972). *Surveillance and Service in Parole*. Washington, D.C.: U.S. Department of Justice.

TONRY, M. (1990). "Stated and Latent Functions of ISP." *Crime and Delinquency, 36*:174–191.

TRAVIS, L., III. (1982). "The Politics of Sentencing Reform." In M. Forst (ed.). *Sentencing Reform: Experiments in Reducing Disparity*. Newbury Park, Calif.: Sage.

VANAGUNAS, S. and D. ENGLAND. (1988). "The Domino Efect—State and Federal Crowding Puts Local Jails on the Receiving End." *Corrections Today, 50* (August):196–199.

VON HIRSCH, A. (1990). "The Ethics of Community-Based Sanctions." *Crime and Delinquency, 36*:162–173.

_____. (1976). *Doing Justice: The Choice of Punishments*. New York: Hill and Wang.

QUESTIONS FOR DISCUSSION

1. Compare the liberal-rehabilitative with the conservative-punitive ideologies of corrections and sentencing practices. Provide examples to support your response.

2. What has been the result of conservative correctional policies? If these policies are continued, what is likely to happen?

3. Discuss three reasons that politicizing issues of crime and punishment are, at least, disconcerting if not socially and economically harmful.

4. Legislators are exploring alternative prisons and intermediate punishments with the hope that these will appeal to conservative voters and cost less than present correctional programs. Discuss these alternatives. Do you believe that these alternatives are viable? Why or why not?

5. In your opinion, what other intermediate sanctions, not mentioned in this article, may be effective sentencing offenders?

20

THE GREATEST CORRECTIONAL MYTH
WINNING THE WAR ON CRIME THROUGH INCARCERATION

Joseph W. Rogers

■ ■ ■ ■ ■ ■ ■ ■ ■ ■ ■ ■ ■ ■ ■ ■ ■ ■ ■

"When the time comes, will there be room enough for your child?" (*Quarterly Journal of Corrections*, Summer, 1977: Front Cover).

Since this poignant inquiry appeared in 1977, this country's prison population has more than doubled from 265,000 to a historic high exceeding 600,000. By the end of 1989 (with turnover), over one million persons will have been incarcerated during the year—1 in 240 Americans, triple the total just two decades ago (*U.S. News and World Report*, November 14, 1988:11; see also Walker, 1989:3-5). To gain some idea of pace, we need go no further than a recent governmental report which shows a 1985 imprisonment growth rate of 8.7 percent. (Bureau of Justice Statistics, December 1987:52). Were we to continue at this annual growth, the prison population would double in less than 9 years! The implications of such acceleration simply cannot be ignored.

Unfortunately, the recent presidential campaign provided little relief from either party or candidate. So many volleys were fired, we can hardly expect any serious attempt to win the "war on crime" by means other than through more concrete, mortar, and metal of additional penal institutions. Indeed, our political leadership seems second to none in seeking "room at the inn" of imprisonment for the Nation's criminal offenders. On the one hand, we have long-standing belief in the powers of imprisonment, no matter how futile; on the other, we have the public's escalating fear of victimization, which seems to turn alternative approaches into perceptions of unforgivable "softness" on offenders. While we could hope this approach will succeed, honesty requires expression of doubt.

The contemporary *wave* of punitiveness is traceable to the mid-sixties. When Garrett Heyns (*Federal Probation*, 1967) wrote that "the 'treat-me-rough' boys are here again," little did he realize they would continue to dominate our justice system for more than two decades. What this former Michigan warden and Washington State director of corrections saw was only the tip of an iceberg. It has since merged as a punishment glacier, composed

---

of the hard ice of fear, hardened further in the cold atmosphere of deterrence and vengeance.

We must not make light of such fear, or the public's motives, for that matter. We have every right to want and seek security in our person and our property. Nor is it useful to advocate "tearing down the walls" or the abolition of maximum-security institutions. The position here concerns the narrowing focus and dependency on imprisonment to the neglect of a larger front in our battle against criminal victimization. Frankly, I am concerned lest the overwhelming success of the Willie Horton campaign waged against presidential candidate, Massachusetts Governor Michael Dukakis, makes cowards of us all. Differences in viewpoint notwithstanding, be assured that all of us are in this together.

THE MYTH OF THE IMPRISONMENT SOLUTION

From the outset we must realize the fundamental weaknesses in the extreme incarceration approach, which must take into account at least several basic factors.

First, 99 percent of those entering prison eventually return to society to become our neighbors in the communities where we live and work. Among the half-million inmates housed in state and federal prisons in 1985 (not including another quarter million in jails), there were only 1,175 recorded deaths (1,148 males, 27 females). Of these, 731 were attributed to natural causes; 112 to suicides; 33 to accidents; 18 to executions; 105 to another person; and 176 to unspecified reasons. These deaths represented less than three-tenths of one percent of the population, not taking into account either turnover or length of stay (Bureau of Justice Statistics, December 1987:71). With few exceptions we can count on those persons entering prison to come out again better or worse for their experience.

Second, the median stay in prison varies from state to state within a range of 15 to 30 months (Bureau of Justice Statistics, June 1984:3). Actual time served (including jail and prison time) is generally much less than the maximum sentence length. For example, while the 1983 admissions reveal a median sentence length of 36 months, the median time served by releases that year was 19 months (Bureau of Justice Statistics, September 1987:7).

Third, there is a yearly turnover involving approximately a half-million prisoners. While 234,496 individuals were exiting state or federal jurisdictions in 1985, even more, 275,366 were taking their places (Bureau of Justice Statistics, December 1987:61-62).

Fourth, as striking as these data are, a crime-prevention policy based primarily on increased imprisonment is at best inadequate; at worst, a clogged pipe of human beings. The problems for criminal justice personnel exist at several junctures in the system, of course; but here our "trouble shooting" must be directed back to the community where the flow begins. Upon so doing, we discover an estimated 40 million victimizations for 1983 alone. In 1982, an estimated 3.2 percent of the Nation's population were victims of rape, robbery, or assault—the equivalent of about 6 million persons (Finn, n.d.:1). Viewed somewhat differently, according to the respected National Crime Survey (NCS), more than 22 million *households* were victimized during 1985 by *at least* one crime of violence or theft. Their estimated total of 35 million individual victimizations is staggering when one considers the possibility of underreporting (Bureau of Justice Statistics, March 1988:11-12).

Fifth, the bulk of offenders are never caught, much less convicted or imprisoned (Ennis, 1967; Clark, 1970; Van den Haag, 1975). During the period 1973–1985 only about one-third of all crimes were reported to the police (Bureau of Justice Statistics, March 1988:34). Further, a review of *Uniform Crime Reports* covering the same time period will reveal an index crime clearance rate approximating 21 percent. In a compelling reanalysis of the President's Crime Commission Task Force Data, Charles Silberman (1978:257-261) provides a reasonable guide beyond this point. Of some 467,000 adults arrested (using rounded figures) 322,000 were punished in some way, with 63,000—about 14 percent— going to prison (Walker, 1988:36-39).

Sixth, prisons can hardly claim any great success when it comes to restoring criminals to law-abiding citizens. Assessments vary from about one-third to two-thirds for recidivism rates of released inmates. In his classic study, Daniel Glaser (1964:13-35) considers the latter figure as mythical, the former as more on target. While I agree with Glaser's cogent analysis, there can be little joy over even this positive claim. For example, Steven Schlesinger (1987:3), Director of the Bureau of Justice Statistics, recently asserted that their studies indicate about half of those released from prisons will return. He also points out that more than two-thirds of the burglars, auto thieves, forgers, defrauders, and embezzlers going to prison have been there before. Half of all the recidivists studied have been out of prison less than 23 months (Schlesinger, 1987:2).

Consider, then, the implications of these six propositions which show that while we keep 600,000 adults locked up, some 35 to 40 million crimes are being committed annually. While all those incarcerated men and women were unable to engage in crime, who were these other people preying upon the public? Many were repeaters, and the Uniform Crime Report Program has been trying to learn more about them and about careers in crime. Doubtless, some were under some alternative form of correctional supervision. For example, in 1985, 254,000 were in jail; 1,870,000 were on probation; and 277,438 were on parole (Bureau of Justice Statistics, December 1987: Front Cover). Some were juveniles, of whom almost 50,000 were in some sort of custodial facility on February 1, 1985 (Bureau of Justice Statistics, September 1987:43).

The above statistics, fragile though they are, underscore the importance of the "war on crime" being waged outside of institutions, not in them. But to the extent we believe in prisons as our justice centerpiece, we must recognize the crucial importance of what we do with (or to) persons during whatever time period they are in custody. Simply put, post-release failure rates are not acceptable.

BYPRODUCTS OF CONTEMPORARY PRISON POLICY

The current emphasis on incarceration should take into account at least eight major prison issues: (1) overcrowding; (2) cost; (3) litigation; (4) race/ethnicity; (5) long-term stays; (6) AIDS; (7) officer stress; and (8) the war on drugs.

Institutional Overcrowding

American prisons have come to resemble bloated sponges. As extra sponges are added, they too become glutted. There are over 700 state and Federal prisons (Innes, December 1986:3; see also Gottfredson & McConville, 1987). The federal government, almost all of the states, and many countries have embarked upon prison and jail construction programs that will remain a legacy of dubious merit from the 1980s. As one observer sees it, "While this expansion will permit incarceration of more people, it is unclear whether the additional facilities will succeed in relieving crowding; there seems to be almost limitless demand for prison beds" (Jacobs: n.d.:1).

One clear indicator is the population density of state prisons which are struggling to keep abreast of national standards. Both the American Correctional Association and the U.S. Department of Justice call for 60 square feet per single cell, provided inmates spend no more than 10 hours per day there; at least 80 square feet when cell confinement exceeds 10 hours daily (Innes, December, 1986:4). As of June 30, 1984, an assessment of 694 prisons revealed an average of 57.3 square feet per inmate: an average of 11.3 hours per day in unit confinement; and 66.5 percent of the inmates in multiple occupancy. This census also disclosed that 33.4 percent were in maximum security; that 11.8 percent of the facilities were over 100 years old, another 22.7 percent 50 to 99 years old; and that 50.8 percent of the institutions held more than 1,000 prisoners (Innes, December 1986:2).

Some jurisdictions are desperate. New York City, for example, is now housing 400 inmates on a five-story barge anchored in the Hudson River. Reminiscent of eighteenth century England, authorities are planning to add two more barges, one with berths for 800 convicts. Their sense of urgency is conveyed by one official, who says bluntly: "We don't have the luxury of waiting five years to build from the ground up" (*U.S. News and World Report*, November 14, 1988:11).

Newspaper releases from the State of Texas have reached near-ludicrous proportions with a cycle of prison "openings" and "closings," as their facilities exceed the allowable 95 percent capacity. Texas prison capacity expanded by 50 percent from 1980 to 1987, while the number of new prisoners increased by 113 percent. During the same period a federal court ordered the State to ease overcrowding through reducing its prison population by 6,500 inmates! Texas is constructing prisons at a pace to increase their capacity by more than 65 percent in just 4 years—a stopgap measure at best. According to their criminal justice director, Rider Scott, the addition of some 26,500 beds will be overly filled by the end of 1990 to the point of again shutting down the institutions, and backing up the overflow in county jails. Even as this was being written, Texas held 38,500 persons in 28 institutions, while another 4,000 state prisoners were serving time in county jails awaiting a prison bed (*El Paso Times*, April 4, 1988:4B).

A third illustration comes from the District of Columbia where prison overcrowding reached a state of crisis in responding to court-imposed population caps by closing the District's prisons to newly sentenced inmates. Imagine a situation (after October 5, 1988) in which some arrivals were distributed to police precinct holding cells: some to the District of Columbia Superior Court cell block which was never designed for feeding people or for overnight incarceration; some to federal prisons outside the District; and some to institutions across the country, e.g., already crowded facilities in Washington State (*Criminal Justice Newsletter*, November 1, 1987:7; see also, Joan Mullen, 1987).

Cost of Imprisonment

Criminal justice is big business, as indicated by its "top 10" status among all government expenditures. Federal, state, and local spending for all such activities in fiscal year 1983 was $39.7 billion—almost 3 percent of all government spending in this country. Approximately $23 billion was spent at the local level, $12 billion by the states, and $5 billion by the federal government. Police protection accounted for the highest amount spent, 52 percent, followed by corrections with 26 percent, and judicial/legal services with 22 percent (Bureau of Justice Statistics, June 1988: front cover).

Among types of justice spending, corrections increased the most—by 15.1 percent from 1982 to 1983; by 50.9 percent from 1980 to 1983 (Bureau of Justice Statistics, September 1987:23). And although estimates vary widely, prison construction costs typically range from $50,000 to $100,000 per cell. The "capital investments" are supplemented by a yearly operating/maintenance expenditure ranging from $10,000 to $25,000 per inmate (Blumstein, n.d.:3; Jacobs, n.d.:1). The Criminal Justice Institute counts 130 prisons for some 53,000 inmates now being constructed at a cost of $2.5 billion, with still another 75,000 convict beds in the planning stage. Moreover, President George Bush is said to favor doubling the current federal prison budget to a new high of $2 billion, about three and one-half times the 1983 figures (*U.S. News and World Report*, November 14, 1988:11).

In short, we are talking big bucks here in an era of budget deficits, and fears of tax increases and, as Clear and Harris (1987:51) point out, proposals often seriously underestimate eventual correctional expenditures. The money being poured into incarceration makes probation, parole, and college education look like great buys, at least on a cost-per-person basis. You can send your son or daughter to your choice of some of the finest private universities in the land—Cornell, Harvard, Stanford—for less! And if you are not too choosy, their entire 4 years of college tuition will cost less at a good state university than will housing a single inmate for 1 year in a typical state prison! And make no mistake, public education must compete for these dollars, just as do public welfare, housing, environment, hospitals, health, highways, and others (Bureau of Justice Statistics, September 1987:22). Given the recent concern with the quality of our public school system, where do you think an extra one billion dollars a year might be well spent to fight crime?

Litigating Prison Conditions

Litigation has become such an American prison way of life that by the end of 1983, eight states had their prison systems declared unconstitutional; 22 had facilities operating under either a court order or consent decree; and nine more were engaged in litigation. By December 1985, only eight states (Alaska, Minnesota, Montana, Nebraska, New York, New Jersey, North Dakota, and Vermont) had remained unencumbered by judicial intervention (Taggart, 1989).

Prison litigation is both intriguing and complex, but prior to the 1960s had been subject to a "hands-off" policy by the federal courts (Bronstein, 1985; see also, Conrad, 1987). However, with the advent of the Warren court, this posture was abandoned through a series of decisions enlarging the federal court's role in prison administration. The stage was set with two key cases: (1) *Jones* v. *Cunningham* (1963) in which the Supreme Court ruled that the state prison could employ a writ of habeas corpus to challenge not only the legality of their imprisonment, but also to contest the conditions of incarceration; and (2) *Cooper* v. *Pate* (1964) in which the Court held that prisoners possessed standing to sue in federal court under the Civil Rights Acts of 1871 (see Taggart, 1989).

These were quickly followed by several other cases expanding inmate legal rights, with filings by state prisoners increasing in the federal courts over 120 percent between 1970 and 1983. Arkansas became the initial state affected by this new "hands-on" stance when its entire prison system was found in violation of the cruel and unusual punishment prohibition of the Eighth Amendment (Holt v. Sarver, 1969). The district court found constitutional deficiencies in such major areas as facilities, safety, medical services, staff practices, and security. Within the next five years Mississippi and Oklahoma were to be found similarly deficient and under court orders (Taggart, 1989). For two instructive state histories, see Hopper, 1985 on Mississippi; Mays and Taggart, 1985 on New Mexico. For a focused discussion of Eighth Amendment litigation, see Ingraham and Welford, 1987.

In a very carefully constructed study of the first 10 states subject to federal court intervention, Taggart (1989) employed a longitudinal model to examine the impact of court-ordered prison reform on state expenditures for corrections. Controlling for the state's prison population, previous expenditures for corrections, and total state expenditures, he found the greater impact on the capital side of the budget than on the operating side. This has significant implications according to Taggart (1989):

> Although the construction of new facilities may function to redress certain problems identified by the courts (e.g., inadequate cell sizes or dormitory living conditions), it is by no means a panacea for compliance. It does not ensure changes in administrative practices or employee behaviors which many times are of equal importance to the bench. Moreover, if capital expenditures are made in response to overcrowded prisons, the lack of concurrent expansion in operating budgets may suggest that some other problem areas are only growing substantially worse (e.g., inmate/staff ratios). It is entirely possible that a capital intensive reform program has helped to make some inmates worse off (Horowitz, 1983).

Certainly, some of these capital outlays would have been spent just as wisely for improving the everyday conditions and programs of existing prisons as for building still more institutions.

Race and Ethnicity

Prisons have long been known for their disproportionate housing of blacks and Hispanics. In 1986 the proportion of blacks in state prisons was 47 percent, almost four times the 1980 proportion of 12 percent in the general United States population; the proportion of Hispanics in these facilities was 13 percent, over twice the 6 percent of the 1980 census

(Bureau of Justice Statistics, March 1988:41; Innes, January 1988:3). The *lifetime* estimate of incarceration is six times higher for blacks (18%) than for whites (3%). After the initial confinement, probability of further commitments is similar for both races: about one-third of each group who have ever been incarcerated will have been confined four times by age 64 (Bureau of Justice Statistics, 1988:47).

Causes are multiple and conventional (e.g., see Hawkins, 1986; Bridges, Crutchfield & Simpson, 1987; Palley & Robinson, 1988). Nevertheless, genuine concern must be expressed about minority youth being incarcerated in juvenile correctional facilities at rates three to four times that of whites. Their numbers are growing even though overall rates of serious youth crime are declining, with minority youth more likely to be arrested and charged than comparably delinquent white juveniles. As Barry Krisberg and his associates (1987:173) see it, "Although further research on these issues is imperative, it is also crucial that public officials begin testing out new strategies to reduce the tragic trend of ever more minority children growing up behind bars."

Long-Term Incarceration

Deborah Wilson and Gennaro Vito (1988) observe that society's response to crime has contributed to several trends resulting in longer prison terms for convicted felons. Determinate and mandatory sentencing, modifications in parole eligibility criteria, enhanced sentences for recidivists, and longer terms for violent offenders have resulted in increased time served plus a subsequent increase in the proportion of long-term inmates in state facilities. These changes result in programmatic and management concerns to correctional administrators which must be addressed.

These authors define a "long-term" inmate as "one who has or will be continuously confined for a period of seven years" (Unger & Buchanan, 1985), given a 1986 average time served of 24.8 months. Survey data from 23 correctional agencies reported the percentage of men serving sentences of 7 years or more in state correctional facilities increased from 20.4 percent in 1979 to 24.8 percent in 1984. Some states reported proportions of long-term prisoners as high as 68 percent for males and 55 percent for females (Unger & Buchanan, 1985, cited in Wilson & Vito, 1988:21). Moreover, the percentage of inmates serving sentences of 20 years or more increased from 13.4 percent of all state inmates in 1983 to 15.7 percent in 1987 (Camp & Camp, 1987 cited in Wilson & Vito:22).

Wilson and Vito (1985:23-24) invoke a vast literature (e.g., Sykes, 1958; Clemmer, 1958; Fox, 1985; Jacobs, 1977) to demonstrate the negative effects of long-term incarceration. They then identify at least eight "demands" which will be created by growing numbers of long-term inmates (Wilson & Vito, 1988:24-25): (1) the need for more bed space; (2) increased financial cost for extended duration of confinement; (3) higher, more costly levels of security; (4) structured activities to fill time voids; (5) specialized mental health services to promote personal adjustment and reduce disciplinary problems; (6) institutional financial assistance to replace diminished outside help; (7) specialized housing and medical services for those becoming elderly; and (8) enhanced pre-release and post-release programs to facilitate readjustment into a changed community after extended absence.

AIDS in Correctional Facilities

Perhaps no one has made a more forceful statement on this issue than National Institute of Justice Director, James K. Stewart (Hammett, April 1987:iii):

> For correctional agencies, the problem of AIDS is a formidable challenge. A substantial percentage of inmates fell within identified high risk groups for AIDS. The presence—or potential presence—of AIDS within the prison is more than a simple health problem; correctional administrators are faced with tough decisions about prevention, institutional management, the best and most equitable means of identifying and treating inmates with AIDS, potential legal issues, and the costs of medical care.

Although data are still lacking, Stewart's concerns are real. As of October 1, 1986, there had been 784 confirmed AIDS cases in 31 state and federal correctional systems—up 72 percent from 455 cases reported as of November 1, 1985, the time of the original survey. This is a large increase in cases, but is actually smaller than the 79 percent national increase from 14,519 cases to 26,002 cases during the same relative time period (Hammett, April 1987:4).

The foregoing figures are *cumulative* totals covering the record-keeping period. Twenty-three state and federal systems reported 174 current cases of AIDS. Further, they reported a cumulative total of 463 prisoners have died from AIDS while in custody. One study of 177 inmate deaths from AIDS in the New York correctional system revealed the following: 97 percent were males; 76 percent were between 25 and 39 years old; 40 percent were Hispanic; 39 percent were black; 86 percent came from New York City; and 92 percent *admitted* to intravenous drug abuse (Hammett, April 1987:4-5).

On the good news side, neither the 1985 nor the 1986 survey identified any AIDS cases among correctional staff attributable to contact with inmates. Ninety-six percent of the federal and state systems have instituted some type of education or training for staff; 86 percent for inmates (Hammett, April, 1987:6). This is especially important in view of fears (some false) of contamination through biting, spitting, knives, inmate wounds, body searches, disposition of deceased persons, etc.

In sum, AIDS has added still another negative factor to diminish the quality of prison life for both inmates and staff through fear, HIV antibody testing, and a host of lawsuits, some of which are already pending.

Correctional Officer Stress

In summarizing the lot of correctional officers, Peter Kratcoski (1988:27) recently asserted:

> The fear of experiencing assaults from prisoners is part of the daily mindset of a prison guard. Morris and Morris (1980:51) state that the prison officer knows only too well that violence is seldom far below the surface of prison life, and Jacobs and Retsky (1977:61) characterize the guard's world as increasingly pervaded by fear and uncertainty. Fogel (1975:70) stated that a guard performs in a world of fear of the unanticipated.

In his study of one federal institution, Kratcoski (1988) found four particular factors related to assaults against staff: (1) more than 70 percent of the assaults occurred in the detention/high security areas; (2) the majority of all assaults occurred during the day shift (8 a.m. to 4 p.m.); (3) staff with less than 1 year received a disproportionate number of assaults (15% of the staff, yet 35% of assaults); and (4) the majority of assaults were committed by inmates age 25 and younger. These, observes Kratcoski, suggest problems of high staff turnover, inadequate training, and questionable staff support.

Gerald Gaes and William McGuire (1985:41-51), in their comprehensive examination of 19 federal prisons over a 33-month period, found crowding by far to be the most influential variable for predicting both inmate-inmate and inmate-staff assaults (without a weapon).

Cullen, Link, Wolfe, and Frank (1985) advocate separate measurement of work and life stress among correctional officers. In their study of a southern correctional system, they found that role problems and perceived danger were related to life stress among the officers. These variables plus six others (being female; location in maximum security prison; more experience as C.O.; and lack of peer, family, or supervisory support) were related significantly to work stress.

Such studies and the excellent literature review by Susan Philliber (1987) underscore the importance of stress factors to both staff and inmate welfare. Other than their peers, the guard is said to be the most important person in the inmate's world. If true, their safety, morale, and even their careers are intimately linked together with a society of captives and keepers (Sykes, 1958).

The Escalating War on Drugs

It was recently announced that William J. Bennett, the former Secretary of Education, has been selected as the new administration's first "Drug Czar." It seems quite certain that drug use, abuse, and distribution will loom larger as incarceration factors as we step up the war on those fronts. A recent signal to this effect was given by the first charges filed under a new federal antidrug law which requires federal judges to impose life sentences without parole on defendants convicted of drug trafficking under certain circumstances (*El Paso Times*, January 5, 1989: 6A; see also Inciardi: 1987).

Drug use is far greater among prison inmates (78%) than in the general population (37%). Moreover, two out of five prison inmates reported they were under the influence of drugs or were very drunk around the time of their incarceration offense (Bureau of Justice Statistics, March 1988:50-51). Yet we have to wonder to what degree drug abuse receives adequate attention in prison. The recent news from Texas is not encouraging when it is reported 67 percent of their drug-abusing inmates are released from prison without receiving any treatment. Reportedly, in 1988 Texas provided only one drug-abuse counselor for 1,667 addicted prisoners; those receiving help averaged only 10 hours of treatment during their confinement. Only 75 inmates received "intensive treatment" during the year (*El Paso Times*, December 19, 1988:4B). The Governor of Texas is asking the 1989 legislature to authorize drug testing of inmates in prison and before they are released on parole (*El Paso Times*, January 9, 1989:4B). Governor Clements is also seeking an additional $343 million for new prison construction to provide 11,000 more prison beds (*El Paso Times*, January 13, 1989:4B). The pressure for space continues.

CONCLUSION

Stephen D. Gottfredson and Sean McConville (1987:9) have recently described this state of affairs as "America's Correctional Crisis," where far-reaching decisions are made with uncertainty and compromise. Instead, they hope "for more informed and balanced debate and for the encouragement of productive and acceptable solutions to problems that can be neglected only at some considerable risk to our nation's future (1987:10)." We should be listening to such counsel which, if anything, seems understated, requiring added emphasis and urgency.

Accordingly, two broad proposals are offered.

First, it is time to convene another President's Commission on Law Enforcement and Administration of Justice (1967). President Lyndon B. Johnson established his Commission on July 23, 1965, almost a quarter century ago. President Bush could initiate the largest scale "brain trust" this Nation has ever known to plan the most comprehensive strategy for crime prevention, treatment, and control in history. So doing is panacea, of course, for many difficulties are attached to such task forces (e.g., see Allen, 1973). But somehow, a concerted collective effort must be made to bring together the vast reservoir of knowledge and ideas accumulating in various disparate forms and places, both here and abroad, during the past three decades.

It would be presumptuous to suggest an agenda here, but no issue should be sacrosanct or beyond debate. From the start it must be recognized that corrections is a component of an interdependent but uncoordinated system of justice which must be understood in relation to the wider structures of social control in American society. This means we must examine criminality in a multilayered fashion—from inception and process to change; from societal ills and malfunctioning to social reform; from community roots to community return. Criminality and delinquency are not unrelated to conditions and problems of other social institutions—family (e.g., domestic violence, runaways); economy (e.g., poverty, unemployment, homelessness); education (e.g., dropouts, drugs); and government (e.g., mismanagement, inadequate funding).

Each of us probably possesses favored issues. For instance, one central probe could (should) be directed at what Shover and Einstadter (1988:204-206) call the "ironies of correctional reform," wherein promising proposals and programs such as diversion or halfway houses become perverted into the much criticized widening effect (Lemert, 1981). Is it possible to prevent a similar fate and abuse of, say a technologically feasible notion such as home incarceration through electronic monitoring (Ball, Huff & Lilly, 1988)? This would also be an excellent forum to sweep aside numerous myths about crime, delinquency, and corrections (for example, see Bohm, 1987; Pepinsky & Jesilow, 1984, 1985; Walker, 1989; Walters & White, 1988; and Wright, 1987). The crime crisis is bad enough without being haunted by widespread misconceptions held by the public, criminal justice practitioners, and professional criminologists.

Second, it would be appropriate to seriously consider William G. Nadel's (1977) advocacy of a moratorium on prison construction. Imagine such a joint state and federal policy effective from, say, 1991 through 1995. The 5-year "savings" could be well invested in the Commission's work; to improving existing prisons; to upgrading community-based corrections; and to fundamental programs involving the health, education, and welfare of the nation's youth.

This last point is particularly important in light of Lamar Empey's (1974:1096) fear that a war on crime could be waged against our country's youth, with a severe loss to basic humanitarian values. Indeed, we must take exception to a social control policy based primarily on measures of exclusion (e.g., isolation, segregation) rather than inclusion (e.g., resocialization, integration) (Cohen, 1985). Shover and Einstadter (1988:208) have stated well the implications.

> ...precisely those conditions which prevent persons from becoming productive, socially conscious members of society, conditions which exclude and cast them out, are the conditions which create the dangerous crime potential we wish to prevent.

> The current direction corrections is taking is exclusionary. Whether the cycle will change in the near future remains an open question, but our ultimate well-being as a democratic society depends on the answer.

There are no easy answers to complex problems (Conrad, 1985). But perhaps we could discover some profound responses through starting the final decade of this millennium with a high-level Commission with the authority, organization, talent, time, and incentives to develop imaginative, innovative, comprehensive policies on behalf of the Nation's citizenry.

REFERENCES

ALLEN, H. E. "The Task Force Model: As a Vehicle for Correctional Change." *Georgia Journal of Corrections.* July 1973, pp. 35–39.

BALL, R. A., G. R. HUFF and J. R. LILLY. (1988). House Arrest and Correctional Policy: Doing Time at Home. Newbury Park, Calif.: Sage.

BOHM, R. M. "Myths about Criminology and Criminal Justice: A Review Essay." *Justice Quarterly* 4 (4). December 1987, pp. 631–642.

BRIDGES, G. S., R. D. CRUTCHFIELD and E. E. SIMPSON. "Crime, Social Structure and Criminal Punishment: White and Nonwhite Rates of Imprisonment." *Social Problems*, 34(4), October 1987, pp. 345–361.

BLUMSTEIN, A. "Prison Crowding" (Crime File Study Guide), National Institute of Justice, no date.

BRONSTEIN, A. J. "Prisoners and Their Endangered Rights." *The Prison Journal*, 65(1). Spring–Summer, 1985, pp. 3–17.

Bureau of Justice Statistics. *BJS Data Report, 1986*. Washington, D.C.: U.S. Department of Justice, September 1987.

Bureau of Justice Statistics. *Correctional Populations in the United States, 1985*. Washington, D.C.: U.S. Department of Justice, December 1987.

Bureau of Justice Statistics. *Justice Expenditure and Employment Extracts: 1982 and 1983.* Washington, D.C.: U.S. Department of Justice, June 1988.

Bureau of Justice Statistics. *Report to the Nation on Crime and Justice*, Second edition. Washington, D.C.: U.S. Department of Justice, March 1988.

Bureau of Justice Statistics. "Time Served in Prison." Washington, D.C.: U.S. Department of Justice, June 1984.

"California 1st to Try No-Parole Drug Law." *El Paso Times*, January 5, 1989, p. 6A.

CAMP, G. M., and C. G. CAMP. *The Corrections Yearbook.* South Salem, N.Y.: Criminal Justice Institute, 1983.

CLARK, R. *Crime in America. Observations on Its Nature, Causes, Prevention, and Control.* New York: Simon & Schuster, 1970.

CLEAR, T. R., and P. M. HARRIS. "The Costs of Incarceration." In S. D. Gottfredson and S. McConville (eds.). *America's Correctional Crisis.* New York: Greenwood Press, 1987, pp. 37–55.

"Clements: Prisons Need 11,000 Beds." *El Paso Times*, January 13, 1989, p. 4b.

"Clements Urges Inmate Drug Testing." *El Paso Times*, January 11, 1989, p. 4b.

CLEMMER, D. *The Prison Community.* New York: Holt, Rinehart & Winston, 1958.

COHEN, S. *Visions of Social Control.* Cambridge, England: Polity Press, 1985.

CONRAD, J. P. "The View from the Witness Chair." *The Prison Journal*, 65(1), Spring–Summer, 1985, pp. 18–25.

Cooper v. Pate, 378 U.S. 546 (1964).

"Court Orders Trigger Closing of D.C. Prisons to New Inmates." *Criminal Justice Newsletter*, 19(21), November 1, 1988:7.

CULLEN, F. T., B. G. LINK, N. T. WOLFE, and J. FRANK. "The Social Dimensions of Officer Stress." *Justice Quarterly* 2(4). December 1985, pp. 505–533.

EMPEY, L. T. "Criminal Prevention: The Fugitive Utopia." In D. Glaser (ed.). *Handbook of Criminology.* Chicago: Rand McNally, 1974.

ENNIS, P. H. "Crime, Victims, and the Police." *Transaction 4,* June 1967, pp. 36–44.

"The Far Shore of America's Bulging Prisons." *U.S. News and World Report*, 105(19), November 14, 1988, pp. 11–12.

FINN, P. "Victims." (Crime File Study Guide). *National Institute of Justice*, no date.

FOGEL, D. *We Are Living Proof.* Cincinnati: Anderson Publishing Co., 1975.

FOX, V. *Introduction to Corrections* (3rd ed). Englewood Cliffs, N.J.: Prentice-Hall, 1985.

GAES, G. G., and N. J. McGUIRE. "Prison Violence: The Contribution of Crowding Versus Other Determinants of Prison Assault Rates." *Journal of Research in Crime and Delinquency.* 22(1). February 1985, pp. 41–65.

GLASER, D. *The Effectiveness of a Prison and Parole System.* Indianapolis, Indiana: Bobbs-Merrill, 1964.

GOTTFREDSON, S. C., and S. McCONVILLE (eds.). *America's Correctional Crisis: Prison Populations and Public Policy.* New York: Greenwood Press, 1988.

HAMMET, T. M. 1986 *Update: AIDS in Correctional Facilities*, Washington, D.C.: National Institute of Justice, April 1987.

HAWKINS, D. F. "Race, Crime Type, and Imprisonment." *Justice Quarterly*, 3(3), September 1986, pp. 251–269.

HEYNS, G. "The 'Treat-em-Rough' Boys Are Here Again." *Federal Probation*. 31(2) June 1967, pp. 6–10.

Holt v. *Sarver,* 300 F. Supp. 825 (E.D. Ark. 1969).

HOPPER, C. B. "The Impact of Litigation on Mississippi's Prison System." *The Prison Journal*, 65(1), Spring–Summer, 1985, pp. 54–63.

HOROWITZ, D. L. "Decreeing Organizational Change: Judicial Supervision of Public Institutions." *Duke Law Journal*, 1983, pp. 1265–1307.

INCIARDI, J. A. *The War on Drugs: Heroin, Cocaine, Crime and Public Policy*. Palo Alto, Calif.: Mayfield, 1986.

INGRAHAM, B. L., and C. F. WELLFORD. "The Totality of Conditions Test in Eighth-Amendment Litigation." In S. D. Gottfredson and S. McConville (eds.). *America's Correctional Crisis*. New York: Greenwood Press, 1987, pp. 13–36.

INNES, C. A. "Population Density in State Prisons." Bureau of Justice Statistics Special Report. Washington, D.C.: National Institute of Justice, December 1986.

INNES, C. A. "Profile of State Prison Inmates, 1986." Bureau of Justice Statistics Special Report. Washington, D.C.: National Institute of Justice, January 1988.

JACOBS, J. B. "Inside Prisons." (Crime File Study Guide) National Institute of Justice, no date.

JACOBS, J. B. *Statesville: The Penitentiary in Mass Society*. Chicago: University of Chicago Press, 1977.

JACOBS, J. B., and H. G. RETSKY. "Prison Guard," in *The Sociology of Corrections: A Book of Readings*. R. G. Leger and J. R. Stratton (eds.). New York: John Wiley and Sons, 1977.

Jones v. *Cunningham*, 371 U.S. 236 (1963).

KRATCOSKI, P. C. "The Implications of Research Explaining Prison Violence and Disruption." *Federal Probation*, 52(1), March 1988, pp. 27–32.

KRISBERG, B. I., I. SCHWARTZ, G. FISHMAN, Z. EISIKOVITS, E. GUTTMAN, and K. JOE. "The Incarceration of Minority Youth." *Crime and Delinquency*, 33(2), April 1987, pp. 173–205.

LEMERT, E. M. "Diversion in Juvenile Justice: What Hath Been Wrought?" *Journal of Research in Crime and Delinquency*. 18(1), January 1981, pp. 34–46.

MAYS, G. L., and W. A. TAGGERT. "The Impact of Litigation on Changing New Mexico Prison Conditions." *The Prison Journal*, 65(1). Spring–Summer 1985, pp. 38–53.

MORRIS, T. P. and P. J. MORRIS. "Where Staff and Prisoners Meet," in *The Keepers—Prison Guards and Contemporary Corrections*. B. M. Crouch (ed.). Springfield, Ill.: Charles C Thomas, 1980.

MULLEN, J. "State Responses to Prison Crowding: The Politics of Change," in S. D. Gottfredson and S. McConville (eds.). *America's Correctional Crisis*, New York: Greenwood Press, 1987, pp. 79–109.

NAGEL, W. G. "On Behalf of a Moratorium on Prison Construction." *Crime and Delinquency*. 23(2), April 1977, pp. 154–172.

PALLEY, H. A., and D. A. ROBINSON, "Black on Black Crime." *Society* 25(5), July–August, 1988, pp. 59–62.

PEPINSKY, H. E., and P. JESILOW. *Myths That Cause Crime*. Cabin John, Md.: Seven Locks Press, 1984, 1985.

PHILLIBER, S. "Thy Brother's Keeper: A Review of the Literature on Correctional Officers." *Justice Quarterly* 4(1), March 1987, pp. 9–37.

President's Commission on Law Enforcement and Administration of Justice. *The Challenge of Crime in a Free Society*. Washington, D.C.: U.S. Government Printing Office, 1967.

SCHLESINGER, S. "Prison Crowding in the United States: The Data." *Criminal Justice Research Bulletin*, 3(1), 1987 pp. 1–3.

SHOVER, N., and W. J. EINSTADTER. *Analyzing American Corrections*. Belmont, Calif.: Wadsworth, 1988.

SILBERMAN, C. *Criminal Violence, Criminal Justice*. New York: Random House, 1978.

"67% of Drug-Abuse Inmates Go Untreated in Prison." *El Paso Times*. December 19, 1988, p. 4B.

SYKES, G. *The Society of Captives*. Princeton, N.J.: Princeton University Press, 1958.

TAGGART, W. A. "Redefining the Power of the Federal Judiciary: The Impact of Court-Ordered Prison Reform on State Expenditures for Corrections." *Law and Society Review* 23(2), 1989, pp. 501–531.

UNGER, C. A., and R. A. BUCHANAN. *Managing Long-Term Inmates*. Washington, D.C.: National Institute of Corrections, 1985.

VAN DEN HAAG, E. *Punishing Criminals: Concerning a Very Old and Painful Question*. New York: Basic Books, 1975.

WALKER, S. *Sense and Nonsense About Crime: A Policy Guide*, 2nd ed. Pacific Grove, Calif.: Brooks/Cole, 1989.

WALTERS, G. D., AND T. W. WHITE. "Crime, Popular Mythology, and Personal Relationship." *Federal Probation* 52(1), March 1988, pp. 18–26.

Wilson, D. G., AND G. F. VITO. "Long-Term Inmates: Special Needs and Management Considerations." *Federal Probation* 52(3), September 1988, pp. 21–26.

Wright, K. N. *The Great American Crime Myth*. Westport, Conn.: Greenwood Press, 1987.

QUESTIONS FOR DISCUSSION

1. At least six basic factors suggest fundamental weaknesses in the overreliance on incarceration. List and discuss these factors.

2. According to the author, the present emphasis on incarceration must consider eight major prison issues. List and discuss these issues.

3. What two broad proposals are offered, by the author, to begin the process of changing policies about incarceration? Do you believe these proposals will be an effective approach?

4. This article states that "we must take exception to a social control policy based primarily on measures of exclusion rather than inclusion." What is meant by this?

21

SERIOUS AND VIOLENT JUVENILE CRIME
A COMPREHENSIVE STRATEGY

John J. Wilson
James C. Howell

■ ■ ■ ■ ■ ■ ■ ■ ■ ■ ■ ■ ■ ■ ■ ■ ■ ■ ■

INTRODUCTION

The office of Juvenile Justice and Delinquency Prevention (OJJDP) has developed a comprehensive strategy for dealing with serious, violent, and chronic juvenile offenders.[1] This program can be implemented at the state, county, or local levels. The program background, principles, rationale, and components are set forth in this article.

Unfortunately, the already stressed juvenile justice system lacks adequate fiscal and programmatic resources either to identify and intervene effectively with serious, violent, and chronic offenders or to intervene immediately and effectively when delinquent conduct first occurs. The Department of Justice and its OJJDP are calling for an unprecedented national commitment of public and private resources to reverse the trends in juvenile violence, juvenile victimization, and family disintegration in our nation.

BACKGROUND

Serious and violent juvenile crime has increased significantly over the past few years, straining America's juvenile justice system.

Juvenile arrests for violent crimes are increasing. During the period 1983 to 1992, juveniles were responsible for 28% of the increase in murder arrests, 27% of rapes, 27% of robberies, and 17% of aggravated assaults (Snyder, 1994). Most of the increase in violent juvenile crimes during the 10-year period from 1983 to 1992 occurred during the second half of that decade. From 1988 to 1992, juvenile violent crime arrests increased 45%. Increases in juvenile arrests for specific offenses were: murder (52%), rape (17%), robbery (49%), and aggravated assault (47%) (FBI, 1993).

The national scope and seriousness of the youth gang problem have increased sharply since the early 1980s. Gang violence has risen drastically in a number of large cities. Youth gangs are becoming more violent, and gangs increasingly serve as a way for members to engage in illegal money-making activity, including street-level drug trafficking (Spergel et al., 1991).

Evidence continues to mount that a small proportion of offenders commit most of the serious and violent juvenile crimes. About 15% of high risk youth commit about 75% of all violent offenses (Huizinga, Loeber, and Thornberry, 1993). Juveniles with four or more court referrals make up 16% of offenders but are responsible for 51% of all juvenile court cases—61% of murder, 64% of rape, 67% of robbery, 61% of aggravated assault, and 66% of burglary cases (Snyder, 1988).

Juvenile court caseloads are increasing, largely as a result of increasing violent delinquency. From 1986 through 1990, the number of delinquency cases disposed by juvenile courts increased 10%. During the same period, juvenile courts disposed of 31% more violent cases, including 64% more homicide and 48% more aggravated assault cases (Snyder, 1993).

Admissions to juvenile detention and corrections facilities are increasing, resulting in crowded facilities with attendant problems such as institutional violence and suicidal behavior. Admissions to juvenile facilities rose after 1984, reaching an all-time high in 1990 with the largest increase in detention (Krisberg et al., 1992). Forty-seven percent of confined juveniles are in detention and correctional facilities in which the population exceeds the facility design capacity. A nationwide study of conditions of confinement in juvenile detention and correctional facilities found crowding to be associated with higher rates of institutional violence, suicidal behavior, and greater reliance on the use of short-term isolation (Parent et al., 1993).

Juvenile cases handled in criminal courts have increased, resulting in increasing numbers of juveniles placed in crowded adult prisons. The number of juvenile cases handled in criminal courts is unknown, but is estimated to be as many as 200,000 in 1990 (Wilson and Howell, 1993). Judicial waivers to criminal court increased 65% between 1986 and 1990 (Snyder, 1993). Between 1984 and 1990, the number of annual admissions of juveniles to adult prisons increased 30% (OJJDP, 1991, 1994).

GENERAL PRINCIPLES

The following general principles provide a framework to guide our efforts in the battle to prevent delinquent conduct and reduce juvenile involvement in serious, violent, and chronic delinquency:

We must strengthen the family in its primary responsibility to instill moral values and provide guidance and support to children. Where there is no functional family unit, a family surrogate should be established and assisted to guide and nurture the child.

We must support core social institutions—schools, religious institutions, and community organizations—in their roles of developing capable, mature, and responsible youth. A goal of each of these societal institutions should be to ensure that children have the opportunity and support to mature into productive law-abiding citizens. A nurturing community environment requires that core social institutions be actively involved in the lives of youth.

We must promote delinquency prevention as the most cost-effective approach to dealing with juvenile delinquency. Families, schools, religious institutions, and community organizations, including citizen volunteers and the private sector, must be enlisted in the nation's delinquency prevention efforts. These core socializing institutions must be strengthened and assisted in their efforts to ensure that children have the opportunity to become capable and responsible citizens. Communities must take the lead in designing and building comprehensive prevention approaches that address known risk factors and target other youth at risk of delinquency.

We must intervene immediately and effectively when delinquent behavior occurs to successfully prevent delinquent offenders from becoming chronic offenders or progressively committing more serious and violent crimes. Initial intervention efforts, under an umbrella of system authorities (police, intake, and probation), should be centered in the family and other core societal institutions. Juvenile justice system authorities should ensure that an appropriate response occurs and act quickly and firmly if the need for formal system adjudication and sanctions has been demonstrated.

We must identify and control the small group of serious, violent, and chronic juvenile offenders who have committed felony offenses or have failed to respond to intervention and nonsecure community-based treatment and rehabilitation services offered by the juvenile justice system. Measures to address delinquent offenders who are a threat to community safety may include placements in secure community-based facilities or, when necessary, training schools and other secure juvenile facilities.

The proposed strategy incorporates two principal components: (1) preventing youth from becoming delinquent by focusing prevention programs on at-risk youth and (2) improving the juvenile justice system response to delinquent offenders through a system of graduated sanctions and a continuum of treatment alternatives that include immediate intervention, intermediate sanctions, and community-based corrections sanctions, incorporating restitution and community service when appropriate.

Target Populations

The initial target population for prevention programs is juveniles at risk of involvement in delinquent activity. While primary delinquency prevention programs provide services to all youth wishing to participate, maximum impact of future delinquent conduct can be achieved by seeking to identify and involve in prevention programs youth at greatest risk of involvement in delinquent activity. This includes youth who exhibit known risk factors for future delinquency; drug and alcohol abuse; and youth who have had contact with the juvenile justice system as nonoffenders (neglected, abused, and dependent), status offenders (runaways, truants, alcohol offenders, and incorrigibles), or minor delinquent offenders.

The next target population is youth, both male and female, who have committed delinquent (criminal) acts, including juvenile offenders who evidence a high likelihood of becoming, or who already are, serious, violent, or chronic offenders.

Program Rationale

What can communities and the juvenile justice system do to prevent the development of and interrupt the progression of delinquent and criminal careers? Juvenile justice agencies and programs are one part of a larger picture that involves many other local agencies and programs that are responsible for working with at-risk youth and their families. It is important that juvenile delinquency prevention and intervention programs are integrated with local police, social service, child welfare, school, and family preservation programs and that these programs reflect local community determinations of the most pressing problems and program priorities.

Establishing community planning teams that include a broad base of participants drawn from local government and the community (for example, community-based youth development organizations, schools, law enforcement, social service agencies, civic organizations, religious groups, parents, and teens) will help create consensus on priorities and services to be provided as well as built support for a comprehensive program approach that draws on all sectors of the community for participation. Comprehensive approaches to delinquency prevention and intervention will require collaborative efforts between the juvenile justice system and other service provision systems, including mental health, health, child welfare, and education. Developing mechanisms that effectively link these different service providers at the program level will need to be an important component of every community's comprehensive plan.

Risk-focused prevention appears to be the most effective approach to preventing delinquency. The major risk factors are found in the community, family, school, and in the individual and peer group. Prevention strategies will need to be comprehensive, addressing each of the risk factors as they relate to the chronological development of children being served.

Research and experience in intervention and treatment programming suggest that a highly structured system of graduated sanctions hold significant promise. The goal of graduated sanctions is to increase the effectiveness of the juvenile justice system in responding to juveniles who have committed criminal acts. The system's limited resources have diminished its ability to respond effectively to serious, violent, and chronic juvenile crime. This trend must be reversed by empowering the juvenile justice system to provide accountability and treatment resources to juveniles. This includes gender-specific programs for female offenders, whose rates of delinquency have generally been increasing faster than males in recent years, and who now account for 23% of juvenile arrests. It will also require programs for special needs populations such as sex offenders, mentally retarded, emotionally disturbed, and learning disabled delinquents.

The graduated sanctions approach is designed to provide immediate intervention at the first offense to ensure that the juvenile's misbehavior is addressed by the family and community or through formal adjudication and sanctions by the juvenile justice system, as appropriate. Graduated sanctions include a range of intermediate sanctions and secure corrections options to provide intensive treatment that serves the juvenile's needs, provides accountability, and protects the public. They offer an array of referral and dispositional resources for law enforcement, juvenile courts, and juvenile corrections officials. The graduated sanctions component requires that the juvenile justice system's capacity to identify, process, evaluate, refer, and track delinquent offenders be enhanced.

The Juvenile Justice System

The juvenile justice system plays a key role in protecting and guiding juveniles, including responding to juvenile delinquency. Law enforcement plays a key role by conducting investigations, making custody and arrest determinations, or exercising discretionary release authority. Police should be trained in community-based policing techniques and provided with program resources that focus on community youth.

The traditional role of the juvenile and family court is to treat and rehabilitate the dependent or wayward minor, using an individualized approach and tailoring its response to the particular needs of the child and family, with goals of (1) responding to the needs of troubled youth and their families; (2) providing due process while recognizing the rights of the victim; (3) rehabilitating the juvenile offender; and (4) protecting both the juvenile and the public. While juvenile and family courts have been successful in responding to the bulk of youth problems to meet these goals, new ways of organizing and focusing the resources of the juvenile justice system are required to effectively address serious, violent, and chronic juvenile crime. These methods might include the establishment of unified family courts with jurisdiction over all civil and criminal matters affecting the family.

A recent NCJFCJ statement succinctly describes the critical role of the court:

> The Courts must protect children and families when private and other public institutions are unable or fail to meet their obligations. The protection of society by correcting children who break the law, the preservation and reformation of families, and the protection of children from abuse and neglect are missions of the Court. When the family falters, when the basic needs of children go unmet, when the behavior of children is destructive and goes unchecked, juvenile and family courts must respond. The Court is society's official means of holding itself accountable for the well-being of its children and family unit (NCJFCJ, 1993).

A decade ago NCJFCJ developed 38 recommendations regarding serious juvenile offenders and related issues facing the juvenile court system. These issues included confidentiality of the juvenile offender and his or her family, transfer of a juvenile offender to adult court, and effective treatment of the serious juvenile offender (NCJFCJ, 1984). OJJDP recently funded the Council's review of the 38 recommendations for the purpose of updating them and making other modifications that might make them more consistent with the Office's Comprehensive Strategy. However, the 38 recommendations were found to be as valid today as ten years ago and also consistent with the Comprehensive Strategy.

DELINQUENCY PREVENTION

The prevention component of OJJDP's comprehensive strategy is based on a risk-focused delinquency prevention approach (Hawkins and Catalano, 1992). This approach incorporates the public health model that has been used so effectively in combating heart disease. Its premise is that in order to prevent a problem from occurring, the factors (risks) contributing to the development of that problem must be identified and then ways must be found (protective factors) to address and ameliorate those factors.

Hawkins and Catalano's review of over 30 years of work on risk factors from various fields has identified four major risk factors for juvenile delinquency, substance abuse, school drop-out, and teen pregnancy. All these problems share the following common risk factors.

Community.   The more available drugs and alcohol are in a community, the higher the risk that young people will use and abuse them. More delinquency and drug problems occur in communities or neighborhoods where people have little attachment to the community, where the rates of vandalism and crime are high, and where there is low surveillance of public places. Children who live in a poor, deteriorating neighborhood where the community perceives little hope for the future are more likely to develop problems with delinquency, teen pregnancy, and drop out of school.

Family.   Children born or reared in a family with a history of criminal activity have a higher risk for delinquency. Poor family management practices, including a lack of clear expectations for behavior, failure to monitor their children, and excessively severe or inconsistent punishment contribute to delinquency and related problems. Child abuse and family violence also increase violent behavior among offspring.

School.   Boys who are aggressive in grades K-3 are at higher risk for substance abuse and juvenile delinquency. Reading problems as early as the first grade predict subsequent delinquency. Beginning in the late elementary grades, academic failure increases the risk of both drug abuse and delinquency. A lack of commitment to school is also associated with academic failure.

Individual/Peer.   Children who engage in antisocial behavior (misbehaving in school, truancy, fighting) are at increased risk for engaging in drug abuse, dropping out and early sexual activity. Youngsters who associate with peers who engage in a problem behavior are more likely to engage in the same problem behavior. The earlier young people drop out of school, begin using drugs, committing crimes and becoming sexually active, the greater the likelihood that they will have problems with these behaviors later.

To counter these causes and risk factors, protective factors must be introduced. Protective factors are qualities or conditions that moderate a juvenile's exposure to risk. Hawkins and Catalano have organized protective factors into three basic categories: (1) individual characteristics such as a resilient temperament and a positive social orientation; (2) bonding with prosocial family members, teachers, and friends; and (3) healthy beliefs and clear standards for behavior. Hawkins and Catalano have organized these elements in a theory called the "Social Development Model." The theory's main premise is that, to increase bonding, children must be provided with *opportunities* to contribute to their families, schools, peer groups, and communities; *skills* to take advantage of opportunities; and *recognition* for their efforts to contribute. Simultaneously, parents, teachers, and communities need to set clear standards that endorse prosocial behavior.

The risk-focused delinquency prevention approach calls on communities to identify and understand what risk factors their children are exposed to and to implement programs that counter these risk factors. Communities must enhance protective factors that promote positive behavior, health, well-being, and personal success. Effective delinquency prevention efforts must be comprehensive, covering the causes of risk factors described above, and correspond to the social development process.

EFFECTIVE/PROMISING PROGRAMS

The following are program models and approaches that have been demonstrated to be effective in addressing the major risk factors for delinquency, that look promising, or appear to be theoretically consistent with the "social development model."

Neighborhood and *community* programs include community policing; safe havens for youth; neighborhood mobilization for community safety; drug-free school zones; community organization—sponsored after-school programs in tutoring, recreation, mentoring, and cultural activities; community and business partnerships; foster grandparents; job training and apprenticeships for youth; neighborhood watch, and victim programs. Community policing can play an important role in creating a safer environment. Community police officers not only help reduce criminal activity but also become positive role models and establish caring relationships with the youth and families in a community. On-site neighborhood resource teams, composed of community police officers, social workers, health-care workers, housing experts, and school personnel, can ensure that a wide range of problems are responded to in a timely and coordinated manner. The private-sector business community can make a major contribution through Private Industry Councils and other partnerships by providing job training, apprenticeships, and other meaningful economic opportunities for youth.

The following programs directly address negative *family* involvement factors and how to establish protective factors: teen abstinence and pregnancy prevention, parent effectiveness and family skills training, parent support groups, home instruction programs for preschool youngsters, family crisis intervention services, court-appointed special advocates, surrogate families and respite care for families in crisis, permanency planning for foster children, family life education for teens and parents, and runaway and homeless youth services.

School-based prevention programs may include drug and alcohol prevention and education, bullying prevention, violence prevention, alternative schools, truancy reduction, school discipline and safety improvement, targeted-literacy programs in the primary grades, law-related education, after-school programs for latchkey children, teen abstinence and pregnancy prevention, values development, and vocational training. School prevention programs, including traditional delinquency prevention programs not related to the school's educational mission, can assist the family and the community by identifying at-risk youth, monitoring their progress, and intervening with effective programs at critical times during a youth's development.

Programs designed to support healthy *individual* development and positive *peer* relations include gang prevention and intervention, conflict resolution–peer mediation, peer counseling and tutoring, self-help fellowship for peer groups, individual responsibility training, community volunteer service, competitive athletic team participation, Head Start Boys and Girls Clubs, scouting, 4–H Clubs, recreational activities, leadership and personal development, health and mental health treatment, and career youth development.

Youth leadership and service programs can provide such opportunities and can reinforce and help internalize in children such positive individual traits as discipline, character, self-respect, responsibility, teamwork, healthy lifestyles, and good citizenship. They can also provide opportunities for personal growth, active involvement in education and vocational training, and life skills development. The components of a youth leadership and service program may include the following types of program activities: Youth Service Corps, adventure training (leadership, endurance, and team building), mentoring, recreational, summer camp, literacy and learning disability treatment, and law-related education.

The OJJDP has provided assistance to NCJFCJ in implementing risk-focused delinquency prevention planning in conjunction with the prevention priority Council President James Farris established for his presidency. OJJDP provided an orientation in risk-focused prevention and resource assessment in conjunction with NCJFCJ's 21st National Conference on Juvenile Justice. This one-day session prepared conference participants to organize delinquency prevention planning efforts for possible funding under the fiscal year 1994 appropriation of $13 million for OJJDP's Title V Delinquency Prevention Program.

The training session on the "Communities That Care" strategy informed participants how to take the lead in organizing their communities to compete for delinquency prevention program funds. Awards will be made to units of local government in 1994 through the state agencies administering Juvenile Justice and Delinquency Prevention Act formula grant funds. Applicants must include a three-year plan describing the extent of risk factors identified in the community and how these risk factors will be addressed through prevention programs.

Beginning in April, a series of training events for local participants in risk-focused prevention will be provided around the country. The first event is an orientation for key community leaders, including judges, prosecutors, lead law enforcement officers, mayors, school superintendents, business leaders, and other civic leaders. The second event is a three-day training session on risk and resource assessment for community planning teams, to provide a foundation for development of comprehensive risk-focused delinquency prevention plans necessary to secure funding under the OJJDP Title V program. These training events will be organized by the state agencies administering the JJDP Act formula grant program, and are to be provided in up to 45 sites across the nation to 5,000 participants during the spring and summer of this year.

GRADUATED SANCTIONS

An effective juvenile justice system program model for the treatment and rehabilitation of delinquent offenders is one that combines accountability and sanctions with increasingly intensive treatment and rehabilitation services. These graduated sanctions must be wide ranging to fit the offense and include both intervention and secure corrections components. The intervention component includes the use of immediate intervention and intermediate sanctions, and the secure corrections component includes the use of community confinement and incarceration in training schools, camps, and ranches.

Each of these graduated sanctions components should consist of sublevels, or gradations, that together with appropriate services constitute an integrated approach. The purpose of this approach is to stop the juvenile's further penetration into the system by inducing law-abiding behavior as early as possible through the combination of appropriate intervention and treatment sanctions. The juvenile justice system must work with law enforcement, courts, and corrections to develop reasonable, fair, and humane sanctions.

At each level in the continuum, the family must continue to be integrally involved in treatment and rehabilitation efforts. Aftercare must be a formal component of all residential placements, actively involving the family and the community in supporting and reintegrating the juvenile into the community.

Programs will need to use risk and needs assessments to determine the appropriate placement for the offender. Risk assessments should be based on clearly defined objective criteria that focus on (1) the seriousness of the delinquent act, (2) the potential risk for reoffending, based on the presence of risk factors, and (3) the risk to the public safety. Effective risk assessment at intake, for example, can be used to identify those juveniles who require the use of detention as well as those who can be released to parental custody or diverted to nonsecure community-based programs. Needs assessments will help ensure that (1) different types of problems are taken into account when formulating a case plan, (2) a baseline for monitoring a juvenile's progress is established, (3) periodic reassessments of treatment effectiveness are conducted, and (4) a systemwide database of treatment needs can be used for the planning and evaluation of programs, policies, and procedures. Together, risk and needs assessments will help to allocate scarce resources more efficiently and effectively. A system of graduated sanctions requires a broad continuum of options.

For intervention efforts to be most effective, they must be swift, certain, consistent, and incorporate increasing sanctions, including the possible loss of freedom. As the severity of sanction increases, so must the intensity of treatment. At each level, offenders must be aware that, should they continue to violate the law, they will be subject to more severe sanctions and could ultimately be confined in a secure setting, ranging from a secure community-based juvenile facility to a training school, camp, or ranch.

The juvenile court plays an important role in the provision of treatment and sanctions. Probation has traditionally been viewed as the court's main vehicle for delivery of treatment services and community supervision. However, traditional probation services and sanctions have not had the resources to effectively target delinquent offenders, particularly serious, violent, and chronic offenders.

The following graduated sanctions are proposed within the intervention component:

Immediate intervention. First-time delinquent offenders (misdemeanors and nonviolent felonies) and nonserious repeat offenders (generally misdemeanor repeat offenses) must be targeted for system intervention based on their probability of becoming more serious or chronic in their delinquent activities. Nonresidential community-based programs, including prevention programs for at-risk youth, may be appropriate for many of these offenders. Such programs are small and open, located in or near the juvenile's home, and maintain community participation in program planning, operation, and evaluation. Community police officers, working as part of Neighborhood Resource Teams, can help monitor the juvenile's progress. Other offenders may require sanctions tailored to their offense(s) and their needs to deter them from committing additional crimes.

The following programs apply to these offenders: Neighborhood Resource Teams, diversion, informal probation, school counselors serving as probation officers, home on probation, mediation (victims), community service, restitution, day-treatment programs, alcohol and drug abuse treatment (outpatient), and peer juries.

Intermediate sanctions. Offenders who are inappropriate for immediate intervention (first-time serious or violent offenders) or who fail to respond successfully to immediate intervention as evidenced by reoffending (such as repeat property offenders or drug-involved juveniles) would begin with or be subject to intermediate sanctions. These sanctions may be nonresidential or residential.

Many of the serious and violent offenders at this stage may be appropriate for placement in an intensive supervision program as an alternative to secure incarceration. OJJDP's Intensive Supervision of Probationers Program Model is a highly structured, continuously monitored individualized plan that consists of five phases with decreasing levels of restrictiveness: (1) Short-Term Placement in Community Confinement, (2) Day Treatment, (3) Outreach and Tracking, (4) Routine Supervision, and (5) Discharge and Follow-up.

Other appropriate programs include drug testing, weekend detention, alcohol and drug abuse treatment (inpatient), challenge outdoor, community-based residential, electronic monitoring, and boot camp facilities and programs.

Secure corrections. Large and congregate-care juvenile facilities (training schools, camps, and ranches) have not proved to be particularly effective in rehabilitating juvenile offenders. Although some continued use of these types of facilities will remain a necessary alternative for those juveniles who require enhanced security to protect the public, the establishment of small community-based facilities to provide intensive service in a secure environment offers the best hope for successful treatment of those juveniles who require a structured setting. Secure sanctions are most effective in changing future conduct when they are coupled with comprehensive treatment and rehabilitation services.

Standard parole practices, particularly those that have a primary focus on social control, have not been effective in normalizing the behavior of high-risk juvenile parolees over the long term, and consequently, growing interest has developed in intensive aftercare programs that provide high levels of social control and treatment services. OJJDP's Intensive Community-Based Aftercare for High-Risk Juvenile Parolees Program provides an effective aftercare model.

The following graduated sanctions strategies are proposed within the secure corrections component:

Community confinement. Offenders whose presenting offense is sufficiently serious (such as a violent felony) or who fail to respond to intermediate sanctions as evidenced by continued reoffending may be appropriate for community confinement. Offenders at this level present the more serious (such as repeat felony drug trafficking or property offenders) and violent offenders among the juvenile justice system correctional population.

The concept of community confinement provides secure confinement in small community-based facilities that offer intensive treatment and rehabilitation services. These services include individual and group counseling, educational programs, medical services, and intensive staff supervision. Proximity to the community enables direct and regular family involvement with the treatment process as well as a phased reentry into the community that draws upon community resources and services.

Incarceration in training schools, camps, and ranches. Juveniles whose confinement in the community would constitute an ongoing threat to community safety or who have failed to respond to community-based corrections may require an extended correctional placement in training schools, camps, ranches, or other secure options that are not community based. These facilities should offer comprehensive treatment programs for these youth with a focus on education, skills development, and vocational or employment training and experience. These juveniles may include those convicted in the criminal justice system prior to their reaching the age at which they are no longer subject to the original or extended jurisdiction of the juvenile justice system.

Transfer to the criminal justice system. Public safety concerns are resulting in increasing demands for transfer of the most violent juvenile offenders to the criminal justice system. These demands will grow as long as American society perceives juveniles to present a disproportionate threat to the public safety. Although state legislatures are increasingly excluding certain categories of juvenile offenders from the jurisdiction of the juvenile court, judicial waiver holds the most promise as the mechanism for determining that a particular juvenile cannot be rehabilitated in the juvenile justice system. This consideration should be paramount, consistent with the original aims of the juvenile justice system and the juvenile court.

Effective/Promising Programs

Recent reviews of all known experimental evaluations of treatment programs have identified effective program approaches (Lipsey, 1992). Interventions that appear to be the most effective include highly structured programs providing intensive treatments over extended periods of time. Juvenile justice system programs that have been effective in treating and rehabilitating serious, violent, and chronic juvenile offenders include intensive supervision programs; day treatment and education programs operated by Associated Marine Institutes (AMI); the Florida Environmental Institute's (FEI) wilderness camp for juveniles and who would otherwise be sent to adult prisons; and intensive family-based, multisystemic therapy (MST) programs, which have been effective with serious juvenile offenders in several localities. OJJDP's Violent Juvenile Offender Program demonstrated that most violent juvenile offenders could be successfully rehabilitated through intensive treatment in small secure facilities. OJJDP has also developed an intensive aftercare model designed to successfully reintegrate high-risk juvenile parolees back into the community.

NCJFCJ has completed a nationwide assessment of promising and effective juvenile justice system programs under OJJDP's new "what works" series. Nearly 1,000 program models were identified. These have been computerized in Pittsburgh, at NCJJ. A comprehensive report is being prepared for Department of Justice distribution.

Under a competitive award, the National Council on Crime and Delinquency (NCCD) is currently reviewing program models to identify the most effective/promising ones for local jurisdictions in implementing OJJDP's Comprehensive Strategy. This review will include programs reported to be effective in the NCJJ "what works" project. The main product of the NCCD program development work: an operations manual, including a blueprint for assessing their present juvenile justice system and for planning new programs that respond to community needs; and a collection of effective promising programs, from which jurisdictions can choose, for implementation.

At the same time, new program models are under development. For example, OJJDP has supported NCJFCJ's development of a domestic violence program model for early intervention in families troubled by domestic violence. This program model, which will complement OJJDP's Comprehensive Strategy, will incorporate policies, programs and practices that serve to coordinate the efforts of police, court, social service agencies, schools, and child protective services in addressing domestic violence through early intervention. This domestic violence model will help preclude the onset of serious, violent, and chronic juvenile offending.

EXPECTED BENEFITS

Jurisdictions that implement OJJDP's Comprehensive Strategy can expect the following benefits.

- *Delinquency prevention.* Effective delinquency prevention will result in fewer children entering the juvenile justice system in demonstration sites. This would, in turn, permit concentration of system resources on fewer delinquents, thereby increasing the effectiveness of the graduated sanctions component and improving the operation of the juvenile justice system.

- *Increased juvenile justice system responsiveness.* This program will provide additional referral and dispositional resources for law enforcement, juvenile courts, and juvenile corrections. It will also require these system components to increase their ability to identify, process, evaluate, refer, and track juvenile offenders.

- *Increased juvenile accountability.* Juvenile offenders will be held accountable for their behavior, decreasing the likelihood of their development into serious, violent, or chronic offenders and tomorrow's adult criminals. The juvenile justice system will be held accountable for controlling chronic and serious delinquency while also protecting society. Communities will be held accountable for providing community-based prevention and treatment resources for juveniles.

- *Decreased cost of juvenile corrections.* Applying the appropriate graduated sanctions and developing the required community-based resources should reduce significantly the need for high-cost beds in training schools. Savings from the high costs of operating these facilities could be used to provide treatment in community-based programs and facilities.

- *Increased responsibility of the juvenile justice system.* Many juvenile offenders currently waived or transferred to the criminal justice system could be provided for intensive services in secure community-based settings or in long-term treatment in juvenile training schools, camps, and ranches.

- *Increased program effectiveness.* As the statistical information presented herein indicates, credible knowledge exists about who the chronic, serious, and violent offenders are, that is, their characteristics. Some knowledge also exists about what can effectively be done regarding their treatment and rehabilitation. However, more must be learned about what works best for whom under what circumstances to intervene successfully in the potential criminal careers of serious, violent, and chronic juvenile offenders. Follow-up research and rigorous evaluation of programs implemented as part of this strategy should produce valuable information.

• *Crime reduction.* The combined effects of delinquency prevention and increased juvenile justice system effectiveness in intervening immediately and effectively in the lives of delinquent offenders should result in measurable decreases in delinquency in sites where the above concepts are demonstrated. In addition, long-term reduction in crime should result from fewer serious, violent, and chronic delinquents becoming adult criminal offenders.

NEXT STEPS

Implementing this comprehensive strategy for serious, violent, and chronic juveniles is a major program priority for OJJDP. Awards were made to two jurisdictions last year for communitywide assessment and planning toward implementing the strategy. The Office anticipates awarding competitive grants to two more jurisdictions in fiscal year 1994 to carry out the assessment, planning, and implementation process. Training and technical assistance will be provided to participating communities. Additional resources are expected to be available in fiscal year 1995 to support further implementation of the Comprehensive Strategy.

NOTES

1. OJJDP has developed the following definitions of serious, violent, and chronic juvenile offenders for purposes of this program. *Serious juvenile offenders* are those adjudicated delinquent for committing any felony offense, including larceny or theft, burglary or breaking and entering, extortion, arson, and drug trafficking or other controlled dangerous substance violations. *Violent juvenile offenders* are those serious juvenile offenders adjudicated delinquent for one of the following felony offenses—homicide, rape or other felony sex offenses, mayhem, kidnapping, robbery, or aggravated assault. *Chronic juvenile offenders* are juveniles adjudicated delinquent for committing three or more delinquent offenses. These definitions include juveniles convicted in criminal court for particular offense types.

2. To reserve spaces for your key community leaders and community planning team at these important events, state Juvenile Justice Specialists must be contacted immediately. (These persons' names and phone numbers can be obtained by calling OJJDP's Juvenile Justice Clearinghouse at 800-638-8736).

REFERENCES

Federal Bureau of Investigation. (1993). *Uniform Crime Reports: 1993.* Washington, D.C.: U.S. Department of Justice.

HAWKINS, DAVID, and RICHARD CATALANO, JR. (1992). *Communities That Care.* San Francisco: Jossey-Bass.

HUIZINGA, DAVID, ROLF LOEBER, and TERENCE THORNBERRY. (1993). *Urban Delinquency and Substance Abuse: Initial Findings Report.* Washington, D.C.: OJJDP.

KRISBERG, BARRY, et al. (1992) *National Juvenile Custody Trends 1978–1989*. Washington, D.C.: OJJDP.

LIPSEY, MARK W. "What Do We Learn From 400 Research Studies on the Effectiveness of Treatment with Juvenile Delinquents?" Presented at the 1992 What Works Conference, University of Salford, Great Britain, September 1992.

National Council of Juvenile and Family Court Judges. (1984). *Children and Families First, A Mandate for Change*. Reno, Nevada. NCJFCJ.

_____. (1984). "The Juvenile Court and Serious Offenders: 38 Recommendations," *Juvenile and Family Court Journal*.

Office of Juvenile Justice and Delinquency Prevention. *Juveniles Taken Into Custody: Fiscal Year 1990 Report*. Washington, D.C.: OJJDP, September 1991.

_____. (1994). *Juveniles Taken Into Custody: Fiscal Year 1992 Report*. Washington, D.C.: OJJDP.

PARENT, DALE, et al. *Conditions of Confinement: A Study to Evaluate Conditions in Juvenile Detention and Corrections Facilities*. Final report submitted to the OJJDP. April 1993.

SNYDER, HOWARD. (1988). *Court Careers of Juvenile Offenders*. Washington, D.C.: OJJDP.

_____. et al. (1993). *Juvenile Court Statistics: 1990*. Washington, D.C.: OJJDP.

_____. (1994). *Are Juveniles Driving the Violence Trends?* OJJDP Fact Sheet.

_____. et al. (1993). *Arrests of Juveniles 1991*. Washington, D.C.: OJJDP.

SPERGEL, IRVING, et al. (1991). *Youth Gangs: Problems and Response*. Final Report submitted to OJJDP. See the "Executive Summary," Stage I: Assessment.

WILSON, JOHN J. and JAMES C. HOWELL (1993). *A Comprehensive Strategy for Serious, Violent, and Chronic Juvenile Offenders*. Washington, D.C.: OJJDP.

QUESTIONS FOR DISCUSSION

1. There are six indicators, presented by the authors, that juvenile crime has increased significantly in frequency and seriousness. List and discuss these indicators.

2. Five general principles are presented as a framework to guide efforts at preventing and reducing juvenile delinquency. List and discuss these principles.

3. According to the authors, juvenile delinquency, substance abuse, school dropout, and teen pregnancy share a common set of four risk factors. List and discuss these risk factors.

4. List and discuss several programs that may be effective when addressing each of the four identified risk factors.

5. What are the expected benefits of OJJDP's Comprehensive Strategy? In your opinion, will this approach be effective?

22

YOUTH GANGS AND PUBLIC POLICY

C. Ronald Huff

■ ■

THE STUDY

The research on which this article is based took place from April 1986 to May 1988. The research project included in-depth case studies of youth gangs in Cleveland and Columbus, as well as secondary surveys of Ohio's five other large cities (Cincinnati, Toledo, Dayton, Akron, and Youngstown).

Data for the study were collected via the following methods:

1. Interviews with gang members, former gang members, police officers, representatives of community and social service agencies, and school officials in Cleveland and Columbus. To ensure a more representative sample of gang members, some of the interviews were conducted with gang members who had not been apprehended. These interviews generally took place either in members' housing projects or neighborhoods or in neutral locations. They were facilitated by trusted intermediaries who arranged them and accompanied the researchers.[1] Some of these interviews were recorded on audiotape whereas others, to reduce the interviewee's apprehensions, were summarized by handwritten notes.

2. Field observations of police operations targeting youth gangs and youth violence.

3. Analyses of secondary data from the Cleveland and Columbus police departments concerning arrests believed to be gang related.

4. Surveys of all 88 county juvenile courts in Ohio, as well as the 7 chiefs of police of Ohio's largest cities and the principals of 66 junior and senior high schools (35 in Cleveland and 31 in Columbus).

PRINCIPAL FINDINGS

The surveys of school principals in Cleveland and Columbus revealed a moderate level of concern about gangs; little consensus on how to deal with the problem; and much agreement on the role of law enforcement, which is perceived as vitally important in

C. Ronald Huff, "Youth Gangs and Public Policy," *Crime and Delinquency* (Vol. 35, No. 4), pp. 524–537, copyright © 1989 by Sage Publications, Inc. Reprinted by permission of Sage Publications, Inc.

controlling gang behavior in the two cities (law enforcement is viewed as having the primary responsibility).

The surveys of police chiefs of the largest cities in Ohio indicate that several chiefs currently acknowledge some problems with gangs; nearly all state that gangs have been a problem in the past, and all estimate that offenses by youth gangs represent less than 1% of all crime and less than 2% of all juvenile crime.

The case studies confirmed that youth gangs exist in both Cleveland and Columbus. During the course of this study, the primary and secondary data identified more than fifty separately named gangs in Cleveland, some of which undoubtedly were "splinter groups" or "groupies" rather than truly separate and unique gangs. Many of these gangs have either dissipated or merged with each other, leaving fifteen to twenty separate, viable gangs. In Columbus, the study identified more than twenty separately named gangs. However, with the same qualifications noted above, the number of truly separate, viable gangs at present is approximately fifteen. Cincinnati, though not a case study site, also has experienced youth gang problems during the course of this research including incidents involving the neo-Nazi "Skinheads."

In terms of racial and ethnic identity, it is probable that about 90% of the members of Cleveland and Columbus gangs are black, whereas the remaining 10% are white and Hispanic. The study identified two Hispanic gangs (on Cleveland's west side). Statewide, police chiefs surveyed also reported that gang membership was more than 90% black, according to their own information.

The age of gang members ranges approximately from ten to thirty (with the most common age range being 14–24), and the larger gangs are stratified by age and sophistication. That is, until one is 16 or 17 years old, he is likely to be in a junior division of the gang. These divisions have their own leadership structures.

Several female "gangs" were identified in Cleveland and Columbus. However, upon closer investigation, these "gangs" were actually more similar to "groupies" whose identity was closely tied to that of male gang allies. Gang membership in Ohio is more than 90% male, according to data generated by this study.

Gangs in Columbus and Cleveland originated in the following ways:

1. Breakdancing/"rappin'" groups evolved into gangs as a result of intergroup conflict involving dancing, skating, and/or rappin' competition. This competition would sometimes spill over into the parking lots of skating rinks, where members frequently had concealed weapons in their cars.

2. Street corner groups similarly evolved into gangs as a result of conflicts with other "corner groups." These groups were more typical of distinctive neighborhoods, such as housing projects. In Cleveland, these groups had a much longer history than in Columbus, although that history has been uneven. Nonetheless, both cities have histories of street corner groups and "street hustling" that predate the current generation of street gangs.

3. Street gang leaders already experienced in gang life moved to Ohio from Chicago or Los Angeles. These more sophisticated leaders were often charismatic figures who were able to quickly recruit a following from among local youths.

Despite rumors to the contrary, this study produced no solid evidence that any Ohio youth gang is a "chapter" or direct affiliate of a gang in any other city (Chicago, Detroit, or Los Angeles, in particular). It is likely that this confusion stems from the "out of state" identities of some gang leaders who moved to Ohio from other states. For the most part, this reflects our society's extensive geographic mobility, coupled with our historic tendency to blame "outsiders" for local problems rather than focus on the root causes (especially poverty and unemployment). However, in the past year Ohio's cities have witnessed the in-migration of "crack" cocaine traffickers from Detroit, Los Angeles, and even Jamaica.

Members of the gangs identified in this study are overwhelmingly drawn from the "urban black underclass" described so well by Wilson (1987) and by Duster (1987). This is true of both Cleveland and Columbus, though for somewhat different reasons. Cleveland, a more heavily industrialized "rust belt" city, has been adversely impacted by the loss of many of its manufacturing jobs and the high unemployment rates it has experienced in the 1980s. Table 1 reflects changes in the poverty status of Cleveland families (including those with children under 18 years of age) from 1970 to 1980, and Table 2 presents the unemployment trend and the loss of manufacturing jobs during that period. Tables 3 and 4 present similar data for Columbus, widely known for its stable, high-tech, service-oriented economy.

What is compelling about these tables is this: An economically and socially marginal youth who has dropped out of or been expelled from school, and/or is without job skills, is in deep trouble in either Cleveland or Columbus. In Cleveland, he is competing for a rapidly shrinking pool of manufacturing jobs (more than 36,000 of these jobs were lost between 1970 and 1980 alone) and cannot qualify for other jobs. In Columbus, there never were that many manufacturing jobs (in 1970 Columbus had less than one-half as many manufacturing jobs as Cleveland), and the jobs that exist require higher levels of

TABLE 1   POVERTY STATUS OF FAMILIES (CLEVELAND), 1970–1980

| | Year | | Change | Percent of Change |
	1970	1980	1970–1980	1970–1980
Number of families	184,645	143,588	-41,057	-22.2
Number of families below poverty level	24,817	26.926	2,109	8.5
Percent of families below poverty level	13.4%	18.8%		5.4
Families below poverty level with children under 18 years	18,227	21,754	3,527	19.4
Percent of families below poverty level with children under 18 years	9.9%	15.2%		5.3

Source: U.S. Bureau of the Census

TABLE 2   TOTAL UNEMPLOYMENT AND LOSS OF MANUFACTURING JOBS (CLEVELAND), 1970–1980

	Year		Change	Percent of Change
	1970	*1980*	*1970–1980*	*1970–1980*
Civilian labor force	303,146	240,538	-62,608	-20.7
Unemployed	15,730	26,359	10,629	67.6
Unemployed as percent of civilian labor force	5.2%	11.0%		5.8
Work force employed by manufacturing	107,477	71,055	-36,422	-33.9
Manufacturing workers as percent of civilian labor force	35.5%	29.5%		-6.0

Source: U.S. Bureau of the Census

education and job skills. To make matters worse, the military, a traditionally available alternative career path for the poor, is increasingly inaccessible due to the higher quality of applicants generated by an economy with relatively few attractive entry-level positions for unskilled workers.

As these tables reveal, poverty is increasingly victimizing families with children under 18 years of age. With little income to buy flashy clothes and other consumer goods advertised throughout our society, a poor minority youth may find the "illegitimate opportunities"

TABLE 3   POVERTY STATUS OF FAMILIES (COLUMBUS), 1970–1980

	Year		Change	Percent of Change
	1970	*1980*	*1970–1980*	*1970–1980*
Number of families	128,594	136,625	8,031	6.2
Number of families below poverty level	12,551	16,482	3,931	31.3
Percent of families below poverty level	9.8%	12.1%		2.3
Families below poverty level with children under 18 years	9,096	13,265	4,169	45.8
Percent of families below poverty level with children under 18 years	7.1%	9.7%		2.6

Source: U.S. Bureau of the Census

TABLE 4   TOTAL UNEMPLOYMENT AND LOSS OF MANUFACTURING JOBS (COLUMBUS), 1970–1980

	Year		*Change*	*Percent of Change*
	1970	*1980*	*1970–1980*	*1970–1980*
Civilian labor force	227,330	279,727	52,397	23.0
Unemployed	8,647	17,894	9,247	106.9
Unemployed as a percent of civilian labor force	3.8%	6.4%		2.6
Work force employed by manufacturing	50,270	43,709	-6,561	-13.1
Manufacturing workers as a percent of civilian labor force	22.1%	15.6%		-6.5

Source: U.S. Bureau of the Census

(Cloward and Ohlin, 1960) available through gangs, crime, and drug sales more compelling than the legitimate options available to him.

The gangs identified in this study correspond to several loosely knit typologies:

1. Informal, *hedonistic gangs* whose focal concerns seem to be "getting high" (usually on alcohol and/or marijuana and other drugs) and "having a good time." These gangs occasionally engage in some minor property crime, but tend not to be involved in violent personal crime.

2. *Instrumental gangs* whose focal concerns are more economic and who commit a higher volume of property crimes for economic reasons. Most of these gang members also use alcohol and marijuana; some use "crack" cocaine. In addition, some *individual* members of these gangs sell drugs, but this is not an organized *gang* activity.

3. *Predatory gangs* that commit robberies, street muggings, and other crimes of opportunity (including at least one known group rape). Members of these gangs are more likely to use highly addictive drugs such as "crack" cocaine, and these drugs contribute significantly to their labile, assaultive behavior. Members of these gangs may also sell drugs to finance the purchase of more sophisticated weapons. Although this study produced no hard evidence that any of these gangs is currently a "drug distribution network," they represent a ready-made "target of exploitation" for organized crime or other criminal groups.

Gang members actually spend most of their time engaging in exaggerated versions of typical adolescent behavior (rebelling against authority by skipping school, refusing to do homework, and disobeying parents; wearing clothing and listening to music that sets them apart from most adults; and having a primary allegiance to their peer group instead of their parents or other adults). They appear to "drift" into and out of illegal behavior, as described by Matza (1964), and the frequency and seriousness of their law-violating behavior appear to fit the three loose gang typologies above. The older the members of a gang, the more they seem to drift toward criminality and away from typical adolescent focal concerns.

Law-violating activities committed by youth gangs during the course of this study include theft, auto theft, intimidation and assault of school and on the street, robbery, burglary, rape, group rape, drug use, drug sales, and even murder. To be sure, the more serious the offense, the less frequently it occurs, but gang members do commit all of the above—and more. As one gang member said during his interview, "People may say there's no gangs 'cause they don't see no colors, but if they be robbin' people, shootin' people, and killin' people, they still a gang" (Field Notes, 1987).

While three of Ohio's largest cities have youth gangs, until recently only one (Columbus) had officially acknowledged their existence. This research, along with other national studies, suggests that cities experiencing problems with gangs pass through distinct and recognizable stages, and both Cincinnati and Cleveland (until recently) could best be characterized as being in the "official denial" stage. For a variety of reasons, not the least of which is protection of a city's "image," political leaders and others in key leadership roles are reluctant to acknowledge the existence of gangs.

Columbus's emergence from its own denial stage was probably accelerated by several gang-related incidents in 1984 and 1985, including: (1) a challenge issued by a gang leader on a local television news show, followed by his death several days later in a "drive-by-shooting" carried out by a rival gang; (2) a gang-related assault on the governor's daughter; and (3) a gang-related assault on the mayor's son.[2]

Officials denial of gang problems appears to facilitate victimization by gangs, especially in the public schools. School principals in several Ohio cities are reluctant to acknowledge "gang-related" assaults for fear that such problems may be interpreted as negative reflections on their management abilities. This "political analysis" appears to encourage gang-related assaults and may send the wrong signals to gang members, implying that they can operate with impunity within the vacuum it creates.

Contrary to much "common wisdom," teachers who demonstrate that they care about a youth and then are firm but fair in their expectations are rarely, if ever, the victims of assault by gang members. Rather, it is those teachers who "back down" and are easily intimidated who are more likely to be the victims of assault. During two years of interviews, *not one* gang member ever said that a teacher who insisted on academic performance (within the context of a caring relationship) was assaulted. Such teachers are respected far more than those perceived as "weak," and "weakness" generally represents a quality to be exploited by gang members in an almost Darwinian fashion, much as they select targets on the street.

On the other hand, *overly* aggressive behavior directed at gang members appears to backfire. Interviews reveal that gang members have an intense dislike for police officers who use unnecessary "strong-arm tactics" in making arrests or questioning them, for example. Gang members indicated that they feel nothing but anger and vengefulness when a police officer behaves "unprofessionally" and that they will seize any subsequent opportunity to "get even."

When asked what they think an officer should do when "baited" in front of other gang members or onlookers, gang members typically respond that an officer should "be professional," perhaps "laugh at him" and walk away rather than fight when challenged. Gang members admit grudging respect for such officers, and this respect appears to be even greater for officers who demonstrate some personal concern for the gang members (asking how they're doing when they see them on the streets or admonishing them to stay out of trouble, for example).

Having moved through its "denial stage" rather quickly, Columbus reacted by implementing a comparatively well-balanced, two pronged approach to the gang problem: (1) active and aggressive enforcement against gang leaders and hard core gang members via the Youth Violence Crime Section, a special 18-officer unit in the Columbus Police Department; and (2) prevention directed at marginal gang members and would-be members via the Youth Outreach Project, supported by United Way, the Columbus Public Schools, and the Columbus Department of Parks and Recreation. Columbus's approach is perhaps as well-balanced and well-coordinated as any in the nation, though much remains to be accomplished. Two keys to its effectiveness are its unique centralization of all four major gang control functions (intelligence, prevention, enforcement, and investigation) in one police unit (the Youth Violence Crime Section) and that unit's close cooperation with the schools, the courts, the prosecutor's office, the Youth Outreach Project, and other community agencies.

An unanticipated consequence of court-ordered busing in Cleveland and Columbus has been exacerbation of gang conflict in certain schools. Prior to mandatory busing, the gangs that existed were largely neighborhood, "turf"-oriented gangs. As a result of busing, there are now rival gangs at the same schools. Schools were not planned and organized with security in mind and do not readily lend themselves to such concerns. As a result, intimidation and assaults have occurred in certain schools where rival gangs find themselves together.

Busing, along with the ready availability of automobiles and improved freeway systems in our metropolitan areas, has also provided gang members with vastly increased geographic mobility. Gang members described in detail the planning and execution of auto thefts in suburban shopping malls far away from their own homes, for example. The implications for law enforcement are clear: to effectively contain these gang-related offenses, police must have some centralized unit or, at the very least, must share intelligence on gang members and their activities. Whether a department has a gang unit, a juvenile bureau, or a highly decentralized organizational structure, it must identify and be able to recognize gang leaders and members who criss-cross the metropolitan area at will and who may show up at citywide events, such as rock concerts, to "shake down the squares" from the suburbs (intimidate and rob suburbanites coming into the city for such events).

Finally, busing has dramatically changed the meaning of "neighborhood." Forerunners of the current gangs in Cleveland and Columbus were neighborhood street corner groups and turf-oriented gangs who fought one another over turf, ethnic and racial conflict, and other issues. Interviews with gang members in both Cleveland and Columbus revealed that "neighborhood" no longer conveys the same kind of meaning, nor does it seem to have much importance to these youths. If still in school, they attend schools with pupils from various neighborhoods. Gang membership is no longer confined to the neighborhood, but involves confederates recruited at school, at skating rinks, and elsewhere throughout the city.

PUBLIC POLICY RECOMMENDATIONS

Youth gangs may best be viewed as a symptom of underlying social and economic problems that go far beyond the usual alienation found in youth subcultures in Western nations. The existence of an urban underclass, with its attendant socially disorganized and fragmented living conditions, gives rise to many social pathologies and the gang problem is just one of them. Primary prevention should be heavily emphasized in any strategy addressing youth gangs, yet it is probably the most neglected type of intervention. As a number of police officers have said during this study, "Simply arresting them and locking them up is not the whole answer. We have to figure out a way to reach young kids *before* they get involved with these gangs" (Field Notes, 1988). Given the obstacles confronting poor and minority inner city youths, primary prevention programs must address both economic opportunity and neighborhood and family social structures.

For this reason, a two-stage strategy for states is recommended. This strategy, which will require federal assistance, is as follows:

1. In Phase One, a state would commission a study to identify *by zip code* those areas of our cities producing disproportionate numbers of commitments to prisons, youth correctional facilities, and mental health facilities, as well as those generating high numbers of public assistance recipients.[3] The total cost of these indicators of social and economic pathology would then be listed for each zip code area. These zip code areas, though not synonymous with "neighborhoods,"[4] would constitute the target areas for special primary prevention efforts.

2. In Phase Two, the state would issue a Request for Proposals for innovative primary prevention approaches to the multiple problems of these zip code areas. Such proposals would address methods of strengthening families and social institutions, improving job opportunities, and otherwise reducing the overwhelming obstacles confronting area residents. Our current failures in these areas of our cities are costing us a great deal of money and even more in human misery and wasted lives. This approach could offer some hope for innovation.

Schools and teacher preparation programs in our colleges and universities should move purposefully to develop teachers who are capable of teaching about and discussing situational ethics in general classrooms. Ethics should not be a special, isolated course, but rather should be integrated at appropriate points during the day as it relates to student dilemmas, student behaviors, history lessons, and so on. This proposal is not meant to violate the separation of church and state; the instruction should not be in religion. Rather, it is analogous to the British "Lifeline" series on situational ethics. Other programs, such as Quest, that focus on values and ethics in the school context should also be considered.

Also, schools and teacher preparation programs should heed the findings of this study with respect to gangs' impact in schools. Teachers (and perhaps principals) need to have better assertiveness training and deeper understanding of some guiding principles such as Glasser's Reality Therapy, which emphasizes holding students accountable for their behavior.

As *preventive* measures, states should consider establishing statewide intergovernmental task forces on gangs, organized crime, and narcotics. The enormous profits to be made by selling drugs will be difficult for poor youths to resist. Some of the gangs that now exist may also be easy targets for exploitation by organized crime seeking new narcotics markets. If prevention is to be successful, it will require statewide coordination.

In addition, each large city should establish a local task force that brings together the following components (where they exist): juvenile bureau, youth gang unit, narcotics unit, organized crime unit, school security division, youth outreach project or other social service coordinating program, and juvenile court. Information must be shared on a regular basis if prevention efforts are to be successful in dealing with the potential drug/gang connection.

The increased mobility of gang members requires that police agencies reassess their organizational structures and strongly consider establishing some citywide unit for monitoring gangs and collecting intelligence information. Ideally, the four major gang control functions identified should be centralized in that unit as much as possible.

Police should be aggressive but professional in dealing with gangs. Gangs must learn that they cannot operate with impunity and that their sense of "invisibility" (which may be a carryover from the well-documented sense of invisibility described by many black citizens in a white-dominated society) is a false one. These aggressive police actions should, however, be targeted solely at the leaders and hard-core members. The marginal members and "wanna be's" can be influenced to redirect their behavior in more positive ways.

For leaders and hard-core gang members who are found delinquent (or, if adults, are found guilty of crimes), but who do not pose threats to public safety, the courts should consider the use of intensive probation supplemented by either random, unannounced visits and telephone monitoring or by electronic monitoring. The purpose of this sanction would be to break up street gangs by requiring that hard-core members and leaders be at home unless they are at school or at work.

School boards should develop very clear policies forbidding weapons of any kind to be brought into schools, and these policies should be explained to all students and enforced without exception. Also, there should be a close working relationship between the schools and the local police, and students should be informed that schools are not "islands" where unlawful behavior is both "invisible" and immune from arrest and prosecution. Weapons offenses, violent assaults, and other serious offenses should be reported to the police.

Schools must make it clear to all that their first obligation is to ensure an environment conducive to learning, and that means one free from intimidation and assault. In some urban schools, administrative concern with school "image" and the administrators' careers, along with some of the other dynamics of official denial, seem to take precedence over the protection of children.

Traditionally, the school was a place that gang members treated with some respect—a sort of "neutral zone" where gang warfare was largely taboo. In part, this reflected tradition and neighborhood loyalties toward neighborhood schools. The demise of neighborhood schools seems to have significantly dissipated this sense of respect. It also has greatly complicated after-school extracurricular activities since many students who might want to participate in those activities may have difficulty finding transportation home afterward. Finally, it has reduced the school's perceived importance as a neighborhood center where other kinds of activities occur (parent effectiveness training, continuing education classes, GED classes, job skills workshops, and so on) since the "common denominator" is no longer as clear to many residents.

Urban communities need to reestablish strong neighborhood-based centers and programs to tie the residents of inner city areas together in the pursuit of their common concerns. To rebuild a sense of community and collective responsibility, we must begin at the family and neighborhood levels.

Finally, several programs now operating in Ohio and elsewhere offer positive examples of programmatic efforts to address the hopelessness and despair confronting the urban underclass. These include Cleveland's "Scholarship in Escrow" Program. This program was begun because of a concern that about half of all students were dropping out of school, in part because they could see no tangible (job-related) benefits of a high school diploma. They often had siblings who *had* completed high school, but to no apparent avail; they still had no jobs, and none of them could afford college or job training programs.

To counter this lack of incentive, the "Scholarship in Escrow" Program was created by a partnership between the Cleveland Public Schools and representatives of the private sector in metropolitan Cleveland. The program essentially creates a trust fund ($16 million thus far) for all students enrolled in grades 7–12 and credits each of their accounts with ten dollars for every C, twenty dollars for every B, and forty dollars for every A earned in school. The money goes into a scholarship fund, where it earns interest. Each student earning money for grades receives a certificate (somewhat like a stock certificate) indicating the amount earned. Students who graduate from Cleveland public high schools have up to eight years to use their scholarship monies at any Pell Grant-certified college or technical school. The program is based on two rationales: (1) If wealthy families can create trust funds for the future of their children, why cannot we as a society create trust funds for *all* kids? and (2) Since their *future* income will be highly correlated with their educational achievement, why not pay kids for doing well in school now, as an intermediate reinforcement? The program is in its first year of operation, and thus far the superintendent reports that about half of the eligible students are earning money; the other half are earning nothing.

Youth gangs are symptomatic of many of the same social and economic problems as adult crime, mental illness, drug abuse, alcoholism, the surge in homelessness, and multigeneration "welfare families" living in hopelessness and despair. While we are justly concerned with the replacement of our physical infrastructure (roads, bridges, sewers) our *human* infrastructure may be crumbling as well. Our social, educational, and economic infrastructures are not meeting the needs of many children and adults. Increases in the number of women and children living in poverty (the "feminization" and "juvenilization" of poverty) are dramatic examples of this recent transformation.

To compete with the seductive lure of drug profits and the grinding despair of poverty, we must reassess our priorities and reaffirm the importance of our neighborhoods by putting in place a number of programs that offer hope, education, job skills, and meaningful lives. It is worth the cost of rebuilding our human infrastructure since it is, after all, our children whose lives are being wasted and our cities in which the quality of life is being threatened.

NOTES

1. I am especially indebted to Akil Ogbanna, a caseworkers with the Home Detention Project of the Cuyahoga County Juvenile Court (Cleveland), and the staff of the Youth Outreach Project (Columbus) for facilitating these interviews, which would otherwise have been impossible.

2. It appears that one of the factors often responsible for moving cities out of the "denial" stage is, unfortunately, a highly publicized assault or homicide involving a highly visible "V.I.P." in the community (for example, the governor's daughter and the mayor's son in Columbus; an affluent Asian woman in the Westwood theater district of Los Angeles; a Honolulu police officer). Generally, the victimization of the poor has not been sufficient to cause this issue to "bubble up" on the political agendas of most American cities.

3. This idea was formulated after learning that the Ohio Department of Youth Services had conducted an internal study analyzing commitments by zip codes. The idea seemed worthy of broader application across multiple social control "systems" (crime, welfare, mental illness, and so on), since zip code information is one of the few common denominators among state government databases, if not the only one.

4. There are several problems inherent in using zip code information; among other things, zip code areas are not uniformly defined, and the populations of those areas are nonuniform. Therefore, any application of this strategy would necessitate some further efforts to standardize these indicators of social pathology on the basis of population size for the purpose of comparing seriousness and developing priority "targets."

REFERENCES

CHIN, KO-LIN. (1986). "Chinese Triad Societies, Tongs, Organized Crime, and Street Gangs in Asia and the United States." Ph.D. dissertation, Wharton School, University of Pennsylvania, Philadelphia.

CLOWARD, RICHARD A. and LLOYD E. OHLIN. (1960). *Delinquency and Opportunity: A Theory of Delinquent Gangs*. New York: The Free Press.

DUSTER, TROY. (1987). "Crime, Youth Unemployment, and the Black Urban Underclass." *Crime & Delinquency* 33: 300–16.

FAGAN, JEFFREY. (1988). "The Social Organization of Drug Use and Drug Dealing Among Urban Gangs." Paper presented at the Ohio Conference on Youth Gangs and the Urban Underclass, Ohio State University, Columbus, May 1988. *Criminology 27*: 633–669, 1989.

Field Notes. (1987). Interview with anonymous juvenile gang member. Cleveland.

Field Notes. (1988). Interview with anonymous police officer. Columbus.

HAGEDORN, JOHN M. (1988). *People and Folks: Gangs, Crime and the Underclass in a Rustbelt City*. Chicago: Lake View Press.

KLEIN, MALCOLM W. and CHERYL L. MAXSON. (1985). "'Rock Sales' in South Los Angeles." *Sociology and Social Research* 69: 561–565.

MATZA, DAVID. (1964). *Delinquency and Drift*. New York: John Wiley and Sons.

WILSON, WILLIAM JULIUS. (1987). *The Truly Disadvantaged*. Chicago: University of Chicago Press.

QUESTIONS FOR DISCUSSION

1. In surveys conducted for this research, the author found that the public views law enforcement as having the primary responsibility for curbing gang activity. How is this view, of the public, faulty?

2. How has geographic mobility influenced the perpetuation of gangs?

3. List and discuss the gang typology presented by the author.

4. Why do gangs assault some teachers and not others?

5. List and discuss the two-stage, public policy strategy presented by Huff.

23

A POLICY MAKER'S GUIDE TO CONTROLLING DELINQUENCY AND CRIME THROUGH FAMILY INTERVENTIONS

Kevin N. Wright
Karen E. Wright

■ ■ ■ ■ ■ ■ ■ ■ ■ ■ ■ ■ ■ ■ ■ ■ ■ ■ ■ ■

For the past two decades, the trend in juvenile justice has been toward more punitive policies and laws. Implicit in these policies is a belief that children are cognizant of and wholly responsible for their behaviors, and therefore deserve the punitive responses they receive. The actions of people and institutions who surround children, however, play vital roles in their development. Therefore families appear to be a crucial, potentially productive point of intervention at which to reduce the likelihood of delinquency. This paper explores the relationship of family life to delinquency and derives five policy strategies to reduce delinquency: (1) prenatal and early childhood health care, (2) early intervention, (3) comprehensive family policy, (4) family treatment for troubled youths, and (5) parent training.

Most activities aimed at controlling crime and delinquency in the United States focus on offenders. Arrest, conviction, and punishment are sought to deter and incapacitate. At best these efforts have proved to be only marginally effective. Despite various attempts to improve the success of the criminal justice system in detecting, apprehending, and bringing to justice adult and juvenile offenders, crime rates remain high.

On the basis of examinations of the association between family life and delinquency, it appears that strengthening families may be an effective method of controlling crime. Research demonstrates clearly that families contribute to the development of delinquent and criminal patterns of life. Studies conducted during the last two decades have found, with considerable consistency, that what occurs in families is related to family members' subsequent delinquent and criminal behavior (for reviews of this literature, Henggeler, 1989; Loeber and Dishion, 1983; Loeber and Stouthamer-Loeber, 1986; Snyder and

Kevin N. Wright and Karen E. Wright. "A Policy Maker's Guide to Controlling Delinquency and Crime Through Family Interventions." *Justice Quarterly* 11: (2): 189–206. Reprinted with permission of the Academy of Criminal Justice Sciences.

Patterson, 1987). Thus, strengthening families appears to be a viable option for improving crime control.

Barry Krisberg (1991:141), president of the National Council on Crime and Delinquency, suggests that policy leaders have not heeded recent advances in criminological research. Instead he notes that they have opted to continue allocating resources to deter and incapacitate offenders, although addressing the origins of delinquent behavior among children and within families might produce more fruitful results with substantially lower human costs. Similarly, Sampson (1987b:378), a sociologist who has spent considerable time studying the relationship of family life to crime and delinquency, suggests that a "coherent family policy" would be more likely to reduce crime than present policies that lead to an ever-increasing prison population.

In this paper we outline policy responses to reduce delinquency through family intervention. These actions are grouped into five categories: (1) prenatal and early childhood health care, (2) early intervention, (3) comprehensive family policy, (4) family treatment for troubled youths, and (5) parent training.

A CAUTIONARY NOTE

We caution readers not to look to family interventions as a panacea. The causes of crime are complex; even the role of family life in the etiology of criminal behavior has been shown to be multifaceted. Although family variables consistently are found to be related to delinquency, they explain only modest amounts of the variation in delinquent outcomes.

Furthermore, programs aimed at intervening in children's lives with the expectation of reducing the risks of future delinquency and criminality have not always produced the hoped-for results. Zigler, Taussig, and Black (1992:997) observe, "Few programs directed at reducing delinquent behavior have shown lasting effects." Similarly, programs intended to prevent delinquency have generally produced few long-term successes (also see Gottfredson, 1986).

Even more disturbing, at least one study (McCord, 1978) discovered harmful effects of intervention in the lives of at-risk children. The Cambridge-Somerville Youth Project was initiated in 1939 to assist delinquency-prone boys and their families. Counselors worked with the boys and their families; many of the youths received academic tutoring; a significant proportion of the boys were provided with medical and psychiatric care; and some boys, who otherwise might not have participated, were brought into community programs. Involvement in the Project lasted five years on the average. A 30-year follow-up found that men who had been in the program were more likely than a control group to have sustained criminal careers, to have mental health and alcoholism problems, to have died, to have suffered stress-related diseases, to have lower-status occupations, and to be less satisfied with their jobs.

Why, asked McCord (1978:288–289), could this well-intended program have produced such subtle and unexpected effects? One explanation is that interactions with adults who possessed a different set of values from those of their families may have produced conflicting expectations in the boys. Involvement in the program may have fostered dependency on outside assistance that persisted throughout the participants' adult lives. Furthermore, the program may have raised expectations among the boys that subsequently could not be fulfilled. Finally, participation in the program may have become a self-fulfilling prophecy: receiving help led to a self-perception of needing help.

These findings led McCord to conclude, "Intervention programs risk damaging the individuals they are designed to assist" (1978:289). Even so, she did not call for the cessation of programs for at-risk youths; instead she admonished practitioners and policy makers alike to proceed cautiously, to remain aware of potential harm of programs to children, and to evaluate outcomes.

We share McCord's concern about the risks of intervention, but, like her, we maintain a commitment to exploring new and we hope more successful practices. We are encouraged by recent advances in knowledge and findings about successful programs. In the following pages we outline several strategies for working with families that have the potential to reduce the incidence of delinquency and criminality. With one exception, the interventions do not deal directly with delinquents and their families; rather, they constitute early interventions in children's lives with the potential for lifelong educational, social, and behavioral effects.

These programs incorporate an ecological view of children and family life. Families are the first and among the most important institutions affecting children's development, but the interaction between parents and children takes place in a broader social and cultural environment. Schools, workplaces, community organizations, child care facilities, and health care systems play important roles in developmental processes. Zigler et al. (1992) state that "[b]y improving parents' interactions with these systems, and by helping them to support their child's physical, cognitive, and socioemotional development" (p. 997), programs can enhance the likelihood of competence in a variety of contexts during childhood and into later life.

PRENATAL AND EARLY CHILDHOOD HEALTH CARE

One way in which public policy can begin to support children's physical, cognitive, and socioemotional development is by ensuring that all families have access to maternal and child health care. Researchers have found considerable stability in aggressive and antisocial behavior, particularly when that behavior is extensive and begins at an early age (Huesmann et al., 1984; Loeber, 1982; Olweus, 1979). This evidence has led some researchers to postulate a predisposition toward impulsive, aggressive, and antisocial behavior which may be attributable to both genetic (Anderson, Lytton, and Romney, 1986; Lytton, 1990:693; Schulsinger, 1980) and biological factors (Loeber, 1991; Werner, 1987). Many of the biological factors can be addressed directly through adequate health care.

Growing evidence suggests that low birth weight, poor nutrition, drug and alcohol abuse during pregnancy, exposure to toxins, and various other health-related factors have profound influences on children's development. They affect intelligence, impulsiveness, and aggression, all known to be related to delinquent and criminal behavior. The National Health/Education Consortium (1991) calls for a program to provide every mother and baby with early, comprehensive, preventive health care: "Unless the commitment exists to provide adequate access to comprehensive maternity and infant care, society will be forced to contend with the care and treatment of unhealthy children who, through no fault of their own, grow up with long-term disabilities or have difficulty becoming self-supporting adults" (p. 7). Aggressive outreach programs for pregnant women at high risk of having children with developmental problems are needed to ensure adequate prenatal education and health care. Early identification of children with such problems has been shown to improve their chances for educational and social success. Waiting until they are in school may make intervention too late; early screening, diagnosis, and treatment are essential. Making sure that all children have the preventive and primary care necessary to ensure a good beginning in their developmental processes is the first step toward controlling future delinquency and criminality.

EARLY INTERVENTION

Research consistently has shown that age at onset is the single most accurate predictor of later and continued delinquency and criminality (Bell, 1977; Loeber and Dishion, 1983; Lytton, 1990; Osborn and West, 1978; Tolan, 1987; Tolan and Lorion, 1988; West and Farrington, 1977; Wolfgang, Figlio, and Sellin, 1972). Furthermore, early antisocial behavioral problems tend to be precursors to delinquency (Barnum, 1987; Hanson et al., 1984; Loeber, 1982; Loeber, Stouthamer-Loeber, and Green, 1987).

According to the model developed at the Oregon Social Learning Center, the developmental process leading to delinquency begins in early childhood with maladaptive parent-child interactions. The components of the reciprocal relationship are complex: "The development of the child appears to be multiply determined by what the child brings to the situation, what s/he elicits from the situation, what the environment can offer and what it does offer" (Sameroff and Seifer, 1983:12). Support for this model has been generated in recent years by numerous studies (Dishion, 1990; Dishion et al., 1991; Larzelere and Patterson, 1990; Loeber and Dishion, 1983, 1984; Patterson, 1980, 1986; Patterson and Dishion, 1985; Patterson, Dishion, and Bank, 1984; Patterson and Stouthamer-Loeber, 1984; Synder and Patterson, 1987).

Parents with a difficult child may cease functioning as parents to gain superficial peace in the home. With a particularly unruly child, the parents not only may fail to supervise but actually may come to dislike the child, adding rejection to the already problematic relationship (Loeber and Stouthamer-Loeber, 1986). Among the various aspects of family life, it appears that parental rejection is the most powerful predictor of juvenile delinquency (see Loeber and Stouthamer-Loeber, 1986). Children raised in supportive, affectionate, accepting environments tend to become self-aware adults who can formulate their own long-term goals and can pursue socially and economically fulfilling lives (Borduin, Pruitt, and Henggeler, 1986; Campbell, 1987; Cernkovich and Giordano, 1987; Fox et al., 1983; Henggeler et al., 1985; Johnson, 1987; McCord, 1979; Rodick, Henggeler, and Hanson, 1986; Smith and Walters, 1978; Tolan, 1987, 1988; Tolan and Lorion, 1988). In contrast, children of harsh, unloving, overcritical, and authoritarian parents often become self-absorbed as adults. Their impulsiveness can lead to violence and substance abuse (Bandura and Walters, 1959; Chollar, 1987; Glueck and Glueck, 1950; Gray-Ray and Ray, 1990; Kroupa, 1988; Loeber and Dishion, 1984; McCord, 1983; Nye, 1958; Pfouts, Scholper, and Henley, 1981; Simons, Robertson and Downs, 1989; Stouthamer-Loeber and Loeber, 1986).

As a child grows older and spends more time outside the home, negative behaviors learned at home are likely to appear in other settings. In school, the child's antisocial disposition may interfere with learning and often will cause the child to be disliked by peers. The failing, disliked, and antisocial child will gravitate toward peers and social settings that reinforce his or her behavior, which in turn may further encourage the child's antisocial actions (Patterson, 1982). As the child or adolescent participates or engages in more frequent antisocial behavior while associating increasingly with antisocial peers, his or her bond to conventional society will grow weaker (Hanson et al., 1984; LaGrange and White, 1985; Matsueda, 1982; Matsueda and Heimer, 1987; Paternoster, 1988; Smith and Paternoster, 1987; Steinberg and Silverberg, 1986). The weakening of this bond may be an initial cause of delinquency; continued and/or increased delinquent acts may become their own indirect cause as they further weaken the youth's bond to family, school, and conventional beliefs (Thornberry, 1987:876).

Longitudinal research is beginning to show that early identification of at-risk children and intervention in this process in their lives may hold great promise in preventing future delinquent behavior and criminality (Tremblay et al., 1991; Zigler et al., 1992). Staff members at the Oregon Social Learning Center have developed a procedure called "Multiple gating" to identify potentially troublesome children. The procedure uses teachers' and parents' reports to identify children likely to have later adjustment and conduct problems. This system has identified 56 percent of later delinquents (Loeber, Dishion, and Patterson, 1984).

Once at-risk children have been identified, interventions in the maladaptive parent-child interactions are needed. This step may involve training parents in effective child management practices; in some cases, respite may be needed for parents of particularly unruly children. Preservation of effective parental supervision, the development of social skills, and maintenance of bonds with conventional society become the goals of intervention as the children begin school.

Zigler et al. (1992) have identified four exemplary early intervention programs: the Perry Preschool Project, the Syracuse University Family Development Research Program, the Yale Child Welfare Research Program, and the Houston Parent-Child Development Center. Each of these produced long-term reduction in antisocial and aggressive behavior and delinquency. None of these four programs was started with the stated purpose of reducing delinquency; rather, the goal was to reduce the likelihood of school failure and to improve social competence. Although the programs differed, they all offered multifaceted interventions including educational assistance, health care, parent training and support, and other specific social services. Through early intervention they alleviated some of the risks in young children's lives, which thereby decreased the likelihood of future delinquency and criminality. According to Zigler and his colleagues, "the effects of successful experiences early in childhood snowballed to generate further success in school and other social contexts; the programs enhanced physical health and aspects of personality such as motivation and sociability, helping the child to adapt better to later social expectations; and family support, education and involvement in intervention improved parents' childrearing skills and thus altered the environment where children were raised" (1992:1002).

COMPREHENSIVE FAMILY POLICY

Research consistently has found that inadequate supervision is a key variable in predicting delinquency (Cernkovich and Giordano, 1987; Fischer, 1984; Laub and Sampson, 1988; Loeber and Stouthamer-Loeber, 1986; Loeber, Weiher, and Smith, 1991; McCord, 1979; Synder and Patterson, 1987; Van Voorhis et al., 1988; Wilson, 1987). The elements necessary for effective parental supervision include the following actions: notice what the child is doing, monitor the activities over long periods, model social skills, state house rules clearly, consistently provide punishment for transgressions, provide reinforcement for conformity, and negotiate disagreement so that conflicts and crises do not escalate (Patterson, 1980:81). Monitoring children involves awareness of their companions, whereabouts, and free-time activities. It also includes appropriate communication, the child's accountability to the parents, and the amount of time spent with parents (Larzelere and Patterson, 1990). Monitoring becomes increasingly important as the child progresses into adolescence, when adequate supervision allows parents to influence the child's selection of friends and activities, to express disapproval, and to sanction antisocial and delinquent behavior (Synder and Patterson, 1987:227).

Some analysts advocate enhancing social services through a coherent family policy. The basis for this suggestion is that inadequate housing, a lack of income, and an inability to obtain adequate day care create stress and make it difficult to function effectively as parents and supervise children adequately.

Single-parent families have been identified as particularly in need of a comprehensive family policy. Because most of these families, and particularly those at highest risk of producing delinquents, are headed by women, the needs of mother-only families are of special interest.

A review of 50 studies on family structure and delinquency revealed that delinquency was 10 to 15 percent more prevalent in single-parent than in two-parent families (Wells and Rankin, 1991:87). Experts generally agree that nothing is inherently pathological about single parenthood, but that the situation predisposes a set of conditions that may contribute to delinquency, such as greater autonomy for the adolescent (Dornbusch et al., 1985; Steinberg and Silverberg, 1986), less parental control (Matsueda, 1982; Steinberg, 1986; Van Voorhis et al,. 1988), increased susceptibility to peer pressure (Henggeler, 1989:48), and poorer economic conditions (Morash and Rucker, 1989:83). Furthermore, because their economic status is often poor, mother-only families may live in higher-crime neighborhoods; these may contribute to higher rates of delinquency because of increased exposure to criminal influences (Felson, 1986; Felson and Cohen, 1980; Sampson, 1986a, 1986b, 1987a).

The Education and Human Service Consortium, composed of representatives from organizations such as the Center for Law and Social Policy, the Children's Defense Fund, the National Alliance of Business, the National Alliance of Secondary School Principals, and the U.S. Conference of Mayors, believes that the current system of social services fails children for five reasons: (1) services are crisis-oriented; (2) the system separates the problems of children and of families into categories that do not take into account the interrelated causes and solutions; (3) communication among service agencies is lacking; (4) specialized agencies cannot easily produce comprehensive solutions to complex problems; and (5) existing services are not funded adequately. The Consortium calls for comprehensive delivery of a wide variety of preventive, treatment, and support services, including techniques to ensure that children and families actually receive the services they need. The focus must be on empowering the entire family (Melaville and Blank, 1991).

Research has verified the beneficial effect of increased services. The provision of a coordinated set of medical and social services, including day care, had a significant impact on women and their children 10 years later. In comparison with a control group, the mothers receiving coordinated assistance were more likely to be self-supporting, had attained more education, and had smaller families. Their children performed better academically (Seitz, Rosenbaum, and Apfel, 1985). The evaluators did not compare the delinquency rates of children from supported and from unsupported families; the variables they measured, however, have been linked to delinquency prevention.

In today's economically and socially stressful world, it has become increasingly difficult for all parents, not only those who are single or poor, to supervise their children adequately, to remain active participants in their children's lives, and to be nurturing and supportive caregivers. The availability of high-quality child care—day care for preschool children and after-school care for school-age youths—is essential to assist parents in supervising their children.

FAMILY TREATMENT FOR TROUBLED YOUTHS

We have shown that when parents are harsh, unloving, overcritical, and authoritarian, healthy development is impeded, and children's risk of delinquency increase. Furthermore, inadequate supervision increases the chances of delinquent behavior.

Growing up in homes with considerable conflict, marital discord, and violence also seems to increase the risks of eventual delinquent and/or criminal behavior. Witnessing violence in the home yields a consistent but modest association with delinquency (Widom, 1989:22; also see Bach-y-Rita and Veno, 1974; Borduin et al., 1986; Gove and Crutchfield, 1982; Hanson et al., 1984; Hartstone and Hansen, 1984; Hetherington, Stouwie, and Ridberg, 1971; Koski, 1988; Lewis et al., 1979; Mann et al., 1990; McCord, 1979, 1988b, 1990; Richards, Berk, and Forster, 1979; Roff and Wirt, 1985; Sendi and Blomgren, 1975; Simcha-Fagan et al., 1975; Sorrells, 1977; Straus, Gelles, and Steinmetz, 1981; Tolan, 1987; Tolan and Lorion, 1988; West and Farrington, 1973). Moreover, being abused as a child increases the risk of becoming an abusive parent, a delinquent, or a violent adult criminal. Not only do abused children manifest more aggressive and more problematic behavior at early ages; research also shows that these children are not likely to outgrow the aggressive patterns as they mature (Widom, 1989; also see Howing et al., 1990; Koski, 1988; Lane and Davis, 1987).

Dysfunctional families—those experiencing high levels of disorganization, conflict, dominance, hostility, lack of warmth, and authoritarian disciplinary style—do not allow children to gain insight and understanding into how their misbehavior might hurt others. In such negative family conditions, children cannot develop conventional moral reasoning with roots in acceptance of mutual expectations, positive social intentions, belief in and maintenance of the social system, and acceptance of motives that include duties and respect. Delinquency can be anticipated when children or adolescents cannot see other people's perspective and lack empathy for other people's circumstances (Arbuthnot, Gordon, and Jurkovic, 1987).

Fortunately, research has identified elements of family life which may shield children from otherwise harmful circumstances. Competent mothers—those who are self-confident, consistently nonpunitive, and affectionate, and who have leadership skills—tend to protect children from criminogenic influences (Lytton, 1990; McCord, 1986, 1991). Similarly, the presence of one caring parent buffers children against the effect of rejection by the other parent (Minty, 1988). In homes with high marital discord, the presence of one parent who maintains a warm, positive relationship with the children buffers them from conduct disorders (Rutter, 1978). Although the children of alcoholic fathers are more likely than others to become alcoholics, the chances of becoming alcoholic are diminished if their mothers did not demonstrate approval or respect for the fathers (McCord, 1988a). Furthermore, having a close sibling or being involved in teen sports provides social support that buffers abused children from becoming delinquent (Kruttschmitt, Ward, and Sheble, 1987).

These findings suggest that even in the face of adverse family conditions, resistance to delinquency is possible. Henggeler et al. (1986) report a successful treatment experiment that used the family-ecological approach for inner-city juvenile offenders and their families. This method addressed the multidimensional nature of behavioral problems, exploring individual deficits such as poor social and problem-solving skills, inappropriate child and family interactions, and problematic transactions with extrafamilial systems such as the peer group and the school. Therapy was individualized, and focused on the most important determinants of each child's problem behavior. Observation revealed that parent-child interactions became warmer and more affectionate with treatment. In turn, parents reported a decline in their children's conduct problems, immature behavior, and association with delinquents.

Potentially the most effective response to delinquent behavior is not to treat the individual delinquent as personally responsible for his or her action, as is currently the predominant response in juvenile justice. Rather, it may lie in a more holistic strategy aimed at both the child and the family. A wide array of treatment programs has been designed to reduce family and child disorders (Hawkins et al., 1988). Teaching parents how to manage older delinquent children is one of the most promising approaches (Bank et al., 1991; Greenwood and Zimring, 1985).

TRAINING IN PARENTING

Children learn to be parents from their parents. When children grow up in families where positive parental practices are modeled, they learn how to care properly for their own children. When children are raised by harsh, rejecting, and violent parents, however, inadequate and ineffective parenting may be transmitted from one generation to the next. Even individuals who were raised in caring and supportive family situations, when confronted with an impulsive or overactive child, may find it difficult to maintain effective parenting practices, particularly when they have only limited coping resources because of their familial or economic situation and when they live in relative social isolation. For people who lack parenting skills, training is a promising method for preventing delinquency. There are two possible points of intervention: in one, parents are taught how to manage difficult children; the other consists of training young people in how to be effective parents.

Programs designed for parents try to improve family management skills by teaching parents to monitor their children's behaviors, to use moderate and consistent discipline of inappropriate behavior, and to reward desired behaviors. Most of the systematic research involves programs for parents of young children with conduct problems. Four experimental tests of such programs (Karoly and Rosenthal, 1977; Martin, 1977; Patterson, Chamberlain, and Reid, 1982; Walters and Gilmore, 1973) substantiated significant reductions in problem behaviors among preadolescent children. An experimental study of a parent training program for families of serious delinquents found that the treatment group committed fewer serious crimes than the experimental group during the treatment year and spent less time in institutions. The benefits of the program, however, reportedly were achieved at substantial emotional cost to the staff (Bank et al., 1991).

Another group that might benefit from training in parental skills consists of adolescents who may lack effective role models, such as children in institutional and foster care, youths whose families are under the supervision of a family court, pregnant teenagers who choose to keep their babies, and delinquents. Some experts advocate parent training for all high school students (Farrington and West, 1981).

CONCLUSIONS

Delinquent youths do not experience a set of common events that lead to delinquency; rather, multiple pathways steer some youths to inappropriate behavior. Some adolescents run away because of a bad situation in the home; some parents push their children out; some teenagers leave for the thrill; still others escape from overprotective parents (Huizinga, Esbensen, and Weiher, 1991:84–85). The same apparently is true for delinquents: no certain or direct pathway emerges for all children growing up at risk (Huizinga et al., 1991).

In the lives of children most at risk of becoming delinquent, however, some or all of the following circumstances may be operating: (1) they receive little love, affection, or warmth, and are physically or emotionally rejected and/or abandoned by their parents; (2) they are inadequately supervised by parents who fail to teach them right and wrong, who do not monitor their whereabouts, friends, or activities, and who discipline them erratically and harshly; and (3) they grow up in homes with considerable conflict, marital discord, and perhaps even violence (Farrington, 1990:94; Leitenberg, 1987). Families at greatest risk of delinquency are those suffering from limited coping resources, social isolation, and (among parents) poor child-rearing skills (Loeber and Stouthamer-Loeber, 1986:97). The presence of any one of these family circumstances increases the chances of raising a delinquent child. The presence of more than one factor increases the odds further (Farrington, 1990; Farrington et al., 1988; Kruttschmitt et al., 1987; Loeber and Stouthamer-Loeber, 1986; Lytton, 1990; McCord, 1990; Minty, 1988).

In this paper we have advocated five strategies for strengthening families to reduce the factors in children's lives that place them at higher risk of delinquency and criminality: (1) prenatal and early childhood health care, (2) early intervention, (3) comprehensive family policy, (4) family treatment for troubled youths, and (5) parent training. Traditional approaches to juvenile delinquency attempt to control behavior after it has become entrenched. The five strategies offered here differ in that they attempt to prevent delinquent behavior before it begins by altering the family circumstances that lead to it. The goal of this approach is not delinquency prevention as such but the development of socially competent adults. Delinquency prevention simply becomes a by-product of that process.

We have presented these five strategies separately, but attention to all five is needed. A healthy start in life is essential for educational and social success. Parent-child relations in early childhood begin the process by which children develop healthy self-concepts, confidence, motivation, and sociability. Children who are prepared socially and academically when they begin school will be more successful and will interact more positively with teachers and peers; this point, too, has implications for continued successful development into adolescence and adulthood. Parents who have adequate social and economic support clearly would be more able to function effectively as parents than individuals who are stressed and alienated by their social and economical disadvantages and isolation. Furthermore, child-rearing skills are not a given. Some parents had successful role models, but those raised by harsh, unloving, overcritical, and authoritarian parents never had the opportunity to acquire the skills they need for effective child rearing.

To meet these requirements demands a comprehensive rather than a narrow approach. The current fragmentation in social services impedes the provision of integrated preventive approaches. Furthermore, because child development is an ongoing process, intervention also must be ongoing. It would be naive to expect a program that briefly influences children's development to alter the course of their lives. If families in fact play significant roles in the developmental processes that lead to delinquency, isn't it time to intervene systematically and comprehensively in those processes which serve as the root causes of delinquency?

REFERENCES

ANDERSON, K. E., H. LYTTON, and D. M. ROMNEY. (1986). "Mothers' Interactions with Normal and Conduct-Disordered Boys: Who Affects Whom?" *Developmental Psychology* 22(5):604–609.

ARBUTHNOT, J., D. A. GORDON, and G. J. JURKOVIC. (1987). "Personality." In H. C. Quay (ed.), *Handbook of Juvenile Delinquency*, pp. 139–183. New York: Wiley.

BACH-Y-RITA, G. and A. VENO. (1974). "Habitual Violence: A Profile of 62 Men." *American Journal of Psychiatry* 131:1015–1017.

BANDURA, A. and R. H. WALTERS. (1959). *Adolescent Aggression*. New York: Ronald Press.

BANK, L., J. H. MARLOWE, J. B. REID, G. R. PATTERSON, and M. R. Weinrott (1991) "A Comparative Evaluation of Parent-Training Interventions for Families of Chronic Delinquents." *Journal of Abnormal Child Psychology* 19:15–33.

BARNUM, B. (1987). "Biomedical Problems in Juvenile Delinquency: Issues in Diagnosis and Treatment." In J. Q. Wilson and G. C. Loury (eds.), *From Children to Citizens. Vol. 3: Families, Schools and Delinquency Prevention*, pp. 51–84. New York: Springer-Verlag.

BELL, R. Q. (1977) "Socialization Findings Re-Examined." In R. Q. Bell and R. V. Harper (eds.), *Child Effects on Adults*, pp. 53–84. Hillsdale, N.J.: Erlbaum.

BORDUIN, C. M., J. A. PRUITT, and S. W. HENGGELER. (1986). "Family Interactions in Black, Lower-Class Families with Delinquent and Nondelinquent Adolescent Boys." *Journal of Genetic Psychology* 147(3):333–342.

CAMPBELL, A. (1987). "Self-Reported Delinquency and Home Life: Evidence from a Sample of British Girls." *Journal of Youth and Adolescence* 16(2):167–177.

CERNKOVICH, S. A. and P. C. GIORDANO. (1987). "Family Relationships and Delinquency." *Criminology* 25(2):295–321.

CHOLLAR, S. (1987). "We Reap What We Sow." *Psychology Today* 21:12.

DISHION, T. J. (1990). "The Family Ecology of Boys' Peer Relations in Middle Childhood." *Child Development* 61:874–892.

DISHION, T. J., G. R. PATTERSON, M. STOOLMILLER, and M. L. SKINNER. (1991). "Family, School, and Behavioral Antecedents to Early Adolescent Involvement with Antisocial Peers." *Developmental Psychology* 27(1):172–180.

DORNBUSCH, S. M., J. M. CARLSMITH, S. J. BUSHWALL, P. L. RITTER, H. LEIDERMAN, A. H. HASTORF, and R. T. GROSS. (1985). "Single Parents, Extended Households, and the Control of Adolescents." *Child Development* 56:326–341.

FARRINGTON, D. P. (1990). "Implications of Criminal Career Research for the Prevention of Offending." *Journal of Adolescence* 13:93–113.

FARRINGTON, D. P., L. MORLEY, R. J. ST. LEDGER, and D. J. WEST. (1988). "Are There Any Successful Men from Criminogenic Backgrounds?" *Psychiatry 51* (May):116–130.

FARRINGTON, D. P. and D. J. WEST. (1981). "The Cambridge Study in Delinquent Development." In S. A. Mednick and A. E. Baert (eds.), *Prospective Longitudinal Research: An Empirical Basis for Primary Prevention*, Oxford: Oxford University Press.

FELSON, M. (1986). "Linking Criminal Choices, Routine Activities, Informal Control, and Criminal Outcomes." In D. B. Cornish and R. V. Clarke (eds.), *The Reasoning Criminal: Rational Choice Perspectives on Offending*, pp. 119–128. New York: Springer-Verlag.

FELSON, M. and L. E. COHEN. (1980). "Human Ecology and Crime: A Routine Activity Approach." *Human Ecology* 8(4):389–406.

FISCHER, D. B. (1984). "Family Size and Delinquency." *Perceptual and Motor Skills* 58:527–534.

FOX, R., A. F. TOATORI, F. MACKLIN, H. GREEN, and T. FOX. (1983). "Socially Maladjusted Adolescents' Perceptions of Their Families." *Psychological Reports* 52:831–834.

GLUECK, S. and E. GLUECK. (1950). *Unraveling Juvenile Delinquency*. Cambridge, Mass.: Harvard University Press.

GOTTFREDSON, D. C. (1986). "An Empirical Test of School-Based Environmental and Individual Interventions to Reduce the Risk of Delinquent Behavior." *Criminology* 24:705–731.

GOVE, W. R. and R. D. CRUTCHFIELD. (1982). "The Family and Juvenile Delinquency." *Sociological Quarterly 23* (Summer):301–319.

GRAY-RAY, P. and M. C. RAY. (1990). "Juvenile Delinquency in the Black Community." *Youth and Society* 22(1):67–84.

GREENWOOD, P. W. and F. E. ZIMRING. (1985). *One More Chance: The Pursuit of Promising Intervention Strategies for Chronic Juvenile Offenders*. Santa Monica, Calif.: RAND.

HANSON, C. L., S. W. HENGGELER, W. F. HAEFELE, and J. D. RODICK. (1984). "Demographic, Individual, and Family Relationship Correlates of Serious and Repeated Crime among Adolescents and Their Siblings." *Journal of Consulting and Clinical Psychology* 52(4):528–538.

HARTSTONE, E. and K. V. HANSEN. (1984). "The Violent Juvenile Offender: An Empirical Portrait." In R. A. Mathias (ed.), *Violent Juvenile Offenders: An Anthology*, pp. 83–112. San Francisco: National Council on Crime and Delinquency.

HAWKINS, J. D., J. M. JENSON, R. F. CATALANO, and D. M. LISHNER. (1988). "Delinquency and Drug Abuse: Implications for Social Services." *Social Service Review* (June): 258–284.

HETHERINGTON, E. M., R. STOUWIE, and E. H. RIDBERG. (1971). "Patterns of Family Interaction and Child Rearing Related to Three Dimensions of Juvenile Delinquency." *Journal of Abnormal Psychology* 77:160–176.

HENGGELER, S. W. (1989). *Delinquency in Adolescence*. Newbury Park, Calif.: Sage.

HENGGELER, S. W., C. L. HANSON, C. BORDUIN, S. M. WATSON, and M. A. BRUNK. (1985). "Mother-Son Relationships of Juvenile Felons." *Journal of Consulting and Clinical Psychology* 53(6):942–943.

HENGGELER, S. W., J. D. RODICK, C. M. BORDUIN, C. L. HANSON, S. M. WATSON, and J. R. UREY. (1986). "Multisystemic Treatment of Juvenile Offenders: Effects on Adolescent Behavior and Family Interaction." *Development Psychology* 22(1):132–141.

HOWING, P. T., J. S. WODARSKI, P. D. KURTZ, J. M. GAUDIN JR., and E. N. HERBST. (1990). "Child Abuse and Delinquency: The Empirical and Theoretical Links." *Social Work* (May):244–249.

HUESMANN, L. R., M. M. LEFKOWITZ, L. D. ERON, and L. O. WALDER. (1984). "Stability of Aggression over Time and Generations." *Developmental Psychology* 20(6):1120–1134.

HUIZINGA, D., F. A. EBSENSEN, and A. W. WEIHER. (1991). "Are There Multiple Paths to Delinquency?" *Journal of Criminal Law and Criminology* 82(1):83–118.

JOHNSON, R. E. (1987). "Mother's versus Father's Role in Causing Delinquency." *Adolescence* 22(86) (Summer):305–315.

KAROLY, P. and M. ROSENTHAL. (1977). "Training Parents in Behavior Modification: Effects on Perceptions of Family Interaction and Deviant Child Behavior." *Behavior Therapy* 8:406–410.

KOSKI, P. R. (1988). "Family Violence and Nonfamily Deviance: Taking Stock of the Literature." *Marriage and Family Review* 12(1-2):23–46.

KRISBERG, B. (1991). "Are You Now or Have You Ever Been a Sociologist?" *Journal of Criminal Law and Criminology* 82(1):141–155.

KROUPA, S. E. (1988). "Perceived Parental Acceptance and Female Juvenile Delinquency." *Adolescence* 23(89) (Spring):171–185.

KRUTTSCHMITT, C., D. WARD, and M. A. SHEBLE. (1987). "Abuse-Resistant Youth: Some Factors That May Inhibit Violent Criminal Behavior." *Social Forces* 66(2):501–519.

LAGRANGE, R. L. and H. R. WHITE. (1985). "Age Differences in Delinquency: A Test of Theory." *Criminology* 23(1):19–45.

LANE, T. W. and G. E. DAVIS. (1987). "Child Maltreatment and Juvenile Delinquency: Does a Relationship Exist?" In J. D. Burchard and S. N. Burchard (eds.) *Prevention of Delinquent Behavior*, pp. 122–138. Newbury, Park, Calif.: Sage.

LARZELERE, R. E. and G. R. PATTERSON. (1990). "Parental Management: Mediator of the Effect of Socioeconomic Status on Early Delinquency." *Criminology* 28(2):301–323.

LAUB, J. H. and R. J. SAMPSON. (1988). "Unraveling Families and Delinquency: A Reanalysis of the Gluecks' Data." *Criminology* 26(3):355–379.

LEITENBERG, H. (1987). "Primary Prevention of Delinquency." In J. D. Burchard and S. N. Burchard (eds.), *Prevention of Delinquent Behavior*, pp. 312–331. Newbury Park, Calif.: Sage.

LEWIS, D. O., S. S. SHANOK, J. H. PINCUS, and G. H. GLASER (1979) "Violent Juvenile Delinquents: Psychiatric, Neurological, Psychological, and Abuse Factors." *Journal of the American Academy of Child Psychiatry* 18:307–319.

LOEBER, R. (1982). "The Stability of Antisocial and Delinquent Child Behavior: A Review." *Child Development* 53:1431–1446.

_____. (1991). "Antisocial Behavior: More Enduring Than Changeable?" *Journal of the American Academy of Child and Adolescent Psychiatry* 30:393–397.

LOEBER, R. and T. J. DISHION. (1983). "Early Predictors of Male Delinquency: A Review." *Psychological Bulletin* 94(1):68–99.

_____. (1984). "Boys Who Fight at Home and School: Conditions Influencing Cross-Setting Consistency." *Journal of Consulting and Clinical Psychology* 52(5):759–768.

LOEBER, R., T. J. DISHION, and G. R. PATTERSON. (1984). "Multiple Gating: A Multistage Assessment Procedure for Identifying Youths at Risk for Delinquency." *Journal of Research in Crime and Delinquency* 21:7–32.

LOEBER, R. and M. STOUTHAMER-LOEBER. (1986). "Family Factors as Correlates and Predictors of Juvenile Conduct Problems and Delinquency." In M. Tonry and N. Morris (eds.), *Crime and Justice: An Annual Review of Research*, Vol. 7, pp. 29–149. Chicago: University of Chicago Press.

LOEBER, R., M. STOUTHAMER-LOEBER, and S. M. GREEN. (1987). "Age of Onset of Conduct Problems, Different Developmental Trajectories, and Unique Contributing Factors." Paper presented at the annual meetings of the Society for Research in Child Development, Baltimore.

LOEBER, R., A. W. WEIHER, and C. SMITH. (1991). "The Relationship Between Family Interaction and Delinquency and Substance Use." In D. Huizinga, R. Loeber, and T. P. Thornberry (eds.), *Urban Delinquency and Substance Abuse: Technical Report*, Vol. 1, Washington, D.C.: Office of Juvenile Justice and Delinquency Prevention.

LYTTON, H. (1990). "Child and Parent Effects in Boys' Conduct Disorder: A Reinterpretation." *Developmental Psychology* 26(5):683–697.

MANN, B. J., C. M. BORDUIN, S. W. HENGGELER, and D. M. BLASKE. (1990). "An Investigation of Systemic Conceptualizations of Parent-Child Coalitions and Symptom Change." *Journal of Consulting and Clinical Psychology* 58(3):336–344.

MARTIN, B. (1977). "Brief Family Therapy Intervention: Effectiveness and the Importance of Including the Father." *Journal of Consulting and Clinical Psychology* 45:1001–1010.

MATSUEDA, R. L. (1982). "Testing Control Theory and Differential Association: A Causal Modeling Approach." *American Sociological Review* 47 (August): 489–504.

MATSUEDA, R. L. and K. HEIMER. (1987). "Race, Family Structure, and Delinquency: A Test of Differential Association and Social Control Theories." *American Sociological Review* 52 (December):826–840.

McCORD, J. (1978). "A Thirty-Year Follow-Up of Treatment Effects." *American Psychologist* 33:284–289.

_____. (1979). "Some Child-Rearing Antecedents of Criminal Behavior in Adult Men." *Journal of Personality and Social Psychology* 37:1477–1486.

_____. (1983). "A Forty Year Perspective on Effects of Child Abuse and Neglect." *Child Abuse and Neglect* 7:265–270.

_____. (1986) "Instigation and Insulation: How Families Affect Antisocial Aggression." In D. Olweus, J. Block, and M. R. Yarrow (eds.), *Development of Antisocial and Prosocial Behavior*, New York: Academic Press.

_____. (1988a). "Alcoholism: Toward Understanding Genetic and Social Factors." *Psychiatry 51* (May): 131–141.

_____. (1988b). "Parental Behavior in the Cycle of Aggression." *Psychiatry 51* (February):14–23.

_____. (1990). "Crime in Moral and Social Contexts—The American Society of Criminology, 1989 Presidential Address." *Criminology* 28(1):1–26.

_____. (1991). "Family Relationships, Juvenile Delinquency, and Adult Criminality." *Criminology* 29(3):397–418.

MELAVILLE, A. I. and M. J. BLANK. (1991). "What It Takes: Structuring Interagency Partnerships to Connect Children and Families with Comprehensive Services." Washington, D.C.: *Education and Human Services Consortium.*

MINTY, B. (1988). "Public Care or Distorted Family Relationships: The Antecedents of Violent Crime." *Howard Journal* 27(3):172–187.

MORASH, M. and L. RUCKER. (1989). "An Exploratory Study of the Connection of Mother's Age at Childbearing to Her Children's Delinquency in Four Data Sets." *Crime and Delinquency* 35(1):45–93.

National Health/Education Consortium. (1991). "Healthy Brain Development: Precursor to Learning." Washington, D.C.: National Commission to Prevent Infant Mortality.

NYE, F. I. (1958). *Family Relationships and Delinquent Behavior.* New York: Wiley.

OLWEUS, D. (1979). "Stability of Aggressive Reaction Patterns in Males: A Review." *Psychological Bulletin* 86(4):852–875.

OSBORN, S. G. and D. J. WEST. (1978). "The Effectiveness of Various Predictors of Criminal Careers." *Journal of Adolescence* 1:101–117.

PATERNOSTER, R. (1988). "Examining Three-Wave Deterrence Models: A Question of Temporal Order and Specification." *Journal of Criminal Law and Criminology* 79(1):135–179.

PATTERSON, G. R. (1980). "Children Who Steal." In T. Hirschi and M. Gottfredson (eds.), *Understanding Crime: Current Theory and Research*, pp. 73–90. Beverly Hills, Calif.: Sage.

_____. (1982). *Coercive Family Process. Eugene*, Oreg.: Castalia.

_____. (1986). "Performance Models for Antisocial Boys." *American Psychologist* 41(4):432–444.

PATTERSON, G. R., P. CHAMBERLAIN, and J. B. REID. (1982). "A Comparative Evaluation of a Parent Training Program." *Behavior Therapy* 13:638–650.

PATTERSON, G. R. and T. J. DISHION. (1985). "Contributions of Families and Peers to Delinquency." *Criminology* 23(1):63–79.

PATTERSON, G. R., T. J. DISHION, and L. BANK. (1984). "Family Interaction: A Process Model of Deviancy Training." *Aggressive Behavior* 10:253–267.

PATTERSON, G. R. and M. STOUTHAMER-LOEBER. (1984). "The Correlation of Family Management Practices and Delinquency." *Child Development* 55:1299–1307.

PFOUTS, J. H., J. H. SCHOLPER, and H. C. HENLEY JR. (1981). "Deviant Behaviors of Child Victims and Bystanders in Violent Families." In R. J. Hunter and Y. E. Walker (eds.), *Exploring the Relationship between Child Abuse and Delinquency*, pp. 79–99. Montclair, N.J.: Allanheld.

RICHARDS, P., R. A. BERK, and B. FORSTER. (1979). *Crime As Play: Delinquency in a Middle Class Suburb.* Cambridge, Mass.: Ballinger.

RODICK, J. D., S. W. HENGGELER, and C. L. HANSON. (1986). "An Evaluation of the Family Adaptability and Cohesion Evaluation Scales and the Circumplex Model." *Journal of Abnormal Child Psychology* 14(1):77–87.

ROFF, J. D. and R. D. WIRT. (1985). "The Specificity of Childhood Problem Behavior for Adolescent and Young Adult Maladjustment." *Journal of Clinical Psychology* 41(4):564–571.

_____. (1978). "Family, Area and School Influences in the Genesis of Conduct Disorders." In L. A. Hersov, M. Berger, and D. Shaffer (eds.), *Aggression and Antisocial Behavior in Childhood and Adolescence*, Oxford: Pergamon.

SAMEROFF, A. and R. SEIFER. (1983). "Sources of Community in Parent-Child Relations." Paper presented at the meetings of the Society for Research in Child Development, Detroit.

SAMPSON, R. J. (1986a). "Crime in Cities: The Effects of Formal and Informal Social Control." In A. J. Reiss Jr. and M. Tonry (eds.), *Crime and Justice Series, Communities and Crime*, Vol. 8, pp. 271–311. Chicago: University of Chicago Press.

_____. (1986b). "Neighborhood Family Structure and the Risk of Personal Victimization." In J. M. Sampson and R. J. Byrne (eds.), *The Social Ecology of Crime*, pp. 25–46. New York: Springer.

_____. (1987a). "Does an Intact Family Reduce Burglary Risk for Its Neighbors?" *Social Science Review* 71(3):204–207.

_____. (1987b). "Urban Black Violence: The Effect of Male Joblessness and Family Disruption." *American Journal of Sociology* 93(2):348–382.

SCHULSINGER, F. (1980). "Biological Psychopathology." *Annual Review of Psychology* 31:583–606.

SEITZ, V., L. K. ROSENBAUM, and N. H. APFEL. (1985). "Effects of Family Support Intervention: A Ten-Year Follow-Up." *Child Development* 56:376–391.

SENDI, I. B. and P. G. BLOMGREN. (1975). "A Comparative Study of Predictive Criteria in the Predisposition of Homicidal Adolescents." *American Journal of Psychiatry* 132:423–427.

SIMCHA-FAGAN, O., T. S. LANGER, J. C. GERSTEN, and J. G. EISENBERG. (1975). "Violent and Antisocial Behavior: A Longitudinal Study of Urban Youth." Unpublished report, Office of Child Development, Washington, D.C..

SIMONS, R. L., J. F. ROBERTSON, and W. R. DOWNS. (1989). "The Nature of the Association between Parental Rejection and Delinquent Behavior." *Journal of Youth and Adolescence* 18(3):297–310.

SMITH, D. A. and R. PATERNOSTER. (1987). "The Gender Gap in Theories of Deviance: Issues and Evidence." *Journal of Research in Crime and Delinquency* 24(2):140–172.

SMITH, R. M. and J. WALTERS. (1978). "Delinquent and Non-Delinquent Males' Perceptions of Their Fathers." *Adolescence 13* (Spring):21–28.

SNYDER, J. and G. R. PATTERSON. (1987). "Family Interaction and Delinquent Behavior." In H. C. Quay (ed.), *Handbook of Juvenile Delinquency*, pp. 216–243. New York: Wiley.

SORRELLS, J. M. (1977). "Kids Who Kill." *Crime and Delinquency* 23:312–320.

STEINBERG, L. (1986). "Latchkey Children and Susceptibility to Peer Pressure: An Ecological Analysis." *Development Psychology* 22(4):433–439.

STEINBERG, L. and S. B. SILVERBERG. (1986). "The Vicissitudes of Autonomy in Early Adolescence." *Child Development* 57:841–851.

STOUTHAMER-LOEBER, M. and R. LOEBER. (1986). "Boys Who Lie." *Journal of Abnormal Child Psychology* 14:551–564.

STRAUS, M. A., R. J. GELLES, and S. K. STEINMETZ. (1981). *Behind Closed Doors: Violence in the American Family*. Garden City, N.Y.: Anchor.

THORNBERRY, T. P. (1987). "Toward an Interaction Theory of Delinquency." *Criminology* 25(4): 863–891.

TOLAN, P. H. (1987). "Implications of Age of Onset for Delinquency Risk." *Journal of Abnormal Psychology* 15(1):47–65.

_____. (1988). "Socioeconomic, Family, and Social Stress Correlates of Adolescent Antisocial and Delinquent Behavior." *Journal of Abnormal Child Psychology* 16(3):317–331.

TOLAN, P. H. and R. P. LORION. (1988). "Multivariate Approaches to the Identification of Delinquency Proneness in Adolescent Males." *American Journal of Community Psychology* 16(4):547–561.

TREMBLAY, R. E., J. McCORD, H. BOILEAU, P. CHARLEBOIS, C. GAGNON, M. LeBLANC, and S. LARIVEE. (1991). "Can Disruptive Boys Be Helped to Become Competent?" *Psychiatry* 54:148–161.

VAN VOORHIS, P., F. T. CULLEN, R. A. MATHERS, and C. C. GARNER. (1988). "The Impact of Family Structure and Quality on Delinquency: A Comparative Assessment of Structural and Functional Factors." *Criminology* 26(2):235–261.

WALTERS, H. I. and S. K. GILMORE. (1973). "Placebo versus Social Learning Effects on Parental Training Procedures Designed to Alter the Behavior of Aggressive Boys." *Behavior Therapy* 4:311–377.

WELLS, L. E. and J. H. RANKIN. (1991). "Families and Delinquency: A Meta-Analysis of the Impact of Broken Homes." *Social Problems* 38(1):71–93.

WERNER, E. E. (1987). "Vulnerability and Resiliency in Children at Risk for Delinquency: A Longitudinal Study from Birth to Young Adulthood." In J. D. Burchard and S. N. Burchard (eds.), *Primary Prevention of Psychopathology, Vol. 10: Prevention of Delinquent Behavior*, pp. 16–43. Newbury Park, Calif.: Sage.

WEST, D. J. and D. P. FARRINGTON. (1973). *Who Becomes Delinquent?* London: Heinemann.

_____. (1977). *The Delinquent Way of Life: Third Report of the Cambridge Study in Delinquent Development.* New York: Crane Russak.

WIDOM, C. S. (1989). "Does Violence Beget Violence? A Critical Examination of the Literature." *Psychological Bulletin* 106(1):3–28.

WILSON, H. (1987). "Parental Supervision Re-Examined." *British Journal of Criminology* 27(3): 275–301.

WOLFGANG, M. E., R. M. FIGLIO, and T. SELLIN. (1972). *Delinquency in a Birth Cohort.* Chicago: University of Chicago Press.

ZIGLER, E., C. TAUSSIG, and K. BLACK. (1992). "Early Childhood Intervention: A Promising Preventative for Juvenile Delinquency." *American Psychologist* 47:997–1006.

QUESTIONS FOR DISCUSSION

1. Discuss the circumstances that may be operating in the lives of children most at risk of becoming delinquent.

2. The authors provide a cautionary note to "not look at family interventions as a panacea" for crime and criminal behaviors. Explain.

3. The authors discuss five strategies for strengthening families to reduce the factors that place children in a higher risk of becoming delinquent and subsequently moving into adult criminality. List and discuss these factors.

4. List and discuss the characteristics of a dysfunctional family.

5. If the primary responsibility for preventing delinquency and producing socially competent adults belongs to parents and families, then what have the government and the criminal justice system to do, ultimately, with the prevention and reduction of crime?

24

EMERGING TRENDS AND ISSUES IN JUVENILE JUSTICE

Michael F. Aloisi

■ ■ ■ ■ ■ ■ ■ ■ ■ ■ ■ ■ ■ ■ ■ ■ ■ ■ ■ ■

The juvenile justice system is experiencing a period of uncertainty and has been for some time now. Since about the middle 1960s, when juvenile arrests went soaring, there have been attacks on the system's ineffectiveness and its failure in meeting the goals of its *parens patriae* philosophy—protecting children. Many states have modified their juvenile justice codes since the 1970s in response to perceived shortcomings of the system. These changes reflect competing visions of what the system should look like and the interests and purposes it ought to serve. While states struggle to achieve the reforms pronounced in the late 1960s, many feel constrained by a need to deal more effectively with violent and chronic juvenile offenders. The future direction of the juvenile justice system, in short, remains unclear.

One unwelcome result of recent (and conflicting) trends has been a bifurcated response to juveniles centered in legislative change. Policymakers in most states have been reluctant to give up the *parens patriae* vision and rehabilitative focus toward minor offenders and nonoffenders. At the same time, there is a clear trend toward viewing the serious and chronic offender as a willing perpetrator rather than as a youthful victim of circumstance (Shireman and Reamer, 1986, pp. 1–30). Consequently, policymakers increasingly view juvenile justice system "clients" in two very different ways—children to be helped and protected versus offenders to be punished or from whom the community must be protected. Responses are shaped accordingly. I will argue that this situation has had a negative impact on the system.

RECENT DELINQUENCY TRENDS

Juvenile justice policy decisions and the day-to-day decisions of system actors are shaped by broader contexts. Economic, political, organizational, and philosophical considerations play an important role in these deliberations (Mahoney, 1987; McGarrell, 1988). Changing perceptions of the extent of juvenile involvement in crime, especially violent crime (and, more recently, drug violations), have had a clear impact on legislation

---

Reprinted by permission of the publisher.

and policy reform. The fear of crime among the public (sometimes more, sometimes less realistic) remains high.

Juvenile arrests soared in the 1960s and continued to increase well into the 1970s, fueled in part by a growing youth population. A look at the fifteen-year period from 1960 to 1974 reflects the enormity of the rise (U.S. Department of Justice, 1975). Juvenile arrests rose nearly 140 percent. The increase was slightly greater for the generally more serious index offenses. For violent index offenses alone (murder, manslaughter, rape, robbery, and aggravated assault), arrests rose by a staggering 254 percent. Then, as now, serious violent crime accounted for a small portion of all juvenile arrests, now more than 5 percent. Such serious offending was and continues to be troubling, nonetheless.

The steep rise in juvenile arrests leveled off and began to decline in the mid-1970s. More recently, juvenile arrests continued to decline during the ten year period of 1979 through 1988. This included a 17 percent drop in arrests for index offenses, with a 7 percent decline for serious violent offenses (U.S. Department of Justice, 1989, p. 172). However, arrests increased somewhat between 1984 and 1988. During that five-year period, total juvenile arrests rose 6 percent, while arrests for index offenses increased 5 percent (with a 9 percent rise for violent index offenses).

Juvenile populations began to decline in the mid-1970s and have continued to decline (Cook and Laub, 1987, p. 124). Taking population change into account, juvenile arrest *rates* peaked in 1974 and have declined more recently (Cook and Laub, 1987, pp. 114–118; Strasburg, 1984, pp. 8–12). The pattern for violent index rates, however, has generally persisted at, or near, the relatively high level of 1974.

A NATIONAL FOCUS OF JUVENILE JUSTICE

Widespread dissatisfaction with the discrepancy between juvenile justice goals (foremost, the rehabilitative ideal) and the actual operation of the system led to what some have called a revolution in juvenile justice that has spanned over twenty years. The federal government has taken an active role throughout this period in the revolution and "counter-revolution" we have experienced.

The year 1967 was a focal point for change. This was the year of the highly influential President's Commission Report. Later that year came the landmark Gault decision extending due process rights in juvenile court proceedings (President's Commission on Law Enforcement and the Administration of Justice, 1967).[1]

Central to the reform agenda of the President's Commission Report were four reforms that have come to be known as the 4Ds: diversion from formal system handling, decriminalization of status offenses (for example, running away from home), deinstitutionalization (development of noninstitutional alternatives to training schools), and extension of due process rights. These four strategies continue to inform public policy today although in modified form. Each of these reforms reflected a growing skepticism about the fairness and effectiveness of the juvenile justice system's attempt to deal with troubled youths. In large part, they reflected a belief that involvement in the system might do more harm than good.

While the report viewed the process of formal delinquency adjudication as a last resort and sought community-based responses where possible, it also suggested that the juvenile court should not have an "exclusive preoccupation" with rehabilitation (1967, p. 81). Instead, it called for the "frank recognition" of society's claim to protection and the condemnation of unacceptable behavior, in cases reaching this formal stage. This recognition of a punitive response, in turn, provides a rationale for mandating the extension of basic principles of due process in juvenile court.

The President's Commission Report, along with the Gault decision (and the recommendations of a series of government and private commission reports that have followed), precipitated a wave of national and state legislative reform. The reform goals were fundamental to the Juvenile Justice and Delinquency Prevention Act of 1974. Its passage reflected the federal government's resolve to encourage states' implementation of the ideas of the reform movement. Among other things, the JJDP Act tied federal grants to state compliance with its call to deinstitutionalize status offenders and nonoffenders (that is, dependent and neglected youths) and to remove juveniles from adult jails and institutions.

There has been substantial but uneven movement toward achieving these reform goals, with some modification in recent amendments to the JJDP Act. Almost all state legislatures have moved to create a nondelinquent status offender designation (for example, juveniles or children in need of supervision, "JINS" or "CHNS") for juveniles who commit acts that would not be considered criminal if committed by adults (for example, incorrigibility, truancy, running away) (King, 1987, pp. 14–20; Rubin, 1986, p. 26). There has, as a result, been a significant decline in the national rate of status offense dispositions in juvenile court (Miller, 1986, p. 113). Incarceration of status offenders has also dropped markedly, with a large majority of states now considered to be in full compliance with the JJDP Act's deinstitutionalization mandate. The call for deinstitutionalization in *delinquency* cases, however, has met with more mixed results with great variation from state to state in their continued utilization of large training schools.

Also, there has been extensive development of diversion programs nationwide for less serious offenses, at both the police and the court levels, to avoid potential stigmatization of formal court involvement and to focus resources on more serious offenders. A number of formal programs, however, initiated with federal funds in the early 1970s, notably youth service bureaus, began to disappear after federal funding ceased. Finally, states have widely extended due process rights in juvenile court, a few even allowing jury trials.

Despite the gains, some argue that this reform movement has had its "down side." For example, diversion critics feel that diversion, while it may help juveniles avoid stigmatization that can be associated with court involvement, often leads to a "widening of the net" of social control (Austin and Krisberg, 1981). That is, diversion programs are likely to handle (or refer for further services) juveniles who otherwise would have been simply released from the formal system.

The decriminalization of status offenders has come under increasing criticism. Although status offenders are much less likely to be found in detention centers or training schools today, there is evidence that the reform movement resulted in the relabeling and placement of many youths in private mental health and other child care institutions. (Lerman, 1980; Shireman and Reamer, 1986, pp. 136–139). Thus, Weithorn suggests, the result has been, not deinstitutionalization, but "transinstitutionalization," substituting often unnecessary hospital stays for commitments to training schools (Weithorn, 1988).

A separate critique is that the deinstitutionalization of status offenders has left a void in the care of troubled juveniles, especially where alternative services have been slow to develop, following the lead of the earlier deinstitutionalization movement in mental health (McCorkell, 1987, pp. 22–30). The well-publicized exodus of mentally ill patients from state mental institutions in the 1960s and 1970s is judged by many to have contributed to the ranks of the homeless in many urban areas. This is because cities failed to respond by developing the hoped for network of community-based mental health services.

A major focus has been the difficulty in providing adequate care for runaways within the present policy environment (Regnery, 1984). Going beyond the issue of deinstitution-alization of status offenders, several highly regarded national groups have recommended that status offense cases be totally removed from the juvenile court's jurisdiction. Only a few states (for example, Washington, Pennsylvania) have actually abolished or seriously curtailed court jurisdiction over these cases, leaving responsibility for care in the hands of private or government human service agencies. Critics argue that the loss of the court's threat of coercion, even if largely symbolic in status offense cases, is a serious mistake. They argue, further, that in this policy void juveniles have been left to the exigencies of the streets—often leading to sexual victimization and other serious threats to health and safety of chronic runaways (Kearon, 1989). Certainly, the human service community has been slow to fill the void. The issue continues to be hotly debated (Bearrows, 1987).

A SHIFT IN FOCUS: "GETTING TOUGH"

The main focus of the nationwide reform movement in juvenile justice in the mid-1960s and early 1970s was on first-time and minor offenders, status offenders, and nonoffenders. These federal efforts at reform largely failed to direct address a rising concern throughout the nation—what to do with serious, violent, and repetitive juvenile offenders.[2] Beginning in the late 1970s and continuing in recent years, widespread state legislative reform has rushed to fill the void. By 1979, at least six states (California, Florida, New York, Colorado, Delaware and Washington) had legislated a more punitive response to the serious juvenile offender (Smith, Alexander, Kemp, and Lembert, 1980). With adoption of its Juvenile Offender Law in 1978, New York became perhaps the most dramatic example at that time of the rejection of the *parens patriae* approach. Among its provisions were:

> automatic placement in criminal court, long sentences, mandated secure confinement, low age jurisdiction, and overall community protection emphasis. (McGarrell, 1988, p. 178)

Since that time, many other states have either adopted or introduced various "get tough" policies for serious juvenile offenders (Miller, 1986, pp. 106—110). While the concept of rehabilitation and concern for the juvenile's welfare remains central to the juvenile system in the great majority of states, many now see it as only one of several legitimate purposes to be served by the juvenile justice system (for example, protection of the community, punishment or accountability).

The *new* reform agenda was spurred on by several catalysts: continuing high rates of violent crime; continuing reports that rehabilitative efforts were, largely, failing; and research that, for the first time, revealed the extent of the chronic offender problem. The influential cohort study of Philadelphia youths conducted by Wolfgang and his colleagues found that 6 percent of the cohort had five or more contacts with the police. These "chronic delinquents" were responsible for 52 percent of the cohort's police contacts and 63 percent of the contacts for UCR index offenses (Wolfgang, Figlio, and Sellin, 1972). Research following cohorts into adulthood reveals that many of them go on to commit offenses as adults (U.S. Department of Justice, 1985a, p. 20; Wolfgang, Thornberry, and Figlio, 1987, p. 33).[3]

States' "get tough" strategies have taken several forms with two main goals: removing certain categories of juveniles from the jurisdiction of the juvenile court and decreasing the broad discretion of judges and other juvenile justice personnel. All states have some provision through which specified juveniles can be transferred to adult criminal court. Juvenile offenders are transferred to criminal courts primarily through statutes that mandate exclusion of certain offenses from the juvenile court's jurisdiction and through judicial waiver of serious and/or repetitive offenders.

Over the past fifteen years or so, almost every state has either made it easier to waive cases, lowered the age of judicial waiver, or excluded additional offenses from jurisdiction (Hamparian, 1987, p. 134). As of 1987, eighteen states excluded certain serious offenses from juvenile court jurisdiction; 48 states have judicial waiver provisions tied to particular offenses and prior offense history (U.S. Department of Justice, 1988a, p. 79). It should be pointed out, though, that handling serious and repetitive (including violent) offenders through waiver and other transfer provisions continues to be the exception and not the rule.

Since the late 1970s, a number of states have initiated mandatory minimum terms of incarceration or minimum lengths of stay, or developed presumptive sentencing guidelines (Krisberg, Schwartz, Litsky, and Austin, 1986, p. 9; U.S. Department of Justice, 1988a, p. 95). Finally, several states (most notably, Washington) have modified the purpose clause of their juvenile codes to reflect increased concern for the goal of holding juveniles accountable for their offenses (Hamparian, 1987, p. 135). The clear emphasis of the recently issued "Model Code," developed under OJJDP funding, is accountability (Rossum, Koller, and Manfredi, 1987).

SOME APPARENT CONSEQUENCES OF "GETTING TOUGH"

The "get tough" policies emerging in recent years appear to have contributed to two trends: rising public custody rates for juveniles and the increasingly disproportionate number of minorities held in public institutions.

National youth populations have been declining since the early 1970s. More recently, there was a drop of over 1.5 million juveniles "at risk" between 1983 and 1987 (U.S. Department of Justice, 1986a, 1988b). In addition, as we saw earlier, juvenile arrest rates for serious offenses have dropped or stabilized (for serious violent offenses) since the mid-1970s. Yet, there were 53,503 juveniles held across the country in public juvenile facilities on the day of OJJDP's 1987 Children in Custody Census. This is a 10 percent increase over

1983 (and a 24 percent increase over 1979). The figure represents the highest population in juvenile public facilities since the census began in 1971. The juvenile custody rate (208 per 100,000 juveniles) was up 18 percent.

If we focus on long-term institutional settings only (including training schools), the increase over 1983 was just over 8 percent. In addition, the volume of juvenile admissions to public facilities was up approximately 13 percent, the highest since 1977.

There is some indication that increasing numbers of juveniles in custody are there on less serious offenses. The number held for serious, violent offenses dropped 8 percent between 1985 and 1987; the number for serious property offenses was down by 2 percent. The number held for alcohol or drug law violations, however, increased significantly.

A second apparent consequence of the "get tough" policies, the increasingly disproportionate incarceration of minorities, is of special concern. According to the latest OJJDP Children in Custody report, the 1987 one-day count showed minorities composing 56 percent of the training school and detention center populations. While the nonminority population remained practically unchanged from 1985 to 1987, the number of minorities in custody increased by 17 percent. Further, since 1979 the minority population in custody has increased by more than half, alongside a slight increase for nonminorities. Krisberg and his colleagues estimated that blacks, in 1982, were more than four times as likely to be incarcerated as white non-Hispanics; Hispanics were nearly three times as likely. This disparity had grown in the 1980s (Krisberg et al., 1987, pp. 183–187).

"WATERSHEDS" AND "BELLWETHERS"

The current period in juvenile justice has been described as a "watershed" with much at stake concerning its future direction (Krisberg et al., 1986). The national trend seems to be toward greater punitiveness, departing from much of the reform agenda of the 1960s and early 1970s. Certainly, the federal government's focus has moved onto how to more effectively identify and handle the serious and chronic juvenile offender. Many states, as we have seen, have facilitated transfers of the most serious juvenile cases to adult court and provide for determinate or, at least, more punitive dispositions.

In addition, there are isolated calls for abolishing the juvenile court. More common are efforts to narrow the jurisdiction of the court (that is, remove the most serious cases, as well as status offenders, and abuse and neglect cases) and limit judicial discretion. Washington State's 1977 Juvenile Justice Code most closely embodies this "criminalized" model of the juvenile court (Moore, 1987, pp. 53–55).

Finally, the principle of using the "least restrictive alternative" in delinquency dispositions (a reflection of the earlier reform movement) is considered by some to be dead, replaced by the new call words of just deserts and accountability (Hurst, 1982, p. 62; Moore, 1987, pp. 117–121).

The current juvenile justice scene, however, is far from one dimensional, with no clear "winner" in a battle between advocates of the earlier reform movement and the more recent reform agenda of the 1980s. While some call for a court almost indistinguishable from adult criminal court, others call for a court almost indistinguishable from adult criminal court, others call for the development of a comprehensive family court with expansive authority or influence over juveniles, families, and community institutions (Moore, 1987).

Although more punitive legislation has increased the use of incarceration, overall, states vary greatly in their incarceration practices. For example, among the fifty states and the District of Columbia, the highest rates of commitment to juvenile public facilities in 1987 (based on one-day counts) were found in Washington, D.C. (300 per 100,000), Nevada (288), and California (284). Among the lowest were Massachusetts (16), Utah (21), West Virginia (47), and Pennsylvania (55).[4]

A number of other states have moved to follow the lead of Massachusetts and Utah in either closing or drastically reducing the use of large state institutions, favoring development of a network of community-based programming for juveniles. Blackmore and colleagues describe the "decarceration" process under way in several "bellwether" states that have taken a lead role in what is considered a crucial and progressive direction for change (Blackmore, Brown, and Krisberg, 1988). These states include Colorado, Louisiana, Oklahoma, Oregon, and Pennsylvania. Pennsylvania, for example, (like Massachusetts and Utah) relies heavily on a network of private agencies to provide community-based residential and nonresidential services for juveniles. It provides fiscal incentives for counties by providing a state reimbursement to counties of 75 percent for a range of community-based dispositional services and detention alternatives (up to a set county appropriation cap) (Juvenile Delinquency Commission, 1990b).

Other states have, likewise, taken this route. Delaware has, in a short period of time, reduced its institutional male population from 250 to 70, with further reductions expected (Juvenile Delinquency Commission, 1990b). Correctional placements have been replaced by a comprehensive network of community-based programs that include group homes, specialized foster care, tracking, and intensive supervision programs.

A BIFURCATED RESPONSE TO JUVENILES IN TROUBLE

In addition to juvenile justice policies that vary from state to state, many states maintain an uneasy mix of policies side by side, with no unifying rationale for how they view juveniles in trouble with the law or for how they structure their responses. Rather than choose one set of goals or strategies over the other, it appears that states have attempted to incorporate these competing visions in their juvenile codes and to implement them in their court practices. A bifurcated (or divided) approach to different categories of court-involved youth is, unfortunately, the result.

Minor delinquent offenders and status offenders tend to be looked upon, largely, as victims of circumstances beyond their control, along the lines of the turn of the century juvenile court philosophy. Therefore, the court attempts to understand the social context leading to the juvenile's problem behavior (increasingly viewed in terms of family dysfunction). The court, finally, seeks a community response to remediate the problems through diversion, or it maintains the case under minimal supervision in the community, sometimes providing or ordering the delivery of services.

At the same time, the serious offender (for example, having committed a violent or property "felony" offense) or the repetitive offender is seen not as a victim but as a willing victimizer in need of punishment or of being held accountable for breaking the law. Ironically, although many chronic offenders are more likely to have been the "victims" of an array of undesirable circumstances or to experience greater skills deficits than many minor offenders, the court is less prone to acknowledge limited "blameworthiness" for them. The vision of the most serious offenders is not conducive to seeking truly rehabilitative interventions. Rather, the focus is on transfer to adult court, mandatory sanctions, or longer training school sentences.

As we saw earlier, however, states vary greatly in their espousal of the "get tough" movement and in the degree to which they entertain this split image of delinquent behavior.[5] Nevertheless, there is often a clear distinction between the family and community focus for minor offenders and the image of the serious and chronic wrongdoer in need of punishment. The split image is reflected in the way the recently revised Pennsylvania juvenile code distinguishes between the "delinquent child" and the "dangerous juvenile offender" (Juvenile Court Judges' Commission, 1988).

The split in how juvenile justice systems see juveniles in trouble with the law has some, it would appear, undesirable consequences. By focusing formal court proceedings on "willing perpetrators" of crime, the court has been "criminalized." Taken in concert with the extension of many due process rights to juveniles, this approach potentially facilitates the demise of a separate juvenile justice system. At the least, the bifurcated approach paves the way for increasingly punitive responses and increases the likelihood that more serious offenders will be incarcerated (McGarrell, 1988, pp. 180–181). In addition, despite an escalation in response for serious offenders, it is likely that many minor offenders never get the message, early on, that what they have done is wrong and unacceptable to the community or the system fails to identify and address real needs. In either case, their chances of returning to court have certainly not been diminished (Barnum, 1987).

In place of a bifurcated approach, a more integrated vision of the delinquent youth along with a more integrated system response is required. One such approach would both hold juveniles across the range of offending responsible for their actions *and* commit the system to contributing to juveniles' future growth into healthy and productive adults. Delinquent (and related problem) behavior would be understood in terms of individual decisions that are both, in some sense, freely made and influenced by a wide range of factors—internal to the individual, part of the individual's immediate environment (for example, family, school, and peers), and the results of broader societal forces (Aloisi, 1984; Gottfredson, 1982).

In essence, this is a call to see delinquent youths as both children and offenders, simultaneously. This means that accountability has an important place across the range of offending. One important potential payoff is a rehabilitative one—if punishment is fairly administered. Barnum suggests that while punishment may not instill a sense of guilt,

it may still inform the offender of the wrongfulness of his actions and underscore his responsibility for it....The right solution to the confusion about punishment and treatment is to use both (1987, pp. 74–75, 77).

What this integrated approach also means is tempering the court's coercive response with the goal of serving the special helping purpose of the juvenile justice system, that is, rehabilitation. Zimring suggests two rationales for the more lenient handling of juveniles within a, primarily, accountability context (1978, pp. 71–81). First, regardless of the seriousness of the offense, the court needs to take into account the relative "immaturity" of adolescent decision making. An additional and even more fundamental point is that the court's response should take into account that adolescence is a crucial period of growth:

> One purpose of mitigating the harshness of punishment for young offenders is to enhance the opportunity to survive adolescence without a major sacrifice in life chances....Social policy toward the young offender should be designed, as much as practical, not to diminish the individual's chances to make that transition successfully (Zimring, 1978, pp. 88–89).[6]

Consistent with this approach, Maloney, Romig, and Armstrong (1988) advance what they call "the balanced approach" to juvenile justice. This approach attempts to reconcile the seemingly incompatible values that have caused the "pendulum swings" in federal government and state legislative initiatives and system response in recent decades. The approach would require a balancing of the following objectives: community protection, accountability, and rehabilitation, specifically in the form of competency (life skills) development (1988, pp. 5–8). It would pull the juvenile justice pendulum more to the center away from both a single-minded "get tough" approach and a one-sided rehabilitative bias.

A CONTINUUM OF CARE AND ACCOUNTABILITY

For this integrated vision to have an impact on juvenile justice practice, there needs to be in place a more comprehensive continuum of dispositional options that is currently available in most jurisdictions. This wide range of response must integrate concerns for both care and accountability to allow the juvenile court to truly provide for the most appropriate response for each case. A wide range of dispositional options is already followed by law in many states (National Conference of State Legislatures, 1988). Yet, while it may exist statutorily, many jurisdictions are still faced with the limited choice of "traditional supervision or training school" in practice.

An adequate continuum of response would provide "alternatives to incarceration" for at least some of the more serious and even violent juvenile offenders. In abandoning its use of large training schools, Massachusetts has replaced them with a diverse network of highly individualized options—very small secure treatment programs for the more violent and serious juvenile offenders and a large number of highly structured community-based programs. These community-based programs include group homes, foster homes, a forestry camp, and, for those not requiring residential placements, day treatment programs (providing daily structure and supervision) and outreach and tracking programs providing intensive supervision for juveniles in the community (Krisberg, Austin, and Steele, 1989, pp. 3–6).

A number of other "alternatives to incarceration" have been suggested for juvenile offenders (and utilized in various jurisdictions) including restitution, intensive probation supervision, electronic monitoring, and intermittent or short-term confinement. For example, restitution (financial restitution to the victim or unpaid community service or service to the victim) has been offered as a viable alternative that can both serve accountability purposes and rehabilitate (U.S. Department of Justice, 1985b). According to one researcher, restitution shows promise in reducing recidivism (Schneider, 1986).

While many speak in terms of "alternatives to incarceration," an adequate continuum of care and accountability might better be conceptualized in terms of the development of an array of "intermediate responses."[7] While some alternatives may be appropriate for more serious or chronic offenders, other options are needed at the "lower end of the spectrum," in terms of the type of juvenile offender and his or her needs as well as the degree of restrictiveness of control or intensity of treatment services required.

It is becoming clear that implementing a network of community-based options is one of the most difficult chores facing the juvenile justice system. For example, despite the strong commitment of the "bellwether" states mentioned earlier, to avoid the use of large state training schools and develop community-based options, these states have had varying degrees of difficulty (once they have begun to "decarcerate") putting into place the desired array of community-based programs (Blackmore, Brown, and Krisberg, 1988). The difficulties are largely fiscal although political and competing philosophical visions also impede development.

EXPERIENCES IN ONE STATE—NEW JERSEY'S BIFURCATED APPROACH

New Jersey substantially revised its juvenile justice code at the end of 1988. Along with the new code, a Family Court was created through constitutional amendment. The amendment consolidated jurisdiction over a diverse collection of family matters under one court, making possible a more unified approach to all family law matters (Juvenile Delinquency Commission, 1986, pp. 38–39).

An important thrust of the legislation was a new emphasis on the family and its contributing role in delinquency and other juvenile problem behavior. A major reform reflecting this focus involved how status offenses were to be viewed and handled. No longer was this type of behavior to be seen as an offense. Rather, "status offenses" were to be treated as "juvenile-family crisis" situations. In addition, in lieu of being handled by the court (except as a last resort), newly created family crisis intervention units (FCIUs) in each county were to provide crisis intervention counseling for the juvenile and family, with referral to community service agencies where appropriate. The large majority of cases handled by FCIUs concern family conflict, truancy, or running away (although they also handle other types of cases such as those involving a threat to a child's safety or minor delinquency charges).

Since their inception, FCIUs have been a successful diversion mechanism. The state's Administrative Office of the Courts recently reported that FCIUs are petitioning only about 11 percent of their cases for a family court hearing (Administrative Office of the Courts, 1989).

The increased family focus was, however, only part of a dual reform agenda. The code's bifurcated approach is reflected in the following statement:

This bill recognizes that the public welfare and the best interests of juveniles can be served most effectively through an approach which provides for harsher penalties for juveniles who commit serious acts or who are repetitive offenders, while broadening family responsibility and the use of alternative dispositions for juveniles committing less serious offenses. (Juvenile Delinquency Commission, 1986, p. 14)[8]

"Get tough" measures of the code included provisions to facilitate "waiver" or transfer to adult court. The code expanded the range of offenses and circumstances that can lead to waiver. It also shifted the burden of proof of amenability to treatment to the defense: the defense attorney must now show that rehabilitation is feasible before the age of nineteen.

In addition to revisions concerning waivers, the code provided extended incarceration terms for juveniles meeting certain criteria. For example, the court can sentence a juvenile to an extended term beyond the maximum provided by the code (the maximum for murder is twenty years) if he or she had been adjudicated on two separate occasions for first or second degree offenses and was previously committed to a state correctional facility. The maximum extended term is an additional five years in the case of murder. (Despite code provisions, use of waiver and extended terms continues to be very limited.)

An additional reform involved the expansion of a range of dispositional options open to judges (to 20) along with a call for an increased local role in providing community-based dispositional responses. Not unlike many other states, New Jersey has seen only limited progress in putting into place the local programs and services that would implement the broad range of options allowed by law, despite the creation of local planning and coordinating agencies to establish need and foster program development (Juvenile Delinquency Commission, 1988, pp. 59–61). One major impediment has been that state government has provided limited funding to push the process ahead. To date, county or municipal governments have been provided little incentive to take over responsibility of dispositional options that have largely fallen to state government in the past.

To partially fill the void, the Department of Corrections (DOC) has created a broad network of state-run, community-based group homes and day treatment centers for juvenile offenders, serving more than seven hundred juveniles. Despite these new programs, training school populations have not declined. In fact, despite a decline in juvenile arrests in the 1980s, the average number of juveniles under the jurisdiction of the department rose by more than half (Juvenile Delinquency Commission, 1990a).[9]

CONCLUSION

Incarceration of juveniles has increased in recent years despite the fact that serious juvenile crime has apparently stayed somewhat stable. The broad development and acceptance of a wide range of community-based alternatives to incarceration (both residential and nonresidential) seems unlikely within the context of what was described as a bifurcated approach.

This seems more likely to occur within the context of a more integrated vision of juvenile crime and juvenile justice that attempts to accommodate accountability concerns along with the traditional (and pragmatic) concern to contribute to juveniles' growth into healthy and productive adults. By maintaining a clear link between minor and serious/chronic juvenile offenders, a more coherent rationale can be offered to eschew or minimize responses to the more troubling juvenile offenders that, in many cases, may be inappropriate. Such inappropriate responses include giving up on the rehabilitative goal and transferring to the adult system, or incarcerating when some other response will adequately hold a particular juvenile accountable, protect the community, and not unduly interfere with future opportunities for growth.

NOTES

1. Dissatisfaction with the operation of the juvenile system predated these national initiatives. For example, revision of juvenile codes to provide many of the procedural safeguards later to be guaranteed in Supreme Court cases had already appeared in California (1961) and New York (1962) (McGarrell, 1988, p. 7).

2. A policy shift, however, is evident on the federal level in recent years. This includes both a call for the federal government to take a lead role in developing policies focusing on serious, violent, and chronic offenders, and to modify earlier JJDP Act initiatives (see Krisberg, 1986, pp. 7–10).

3. According to Hamparian and her colleagues, three quarters of the violent and chronic offenders became adult offenders. Tracy, Wolfgang, and Figlio (1985) found that 45 percent of the chronic juvenile offenders went on to become chronic offenders as adults.

4. Commitment rates have been compiled utilizing 1987 information provided by OJJDP. A more discrete breakout of data is provided in their October 1988 Bulletin (U.S. Department of Justice, 1988b). The custody rates above include commitments only, for training schools, ranches, camps, farms and halfway houses/group homes).

5. Armstrong and Altschuler (1982) note the divergent strategies apparent in the handling of serious and violent juvenile offenders across the country.

6. As a result, Zimring argues for a juvenile dispositional policy that includes a presumption against secure confinement for juveniles adjudicated delinquent on property offenses (including most first- and second-time offenders) (1978, pp. 88–89).

7. One emphasis has been on providing a range of intermediate sanctions or punishments between "ordinary" probation and incarceration (see Morris and Tonry, 1990). Yet, broadening the concept to include clearly rehabilitative responses for juveniles seems appropriate. As was alluded to earlier, while we sometimes "overrespond" by incarcerating youths inappropriately (at times because we cannot provide an adequate treatment setting, for example, intensive mental health services), we also "underrespond" in less serious cases by not taking the opportunity to show juveniles that there are consequences to their behavior. In addition, and perhaps more important, at times we wait too long to respond with "treatment," whether that means counseling, drug treatment, or providing for much-needed job skills or other life skills development.

8. This is a quote of a Senate Judiciary Committee statement in February 1982.

9. Juvenile arrests in New Jersey dropped 26 percent from 1980 to 1989. Arrests for index offenses declined, as well (–35 percent), although there was a small increase of 5 percent for violent index offenses (murder, rape, robbery, and aggravated assault) (Juvenile Delinquency Commission, 1990c). Arrests for these serious violent offenses, however, had risen a substantial 73 percent from 1977 to 1983 (the year New Jersey's revised code legislation was passed). This may have contributed to concerns to "get tough" in the early 1980s. In the most recent period (1985–1989), however, even arrests for violent index offenses have dropped (–16 percent).

REFERENCES

Administrative Office of the Courts. (1989). *Report on Juvenile-Family Crisis Intervention Units.* Trenton, N.J.: Administrative Office of the Courts.

ALOISI, MICHAEL. (1984). *Chronological Age and the Differential Impact of Social and Personality Factors in Adolescent Delinquency.* Unpublished doctoral dissertation, Rutgers University, New Brunswick, New Jersey.

ARMSTRONG, TROY, and DAVID ALTSCHULER. (1982). "Conflicting Trends in Juvenile Justice Sanctioning: Divergent Strategies in the Handling of the Serious Juvenile Offender." *Juvenile and Family Court Journal, 33* (4), 15–30.

AUSTIN, JAMES, and BARRY KRISBERG. (1981). "Wider, Stronger and Different Nets: The Dialectic of Criminal Justice Reform." *Journal of Research in Crime and Delinquency, 18.* 165–196.

BEARROWS, THOMAS. (1987). "Status Offenders and the Juvenile Court: Past Practices, Future Prospects." In Francis X. Hartmann (Ed.), *From Children to Citizens, Vol. 2: The Role of the Juvenile Court.* New York: Springer-Verlag.

BLACKMORE, JOHN, MARCI BROWN, and BARRY KRISBERG. (1988). *Juvenile Justice Reform: The Bellwether States.* Ann Arbor, Mich.: Center for the Study of Youth Policy.

BARNUM, RICHARD. (1987). "The Development of Responsibility: Implications for Juvenile Justice." In Francis X. Hartmann (ed.), *From Children to Citizens, Vol. 2: The Role of the Juvenile Court.* New York: Springer-Verlag.

COOK, PHILIP, and JOHN LAUB. (1987). "Trends in Child Abuse and Juvenile Delinquency." In Francis X. Hartmann (Ed.), *From Children to Citizens, Vol. 2: The Role of the Juvenile Court.* New York: Springer-Verlag.

GOTTFREDSON, MICHAEL. (1982). "The Social Scientist and Rehabilitative Crime Policy." *Criminology, 20.* 29–42.

HAMPARIAN, DONNA. (1987). "Violent Juvenile Offenders." In Francis X. Hartmann (Ed.), *From Children to Citizens, Vol. 2: The Role of the Juvenile Court.* New York: Springer-Verlag.

HURST, HUNTER. (1982). "Issues for Resolution in the Eighties: Family Courts and Retribution." *Today's Delinquent, 1,* 57–68.

Juvenile Court Judges' Commission. (1988). *The Juvenile Act.* Harrisburg, Pa.: Juvenile Court Judges' Commission.

Juvenile Delinquency Commission. (1986). *The Impact of the New Jersey Code of Juvenile Justice.* Trenton, N.J.: Juvenile Delinquency Commission.

Juvenile Delinquency Commission. (1988). *Juvenile Justice—Toward Completing the Unfinished Agenda.* Trenton, N.J.: Juvenile Delinquency Commission.

Juvenile Delinquency Commission. (1990a, February 16). "Juvenile Correctional Populations: Looking Back at the Eighties." *JDC Clearinghouse.* Trenton, N.J.: Juvenile Delinquency Commission.

Juvenile Delinquency Commission. (1990b, April 6). "A Backyard Dialogue." *JDC Clearinghouse.* Trenton, N.J.: Juvenile Delinquency Commission.

Juvenile Delinquency Commission. (1990c, June 1). "Looking Back—Juvenile Crime in the '80s." *JDC Clearinghouse.* Trenton, N.J.: Juvenile Delinquency Commission.

KEARON, WILLIAM. (1989). "Deinstitutionalization and Abuse of Children on Our Streets." *Juvenile and Family Court Journal, 40* (1), 21–26.

KING, JANET. (1987). *A Comparative Analysis of Juvenile Codes*. Champaign, Ill.: Community Research Associates.

KRISBERG, BARRY, JAMES AUSTIN, and PATRICIA STEELE. (1989). *Unlocking Juvenile Corrections: Evaluating the Massachusetts Department of Youth Services*. San Francisco: National Council on Crime and Delinquency.

KRISBERG, BARRY, IRA SCHWARTZ, GIDEON FISHMAN, ZVI EISIKOVITZ, EDNA GUTTMAN, and KAREN JOE. (1987). "The Incarceration of Minority Youth." *Crime and Delinquency, 33*, 173–205.

LERMAN, PAUL. (1980). "Trends and Issues in the Deinstitutionalization of Youths in Trouble." *Crime and Delinquency, 26*, 281–298.

MAHONEY, ANNE RANKIN. (1987). *Juvenile Justice in Context*. Boston: Northeastern University Press.

MALONEY, DENNIS, DENNIS ROMIG, and TROY ARMSTRONG. (1988). "Juvenile Probation: The Balanced Approach." *Juvenile & Family Court Journal* 39, 1–63.

McCORKELL, JOHN. (1987). "The Politics of Juvenile Justice in America." In Francis X. Hartmann (Ed.), *From Children to Citizens, Vol. 2: The Role of the Juvenile Court*. New York: Springer-Verlag.

McGARRELL, EDMUND. (1988). *Juvenile Correctional Reform: Two Decades of Policy and Procedural Change*. Albany: State University of New York Press.

MILLER, MARC. (1986). "Changing Legal Paradigms in Juvenile Justice." In Peter W. Greenwood (Ed.), *Intervention Strategies for Chronic Juvenile Offenders*. New York: Greenwood Press.

MOORE, MARK HARRISON. (1987). *From Children to Citizens, Vol. I: The Mandate for Juvenile Justice*. New York: Springer-Verlag.

MORRIS, NORVAL, and MICHAEL TONRY. (1990, January/February). "Between Prison and Probation— Intermediate Punishments in a Rational Sentencing System." *NIJ Reports*, pp. 8–10.

National Conference of State Legislatures (Criminal Justice Program). (1988, July). Legal dispositions and confinement policies for delinquent youth. *State Legislative Report*, p. 13.

President's Commission on Law Enforcement and Administration of Justice. (1967). *The Challenge of Crime in a Free Society*. Washington, D.C.: U.S. Government Printing Office.

REGNERY, ALFRED. (1984). *Runaway Children and the Juvenile Justice and Delinquency Prevention Act: What is the Impact? (Introduction)*. Washington, D.C.: U.S. Government Printing Office.

ROSSUM, RALPH, Benedict KOLLER, and CHRISTOPHER MANFREDI. (1987). *Juvenile Justice Reform. A Model for the States*. The Rose Institute of State and Local Government; The American Legislative Exchange Council. Claremont McKenna College.

RUBON, SOL. (1986). *Juvenile Offenders and the Juvenile Justice System*. New York: Oceana.

SCHNEIDER, ANNE. (1986). "Restitution and Recidivism Rates of Juvenile Offenders: Results from Four Experimental Studies." *Criminology, 24*, 533–552.

SHIREMAN, CHARLES, and FREDERIC REAMER. (1986). *Rehabilitating Juvenile Justice*. New York: Columbia University Press.

SMITH, CHARLES, PAUL ALEXANDER, GARRY KEMP, and EDWIN LEMERT. (1980). *A National Assessment of Serious Juvenile Crime and the Juvenile Justice System: The Need for a National Response, Vol. III: Legislation, Jurisdiction, Program Interventions, and Confidentiality of Juvenile Records*. Washington, D.C.: U.S. Department of Justice.

STRASBURG, PAUL. (1984). "Recent National Trends in Serious Juvenile Crime." In Robert A. Mathias et al. (Eds.), *Violent Juvenile Offenders, An Anthology*. Newark, N.J.: National Council on Crime and Delinquency.

TRACY, PAUL, MARVIN WOLFGANG, and ROBERT FIGLIO. (1985). *Delinquency in Two Birth Cohorts: Executive Summary*. Washington, D.C.: U.S. Department of Justice.

U.S. Department of Justice, Bureau of Statistics. (1986a). *Children in Custody, 1982/83: Census of Juvenile Detention and Correctional Facilities*. Washington D.C.: Government Printing Office.

U.S. Department of Justice, Bureau of Statistics. (1986b). *Children in Custody, Public Juvenile Facilities, 1985*. Washington D.C.: Government Printing Office.

U.S. Department of Justice, Bureau of Statistics. (1988a). *Report to the Nation on Crime and Justice*. (2nd ed.) Washington D.C.: Government Printing Office.

U.S. Department of Justice, Federal Bureau of Investigation. (1975). *Crime in the United States: Uniform Crime Reports*. Washington D.C.: Government Printing Office.

U.S. Department of Justice, Federal Bureau of Investigation. (1989). *Crime in the United States: Uniform Crime Reports*. Washington D.C.: Government Printing Office.

U.S. Department of Justice, Office of Juvenile Justice and Delinquency Prevention. (1985a). *The Young Criminal Years of the Violent Few*. Washington D.C.: Government Printing Office.

U.S. Department of Justice, Office of Juvenile Justice and Delinquency Prevention. (1985b). *Guide to Juvenile Restitution*. Washington D.C.: Government Printing Office.

U.S. Department of Justice, Office of Juvenile Justice and Delinquency Prevention. (1988b). *Children in Custody: Public Juvenile Facilities, 1987*. Washington D.C.: Government Printing Office.

WEITHORN, LOIS. (1988). "Mental Hospitalization of Troublesome Youth: An Analysis of Skyrocketing Admission Rates." *Stanford Law Review, 40*, 773–838.

WOLFGANG, MARVIN, ROBERT FIGLIO, and THORNSTEN SELLIN. (1972). *Delinquency in a Birth Cohort*. Chicago: University of Chicago Press.

WOLFGANG, MARVIN, TERENCE THORNBERRY, and ROBERT FIGLIO. (1987). *From Boy to Man, from Delinquency to Crime*. Chicago: University of Chicago Press.

ZIMRING, FRANKLIN. (1978). *Confronting Youth Crime: Report of the Twentieth Century Fund Task Force on Sentencing Policy Toward Young Offenders (background paper)*. New York: Holmes and Meier.

QUESTIONS FOR DISCUSSION

1. Because of the discrepancy between juvenile justice goals and the actual operations of the system, a revolution in juvenile justice has occurred over the past twenty years. Describe some major features of this revolution.

2. What have been the results of "getting tough" with juvenile offenders? Provide examples to support your response.

3. Many states have approached juvenile justice with a bifurcated response or an "uneasy mix of policies" that are inconsistent and irrational. What are the major problems with this type of response?

4. What are the advantages of creating policies, about juvenile justice, that are more integrated or balanced? Provide examples to support your answer.

PART THREE

TRENDS IN PUBLIC POLICY, CRIME, AND CRIMINAL JUSTICE

■ ■ ■ ■ ■ ■ ■ ■ ■ ■ ■ ■ ■ ■ ■ ■ ■ ■ ■ ■

INTRODUCTION

Crime and the system of justice related to its control are inevitably influenced by historical as well as current public policies; each designed to create, at least through stated intent, a safer society. A tremendously important social and political issue, public safety surpasses virtually all others as America races into the new century more fearful of crime than of any foreign enemy. This fear, argued by some as a media blitz, and by others as overstated statistics, is perhaps more real to the present generation than to generations past. Historically, crime has always been a major social concern in America, and it runs deep into the psyche and culture of the country. In terms of history, though, crime did not seem as near or as pervasive as it does today. The modern social world seems tattered, torn, and complex to many Americans. The fear of crime is certainly more damaging to our daily social lives than any external enemy, and yet public expectations of government and the criminal justice system revolve around the reduction of the threats that produce this fear. If our existence seems shaken, fragile, and jeopardized by the continuation of violence and disorder, it is truly undermined by the escalation of inconsistent and often conflicting policies regarding crime and criminal justice.

Amazingly, our nation currently spends more money, time, and energy dealing with crime problems through the criminal justice system and other agencies than at any other time in history. In addition, the 1990s has been plagued by a pessimistic attitude that government cannot solve social problems with any consistency. Governmental policies aimed at the reduction of crime in the society are currently under more scrutiny than has been the case in past decades. Obviously, there are no simple solutions to the problems associated with crime and criminal justice; however, underlying all reform efforts is the notion that the crime problem is solvable. If this is indeed the case, successful criminal justice policy must become innovative and imaginative, and it must focus on outcome-based expectations. Safe neighborhoods, stable families, and employment are all vital if the outcome is to be social justice. Credibility must be the standard if the system is to plan and implement policies that lead to greater safety, a lower level of crime, and intelligent action toward those who violate the law.

The provocative nature of the articles in this final section should not overshadow their realism. It has been apparent for some time that many changes are necessary if we are to create a superior system of criminal justice. These changes, however, must be tempered by ideas grounded in the reality of historical events and processes. The recent trends toward incapacitative and punitive correctional policies will not solve the underlying social problems brought on by reactive social policy. As a corpus, the readings suggest collaboration and peacemaking are fundamental to any long-term improvements in our system of justice.

We begin with Joan Petersilia's Presidential Address to the American Society of Criminology in 1990, titled "Policy Relevance and the Future of Criminology." Petersilia points out that the need for policy relevance has never been greater mainly because the criminal justice system is in crisis. There especially must be a bridge between those who set policies and those who make them work.

Criminology may be much better off working for peace rather than war. Robert Elias's article, "Crime Control as Human Rights Enforcement," is an elegant, though urgent, call for the enforcement of human rights. Instead of making war, Elias argues, crime control and criminology should be making peace. The use of war to make peace has been the major crime policy of mainstream criminal justice. It is time to address crime control policy as a peacemaking effort with justice being the centerpiece of a system that would advocate social, economic, and political justice as primary to justice in the criminal justice system.

The twenty-first century springs to mind in this, the mid-1990s. M. Kay Harris asks us to imagine a new century wrapped in a feminist orientation of justice. Harris, in, "Moving into the New Millennium: Toward a Feminist Vision of Justice," argues that equality in sexual, racial, economic, and all other human conditions is essential if justice, and especially criminal justice, is to be achieved. Caring for others and justice for all is much more conducive to solving our societal problems than the continued struggle for power that has dominated our history.

Are we systematically abusing and neglecting the social environment? Elliott Currie, in a very serious-minded article, "Confronting Crime: Looking Toward the Twenty-First Century," claims we are afraid to look at the sources of crime and have instead concerned ourselves with the "downstream" consequences. As we have argued elsewhere, this is a continuation of the reactive approach to crime. The "conservative" approaches to crime and justice have escalated the social problems related to crime into a crisis leading to a collapse of public faith in the abilities of the system to deliver "justice."

Russ Immarigeon, in "Beyond the Fear of Crime: Reconciliation as the Basis for Criminal Justice Policy," argues persuasively that prison expansion and control policies aimed at retribution and deterrence have grown at a staggering rate over the past two decades. Restitution and reconciliation are ideas that are gaining currency among both liberals and conservatives alike. There is a growing body of evidence that restitution and victim–offender reconciliation programs are more effective at deterring crime than incapacitative and punitive penalties.

We conclude this anthology with "A Life of Crime: Criminology and Public Policy as Peacemaking" by Richard Quinney. Without doubt, Richard Quinney has become one of the foremost criminologists of our time, and his suggestions that we engage in a "compassionate criminology" resonates loudly in a social world filled with the noises of social upheaval and injustice.

25

POLICY RELEVANCE AND THE FUTURE OF CRIMINOLOGY

THE AMERICAN SOCIETY OF CRIMINOLOGY 1990 PRESIDENTIAL ADDRESS

Joan Petersilia

■ ■

This is the American Society of Criminology's fiftieth year as a professional organization. In this signal year, I think it is appropriate to take stock of how far we have come and where we would like to go as an organization—and as a discipline.

Since its founding, the ASC has helped criminology become a respected academic discipline and an influence on criminal justice policy and practice. However, several signs suggest that this influence is weakening and that our research and analysis may be coming less relevant to the practical workings and problems of the system than they used to be. My purpose is to discuss these developments and to ask why this has happened, why we should care, and what, if anything, we can do about it.

CRIMINOLOGY AND THE ASC: COMING OF AGE TOGETHER

A brief history will help to illuminate the issues. As an academic discipline, criminology is a relative newcomer. Fifty years ago, it was a fledgling field with little academic status. Universities didn't even offer courses labeled *criminology* until the 1930s and didn't permit a major in criminology until 1933.[1] Not until 1950 was the nation's first, formally designated School of Criminology established at the University of California, Berkeley.

The establishment of that school is an impressive example of how interwoven the fortunes of the ASC and the discipline of criminology have been. The ASC had been founded only 10 years earlier, but it was largely through the efforts of its founders that the Berkeley School of Criminology came to be.

The ASC grew out of an informal meeting at the house of August Vollmer, a former Berkeley police chief. Vollmer was also a part-time professor at the university, and he was joined by seven other men, most of them current or former policemen also interested in teaching. They wanted to help develop a special curriculum for students who would enter policing and to bring practical experience to bear on what the university taught. In other words, they believed their perspective could make the university's offerings more relevant to practice. In turn, being part of the university would make their research richer and more rigorous. To pursue these and other goals, the ASC was founded and held its first meeting in Berkeley in 1941.

As many of you know, in those early days, the discipline and the ASC were strongly grounded in practical concerns of the criminal justice system. Most of the faculty were or had been practitioners. Many of the students worked in police and correctional agencies, going to school part time to see if anything the universities had to teach would help in their jobs. During the 1950s and 1960s, the core group of ASC founders worried that the membership was restricted too narrowly to policing, and they actively encouraged others to participate. Still, most of the expanding membership came from the ranks of practitioners who were also involved in teaching.

As the early criminologists found, coming into the university was one thing, getting academic recognition was another. Their discipline and its outputs didn't get much scholarly or scientific respect in academic circles generally or in the sociology departments where they usually resided.[2] As they soon learned, their practical experience and concerns actually worked against them in gaining academic "respectability."

In academia, science is primary, practical applications secondary. I don't mean to denigrate the importance of basic science. It is simply a fact that the academic model of recognition and respect is based on "pure" disciplines, such as philosophy, economics, or physics, not on "applied" disciplines, like criminology or education. The former can be applied to various substantive problems, but their concepts and methodologies transcend those subjects. The latter are focused on social phenomena and have a given subject. Their concepts and methodologies are largely adopted from other fields and applied.

Under the academic model, recognition goes much more often to those who advance science than to those who are primarily concerned with solving society's problems. Consequently, to gain academic recognition and respect, criminologists had to develop and rigorously apply the scientific tools for studying criminal justice—and emphasize the scientific aspects of their work.

We have done so, and the field has changed. Criminology is now a respected academic field, rigorous in research, discriminating in its hiring and advancement criteria, and highly productive. Thousands of undergraduates now major in the field. Ninety universities now have graduate programs in criminal justice, and 16 have doctoral programs (Academy of Criminal Justice Sciences, 1990). Gone is the practitioner-student of the past, largely replaced by full-time graduate student who intends to pursue a teaching or research career and is steeped in concepts and methodologies. And these students are in great demand: Ads in *The Criminologist* have increased significantly, and at this year's annual ASC meeting, there were only 50 candidates for the 150 positions advertised.

Our academic coming-of-age is also signaled by the outpouring of a scientifically rigorous literature and the proliferation of professional journals in which it can be published. The latest count shows more than 20 journals devoted to criminal justice.

The ASC has also changed: It has gone from the original 8 planners to nearly 2,500 members. As its numbers have grown, the nature of its membership has changed. It now represents virtually every area related to the control and treatment of crime and delinquency, far beyond the early focus on policing. At the same time, the balance has shifted from practitioners to researchers and, to a lesser degree, policymakers.

The ASC has clearly emerged as the premier organization of its kind, not only for the United States but for the international community as well: 20 foreign countries are represented at this year's meeting. Our journal, *Criminology*, is now a widely recognized, highly regarded research journal. ASC members now compete successfully for research grants from traditional academic funding sources, such as the National Science Foundation (NSF), the National Institute of Justice (NIJ), and the National Institute of Drug Abuse (NIDA).

In short, we can be justly proud of the growth and accomplishments of our discipline and our society. We owe a particular debt to the ASC founders, the leaders who saw it through its infancy and its adolescence, if you will.

HAS CRIMINOLOGY LOST ITS RELEVANCE TO POLICY?

Despite these accomplishments, I believe it is vital to consider whether our academic momentum is pulling us loose from our roots and the ASC's original purposes.

Part of our stated mission is to be a forum for the exchange of practical information between researchers and the field—those who set policies and those who make them work. That seems especially compelling at a time when crime is a major public concern and the criminal justice system is, quite literally, in crisis. In the early days, the link between research and the system was virtually embodied in the faculty and students, and the influence went both ways. But since the academic has largely replaced the practitioner in the classroom and in research, the link has grown weaker and, with it, that kind of immediate influence.

Everyone has 20–20 hindsight, but it seems to me that the research community either failed to notice or did not consider what the loss of that link meant. As researchers, we simply continued taking the influence for granted. Yet, several signs indicate that our research is not influencing policy and practice the way a prolific and scientifically rigorous body of work should.

What are those signs? The three that strike me as most compelling are the following:

- A pervasive, often-voiced felling among us that policymakers and practitioners largely ignore our findings or, worse, sometimes act counter to what our best science tells us about the system.

- Some policymakers' and practitioners' lack of awareness that research has influenced the system.

- The scope and changing nature of research funding.

Concerning the first sign, I could simply say: "Consult your perceptions." Over the past 10 years at ASC and other professional meetings, formal and informal, I have repeatedly heard criminologists say that our research and analysis does not affect policy and practice. That belief was implied by the past five ASC presidents, who said in their statements that, if elected, one of their highest priorities would be to bring the prestige of our organization to bear on national and state policymaking.

From what I gather, few of us would argue that the system's basic approach to crime is informed by what our analytic studies say. However, I could argue that our sense of frustration results partly from an ideal, not a real, sense of how research affects policy and practice.

When criminologists complain that their work is not being used, they evidently have in mind an "instrumental" model of use (Rich, 1981). In its most simplistic terms, the model is roughly this: (1) here is a problem, (2) there is a study of the problem, (3) here is what the study says we should do about the problem, (4) we will do it. In criminal justice, "we will do it" could mean, for example, adopting a policing practice, diverting resources from one part of corrections to another, or passing a law about mandatory sentencing.

This model suggests that the effects of research on subsequent events or actions should, at least, be traceable. However, experience shows that this model is not appropriate for the social sciences, and that the true test of research influence is not whether a law has been passed or a practice changed. Using that test, how many of us can say we have directly influenced the policy process?

According to knowledge utilization research, conceptual use is the more appropriate model for the social sciences (Weiss and Buchuvalas, 1980). In that model, research affects policy and practice indirectly: It influences how policymakers think about issues, problems, and the range of viable solutions. It works more on the conceptual than on the instrumental level. Paradoxically, it is also likely to have a more lasting effect, but it is hard to trace or measure how research influences thinking.

Further, even if the policy implications of research are apparent and a decision maker is impressed with them, research cannot be an unambiguous guide to policy. Criminologists can point out, for example, the trade-offs among policy alternatives, but empirical results must be weighed against political and economic constraints. Little wonder, then, that research is more likely to influence the way policymakers think about problems than to provide solutions "off the shelf."

I am not suggesting that criminal justice research has had no traceable effects on the system. Rather, I am suggesting that perceptions of the effect are distorted by an inappropriate model. Perhaps that is also why many in the policy community, especially the funders, question how relevant and useful research has been for the criminal justice system—the second sign I identified above.

Several years ago, the National Institute of Justice asked me to investigate how much the research it funded has actually affected policy and practice. I found convincing evidence of research effect.[3] Here is a sample:

- Research has helped shape the way police are deployed in our nation's cities and how they handle calls for service from the public.

- Research has also identified the existence of career criminals, provided information about the patterns of their criminality, and demonstrated the effectiveness of career criminal programs in prosecutors' offices and repeat offender projects in police departments.
- Research has improved the ability to classify offenders and to predict recidivism. Prediction models and the classification systems they are based on are now routinely used in bail, prosecution, sentencing, and parole decision making.
- Research has provided information about the relationship between drug abuse and crime: We now know that drug-abusing criminals commit twice as much crime as other offenders—up to six times more when they are abusing heavily. Testing has found that half the people arrested in some cities are under the influence of one or more drugs.
- And, of course, research confirmed that no one has found empirical evidence that participation in rehabilitation programs necessarily reduces recidivism.

Given the range and significance that even this brief sampling suggests, it seems strange that researchers or policymakers should perceive that research has not contributed much. I can offer one speculation about the latter's perceptions: During the NIJ project, I found that many of the concepts and conclusions of research have been so thoroughly assimilated into policy and practice that some of the people I interviewed had forgotten where those ideas originated. If that does explain their perception of research influence, I could ask if we should really care. After all, as long as our work is improving the system, do we need the glory? I think we should care because their perceptions affect the reception and support of research. For example, how receptive and supportive does William Bennett, former director of the Office of National Drug Control Policy, sound? In a speech he made at Harvard (Bennett, 1990), he said:

> In the great public-policy debate over drugs, the academic and intellectual communities have, by and large, had little to contribute, and little of that has been genuinely useful, or for that matter, mentally distinguished. The field of national drug policy is wide open for serious research and serious thinking on both the theoretical and practical levels.

Granted, Bennett may be an extreme case. There has, in fact, been very thoughtful research by criminologists on this subject.[4] But it has not said many things that support the administration's favored strategies in the "war on drugs," and the call for *serious* research should be read accordingly.

Still, reservations about the relevance and benefits of research do appear to affect funding—the third sign I listed. Both the scope and changing nature of support suggest that the research funding community does not believe it is getting much of what it needs and wants from criminologists.

If money spent is an indicator of perceived effect and value, criminal justice research gets relatively low ratings. The federal government is, by orders of magnitude, the largest funder of research on criminal justice policy. The National Science Foundation recently published the following chart comparing the research funds allocated to various domestic areas. Clearly, criminal justice gets very low priority. For every U.S. citizen, federal funders spend $32 on health research, but only 13 cents on criminal justice research (Figure 1).

Another way to look at this issue is to compare the research budgets of a number of institutes with NIJ's budget (Table 1). I am sure these organizations produce services valuable to the public. Still, this allocation hardly accords with priorities of the American public, for which crime is a matter of most serious concern.

Reservations about criminal justice research are also implied by a change in funding mechanisms. In the early days of the National Institute of Law Enforcement and Criminal Justice (NIJ's predecessor), most funds were dispersed through block grants or core funding. As you know, under that mechanism a research group receives funds over a given period (say five years) with a mandate to conduct research in a broadly defined area of study. The researchers themselves choose the actual research topics.

Through the mid-1980s, that method of funding was gradually replaced. Criminal justice agencies shifted to contact or grant funding of specific projects on defined research topics, but still left room in each area for researchers to submit "unsolicited proposals." Now, the most recent (1990) NIJ Program Plan, for example, has no place for unsolicited proposals. There is a specific list of research topics for which they will fund projects.

FIGURE 1   Domestic Research Priorities: Expenditure per Capita

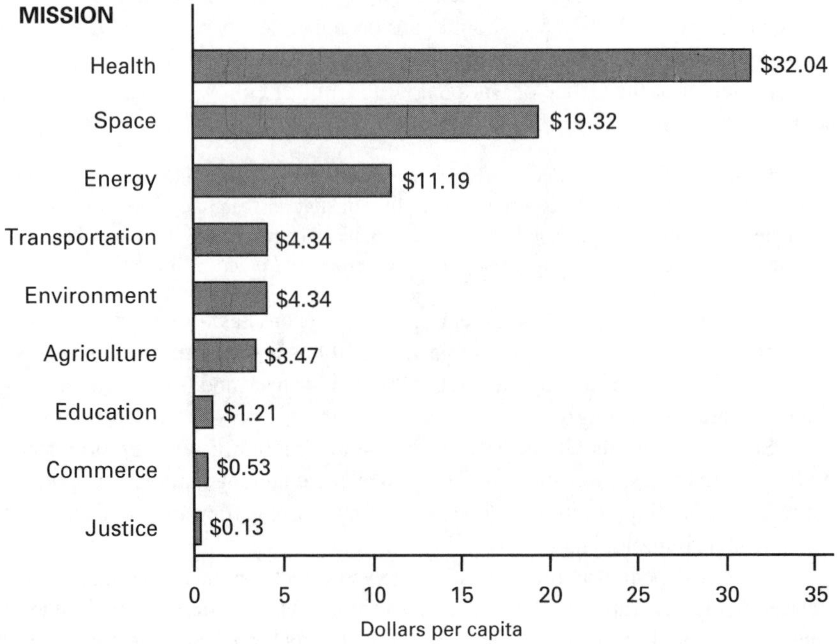

Source: National Science Foundation, April 1988.

TABLE 1   DOMESTIC RESEARCH COMMITMENT (MILLIONS) (BUDGET OF THE U.S. GOVERNMENT-FY 89)

National Eye Institute	229
National Institute on Aging	205
National Endowment for the Arts	167
National Endowment for the Humanities	140
National Institute for Dental Research	127
Institute of Museum Services	22
National Institute of Justice	21

Further, they are now even defining the method projects must use to study issues (for example, field experiments to study drug testing, ethnography to study deterrence).

Discussions with agency heads suggest that these restrictions are growing precisely because they are not confident that researchers will produce relevant information—if we are left to our own devices. In other words, they feel compelled to take the initiative in setting the agenda for federally funded research. Either this change has gone largely unnoticed by the research community or no one has commented on it publicly. However, I think it has serious implications for criminal justice research, to which I'll return later.

WHY HAS THIS HAPPENED?

If I am right about these signs, we need to understand why this has happened before we can think about solutions. This is a complex challenge because people may well, and reasonably, disagree about the causes.

In some sense, the very marks of academic status may help explain what has happened. The potential for policy "irrelevance" is inherent in the scientific management of which we are justly proud. It is also inherent in how we are trained, how we do our research, how we communicate our results, and how we are rewarded.

I think we would all agree that criminological research is more credible and rigorous than ever before. Paradoxically, as research gets better, it generally leads to greater complexity and involves a more complicated view of problems and solutions. The progress of research often reveals the inadequacy of accepted ideas about solving problems. It is quite common for social science research, particularly evaluations, to yield only "negative knowledge"; it tells a policymaker what does not work but gives little guidance about what to do. As Cohen and Weiss (1977:68) write:

> what researchers understand by improvement in their craft leads not to greater consensus about research problems, methods, and interpretation of results but to more variety in the way problems are seen, more divergence in the way studies are carried out, and more controversy in the way results are interpreted.

To us, this complexity is a necessary concomitant of rigorous, thoughtful research. To policymakers and practitioners, it may seem like unnecessary complication of issues.

How criminologists are trained may also encourage "irrelevance" to policy and practice. I recruit and interview researchers for RAND's Criminal Justice Program, and I am impressed by the increasingly strong analytic skills of many applicants. They can go on at length about beta coefficients, log-normal distributions, and whether their data are appropriately analyzed using probit or logit regressions. But ask them about the policy implications of their findings, how their "solutions" might be constrained by politics or resources, or even who in the world should be interested in their research—and they often come up blank. Not their fault, they are clearly bright and competent. They are simply products of their academic training.

To succeed under the academic model I mentioned at the beginning, graduate schools must place science first and application a weak second. But our graduate schools are not (with some notable exceptions) giving criminologists-in-training much sense at all about the world in which their work can be applied. I know this sounds like the old-timer cliché, but in the "old days" graduate programs often had internships that made students very aware of criminal justice realities. During my master's program, I lived two days a week in a halfway house for women parolees, interviewing them about their adjustment difficulties, and so on. That experience influenced me in a way that analyzing a computer tape never could. It gave me a keen sense of the world described by the term *community corrections*, and a concern for that world that has stayed with me.

Once out of graduate school, we increasingly conduct our research in isolation from the system. It becomes ever easier to study problems outside their context. Simply get a computer tape of large data files. No need to spend months, pad and pencil in hand, taking notes in field offices. This creates a situation in which researchers are even less likely to interact with practitioners than they have been in the past.

Dissection from afar makes it unlikely that the real concerns of practitioners will be recognized and addressed, and that research results will meet their practical needs. The further we move into computer analysis of large data files with more sophisticated methods, the harder it becomes for practitioners and policymakers to follow.

We make it even harder through the means we choose to disseminate our findings, both where we publish and what we say. In the NIJ study mentioned earlier, I noted that most academic researchers think of dissemination as publishing in academic journals. Even when policymakers and practitioners are aware of those journals, they generally don't consult them. Little wonder, because in those journals we generally talk for and to each other, not to them. Given how we talk to each other, how evident is it to them that what we're saying is relevant to their problems?

Many of the policymakers I interviewed made it clear that it wasn't at all evident, and they had simply stopped trying to infer the relevance on their own. We are unlikely to be published in academic journals unless we follow the reporting conventions of social science, but most of them were put off by those conventions. They especially disliked being led step by step through the research process, never to find any conclusions or implications they could apply to critical issues. Or they found conclusions too hedged with caveats to be useful in policy deliberations. Their ultimate exasperation was expressed in this charge: "Analysts are more interested in impressing their colleagues than informing policy or practice."

If I suggested that we should stop writing for journals that only other researchers read, I know what would go through most minds: "How would that look on my résumé?" Put another way, journal publication is the surest route to professional recognition—including tenure.

That brings me to the strongest academic reinforcement of "irrelevance": the reward structure. Most criminal justice research is conducted in universities, and university departments rarely reward people for concern with policy relevance, especially if the pursuit of relevance leads to time in the field. Much of what I have said implies that our perceived irrelevance is a concomitant of our growing isolation from what goes on "out there"—in policing, the courts, and corrections. However, when researchers spend time out there trying to understand problems or help solve them, review committees are likely to dismiss the effort as "community service." The strongest academically respected reason for field work is collecting primary data for scientific analysis.

Those of you who know my background may wonder how much insight I can have into the academic model and its effects—since I am not in a university department. Perhaps that's why I am in a position to see just how much of a quandary "service to the field" creates under the academic model. I am frequently asked to sit on tenure committees when this is an issue.

In a recent case, the dean of a leading criminal justice department asked me to review the tenure application of a faculty member. The department couldn't reach consensus on tenure for this person, primarily because they didn't know how to weight the training, technical assistance, and trade-journal publications that had contributed significantly to making this individual well known in the system. Was this scholarship? Was it less or more important than academic journal publications? In short, how should these policy-relevant activities be evaluated? Was this individual really a criminological scholar, or more of a consultant/trainer?

In short, under the academic model, criminology has moved away from its concern with relevance to the system it studies. I know that I have stated this case in its most extreme terms, but if that is necessary to bring home the implications of our current situation, I think the extremity is justified. If we fail to recognize the seriousness of the implications, our work is likely to have increasingly less influence on policy and practice in the future.

WHY SHOULD WE CARE?

Earlier I asked whether we should care about perceptions of relevance as long as our research is influencing the system. I said yes then, largely on the basis of our professional self-interest: The low level of funding and contract restrictions both imply that our research is not perceived as sufficiently relevant or beneficial to the system. However, I believe we should also be concerned on a deeper level that is not wholly self-interested and on an ethical basis, as well.

Let me address the ethical issue first. Ultimately, our support comes from the public. Few of us are employed, or fully supported in our research, by private firms or privately endowed universities. Most of our paychecks are paid, one way or another, with tax dollars. Given that, it seems incumbent upon us to respond to public concerns as fully as possible.

Polls continue to show crime and its effects high on the list of those concerns. The public is frightened and pressuring government to "do something" about the problem. It seems to me that federal, state, and local decision makers have every right to expect our help in addressing the problems *as they see them*. We are not being responsive if we insist on treating crime and criminal justice only as the occasion to study "academically interesting" issues and problems.

However, I think that this obligation needs some qualification. Implicitly, I have been talking about *relevance* and *responsiveness* as wholly positive objectives of research. In fact, if we pursued either to the exclusion of other research obligations, we would be serving neither the public's nor our own best interests.

Policymakers and practitioners operate under tremendous political, fiscal, and social pressures and constraints. Those conditions put them in a problem-solving mode: Find out what is wrong with some part of the system and fix it. However, if researchers limit themselves to that kind of problem solving, they are not being true to their higher research mandate, professionally or socially. We *should* understand and address particular problems, but we have other, equally strong obligations.

One is to look beyond the moment, the particular problem, and the options for solving it. Problems generally develop over time, their cases are complex and, often, not immediately apparent, and expedient solutions can have unforeseen and unintended effects—some of which can be harmful. For example, every state is trying to cope with prison crowding. Many are trying to ease the crowding through intensive supervision programs (ISPs) for probationers and parolees. However, with electronic monitoring and frequent drug and alcohol testing, these programs have instead, and unexpectedly, had higher reincarceration rates than traditional probation and parole programs have. The result: Instead of helping solve the prison-crowding crisis, ISPs may contribute to it.

Another obligation is to question continually the basic assumptions underlying policies, programs, and operational strategies. The system has many problems that are verging on crisis because policies and operations are based on faulty assumptions or a narrow focus. Taking ISPs as an example again: Monitoring and substance testing reflect an assumption about deterrence: if individuals know that they will be punished severely, they will not violate program conditions. Monitoring and testing make it likely that violations will be detected. Therefore, they intensify the deterrent effect. That hasn't proved true, and research suggests that ISPs are unlikely to change behavior unless they include rehabilitative efforts (Petersilia and Turner, 1990).

If no one is thinking about the larger conceptual issues, problem solving will continue to be fire fighting, at best, and triage, at worst. We have an obligation to keep research from settling into either mode. However, the level and mechanisms of current research funding are making it hard for us to pursue the larger conceptual and scientific objectives of research (for a complete discussion see Hawkins and Harris, 1988). Over the past decade, we had have less support and autonomy to undertake the kinds of work that meeting those obligations requires: for example, long-term, empirical studies that address basic assumptions; qualitative studies; syntheses of research; and sustained study of particular areas and issues of the system. If this continues, it will begin to undermine our academic status and, paradoxically, our effectiveness as criminal justice problem solvers, as well.

WHAT CAN WE DO?

Given these caveats, what can we do? The first step is to open a discussion about two basic objectives: first, addressing public concerns about crime and helping improve the criminal justice system; second, making policymakers (including funders) and practitioners confident that our research is relevant and responsive to their needs—without compromising the higher objectives of research.

I would like to open that discussion and to suggest several means of serving those objectives. Some of these things we can accomplish as individuals. However, most require support and cooperation from our research institutions, the funding agencies, policymakers, and practitioners. I believe the ASC can play a central role in furthering the objectives and the means for accomplishing them. These means include:

- Establishing a collaborative framework that involves researchers, policymakers, and practitioners in focusing, brokering, and utilizing research.

- Reporting and disseminating our work more effectively than in the past.

- Defining our research mission to include assistance in the field.

- Tailoring the academic model to accommodate the mission of criminal justice research.

Let me touch just briefly on these four points.

First, I have argued that criminology should not be concerned with real-world applications of its research—but not at the expense of its larger obligations. One way around this potential standoff is to establish and maintain a framework and forums for ongoing dialogue among researchers, policymakers, and practitioners. In this framework, researchers could get advice from the policy community in framing research questions, challenge the assumptions informing those questions, and if appropriate, cooperate in reformulating the questions. Practitioners could help focus the agenda, widen dissemination of research, and increase its utility by making their needs and priorities known to researchers and policymakers.

Researchers will have to take the initiative in this, but we will need cooperation from professional societies, our research institutions, and funding agencies to identify, establish, and maintain the most effective forums for this collaboration. The ASC could take a leading role in this effort.

Second, as I argued earlier, how and where we publish our research has helped make it seem irrelevant to high-level policymakers. Policymakers are not resistant to using research, but we make their access to relevant findings difficult. It isn't just that we publish in journals they seldom read; it is also the nature of our reporting. As a discipline, we need to develop publications and other forms of communication tailored for those audiences. Exemplars are the NIJ *Research in Brief* series, aimed at policymakers, and its *Crime File* videotapes, which have been praised by the practitioner community.

Wherever we write or give presentations, we need to remember several things: For one, it is our responsibility to make the policy and practical implications of our findings clear. The facts don't speak for themselves. I have had heated arguments with some colleagues over this point. They believe the opposite: Tables and figures will reveal "the obvious."

For another, we should give the same explicit attention to the implications of our research as we do to reporting our data and methods. In fact, in writing for policymakers and practitioners, we should give much more attention to the bottom line, clearly articulating the findings' policy relevance. This kind of writing has to be informed by an understanding of those audiences and what they care about, something we can get from the collaborative efforts I just described.

Third, we need to consider whether our responsibility ends with giving a presentation, publishing an article, or putting a document in the mail. An NIJ survey in the early 1980s indicated that practitioners wanted researchers to help put research results into practice. They believed we should take some responsibility for the training needed to implement programs or practices we recommend.

Whether or not we agree with that, I believe research would have more utility and benefit for the system if we had the interest, funds, and incentives to provide hands-on assistance in the field. Obviously, that would require the support of agencies that funded the research, relevant parts of the system, and our research institutions.

That brings me to the fourth, and final, point. I can imagine one response to these suggestions: "We don't have the time or the resources and we aren't rewarded professionally for such efforts—in fact, we could well be penalized for them. Time on these efforts is time away from research. And what about the advancement of science and researchers' basic scientific interests?"

We have prospered by following the time-honored academic model. But criminology has reached a point at which we need to rethink what is valued in the academic scheme of things. As I said earlier, our field is defined by a major social phenomenon—crime—and the system and agencies established to address that phenomenon. That is not true of the basic academic fields that generated the model. I think the time has come to tailor that model rather than emulating what is more appropriate to less-applied fields. Review committees should accept so-called community service as a valid contribution to criminology—or at the very least not penalize those who engage in it.

Further, I am not suggesting that every researcher should be concerned with informing public policy. I am suggesting that the reward structure should be modified to capitalize on people's comparative strengths and interests. Those who have the interest in and abilities to engage in those efforts should have the character to do so. Those whose greater interests and strengths lie in the lab, as it were, will benefit, too, because their work will also have a greater effect. Many ASC members are very senior faculty in the universities and could influence the incentive/disincentive structures that now inhibit such flexibility.

In closing, let me say I recognize that my premises and my suggestions may be controversial and that the issues are complex and politically sensitive. Further, I have not meant to lay responsibility for the situation described on researchers, policymakers, or practitioners—individually or collectively. If the problem is as I describe, like other problems of the larger criminal justice system, it has a complex etiology. Like the alternatives for solving those other problems, the intended and unintended effects of my suggested responses also need to be carefully considered.

In opening this discussion, I am hoping that the ASC may be a catalyst, as it has in the past, for strengthening and enriching our discipline.

NOTES

1. This historical account of academic criminology was informed by Albert Morris (1975).
2. Discussions of the dominance of criminology by sociologists are contained in Binder (1988) and Laub (1983).
3. Complete results are contained in Petersilia (1987).
4. A recent compilation of such research is contained in Tonry and Wilson (1990).

REFERENCES

Academy of Criminal Justice Sciences. (1990). *Guide to Graduate Programs in Criminology, 1989–1990*. Highland Heights, Ky.: Academy of Criminal Justice Sciences.

BENNETT, WILLIAM. (1990). Speech. International Journal on Drug Policy, June 1990:16.

BINDER, ARNOLD. (1988). "Criminology and Interdisciplinarity." *Issues in Integrative Studies* 5:41–67.

COHEN, D. D., and J. A. WEISS. (1977). "Social Science and Social Policy: Schools and Race." In Carol Weiss (Ed.), *Using Social Research in Public Policy Making*. Lexington, Mass.: Lexington Books.

HAWKINS, KEITH, and DONALD HARRIS. (1988). "Policy, Research, and Funding: Socio-Legal Studies in a Changed Political Climate." *Law and Policy 10*:167–200.

LAUB, JOHN. (1983). *Criminology in the Making: An Oral History*. Boston: Northeastern University Press.

MORRIS, ALBERT. (1975). "The American Society of Criminology: A History, 1941–1974." *Criminology 13*:122–166.

PETERSILIA, JOAN. (1987). "The Influence of Criminal Justice Research." R-3516-NIJ. Santa Monica, Calif.: RAND.

PETERSILIA, JOAN, and SUSAN TURNER. (1990). "Intensive Supervision for High-Risk Probationers: Findings from Three California Experiments." R-3936-NIJ/BJA, Santa Monica, Calif.: RAND.

RICH, R. F. (1981). *Social Science Information and Public Policy Making*. San Francisco: Jossey-Bass.

TONRY, MICHAEL, and JAMES Q. WILSON. (1990). *Drugs and Crime*. Chicago: University of Chicago Press.

WEISS, CAROL, and M. J. BUCHUVALAS. (1980). "Trust Tests and Utility Tests: Decision-Makers' Frames of Reference for Social Science Research." *American Sociological Review 45*:302–313.

QUESTIONS FOR DISCUSSION

1. The author cites three signs that criminological research is not influencing policy and practices in criminal justice. List and discuss these signs.
2. Even if research is convincing and the conclusions undisputable, why do policy makers often choose not to base policy on research findings? Provide examples to support your response.
3. The way in which criminologists are trained may encourage "irrelevance" in policy and practice. Explain.
4. The criminal justice system is verging on a crisis because policies and operations are based on faulty assumptions or a narrow focus. Explain.

26

CRIME CONTROL AS HUMAN RIGHTS ENFORCEMENT

Robert Elias

■ ■

Crime threatens the social order in the same way as totalitarianism

—CHARLES SILBERMAN

You will not eliminate crime by eliminating poverty, ignorance, poor health, and ugly environments. But it is clear that such conditions are demonstrably responsible for most crime

—RAMSEY CLARK

...the crimes committed in the name of the state, unfortunately, have...been so great that we cannot shun the obligation to examine the grounds of its authority and subject them to rigorous critique

—ROBERT PAUL WOLFF

WAR AND PEACE

When the government declares another of its countless wars on crime or on drugs, criminology often provides logistical support for the resulting battles. This happens even though these wars are never won; indeed, we can easily predict that they'll be lost. Why do we pursue predictably ineffective crime policies? Why does criminology so often support those wars, thus promoting its own, professional failure? Instead of making *war*, crime control and criminology should be making *peace*.

The government has perhaps a strategic sense of this, having already appropriated the word *peace*: At U.S. military bases, the new motto is "Peace" Is Our Profession. Likewise, in many areas, police officers are now "peace" officers. Nevertheless, military and law-enforcement policies remain virtually the same: they're still pursuing war not peace.

What would crime control or criminology as peacemaking look like? What do we mean by peace? Over the four-decade history of peace studies, peace has come to mean

Robert Elias, "Crime Control as Human Rights Enforcement," *Criminology as Peacemaking*, pp. 69–79. Reprinted by permission of Indiana University Press.

two things: *positive* peace and *negative* peace (Galtung, 1980). We're most familiar with the commonsense notion of negative peace, meaning an absence of violence and war. Here, crime control as peacemaking might resemble conventional crime policy (put with significantly different tactics): fighting crime either to prevent personal violence or to prevent crime "wars" such as those fought among drug dealers or mafia families. Crime policy typically fails to provide this kind of peace, perhaps because officials don't seriously want it (Reiman, 1984), but also because it makes the wrong diagnosis and pursues the wrong strategies (Anderson, 1988; Pepinsky and Jeslow, 1984; Walker, 1985).

In part, crime policy fails because it ignores the second notion of peace. Positive peace describes not what government should prevent, but what government or the society should provide—*justice*: and not just criminal justice, but also political, economic, and social justice. You can't have peace if you don't have justice. Injustice is not merely unpeaceful in itself. It's also the source of further violence and war in any society, and it's the major source of the kind of violence and war we commonly call *crime*.

Most crime results from political, economic, and social injustices that the government or the society has failed or refused to prevent. In some circles, that injustice is called "repression": a violation of human rights. Thus, promoting peace is a matter of the government not merely refraining from its own violence and war (and crime) but providing the conditions to persuade others against launching their own violence and war (and crime). Crime control can be successful only by taking human rights enforcement seriously.

CONVENTIONAL CRIME CONTROL

Mainstream crime policy uses war purportedly to create peace. Yet as a process, its wars undermine both negative and positive peace: they use violence and rights' violations as their major tactics. The need to win these wars rationalizes the use of illegitimate, but supposedly more effective, methods: We're told the police should no longer be "handcuffed"; rights must be sacrificed; our enforcement and punishments must be more violent. In the long run, crime will decline and peace will reign (President's Task Force, 1982). Yet the peace never comes: criminal violence keeps pace with escalating official violence.

Despite the wars, criminal victimization continues because conventional crime policy either ignores or misdiagnoses crime's sources (Wilson and Hernnstein, 1985). Officials argue that we don't or can't know the causes of crime, or they attribute it to what might better be viewed as crime symptoms. They blame offenders and institutions, even victims. Offender-blaming attributes crime to evil individuals or their inadequate families. Institution-blaming focuses on lax enforcement, inadequate resources, excessive rights, and judicial softness as the causes of crime. Victim-blaming faults victims for not taking precautions sufficient to deter crime. Predictably, crime-control strategies follow from these diagnoses. They're pursued; they fail.

Nevertheless, officials return to these diagnoses and strategies time and again (Elias, 1990b). Criminology largely follows suit, adopting official definitions and perspectives. When officials go to war, criminology goes to war too. When confronting crime, government limits its scope; criminology does so too (Elias, 1985). The diagnoses made of what causes crime necessarily constrict the options for fighting it; make the wrong diagnoses and you'll likely pursue the wrong strategies. Conventional crime policy's repeated failure would seem reason enough to consider alternatives. Better yet, alternative diagnoses and strategies already exist (Brady, 1981; Currie, 1985; Elias, unpublished manuscript).

ALTERNATIVE CRIME POLICY

Blaming the System

An alternative crime policy would wage peace not war. It would begin with a different diagnosis: Crime primarily results not from inherently or inevitably evil offenders, nor from institutional inefficiencies, nor from victim complacency. Rather, it's caused by adverse or destructive political, economic, and social conditions that induce crime across the spectrum of classes and races in American society. Instead of blaming offenders, institutions, or victims, this diagnosis blames the system, the existing set of U.S. political and economic arrangements. Inadequacies in the American political economy provide the breeding ground for most crime (Elias, 1986; Quinney, 1980).

The economic system, for example, produces poverty, inequality, homelessness, hunger, and other victimization. It's not surprising that many poor people turn to crime, for economic gain or merely to vent their frustrations (Barlow, 1988; Braithwaite, 1979; Michalowski, 1985; Silberman, 1978; Wideman, 1984). The economy also promotes excessive materialism, competition, and consumerism. To get ahead and keep ahead, middle- and upper-class people commit crime too. If their wrongdoing was measured or enforced like poor people's crimes, it would amount to far more criminality and damage than the conventional crime we worry so much about (Frank, 1985; Green and Berry, 1985; Horchstedler, 1984; Mokiber, 1988; Reiman, 1984).

The political system has its own inadequacies, induced partly by the economic system. Government officials widely commit crimes themselves, usually with little or no accounting, the Iran-Contra episode being only the latest example (Chambliss, 1987; Foraker-Thompson, 1988; Kelman and Hamilton, 1989; Kwitny, 1987; Ratner, 1987; Tushnet, 1988). Access to meaningful political participation is blocked for almost all but the very wealthy. Elections function more to tame the masses than to empower them. Despite talk about getting government off our backs, it steadily centralizes and grows. We're overwhelmed and alienated by our various public and private bureaucracies, including most of our workplaces. Government pays lip service to equality while tolerating or promoting racism, sexism, and classism (Dunbar, 1984; Gross, 1980; Marable, 1983; Parenti, 1988; Russell and Van den Ven, 1984). Whether in its domestic policy or its foreign policy, we learn by the government's official actions, if not by its pious rhetoric, that violence is legitimate (Herman, 1982; Rubin, 1986; Wolfe, 1978).

In practice, we lack both political and economic democracy. Our system produces problems and conditions that breed crime far more than the things we usually blame. Societies with greater political and economic democracy have less crime and victimization. Even nations like those in Eastern Europe or like Cuba, which has little political democracy but greater economic democracy, have much lower crime rates than our nominally democratic capitalism (Clinard, 1978; Los, 1982).

Crime and Repression

But the problems of failed political and economic democracy are the sources of more than merely criminal victimization; the problems are themselves victimization. Human rights advocates would call these problems repression. International law requires nations to prevent or deal with these problems; and nations which fail to do so (particularly if, like the United States, they have the means) are human rights violators. These are crimes against humanity. Repression is crime. Crime is a human rights violation. Crime results from the violation of human rights produced by unjust political and economic arrangements (Meier and Geis, 1978; Reasons, 1982).

Criminals are also victims, and, of course, offenders bear some responsibility for their crimes. But viewing criminals as passive automatons shaped by monolithic forces degrades offenders every bit as much as our conventional criminal process. And recognizing offender motivation does not excuse their crimes. Nevertheless, offenders act within an environment that often makes crime a viable alternative, a likely possibility, even a necessity. It's not an environment of lenience, as "law and order" advocates argue. (The United States has long had one of the world's highest incarceration rates and severity of punishments.) Rather, it's an environment of victimization, which beats people down, robs them of opportunities, and provokes their rage, frustration, and desperation. In response, they attack others; but their victims are much like themselves: Most victims come from the same backgrounds, and many of them have omitted their own crimes for similar reasons (Elias, 1986).

It's politically convenient for officials to pit criminals and victims against each other. Protecting victims has justified our growing fortress mentality: increasing government powers and declining individual rights. Yet victim policy does not reduce crime; and arguably, pursuing crime and control strategies that routinely fail, even encourage crime, makes victimization even more likely (Elias, 1990c). Successful crime control relies not on promoting victims over offenders, but on recognizing how both are victimized and how the rights of both must be protected. Victims and criminals have the same interest: the protection of their human rights.

Alternative crime control strategies would follow from this diagnosis. It would require us to reduce or eliminate crime's systemic sources. We'd have to significantly restructure our political and economic system, bringing both much closer to democracy and justice. Thereby, we'd be promoting both positive and negative peace: a reduction in the violence the system and its major institutions directly produce, and a reduction in the violence committed by others in the society in reaction to injustice. By pursuing justice, we'd be pursuing peace; and we'd also be reducing the crime that now significantly impedes that peace.

RESISTING PEACE

Why does mainstream crime policy, which routinely fails, shun this alternative? It does so because it would clash dramatically with the American system's conventional political and economic practice both at home and abroad. To adopt alternative crime policies, we'd have to pursue crime control that really reduces crime rather than merely overseeing it. We'd have to stop manipulating or blaming victims, and take victimization (criminal and otherwise) seriously. We'd have to reject "democracy for the few" in favor of a more just political economy. We'd have to renounce our isolation from the world community and our rejection of international human rights standards (Chomsky, 1988; Elias, 1990c; Falk, 1981; Parenti, 1988; Reiman, 1984).

Rogue Society

Let's examine, for example, U.S. human rights policy. The United States has long crusaded as democracy's champion at home and abroad. It's held up its own system as the democratic ideal and justified its foreign policy as helping others become more democratic. By now, it's hardly controversial to suggest that in practice the United States does neither. Even the pretensions of real democracy largely evaporated with Jimmy Carter, who at least pursued human rights rhetorically if not very vigorously in practice. Whether it's our increasing poverty, homelessness, inequality, and violence at home, or our promotion of brutal repression abroad, the victimization produced by the U.S. government and our other institutions hardly makes our commitment to human rights credible (Chomsky and Herman, 1979; Goldstein, 1978; Gross, 1980; Klare and Arnson, 1981; Lappe et al., 1980; Scherer and Shepard, 1983; Special Issue, 1989; Weisband, 1989).

The United States is out of step with the world community (Boyle, 1988; Frappier, 1984; Weston, 1987). We pull out of United Nations' agencies while other nations commit themselves more fully. We're practically alone in rejecting the Law-of-the-Sea-Treaty's cooperative exploration of the oceans in favor of competitive exploitation. We defend the unconscionable marketing of infant baby formula while the rest of the world deplores it. We support pariah states like Chile, Israel, and South Africa while the international community condemns them. We increasingly reject and violate international law (and the jurisdiction of agencies like the World Court) while the rest of the world increasingly embraces it. We substitute military intervention for diplomacy when even the Soviet Union has rejected the practice. George Bush asks the U.S.S.R. to intervene in Rumania, and Mikhail Gorbachev says they don't do that kind of thing anymore. A few days later, the United States illegally invades Panama; and the Latin American nations, no lovers of Manuel Noriega, rightfully condemn us.

Human Rights Standards

Likewise, the United States exhibits a limited commitment to international human rights standards (Claude and Weston, 1989; Forsythe, 1989). By now, the world's nations have recognized, and most have ratified, three "generations" of human rights: political and civil rights; economic, social, and cultural rights; and peace, development and environmental rights. The United States has ratified none of these standards. We've even shunned the Covenant on Political and Civil Rights, which comes closest to our narrow human rights definitions. Although this covenant embodies many of the things already in our own Bill of Rights, it adds other rights and, more menacing, threatens to make the rights substantially enforceable and not merely rhetorical. We'd have an international obligation to take these rights seriously. And instead of piecemeal, impermanent, and often unenforced rights protections (Scheingold, 1974), we'd be responsible for more honestly and equitably guaranteeing freedom of expression, political access, privacy, due process for suspects and defendants, and race and gender equality—rights that have instead declined in the last two decades (faster than they can be promoted) and are threatened even further by the recently inaugurated Rehnquist Court (Curry, 1988; Dorsen, 1984; Karp, 1988; Lobel, 1988; Marx, 1988; Pell, 1984; Spence, 1989).

Even more ominous for the American system would be accepting and protecting the second and third generations of human rights. Embracing economic, social, and cultural rights, for example, would force the United States to fundamentally change its political economy, which now acts systematically to deprive these rights for vast portions of the population. We can imagine why officials won't recognize the right to housing, employment, quality education, nutrition, good working conditions, comprehensive health care, and social and cultural equality. Similarly, the newest generation of human rights—the rights to peace, development, and a clean environment—also clashes with the American system since this generation would condemn our persistent and far-flung military and economic interventionism, reject vast nuclear stockpiles, and indict the corporate pollution of our environment.

Human rights covenants are treaties in U.S. and international law. If we were to ratify these treaties, they would become the law of the land under the U.S. Constitution. As such, the rights they contain would be legally enforceable in U.S. courts. We can imagine the threat posed to the American system by suits brought to demand that these rights be protected. Suppose claims were brought by our four million homeless Americans for their housing rights, or by our 60 million illiterates for their educational rights, or by our millions of jobless (50 percent in our ghettos) for their employment rights, or by our 30 million underfed for their nutrition rights, or by our millions of uninsured (50 percent of the population) for their health care rights, or by even millions more (such as those living near our 75,000 toxic dump sites) for their environmental rights. Or suppose U.S. citizens or foreigners sued to protect the rights of the millions of people victimized by the repression and economic deprivation our foreign policy exports to nations like El Salvador, Lebanon, Chile, South Africa, and many others.

Rights as Threats

Despite the rhetoric, the United States has been only minimally committed to protecting human rights. The few exceptions are politically motivated, such as the "demonstration elections" we've sponsored to help sanitize our client states (Brodhead and Herman, 1987). When we back away from the endless dictators we've either sponsored or installed, it's only after they've outlived their usefulness (such as Noriega in Panama) or where their population overthrow is inevitable (such as Marcos in the Philippines). If popular revolution (such as Nicaragua) threatens to seriously protect human rights and promote real political and economic democracy, we attack it.

A nation which tolerates and even promotes the victimization caused by repression can hardly be expected to respond differently to victimization caused by crime. Wars on crime and drugs, government-backed victim movements, and pious rhetoric about the "forgotten" victim in the criminal process achieve little for crime victims in practice. There's little evidence that officials ever thought they would (Elias, 1983, 1990a, 1990b).

We don't take crime and its victims seriously for the same reasons we don't take repression and its victims seriously; to do so would require fundamental changes in the American system, which would upset its prevailing concentration of power and resources. Undoing that concentration is the only hope for genuinely protecting and providing human rights; and short of that, crime and other victimization will continue unabated. The United States can't achieve peace if it's only willing to fight wars, especially since they're often launched not just against innocent foreigners, but also against its own people. Are U.S. wars, whether against domestic crime or foreign enemies, fought to promote democracy for the many or to preserve democracy for the few?

Taking Rights Seriously

Real crime control would consider rights not as an obstacle but rather as its major objective (Walker, 1982). Now, to fight crime, our "law and order" policy restricts and violates the rights of suspects, defendants, and the public; it further victimizes purportedly to end victimization. Indeed, alternative crime control would promote human rights fully: not just for suspects and defendants, not just to stem a growing police state, but also for the kind of political, economic, and social justice that would significantly eliminate crime's sources in the first place. An effective crime policy would recognize the relationship between crime victimization and human rights victimization, not treat the two as separate and unconnected, and pursue a joint strategy designed to alleviate them both simultaneously.

How can this be done? We can begin, perhaps, by taking the lead offered by the recently passed United Nations Declaration of the Victims of Crime and Abuses of Power (Lamborn, 1987; U.N. Secretariat, 1980). Here the link has been made, despite U.S. resistance, between crime and repression. Like other declarations, its effectiveness depends first on getting as many nations as possible to ratify it; and the United States should be pressured to do so. Next, the U.N.'s Crime Prevention and Criminal Justice Branch must devise standards for the declaration's implementation; and criminologists, victimologists, and human rights advocates should contribute to this process (Geis et al., 1985). More generally, the United States should be pushed to get in step with the international community: It must ratify the human rights covenants. It must respect the sovereignty of other nations and peoples. It must recognize international law (Bassiouni, 1985; DeCataldo Neuberger, 1985; Hertzberg, 1981; Johnston, 1974, 1978; Lopez-Rey, 1985; Lynch et al., 1988; Schaaf, 1986).

At home, the United States must take human rights serious, implementing and enforcing them in both the political and economic realms. To do so requires not merely a more just legal system and less criminal government, but fundamental changes in the American system to undo its many obstacles to political and economic democracy. The United States must be held more accountable. Criminology and victimology can contribute by challenging prevailing assumptions about official benevolence and by adopting alternative definitions and perspectives on crime and victimization (Elias, 1986; Snider, 1988).

Of course, these objectives will not come easily. By now it should be obvious that formidable and fundamental changes will be needed to significantly reduce crime. A human rights perspective, however, gives us a new way of approaching the task ahead and, perhaps, a more powerful and symbolically acceptable mechanism for accomplishing it.

No doubt the obstacles will be compounded by official resistance to a substantive human rights movement. Rights will likely remain a threat to those unwilling to relinquish political and economic power, both at home and abroad. Our archconservative Supreme Court and foreign policy will be further impediments to taking rights seriously. Nevertheless, one wonders how long the United States can resist our rapidly changing world. With the walls of repression falling in Eastern Europe, and with incipient signs of democratic renewal in Latin American (despite U.S. policy), now is perhaps a historic opportunity. With renewed determination, perhaps we can launch a real human rights movement, beyond mere rhetoric, which emphasizes substantive protections of all human rights—a movement which will help reduce not only human rights victimization, but criminal victimization as well (Eide, 1986; Kim, 1983).

How can criminology work for peace? It can promote human rights—*justice*: the only effective path to peace, whether in our streets or among our nations (Alston, 1981).

REFERENCES

ALSTON, PHILIP. (1981). "Peace As A Human Right." *Bulletin of Peace Proposals 11*: 319–326.

ANDERSON, DAVID. (1988). *Crimes of Justice*. New York: Times Books.

BARLOW, DAVID E. (1988). "Economic Crisis and the Criminal Justice System." Paper presented at Annual Meeting of American Society of Criminology, Chicago.

BASSIOUNI, M. C. (1985). "The Protection of 'Collective Victims' in International Law." *New York Law School Human Rights Annual* 2 (Spring): 239–257.

BOYLE, FRANCIS A. (1988). "International Law, Citizen Resistance, and Crimes By the State." Paper presented at Annual Meeting of American Society of Criminology, Chicago.

BRADY, JAMES. (1981). "Towards Popular Justice in the U.S." *Contemporary Crises 5*: 155–194.

BRAITHWAITE, JOHN. (1979). *Inequality, Crime and Public Policy*. New York: Routledge and Kegan Paul.

BRODHEAD, FRANK, and EDWARD HERMAN. (1987). *Demonstration Elections: U.S. Staged Elections*. Boston: South End Press.

CHAMBLISS, WILLIAM. (1989). "State-Organized Crime." *Criminology* 27: 183–208.

CHOMSKY, NOAM. (1988). *The Culture of Terrorism*. Boston: South End Press.

CHOMSKY, NOAM, and Edward HERMAN. (1979). *The Washington Connection and Third World Fascism*. Boston: South End Press.

CLAUDE, RICHARD, and BURNS WESTON. (Eds.). (1989). *Human Rights in the International Community*. Philadelphia: University of Pennsylvania Press.

CLINARD, MARSHALL. (1978). *Cities With Little Crime*. New York: Cambridge University Press.

CURRIE, ELLIOT. (1985). *Confronting Crime*. New York: Pantheon.

CURRY, RICHARD (Ed.). *Freedom At Risk: Secrecy, Censorship and Repression in the Eighties*. Philadelphia: Temple University Press.

DeCATALDO NEUBERGER, LUISA. (1985). "An Appraisal of Victimological Perspectives in International Law." *Victimology 10*: 700–709.

DORSEN, NORMAN. (1984). *Our Endangered Rights*. New York: Pantheon.

DUNBAR, LESLIE (Ed.). (1984). *Minority Report*. New York: Pantheon.

EIDE, A. (1986). "The Human Rights Movement and the Transformation of the International Order." *Alternatives* 11: 367–402.

ELIAS, ROBERT. (1983). *Victims of the System*. New Brunswick, N.J.: Transaction Books.

_____. (1985). "Transcending Our Social Reality of Victimization." *Victimology 10*: 6–25.

_____. (1986). *The Politics of Victimization: Victims, Victimology and Human Rights*. New York: Oxford University Press.

_____. (1990a). "The Conflicting Politics of Victim Movements." *Victimology 14*: 25–37.

_____. (1990b). "Wars on Drugs and Crime as Historic Propaganda." Unpublished paper.

_____. (1990c). "Which Victim Movement? The Politics of Victim Policy." In Wesley SKOGAN, et al., *Victims and Criminal Justice*. Newbury Park, Calif.: Sage.

FALK, RICHARD. (1981). *Human Rights and State Sovereignty*. New York: Holmes and Meier.

FORAKER-THOMPSON, JANE. (1988). "Crime and Ethics in Government: Constitutional Crisis." Paper presented at Annual Meeting of American Society of Criminology, Chicago.

FORSYTHE, DAVID. (1989). *Human Rights and World Politics*. Lincoln, Nebr.: University of Nebraska Press.

FRANK, NANCY. (1985). *Crimes Against Health and Safety*. Albany: Harrow and Heston.

FRAPPIER, JAN. (1984). "Above the Law: Violations of International Law by the U.S. Government." *Crime and Social Justice 23*: 1–45.

GALTUNG, JOHAN. (1980). *The True Worlds*. New York: Free Press.

GEIS, GILBERT, DUNCAN CHAPPELL, and MICHAEL AGOPIAN. (1985). "Toward the Alleviation of Human Suffering." Dubrovnik: Rapporteurs' Report of the 5th International Symposium on Victimology.

GOLDSTEIN, ROBERT. (1978). *Political Repression in Modern America*. Cambridge, Mass.: Schenkman.

GREEN, MARK, and JOHN F. BERRY. (1985). *The Challenge of Hidden Profits: White Collar Crime as Big Business*. New York: William Morrow.

GROSS, BERTRAM. (1980). *Friendly Fascism*. New York: M. Evans.

HERMAN, EDWARD. (1982). *The Real Terror Network*. Boston: South End Press.

HERTZBERG, SANDRA. (1981). *The Protection of Human Rights in the Criminal Process Under International Instruments and National Constitutions*. Amsterdam: Eres.

HOCHSTEDLER, ELLEN, (Ed.) (1984). *Corporations as Criminals*. Beverly Hills, Calif.: Sage.

JOHNSTON, STANLEY. (1974). "Toward A Supra-National Criminology: The Right and Duty of Victims of National Government to Seek Defense Through World Law." In Israel Drapkin and Emilio Viano (Eds.), *Victimology: Theoretical Issues*. Lexington, Mass.: Lexington Books.

_____. (1978). "Instituting Criminal Justice in the Global Village." In Emilio Viano (Ed.), *Victims and Society*, Washington, D.C.: Visage Press.

KARP, WALTER. (1988). "Liberty Under Siege." *Harper's Magazine* (November): 53–67.

KELMAN, HERBERT, and V. LEE HAMILTON. (1989). *Crimes of Obedience*. New Haven, Conn.: Yale University Press.

KIM, SAMUEL. (1983). *The Quest for A Just World Order*. Boulder, Colo.: Westview.

KLARE, MICHAEL, and CYNTHIA ARNSON. (1981). *Supplying Repression*. Washington, D.C.: Institute for Policy Studies.

KWITNY, JONATHAN. (1987). *The Crimes of Patriots*. New York: Simon & Schuster.

LAMBORN, LEROY. (1987). "The United Nations Declaration on Victims: Incorporating 'Abuse of Power.'" *Rutgers Law Journal* 19: 59–95.

LAPPE, FRANCES MOORE, JOSEPH COLLINS, and DAVID KINLEY. (1980). *Aid As Obstacle*. San Francisco: Institute for Food & Development Policy.

LOBEL, JULES. (1988). *A Less Than Perfect Union*. New York: Monthly Review Press.

LOPEZ-REY, MIGUEL. (1985). *A Guide to United Nations Criminal Policy*. New York: United Nations.

LOS, MARIA, (1982). "Crime and Economy in the Communist Countries." In Peter Wickman and Timothy Dailey (Eds.), *White Collar and Economic Crime*. Lexington, Mass.: Lexington Books.

LYNCH, MICHAEL, DAVID MCDOWALL, and GRAEME R. NEWMAN. (1988). "Crime in the World System." Paper presented at the Annual Meeting of American Society of Criminology, Chicago.

MARABLE, MANNING. (1983). *How Capitalism Underdeveloped Black America*. Boston: South End Press.

MARX, GARY T. (1988). *Under Cover: Police Surveillance in America*. Berkeley: University of California Press.

MEIER, ROBERT, and GILBERT GEIS. (1978). "The Abuse of Power as a Criminal Activity." In Gilbert Geis (Ed.), *On White Collar Crime*. Beverly Hills, Calif.: Sage.

MICHALOWSKI, RAYMOND. (1985). *Order, Law and Crime*. New York: Random House.

MOKIBER, RONALD. (1988). *Corporate Crime and Violence*. San Francisco: Sierra Books.

PARENTI, MICHAEL. (1988). *Democracy for the Few*. New York: St. Martin's.

PELL, EVE. (1984). *The Big Chill*. Boston: Beacon Press.

PEPINSKY, HAROLD E., and PAUL JESILOW. (1984). *Myths That Cause Crime*. Cabin John, Md.: Seven Locks Press.

President's Task Force on Victims of Crime. (1982). *Final Report*. Washington, D.C.: U.S. Government Printing Office.

QUINNEY, RICHARD. (1980). *Class, State and Crime*. New York: Longman.

RATNER, MICHAEL. (1987). "Contragate, Covert Action and the Constitution." *Social Policy* (Summer): 43–47.

REASONS, CHARLES. (1982). "Crime and the Abuse of Power." In Peter Wickman and Timothy Dailey (Eds.), *White Collar and Economic Crime*. Lexington, Mass.: Lexington Books.

REIMAN, JEFFREY. (1984). *The Rich Get Richer and the Poor Get Prison*. 2d ed. New York: J. Wiley.

RUBIN, LILLIAN. (1986). *Quiet Rage: Bernie Goetz in A Time of Madness*. New York: Farrar, Straus & Giroux.

RUSSELL, D. E. H., and N. VAN DEN VEN. (1984). *Crimes Against Women*. East Palo Alto, Calif.: Frog In the Well Press.

SCHAAF, R. W. (1986). "New International Instruments in Crime Prevention and Criminal Justice." *International Journal of Legal Information* 14 (June): 176–182.

SCHEINGOLD, STUART. (1974). *The Politics of Rights*. New Haven, Conn.: Yale University Press.

SCHERER, JACQUELINE, AND GARY SHEPARD (Eds.). (1983). *Victimization of the Weak*. Springfield, Ill.: C. Thomas.

SILBERMAN, CHARLES. (1978). *Criminal Violence, Criminal Justice*. New York: Vintage.

SNIDER, LAURA. (1988). "The Potential of the Criminal Justice System to Promote Feminist Concerns." Paper presented at Annual Meeting of American Society of Criminology: Chicago.

Special Issue. (1989). "Domestic Surveillance." *Covert Action Information Bulletin* 31 (Winter): 1–74.

SPENCE, GERRY. (1989). *With Justice for None*. New York: Times Books.

Tushnet, Mark. (1988). *Central America and the Law*. Boston: South End Press.

United Nations Secretariat. (1980). "Crime and the Abuse of Power: Offenses and Offenders Beyond the Reach of the Law." U.S. Doc. A/CONF/87/6.

Walker, Samuel. (1982). "What Have Civil Liberties Ever Done for Crime Victims? Plenty!" *Academy of Criminal Justice Sciences Today* (October) 4.

_____. (1985). *Sense and Nonsense About Crime*. Belmont, Calif.: Brookes-Cole.

Weisband, Edward (Ed.). (1989). *Poverty Amidst Plenty*. Boulder, Colo. Westview, 1989.

Weston, Burns. (1987). "The Reagan Administration Versus International Law." *Case Western Reserve Journal of International Law*. 19: 295–302.

Wideman, John Edgar. (1984). *Brothers and Keepers*. New York: Penguin.

Wilson, James Q., and James Hernnstein. (1985). *Crime and Human Nature*. Cambridge, Mass.: Harvard University Press.

Wolfe, Alan. (1978). *The Seamy Side of Democracy*. New York: Longman.

QUESTIONS FOR DISCUSSION

1. Compare positive peace to negative peace.

2. The author asserts that crime is "caused by adverse or destructive political, economic, and social conditions that induce crime across a spectrum of classes and races in American society." Explain.

3. Discuss the relationship of crime and repression. Provide examples to support your answer.

4. According to the author, mainstream crime policy, which has continually failed, shuns the notion of reducing or eliminating crime by restructuring the political and economic system. Why?

5. Discuss why a basic commitment to human rights would cause a significant change in crime policy. Why might a commitment to human rights pose a threat to the existing political and economic system? Provide examples to support your answer.

27

MOVING INTO THE NEW MILLENNIUM

TOWARD A FEMINIST VISION OF JUSTICE

M. Kay Harris

■ ■ ■ ■ ■ ■ ■ ■ ■ ■ ■ ■ ■ ■ ■ ■ ■ ■ ■ ■

The approach of the twenty-first century tends to inspire future-oriented thinking. With respect to criminal justice policies and practices, it is disheartening to imagine what the future holds if the current course is maintained. This article argues that moving toward a significantly brighter future requires abandoning conventional frames of thought and practice and adopting a fundamentally different way of thinking and acting. The focus is on exploring what the next century might look like if a feminist orientation toward justice were embraced.

CONVENTIONAL APPROACHES TO CRIMINAL JUSTICE REFORM

Most proposals for change in policies directed at crime and criminal justice concerns fall within one of two types. Many proposals are developed from a systems-improvement orientation. This orientation takes for granted existing political, economic, and social institutional structures as well as the values that undergird them, assuming that they are proper or, at least, unlikely to be changed within the foreseeable future. Reform proposals generated from a systems-improvement perspective characteristically are framed as if crime were primarily an individual problem best addressed through more effective or more rigorous enforcement of the law. Thus, they focus on trying to find better means of identifying and intervening with individual offenders and of strengthening and increasing the efficiency of existing criminal justice institutions and agencies.

The other familiar way of framing reform proposals involves a broader crime-prevention/social-reform orientation. Reformers with this orientation emphasize the social and economic underpinnings of crime and the need to address them through policies and programs focused on families, neighborhoods, schools, and other institutions. In recent years, advocates of a prevention/social-reform approach have moved considerably beyond the ameliorative strategies of the 1960s toward proposals for more sweeping social and

Reprinted by permission of the author.

economic reconstruction, stressing that policies aimed at strengthening families and communities need to be coupled with efforts to promote economic development and full employment.[1] Although they do not excuse individual offenders or ignore possible advances to be made by improving criminal justice practices, these reformers tend to view interventions with identified offenders more as last lines of defense than as promising avenues for reducing crime.

There are significant problems associated with trying to formulate recommendations for the future on the basis of either of these two conventional ways of framing the issues. The systems-improvement approach has the apparent advantage of offering advances in the identification, classification, control, or treatment of offenders and in the operation, efficiency, effectiveness, or accountability of criminal justice agencies. However, this approach ignores the political, economic, and social aspects of crime and has little or nothing to contribute to the overall, long-term development of social life. Furthermore, it offers, at best, only limited, short-term utility in dealing with crime.

Many systems-improvement advocates promise dramatic increases in crime control if only sanctions can be made more frightening, severe, certain, restrictive, or corrective. But such promises lack both theoretical and scientific support. Current knowledge provides little basis for expecting significant reductions in crime through reshaping policies in hopes of achieving greater deterrent, incapacitative, or rehabilitative effects. Other systems-improvement supporters concede that notable increases in domestic tranquillity are unlikely to be secured at the hands of crime-control agents, but argue that until more fundamental changes have been made in social relations and policies, there is no alternative but to continue working toward whatever marginal increases in efficiency, effectiveness, or evenhandedness might be achievable.

To date, prevention/social-reform advocates have made scant progress in overcoming the notion that their proposals already have been tried in the War on Poverty/Great Society era and found ineffective. Many who agree that the measures championed by these advocates are prerequisites for dramatic shifts in crime and social relations doubt that the massive changes envisioned are economically or politically feasible. Furthermore, prevention/social-reform advocates have had little influence in ongoing criminal justice policy debates because their recommendations concerning interim criminal justice policies have been meager and uncompelling. They have offered little more than echoes of systems-improvement reform proposals, accompanied by warnings about the risk of simply reinforcing the underclass and increasing the social divisions in society if repressive measures targeted on offenders are pursued too zealously.

Thus, despite widespread dissatisfaction with the results of current policies and their burgeoning costs, it is difficult to find grounds for believing that the future toward which we are heading holds much promise of anything beyond more of the same. If current trends hold the key to seeing what the criminal justice system will look like in the next few decades, we face the prospect of maintaining a punishment system of awesome proportions without being able to expect much relief from the problems it supposedly exists to address.

CURRENT TRENDS

Over the last decade, approximately 200,000 beds have been added to state and federal prisons across the United States, increasing their confinement capacity by more than two-thirds (Bureau of Justice, *Bulletin* 1986, 1987). In a recent random sample survey of local jails, officials in 44 percent reported that facility construction or renovation was underway (Bureau of Justice, *Compendium*, 1986). And even though at least 22 states had to make spending cuts in their fiscal-1987 budgets and 23 states passed or considered increases in gasoline, cigarette, or sales taxes, a review of spending proposals by governors across the country suggests that substantial additional increases in institutional networks are being planned (Pierce, 1987).

If the average annual growth during the 1980s in the number of federal and state prisoners continues through 1987, the nation's prison population will have tripled over the last fifteen years.[2] But the recent expansion of the punishment sector of the system has not been limited to prisons and jails. At the most drastic extreme, there are now more than 1,800 persons awaiting state execution across the United States (*Lifelines*, 1987). At the other end of the penal spectrum, the adult probation population has been increasing even more rapidly in the 1980s than the incarcerated population.

As of the end of 1985, the total population under the control or supervision of the penal system has risen to 2.9 million persons, representing fully 3 percent of the adult males in the country.[3] An estimated one in every ten black adult men was on probation or parole or in prison or jail.[4] The proportion of Hispanics under penal control is not fully reported, but the number of Hispanics in the nation's prisons reportedly has doubled since 1980, a rate of growth that could result in Hispanics constituting one-fourth of the incarcerated population by the year 2000 (Woestendiek, 1987).

Not only have the numbers and mix of persons under penal control been changing, but the nature of that experience has been changing as well. For those incarcerated, such forces as overcrowding, de-emphasis on programs and services, mandatory sentences, and other reflections of an increasingly harsh orientation toward offenders have worked to offset gains made through litigation and other efforts to improve the situation of those confined. Idleness, demoralization, isolation, danger, and despair permeate the prison and the jail.

For those subject to nonincarcerative penalties, levels of intervention and control, demands for obedience, and the sheer weight of conditions never have been heavier. As of the spring of 1986, intensive supervision programs were operating in at least 29 states, and an additional eight states reportedly were planning to implement such programs in the near future (Byrne, 1986). Typical requirements in such programs include not only increased contact and surveillance, but also mandatory restitution and community service obligations; payment of supervision fees, court and attorney costs, and fines; curfews and periods of house arrest; urinalysis, blood tests, and other warrantless searches; and even periods of incarceration. The latest popular addition to these and other nonincarcerative sanctions is electronic surveillance. There are now more than 45 programs in 20 states using electronic devices to monitor the whereabouts of convicted offenders of defendants awaiting trial (Yost, 1987).

IRON BARS AND VELVET ANKLE BRACELETS: THE NEED FOR NEW APPROACHES

Many common citizens, scientists, futurists, and leaders are predicting that the next 25 years portend a series of collisions, conflicts, and catastrophes. Recent world experience with increasing interpersonal violence, terrorism, social injustice, and inequality—along with such growing problems as overpopulation, ecological damage, resource shortages, the continuing arms buildup, and the specter of nuclear holocaust—has generated heightened awareness of the need to think globally and much more creatively about the future. To begin to adequately envision what criminal justice should look like in the year 2012, we need to step outside of the traditional ways of framing the issues and consider approaches that transcend not only conventional criminological and political lines, but also national and cultural boundaries and other limiting habits of the mind. At the same time, "focusing on the principles and tools of punishment" can help us "understand the most prevalent way we have chosen to relate to each other in the twentieth century" (Sullivan, 1980:14).

Just as the velvet glove only thinly cushions and screens the iron fist, it is important to recognize that "the velvet ankle bracelet" and its ostensibly more benign brethren "community penalties" are facilitating the diffusion and expansion of social control through the penal system and augmenting the iron bars rather than replacing them. With little fanfare or protest, we have come to accept levels of state intrusiveness into individual lives, remarkable in a society that professes to value liberty. The nature and direction of the bulk of changes undertaken in the criminal justice system in recent years are such that the most pressing tasks in the coming years necessarily will involve damage control. Massive efforts will need to be devoted to coping with, undoing, and trying to ameliorate the effects of the present blind, determined push for greater punishment and control. Pursuing a more hopeful future requires exploration of alternative visions of justice.

A number of movements, models, and philosophies in various stages of development have arisen in response to the critical problems of the day, ranging from those focused on world order or global transformation to pacifism or peace studies, reconciliation, humanism, feminism, and a wide range of other visions of a better world and a better future. While few have been focused on criminal justice problems, they offer a rich resource for a fundamental rethinking of our approach to crime and justice.

In seeking to escape the fetters on my own thinking and aspirations for the future, I have found much of value in a number of orientations. Indeed, I have been struck by the common themes that emerge across a variety of perspectives with a wide range of labels. This suggests the possibility of articulating a new direction for the future by drawing from many orientations and avoiding attaching any label to the values and concepts discussed. Such an approach would help prevent burdening the ideas with unnecessary baggage or losing the attention of people put off by the images any particular school of thought raises in their minds. For me, however, the most significant breakthroughs in thought and hope came when I began to apply myself to considering what the values and principles of one particular orientation—feminism—would mean in rethinking crime and justice issues. Thus, the rest of this article shares ideas that emerged from this path of exploration, a path that continues to hold increasing meaning and inspiration for me and one that I hope will attract interest from a variety of people who otherwise might not devote attention to these issues. At the same time, it is my hope that people who find themselves more attuned to other orientations, or who see feminism differently, may find it useful to consider how the values described fit with theirs and what a future based on these values might look like, no matter what terms are used to describe it.

VALUES CENTRAL TO A FEMINIST FUTURE

Feminism offers and is a set of values, beliefs, and experiences—a consciousness, a way of looking at the world. Feminism should be seen not merely as a prescription for granting rights to women, but as a far broader vision. There are a number of varying strands within feminism thought, but there are some core values that transcend the differences. Among the key tenets of feminism are three simple beliefs—that all people have equal value as human beings, that harmony and felicity are more important than power and possession, and that the personal is the political (French, 1985).

Feminist insistence on equality in sexual, racial, economic, and all other types of relations stems from recognition that all humans are equally tied to the human condition, equally deserving of respect for their personhood, and equally worthy of survival and of access to those things that make life worth living. This is not to argue that all people are identical. Indeed, feminism places great emphasis on the value of difference and diversity, holding that different people should receive not identical treatment, but identical consideration. Feminists are concerned not simply with equal opportunities or equal entitlements within existing social structures, but with creating a different set of structures and relations that are not only nonsexist, but also are nonracist and economically just.

In the feminist view, felicity and harmony are regarded as the highest values. Viewing all people as part of a network on whose continuation we all depend, feminists stress the themes of caring, nurturing, and loving. This contrasts sharply with an orientation that values power and control above all else. Where the central goal is power, power conceived as "power over" or control, people and things are not viewed as ends in themselves but as instruments for the furtherance of power. Hierarchical institutions and structures are established both to clarify power rankings and to maintain them. The resulting stratifications create levels of superiority and inferiority, which carry differential status, legitimacy, and access to resources and other benefits. Such divisions and exclusions engender resentment and revolt in various forms, which then are used to justify greater control.

Feminists believe that it is impossible to realize humane goals and create humane structures in a society that values power above all else. A major part of feminist effort involves better identifying and confronting characteristics and values—the political, social, economic, and cultural structures and ideologies—that are not conducive to the full realization of the human potential in individuals or society, the negative values that underlie stereotypes, rationalize discrimination and oppression, and serve only to support the groups in power.

Feminist belief is that the personal is the political, which means that core values must be lived and acted upon in both public and private arenas. Thus, feminists reject the tendency to offer one set of values to guide interactions in the private and personal realms and another set of values to govern interactions in the public worlds of politics and power. Empathy, compassion, and the loving, healthy, person-oriented values must be valued and affirmed not only in the family and the home but also in the halls where public policy-making, diplomacy, and politics are practiced.

MODES OF MORAL REASONING

Research on moral development and on how people construe moral choices has identified two orientations that reflect significant differences (Gilligan, 1982, April 1982). In a *rights/justice* orientation, morality is conceived as being tied to respect for rules. It is a mode of reasoning that reflects the imagery of hierarchy, a hierarchy of values and a hierarchy of power. It assumes a world comprised of separate individuals whose claims and interests fundamentally conflict and in which infringements on an individual's rights can be controlled or redressed through rational and objective means deducible from logic and rules.

In a *care/response* orientation, morality is conceived contextually and in terms of a network of interpersonal relationships and connection. This mode of reasoning reflects the imagery of a web, a nonhierarchical network of affiliation and mutuality. It assumes a world of interdependence and care among people, a world in which conflicts and injuries can best be responded to by a process of ongoing communication and involvement that considers the needs, interests, and motivations of all involved.

At present, the care/response mode, with its emphasis on contextuality, relationship, and the human consequences of choices and actions, tends to be viewed as representing a lesser stage of moral development—less broadly applicable—than the rights/justice orientation, with its emphasis on standards, rights, and duties (Scharf et al., 1981:413). This tendency to contrast and rank the differing modes of reasoning has limited the moral and conceptual repertoires with which problems are approached in the worlds of government, science, and world power. Devotion to peacekeeping and nonviolent conflict resolution often are dismissed as irrelevant or less important than devotion to the "rules of the game" or abstract notions of rights and responsibilities. Thus, the potential contributions of a care/response orientation to dealing constructively with the major global crises of security, justice, and equity have hardly begun to be tapped (Reardon, 1985: 89–90).

There is a need for a massive infusion of the values associated with the care/response mode of reasoning into a wide range of contexts from which they have been excluded almost entirely. It would be a mistake, however, to try to simply substitute a care/response orientation for one focused on justice and rights. Especially at present, when there are such vast differences in power among people, we are not in a position to trust that the interests of the less powerful will be protected in the absence of rules designed to insure that protection.

Studies by Carol Gilligan suggest that although most people can and do understand and use both modes of reasoning, they tend to focus more on one or the other in confronting moral issues.[5] In her research, the mode of reasoning around which people tended to center was associated with gender. Men were more likely to employ a rights/justice orientation and women were more likely to reflect a care/response orientation, although responses from women were more mixed than those for men. Given the capacities of both men and women to use both modes of moral reasoning, and because there is no reason to believe that differing emphases or priorities in moral reasoning are innate or biological (see Bleier, 1984), we have an opportunity to explore more fully the contributions each can make to resolving moral dilemmas of all kinds.

Thus, the challenge involves searching for a more complete vision of justice and morality, a vision that encompasses concern for process and outcomes, as well as principles and rules, and for feelings and relationships, as well as logic and rationality. We need to labor to find ways of more fully integrating abstract notions of justice and rights with contextual notions of caring and relationship in both public (political) and private (personal) realms.

THE CRIMINAL JUSTICE CONTEXT: THE DILEMMAS OF DEFENSE AND PROTECTION

The criminal justice system provides a clear picture of the challenges ahead. In the criminal justice arena, there is no attempt to disguise the fact that the goal and purpose of the system is power/control. The stated goal is control of crime and criminals, but it is widely recognized that the criminal justice system serves to achieve social control functions more generally. Law is an embodiment of power arrangements: it specifies a set of norms to be followed—an order—and also provides the basis for securing that order coercive force. Coercive force is seen as the ultimate and the most effective mechanism for social defense. And once the order to be protected and preserved is in place, little attention is given to whether the social system to be defended is just or serves human ends.

It is important to bear in mind that penal sanctions, like crimes, are intended harms. "The violent, punishing acts of the state…are of the same genre as the violent acts of individuals. In each instance the acts reflect an attempt to monopolize human interaction to control another person as if he or she were a commodity" (Sullivan, 1980). Those who set themselves up as beyond reproach define *the criminal* as less than fully human. Without such objectification, the routine practice of subjecting human beings to calculated pain infliction, degradation, domination, banishment, and execution clearly would be regarded as intolerable.

Feminist analysis of the war system can be applied to the criminal justice system; the civil war in which we are engaged—the war on crime—is the domestic equivalent of the international war system. One has only to attend any budget hearing at which increased appropriations are being sought for war efforts—whether labeled in defense of criminals, communists, or other enemies—to realize that the rationales and the rhetoric are the same. The ideologies of deterrence and retaliation; the hierarchical, militaristic structures and institutions; the incessant demand for more and greater weaponry, technology, and fighting forces; the sense of urgency and willingness to sacrifice other important interests to the cause; the tendency to dehumanize and objectify those defined as foes; and the belief in coercive force as the most effective means of obtaining security—all of these and other features characteristic of both domestic and international so-called defense systems suggest not just similarity, but identify. People concerned with international peace need to recognize that supporting the "war on crime" is supporting the very establishment, ideology, structures, and morality against which they have been struggling.

We are caught in a truly vicious cycle. Existing structures, institutions, relations, and values create the problems that we then turn around and ask them to solve—or rather, control—using the very same structures, forms, and values, which in turn leads to more problems and greater demand for control. We all want to be protected from those who would violate our houses, our persons, and our general welfare and safety; but the protections we are offered tend to reinforce the divisions and distorted relations in society and to exacerbate the conditions that create much of the need for such protections. The complicated issues surrounding self-defense—whether in an immediate personal sense (as when confronted by a would-be rapist or other attacker), in a penal policy sense (as when deciding how to deal with known assaulters), or in even broader terms (as when confronted by powers and structures that seem bound to destroy us)—vividly illuminate the dilemma.

Sally Miller Gearhart vividly describes the dilemma surrounding trying to work toward the future we dream of while living in the present world by citing a science fiction work, *Rule Golden*, in which Damon Knight wipes violence from the face of the earth by having every agent feel in his/her own body and physical action what she/he delivers. "Kick a dog and feel the boot in your own rib: commit murder and die yourself. Similarly, stroking another in love results in the physical feeling of being lovingly stroked" (Gearhart, 1982:266). Such imagery highlights:

> ...the necessary connection between *empathy* and *nonviolence*, [the fact that] *objectification* is the necessary, if not sufficient component of any violent act. Thinking of myself as separate from another entity makes it possible for me to "do to" that entity things I would not "do to" myself. But if I see all things as myself, or empathize with all other things, then to hurt them is to do damage to me...

> But empaths don't live if the Rule Golden is not in effect. Our world belongs to those who can objectify...and if I want to protect myself from them I learn to objectify and fight back in self-defense. I seem bound to choose between being violent and being victimized. Or I live a schizophrenic existence in which my values are at war with my actions because I must keep a constant shield of protectiveness (objectification) intact over my real self, over my empathy or my identification with others; the longer I keep up the shield the thicker it gets and the less empathetic I am with those around me. So every second of protecting myself from violence makes me objectify more and ensures that I am more and more capable of doing violence myself. I am caught always in the violence-victim trap. (Gearhart, 1982: 266)

Clearly, the standard approach in recent years has been to seek more control—more prisons, more time in confinement for more people, more surveillance and restriction of those not confined. Our willingness to cede greater and greater power to the institutions of social control is a reflection of a desperate society. But "no amount of police, laws, courts, judges, prisons, mental hospitals, psychiatrists, and social workers can create a society with relative harmony. The most institutions can do is impose the appearance of relative harmony..." (French, 1985). To the extent that we acquiesce to continuing escalation of social controls, agents of the state, we reduce correspondingly the prospects for the kind of safety that cannot be achieved through force.

It will not be easy to escape from the cycle in which we find ourselves swirling. Legitimate concerns for safety and protection pose difficult dilemmas for feminists. How can we meet the serious and all-too-real need for protection against violence without violating our peaceful values and aspirations? How can we respond effectively to people who inflict injury and hardship on others without employing the same script and the same means that they do? How can we satisfy immediate needs for safety without elevating those needs over the need to recreate the morality, relations, and conception of justice in our society?

As Marilyn French has put it, "The major problem facing feminists can be easily summed up: there is no clear right way to move" (French, 1985). However, we can expand the conceptual and practical possibilities for change in criminal justice by re-examining our assumptions and expectations.

> [W]e need to begin picturing the new order in our minds, fantasying it, playing with possibilities....An exercise in first stepping into a desired future in imagination, then consciously elaborating the structures needed to maintain it, and finally imagining the future history that would get us there, is a very liberating experience for people who feel trapped in an unyielding present....[S]ocieties move toward what they image. If we remain frozen in the present as we have done since World War II, society stagnates. Imaging the future gives us action ideas for the present. (Boulding, 1987).

EMERGING GUIDES FOR THE FUTURE

Identifying values central to feminist belief does not automatically yield a specific formula for better responding to crime and other conflicts, or for resolving the dilemmas with which we are confronted. Indeed, feminists do not see the best way of moving toward a more positive future as involving primarily analytic and abstract efforts to describe specific structures and processes. Such approaches almost never encompass any explicit element of human relations or affective, emotional content, and few display any cultural dimension (Reardon, 1985: 89–90). "We need theory and feeling as rough guides on which to build a next step and only a next step: flexible, responsive emotional theory capable of adjusting to human needs and desires when these create contradictions" (Reardon, 1985: 89–90).

Feminist values do offer, however, some beginning guides for approaching the future. A key standard to help in making choices is to ask: What kinds of behavior and responses will achieve the goal of the greatest possible harmony? Thus, the task is not to discover how to eradicate crime, but to discover how to behave as befits our values and desires for harmony.

Acceptance of human equality and recognition of the interdependence of all people requires rejection of several current common tendencies. We need to struggle against the tendency toward objectification, of talking and thinking about crime and criminals as if they were distinct entities in themselves. We also need to reject the idea that those who cause injury or harm to others should suffer severance of the common bonds of respect and concern that bind members of a community. We should relinquish the notion that it is acceptable to try to "get rid of" another person, whether through execution, banishment, or caging away people about whom we do not care. We should no longer pretend that conflicts can be resolved by the pounding of a gavel or the locking of a cell door.

A feminist orientation leads to greater awareness of the role and responsibility of society, not just the individual, in development of conflict. This suggests that individuals, groups, and societies need to accept greater responsibility for preventing and reducing those conditions, values, and structures that produce and support violence and strife. Removing the idea of power from its central position is key here, and this requires continually challenging actions, practices, and assumptions that glorify power, control, and domination, as well as developing more felicitous alternatives.

Commitment to the principle of equality means striving for interactions that are participatory, democratic, cooperative, and inclusive, characteristics that are incompatible with hierarchy, stratification, and centralized decision making. Thus, rules, which often are substituted for sensitive, respectful engagement of persons in cooperative problem solving, should not be regarded as sacrosanct. And because people learn from the nature of the processes in which they participate, as well as from the objectives of those processes, we should give greater attention to what the process teaches and how it is experienced.

It may be difficult to imagine how some conflicts could be resolved amicably. Especially while we are in the process of transition, we have to contend with all of the effects that our present structures, values, and stratifications have had on people. Thus, we are likely to reach soon a stage in which we can expect never to feel the need to resort to exercising control over another person. But we can greatly reduce our current reliance on repressive measures, and we should aim or move continually in the direction of imposing fewer coercive restraints on other people.

Indeed, we need to question and rethink the entire basis of the punishment system. Virtually all discussion of change begins and ends with the premise that punishment must take place. All of the existing institutions and structures—the criminal law, the criminal-processing system, the prisons—are assumed. We allow ourselves only to entertain debates about rearrangements and reallocations within those powerfully constraining givens. We swing among the traditional, tired philosophies of punishment as the weight of the inadequacies of one propels us to turn to another. We swing between attempting *to do something with lawbreakers*—changing controlling, or making an example of them—and simply striving *to dole out a just measure of pain*. The sterility of the debates and the disturbing ways they are played out in practice underscore the need to explore alternative visions. We need to step back to reconsider whether or not we should punish, not just to argue about how to punish.

We may remain convinced that something is needed to serve the declaratory function of the criminal law, something that tells us what is not to be done. We may conclude that there is a need for some sort of process that holds people accountable for their wrongful actions. We may not be able to think of ways to completely eliminate restraints on people who have done harmful things. But we should not simply assume that we cannot develop better ways to satisfy these and other important interests as we try to create our desired future.

While we are in the transition process, and where we continue to feel that it is necessary to exercise power over other people, we should honor more completely certain familiar principles that are often stated but seldom fully realized. Resort to the restriction of liberty, whether of movement, of association, or of other personal choices, should be clearly recognized as an evil. Whenever it is argued that it is a necessary evil, there should be a strong, nonroutine burden of establishing such necessity. And where it is accepted that some restriction is demonstrably necessary, every effort should be made to utilize the least drastic means that will satisfy the need established, Thus, we should approach restriction and control of others with trepidation, restraint, caution, and care.

In addition, we should recognize that the more we restrict an individual's chances and choices, the greater is the responsibility we assume for protecting that person and preserving his or her personhood. We should no longer accept the routine deprivations of privacy, healthful surroundings, contacts, and opportunities to exercise choice and preference that we have come to treat as standard concomitants of restriction of liberty. Such deprivations are not only unnecessary but also offensive to our values and destructive to all involved.

These principles make it apparent that we should abandon imprisonment, at least in anything like the way we have come to accept the meaning of that word. There is no excuse for continuing to utilize the dungeons of the past nor for replicating the assumptions, ideology, and values that have created their newer, shinier, more modern brethren, those even now being constructed on an astonishing scale. While tiers of human cages stacked one upon another are the most apparently repugnant form, all institutions erected for the purpose of congregate confinement need to be acknowledged as anachronisms of a less felicitous time.

How should be deal with people who demonstrate that, at least for a time, they cannot live peacefully among us unrestrained? Although the answers to that question are not entirely clear, feminist values suggest that we should move toward conceiving restriction of liberty as having less to do with buildings, structures, and walls and more to do with human contacts and relations. Few if any creatures are dangerous to all other creatures at all times, especially to those with whom they are directly and closely connected on an ongoing basis. Perhaps we can fashion some variant of jury duty and of citizens standing up for one another in the tradition of John Augustus, in which a small group of citizens would be asked to assume responsibility for maintaining one person safely for a period of time. A range of compassionate, constructive, and caring arrangements needs to be created. And we should not allow the most difficult cases to stand in the way of more rapidly evolving, better approaches for the rest.

At the same time, we need to stop thinking about issues related to how best to respond to those who caused harm as if they were totally separate from, or in competition with, issues related to how best to respond to those who have been harmed. There is not a fixed quantity of compassion and care, or even of rights, that will be diminished for those who have been victimized as they are extended to those who victimized them.

Many of these ideas may seem foreign, naive, or beyond our abilities. If they seem foreign, that may be because the ideas of care, community, and mutuality seem foreign. If these dreams for the future seem naive or out of reach, that may be because we have lost confidence in our capacity to choose, to recreate relations, and to realign priorities. It may be tempting to conclude that no efforts in the directions suggested here will be worthwhile, that nothing can be done until everything can be done, that no one can confront crime humanely until everyone is willing to do so. And it is true that we will never approach making such a vision reality if we focus only on issues of criminal justice. Our energies must be focused on the full panoply of global-peace and social-justice issues. But when we turn our attentions to criminal justice, we should choose and act according to the values and aims we seek more generally and not to increase division, alienation, bitterness, and despair. And every day, we should try to act as we believe would be the best way to act— not just in the future, but in the present.

What is advocated here is radical, but hardly novel. It simply echoes themes that have been heard through the ages, if rarely lived fully. We should refuse to return evil with evil. Although we have enemies, we should seek to forgive, reconcile, and heal. We should strive to find within ourselves outrageous love, the kind of love that extends even to those it is easiest to fear and hate. Love frequently is seen as having little relevance outside the personal realm. Yet the power ethic has failed to serve human happiness. To have a harmonious society, we must act in ways designed to increase harmony, not to further fragment, repress, and control. There is no other way. The means and the ends are the same.

NOTES

1. A collection of articles that well exemplifies this approach is assembled in a book designed to provide an update of the report of the National Commission on the Causes and Prevention of Violence, commonly referred to as the Eisenhower Commission after its chair, Milton S. Eisenhower. See *American Violence and Public Policy: An Update of the National Commission on the Causes and Prevention of Violence*, ed. Lynn A. Curtis (New Haven: Yale University Press, 1985).

2. In 1972, there were 196,183 state and federal prisoners. See Mullen et al., *American Prisons and Jails, Vol. I: Summary and Policy Implications of a National Survey* (Washington, D.C.: U.S. Department of Justice, 1980). At year-end 1986, there were 546,659 state and federal prisoners according to the Bureau of Justice *Statistics Bulletin*, "Prisoners in 1986," May 1987. If the average annual growth rate of the 1980s of 8.8 percent continues through 1987, the total will exceed 590,000 state and federal prisoners.

3. These numbers are reported only for males, presumably because men make up most of the correctional population. See "Criminal Justice Newsletter," 16 January 1987, p. 5. It should be noted, however, that the number of women in state prisons has more than doubled since 1981, up to 26,610 from 11,212 in 1981; and the rate of growth in the population of female prisoners has been faster in each of those years than that of male prisoners. See Peter Applebome, "Women in U.S. Prisons: Fast-Rising Population," *New York Times*, 15 June 1981.

4. Given that nearly 87 percent of the adult correctional population was male and 34 percent was black, an estimated 850,000 adult black men were under correctional control at year-end 1985 according to the Bureau of Justice *Statistics Bulletin*, "Probation and Parole 1985," January 1987. The Census Bureau estimates that there were 8,280,000 black adult male residents in the United States at midyear 1985. See U.S. Bureau of the Census, *Estimates of the Population of the United States, by Age, Sex, and Race: 1980 to 1986*, Current Population Reports, Population Estimates and Projections, ser. P-25, no. 1000, p. 24. At year-end 1985, there were approximately 1,617,492 white adult males under some form of correctional control, out of approximately 72,780,000 white adult male residents in the United States, representing a correctional control rate for white adult males of about 1 in 45. Neither the Bureau

of Justice nor the Census Bureau data report separate figures for Hispanics or other specific ethnic or racial groups.

5. This discussion is based on an oral presentation by Carol Gilligan at the Community College of Philadelphia in April 1984. See also other Gilligan works cited in this article.

REFERENCES

BLEIER, RUTH. (1984). *Science and Gender: A Critique of Biology and its Theories on Women*, New York: Pergamon Press.

BOULDING, ELISE. (1987). "Warriors and Saints: Dilemmas in the History of Men, Women, and War." Paper presented at the International Symposium on Women and the Military System, Siuntio Baths, Finland, 22–25 January. On file with author.

BRYNE, JAMES M. (1986). "The Control Controversy: A Preliminary Examination of Intensive Probation Supervision Programs in the United States." *Federal Probation 50*: 9.

Bureau of Justice. (1986). "Prisoners in 1985." *Statistics Bulletin* (June).

_____. (1986). "Prisoners in 1986." *Corrections Compendium*, November–December 1986.

FRENCH, MARILYN. (1985). *Beyond Power: On Women, Men and Morals*. New York: Summit Books.

GEARHART, SALLY MILLER. (1982). "The Future—if There Is One—Is Female." in Pam McAllister (Ed.), *Reweaving the Web of Life: Feminism and Nonviolence*. Philadelphia: New Society Pub.

GILLIGAN, CAROL. (1982). *In a Different Voice: Psychological Theory and Women's Development*. Cambridge, Mass.: Harvard University Press.

_____. (1982). "New Maps of Development: New Visions of Maturity." *American Journal of Orthopsychiatry* (April).

Lifelines. Newsletter of the National Coalition Against the Death Penalty. January–February 1987, p. 8.

PIERCE, NEAL. (1987). "Prisons Are Proving Costly to the States." *The Philadelphia Inquirer*, p. 11a.

REARDON, Betty A. (1985). *Sexism and the War System*. New York: Teachers College Press, Columbia University.

SCHARF, PETER, LAWRENCE KOHLBERG, and JOSEPH HICKEY. (1981). "Ideology and Correction Intervention: The Creation of a Just Prison Community." In Peter C. Kratcoski (Ed.), *Correctional Counseling and Treatment*. Monterey, Calif.: Duxbury.

SULLIVAN, DENNIS. (1980). *The Mast of Love: Corrections in America (Toward a Mutual Aid Alternative)*. Port Washington, N.Y.: Kennikat Press.

WOESTENDIEK, JOHN. (1987). "An Influx of Hispanics is Challenging the Prisons." *The Philadelphia Inquirer*, p. 1a.

YOST, PETE. (1987). "Electronic Alternative to Prison is in 20 States." *The Philadelphia Inquirer*, p. 5a.

QUESTIONS FOR DISCUSSION

1. The author identifies two types of proposals for changes in policies targeted at crime and criminal justice. List these two types of proposals. What are the weaknesses of these proposals?

2. How do the central values of feminism offer a new way of approaching public policy and peacemaking? Provide examples to support your answer.

3. List and discuss the modes of "moral reasoning."

4. Harris says that "in criminal justice…the goal and purpose of the system is power/control." Cite specific examples that the author provides to support this claim.

5. What "emerging guides" does the author suggest for the future regarding the contributions of a feminist orientation and obtaining a more peaceful society? Provide examples to support your answer.

28

CONFRONTING CRIME
LOOKING TOWARD THE TWENTY-FIRST CENTURY

Elliott Currie

■ ■

We have reached what may be an important turning point in the development of criminological thought and of social policy toward crime. The "conservative revolution" in criminology has lost considerable credibility, along with the entire set of minimalist strategies toward the disadvantaged that dominated social policy throughout much of the recent past. A space has opened for the development of a "social environmental" or "human-ecological" approach to crime, which combines a variety of interventions on the individual and family level with an array of broader policies aimed at controlling the social and economic forces that place individuals, families, and communities at risk in the first place.

In this paper I'd like to talk about an agenda for social policy toward crime as we move toward the twenty-first century. I'm aware that this is a very big order, and I hasten to stress that these remarks make no pretense of being definitive; my aim is only to help spark what I hope will become a fruitful and continuing debate. But I think it's important to step back periodically and ask where we have been and where we want to go. I believe that forward look is especially important now, for unless I'm greatly mistaken, we have reached a turning point in our approach to crime in the United States. We are poised uneasily at the end of one criminological era and the beginning of a new one, and it will be up to us to define just what the new one will look like.

The last such turning point took place around the beginning of the 1970s with the emergence of what we could fairly call the "conservative" revolution in criminology. (I use "conservative" here not in the narrow political sense, but in a broader philosophical one). The conservative revolution in criminology was only one facet of a much broader transformation in American social thought and policy generally—one with particular significance for the interconnected problems of the inner cities. It had a major impact on the way in which we approached crime in the United States, both in theory and in practice. It dethroned social explanations of the causes of crime, cast the idea of rehabilitating offenders into the category of the antique and faintly disreputable, relegated to the margins of public

Elliott Currie. "Confronting Crime: Looking Toward the Twenty-First Century." *Justice Quarterly* 6:(1): 5–25. Reprinted with permission of the Academy of Criminal Justice Sciences.

disclosure the idea that social programs might help prevent crime, and simultaneously elevated some combination of deterrence and incapacitation to a central, even a commanding place in anticrime policy.

But I think that this revolution has nearly run its course. I'm not suggesting that there's no life in it at all; many of its basic themes are very much alive in some quarters, not least in the recent presidential campaign. But I believe that the conservative revolution in criminology has lost much of its *intellectual* hegemony—its power to persuade and to convince and, above all, its credibility as a guiding vision for the future. In particular, there is no longer much compelling intellectual justification for its two main and intertwined themes: the wholesale rejection of the usefulness of social intervention to prevent crime and delinquency, and the expanded use of the criminal justice system to contain the consequences of social and economic neglect and disarray.

The reason for this decline is simple: the conservative model has run up against stubborn reality. It has suffered its own version of what the British criminologist Jock Young (1988: 138–141) calls the "etiological crisis," which undercut the outlook that dominated American criminology until the 1970s; the view that, with desperate simplification, I've called "liberal criminology" (Currie, 1985). By "etiological crisis" Young means that the liberal view of the causes of crime, and of appropriate remedies, was undermined by the apparent paradox that crime rates rose just when a number of things which (according to this view) ought to have reduced crime were improving substantially, at least on paper and in the aggregate. Incomes were rising; unemployment (on the national level) was falling; and we were beginning to devote significant governmental attention to social programs for the education and training of the disadvantaged. If the liberal view had been correct, conservatives argued gleefully, the crime rate should have fallen; that it did not fall opened the door to a view that blamed the rise in crime primarily on the leniency of the criminal justice system (and to a lesser extent the family and the schools) while arguing that liberal programs were at best irrelevant and at worst part of the deepening culture of permissiveness and indulgence that bred crime.

But the conservative revolution began likewise to sputter in its tracks in the mid-1980s, when it became apparent to all but the most ideologically stalwart that the model wasn't working. Despite the huge increases in incarceration in the 1970s and 1980s, the rate of criminal violence remained devastatingly high, and increased in some places; whole communities were shredded and turned nightmarish by drugs and gang violence. After all, this was one of the largest experiments in social engineering ever undertaken in the United States (though it was rarely acknowledged as such); thus its failure was an event of considerable moment. The prison population tripled nationally from the early 1970s to the present—a rate of increase that far outstripped the crime rate itself (Irwin and Austin, 1987). Yet no one needs to be reminded of the tragic, sometimes nearly incomprehensible social disintegration and violence that still confront us in the streets and homes of so many of our cities.

Jock Young calls the resulting crisis in the credibility of the conservative model the "crisis of penality." Whatever we choose to call it, it is real, and it is not confined within the narrow perimeter of public policy toward crime and criminal justice. The twilight of the conservative model of crime is only one aspect of what the conservative columnist George Will (1988) calls the "dusk" of the conservative era.

I think we should make allowances here for exaggeration. Surely there is a great deal of political steam left in the conservative revolution, and its legacy in social policy will doubtless be with us for some time. But it's certainly true that the continuing crisis in urban America has begun to undercut the intellectual foundations of the entire range of conservative social policies toward those "at risk" that emerged during the 1970s and flowered during the 1980s. We might regard this set of strategies as the social equivalent of the "let it burn" policy of the U.S. National Park Service, as practiced at Yellowstone Park and elsewhere. We withdrew services and public support from the most distressed communities and the highest-risk families and individuals in America, in the vague expectation that this would free the forces of the market economy to work their supposed magic. But it has now become widely apparent, across a broad spectrum of informed opinion, that this course of action hasn't, after all, revitalized the cities or transformed and motivated the urban underclass. On the contrary, it has exacerbated the social disintegration of the cities, and in the process it has produced another generation of increasingly damaged and alienated young people. In short, it has accelerated a human-ecological disaster of almost unprecedented proportions. Our cities are in a terrible mess; and it is no longer possible to hide that fact, or to blame it credibly on the leniency of our justice system or on the demoralizing largesse of an overactive government.

These hard realities have not been lost on those whose job it is to govern the cities or to do business in them. They have rocked the intellectual and cultural foundations of the minimalist model of the 1970s and early 1980s; and they have ushered in a period in which the conventional wisdom, the moral and conceptual language in which these issues are discussed, has begun to shift in important ways. So far this shift has taken place mainly on the symbolic level, without an accompanying commitment of resources to back it up; but that doesn't mean that it's unimportant.

Thus *Business Week* magazine, in a major cover story on what it calls the crisis of "human capital" in America, gently rebukes the neglectful social policies toward the disadvantaged of the past eight years, and warns that "the U.S. may now be entering an era when neglect of the bottom half of society begins to threaten the welfare of the entire nation" (1988:103). The magazines goes on to propose substantially increased public spending for such services as preschool education and prenatal care, as well as intensive job training for the disadvantaged young.

Nor is this an isolated statement. A recent issue of *U.S. News and World Report* (1988)—like *Business Week*, a magazine not noted previously for its bleeding-heart sympathies—headlined its cover story "Save the Children" and chided government for offering "too many promises, too little help." Indeed, a more activist social policy—particularly toward children and families—has emerged suddenly as something close to a "motherhood" issue, at least on the level of political rhetoric. Both presidential candidates came out for social programs to benefit children and families: George Bush called on the nation to "invest in children," and the Republican party platform called for "large" increases in funding for Head Start. Similarly, the well-known corporate policy organization, the Committee for Economic Development (1986), urges billions of dollars in new funding for Head Start, child health care, and other active public policies for high-risk children. As the economic columnist Robert Samuelson (1988) notes, "a crude consensus" has emerged; its message is that "government should do more." Even some noted criminologists of a decid-edly conservative bent, who in earlier incarnations ridiculed those colleagues who imagined that government could do much of anything about the conditions affecting families and children, can now be heard to suggest that limited experiments with parenting or Head Start-type programs just might be worth exploring (Wilson, 1988).

Skepticism about the depth of some of these claims is in order, especially those claims made in the heat of a presidential election campaign. Nevertheless, I believe that this shift is both real and encouraging. The climate was very different as recently as the early 1980s. If you dared to suggest in those days that early childhood education or family-support programs (much less a serious employment and training policy) might play a significant role in reducing crime and delinquency, or if you hinted that we might be able to do something constructive with young offenders in the juvenile justice system so that their life chances were slightly better when they left the system than when they entered it, you were likely to be ignored or dismissed as a naive if well-meaning peddler of the stale and discredited ideas of the 1960s. In vain you might protest that pinning historical labels on these efforts was far less important than the growing evidence that some of them *worked*.

In those days such was the power of the 1970s model that mere evidence didn't stand much of a chance. (As John Kenneth Galbraith once wrote, it is far more comforting to have a firm anchor in nonsense than to put out upon the troubled seas of thought ([1970: 145]). Today, however, at the close of the 1980s, the short-lived conventional wisdom of that era—that "nothing works," that all social intervention is futile or counterproductive—begins to seem like ancient history, or a bad dream.

To sum up, I believe that a new intellectual and political space has been forced open by the widespread and often frightening failures of the neglectful strategies that came before. In this space, a new criminological vision and a new public policy toward crime may take root, even flower. Having said that, however, I'm not certain what exactly will emerge to fill that space. There is a spectrum of possibilities, not all of them pleasant.

I

One troubling possibility is that we might go backward. We might adopt the view that the failure of our recent strategies toward crime and toward the more general problems of those "at risk" tells us that the problems are much more intractable than we had supposed—so intractable that it isn't worth the effort to do anything but contain them. In turn, we might locate the source of this intractability in the biological insufficiencies or cultural inferiorities of those who continue to fail to "make it" into the increasingly elusive mainstream of American society. We might use that explanation to justify what would amount to urban triage: an even greater withdrawal of resources from the most problematic communities and a *de facto* policy of allowing them to spiral downward still further. I don't think that will happen; I think the potential social costs are too great and too widely understood. But I don't think it's inappropriately alarmist to suggest it as a possibility. After all, it is not all that far from the strategy of omission that we have followed for some years.

More likely, I think, is a more positive and more humane approach that simply doesn't go far enough. This is what troubles me about the otherwise encouraging recent revival of interest in early intervention strategies with children and families. Again, I can't emphasize too often that I think this revival is positive and is moving in the right direction. But sometimes it seems to place too many expectations on approaches to individual and family problems which do not confront the larger social and economic context in which those problems originate. It also shares a certain quintessentially American tendency to over-promise results on essentially educational solutions to social problems. I think that the results of such programs as the Perry Preschool project (Beruetta-Clement, Schweinhart, Barnett, and Weikart, 1987) are inspiring, but they are also partial.

Similar concerns have been voiced recently by careful students and practitioners of early intervention (Woodhead, 1988, Zigler, 1987). As the British scholar Martin Woodhead has written, "Expectations are becoming narrowly focused on the apparent power of early intervention to tackle social problems single-handedly"; but since "such expectations are unlikely to be realized in practice," the long-term result could be to "undermine public sympathies toward early childhood programs" (1988: 452). A preschool on every ghetto corner won't overcome the structural disintegration of the surrounding communities—a disintegration whose sources lie well beyond the disadvantaged child and family, beyond the local community, and beyond the reach of the school, and which may well intensify in the coming decades. I think we must face squarely the unhappy fact that the level of social devastation in many American communities that have been affected most seriously by the destruction of solid adult labor markets, the retreat of preventive social services, and the flood of hard drugs is now beyond anything we've ever seen in this country; and that it will require responses of a breadth and depth we have not yet contemplated seriously in the United States. We will not address these problems effectively on the cheap, simply by trying to fix up poor kids. That's a very important part of what we need to do, but it's only a part.

II

I suggest that the approach we need toward crime in the coming decades might be called "social-environmental"—or, to resurrect an older term, "human-ecological." But that I mean a strategy which includes interventions on the level of individuals and families "at risk," but also moves beyond that level to exert social control over those larger forces which now are increasingly undermining communities and placing families at risk in the first place. Those forces are aggravating an already fundamental imbalance in our society that has enormous consequences for crime and for much else; these consequences, I believe, are confirmed increasingly by an accumulating body of empirical research. Such an approach, moreover, should raise questions not simply about *what* forces in our society need controlling, but also about *who* may decide and who is held responsible for the consequences of those decisions. If we think of the era of liberal criminology as the first stage of recent criminological thinking and consider the conservative revolution as the second, such a social-environmental vision can serve as the bedrock for a third, more sophisticated stage which both builds upon and transcends the stages that came before.

For the present, let me simply sketch out a few components of such a strategy which I believe to be most crucial. Some of these elements involve interventions on the level of families and high-risk individuals; others entail addressing more complex and longer-range issues of community stability, of political economy, and even of culture. The list is meant to be illustrative, not exhaustive; I want simply to note, in broad brush-strokes, what I think ought to be some guiding themes of a twenty-first century crime policy.

First, we should expand high-quality, intensive *early education* along the model of Head Start and the Perry Preschool project. I've just argued that these programs shouldn't be viewed as panaceas, but they do make a difference (Beruetta-Clement, et al., 1987). Indeed there is some evidence that these programs have a strong positive effect on the psychological well-being and social functioning of *parents* as well as of children (Parker, Piotrowski, and Peay, 1987). Yet the proportion of eligible children served by such programs is now about 18 percent (*Business Week*, 1988), and not all of those programs are good ones. I've heard no credible intellectual or fiscal argument against increasing that proportion and simultaneously raising the quality of existing programs. There is an intriguing debate about *how* early educational intervention works (Woodhead, 198), but there is little question that these programs, done properly, produce results on a variety of crucial measures of development and behavior. They're also cost-efficient. It's difficult to see how we could lose by putting more resources into them.

Second, we should expand *health and mental health services* for high-risk children and youth and for their parents, including high-quality prenatal and postnatal care. We should do this anyway, but there's reason to believe that it can be a meaningful part of a comprehensive, "ecological" strategy against crime and delinquency. The evidence is complex, but highly suggestive, that such conditions as early childhood traumas of the central nervous system, early severe psychiatric problems, and perhaps low birth weight may be implicated in some kinds of delinquency, including some of the most troubling and most destructive. (See especially the work of Dorothy O. Lewis and her colleagues [1985, 1988].) The evidence also suggests that many—perhaps most—children who most need early and intensive help to address these problems aren't getting it, with the predictable result that the problems are worked out on the bodies of other people. In their study of 14 juveniles condemned to death in the United States for especially brutal crimes, Dorothy Lewis and her colleagues conclude that these children typically are "multiply handicapped": they "tend to have suffered serious CNS injuries, or have suffered since early childhood from a multiplicity of psychotic symptoms, and to have been physically and sexually abused." At the same time, "the clinical and legal services necessary to try to uncover these vulnerabilities are *routinely unavailable* to this population of juveniles" (1988: 587, 598; emphasis added)—not to mention the services necessary even to begin to treat them.

Third, in a related vein, we need a much greater commitment to *family support programs*, especially real rather than rhetorical support for comprehensive programs against child abuse and domestic violence. The debate over the family's role in crime and delinquency has been shaped, even more strongly than most criminological issues, by the shifting ideological currents of recent years. The liberal criminology of the 1950s and 1960s tended to avoid acknowledging the family's importance as a crucible of character formation and hence as a critical area for the development of delinquency—or of "prosocial" behavior.

The conservative criminology of the 1970s and 1980s revived interest in the family's role in developing character and competence, but also detached the family and its functioning from the social and economic forces that shaped it powerfully. In a third stage, social-environmental criminology for the coming century must recognize that the family is both a crucial shaping force and one that is shaped in turn by forces far larger than itself. Accordingly we will need both a genuinely pro-family economic policy at the national level (about which more below) and far greater attention to interventions at the level of individual families.

On the latter level, I'd like to see violence in the home become the kind of political issue in the twenty-first century that crime in the streets has been in the last third of the twentieth. In *Confronting Crime* (1985), I pointed to some encouraging improvements in child-rearing skills resulting from the federally funded family-resource programs in the 1970s; to these I'd add encouraging results from innovative interventions with child-abusing families (Wolfe, 1987).

Once again, however, if the emerging empirical evidence on what we *could* do is encouraging, the level of implementation is not. In the case of child abuse in particular, it is pitifully weak: we are quite simply allowing a massive and at least partly preventable tragedy to play itself out in soul-shattering ways, on children whose other social and economic disadvantages render them both vulnerable and largely invisible. This is not only a major crime in itself, but one which tends disturbingly often to perpetuate itself as many abused children become abusive parents in their turn (Gelles and Straus, 1988). There is nothing inevitable about that progression, as the developmental psychologists Joan Kaufman and Edward Zigler (1987) remind us, but even their own best estimate suggests that about one-third of severely abused children are likely to become severely abusive parents—a rate six times that of the rest of the population (1987: 190).

All of these suggestions are aimed at preventing delinquency and crime before they happen, but we also need to take a fourth step: to reassert the importance of doing something constructive with people after they've broken the law. This common-sense idea fell out of favor, almost into oblivion, in the 1970s, despite some evidence for a more encouraging view (Cullen and Gilbert, 1982; Gendreau and Ross, 1987). But no one today can deny seriously that we could be doing much more than we have done.

On the most immediate level, we can begin to deliver more consistently the basic services that many young offenders often need. Within the juvenile justice system in particular, we should insist finally that the time when young offenders are under our care be used more constructively. We ought to consider that time as a resource, which we may use profitably to ensure that they leave a little smarter, a little healthier, a little more sober than they came in. We ought to establish a higher floor of expectations about what institutions for the young should accomplish. For now I'm not talking about remaking personalities, but simply about improving basic skills and competencies. This is particularly important in view of what some research suggests about the links between low skills and poor verbal abilities and serious delinquency (Berlin and Sum, 1988; Denno, 1986). We know how to do these things; we should do them more seriously and more consistently, so that by the year 2000 no young person is languishing idle and illiterate in any juvenile institution in the country.

Finally, we need a commitment (again, real rather than rhetorical) to accessible, non-punitive drug abuse treatment for those who need it. Like our approach to the family, our views about hard drugs have been shaped deeply, and for the most part unfortunately, by broader ideological agendas rather than by a levelheaded reading of the evidence. Liberal criminology often failed to take the drug problem seriously; occasionally, it found more to worry about in the public distress over drug abuse than in the effects of hard drugs on communities and individuals—particularly the disadvantaged, who were (and are) the chief victims of the spread of hard drugs. Conservatives put most of their money on strategies—especially interdiction and harsh mandatory sentencing—that did not work, probably cannot work, and certainly would not work in the face of the simultaneous depletion of antidrug budgets by a conservative administration.

Once again, however, things have begun to show some improvement—at least on the level of political awareness. After several years of empty rhetoric about warring on drugs, national legislation has shown a moderately encouraging tilt away from overreliance on interdiction, deterrence, and incapacitation and toward moderately serious attention to treatment and prevention. That shift, however, will remain merely symbolic without a serious commitment of funds to back it up.

Beyond the problem of financing is a deeper concern. We must take great care that in the rush to leap on the political bandwagon we do not simply throw new money at the existing treatment system. I've worked in that system, and I think we must insist that it be reformed as well as supported. We must ensure that treatment is intensive and of high quality; it must be accompanied by serious outreach to hard-to-reach abusers, by aftercare that supports abusers after they leave treatment, by advocacy in the community for their broader needs with respect to housing, health care, and employment. We've learned that it's not that hard to get people off drugs; what's hard is to *keep* them off, and that tougher goal must be a main objective of twenty-first-century drug policy.

The accumulating evidence suggests that all of these steps can be important in reducing crime and delinquency if they are taken with the necessary seriousness and intensity. They also have many other positive outcomes, which we ought to support in any case. But it will take a long, hard political effort to get the bold, creative commitment of public resources that we need in order to do any of these things well. It's easy to be abstractly in favor of more and better drug treatment or preschool education or mental health services for children; it's harder to insist that we ought to *pay* for them as well. Nevertheless, I'm convinced that the time is right for making a strong effort to develop the political momentum to put programs that we know can be effective into practice; we should seize it. Speaking very personally for a moment, I am sick of the recurrent frustration of seeing us lock up kids who have remediable problems which we know how to address—locking them up because we have no place else to put them. I'm sick of seeing whole communities besieged by drug abusers who can't find treatment. I'm sick of looking again and again at the histories of violent kids and predictably finding abusive families that we might have been able to help.

III

But we must also work on the longer-range and more complex issues without which all of these interventions on the level of families and individuals will be frustrated and compromised; issues that will become increasingly crucial in view of the economic and demographic changes that we may expect in the next century. By that time, we should finally have come to grips with the simple (but, for some, difficult-to-grasp) fact that the level of crime is a social-structural problem. It is not by accident that the United States has the highest rates of serious crime in the developed world while standing out among other industrialized societies on a host of other troubling measures: child poverty, infant mortality, inadequate public services, economic inequality. It's no exaggeration to say that we've reached a point where the future of civilized life in the cities has been imperiled by generations of social neglect and economic havoc. A great many chickens have come home to roost, and at this late hour it will be extraordinarily difficult to reverse the disintegration we've allowed to continue for so many decades.

That is only the bad news, however, The good news is that at least we've begun—although haltingly and so far not very successfully—to address some of these issues on the level of national legislation. But the tentativeness of that legislation, and the bitterness with which it is resisted, tell us how far we have to go. Here are four goals for the twenty-first century. All of them are important for many reasons, not least because they have the potential to alter the context of individual and family development in ways that promise to diminish criminality.

First, we must move to *reduce inequality and social impoverishment.*

We know that the gap between affluent and poor has been increasing in the United Sates, in part because of widening differences in earnings among people who work (Currie, Dunn, and Fogarty, 1988; Harrison, Tilly, and Bluestone, 1986). And the bare income figures understate the growth in inequality because they mask the bifurcation of social services that also is taking place—the withdrawal of the public sector from the lower 30 percent or so of the population, especially the young. We need to reverse this trend, not least because the evidence continues to grow, from both crossnational and domestic studies, that violent crime is generated by extremes of inequality, especially when coupled with excessive mobility and the fragmentation of community and family life (Avison and Loring, 1986; Brownfield, 1986). Granted, reducing inequality is a tall order, but it's not impossible. Many other nations have done it. And though we can't simply transfer their approaches to our very different social and historical context, we can learn much from their experience that is vital to our own efforts to create a more just and more secure society.

The deliberate reduction of social inequality therefore, ought to be one of the primary goals of social policy in the twenty-first century. In this country, we've barely begun to address this issue. Witness the current, fiercely fought legislative battle over efforts to restore some of the value of the minimum wage, which has fallen almost 30 percent in real terms since the early 1980s. We need to continue to press for a decent floor on earnings, but we also need to do much more: ultimately to move toward what in Scandinavia is called a "solidaristic" wage policy (Rehn, 1985)—one that raises the floor not merely from $3.35 to $4.55 an hour but enough to ensure every working adult the means to a dignified livelihood—and enough to narrow the demoralizing and criminogenic abyss between affluent and poor. Such a move should include an explicit effort—as it has in Sweden, for example—to raise women's earnings closer to those of men, in order to reduce the now-intolerable deprivations and stresses inflicted on families headed by single women in the United States.

Second, and closely related to the reduction of inequality and deprivation, we should move toward an *active labor market policy* aimed at upgrading the work available to disadvantaged Americans. I think that the evidence gives strong support for a link between poor jobs—unstable, dead-end, with low wages—and many kinds of crime. And I believe that the effects tend to accumulate when several generations remain trapped with few opportunities beyond those jobs, partly because of long-term, corrosive effects on the mediating institutions of family and community (Currie, 1985; Sviridoff and McElroy, 1985). That being the case, it's difficult to be sanguine about the much-touted high rate of job creation in recent years in the United States; it's painfully clear that increasing proportions of those jobs are low-paying (Bluestone and Harrison, 1987) and often part-time (Levitan and Conway, 1988). This kind of economic "growth" can do little or nothing to address the roots of social pathology among those now disadvantaged by low earnings and by the shattering of links to more sustaining and more stable livelihoods.

As we move toward the next century, we must acknowledge—as some European countries have long done—that a more rewarding structure of employment does not flow automatically from the operation of the private market, but requires strategic, active intervention by government. In the United States, the most critical need is for public supported, community-oriented job creation, particularly in providing essential public services to disadvantaged communities. Among other things, a full-scale policy to create those jobs can help us accomplish some of the key strategies I've just suggested—early education, childhood mental health services, family support programs, drug treatment for all who require it. *Without* a public policy to create community-sustaining jobs, on the other hand, it's hard to see how we could put those expanded services in place. With such a policy, we could contribute to the rebuilding of a viable economic infrastructure in "high-risk" communities; and simultaneously, we could deliver the basic reparative and socializing services without which neither social peace nor economic development in those communities will be possible.

Let me emphasize again that this task is much more difficult and more long-term than most criminologists have been willing to acknowledge. Liberal criminologists have sometimes seemed to imply that simply reflating the national economy to bring down the overall unemployment rate or launching another summer job program for ghetto kids will do the trick. It would be nice if that were so, but the evidence tells us that the problems are much deeper. Again, I can't stress too often that we are dealing now with several generations of the accumulated effects of long-term economic deprivation and social impoverishment on family and personality. I believe that there is still time to reverse those effects, but no one should underestimate how hard it will be. Conservatives, for their part, consistently have obscured the importance of the connection between inadequate labor markets and crime, in part by focusing too narrowly on the immediate effects of job loss on crime (where evidence is relatively weak) and ignoring the long-term effects of persistent labor-market disadvantage (where evidence is quite strong). By now, however, all of us should have learned that we can't have it both ways: we can't simultaneously have orderly and secure communities *and* an economy that routinely condemns some people to deepening economic insecurity, social impoverishment, and communal disruption while visibly enriching others.

Third, we should work toward a genuinely *supportive national family policy*.

We talk a great deal about this in the United States: nobody is against the family and nobody would be caught dead acknowledging that the economic and social policies they favor are *bad* for families and children. But that consensus is largely superficial, and it masks the ongoing disaster that has afflicted families, especially in the bottom 30 percent or so of the income distribution (Children's Defense Fund, 1988). As things stand now, we allow a large and perhaps growing segment of American families to remain at the mercy of an essentially destabilizing and destructive economic and social environment. I've just argued that we should put more resources into supportive programs for high-risk children and families, but if we make no simultaneous effort to control the forces that wreck families in the first place, we'll be forever stuck at the level of picking up the pieces.

In particular, as we move toward the next century, we should finally become serious about adapting the nature of work to the imperatives of family life. The United States is one of the few remaining industrialized countries that doesn't officially recognize the human, social, and even economic value of freeing time for working parents to spend with their families (Hopper and Zigler, 1988). Our traditional practice has been to squeeze every minute of paid working time out of parents in the name of private economic gain and to scream bloody murder that the rather innocuous idea that private businesses have some responsibility for this aspect of their employees' welfare. Witness the fate of our stunningly timid first effort at national legislation in this direction: the Dodd Bill, which would mandate companies to provide parents with up to 10 weeks of *unpaid* leave over two years, at the birth of a child or in the event of a child's illness (some European countries mandate a *paid* leave of up to several *months*). That bill was filibustered to temporary death in the Senate, a casualty of the view (promoted by some of the business community) that it represented unwarranted interference by government in the private economy.

The reality, of course, is that our lack of a humane national policy concerning family and work—a lack which distinguishes us from virtually every other industrialized society— amounts to a massive subsidy to private business. It requires the rest of us to pay for the social costs of the resulting strains on families and for the consequences of these strains for physical and mental health, domestic violence, and delinquency. We need to push for family leaves, and more broadly, for the idea that Americans who work have a fundamental right to sufficient family time, in order to make possible (among other things) the attentive and unharried care of the young.

Fourth, just as we should move toward assuming greater responsibility for the conditions affecting the stability and functioning of families, so we need to begin assuming greater *responsibility for the economic and social stability of local communities*. One of the great (through sometimes subtle) social disasters of the past 30 years is the extent to which the often sudden and capricious movement of capital and employment opportunities has forced families to move in order to chase jobs and income. This process has deepened and accelerated in the face of intensified international economic competition in the past several years, and has increasingly fractured the stability and the sustaining power of families and communities across the country. This means (among other things) that often there is no larger network of people available to be there when parents cannot be, to take on some of the burden of the care and supervision of the young.

This is an important, and I think deepening, change in the fundamental character of the local community in America. Sociologists have long stressed the importance of local, "informal" institutions in providing the dense network of supports and controls that can help prevent delinquency and crime, especially in communities suffering other economic disadvantages (Smith and Jarjoura, 1988). But those institutions have been eroded steadily through economic decisions made, most often, outside the community and without reference to its needs. Our first very tentative national legislation to address this issue, the provision for notification of plant closing in the recent trade bill, was initially voted by President Reagan after passing both houses of Congress. Yet, like 10 weeks of unpaid leave or a restoration of a minimum wage, it's only a single step toward recognition of the larger principle that we need to place on the national agenda: in this case, making the stability of local communities, and thereby their capacity to serve as nurturing settings for the young, a central consideration in economic decision making.

IV

Finally, a *research* agenda accompanies these policies. Without presuming to dictate what criminologist ought to study, let me offer some brief and necessarily subjective thoughts about priorities for research in the coming years. The broad emphases of criminological research, like those of criminal justice policy, are shaped in part by the subtle pressures of the dominant social attitudes of their time. In the era of the conservative ascendancy in criminology, the research balance was tipped heavily toward the issues of deterrence and incapacitation—pro or con. This research emphasis was prompted in part by an underlying pessimism—ungrounded in hard empirical evidence—about the possibility of doing anything *else* to prevent crime, either on the level of changing individual offenders or of altering the criminogenic character of the communities from which they came. We learned a great deal from that outpouring of research, much of it of enduring value, but probably by now it has probably reached a point of diminishing returns. We need a less constrained agenda for research in the coming decades: an agenda that shifts the balance toward clarifying what we might do rather than assuming at the outset that we can do very little. I see at least three priorities within that agenda, all of which are implicit in the suggestions I've just made for social policy.

First, we need much more careful research into what works with individuals "at risk." We've made an important beginning in this regard in the last several years; by now the accumulating evidence should have banished the last vestiges of the simplistic idea that nothing works. But at the same time, there have been so few solidly designed and strongly implemented efforts to intervene with high-risk people that we've barely begun to test the possibilities. There has been considerable interest of late in launching yet further studies to track the careers of children longitudinally in order to see who goes wrong. I'm more interested in developing strong programs with sufficient resources and staff to insure "therapeutic integrity" (Gendreau and Ross, 1987) designed to keep children from going wrong to begin with and to help steer them toward a more contributive life if they break the law. We should then evaluate these programs thoroughly and creatively, and translate the results of that evaluation into ongoing improvements in the programs in order to ensure that we build on the lessons learned.

Second, and in a similar vein, we need to learn more about how to create comprehensive preventive strategies for "high-risk" *communities*. We're beginning to learn something about which programs show the most promise in regenerating severely disadvantaged neighborhoods (Curtis, 1987). Once again, however, it's obviously difficult to assess the effectiveness of community-based programs unless they are implemented with enough depth and continuity to make real evaluation possible; and that, in turn, requires a level of resources that has rarely been available in the past 15 years of minimalist social policy. Therefore a key research priority for the next decades should be the development of comprehensive community prevention programs of sufficient resource intensity and staying power to do what they set out to do, and, hence, to be capable of being evaluated meaningfully, and, given encouraging results, to be replicated.

Third, we have unduly neglected what ought to be one of our most urgent research concerns: understanding more about why some societies have low or relatively low crime rates while others, including our own, suffer such pervasive violence. One of the more curious products of criminology's recent conservative past was the idea that crime is virtually the same in all societies, or that it is more important to learn what is common in the experience of crime among the world's societies than to learn what is different. Yet the vast differences in serious crime—especially violent crime—among different societies are both inescapable and potentially enormously illuminating. And though there have been some attempts, my own included (Currie, 1985; cf. Clinard, 1978), to explore the roots of those glaring differences, much more remains to be done. Learning more about how some societies manage to avoid the extremes of violence that wrack us in the United States is critical if we want to move toward a more fruitful anticrime policy and a more secure, more humane society.

V

There is much more to be said. I've said nothing, for instance, about a serious housing policy to begin to cope with the situation of the homeless, especially homeless children, who could become a criminological time bomb in the next decades. I haven't talked much about the schools. Still, even this much amounts to a very tall order, and it engages many issues that are generally considered far beyond the customary boundaries of criminology. But that's just the point. A social policy toward crime and delinquency that has even a prayer of meeting the social and economic challenges of the next century must transcend the disciplinary and bureaucratic fragmentation that now characterizes our approach to crime, even at best. And it must begin to take seriously what most of us know already: that in human societies, as in the natural environment, things are connected to each other. What we do (or don't do) in the realm of economic policy in particular has a profound impact on the basic social institutions through which individuals are brought up healthy or damaged, compassionate or unfeeling, contributive or predatory. Making a serious attack on criminal violence, in the home as on the street, involves restoring the integrity of that social environment by harnessing our material and technological resources to ends more supportive and more sustaining of community, family, and human development.

Let me take this argument one step farther. Along with and underpinning these institutional changes, in the next century we will need accompanying changes in what we loosely and vaguely call *culture*. There are those who think deliberate cultural change is difficult, if not impossible; who invoke the idea of cultural rigidity as a way of downplaying altogether the possibility of conscious social change (Jencks, Currie, and Herrnstein, 1988). But that approach betrays a narrow and static view of culture. After all, in the last generation alone we've seen several major—even epochal—normative changes in American society: in the way we think about the social role of women, or about the status of people of color; in the way we think about our relationship to the natural environment; increasingly, too, in the way we think about health and nutrition. On all of these planes, as a culture, we are very different than when I was growing up.

By the time my own daughter is my age, toward the end of the second decade of the twenty-first century, we may hope to have fostered some comparable changes in aspects of American culture that now may seem to be set in stone: the degree of social deprivation and inequality we tolerate; the amount of violence we consider normal and acceptable in the course of child rearing or of marriage; the level of access to social and health services we deem the minimum responsibility of civilized society; the relative importance of private gain and of cooperative endeavor as esteemed personal motives, or of private economic "choice" versus the stability and socializing competence of communities and families.

Just as we have begun now—belatedly and perhaps in the nick of time—to understand that we cannot systematically spoil and neglect the natural environment, or our bodies, without destructive and self-defeating consequences, so we must come to understand that the *social* environment requires a level of sustenance and stewardship far beyond what can be provided as a residual product of economic growth. The big job for twenty-first-century criminology—and for twenty-first-century social policy generally—will be to place the integrity of the social environment firmly at the top of the political and intellectual agenda, and to keep it there.

But as the recent history of environmental policy itself attests, that goal will not be accomplished without a considerable and protracted struggle. Criminologists and criminal justice practitioners can play a very important part in that struggle by pointing out continually the many links between the problems that confront us daily and the larger forces that shape them; between economic violence and interpersonal violence; between the erosion of communal life and livelihood and the deterioration and distortion of individual personality. We cannot concern ourselves only with the "downstream" consequences of the systematic abuse and neglect of the social environment; we must be bold enough to look unflinchingly at the source.

REFERENCES

AVISON, WILLIAM R., and PAMELA L. LORING. (1986). "Population Diversity and Cross-National Homicide Patterns: The Effects of Inequality and Heterogeneity." *Criminology 24* (No. 4).

BERLIN, GORDON, and ANDREW SUM. (1988). *Toward a More Perfect Union: Basic Skills, Poor Families, and Our Economic Future.* New York: Ford Foundation.

BERUETTA-CLEMENT, J. R., L. J. SCHWEINHART, W. S. BARNETT, and D. P. WEIKART. (1987). "The Effects of Early Educational Intervention on Crime and Delinquency in Adolescence and Early Adulthood," in John D. Burchard and Sara N. Burchard (Eds.), *Prevention of Delinquent Behavior.* Beverly Hills, Calif.: Sage.

BLUESTONE, BARRY, and BENNETT HARRISON. (1988). "The Grim Truth about the Job Miracle." *New York Times*, February 1.

BROWNFIELD, DAVID. (1986). "Social Class and Violent Behavior." *Criminology 24* (No. 3).

Business Week. (1988). "Human Capital." September 19, p. 103.

Children's Defense Fund. (1988). *Vanishing Dreams: The Growing Economic Plight of America's Young Families.* Washington, D.C.: Children's Defense Fund.

CLINARD, MARSHALL. (1978). *Cities With Little Crime*, Cambridge: Cambridge University Press.

Committee for Economic Development. (1987). *Children in Need: Investment Strategies for the Educationally Disadvantaged.* New York: Committee for Economic Development.

CULLEN, FRANCIS T. and KAREN E. GILBERT. (1982). *Reaffirming Rehabilitation.* Cincinnati: Anderson.

CURRIE, ELLIOTT. (1985). *Confronting Crime: An American Challenge.* New York: Pantheon.

CURRIE, ELLIOTT, ROBERT DUNN, and DAVID FOGARTY. (1988). "The Fading Dream: Economic Crisis and the New Inequality." In Elliott Currie and Jerome H. Skolnick (Eds.), *Crisis in American Institutions.* 7th edition. Glenview, Ill.: Scott, Foresman/Little Brown.

CURTIS, LYNN (Ed.) (1987). "Policies to Prevent Crime: Neighborhood, Family, and Employment Strategies," *Annals of the American Academy of Political and Social Science*, p. 494.

DENNO, DEBORAH. (1986). "Victim, Offender, and Situational Characteristics of Violent Crime." *Journal of Criminal Law and Criminology 77* (No. 4, Winter).

GALBRAITH, JOHN KENNETH. (1970). *The Affluent Society.* New York: New American Library.

GELLES, RICHARD J., and MURRAY A. STRAUSS. (1988). *Intimate Violence.* New York: Simon and Schuster.

GENDREAU, PAUL, and ROBERT R. ROSS. (1987). "Revivification of Rehabilitation: Evidence from the 1980s." *Justice Quarterly 4* (No. 3, September).

HARRISON, BENNETT, CHRIS TILLY, and BARRY BLUESTONE. (1986). "Rising Inequality." In David Obey and Paul Sarbanes (Eds.). *The Changing American Economy.* New York: Basil Blackwell.

HOPPER, PAULINE, and EDWARD ZIGLER. (1988). "The Medical and Social Science Basis for a National Infant Care Leave Policy." *American Journal of Orthopsychiatry 58* (No. 3, July).

IRWIN, JOHN, and JAMES AUSTIN. (1987). *It's About Time: Solving America's Prison Crowding Crisis.* San Francisco: National Council on Crime and Delinquency.

JENCKS, CHRISTOPHER, ELLIOTT CURRIE, and RICHARD HERRNSTEIN. (1987). "Genes and Crime: An Exchange." *New York Review of Books*, June 11.

KAUFMAN, JOAN, and EDWARD ZIGLER. (1987). "Do Abused Children Become Abusive Parents?" *American Journal of Orthopsychiatry 57* (No. 2, April).

LEVITAN, SAR A., and ELIZABETH CONWAY. (1988). "Shortchanged by Part-Time Work." *New York Times*, February 27.

LEWIS, DOROTHY O., E. MOE, and L. D. JACKSON. (1985). "Biopsychosocial Characteristics of Children Who Later Murder: A Prospective Study." *American Journal of Psychiatry 142* (No. 10, October).

LEWIS, D. O., J. H. PINCUS, B. BARD, E. RICHARDSON, L. S. PRICHEP, M. FELDMAN, and C. YEAGER. (1988). "Neuropsychiatric, Psychoeducational, and Family Characteristics of 14 Juveniles Condemned to Death in the United States." *American Journal of Psychiatry* 145 (No. 5, May).

PARKER, FAITH LAMB, CHAYA S. PIOTROWSKI, and LENORE PEAY. (1987). "Head Start as a Social Support for Mothers: The Psychological Benefits of Involvement." *American Journal of Orthopsychiatry 57* (No. 2, April).

REHN, GOSTA. (1985). "Swedish Active Labor Market Policy: Retrospect and Prospect." *Industrial Relations* 24 (Winter).

SAMUELSON, ROBERT. (1988). In *Newsweek*, November 14, p. 559.

SMITH, DOUGLAS A. and G. ROGER JARJOURA. (1988). "Social Structure and Criminal Victimization." *Journal of Research in Crime and Delinquency 25* (No. 1, February).

SVIRIDOFF, MICHELE, and JEROME E. McELROY. (1985). *Employment and Crime: A Summary Report.* New York: Vera Institute of Justice.

U.S. News and World Report. (1988). "Save the Children." November 7.

WILL, GEORGE. (1988). "The Prop. 13 Pendulum Swings Back." *Los Angeles Times*, June 5, p. 5.

WILSON, JAMES Q. (1988). Address to Western Society of Criminology, Monterey, Calif.: February 26 (mimeo).

WOLFE, DAVID A. (1987). "Child Abuse Prevention with At-Risk Parents and Children." In John D. Burchard and Sara N. Burchard (Eds.), *Prevention of Delinquent Behavior.* Beverly Hills, Calif.: Sage.

WOODHEAD, MARTIN. (1988). "When Psychology Informs Public Policy: The Case of Early Childhood Intervention." *American Psychologist 43* (No. 6, June).

YOUNG, JOCK. (1988). "Recent Developments in Criminology." In M. Haralambos (Ed.), *Developments in Sociology.* London: Causeway.

ZIGLER, EDWARD. (1987). "Formal Schooling for Four-Year-Olds? No." *American Psychologist 42* (March).

QUESTIONS FOR DISCUSSION

1. Currie believes that the conservative model that has dominated public policy for the past twenty years is beginning to decline. What evidence does he present to support this claim?

2. What are the major components of the "social-environmental" approach presented by Currie? Provide examples of each of the major components.

3. Perhaps a bigger and more long-range problem is that of the social structure. What suggestions are made about how this structure must change for an enduring improvement in the crime problem? Cite specific examples of such changes.

4. What role should research play when formulating policies for criminal justice?

5. What cultural changes are necessary for American society to realize an improvement in all social problems? Provide examples to support your answer.

29

BEYOND THE FEAR OF CRIME
RECONCILIATION AS THE BASIS
FOR CRIMINAL JUSTICE POLICY

Russ Immarigeon

■ ■

> *If perceptions of certainty and severity of punishment influence inten-*
> *tions regarding reoffending, but have little or nothing to do with subse-*
> *quent criminal behavior, then it is unlikely that programs emphasizing*
> *the fear factor will be effective. These programs may seem to hold the*
> *promise of reducing delinquency because they are believed to induce an*
> *immediate intent of avoiding crime; but the context within which actual*
> *decisions to commit crimes are made differs substantially from the con-*
> *text in which those intentions are shaped by programmatic experiences.*
>
> —Anne L. Schneider (1990)

> *Have I romanticized these kids, made them more "human" so the world*
> *will understand them and the problem they represent? That has certain-*
> *ly not been my intention. I have tried to present the reality behind the*
> *newspaper and television version of teenagers selling cocaine on New*
> *York City streets. yes, there is violence and death on those streets, but*
> *there are also struggling young people trying to make a place for them-*
> *selves in a world few care to understand and many wish would go away.*
>
> —Terry Williams (1989)

> *The most effective peacemakers are those who have experienced the*
> *healing of their own fears and can now help lead others out of theirs.*
>
> —Jim Wallis (1983)

Criminal justice policy on the relative use of imprisonment and nonincarcerative sanctions in the 1990s is being shaped, initially at least, by perspectives and circumstances that have emerged over the past twenty years. In this period, prison use and the expansion

Russ Immarigeon, "Beyond the Fear of Crime," *Criminology as Peacemaking*, pp. 251–262. Reprinted by permission of Indiana University Press.

of social control networks has grown at a staggering rate. Between 1970 and 1988, for instance, prison populations in the United States have more than tripled, from 196,441 to 627,402 inmates (Bureau of Justice Statistics, 1988, 1989). Disproportionality has also become a serious factor. The number of women in local jails across the country has increased 93 percent between 1983 and 1988 while the male population in these facilities *only* increased 51 percent in the same period (Bureau of Justice Statistics, 1990). Nearly one in four African-American men between the ages of twenty and twenty-nine are either imprisoned or under community supervision on any given day (Mauer, 1990). Probation and parole case-loads have also reached record levels, and never in our history have so many probation and parole violators been returned to prison for technical as well as "new crime" reasons.

But changes in how local, state, and federal jurisdictions are reacting to crime are even more telling than those distressing statistics. Simply stated, rehabilitation has been replaced by retribution as the dominant paradigm for criminal justice intervention. Criminal sentences are more generally intended to punish than reform.

However, bubbling under the surface of this significant change are some different perspectives on how criminal sanctions can respond to criminal behavior and victimization. In particular, restitution and reconciliation are concepts that are gaining currency among conservatives and liberals alike. More important, studies are finding that reparative sanctions such as restitution and victim–offender reconciliation are more effective at deterring crime than incapacitative and punitive penalties.

In *Deterrence and Juvenile Crime*, Anne L. Schneider recently reported in a national study of six juvenile restitution programs that:

> restitution is more effective (than probation) in reducing recidivism because it provides the juveniles with immediate and continuing success in the program. In other words, the juveniles can quickly develop a sense of being successful by obtaining employment and beginning to make their restitution payments or perform their community service. The data suggest that this reduces the offense activity during the time they are in the program. The sense of success and the reduced in-program offense rate both enhance the juvenile's sense of citizenship as well as reduced intentions to reoffend and actual recontacts with the court. (Schneider, 1990:111)

At the same time, a study of the effectiveness of selective incapacitation, a much proposed remedy for escalating crime rates, suggested, like a number of studies before it, that any hope of significantly reducing crime through incapacitation, whether collective or selective, would seem to be remote (Haapanen, 1990: 136–137).

The 1990s began in a state of massive correctional crowding. But as one decade tumbled over into another, policies based on longer sentences and longer periods of time served were cascading out of control. In Minnesota, for example, the number of women incarcerated in what many people feel is our most progressive state on correctional issues increased from approximately 120 to 180 in less than two years.

Nonetheless, despite an escalating drug war complete with steady Bush-administration volleys for more prisons and more prisoners, strong interests exist for the use of nonincarcerative sanctions. The Judicial Conference of the United States, for instance, in a March 1989 report on the impact of drug-related criminal activity on the federal courts, supported the use of substance-abuse treatment programs, restitution, fines, and electronic monitoring as alternatives to incarceration. The report also requested more funds for pretrial, probation, and defender services staff to prepare and implement alternative sanctions (Federal Judicial Center, 1989: 53–54).

Shortly thereafter, the Police Foundation released the findings of its National Symposium on Community Institutions and Inner-City Crime Project. This project, too, supported alternatives to incarceration. "Judges should continue to tailor sentences to individual offenders rather than rely totally on sentencing alternatives," the report argued. "Judges should use alternatives to incarceration, particularly when the offender is nonviolent. Community service, restitution, drug treatment, and house arrest can be effective sanctions" (Sulton, 1990: 108–109). Other sections of this report supported the use of halfway houses and discouraged returning parole violators to prison when they have not committed a new crime.

At the start of the decade, then, criminal justice policy in the country relies heavily on repressive measures, but there are numerous cracks in this armor. An opening therefore exists to challenge and organize against the prevailing paradigm of justice. The relationship between criminal justice policies and criminology is generally ill-defined and uncertain. Often, this relationship, or lack of relationship, is glossed over rather than confronted. Rarely is the process studied in organized fashion. Peacemaking criminology has an important role in developing these inquiries. In this essay, I will briefly refer to some directions for this budding perspective.

In "Conflicts as Property," a paper originally given as the Foundation Lecture of the Centre for Criminological Studies at the University of Sheffield in March 1976, Norwegian criminologist Nils Christie vented his suspicion that "criminology to some extent has amplified a process where conflicts have been taken away from the parties directly involved and have thereby disappeared or become other people's property." Both situations were deplorable, he said. "Conflicts ought to be used, not only left in erosion. And they ought to be used, and become useful, for those originally involved in the conflict" (Christie, 1977:1).

When applied to ordinary criminal cases, Christie's argument suggests that the interests, perspectives, and concerns of both victims and offenders are "disappeared" or lost when criminal justice officials—police, prosecutors, defense attorneys, probation officers, prison administrators, and even reform advocates—speak or act on their behalf. In short, Christie posits that "professionals" (rather than direct participants) seize control and define (or redefine) what has taken place and what must be done about it. Prosecutors, for instance, may be more interested in convictions with stiff penalties than victim restitution while the victim's main concern, to use a simple example, is that she get her purse and its contents returned to her. Defense attorneys, to use another example, may be well satisfied that a full package of sentencing alternatives that includes restitution, community service, strict supervision, and the like is to the benefit of the clients they represent when, in fact, they may be "widening the net of social control" for their clients to plunge through while perhaps going far beyond the needs of the victims involved.

Damon Runyon, the writer, once touched on part of what Christie spoke about in observations he once made about murder trials. "A big murder trial possesses some of the elements of a sporting event," Runyon suggested. "There is the same conversational speculation of the probable result. The trial is a sort of game, the players on the one side attorneys for the defense, and on the other side the attorneys for the State. The defendant figures in it merely as the prize" (Pollack, 1972:27).

More to the point, numerous examples of such thievery can be found in almost any courtroom on any day one chooses to attend local criminal proceedings. For the sake of brevity, let me describe only two such instances which I return to later in this essay.

Several years ago, the Vera Institute of Justice was generous enough to allow me to follow a court representative in its community service program through his daily round of work. At one point, we entered the bullpen, a squalid series of short-term holding cells for detained prisoners awaiting a court appearance, to speak with a defendant who was soon to appear before the bench. Earlier, the court rep had identified this one fellow as a likely candidate for Vera's community service program after a brief review of court papers on file in the courtroom. The court rep spoke to the prisoner for less than five minutes but obtained a staggering amount of information about him, including his drug-use history (McDonald, 1986).

At the bench, the court rep asked the court to sentence the defendant to the Vera program. The Vera program consisted of six weeks of unpaid public-service labor at a community work site supervised by Vera staff. A straightforward sentence. But the judge was interested in the offender's drug-use history. He looked first toward the prosecutor, then toward the defense attorney, and asked whether the offender used drugs. Neither one knew. The court rep was not asked, and he did not volunteer what he knew because while the program helps offenders find treatment services for their addictions, such rehabilitative programming is not a formal part of the services they provide. Meanwhile, the defendant, who may or may not have told the court what it wanted to know, was standing several yards away. A certain source of some information. Yet no one asked him.

More recently, a tragic homicide in Tennessee occurred when a drifter assaulted and murdered a well-known, elderly community volunteer. The drifter was soon caught, and brought to trial. Before his identification and arrest, however, the victim's brother, a Catholic priest, asked, on behalf of the victim's family, that the prosecutor not seek the death penalty in this case. When the drifter was caught, the family met with the prosecutor to repeat their deeply felt request. The woman killed did not believe in the death penalty, and she would not want further violence to result even when she had been the victim of senseless violence.

In a letter to the prosecutor, the victim's family wrote:

> The cruelty of her death, as devastating as it is, does not diminish our belief that God's forgiveness and love, as our mother showed us, is the only response to the violence we know. If the suspect is guilty as alleged, it is clear that he is deeply troubled and needs all the compassion that our society and its institutions can offer.

Although this was the sense of justice the victim's family wanted pursued by those who represented their interests (the state of Tennessee), the prosecutor nonetheless asked for the death penalty (Loggins, 1989).

Over twenty years ago, sociologist Ned Polsky gave a ground-breaking critique of criminological methods in an essay in his collected works, *Hustlers, Beats, and Others.* Central to Polsky's critique was the charge that:

> experience with adult, unreformed, serious criminals in their natural environment—not only those undertaking felonies in a moonlighting way, such as pool hustlers, but career felons—has

convinced me that if we are to make a major advance in our scientific understanding of criminal lifestyles, criminal subcultures, and their relation to the social system, we must undertake genuine field research on these people. (Polsky, 1967: 117)

In at least one important way, Polsky's critique mirrors Christie's complaints: Both men fault the common characteristic of avoiding the people who criminologists and criminal justice practitioners are supposed to be dealing with—criminals and victims. American criminology has grown dramatically since the days of Polsky's critique, but too little evidence exists that the field has learned very much.

Crime problems, prison problems, and justice problems are rapidly changing. Definitions of what is criminal are altered in a wink of the eye. In the late 1970s and early 1980s, for instance, the National Coalition for Jail Reform coordinated a broad coalition of disparate criminal justice agencies that agreed that public inebriates (common drunkards) should not be jailed. Within years, however, Mothers Against Drunk Driving and other victim groups helped establish an environment within which legislators swiftly enacted laws that criminalized and imprisoned hundreds of thousands of drinking drivers. At the beginning of this sea change, restrictive measures, such as loss of license and incarceration, were the most frequently mandated remedies. More recently, victim participation, victim impact statements, and victim testimony are lending a reconciliatory, community-building edge to the form of changing responses to this serious social issue.

Criminologists have not investigated these changes very adequately. More often than not, they are too accepting of whatever "official discourse" permeates either from governmental fund givers or from ideological restrictions. At an international crime prevention conference in Montreal recently, local and national officials from different countries met to examine different strategies toward crime prevention. Western European and Canadian representatives spoke eloquently about getting to the root causes of deviant behavior. The American response, one observer noted, was drugs, drugs, drugs—the implication being that Americans had lost any tangible grasp of even looking under the surface at what the problem was and, thus, what to do about it. Helplessness, not involvement, becomes our response to social problems.

Crime and fear have many associations. Some of these we are well familiar with. Public opinion polls, for instance, commonly tell us that people in our communities fear crime. How widely crime is feared and how this fear affects our lives varies from one period of time to another and from one community to another.

The relationship of crime and fear is not without its ironies. Victimization surveys, for example, frequently show us that people who have not been victims of crime are more fearful of crime than those who have been attacked or robbed. Old people and women, statistically less likely to be victimized than young men, nonetheless have higher levels of fear. It is far less clear, however, how these findings translate into cogent public policy.

One thing is certain. The fear of crime affects more than how we walk down the street, or even whether we walk down the street, at night. The fear of crime affects the way we determine how we as a society respond, as a matter of social policy, to crime. Part of this shameful situation arises because we as criminologists too frequently avoid many serious issues in criminal justice policy making.

One example. Several years ago, Gottfredson and Taylor reported that legislative policymakers in Maryland thought that their constituency was far more punitive-oriented than they found out was actually the case. No replications of this study have been done, but it is probable that similar findings would be found elsewhere. What these findings suggest is that instead of finding out what people really think and feel, policymakers avoid this issue, avoid it perhaps because they are lazy, because they are too busy, or because they really do not want to know.

The process of finding out what people really think has further complications. The Public Agenda Foundation recently completed both a national survey and a state-specific survey of public opinion on crime and punishment issues. What they, and several other similar surveys, have found is that people's opinions change when given information that educates them about the topic being discussed. In short, people's opinion can change in rather a short time.

These studies successfully uncover social facts that more comfortably fit into criminological thought than in legislative dialogue. Peacemaking criminology needs to bridge this gap.

CASE STUDY 1: HOMELESS MAN STABS SUPERMARKET MANAGER

A forty-year-old Cuban man, homeless, has a job gathering shopping carts from a supermarket parking lot. He gets paid ten dollars a day. One day, the store manager says he deserves only five dollars. Angered, a struggle ensues and the man stabs the store manager in the knee. The man spends four months in pretrial detention. At his sentencing, the judge receives an alternative sentencing plan that provides for literacy training, work, a place to stay, and so on. A community agency has a place ready for him.

Instead of making a decision, however, the judge listens to the prosecutor, who wants a three-year prison term, and to the defense attorney, who wants leniency. Since these two professionals are in conflict, the judge, who is leaning toward the community sentence, holds the sentencing over for another month. This "cooling" periods allows both professionals to gain something. The prosecutor gets more punishment. The defense attorney gets some rehabilitation for his client. But the main party—the Cuban man—needlessly loses more time in confinement.

This scenario is very common in American courtrooms. It is a classic example of adversary justice as work. Notice, however, the missing pieces. The victim was not involved in any of the courtroom proceedings. Nor was he mentioned in any of the deliberations. His injury was minor, and no one thought to ask him what sentence he would like to see imposed. No one asked if the victim and offender wanted to get together to work things out for themselves. The criminal justice system seemed satisfied with the case's outcome even though it eventually paid for the cost of two attorneys' time and the price of five months' imprisonment.

CASE STUDY 2: PRISONER RECEIVES TREATMENT LONG AFTER NEED DISSIPATES

Every once in a while, a sheriff or warden says that the jail or prison they manage is so overcrowded that they simply would not accept any more prisoners. These correctional administrators know they do not have any legal authority to do this sort of thing; but frequently they are exasperated, and they are seeking dramatic ways to make a point to the general public that they are in dire straits. One remedy to this situation would be to have courts delay the start of a prisoner's term of incarceration until space is available. When space becomes available, then the prisoner can begin to serve time. The Dutch do this; those awaiting incarceration are called "walking convicts." It is a method of planning and it seems to work. In the United States, however, such a remedy would catch only derisive comments and political rejection.

In the United States, offenders are forced to go directly to jail or prison even when suitable space is not available. Are they ever forced to participate in treatment options when space in these programs is not available? Recently, a New York prisoner captured the double standard that exists in sentencing practice in this country:

> It is ironic that while I was at liberty on the streets and sought a residential treatment program for my cocaine addiction I was told there was a waiting list for such programs and I should keep in contact with the referral agency each month until a space for me opened up. I responded that I was severely addicted and needed help right at that moment, that I was not sure where I would be month to month or what bizarre behavior and crimes my addictions would drive me to or whether I would be alive to benefit from any such program in the future. My will to straighten out was strong at that moment, but there was no help available. Now as a prisoner of the state, I am not only given such a residential program—long after the exigencies of my former condition have subsided due to over four years incarceration—but I am compelled to partake of such a program as a requirement of earned eligibility (a form of early release in New York State) certification. (Anonymous, 1990: 1)

CASE STUDY 3: TOWN PROTESTS STATE PLANS FOR PRISON

If a town does not want a prison in its backyard, is it being selfish or reactionary? Or can a town raise legitimate planning issues not only about corrections policy but also about town development? The small New England farm community of New Braintree is still fighting a five-year battle to prevent the Commonwealth of Massachusetts from converting an empty school into a medium-security prison. This case is particularly interesting because, except for local and regional support, the town has received only conservative backing from statewide leaders. Liberal leaders have abandoned a "cause" that in other times would be a natural target for their interests.

In the late 1960s, New Braintree residents battled successfully to close a private landfill operation that was dumping pollutants, with no environmental protections, just behind where the commonwealth is now in the process of building a prison. "For the first time in its history," one resident wrote the local paper, "New Braintree is in danger of losing its wholesome country atmosphere" (Immarigeon, 1987: 16). Sometime afterward, the town also acted to deny a private investor from building a large mobile-home park because it would have exhausted the town's fragile water supply.

With its history of environmental concern, townspeople were reasonably interested in future state plans when the commonwealth began exploring the possibility of converting the empty school into a jail for drunk drivers. Initially, the townspeople were simply looking for assurances that this facility would not grow into something larger, an institution that would overtax local resources. Townspeople were stopped short by state officials who preferred to stonewall them rather than inform them. Townspeople, who knew a great deal about stone walls, began to dig in deep.

When New Braintree residents found out that the commonwealth was planning to build a prison at the school site located squarely in the middle of town, they felt that their worst fears were realized. Their organization and political mobilization increased. State officials became more surly in the dealings with townspeople. At different points, state representatives either dismissed the inquiries of the residents out of hand or they insisted on telling them that they were concerned about things such as diminishing land values, higher crime rates, and the like. They in fact were not concerned. The town eventually sued the commonwealth over violations of its own administrative procedures for starting construction projects. The town lost. The commonwealth seized by eminent domain the land on which the empty school rested and then, with guards posted outside, placed a perimeter fence around the site and started to renovate the facility—even though (at this writing) there were no funds available to actually house prisoners in the prison.

CASE STUDY 4: PRISON FURLOUGHS, THE PRESIDENTIAL CAMPAIGN OF 1988, AND MORE PRISON FURLOUGHS

Other articles in this volume comment on the Willie Horton affair. Briefly, Willie Horton skipped the Commonwealth of Massachusetts while on furlough release. This highly successful state program was brought into question when Horton violently assaulted a Maryland couple. A local campaign—started by several Andover housewives who wanted to find answers to some of their questions about why Horton was on the streets—escalated into a statewide initiative to abolish furloughs for all first-degree, and eventually second-degree, murder offenders. As in New Braintree, a central factor in the development of this campaign was the intransigence of executive-branch officials to address citizen concerns directly.

In the Bush–Dukakis presidential campaign of 1988, President Bush used the Horton case for his own political ends. Dukakis himself also chose a political approach to the issue. Instead of defending the program—Massachusetts corrections officials were chomping at the bit to show not only that the program was tightly managed but also that it was benefiting offenders and citizens alike—Dukakis decided to avoid discussing it.

In the wake of this debacle, in state after state, furlough programs were watered down or eliminated. Regardless of the efficacy of individual programs, furloughs became politically incorrect and were increasingly defined as unacceptable in themselves.

Ironically, in the midst of many states opting to reject the use of conditional-release programs as preparation for full release, support for prerelease still holds credibility for at least some state policymakers. In Virginia, for example, Governor Baliles's Commission on Prison and Jail Overcrowding argued in December 1989 for greater use of work-release and prerelease programs as a method of reducing recidivism. The commission's final report stated: "By gradually providing greater contact and interaction with society, while retaining considerable control of inmate's time and activity, and by enforcing values of work and responsibility, these options may also serve to reduce an offender's likelihood to recidivate" (Ferguson, 1989: 59).

CASE STUDY 5: BARLINNIE SPECIAL UNIT

The Barlinnie Special Unit, established in February 1973, is a Scottish prison unit that houses seriously disruptive prisoners. These are men the prison officials have determined are unmanageable elsewhere in the system.

Various factors may have brought about these changes, but several particular items are noteworthy. Prisoners in the Barlinnie Special Unit are given advantages not afforded other prisoners in the system. Especially, prisoners at Barlinnie are allowed a participatory role in deciding routines within the facility. Community meetings are set up to determine appropriate and inappropriate behavior. Early in the experiment, prisoners decided that all forms of violence were unacceptable. Prisoners are encouraged by prison officers and other staff to verbalize aggressive feelings. Prisoners are held accountable for their behavior as well as the behavior of their fellow inmates. Among the benefits they experience are frequent visits from family and friends, the right to work or not work, and the ability to cook their own food.

The only empirical investigation of this unit to date examined the prison and post-unit behavior of the twenty-five men who had participated in this regime by November 1986. Seventy-two percent of this small population had one or more murder or attempted murder convictions. Sixty percent were serving life sentences. Only three prisoners were serving terms of less than ten years. Results of this study suggest that "transfer to the Special Unit results in a significant and substantial change in the number of physical assaults and the level of disruptive behavior within the unit and following transfer from the unit" (Cooke, 1989; Whitmore, 1987).

In this essay, I have used the term *criminology* in very broad terms. One could reasonably argue that I have included political scientists, corrections administrators, sociologists, criminal justice practitioners, and many others under a single, unclearly defined rubric. This is true. But criminology as a field has become disoriented. Polsky's assaults on the field more than twenty years ago are still applicable today. Criminologists are more ready to see what officially processed data say than to find out what criminals, victims, policymakers, and administrators themselves have to say. Criminology's growth, therefore, does not necessarily mean its expansion as a field of inquiry.

Contemporary criminologists are still too rarely out in the field. Peacemaking criminologists, however, are susceptible to the same mistakes that traditional, radical, and other criminologists have made. In particular, we can become more enmeshed in our visions than in people's real-life experiences.

REFERENCES

Anonymous. (1990). "A.S.A.T.A. Prisoner's Perspective." *Justicia* (February): 1–4.

Bureau of Justice Statistics. 1988. *Historical Statistics in State and Federal Institutions, Yearend 1925–1986*. Washington, D.C.: U.S. Department of Justice.

_____. (1989). "Prisoners in 1988." Washington, D.C.: U.S. Department of Justice.

_____. (1990). "Census of Local Jails, 1988." Washington, D.C.: U.S. Department of Justice.

Christie, Nils. (1977). "Conflict as Property." *The British Journal of Criminology 17* (1): 1–14.

COOKE, DAVID J. (1989). "Containing Violent Prisoners: An Analysis of the Barline Special Unit." *British Journal of Criminology* 29 (2): 129–143.

Federal Judicial Center. (1989). "Impact of Drug Related Criminal Activity on the Federal Judiciary." Washington, D.C.: Federal Judicial Center.

FERGUSON, JACK H. (1989). *1989 Commission on Prison and Jail Overcrowding*. Richmond: Governor of Virginia.

HAAPANEN, RUDY A. (1990). *Selective Incapacitation and the Serious Offender: A Longitudinal Study of Criminal Career Patterns*. New York: Springer-Verlag.

IMMARIGEON, RUSS. (1987). "Saving a Small Town." *Boston Herald Sunday Magazine*, 5 July, 4–7, 16–18.

LOGGINS, KIRK. (1989). "DA Asking Judge to Bar Strobels' Death Penalty View." *The Tennessean*, 7 September.

McDONALD, DOUGLAS CORRY. (1986). *Punishment without Walls: Community Service Sentences in New York City*. New Brunswick, N.J.: Rutgers University Press.

MAUER, MARC. (1990). *Young Black Men and the Criminal Justice System: A Growing National Problem*. Washington, D.C.: The Sentencing Project.

POLLACK, JACK HARRISON. (1972). *Dr. Sam: An American Tragedy*. Chicago: Henry Regnery Company.

POLSKY, NED. (1967). *Hustlers, Beats, and Others*. Chicago: Aldine.

SCHNEIDER, ANNE L. (1990). *Deterrence and Juvenile Crime: Results from a National Policy Experiment*. New York: Springer-Verlag.

SULTON, ANNE THOMAS. (1990). *Inner-City Crime Control: Can Community Institutions Contribute?* Washington, D.C. Police Foundation.

WALLIS, JIM. (1993). *Revive Us Again: A Sojourner's Story*. Nashville, Tenn.: Abingdon Press.

WHITMORE, PETER B. (1987). "Barlinnie Special Unit: An Insider's View." In Anthony E. Bottoms and Roy Light (Eds.), *Problems of Long-Term Imprisonment*. Brookfield, Vt.: Gower.

WILLIAMS, TERRY. (1989). *The Cocaine Kids: The Inside Story of a Teenage Drug Ring*. Reading, Mass.: Addison-Wesley.

QUESTIONS FOR DISCUSSION

1. The author asserts that the "interests, perspectives, and concerns of both victims and offenders are disappeared or lost when criminal justice officials speak, or act on their behalf." Explain.

2. What is meant by the "thievery" that can be found in any courtroom on any day one chooses to attend a local criminal proceeding? Provide examples to support your answer.

3. Criminologists "more often than not…are too accepting of whatever 'official discourse' permeates either from government fund givers or from ideological restrictions." What is meant by this statement? Provide examples to support your answer.

4. Choose three to five cases of the studies presented, and discuss how these studies uncover social facts that shed light more on criminology than legislative exchange. Why may it be more important to take this approach rather than an approach used in typical criminological research?

30

A LIFE OF CRIME
CRIMINOLOGY AND PUBLIC POLICY AS PEACEMAKING

Richard Quinney

■ ■

The focus of this paper is on criminology and public policy as peacemaking. It offers a challenge to criminologists to reexamine their personal and professional agenda. Criminologists are encouraged to support and engage in a "compassionate criminology" that recognizes the interrelatedness of everything; that everyone is connected to each other and to their environment. Compassion, wisdom, and love are essential to understanding the suffering of which we are all a part and to practicing a criminology of nonviolence. A compassionate criminology advocates cooperation and compassion rather than competition, exploitation, and greed.

I

We have heard it said that economics is the dismal science. In these times of dismal economy, any discipline connected to that economy is self-evidently dismal. And cannot the same be said of a discipline that makes crime today a subject of its discourse? Criminology may easily join economics as a dismal science. If not a dismal science, certainly much of criminology is a science for a mean-spirited time.

A prerequisite for considering the role of criminology in public policy, then, is an examination of our livelihood as criminologists. We might ask, are we doing a criminology that is worthy of an enlightened public policy? And then the related questions: What do we mean by public policy; what do we do when we engage in public policy?

My considerations are framed clearly in a perspective of peace and social justice. This tempered at all points by the ancient text: "All that we are is a result of what we have thought." That is, our actions follow our thoughts. Hatred begets hatred; love makes us loving. How we think as criminologists has consequences for our lives and for the world.

II

The mind is made of thoughts. Thoughts live, and they travel far. Thus, great care must be taken about what we think. Likewise, care is to be taken in how we speak, in the language that we utter. Certainly it is not in how much we say—in how many articles and books we write, but in how we say it, in what words we use. All this coming from the way we have taught ourselves to think.

Richard Quinney, "A Life of Crime: Criminology and Public Policy as Peacemaking," *Journal of Crime and Justice*, Vol. 16, No. 2, pp. 3–9, copyright © 1993. Reprinted with permission of the publisher.

I am inspired by the lines from the 8th chapter of the *Dhammapada*: "A single wise word, bringing peace to the listener is worth more than a thousand speeches full of empty words." By extension, to criminology, and to public policy, a few correct ideas, spoken in a language of care, can bring peace to the listener and social justice to the world. What is required, in our work as criminologists, is not only an academic literature and a professional organization, but ways of thinking, speaking, and writing that foster peace. This is a compassionate criminology, a criminology of peacemaking.

We are what we eat; we are what we think. When we engage in a mean-minded criminology—a criminology of prejudice and punishment—we become the lives that we lead. And we help create, or at least we are collaborators in, the policies and structures that deny justice and perpetuate a social order based on crime.

Such a criminology—as a daily diet—can make us uncaring and unloving, just as it helps to maintain a social ethos of hate, selfishness, and violence. If we want to reduce crime—and yes, even eliminate crime—we need first to live personal lives of loving kindness, of loving others, including our neighbors in crime. Transforming our criminology, our policies and our society, begins very close to home. In our own minds, in our own hearts, in what we think and how we speak.

III

We are currently in the depths of an era that began twenty-five years ago. It is an era that started with the hopes of a good society, a great society, a new society of equality, job security, health care, the ending of poverty, and the reduction of crime. But the war in Vietnam was pursued with obsession by successive Presidents. The Great Society advances of Lyndon Johnson were to falter and fail in the determined continuation of an immoral and illegal war. War and violence took precedence over the humane values of peace, equality, and prosperity.

Practically all of the anti-poverty programs were scrapped (both guns and butter could not prevail). As criminologists we know well the demise of the social programs dealing with crime. We continue to be in the grip of the conservative response to crime, brought about with a vengeance by the Republican administrations of Nixon, Reagan, and Bush.

No wonder that the students in our criminology courses today, the students born after the late 1960s, come to us entrenched in a conservative ideology of crime. The anti-crime thought which they have grown up with, particularly in media presentations, but in the home and community as well, is that of stricter law enforcement, more prisons, and inevitably, the death penalty. To advance an alternative, a non-violent and humane approach to crime, is met with considerable dismay and resistance. A peacemaking, compassionate criminology is clearly against the grain in these times. Our work as teachers is particularly challenging, demanding the best in us.

IV

In the classroom, in our studies, or on the street, we begin with the awareness that this country has one of the highest crime rates in the world. And that our official ways of responding to crime are similar to those of the most repressive nations. We have a tremendously high homicide rate. If the United States were involved in an international war that resulted in an annual casualty figure of 25,000 dead, we as a nation would regard this as outrageous and intolerable.

Yet, more than this number die each year in a time of "peace" in this country. There is, to be exact, a war taking place every day in the United States—a domestic war.

To be aware of the violence in our everyday life is a beginning in the move to a peace-making criminology. But the outrage and anger that we feel in this realization must be turned into an energy that promotes thoughts—and actions—of peace and goodwill. Otherwise, we are in the spirit of the criminology from which we are trying to remove ourselves.

V

A compassionate criminology begins with the awareness of the interpenetration of all things, animate and inanimate. A Zen master notes (Aitken, 1984, p. 10): "We are all of us inter-related—not just people, but animals too, and stones, clouds, trees." All phenomena—of which we are an integral part—are transparent, ephemeral, and totally one in the great void of existence.

Nothing exists by itself; nothing has a separate existence, a separate self. Everything is everything else. As human beings we are part of all things, we are of nature, we are nature. As human beings we are connected intimately to one another—in all the joy and all the suffering of the world. "Everyone," Thich Nhat Hanh observes (1988, pp. 51–52), "is responsible for everything that happens in life." We are one. The truth is in our interbeing, beyond the dualistic thought of Western philosophy.

Where does this lead in our criminology? The objective is quite simple: to be kind to one another, to break down the barriers that separate us from one another, to live moment-to-moment our connection to all that is. The peace and social justice we seek comes in the realization of our interconnectedness—our oneness. Returning to the source, as in the Zen search for the ox (see Sekida, 1975, pp. 223–237), we are fully in the wonder of our existence. We go to town—we enter the marketplace—with helping hands, serving others with great compassion. The oneness of all, I do not know its human name: let us call it love.

VI

Compassion opens us to all the suffering in the world. With unconditional compassion, we have no need to close our hearts and minds to the suffering of others, or to deny our own suffering. We do not retreat to the violence of denial or to the harm of violent deeds.

But compassion must be accompanied by insight, by wisdom. Wisdom into the interconnectedness—and the interconnected suffering—of all beings is essential to a peacemaking criminology. Wisdom provides us with the awareness that the division is not between the bad and the good, the criminal and the noncriminal. Wisdom teaches interbeing.

With compassion and with wisdom, we are capable of understanding. Compassion, wisdom, and understanding, using these we practice a criminology of nonviolence. And in the practice, we in turn become more compassionate, wiser, and more understanding in our own daily lives. We are what we practice.

We are, then, truly in the world. We have become one with that which we now understand. We have entered, we have participated in, the world in the course of our understanding (see Hanh, 1988, pp. 11–13). To know, we become one with the known. No longer is there a distinction—a duality—between the observer and the observed.

In our effort to understand crime—and to do something about it—we must do the same. We have to become one with all who suffer from lives of crime and from the sources that produce crime. Only then can we really understand. And only then can we love. Loving the world as we come to understand it.

Great care is then taken in our response to crime. Our actions—our public policies—are consistent with our understanding. And cannot it be noted that understanding, itself, is action, and may be the best policy?

VII

A compassionate criminology ceases to make the dualistic distinction between the outer world and the inner world. This is a distinction that has been created solely by our thought, separating our inner being from the social and political world. Until we realize the reality of the interconnectedness, the oneness, of mind and society, we will continue to perpetuate a kind of thinking that is divisive and a cause of strife and trouble. There can be no peace in the world, including peace in the streets and peace in the home, without peace in our mind. What happens within us, happens outside of us. The inner and the outer are one.

A society of meanness, of competition and greed, of injustice, is created by minds that are greedy, selfish, filled with fear and hate, and crave for power over others. Suffering on the social level can be ended only with the ending of suffering on the personal level—the two realms are really one and the same. Peace at home and peace abroad are of the peace that is within us. One kind of peace cannot come without the other.

This is to say to us as criminologists that we are involved simultaneously in creating a better society and a transformed human being. Our struggle is for social justice in the world and peace in the hearts and minds of us all. The words of the Dalai Lama of Tibet, shortly before receiving the Nobel Peace Award, are a guide to us as criminologists: "What is required is a kind heart and a sense of community, which I call universal responsibility" (quoted in the *Buddhist Peace Fellowship Newsletter*, Fall 1989, p. 4). A criminology that can end suffering and thereby reduce crime requires criminologists of sound mind and gentle heart, peacemakers of the world.

VIII

Let us conclude these thoughts on peacemaking in criminology with some reflection on public policies of crime and criminal justice. We have observed that the policies of the last twenty-five years have been founded on a conservative ideology and administration. The funds that have been allocated to crime have gone to fighting those who suffer from the harms of a mean-spirited capitalist economy. Criminal justice at home has paralleled the violence of warfare abroad. Our criminology has too often served the violence of criminal justice.

We know there are alternatives to a conservative criminal justice. Some of these alternatives have to do with policies and procedures within the criminal justice system, such as mediation, probation, and rehabilitation. But there must be alternatives that go beyond the criminal justice system: quality education for children, physical and mental health services, family support programs, employment and job security, and the allocation of resources for the reduction of poverty. Elliott Currie (1985) has shown us that once, before the Vietnam War drained the nation, there were liberal policies and programs that would have worked in reducing crime, if they had been allowed to continue. Mark Colvin (1991) recently has described similar and related alternatives. It is a commentary on our times that such proposals are termed "outrageous." Instead of a war on crime (on "criminals"), we need to be waging peace on the economy, in the society, and within ourselves.

What is being said is that public policy is to be peacemaking. If the objective is to end suffering and reduce or eliminate crime, there can be no other path than peace and social justice.

A compassionate public policy is a natural, effortless consequence of a compassionate criminology. If we pursue a peaceful, peacemaking criminology, whenever and however we engage in public policy, we will think and act in the ways of wisdom, love, and compassion. Out of an understanding so informed, we know what is to be done.

Finally, let us remember that the original project still guides us: the creation of a better world, a world which we are capable of forming as human beings. This will be a world of cooperation and compassion, rather than one of competition, exploitation, and greed. The forms and processes will be democratic and socialist, a democratic socialist reality that we will create as never before. A humane and universal order founded on the natural interdependence and harmony of the universe. As criminologists, we are part of this movement of history.

REFERENCES

AITKEN, R. (1984). *The Mind of Clover: Essays in Zen Ethics*. San Francisco: North Point Press.

Buddhist Peace Fellowship Newsletter. (1989 Fall).

COLVIN, M. (1991). "Crime and Social Reproduction: A Response to a Call for 'Outrageous' Proposals." *Crime and Delinquency*, 37:436–447.

CURRIE, E. (1985). *Confronting Crime: An American Challenge*. New York: Pantheon.

The Dhammapada. (1985). Translated by Eknath Easwaran. Petaluma, Calif.: Nigiri Press.

SEKIDA, K. (1975). *Zen Training: Methods and Philosophy*. New York: Weatherhill.

QUESTIONS FOR DISCUSSION

1. Discuss what is meant by a "compassionate criminology." Provide examples.

2. What are several alternatives, presented by the author, to typical conservative criminal justice that will effectively address crime and, more importantly, social justice? Cite examples.

3. Suffering on the social level will end when suffering on a personal level ends. Explain.

4. What is meant by public policy as "peacemaking"? Discuss.

EPILOGUE

■ ■ ■ ■ ■ ■ ■ ■ ■ ■ ■ ■ ■ ■ ■ ■ ■ ■ ■ ■

As you have discovered from this collection, crime policies are often ineffective because of the plethora of countervailing political, economic, and social influences that determine their outcome. Most often, the reactive sociopolitical environments within which policies are initiated do not focus on the results of policy as an integrated whole, but instead on individual components of the criminal justice system as if these parts were nonsystemic. These problems aside, the basic issues in crime and criminal justice remain fundamental for most Americans. The majority of citizens simply want the amount of crime to lessen and for the criminal justice system to act systematically toward the achievement of enhanced public safety. This demand is made with the stipulation that our liberty, freedom, and rights will be respected and upheld. These desires draw a fine line between due process and crime control—a line that is really at the heart of all public policy regarding crime.

The nation, in an increasingly rapid era of change, must take control of crime problems by refining the system of justice to carry out a public mandate for a safer society. Major changes in the direction of public policy do not happen often in crime or other areas such as energy, environment, or education. Although change has come slowly to criminal justice, the contradictory outcomes have lead to a crisis of faith in the system. Along with record levels of homicide and the number of persons incarcerated, the level of fear has increased rather than abated. More than simply a lack of will, the underlying problems have to do with a system that has lacked congruent, measurable, and nonpolitized goals for reducing crime and thus the American mindset of the fear of crime. If we are to overcome the problems of our justice system, we must begin to eradicate the processes that produce the problems. Our nation should consider the immediate safety of the citizenry first and then deal with the landmines that have contributed to the broader social injustices. A system of simplified rules and regulations that deals with the most serious crimes in a rational manner and then deals with the less serious crimes is not too much to ask of our government. The current incarceration binge, if not slowed, could cost the nation more money than could ever be justified. The contradictions found in the correlation of record levels of spending and record homicide rates are clear indictments of a system bent on spending without outcome-based objectives.

In essence, a safer society should not be a dream the nation has, only to awaken to a living nightmare of violence and disorder. The real enemies of the 1990s are not to be found outside the borders of our great nation, but within the belly of the beast. The credibility of the justice system in America is to be found in the effects it has on restoring faith in itself and in reducing the threats to our democracy.